THE KOWOJ

Mesoamerican Worlds: From the Olmecs to the Danzantes

IDENTITY, MIGRATION, AND GEOPOLITICS

THE KOWOJ

IN LATE POSTCLASSIC PETÉN, GUATEMALA

EDITED BY **Prudence M. Rice and Don S. Rice**

UNIVERSITY PRESS OF COLORADO

© 2009 by the University Press of Colorado

Published by the University Press of Colorado
5589 Arapahoe Avenue, Suite 206C
Boulder, Colorado 80303

 The University Press of Colorado is a proud member of
the Association of American University Presses.

The University Press of Colorado is a cooperative publishing enterprise supported,
in part, by Adams State College, Colorado State University, Fort Lewis College,
Mesa State College, Metropolitan State College of Denver, University of Colorado,
University of Northern Colorado, and Western State College of Colorado.

∞ The paper used in this publication meets the minimum requirements of the
American National Standard for Information Sciences—Permanence of Paper for
Printed Library Materials. ANSI Z39.48-1992

Library of Congress Cataloging-in-Publication Data

The Kowoj : identity, migration, and geopolitics in late postclassic Petén, Guatemala /
Prudence M. Rice and Don S. Rice, editors.
    p. cm. — (Mesoamerican Worlds)
  Includes bibliographical references and index.
  ISBN 978-0-87081-930-8 (alk. paper)
  1. Kowoj Indians—Guatemala—Petén (Dept.)—History. 2. Kowoj Indians—Ethnic
identity. 3. Kowoj Indians—Antiquities. 4. Zacpetén Site (Guatemala) 5. Indian
pottery—Guatemala—Zacpetén Site. 6. Excavations (Archaeology)—Guatemala—
Zacpetén Site. 7. Petén (Guatemala : Dept.)—Antiquities. 8. Ethnology—
Guatemala—Petén (Dept.) I. Rice, Prudence M. II. Rice, Don Stephen.

  F1465.2.K68K68 2009
  972.81'201—dc22

                                                              2008048209

Design by Daniel Pratt

18 17 16 15 14 13 12 11 10 09   10 9 8 7 6 5 4 3 2 1

It is with the greatest affection that we dedicate this volume to two dear friends and mentors of our work in Guatemala, the late Edward S. Deevey Jr. and (the living!) Roberto C. Dorion

Contents

Figures

Tables

Proyecto Maya Colonial is the most recently completed subproject of long-term archaeological fieldwork we have pursued in the Petén lakes region since 1973–1974. At that time we had the great fortune to participate in the Central Petén Historical Ecology Project directed by the late Edward S. Deevey Jr., which focused on Lakes Yaxhá and Sacnab at the eastern end of the Petén lakes chain. Since that project, our work has moved westward through the lake basins and has taken on a more historical direction as we have collaborated with ethnohistorian Grant D. Jones. Grant's studies of documents relating to the final Spanish conquest of the Itza (Jones 1998) revealed that numerous seventeenth-century toponyms were reflected in local twentieth-century place names, some of which corresponded to archaeological sites. His work also indicated that the Itza in the Lake Petén Itzá basin were not the only ethno-political group in the Petén lakes region at the time of conquest; another group, poorly known until his archival work, existed in eastern Petén. These were the Kowoj.

This revelation clarified a few issues that had vexed us for decades (such as, why are Arlen's sherds from Tayasal so different from Pru's from Topoxté?

And why are there temple assemblages in the east and not in the west?). It also stimulated us to carry out a more systematic, on-the-ground examination of sites in the lakes region to try to verify Grant's model of political territories and locations of capitals. The result was Proyecto Maya Colonial, which we carried out with funding from the National Science Foundation primarily from 1994 through 1999.

Our field efforts came to be concentrated on the Postclassic- and Contact-period site of Zacpeten in Lake Salpetén, which lies within what can now be described as "Kowoj territory." This work allowed us to identify what we believe are ethno-specific identifiers of the Kowoj peoples, as distinct from the Itza, which consist of distinctive characteristics of pottery, architecture, and mortuary practice. Much of the data from our project has already been presented in various venues, including dissertations, journal articles, chapters, and papers presented at meetings. At the project's conclusion, however, we realized it would be advantageous for the growing numbers of researchers interested in the lowland Maya Postclassic period if we were to compile the syntheses of our findings into a single volume. The outcome of that realization is this book.

Regrettably, our analyses of the Zacpetén data are still incomplete. The lithics are being analyzed by Matt Yacubic, a doctoral candidate at the University of California–Riverside, but we have not yet carried out analyses of faunal remains or ground stone artifacts. Nonetheless, we felt it was more important to publish relatively promptly our current syntheses than to wait until "all of the data are in."

Most publications on the Maya need to be prefaced with a comment on orthography because the spelling and diacritics of words in various Mayan languages frequently change or are subject to disagreements and different practices among specialists. Except for two chapters, Andy Hofling's Chapter 4 on the *Books of Chilam Balam* and David Stuart's Chapter 13 on the text of Altar 1 at Zacpetén, very few Mayan words are used here. Probably the most confusing issue is the spelling of Itza, which is also seen in the literature as Itzá and Itzaj. Except in direct quotations, we use Itza, reserving Itzaj for the language.

How to begin? The scholarship most directly represented by the chapters in this volume was carried out between 1994 and 2002 by the chapters' authors, but the perspectives and interpretations presented here were developed over decades of fieldwork in Petén beginning in the 1970s. During this time we experienced the joy of developing enduring friendships with innumerable Guatemalan and American individuals and families who have inspired us, supported us, entertained us, and helped us learn what an enormous privilege it is to be able to work in Petén. It was the best of times and it was the worst of times . . . but our affection for Petén and Peteneros remains undiminished.

Our research in Guatemala was initiated in 1973 under the auspices of the late eminent ecologist and limnologist Edward S. Deevey Jr., who remains a source of inspiration to us and to whom we dedicate this volume. Ed was one of the last Renaissance men, and we will always remember, with great fondness and amusement, his and Georgie's quasi-parental visits to us in the field. We'd gather for breakfast at the Hotel Maya Internacional restaurant, and in the calm brilliance of an early Petén morning, before the sun gathered all its strength, Ed would placidly deliver disquisitions on jumping spiders or the song of the red-winged blackbird, all the while puffing thoughtfully on his pipe. We will never forget that Ed cashed in a life-insurance policy when we ran out of money to complete our fieldwork.

We also dedicate this volume to Roberto Dorion of Guatemala City. We met Bobby at the start of our fieldwork in the 1970s, with an introduction through Ed, and he has been a steadfast (if mildly flaky) source of support for us throughout all these years, especially on those many occasions of gringo befuddlement at the maze of Latin American bureaucracy. Bobby and his beautiful wife, Ana, have shown us what a gracious life truly is.

Beyond these dedicatory statements, we direct the remainder of our acknowledgments to the academic and non-academic support systems we have been fortunate to count upon, recognizing that these are often rather artificial distinctions.

On the academic side, we take enormous pleasure in acknowledging our long-standing collaboration with Grant D. Jones. His pioneering ethnohistoric investigations into the immediate pre-conquest situation in the central Petén lakes, and the subsequent decades of our give and take on matters historical and archaeological, have been a source of unparalleled insight into the potsherds and stone fragments that emerge from our excavations in the eastern Petén lakes. Grant's findings have guided our work for well more than a *k'atun*.

We have been privileged throughout our research in Petén, past and present, to count on the moral and logistical support of many local friends and families. Among the most long-standing of these are Tono and Aura Ortiz and their family. Tono's greatest contribution to our careers is that he taught us to appreciate Red Label without ice. We gratefully acknowledge the unfailing generosity and friendship of Rafael and Clemencia Sagastume ("*nuestros primos del sur*") in Petén and Guatemala City. They provided convenient and luxurious lodging and lab space at the Hotel Maya International and the Villa Maya and unrestricted permission to work on their land around Lake Petenxil. During the last few years of our project we lived on Flores Island, renting a house and a lab from Doña Esperanza Diaz de Tager; a kinder and more supportive "landlady" could not possibly exist.

Lic. José Rómulo Sánchez Polo was our co-PI and co-field director for Proyecto Maya Colonial, and we and our students literally could not have carried out any of this fieldwork without him (and his delightful family). We are particularly grateful that Rómulo arranged for many of his students at the Centro Universitario del Petén (CUDEP) to work with our project. This has been a win-win situation for all concerned, and we are particularly grateful for the long-standing participation of one former student, Miriam Salas, in past and present project lab work. We also thank two other archaeological colleagues in Petén who have generously shared their time, data, and expertise with us: Bernard Hermes, with respect to the Topoxté excavation data, and Rolando Torres. The Cervantes family of Ixlú allowed us to rent storage space for our artifacts, and we appreciate their carefully guarding them and our broken-down van and boat for several years.

Proyecto Maya Colonial could not have been carried out without the past and present permissions and oversight of the directors and staff of the Instituto de Antropología e Historia (IDAEH) in Guatemala City. We also gratefully acknowledge financial support for our fieldwork from the National Science Foundation: grants DBS-9222373 and SBR-9515443 to D. S. Rice, P. M. Rice, and G. D. Jones. In addition, we and our students have been fortunate to receive NSF Dissertation Improvement Grants: SBR-9816325 to P. Rice and L. Cecil, BCS-0002831 to D. Rice and K. Schwarz, and BCS-0125311 to P. Rice and W. Duncan. Leslie's fieldwork was also supported by a Sigma Xi Grant-in-Aid of Research and by Southern Illinois University Carbondale (SIUC) in the form of a University Fellowship and a Dissertation Research Award. Tim's fieldwork was funded by a grant from the Foundation for the Advancement of Mesoamerican Studies, Inc.

This volume owes an immeasurable debt to a very thorough, thoughtful, and detailed review of the initial manuscript by Marilyn Masson, as well as ongoing informal collaborations with her, and we acknowledge with gratitude her generous sharing of data and interpretations. Finally, words cannot express our thanks for the enthusiasm, encouragement, and truly infinite patience of Darrin Pratt of the University Press of Colorado.

THE KOWOJ

PART I

INTRODUCTION to the POSTCLASSIC- and CONTACT-PERIOD KOWOJ

Prudence M. Rice

INTRODUCTION TO THE KOWOJ
AND THEIR PETÉN NEIGHBORS

 Prudence M. Rice and Don S. Rice ————————————————

The Postclassic period (ca. A.D. 950/1000–1525) in the Maya lowlands of eastern Mesoamerica was long disparaged as one of "decline, decadence, and depopulation" (Chase and Rice 1985a: 1), disdained by archaeologists except for the sites of Chich'en Itza and Mayapán in Mexico's northern Yucatán peninsula (Map 1.1). To the south, in the dense tropical forests of the modern political unit known as the Department of El Petén, in northern Guatemala, the Postclassic was reconstructed almost solely with reference to a group identified as the "Itza." Both of these viewpoints were discarded by the end of the twentieth century with recognition of significant complexity and variability in the Postclassic historical and archaeological records. The chapters that follow were compiled with the goal of illuminating one heretofore relatively unknown component of late Maya history: that of the Kowoj in the eastern lakes region of Petén.

As prelude to the Kowoj story, we note that Classic lowland Maya civilization—renowned today for its towering pyramids, carved texts on limestone monuments, exquisite polychrome-painted pottery, and sumptuous

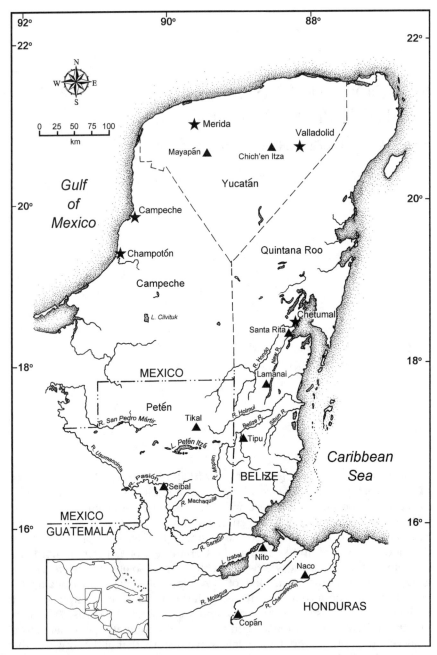

Map 1.1. The Maya lowlands, showing modern political boundaries and cities (stars),
major archaeological sites (triangles), and geographic features mentioned in this volume.

royal burials—flowered in the Yucatán peninsula between about A.D. 200 and 820. During the Terminal Classic period (ca. A.D. 820 to 950/1000), the southern lowlands experienced a series of transformations simplistically (mis)characterized as the civilization's "collapse," marked by the demise of divine kingship and royal dynasties, the abandonment of large elite ceremonial centers, and the depopulation of Petén (Aimers 2007; Culbert 1973, 1983; Demarest, Rice, and Rice 2004; Webster 2001). Centuries later, however, when the Spanish conquistador Hernán Cortés and his army traversed Petén in 1525, en route from the Gulf coast to what is now Honduras, he reported numerous settlements. According to Cortés (1976), much of the territory was controlled by a people known as Itza. Obviously, Petén had been neither permanently nor completely depopulated, but what actually transpired in this isolated area between 820 and 1525?

Archaeological and historical study of the "post-Classic" period following the "collapse" began as a rather obscure endeavor undertaken only sporadically through the 1960s (Guthe 1921–1922; Cowgill 1963). The Postclassic and Contact periods in Petén (950/1000–1525 and 1525–1700, respectively)[1] were denigrated as of little intrinsic archaeological or ethnohistoric interest in comparison to both the Classic period in Petén (cf. Hellmuth 1972, 1977) and the Postclassic and later periods in Yucatán, which boasted the great cities of Chich'en Itza (Morris, Charlot, and Morris 1931) and Mayapán (Pollock et al. 1962).

By the 1980s, however, the archaeology of the Postclassic period throughout the Maya lowlands was conceded new respectability (Chase and Rice 1985b; Graham, Jones, and Kautz 1985; Pendergast 1986; Sabloff and Andrews V 1986), and much has been illuminated about the late Maya through the last decades of archaeological investigations. Our own most recent project, carried out in the 1990s, was prompted by ethnohistorian Grant D. Jones's (1998) explication of the 1697 Spanish conquest of the Itza in Petén, the last indigenous kingdom in the Americas to fall to European dominion. The role of a people known as Kowoj, the subject of this volume, is a major new ingredient to add to the mix of recent Maya history in Petén.

The Petén Lakes Region

We and our students and colleagues have conducted archaeological, ecological, and historical investigations into Maya occupation of the lake basins of northeastern Petén since 1973. Although these lakes lie within what is usually described as the heartland of Classic-period southern lowland Maya civilization, they are actually on the southern margins of the distribution of the spectacular cities such as Tikal and Calakmul that are that civilization's hallmark.

Geologically, the area occupied by the lowland Maya is the low, karstic limestone plateau that forms the Yucatán peninsula. This peninsula increases in elevation from sea level on the northern (Gulf of Mexico) coast to ca. 500 meters in southern Petén, where it meets the deformed Paleozoic metamorphic rocks at the northern edge of the highlands of southern Guatemala.

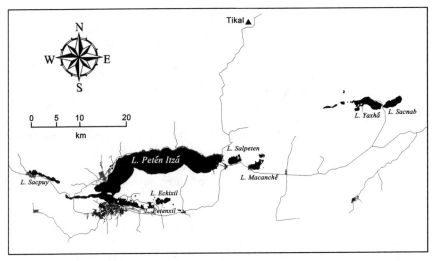

Map 1.2 The central Petén lakes region showing modern towns and roads.

Geographically, the focus of interest here is the "central Petén lakes region" (Map 1.2), defined by an east-west chain of lakes known (from west to east) as Lake Perdida, Lake Sacpuy, Lake Petén Itzá (with tiny Lakes Petenxil and Quexil south of its large main arm), Lake Salpetén, Lake Macanché, Lake Yaxhá, and Lake Sacnab. These bodies of water lie along a fault line at roughly 17° North latitude, the approximate boundary between Paleocene limestones to the north and Late Cretaceous deposits to the south (Hodell et al. 2004: figure 1). They were formed in part by karstic drainage and sinkhole formation. As a consequence of these processes, the levels of the lakes fluctuate dramatically, the most recent perturbation being a rise of 4 meters of Lake Petén Itzá beginning in 1978; by 2008 it had returned to its former level. During these later years, the level of Lake Yaxhá to the east dropped several meters such that the Topoxté Islands are no longer islands but part of a greatly expanded southern shore.

The topography of the central Petén lake basins differs markedly on their northern versus their southern shores (Map 1.3). The north sides of the basins are extremely steep, climbing abruptly 90–200 meters above the lakes' water levels (which lie approximately 100–110 meters above mean sea level). The southern shores are low wetlands with a very gradual rise over a distance of a kilometer or so until they meet the low karst hills characteristic of the southern Department of Petén.

The lake basins have only internal drainage, with a few small and often seasonal streams feeding into their southern shores. They are commonly characterized by small islands and peninsulas jutting out from their margins, which are particular foci of Postclassic-period settlement. The sixteenth-century Franciscan bishop of Yucatán, Diego de Landa, characterized the Itza region of the southern Yucatán peninsula by its rivers—"the rivers of Taiza"

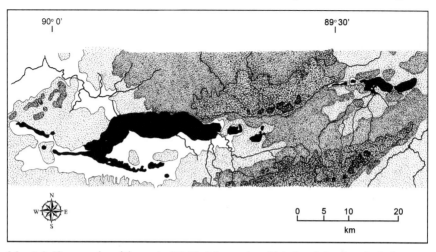

Map 1.3. Topography of the central Petén lakes region. Note low-lying terrain to the south and northwest of Lake Petén Itzá and the higher elevations to its northeast and southeast.

(in Tozzer 1941: 5) — rather than its lakes, which were the locations of its towns and cities. One wonders if this is because of the lack of rivers in the north or because the movement of Spaniards (and trade?) primarily followed riverine routes.

Archaeological Investigations in the Petén Lakes Region

Our interest in the occupational history of the lake basins, particularly their Postclassic settlement, arose out of the Central Petén Historical Ecology Project (CPHEP; 1973–1974), an archaeological and ecological investigation of Maya settlement and land use in the basins of the easternmost lakes, Yaxhá and Sacnab. Under the direction of the late Edward S. Deevey Jr., who addressed the impact of human settlement on a tropical lacustrine environment, the archaeological portion of the project involved test excavations of structures mapped in ten survey transects around the lakes, as well as on the Topoxté Islands in Lake Yaxhá (Deevey et al. 1979; D. Rice 1976; Rice and Rice 1980).

Proyecto Lacustre (1979–1981) continued this work, investigating occupation of the basins of Lakes Macanché and Salpetén, roughly twenty-five kilometers west of Lakes Yaxhá and Sacnab and east of the large northern arm of Lake Petén Itzá, and Lakes Quexil and Petenxil east of its small southern arm. This provided our first encounter with the peninsular site we named Zacpetén in Lake Salpetén, which we mapped and tested — quickly discovering that it, like the Topoxté Islands, had a substantial Postclassic component. We began to question the "demographic collapse" model of the southern lowlands, and, building on the earlier work of George L. Cowgill (1963) and William R.

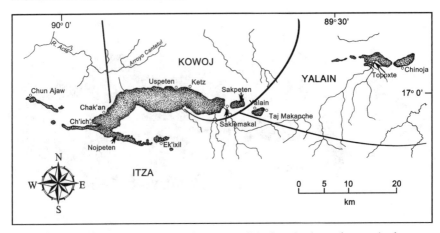

Map 1.4. Late-seventeenth-century indigenous political territories and towns in the central Petén lakes region. Modified from Jones 1998: map 3.

Bullard Jr. (1970, 1973), we regularly deviated from our randomized sampling protocols thereafter to map and test-excavate the lakes' islands and peninsulas so as to investigate Postclassic occupation.

In the 1980s our interest in the Postclassic period gained new impetus through Grant Jones's ethnohistorical studies of sixteenth- through eighteenth-century archived accounts of Spaniards' contacts with Maya inhabitants of Petén (Rice, Rice, and Jones 1993). These documents included names of rulers, titles, towns, regional settlements, and lineage territories. Jones's magisterial synthesis, *The Conquest of the Last Maya Kingdom* (1998), exposed enormous complexity in Petén's demographic situation: in the sixteenth and seventeenth centuries the area was occupied by several Maya groups embroiled in civil war. These conflicts were the consequence of many generations of political intrigue and factionalism, ethnic rivalries, calendrical disagreements, territorial disputes, stresses brought on by Spanish contact, conquest, diseases, taxation, labor demands, demographic flux, and myriad other causes. Jones's analyses revealed that—unlike earlier interpretations of Contact-period Petén history, which suggested occupation and control of a broad region by a large, relatively undifferentiated sociopolitical unit known as "Itza"—numerous groups distinguished by social (lineage), ethnic, and linguistic differences occupied Petén during the period of Spanish contact.

Jones's findings led to Proyecto Maya Colonial (1994–1999), an archaeological and historical project initiated to investigate his model of indigenous Maya lineage distributions and political geography. The goal was to locate sites that could be correlated with named Postclassic- and early Colonial-period settlements and territories identified in the Spanish accounts, particularly three political provinces or territories (Map 1.4): Kowoj, Yalain, and Kan Ek'. It was the Kan Ek' and their allied lineages in the Lake Petén Itzá region who were known to the Spaniards as the "Itza."

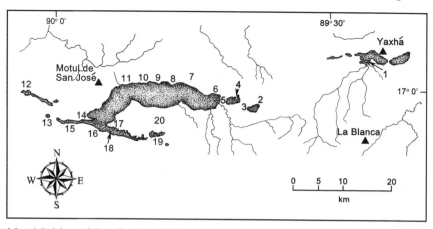

Map 1.5. Mapped Postclassic- and Contact-period sites in the central Petén lakes region: (1) Topoxté Islands; (2) Muralla de León; (3) Yalain; (4) Zacpetén; (5) Ixlú; (6) Piedra Blanca; (7) Jobompiche I; (8) El Astillero; (9) Uxpetén; (10) San Pedro; (11) Chachaclún; (12) Sacpuy; (13) Picú; (14) Nixtun-Ch'ich'; (15) Pasajá; (16) Colonia Itzá; (17) Tayasal; (18) Flores; (19) Quexil Islands (Ek'exil); (20) Cenote.

The first stage of Proyecto Maya Colonial, "The Seventeenth-Century Political Geography of Central Petén, Guatemala," consisted of archaeological reconnaissance in 1994 and 1995 in six lake basins (Macanché, Salpetén, Petén Itzá, Quexil, Petenxil, and Sacpuy) and included survey, mapping, and small-scale excavations. Jones's data on specific toponyms and socio-ethnic (or ethno-political) groups, along with distinctive Postclassic architecture known from our earlier projects in the eastern lakes region, focused project surveys on eighteen Postclassic- and/or Contact-period settlements: thirteen newly mapped and five remapped (Map 1.5). The density and location of these sites readily conform to Spanish descriptions of specific seventeenth-century Maya towns, and we believe at least ten are mentioned in the documentary records. This correspondence, plus the nonrandom distribution of architectural complexes and ceramics, established the context for the next stage of field research from 1996 through 1999: comparative investigation of sites immediately east of Lake Petén Itzá, specifically Zacpetén, Ixlú, and Yalain. This volume presents our findings on the Postclassic and later occupation at the site we studied most intensively: Zacpetén.

Although our questions in these projects were directed primarily to the Postclassic and Contact periods, our investigations uncovered continuous Maya settlement in the lakes area from the Middle Preclassic period (beginning ca. 800–700 B.C.) through the seventeenth century of this era and revealed important insights into the region's late occupational history. For example, contrary to early assumptions underlying reconstructions of a catastrophic demographic collapse in the southern lowlands, the region was never completely abandoned. Instead, during the Terminal Classic period, reduced

9

populations began reorganizing themselves in and around the basins of the central Petén lakes (Chase 1990; Rice and Rice 1990).

Second, a heretofore virtually unknown "post-Classic" archaeological period in central Petén was revealed as a culturally vibrant episode, with residential occupation and ceremonial construction concentrated on the easily defended islands and peninsulas in the region's lakes.

Finally, the well-watered and underpopulated lakes district seems to have attracted immigrants from adjacent regions beginning in the Late and Terminal Classic and continuing through the Postclassic and into the Contact period. Terminal Classic in-migration is evidenced by the introduction of ceramic types and architectural forms, better and earlier known in the Petexbatun region to the southwest (Demarest 2004; O'Mansky and Dunning 2004), found particularly at sites around Lake Petén Itzá but also in the Salpetén and Macanché basins. Postclassic Maya migrations, especially the arrival of the Itza in Petén, are long known through the indigenous "prophetic histories" of northern Yucatán but have not been well attested archaeologically. For a millennium, from the ninth through the eighteenth centuries—archaeologically differentiated into the Terminal Classic, Postclassic, and Contact periods—the Petén lakes region served as a refuge for groups of Maya forced into exile by the waning sociopolitical fortunes of towns and regional hegemonies to the north, south, east, and west (Caso Barrera 2002; Farriss 1984; Jones 1998; P. Rice and D. Rice 2005).

Socio-Ethno-Politico-Linguistic Groups in Postclassic Petén

Postclassic- and Contact-period Petén was inhabited by numerous groups that varied to greater or lesser degrees in terms of social formations, ethnicity, political organization, and language (see Hofling, Chapter 4, this volume, Map 4.1; Thompson 1977). Of these, the more centrally located spoke related and mutually intelligible dialects of the Yukatekan branch of the Maya language family. The Classic lowland Maya are believed to have spoken Yukatekan in the north and Ch'olan Maya in the south; occupants of the lakes area might have been bilingual. Postclassic linguistic reconstructions (Hofling 2006b) indicate that the later languages began to differentiate sometime around 1000, likely as a consequence of the population shifts attendant to the Terminal Classic transition. In nearly all cases, the history and archaeology of these groups are relatively little known, although the late centuries of the central Petén Postclassic and Contact periods have been framed solely in terms of the Itza.

Our attention here is on the Postclassic- and Contact-period Maya in the basins of the eastern lakes, that is, those east of the main arm of Lake Petén Itzá: Lakes Salpetén, Macanché, Yaxhá, and Sacnab. At the time of European conquest, this region was occupied by a little-known group: the Kowoj. As Jones explains (Chapter 3, this volume; also Rice, Chapter 2, this volume), scholars generally did not know of or understand the Kowoj as significant "players" in Contact-period Petén until his analysis of previously unstudied documents illuminated their role. The Kowoj claimed to have migrated to Petén from Mayapán, but the Kowoj in Yucatán are also poorly known archaeologically and historically, and their role in events can only have been confused by the idiosyncrasies of sixteenth- and seventeenth-century Spanish orthography. For various reasons, discussed in subsequent chapters, we believe the Kowoj in Yucatán were a Xiw-affiliated elite lineage group. And as detailed in numerous contributions to this volume, project excavations at the peninsular site of Zacpetén in Lake Salpetén confirmed strong cultural and historical connections with Mayapán, consistent with the Kowoj claim of descent from that city.

We consider the Kowoj in Petén to have maintained a distinct ethno-political identity (vis-à-vis the Itza) and to have spoken a Yukatekan Mayan dialect. As with the Itza in Petén, a major issue concerning the Kowoj is the date when they arrived in the lakes region. Jones (1998: 11, 16, 430n24) indicates that the Kowoj migrated from Mayapán at the time of the initial wave of Spanish conquest, roughly between 1520 and 1543. For various reasons (see Rice, Chapter 2, this volume; Pugh and Rice, Chapter 5, this volume), we believe the migration occurred earlier and that there were likely multiple episodes of migration of Xiw-related groups into Petén, of which the Kowoj proper were (one of) the last.

Of the several groups occupying Petén during the Contact period, the Spaniards most frequently mentioned the Itza. Through repeated contacts, the Spaniards apparently mistakenly believed that much of Petén was dominated by a unitary, centralized monarchy—much like that in their own post-medieval homeland and in the large civilizations they encountered in highland Mexico and Peru, headed by a ruler known since Cortés's visit as Kan Ek'. However, it is now clear that by the time of final Spanish conquest in 1697, the Itza controlled a more restricted area limited to the west and south of what is now called Lake Petén Itzá from their island capital Nojpeten ("great island").

Fray Bartolomé de Fuensalida, who visited Nojpeten in 1618 and 1619, reported that the Itza in Petén had fled from Chich'en Itza a century before the Spaniards arrived in Yucatán (cited in López de Cogolludo 1971 [vol. 2, bk. 9, ch. 14]: 256–257). The ruler of Nojpeten at the time of the 1697 conquest, Ajaw Kan Ek', claimed descent from that city through his mother (Jones 1998: 11). Clearly, during the Postclassic period the Itza were among many groups translocating between the settled north and the more sparsely occupied territory of central Petén. Once there, they pursued an expansionist strategy, carrying out raids, wars, and resettlements and fomenting rebellion in all four quarters of their territory (D. Rice and P. Rice 2005; P. Rice and D. Rice 2005).

Jones tentatively postulated the existence of a third late territory and ethnic group in the lakes region, the Yalain. A town called Yalain was described by Franciscan Fray Andrés de Avendaño y Loyola in 1696 (in Jones 1998: 216, 443n11) as "a town of very few houses clustered together, but of many well-populated *milperías* [food cultivations]" occupied by people from Nojpeten who had agricultural plots there. Yalain was said to lie east of Lake Petén Itzá, and Jones (1998: 19, map 6; Jones, Chapter 3, this volume) proposed that the town lay in the Lake Macanché basin; the territory extended east to the basins of Lakes Yaxhá and Sacnab, over former Kowoj lands, and was controlled by the Itza after their aggressive expansion in the 1630s. We are somewhat less persuaded of this possibility, which supposes a remarkable distance for Nojpeten farmers to cultivate their fields. Instead, we are inclined to place Yalain east of the small southern arm of Lake Petén Itzá where, within sight of Nojpeten, a system of canals and raised fields joins (or joined, before modern road building) Lakes Quexil and Petenxil with Lake Petén Itzá (Rice 1996).

We believe the site of Ixlú corresponds to Saklemakal, known in archival accounts as a port town on the eastern end of Lake Petén Itzá and later named Puerto Nuevo de San Antonio del Itzá (Jones 1998: 371). The Spaniards noted that Saklemakal was a contested site in the late seventeenth century, with the Yalain/Itza and Kowoj vying over its control and the latter seizing the port in the turmoil that followed the Spanish conquest of Nojpeten. Mapping and excavation confirm in part that the site was contested: a late pre-conquest Itza presence at Ixlú/Saklemakal may be detected in the construction of a small central shrine in the site's main plaza and in a pattern of caching skulls in pairs around the shrine (paired skulls were also found at Flores; Cowgill 1963: 20–22), one pair of which overlay earlier cached skull lines (Duncan 2005a: 202), also known from our excavations on the eastern Lake Macanché mainland.

Other groups in Postclassic- and Contact-period Petén were the Kejach, Mopan, and Lacandon. These groups probably all had a long ancestry in central Petén but were pushed out into the peripheries by Itza expansionism (Jones 1998: 19–28; P. Rice and D. Rice 2005). The Kejach (or Cehache 'place of deer') occupied the area north and northwest of the Itza (Thompson 1977: 11–12), and the two groups were apparently separated by an empty no-man's land. Unlike the Itza, the Kejach lacked centralized political authority and hierarchical sociopolitical organization (Alexander 2000: 387). Reportedly, the Itza and Kejach were frequently at war, and when Cortés passed through this area in 1525 on his way to Honduras he found that the towns were often fortified and situated in easily defendable locations. The sharing of surnames between the Kejach and the Itza suggests that they may have had a common origin (Jones 1998: 23), although by the time of European contact they were clearly not on good terms. The Spanish-constructed road leading south into Petén from the western Yucatán port of Campeche passed through Kejach territory, and several small Spanish missions (Ichbalché, Tzuktok) were briefly occupied there. Unfortunately, to our knowledge, no archaeological fieldwork has been undertaken in the Kejach area of Petén (but cf. Alexander 2000 for Lake Cilvituk in Campeche).

The Mopan-speaking Maya occupied the valley of the Río Mopán in southeastern Petén and Belize, east and southeast of the Kowoj region; the Belize River may have been their northern boundary (see Thompson 1977: 5). In 1618 Mopan territory extended northward to just south of Kowoj-occupied Lake Yaxhá, between Itza territory and the site of Tipu (or Negroman-Tipu), on the western bank of the Macal River—a tributary of the Belize River—in western Belize. During Colonial times Tipu served as the staging point for Spanish efforts to evangelize the "heathen" Itza in Petén.[2] Included among the Mopan are groups known as the Chinamitas in eastern Petén and Belize, with a fortified town named Tulumki ('agave-walled fortress'), and the Musules (Jones 1998: 20–21). Reportedly, the Mopan were constantly at war with the Itza, who had pushed them to the margins of Petén by pursuing their own strategies against the Spaniards; such Itza aggression likely predated Spanish documentation. The town of Mopan (now San Luis) in southeastern Petén was briefly a mission town, but it was attacked by the Itza and "incorporated into the Itza political system as an outlying colony whose duty was to monitor the frontier with Verapaz" (ibid.: 58), which was dominated by Dominican missionaries. By the end of the seventeenth century the Spaniards considered the Mopan political "dependents" of the Itza (ibid.: 19–22). Research by Guatemalan archaeologists in the southern part of Mopan territory, while focusing on the Classic rather than the Postclassic period, has identified at least two sites with Postclassic occupation (Laporte 1996, 2004).

The Lacandon Maya, numbering only about 500 people in eastern Chiapas, Mexico (southwest of the Petén lakes), represent the remnants of a larger group(s) that remained isolated from Christianity and Western influences until relatively recently (Boremanse 1998; Duby and Blom 1969; McGee 1990; Palka 1998, 2005a, 2005b; Thompson 1977: 14–19). They consist of two separate populations with different geographical origins (Boremanse 1998: 4). The southern group fled Yucatán, while the Northern Lacandon — perhaps descendants of the Kowoj (Pugh, Chapter 16, this volume) — may have been pushed out of Petén by the Itzá.

To judge from the historical documentation, then, in the seventeenth century a number of Maya socio-ethno-politico-linguistic groups in Petén were in some state of hostilities, if not active warfare, with each other. Central Petén, a distant and isolated refuge zone for Maya clinging to traditional ritual practices, was receiving scores of immigrants fleeing the oppressive conditions of the Spanish *encomiendas* (grants of labor and, by extension, land) to the north. Once a vast but relatively sparsely occupied forested terrain, Petén not only was increasingly populated by a motley assortment of refugees and fugitives, but this "safe zone" was simultaneously shrinking as Spanish missionaries and military forces steadily encroached on all sides. By the late seventeenth century, Itza expansionism had pushed ethno-linguistic groups of long standing in Petén into the peripheries (P. Rice and D. Rice 2005). The Postclassic archaeology of the Kejach, Mopan, Manche Ch'ol, and other distant neighbors of the Itza is poorly known, such that it is not possible to specify to what extent their nonperishable material culture might have displayed resistance to their Itza oppressors.

Within this broader environment, the Petén lakes region was wracked by powerful factions in the Late Postclassic and Contact periods, and by the seventeenth century the lines were drawn over issues of capitulation to the Spaniards and acceptance of Christianity. The Itza under Ajaw Kan Ek' were on one side of this conflict; the Kowoj, with their late "capital" at Zacpetén, along with an allied faction of Itza on the northwest shore of Lake Petén Itzá, were on the other.

Organization of this Volume

In this book we focus on the ethno-political group known as "Kowoj" in seventeenth-century Spanish documents, and we ask two questions about them: (1) Who were the Kowoj, in the sense of both their archaeological visibility and their cultural or socio-ethno-political identity, and (2) what was their history in Petén? That is, we seek to characterize the Kowoj as they identified themselves and as they can be identified through their recoverable material remains, primarily those from the site of Zacpetén but supplemented by data from other sites such as Topoxté. We also try to determine when and how they came to be distinguishable from the better-known (at least in documentary sources) Itza in Petén. Given our focus on what can be studied through archaeological investigations, the primary data sets explored in detail to date are architecture, pottery, and mortuary patterns. These data sets constitute the bulk of this volume.

The book is organized into six sections. This first part, Chapter 1, provides a brief and general introduction to the volume, the history of our archaeological investigations in Petén, and an overview of the social, political, and "ethnic" context of Maya groups in Contact-period Petén. The most important components of this context are that (1) multiple groups speaking variant dialects within the Yukatekan branch of the Maya language family occupied Petén in the Postclassic and later periods, and (2) by the late seventeenth century they all existed in a state of mutual hostilities.

Part II introduces the Kowoj of Petén from several largely non-archaeological perspectives, because they need to be understood within the complex historical context of feuding and factional competition between the two major elite lineage alliances of Yucatán — the Itza and Xiw — and the large cities of Chich'en Itza and Mayapán. Chapter 2 seeks to place the Kowoj within this broader spatio-temporal and cultural context, with discussion of indigenous documents (and archaeological data) concerning the Postclassic Maya lowlands and the ties between the Kowoj and the better-known Xiw in the north. This is followed by Grant Jones's summary of the ethnohistorical research that led to recognition of the Kowoj as a political entity from data in archived documents and Charles Andrew Hofling's chapter on linguistic differences between Itza and Xiw as evidenced in the *chilam b'alam* books. The most critical issue here is the history and dating of the Kowoj in Petén, an issue that cannot be definitively settled although we believe we have the outline of a satisfactory resolution. In Chapter 3, Jones notes that a Kowoj informant reported to a Spanish military man that the Kowoj had origins in Mayapán and fled northern Yucatán and arrived in Petén in the second quarter of the sixteenth century. While we cannot argue with this testimony, we have a difficult time squaring that late date with the long Postclassic archaeological sequence in eastern Petén. We propose that the Kowoj were one of several elite lineages affiliated with the Xiw in Yucatán, and, more specifically in Petén, the "Kowoj proper" were probably the last in a series of these lineages to flee Yucatán and migrate to Petén during the several centuries of the Postclassic period.

Parts III, IV, and V address various categories of archaeological data from our excavations at Zacpetén. Part III surveys the architecture and settlement patterns of the Kowoj (or Xiw affiliates) in Petén. Of particular importance are the two largely contemporaneous Mayapán-style architectural complexes known as "temple assemblages" at Zacpetén. Existing only in the eastern part of the Petén lakes district (and not in the Itza-controlled west), the temples and open hall structures of these assemblages yielded large quantities of primarily ritual artifacts in situ, suggesting that they were abandoned in haste. Several domestic structures were also investigated at Zacpetén, the most unusual of which was Structure 719 (Chapter 9), which may have been a very late-occupied council house.

The three chapters in Part IV add ceramic data to the mix. These chapters combine technological analyses of paste and pigment constituents and design elements of the slipped and decorated Postclassic pottery at Zacpetén and the lakes area plus descriptions of the incense burners and other ritual pottery found in the temples and elsewhere at Zacpetén. The Kowoj and their Xiw-related allies in Petén made and used the distinctive Clemencia Cream Paste-ware pottery, which we believe was produced in or near the Topoxté Islands in Lake Yaxhá, although similar stylistic attributes of decoration (and also incensarios) were copied in other clay pastes found at Zacpetén.

Part V's chapters provide additional information on the history of the Kowoj and their Xiw-related allies at Zacpetén, as well as distinguishing them from other groups in broader spatial and temporal contexts. These contexts include information from a carved Classic altar at Zacpetén, their patterns of access to obsidian, data on mortuary patterns—a mass grave of ~thirty-seven individuals—and possible relations between the Kowoj and the Northern Lacandon in Chiapas, Mexico.

Part VI, the concluding Chapter 17, summarizes the varying interpretations and often contradictory evidence, especially concerning dating, while highlighting what we consider our successes in relating the Kowoj and their Xiw-related antecedents to Mayapán and in distinguishing ethnicity (or some ethno-linguistico-political variant thereof) in the archaeological record of central Petén.

Notes

1. Norman Schwartz (1990: 2) divides the post-conquest history of Petén into these periods: Early Colonial 1697–1720s; Late Colonial, 1720s–1821; Independence, 1821–1890s; Enclave Economy, 1890s–1970s; and Modern Colonization, since the 1970s.

2. Tipu had close relations with the Petén lakes region during the Postclassic period, as evidenced by ceramic exchange—approximately 40 percent of the Postclassic pottery (by sherd count) from early excavations was Snail-Inclusion Paste ware or Clemencia Cream Paste ware in roughly equal amounts (Rice 1984c)—and intermarriage (the presence of Itza surnames; Jones 1998: table 1.1).

PART II

WHO WERE THE KOWOJ?

Prudence M. Rice

The primary question framing the chapters in this volume is, who were the Kowoj Maya? We approach this question from various starting points with respect to methods and data, emphasizing archaeological data from the site of Zacpetén.

The simplest and most straightforward response to our question is to say who the Kowoj were *not*: the Kowoj were not the Itza. Until Grant D. Jones's pioneering exegesis of the late-seventeenth-century conquest of the Petén Itza at Nojpeten, the Kowoj were little differentiated from them. With publication of *The Conquest of the Last Maya Kingdom* (Jones 1998), however, this situation has been rectified and the Kowoj have emerged as a significant social and political presence in the region, particularly in the context of their maneuvering against both the neighboring Itza and the encroaching Spaniards in the bitter circumstances of impending conquest.

The Kowoj are one of numerous groups in Postclassic- and Contact-period Petén, groups that can be described as having varying degrees of differentiation in their social, political, ethnic, and linguistic identities. Next to the Petén Itza — who are well-known through documents but not particularly well-characterized archaeologically — we believe the Kowoj were probably the second most powerful and second best-known group in Petén. Others, such as the Mopan, Kejache, Chinamita, Lacandon, Icaiche, and Yalain, remain virtually unknown materially and geopolitically except for documentary references or linguistic reconstructions.

Sir J. Eric S. Thompson made several notable efforts to untangle the multiple ethno-specific threads of Postclassic and later Maya occupation in Petén. One was his (Thompson 1970: 3–47) discussion of the expansion of Chontal Maya—whom he dubbed the "Putun"—into western Petén. On the basis of available ethnohistorical information, he proposed that the Putun, with their homeland in the Gulf coastal area of Tabasco and Campeche and their circum-peninsular trading activities, moved upstream into Petén along the Usumacinta and Pasión rivers. In doing so, they conquered the Classic Maya riverine cities along their route as far south as Seibal and eastward to Ucanal. According to Thompson's proposal, "Putun" was a collective appellation for various groups originating in the Acalan area, including the Itza; they established Chich'en Itza and ultimately became the ancestors of the Lacandon.

A later, similarly sweeping effort to explain the Postclassic and Colonial sociopolitical situation in Petén is Thompson's "Proposal for Constituting a Maya Subgroup . . . in the Petén." In this contribution, Thompson (1977: 4) suggests that the Maya occupying Petén during the Colonial period—"the Mopan Maya, the Cehach, the Chinamita, and the . . . Lacandon"—were a subgroup more closely related to the Mopan Maya in the southeast than to Yukatekan speakers to the north. He refers to them as the "Chan" Maya, on the basis of the prevalence of the Chan surname in documentary sources. The proposed Chan area covers most of modern Belize and north-central Petén: from the northern Belize border, southwest to the Río Usumacinta, south to the Pasión, and southeast to incorporate modern San Luis (ibid.: map 1-1).

Considering the lack of well-contextualized historical data, not to mention the dearth of published archaeological research on the Petén Postclassic through the 1970s, Thompson's efforts at synthesis can only be described as heroic. Nonetheless, given the last several decades of rapidly accumulating knowledge about the Postclassic archaeology of both northern Yucatán and the central Petén lakes region—some of which is reviewed herein—most of his ideas are no longer tenable. For example, historical linguistic studies indicate that the Mopan language was the earliest to separate from the other languages of Yukatekan (see Hofling, Chapter 4, this volume).

Another more recent effort to interpret Petén Postclassic data within a larger pan-Maya synthesis—in some senses an outgrowth of Thompson's Putun model—is John W. Fox's (1987) study of Postclassic state formation. Fox identified shared architectural complexes (the "basic ceremonial group" and radial temples) and iconographic motifs (serpents and mats) as part of a "Chontal diaspora" from the Gulf coast throughout the Maya lowlands and highlands. More encompassing than Thompson's Putun model and informed by substantial archaeological data, Fox's admirably documented model is nonetheless limited by the long-standing lack of recognition of significant sociopolitical variation in the Petén lakes region. This large area was not dominated by a single powerful political entity, the Itza; instead, the Itza were increasingly challenged from within and without by their Maya neighbors, the Kowoj. Our evolving awareness of east-west differences in archaeological remains in central Petén, which first began to emerge in the 1970s, can now, as a result of Jones's archival studies, be explained by authentic east-west socio-ethno-political identity distinctions—Kowoj versus Itza, respectively—in the region.

We feel that the careful interweaving of ethnohistorical and archaeological data, exemplified here by our investigation of the Kowoj in Petén—whom we believe were socially and historically affiliated with the Xiw in northern Yucatán—could be profitably extended to a study of other groups on the peripheries of the lakes region. The history of the Lacandon is currently being investigated archaeologically (Palka 2005a, 2005b), but the Mopan and the Kejach should also be amenable to on-the-ground study. The Kejach, for example, lived in well-fortified towns along the main trade route from Campeche to Lake Petén Itzá; surely some remnant of these towns should still exist. The same might be true of the Chinamitas and the Mopan in southeastern Petén.

The chapters in Part II provide background for answering the question who were the Kowoj by approaching the issue from various perspectives. One comes from native texts (Rice, Chapter 2), another from the writings of early Spaniards in the area (Jones, Chapter 3), and still another from linguistic studies of Yukateko dialect variations (Hofling, Chapter 4). This material establishes the context within which the data from excavations at Zacpetén, reported in the remainder of the book, must be interpreted.

THE KOWOJ IN
GEOPOLITICO-RITUAL PERSPECTIVE

—— Prudence M. Rice ————————————————————————————

The history of the Kowoj in Petén cannot be understood outside of broader relations with other groups in Petén, with groups in Yucatán, and also with the Spaniards. Documentary evidence concerning the latter has been explored by Grant D. Jones (1998, Chapter 3, this volume). Here I situate the Kowoj within a wider historical and geopolitico-ritual landscape by overviewing the practices and events that establish the context of these interrelations.

The northern Yucatán peninsula was dominated geopolitically in the Post-classic and Colonial periods by two alliances of elite lineages known as the Itza in the east and the Xiw in the west. The standard outline of Postclassic Yucatán history derives from analysis of Colonial-period indigenous Maya "prophetic histories" such as *The Book of Chilam Balam of Chumayel* (hereafter *Chumayel*; Roys 1967; Edmonson 1986), *The Book of Chilam Balam of Tizimin* (*Tizimin*; Edmonson 1982), of *Maní* (Craine and Reindorp 1979), of *Oxcutzcab* (Morley 1920), and so on, many unpublished. These books are heavily reworked compilations of oral histories and prophecies originally delivered by the spokesman or speaker (*chilan, chilam*) of the jaguar priest (*b'alam*), who ruled over the calendrically and ritually significant period of nearly twenty Christian years known as a *k'atun*. They were written in Yukateko using Latin script and are now referred to by the towns in which the manuscripts were found.

The veracity of the annals in the *chilam b'alam* books as they relate to Classic-period history has been repeatedly questioned. Part of the reason some scholars mistrust these books is because they, like most histories, were compiled with unstated agendas, or at least authorial and political motives of which we are not always fully aware. For example, the *Chumayel, Maní,* and *Oxcutzcab* are considered chronicles of the Xiw and they denigrate their rivals, the Itza, while the *Tizimin* is a reconstruction of Maya history favorable to the Itza. From a different point of view, however, these books can be apprehended as Xiw and Itza expressions of their own historical consciousness of the processes of ethnic identity formation—ethnogenesis—played out during the Postclassic period. As part of this expression, they also appear to record dialect differences in the languages of the Xiw versus the Itza (Hofling, Chapter 4, this volume).

Another reason the histories outlined in these indigenous books is debated is because of the Maya emphasis on cyclical time. Dating events is problematic because the books give dates according to numbered *k'atuns,* which regularly recurred within calendrical cycles of approximately 256 Gregorian years but cannot be unambiguously pinned to the centuries of the modern calendar (Appendix 2.I). Because lowland Maya Postclassic geopolitical organization was heavily grounded in calendrical cycling and the rest of the book's chapters make reference to these matters, Maya calendars are briefly summarized here.

Maya Cosmology and Calendars

Postclassic Maya worldview, whether in the southern or northern lowlands, was dominated by two overarching concepts: cosmic quadripartition and cyclical time (Rice, in press). For the Maya, "[T]ime is cosmic order" (Farriss 1987: 574). The Maya cosmos had three components: the heavens (with thirteen levels), the natural earthly world, and the Underworld (nine levels). In all components and levels the Maya cosmos was partitioned into four quarters, based roughly on the four cardinal or inter-cardinal directions—or, perhaps more accurately, on the solar solsticial rising and setting points. Worldwide, many prehistoric and non-Western communities have similar quadripartite cosmologies, and the built world or earthly domain frequently repeats that four-part structure (Carlson 1981; M. Coe 1965; Eliade 1979; Marcus 1973; Marcus, Flannery, and Spores 1983: 38–39; Tichy 1981). Among the Maya, individual buildings and architectural complexes, typically with structures arranged to the cardinal directions around open plazas, are often held to represent "cosmograms" and thus constitute sacred landscapes (Ashmore 1989, 1991; Coggins 1980; Guillemin 1968; cf. Smith 2005).

According to an idealized, quadripartite model (M. Coe 1965), ancient Maya communities would have consisted of four wards, each associated with a cardinal direction, a color,[1] and a series of ranked offices; community ritual and political leadership might have rotated through the wards in a four-year counterclockwise cycle. Use of "calendrical permutations to rotate power among equal segments of a community" seems "uniquely Maya" and solved inevitable problems of ruler succession; moreover, the "regular transfer of ascendancy, perhaps purely ritual," by twenty-year *k'atuns* presents "an ideal model of 13 territories" (M. Coe 1965: 109–110).

As for their view of time, the Maya and other Mesoamerican groups, like modern westerners, recognized time as having linear or progressive qualities—as in past, present, and future—but of deeper importance to their cosmology was the concept of cyclical time (Rice 2004a, 2007a, 2008). This was based on their remarkably accurate predictive astronomy that allowed tracking of the movements of the sun, moon, Venus, and other heavenly bodies and interrelated them in interlocking cycles. Through these cycles, astronomers or calendar priests were permitted understanding of celestial events such as solstices, eclipses, and so on, in the past, as well as foreknowledge of such events in the future. They were then able to coordinate earthly events and rituals with cosmic sanctions and auguries that were both validated by past experience and anticipatable in the future (see Farriss 1987).

The fundamental unit of Mesoamerican time was the day. Among the Yukatekan Maya the word for day is *k'in*, a word that means "sun," "day," and "time" but also designates the priests, Aj K'in, in charge of calendrical affairs. The Mesoamerican counting system was base-twenty or vigesimal (unlike western base-ten decimal systems), which meant time's passage was recorded in counts of days that were mostly multiples of twenty.

Mesoamerican peoples recorded events by two concurrently running calendars, one of 260 days and the other of 365 days (for details, see Aveni 1981; Edmonson 1988; Girard 1962; Gossen and Leventhal 1993; Lounsbury 1978; Marcus 1992: 132–140; Milbrath 1999; Sharer 1994: 513–629; Tedlock 1992; Thompson 1960; Vogt 1964, 1969). The basic units of the 260-day calendar (what Mayanist archaeologists call the *tzolk'in*; Nahuatl *tonalpohualli*) were a numerical count from 1 to 13 preceding 1 of the 20 day-names; because of the permutation of 13 and 20, the same number/day-name combination could recur only every 260 days. The 365-day "solar" calendar (Maya *ja'ab'*) consisted of 360 days (a unit called a *tun*) grouped into 18 *winals* or "months," each of which comprised 20 days numbered from 0 to 19. At the end of this period, 5 days were added as a nineteenth "month"; these were deemed unlucky and preceded the first day of the new year, 0 Pop. By means of this system, any given day would be designated by its names and numbers in both calendars, with the day in the 260-day calendar given precedence, as, for example, a Maya day 11 Ajaw 18 Pop.

The simultaneous cycling of these calendars led to two distinctive features of Mesoamerican time keeping. First, a total of 18,980 days, or 52 of the 365-day years, elapsed before any particular number and day in one calendar—say, 12 Ajaw in the Maya 260-day almanac—coincided again with a particular day and month—say, 3 K'ank'in—in the solar calendar. Called the "Calendar

Round," this cycling of the two calendars was completed every 52 years (see Appendix 2.I)—probably only once in most humans' lifetimes. Among the Aztec, this was the occasion of dramatic celebrations involving the dedication of new or remodeled temples and the lighting of new fires (Hassig 2001). The Maya, Classic and Postclassic, also celebrated these cycles; the Christian year 1581, for example, was the ending/beginning of a new Calendar Round (Edmonson 1986: 5).

Second, Mesoamericans personified the first day of the year in the 260-day calendar as a "yearbearer" because it had the responsibility of bearing the "burden" of time for the entire year. Only 4 of the 20 day-names in the 260-day calendar could be yearbearers at any one time because of a feature of the simultaneously running solar calendar: the 5 unlucky days over and above its 360-day *tun* caused an annual forward shift of 5 day-names of the first day of the year in the 260-day calendar. In the Classic period, the Maya yearbearers were the days Ak'b'al, Lamat, B'en, and Etz'nab' (Sharer and Traxler 2006: 109). The Campeche calendar, which entered the southwestern peninsula in the Late Classic, introduced some variations but used the same yearbearers; its senior yearbearer was B'en (Edmonson 1988: 148). The Colonial-period Mayapán calendar, modified in 1539, was derived from the Campeche and continued the same yearbearers (Edmonson 1988: 203).

Other intervals of time are also of interest, particularly multiples of the 360-day "years" known as *tuns*. The most important of the *tun* periods is the *k'atun*, a count of 7,200 days, or approximately 20 Gregorian years. Until 1539, most Maya celebrated these intervals not by their beginnings but by their endings: for example, during the Classic period the Maya recorded the endings of *k'atuns* and 5-year divisions of *k'atuns* within the Long Count by erecting carved, dated stelae.

The Calendrical Basis of Postclassic Maya Geopolitical Organization

In 1695, Franciscan friar Andrés de Avendaño y Loyola (1987: 39) illuminated the hitherto concealed foundations of Yucatecan Maya geopolitical organization, writing that it was based on 13 periods ("ages"): "These thirteen ages are divided into thirteen [spatial] parts, which divide this kingdom of Yucathán, and each age, with its idol, priest, and prophecy, rules in one of these thirteen parts of this land, according as they have divided it." An "age" is the 20-year period of the *k'atun*, and 13 ages or *k'atuns* comprise the key politico-ritual and spatio-temporal unit known as the "*k'atun* cycle." The *k'atun* cycle or round (*u kahlay k'atunoob'*) consists of 260 *tuns*, or 13 *k'atuns* of 7,200 *k'ins* per *k'atun*; phrased differently, it consists of 93,600 days, 160 days short of 256 Western/ solar/Gregorian years (Edmonson 1986: 9). As it relates to geopolitico-ritual affairs, this cycle of approximately 256 years between one *k'atun* and the next, having exactly the same combination of day-names and numbers in the Maya 260-day calendar, is known as the *may* ('cycle').

Because the Maya traditionally commemorated the passage of time by the completion of units, *k'atuns* were always named for a day Ajaw ("Lord"),

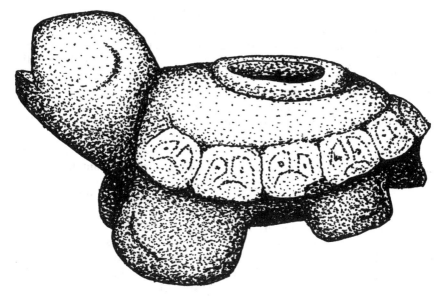

Figure 2.1. Carved stone turtle from Mayapán, with thirteen Ajaw glyphs – presumably a reference to the thirteen k'atuns *in a* may *– around the edge of the carapace. Redrawn from Proskouriakoff 1962b: figure 1.g.*

the last of the 20 day-names in the 260-day calendar. In the Classic calendar, K'atun 8 Ajaw was not only the last number and day-name of a particular *k'atun*, it was also—for reasons too complex to detail here—always the ending of an entire *k'atun* cycle or *may*. In sixteenth-century Yucatán this cycle of 13 *k'atuns* was represented as a wheel divided into 13 sections, and at pre-Hispanic Mayapán a stone turtle had thirteen Ajaw glyphs carved into its carapace (Figure 2.1; Proskouriakoff 1962b: figure 1.g; Taube 1988).

The political significance of calendrical cycling can be appreciated in Postclassic northern Yucatán, where particular cities held ritual and secular power as centers of *k'atun*- and *may*-based ritual. That is, every 260 *tuns* (or ~256 years), as one *may* ended the new *may* cycle was ritually "seated" in a particular city that became that region's dynastic and religious capital. According to Munro Edmonson (1979: 11, 1982: xvi, 1986: 4–5), the seat of the *may* was "Born of Heaven" (*siyaj ka'an*): it was a sacred or holy city, its main temple was the cycle seat proper, and its plaza was the region's religious center. The *may* seat enjoyed power for approximately 256 years, after which the city and its roads and idols were ritually destroyed or "terminated" and the city was "abandoned," although perhaps only by its ruling dynasty or, metaphorically, by ritual demotion.

During the ~256-year period in which a particular city seated the *may*, other important towns within the region seated its 13 *k'atuns*. Every 20 years, as one *k'atun* ended the new *k'atun* was seated in a town that became an important ritual center and home of the chief priest of the *k'atun*. This *k'atun* priest, the *b'alam* or sometimes *aj k'in may*, "sun priest of the cycle" (Edmonson 1986: 4; and perhaps Barbara Tedlock's [1992: 2] "daykeeper"), had a *chilam* who was the official prophet of the *k'atun*. This is the origin of the titles of the indigenous books of the *chilam b'alams*, identified by the Yucatecan towns (probable *k'atun* seats) where they were kept. *K'atun* seats were not only ritual centers. They also had economic powers — controlling tribute rights, land titles, and appointments to public office within the realm for their 20-year duration (Edmonson 1979: 11, 1982: xvii). When *k'atun* seats rotated from one town to another, priestly and secular administration was also transferred. According to the books of the *chilam b'alams*, *k'atun* seatings circulated among multiple towns during a given *may*, typically two or three but sometimes as many as seven; in an idealized model, there were probably thirteen *k'atun* seats. This *may*-based geopolitico-ritual organization can be seen to have existed in the Classic period and has roots in the Preclassic (Rice 2007a). In describing the political organization of the northern lowlands, as reconstructed from the books of the *chilam b'alams*, Edmonson notes that these sources provide considerable agreement about which cities seated and ruled over *k'atuns* during the fifteenth and late sixteenth centuries (Table 2.1).

Early Spanish chroniclers reported pervasive and relatively constant hostilities among towns in northern Yucatán. In the sixteenth century, Bishop Diego de Landa mentioned "great strifes and enmities" among the major ruling lineages and the Mayas' fears of being captured, sold into slavery, or sacrificed as a result of defeat in these wars (in Tozzer 1941: 40–41, 217). Antonio de Herrera y Tordesillas (1941: 217) noted that the Maya "were scattered. And their discords had increased so much that for any little cause they fought. . . . And so they never had peace, especially when the cultivation was over." The reasons for the unrest are complex, related to oppressive colonial circumstances but also to long-existing feuds and rivalries over captive taking, trade relations, and various misdeeds and crimes (see Farriss 1987; Restall 1997; P. Rice and D. Rice 2005; Roys 1972: 65–70). There were also antagonisms related to calendrical matters, such as conflicts among towns competing for the privilege of seating the *k'atun* because of the extensive powers it entailed. This relates to the fact that the word *k'atun* also means "war(rior), battle, combat," and the heads of *k'atun* seats might have served as war captains.

Postclassic Northern Yucatán

The social and political history of the Kowoj in Petén is tied to the northern Yucatán peninsula, to the extent that it can be uncovered in the indigenous histories in the books of the *chilam b'alams*. For this reason it is important to review what is known of the Terminal Classic, Postclassic, and Colonial periods in the northern lowlands. Archaeological, historical, and ethnohistorical data illuminate two groups of elite lineages that have come to be known as the Itza and the Xiw as well as two major cities, Chich'en Itza and Mayapán. A third city, Uxmal, does not figure heavily in the indigenous literature,

Table 2.1. Cities seating the *k'atuns* in the fifteenth through eighteenth centuries according to the *Books of the Chilam Balam* (C = *Chumayel*; K = *Kaua*; M = *Maní*; T = *Tizimín*).

Ajaw	Year	Seat	Ajaw	Year	Seat
Classic Calendar:			*Mayapán calendar:*		
12	1421	Otzmal (C, T)	11	1539*	Colox Peten (C)
10	1441	Coba (C)			Emal (C, T)
		Tan Xuluk Mul (C)			Mérida (C, K, M, T)
		Zizal (C)	9	1559	Mérida (C, T)
8	1461	Chich'en Itza (C, T)			Teabo (C, K, M, T)
		Izamal (C, M, T)	7	1579	Mayapán (C, K, M, T)
		Kan Cab A (C)			Mérida (C, T)
		Tan Xuluk Mul (C, T)	5	1598	Mayapán (M)
6	1480	Hunac Thi (C)			Mérida (T)
		Mérida (C)			Zotz'il (C, K, M, T)
		Teabo (C)	3	1618	Mérida (C, T)
		Uxmal (C, K, M, T)			Zuyua (C, M, T)
4	1500	Atikuhe (C)	1	1638	Emal (C, M, T)
		Bolon Te Uitz (C)			Mérida (C, T)
		Chichen Itza (C, T)	12	1658	Valladolid (C, K, M, T)
		Hol Tun Zuyua (C)	10	1677	Chable (C, K, M, T)
		Kin Colah Peten (C)			Valladolid (T)
		Na Cocob (C)	8	1697	Chable (C, K, M, T)
		Teabo (C, K)	6	1717	Teabo (C, M, T)
2	1520	Chacal Na (C)	4	1737	Bacalar (C)
		Cozumel (C)			Tan Hom (C)
		Tihosuco (T)			Teabo (C, M, T)
		Kin Colah Peten (C)			
13	1539*	Coba (CT)	*Valladolid calendar:*		
		Cozumel (C)	2	1776	Valladolid (C, K, M, T)
		Kin Colah Peten (C)	13	1800	Coba (C, K, M, T)
		Mayapán (C)			
		Mérida (C)			

* 1539 is listed twice because, with the beginning of the Mayapán calendar in that year, *k'atuns* began to be counted from their initial date instead of from the terminal date.
Source: Edmonson 1986: 275–276.

but it was the first capital of the Xiw, so it also played an important early (Terminal Classic and Early Postclassic) role in the northern lowlands political landscape. During the Postclassic period, as disagreements escalated over untold scores of matters, including calendrics, the population seems to have fissioned into numerous and frequently antagonistic towns and lineage (or other kin-based) alliances. Simple dichotomization into two opposing camps, Itza and Xiw, obscures considerable variability in attitudes, beliefs, and practices among these entities, and it is evident that significant factions and fluidity existed within each alliance.

Details of the history of northern Yucatán and especially Mayapán, reconciling architectural and ceramic data with indigenous *k'atun* histories, have recently been presented by art historian Susan Milbrath and Mexican archaeologist Carlos Peraza Lope (Milbrath and Peraza Lope 2003), along with new radiocarbon dates obtained by Peraza Lope, Marilyn Masson, and their archaeologist colleagues working at Mayapán (Peraza Lope, Masson, and Russell 2006). The summary here is based on these remarkable syntheses.

The Itza and Chich'en Itza

The Itza were a group of elite lineages that dominated the northeastern Yucatán peninsula during the Postclassic and Colonial periods. Several theories have been advanced about the origins of the Itza (see Boot 2005; Tozzer 1941: 20n123, 32–33n172). One, originally favored by Ralph L. Roys (1967), is that the Itza were non-Maya "foreigners" or highland Mexicans (Toltecs). Another theory is that they were Chontal-speaking Maya or "Putun" from the Gulf coast region (Kowalski 1989; Thompson 1970). William Ringle, Tomás Gallareta Negrón, and George Bey (1998) identify the Itza with a Quetzalcoatl cult introduced into the northern lowlands in the Postclassic. Yet another possibility is that they were the Mexican Aj Kanuls (*canul* 'guardian') who arrived around 1200, and the nominal "Itza" appearing in the indigenous chronicles was "applied retroactively" (Tozzer 1941: 33n172). "Itza" initially might have been an inclusive identifier for groups with ultimate origins in Late or Terminal Classic central Petén, as suggested by recent epigraphic research (Boot 2005: 35–84), but we are not presently in a position to evaluate that statement with archaeological data. Indeed, "Itza" might have been a toponym rather than an ethnonym (Boot 2005: 12, 37). The Itza in Yucatán are treated ambivalently in the *Chumayel* and elsewhere, described as "those who speak our language brokenly," "foreigners," "people without fathers or mothers," and "tricksters and rascals," but also as "holy men" (see Tozzer 1941: 20n123).

The Itza are particularly associated with the site of Chich'en Itza — 'mouth (*chi*) of the well (*ch'en*) of the Itza' — in the north-central part of the peninsula. According to the *Tizimin*, the people known as Itza claim to have established Chich'en Itza as their "capital" city (or, more accurately, to have "seated the *may*") in a calendrically propitious K'atun 8 Ajaw, presumably that of A.D. 672–692 (Schele and Mathews 1998: 365n31). According to the *Chumayel*, however, the Itza "appeared" in the following *k'atun*, a K'atun 6 Ajaw (692–711), while the *Maní* (Xiw) chronicle puts their arrival even later in a K'atun 11 Ajaw (770–790).[2]

The early elites of Chich'en Itza were literate in hieroglyphic writing, and the inscriptions at the site date from about 800 to 998 (latest date at the Osario structure; Milbrath and Peraza Lope 2003: 21). Although ceramic dating has been a matter of sustained dispute (Andrews, Andrews, and Robles Castellanos 2003; Cobos Palma 2004), two complexes have been identified: Early Sotuta, mixed with some Cehpech pottery associated with the Puuc hills area to the west, 750–900; and Late Sotuta, 900–1000/1050. Chich'en Itza is known for its distinctive architecture, some of which — especially in the southern part of the main civic-ceremonial center — is in the Puuc style, with elaborate stone mosaic facades and Chaak masks. The northern part of the site exhibits features long attributed to "Mexicans" or "Toltecs," including colonnades, eagle and serpent symbolism, and talud-tablero construction and also its deep, sacred *ch'en* (*cenote*, water-filled sinkhole). Active construction appears to have ceased around 1000–1050, with the end of the city's geopolitical power thought to have been around 1100 (Andrews, Andrews, and Robles Castellanos 2003: 152). According to the chronicles, in a K'atun 8 Ajaw (1185–1204) the "Itza's *ch'en*" (i.e., the site of Chich'en Itza) was "destroyed," probably the ritual termination that accompanies the end of the seating of a *may*. The site was never abandoned, however, and continued to be occupied into the Colonial period, with its sacred *cenote* a key pilgrimage destination.

At the demise of Chich'en Itza as a *may* seat, some Itza fled to a place called Chak'an Putun (Chak'anputun), where there were already "houses of those of Itza, holy men" (*Maní*, quoted in Tozzer 1941: 20n123). This destination has been interpreted as lying near Lake Petén Itzá, where there might have been preexisting Itza populations (discussed later). Chak'an Putun was ritually destroyed in a K'atun 8 Ajaw (perhaps 1185–1204?), after which some Itza returned to Chich'en Itza. Roys (1932, quoted in Tozzer 1941: 21n123) proposed a probable "division among the Itzas themselves, one faction of whom conquered some of the more important cities of northern Yucatan during the same generation in which Chakanputun was abandoned. The other faction appears to have been less fortunate for we find that they wandered for two katuns in the wilderness."

An important lineage and faction leader among the Itza in Yucatán was the Kokom. The appellative or patronym Kokom appears as K'ul Kokom in a glyphic text on the Ak'ab Dzib' at Chich'en Itza before 900 (Ringle 1990: 235); and the name Kan Ek', long associated with the Itza in Petén, appears in the Chich'en Itza Great Ballcourt. Another patronym, Kupul, also appears (as Copul) in a Chich'en Itza text (ibid.). As Roys (1962: 81) observed, it is peculiar that the indigenous literature such as the *chilam b'alams* refers to the Itza, but early Spanish writers instead refer to the Kokom. The likelihood of Itza factionalism led Roys (ibid.) to surmise that the Kokom rulers of Mayapán originally considered themselves to be Itza, but after the Xiw-led revolt against the Itza/Kokom in the mid-fifteenth century (see later discussion) the Itza fell into "serious disrepute." Some Itza were killed in the revolt, some congregated around Chich'en Itza, some may have fled to the eastern peninsula or Petén to join relatives, and the Kokom remaining in Yucatán might have wished to avoid association with the Itza identifier. Alternatively, "Itza" may have been a collective term referring to the fluid alliance of lineages rather than to any single one of them. Or, the Spaniards' consistent reference to Kokoms may reflect the influence of one of their major informants, Na Chi Kokom.

By the Colonial period, if not much earlier, the Kokom, with their capital in the Sotuta province, presented themselves as the most powerful group in the Itza alliance, viewing themselves as the "natural lords" of Yucatán Itza territory. According to Torquemada (quoted in Tozzer 1941: 23n126), "They say that the kings of Yucatan, who are called *Cocomes* [*Kokoms*], which means

Oidores [*judges*], were descended from [Quetzalcoatl]." Other groups, perhaps affiliated lineally or merely philosophically with the Itza, in the eastern part of the peninsula remained steadfastly opposed to conversion to Christianity and were poorly controlled by the Spanish overlords (Farriss 1984).

Mayapán

The city of Mayapán, an important Late Postclassic (1200–1450) city seventy kilometers southeast of modern Mérida in northwestern Yucatán, lies at the boundary between Xiw and Itza territory. Archaeologists' understanding of Mayapán has long been informed by native sources (e.g., the books of the *chilam b'alams*) and the comments of Bishop Diego de Landa (in Tozzer 1941) and other early European residents in the area. In addition, an extensive excavation project carried out by the Carnegie Institution of Washington in the first half of the twentieth century (Pollock et al. 1962) integrated textual evidence into the archaeological research design. Mayapán has long been a sort of "index fossil" for the Maya Postclassic and a source of direct historical analogy for analyses of polities outside the northern lowlands (e.g., Jones 1998; Rice 2004a). The city is of considerable importance here because the Kowoj in Petén claimed origins at Mayapán.

As with Chich'en Itza, dating the construction and occupation of Mayapán is a matter of debate, with two chronologies recently propounded. One is a *k'atun*-based model, integrating the events in the prophetic histories of the *chilam b'alams* with archaeological data (Milbrath and Peraza Lope 2003); the other is based on radiocarbon assays of samples primarily from recent excavations at the site (Peraza Lope et al. 2006). Disagreements exist between the two, and neither is absolute. The *k'atun*-based effort is somewhat tautological (and the books themselves differ), and the potential precision of radiometric dating is confounded by the bimodal calibration curve for dates in the Postclassic period.

According to Bishop Landa (in Tozzer 1941: 24n129), Mayapán was occupied for more than 500 years, hinting that its earliest settlement was in the mid-tenth century. The Carnegie excavations recovered scattered Preclassic and Early Classic pottery fragments (Milbrath and Peraza Lope 2003: 3; Smith 1971, 1: 137–141), but the initial occupation that burgeoned into this famous city may have been a small Puuc-related Terminal Classic shrine center around 940–950 near the Itzmal Ch'en Cenote group (Milbrath and Peraza Lope 2003: 8; cf. Peraza Lope et al. 2006, who emphasize the low proportions of Terminal Classic pottery in overall sherd counts). Pottery of this period is affiliated with the western Cehpech sphere, and Terminal Classic Puuc-style architecture (e.g., the distinctive mosaic Chaak masks of Structure Q-151) was later dismantled (Milbrath and Peraza Lope 2003). These western ties suggest that Mayapán may have begun as a Xiw-related settlement.

Textual sources indicate that the early growth of Mayapán was linked to the fall of Chich'en Itza, and this is corroborated by ceramic evidence. According to the *Mani*, the destruction of Chich'en Itza and the downfall of its ruler or chief rain priest, Chaak Xib Chaak, in a K'atun 8 Ajaw (1185–1204) are said to have occurred at the hands of Hunak Keel (Hunac Ceel), the ruler of Mayapán. Pottery from early levels of the Mayapán construction sequence, particularly the black-painted Peto Cream ceramic group, is similar to that found in the upper levels of Chich'en Itza, accompanying its destruction. This has suggested that the same or closely related groups were responsible for both phenomena. Around forty years later, in a K'atun 4 Ajaw (1224–1244), a group of Itza from Chich'en Itza may have avenged the attack by invading Mayapán, an event Milbrath and Peraza Lope (2003: 37) suggest was related to a calendrical dispute and an effort to maintain Chich'en Itza's hegemony as seat of the *may*. Roys (1967: 177–181, 204) interprets both events as a struggle between two factions of Itza.

Indigenous chronicles give prominence to the "founding" of Mayapán but do not agree on dates: the *Tizimin*, for example, says Mayapán was established by (presumably Itza) refugees from Chak'anputun in a K'atun 2 Ajaw (997–1017? 1244–1263?), while the *Chumayel* says the city was established in the next *k'atun*, 13 Ajaw (1017–1037? 1263–1283?) by Itza from Chich'en Itza (Roys 1962: 43, 77; Milbrath and Peraza Lope 2003: 4). Other sources associate the nascence of the city with the "arrival"[3] of the Xiw a cycle or so earlier (discussed in the next section) but do not specify them as founders. The mid-thirteenth-century dates, rather than those in the eleventh century, are generally most widely accepted for the beginning of Mayapán's Late Postclassic peninsular hegemony. Regardless of the differences in dates (see Note 2), the founding refers to Mayapán's becoming a *may* seat dominated by the Itza.

The civic-ceremonial architecture of Mayapán copies that of Chich'en Itza, both having "single-staircase serpent temples, round temples, colon-naded halls," and similar artistic programs (Masson, Hare, and Peraza Lope 2006: 190). Several distinctive structures at Mayapán appear to have been constructed during the early *k'atuns* of turmoil between the Itza and Xiw before the founding events. For example, the first Castillo, a small-scale replica of that at Chich'en Itza, might have been constructed in a K'atun 6 Ajaw (1204–1224) (Milbrath and Peraza Lope 2003), perhaps to celebrate two events: the endings of a Calendar Round in 1217 and of B'ak'tun 11 in 1224. Subsequently, in a K'atun 13 Ajaw, the time of Mayapán's founding according to the *Chumayel*, the earliest round temple, Structure Q-218, was constructed (Milbrath and Peraza Lope 2003: 4), perhaps associated with completion of a Calendar Round in 1269.

The second and final Mayapán Castillo, Structure Q-162, is a radial structure with nine tiers. Like the earlier and larger Castillo at Chich'en Itza, it features a serpent temple on top with exterior and interior structures; the interior structure, facing north, has painted walls and an altar. The plaza floor in front of the Castillo was re-plastered thirteen times, four in association with the earlier structure and nine with the later one (Shook 1954a). Clearly, celebration of each of the thirteen *k'atuns* of the *may* seated at Mayapán occasioned major refurbishing of the main plaza floor.[4]

The city was enclosed by a wall with a nine-kilometer circumference, and its central ceremonial precinct may have been enclosed by another wall. The chronicles refer to the site as "Tankaj Mayapan," which may reference this sacred interior, "inside of which were the temples and the houses of the lords" (Tozzer 1941: 25n131). Sylvanus G. Morley, writing in 1938, noted that nine entrances penetrated the external wall at Mayapán, and nineteen *cenotes* lay within the walled area (in ibid.: 24n131, 25). Edwin Shook (1952: 10), however, identified twelve gates, seven major (one blocked) and five minor.

Although Mayapán's layout has been described as "chaotic" (Proskouriakoff 1954: 102; Brown 1999), upon closer analysis it is evident that site planning was carefully structured. For example, imaginary lines drawn across four of the major gates allowing entrance into the city intersect at the Castillo and divide the site into four quadrants (Brown 1999: 67). As described by Timothy Pugh (2003b: 426), Mayapán represented "an ideal model of the physical and social universe." Although many of its structures were smaller and more poorly constructed copies of prototypes at Chich'en Itza—for example, the Castillo and the Caracol—Mayapán differed most pronouncedly from that earlier *may* seat in lacking ballcourts (Chich'en Itza had thirteen) and *chacmools* (ibid.).

Importantly, Mayapán seems to have revived the Classic practice of erecting stelae to commemorate *k'atun* endings. The third chronicle of the *Chumayel* mentions the erection of "stones" in different towns for each *k'atun*, and thirteen carved stelae have been found at Mayapán (Morley 1920: 574–576; Proskouriakoff 1962a: 134–136). Bishop Landa, writing in the late sixteenth century, noted that in Mayapán's main plaza there were "seven or eight stones, each about ten feet long and rounded on one side, well worked and containing several lines of the characters which they use, and which cannot be read from their having been worn away by water . . . and the natives, when asked about this, reply that they were accustomed to erect one of these stones every twenty years" (in Tozzer 1941: 38–39). All but two of the sculptured stelae were carved in two registers, a glyphic text above a figural scene.

Twenty-five additional monuments have been found at the site, mostly in the main ceremonial group and near other important structures, particularly round buildings such as Structures Q-126 and Q-84 (Proskouriakoff 1962a: 134–137; Milbrath and Peraza Lope 2003: 12). Of the plain monuments, two were erected at the west gate to the city, and some have "an almost pointed, tapering top" (Proskouriakoff 1962a: 135) like those of Puuc sites. The stelae are very difficult to date (Table 2.2) because of erosion, and Tatiana Proskouriakoff (ibid.) contemplated attributing the introduction of the stela cult to the arrival of the Xiw as well as to Uxmal, whose inhabitants also erected stelae on platforms (Milbrath and Peraza Lope 2003: 33). Whatever the source, Mayapán's thirteen-stelae program seems to have emphasized radial/round structures (which may be an Itza rather than a Xiw trait) and carved monument erection to commemorate *k'atun* endings.

Carved Stela 1 gives a date of K'atun 10 Ajaw, which might be either 1165–1185 or 1421–1441. Bruce Love (1994: 11) notes similarities between Mayapán

Table 2.2. Possible dates for Mayapán stelae.

Stela	Ajaw Date	Gregorian Date
5	4 Ajaw	1244
13	2 Ajaw	1263
6	13 Ajaw	1283
Altar	1 Ajaw	1141 or 1401
1	10 Ajaw	1185 or 1441

Source: Andrews, Andrews, and Robles Castellanos 2003: 153; Schele and Mathews 1998: 367.

Stela 1 and the scene on page 11 of the Paris Codex: the lower register shows two figures facing each other, the left one standing on a rectangular platform with a bird above; the right one is seated on an elevated throne. Love favors the later date, near the close of Mayapán's occupation and *may* seating, and believes the Paris Codex was produced in Mayapán around 1450 (Love 1994: 13).

Proskouriakoff (1962a: 132; see Milbrath and Peraza Lope 2003: 35) notes three styles of architecture at Mayapán: "Toltec," Puuc, and "east coastal." The so-called Toltec style is related to the Itza/Kokom of Chich'en Itza; the Puuc style is associated with the Xiw of western Yucatán; and the east coastal style, characterized by colonnaded halls and Peto Cream pottery, might be the earliest. Interestingly, the Kokom and Kupul lineages at Mayapán might have had eastern origins (Milbrath and Peraza Lope 2003: 34, citing Peniche Rivero 1987: 945–946).

The three architectural styles might relate to various arguments (Lincoln 1994) that the political organization of the Postclassic northern lowlands — particularly the so-called League of Mayapán, characterized by "group rule" or "joint government" (*mul tepal*) — was based on agreements among not two (Xiw and Itza) but three major political units/alliances and/or their capitals: Uxmal, Chich'en Itza, and Mayapán. Matthew Restall (1998: 141) suggests that the League of Mayapán was a peace treaty among these three entities that lasted for 200 years, a period Antonio Barrera Vásquez and Morley (1949) date to 997–1194 and Masson (2000) dates to 1000/1100–1200/1300 (Milbrath and Peraza Lope 2003: 24). Milbrath and Peraza Lope (ibid.) associate the league with a period in which "Uxmal and Chich'en Itza were declining and Mayapán was ascending," intervals I would associate with *may* cycling, but of course 200 years does not fit neatly in the ~256-year model. Chich'en Itza declined as a *may* center while Mayapán came to power as a *may* seat between roughly 1050 and 1200.

Regardless of the specific dates of the league, "shared rule" at Mayapán is generally agreed to represent an alliance among numerous (sixteen?) provinces in the Postclassic northern Yucatán peninsula (Map 2.1; Roys 1957). It is unclear to what degree these centers and/or lineages constituted well-defined political units before Mayapán's ceremonial founding or *may* seating. A traditional interpretation is that joint rule at the city was an effort to unite

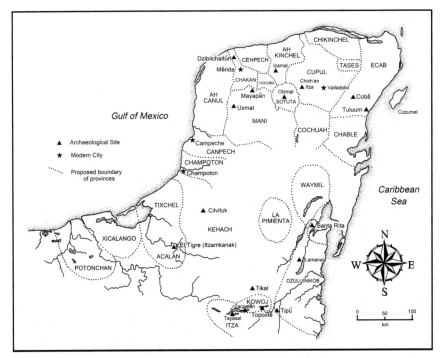

Map 2.1. Indigenous political provinces in Yucatán. After Roys 1957: 2; Edmonson 1982: x; Andrews 1984.

the peninsula's distinct eastern and western cultural spheres. This east-west differentiation is recognizable as early as the Terminal Classic period in the northern peninsula (Robles Castellanos and Andrews 1986: 91) and in ceramic assemblages in Petén (Foias 1996: 572; Rands 1973; Rice and Forsyth 2004; Rice and Rice 2004: 139), where it is also recognized linguistically (Wichmann 2006). However, five of the sixteen territories were only marginally incorporated or not at all: Canpech (Campeche) and Chanputun (Champotón) on the Gulf coast to the southwest, Chikinchel on the north coast, and Ecab and Cozumel on the Caribbean coast to the east (Robles Castellanos and Andrews 1986: 93); a sixth province, Aj Kanul on the northwest coast, may not have existed until after the breakup of Mayapán (see Roys 1957: 11–13, 30). I suspect that these coastal areas remained independent because of their control of lucrative cacao-producing lands and salt beds, plus their key roles in waterborne trade around the peninsula or overland across the base and into Petén. The League of Mayapán, then, might represent an essentially defensive economic alliance of largely land-locked provinces to strengthen their collective negotiating position vis-à-vis coastal groups that controlled trade, salt, and cacao.[5]

New radiocarbon dates (Peraza Lope et al. 2006) support textual evidence that the agreement among the leaders of Mayapán's joint government began disintegrating in the late fourteenth century (K'atuns 3 Ajaw, 1362–1382, and 1 Ajaw, 1382–1402). The Itza/Kokom seem to have strengthened and consolidated their power in K'atun 3 Ajaw, the midpoint of which was a Calendar Round completion, and the earliest effigy censers of Chen Mul Modeled type were recovered under a sealed floor that appears to date to this interval (Milbrath and Peraza Lope 2003: 38; see Masson 2000: 261). Supposedly, the Itza's chief deity or priest, Kukulkan, left Yucatán at this time (Roys 1967: 45–46), an event, whether mythical or real, that doubtless changed the balance of power in their alliance. The succeeding K'atun 1 Ajaw marked a serious schism between the Kokom and the Xiw, although it is not exactly clear what caused it. According to the *Chumayel*, on the last day of a K'atun 3 Ajaw the Itza/Kokom subjected all the head chiefs to obscure questioning in the "language of Zuyua" (Nahuatl? Chontal?).[6] Regardless of whether this was a precipitating event, some Xiw — including the head chief — left Mayapán in K'atun 1 Ajaw, as did some Itza, and the Kokom and Kanul gained greater power.

The Mayapán confederation fell apart in a K'atun 8 Ajaw, 1441–1461, following an uprising against the Kokom led by the remaining Xiw. The Kokom had angered the Xiw for many reasons, among them their leader's apparent agreement to hand over the city to Aztec troops in the garrison at Tabasco and Xicalango (Landa in Tozzer 1941: 32, 36). A Xiw leader, possibly Hunak Keel,[7] conspired with seven other Xiw lords to destroy — perhaps only ritually — the holy *may* seat of Mayapán and its joint leadership. Following these events, Mayapán was largely abandoned and the lineage leaders returned to their home territories, the Itza to Tibolon in Sotuta province and the Xiw to Maní in the province of Maní immediately to the west. This was the situation the Spaniards encountered a half-century later: a strong historical memory of the centralized Mayapán confederacy but the reality of numerous independent provinces throughout the peninsula.

After the fall of Mayapán, Mérida/Mayapán/Xiw/west seated the *may* cycle from 1539 through 1658, at which point the seat shifted to Valladolid/Itza/east. Although this is a period of 120 years, almost half a *may*, it is likely that Mérida, the Maya city of Tihoo, was a *may* seat directly following Mayapán's termination around 1450. There is no mention of *may* seating in Landa's report. The Maya must have kept these calendrical precepts very well hidden from him and other priests, although the latter (e.g., Avendaño) did decipher the geopolitical role of *k'atuns*. Tozzer (1941: 41n206) suggested that after Mayapán fell, there was an "informal alliance between the Xius of Maní and of Uxmal, the Chels of Tecoh, the Pech of Motul and the Cupuls now living in the vicinity of Chichen Itza," with some of these towns possibly *k'atun* seats (Edmonson 1986: 275). Edmonson (1979: 16) suggested that Tixchel (and Tayasal in the south) were also *may* seats. Possible *k'atun* seats in Petén are mentioned almost exclusively in the *Chumayel* and only once in the *Tizimin*. By the mid-sixteenth century, Bishop Landa (in Tozzer 1941: 17–18) commented that northern Yucatán had been "divided into provinces subject to the nearest Spanish towns. The province of Chetumal and Bakalar is subject to Salamanca.

The provinces of Ekab, Cochua and Cupul are subject to Valladolid. Those of Ah Kin Chel, Izamal, Sotuta, Hocabaihomun [Hocaba and Homun], Tutul Xiu, Ceh Pech and Chakan are subject to the City of Mérida. Those of Ah Canul, Campeche, Champotón and Ixchel belong to San Francisco de Campeche."

The Xiw

The western Yucatán peninsula was dominated by peoples referred to in the literature as "Xiw" in the Terminal Classic, Postclassic, and early Colonial periods (Edmonson 1982: xvi). Because there is reason to identify the Kowoj in Colonial-period Petén as having Xiw affiliation if not direct ancestry, it is important to devote some attention to this group.

Among the Maya of Yucatán, the Xiw were generally regarded as "foreigners," with origins in Mexico or a place in contact with Mexico: the "Tutul" or "Toltec" Xiw. The identifier Xiw (or Xiu) is likely from Nahuatl: *xiuh* ('reed') or *xiutl* ('plant, herb, turquoise, blue-green') (Cortez 2002: 203). The Xiw frequently had Nahuatl (Mexican) surnames such as Nahuat or Cuat, although they spoke Yukatekan Maya. Two modern dialects of Yukateko in the western peninsula can probably be linked to Xiw ancestry, one in the northwest around Mayapán and the other in the southwest around Campeche (Hofling, Chapter 4, this volume).

The books of the *chilam b'alams* provide considerable—albeit contradictory—information on the Xiw in Yucatán. Although the Itza-related *Tizimin* claims they arrived in a K'atun 10 Ajaw, the *Maní* states that they were ultimately from a place called Zuyua but stopped in Petén for about 500 years and then arrived at Uxmal in a K'atun 2 Ajaw. Linda Schele and Peter Mathews (1998: 259) place the arrival of the Xiw at Uxmal in 751 (the end of a K'atun 2 Ajaw and the beginning of a 13 Ajaw). If these points—the 751 date, the preceding 500 years in Petén, and the Mexican ancestry—have any historical veracity, they suggest that the Xiw might have been distantly related to central Mexican (Teotihuacano) incursions into Petén in the Early Classic period, around 200–250 (see Stuart 2000). Other interpretations simply claim that the Xiw arrived "from the west," and their original settlement was likely in the Champotón area or farther southwest in the Chontal-speaking region of Tabasco or even Chiapas (Tozzer 1941: 30–40). The Xiw "arrival" in the northern peninsula in the Late or Terminal Classic period coincided with the introduction of new calendars from the Gulf coast (Rice 2004a: 74–75, 239).

The first capital of the Tutul Xiw in Yucatán was established in a K'atun 2 Ajaw, 731–751 (less likely 987–1007), at Uxmal in the Puuc region by an individual named Hunuikilchak, possibly Hun Witzil Chaak or Hun Winkil Chaak (Morley and Brainerd 1956: 148–149; Tozzer 1941: 29–30n159). His wife was from Ticul, in Maní province. From their base at Uxmal, a probable *may* seat, the Tutul Xiw quickly became the principal elite lineage group of western Yucatán.

The Xiw and Itza/Kokom shared rule at Mayapán until 1451 (the middle of a K'atun 8 Ajaw), but their relations were not amicable. A significant incident occurred in a K'atun 1 Ajaw, presumably between 1382 and 1402, when a Xiw revolt against the Kokom resulted in the departure of some Xiw, including the head chief. Recent radiocarbon dating of samples from Carnegie and more recent Instituto Nacional de Antropología e Historia (INAH) excavations at Mayapán has revealed evidence for considerable violence at the city before 1400 and its final collapse, including mass graves and the burning of architecture (Peraza Lope et al. 2006).

For purposes of understanding a Xiw/Kowoj presence in Petén, the destruction of Structure Y-45a, a multi-room elite residence in the south part of the site near the city wall, is informative. Excavation of this structure uncovered debris-filled rooms, with massive quantities of pottery vessels smashed on the floors and offerings burned in the rear rooms, after which the residents abandoned the domicile (Peraza Lope et al. 2006). The calibrated, two-sigma range on a carbon sample recovered over the floor of the passageway of room 2 in Structure Y-45a was 1270–1440 (radiocarbon age 655 ± 30 B.P., with probabilities favoring a one-sigma range of A.D. cal. 1350–1390) (ibid.: 157). This date strongly supports the possibility that the abandonment of this structure was related to the K'atun 1 Ajaw revolt. For us, the key point indicating that Structure Y-45a was likely a Xiw (and, more specifically, a Kowoj-related) residence is the presence of unusually large (for the site) quantities of distinctive decorated pottery stylistically similar to Chompoxté Red-on-cream: Chompoxté variety pottery from Zacpetén and the Topoxté Islands in Petén, which we identify with the Kowoj (see Rice and Cecil, Chapter 11, this volume). Typologically, nineteen of twenty-seven vessels in the structure are Tecoh Red-on-buff and related types Pele Polychrome (black decoration) and Polbox Buff (Masson and Peraza Lope 2005: 414).

The sociopolitical situation in Mayapán after this late-fourteenth-century violence is difficult to ascertain. As discussed, it is thought that the Kokom strengthened their power, ceased erecting carved stelae, and increased the use of effigy censers—perhaps in connection with a new group, the Aj Kanul. According to the *Crónica de Calkini*, the Kanul, like the Xiw, are said to be from Zuyua (Mexico) by way of the Lake Petén Itzá region (Roys 1957: 12), and the appearance of Mexican deities (such as Tlahuizcalpantecuhtli, Tlazolteotl, and Xipe Totec; Milbrath 2007) on censer effigies could indicate Kanul influence (Milbrath and Peraza Lope 2003: 40, citing Pollock 1962: 8). The Xiw in Mayapán may not have been completely silenced, as Milbrath and Peraza Lope (2003: 39) proposed that they reset several damaged monuments (Stelae 5, 6, 7, and 8) on the platform of round temple Structure Q-152. The end of Mayapán came when seven Xiw lords "overthrew" the city and their Itza co-rulers in a K'atun 8 Ajaw, 1441–1461 (Edmonson 1982: 9n119), although this might simply have been the ritual destruction of a *may* seat and its rulers that accompanies the end of a cycle.

Retribution clearly occupied the minds of the Kokom, who decades later exacted their revenge on the Xiw. In 1536 Xiw priests from Maní decided to make a pilgrimage to the rain deities of the *cenote* at Chich'en Itza, east of the Itza-controlled Sotuta province, following a severe drought and famine the previous year. The Xiw leader Ah Dzun Xiw—a great-grandson of Ah Xupan Xiw, who had played a major role in the slaying of the last Kokom ruler of Mayapán—thought it prudent to ask Na Chi Kokom, the Kokom/Itza leader at the capital Tibolon in Sotuta province, for safe passage through Sotuta on the way to Chich'en Itza. Na Chi Kokom granted passage to Ah Dzun Xiw and forty other Xiw leaders/priests, and he and his men met the Xiw group at Otzmal, eight kilometers southeast of Tibolon. After feasting for three days, the Kokom set fire to their guest house, killing nearly all the Xiw (Blom 1928: 253). A second incident occurred not long thereafter, sometime between 1542 and 1545, when three Xiw representatives (Ikeb, Caixicum, and Chuc) accepted an invitation from the Adelantado Francisco Montejo to visit him in Mérida and try to persuade the Kokom to join their side. An embassy of leading Xiw "governors" led by Na Pot Xiw attended a banquet in Otzmal, which ended with the Xiw ambassadors being blinded and returning to Mérida (ibid.; Morley 1920: 482–484). These events certainly encouraged the Xiw to ally with the Spaniards against the Itza/Kokom.

During early Colonial times the Xiw capital was Tiho (also seen as T'ho, Tihoo, Ichcanzihoo), modern-day Mérida, in Maní province. In contrast to the Itza-related or -descended groups in the east, the Xiw were initially "benevolently neutral" toward the Spaniards and, because of their proximity to centers of Spanish control in the western peninsula, more hispanicized than the Itza. By 1542, however, after the Otzmal massacre, the Xiw ruler's adoption of Christianity, and the establishment of Mérida as the Spanish Colonial capital, they and the other western provinces (Chel, Pech) became active allies (Roys 1957: 63). Nonetheless, they continued to observe traditional Maya calendar ceremonies, holding *may* and *b'ak'tun* celebrations in Mérida in 1539 and 1618, respectively (Edmonson 1982, 1985, 1986).

Doubtless because of their close association with the Spaniards, the Xiw produced two surviving European-style pictorial documents, a "family tree" and a "coat of arms." These were created by Gaspar Antonio Chi, an educated young man whose mother was Xiw and who spoke Yukateko Mayan, Nahuatl, Spanish, and Latin (Cortez 2002: 201–202; Blom 1928). The Xiw family tree shows various branches of the family line emerging from the loins of the ancestor Tutul Xiw in a picture that depicts their heritage in the manner of a Christian religious icon but also employs considerable Aztec imagery (Cortez 2002: 206). Constance Cortez (ibid.: 213n1) suggests that it was probably produced around 1558–1560 in connection with the 1557 Maní Land Treaty, accompanying documentation of the ancestral boundaries of Xiw territory to justify to the Spaniards their long-standing claim on the land.

The "coat of arms" shows thirteen human heads representing some of the Xiw priests and nobles killed by the Kokom on their 1536 pilgrimage, arranged in the convention of a *k'atun* wheel (Blom 1928; Cortez 2002: 209–210). Those pictured include Ah Na Pot Xiw (their leader), Zon Kej, Ajaw Tuyu, Xul Cumche, Tucuch, Kit Couat Chumalel, Yluac Chan, Nauat, Kupul, Kan Caba, Pacaj, Yiban Can, and Aj K'in Chi—Gaspar Antonio Chi's father—who had an arrow shot through his eye (Blom 1928; Cortez 2002: 209–210).

Table 2.3. Comparison of calendars and calendrical rituals in Postclassic northern Yucatán.

	Edmonson		*Revised*	
	A	B	C	D
	Xiw	Itza	Xiw	Itza
Calendar	"Classic"			"Classic"
Beginning	6 Ajaw	11 Ajaw	13 Ajaw	6 Ajaw
End	8 Ajaw	13 Ajaw	11 Ajaw	8 Ajaw
Naming	End (8 Ajaw)	Beg. (11 Ajaw)	Beg. (13 A.*)	End (8 A.)
Yearb.[†]				Ix (46)
Ritual	YB, Cal. Round	K'atuns	K'atuns	Cal. Round

* According to Cortez (2002: 211), in the books of *Chumayel* and *Kaua*, the *k'atun* wheel begins with a cross in a K'atun 13 Ajaw.
[†] See Hofling, Chapter 4, this volume, Table 4.1i.
Source: K'atun dates are taken from the *Chumayel* and the *Tizimin*.

Calendrical Disagreements between the Itza and Xiw

Disagreements raged concerning the nature of the calendar in Postclassic northern Yucatán, as the Itza and the Xiw observed different calendrical instruments and rituals. The naming of *k'atuns* by their endings on K'atuns 8 Ajaw, previously described, was a long-standing practice from Classic times (the "Tikal calendar"). According to Edmonson's (1982, 1985, 1986, 1988) reconstruction of Postclassic calendars and associated rituals in Yucatán, the Xiw (and also the Itza in Petén) adhered to the Classic calendar, naming *k'atuns* by their *ending* days in K'atuns 8 Ajaw; that is, their thirteen-*k'atun* cycles ran from K'atun 6 Ajaw through the end of K'atun 8 Ajaw. The Itza in Yucatán, in contrast, counted *k'atuns* from their *initial* dates beginning in a K'atun 11 Ajaw, and their cycles closed in K'atuns 13 Ajaw: "13 Ahau was the ordering of the mat," or the time of reorganization of geopolitical order (Edmonson 1986: 51). His reconstruction can be seen in columns A and B of Table 2.3.

Edmonson (1982: 48n927) claims that Itza calendrical rituals, like those of the Classic Maya, emphasized *tuns* and *k'atuns*, but my reconstruction of Itza and Chich'en Itza history suggests that major events coincided with the celebration of fifty-two-year Calendar Rounds. The Xiw, while adhering to the Tikal calendar, are also said to have emphasized yearbearers and the Calendar Round (Edmonson 1982: 927), perhaps true to their "Mexican" origins. But the *k'atun* dates given for events (Table 2.4), such as the arrival of various groups and the establishment of major centers (or seating of *mays*), do not seem to correspond to the purported affiliations of the lineage groups (see Note 2). In addition, the *Chumayel* mentions the Itza more than the *Tizimin* does, but in disparaging ways. All this leads me to wonder if the *Chumayel* could have been produced by a dissident faction of Itza who observed more Xiw-like calendrical practices and were opposed to a *Tizimin*/Kokom faction.

The contradictions within the prophetic histories in dating major events suggest that calendrical practices in Postclassic and Colonial Yucatán were

Table 2.4. Dating of major events in Postclassic Yucatán (by K'atuns Ajaw) in the books of the *chilam b'alams*.

	Tizimin	*Chumayel*	*Maní*
Arrival of Itza		K6A begin?	K11A
Chich'en Itza established	K8A end		
Mayapán established	K2A end	K13A begin?	

more complicated than the simple binary distinction of Xiw vs. Itza/Kokom. One contributing factor would have been the repeated "arrivals" of groups such as the Xiw and the Itza among existing populations in the northern peninsula. The factionalism in northern Yucatán, with the accompanying formation and dissolution of alliances, makes it likely that by the Colonial period, if not by the time of Mayapán's earlier florescence, varied calendrical beliefs and rituals were practiced that did not fall into two dichotomous sets. Multiple groups of Kokom/Itza lineages were likely involved in the destruction of Chich'en Itza and the founding of Mayapán, and multiple groups of Xiw-affiliated elites likely existed at Mayapán—some of whom were involved in the K'atun 1 Ajaw revolt against the Kokom and some of whom remained at a distance. The most elite of the Xiw were probably the Tutul Xiw, as this is the name of the apparent founding lineage and also the title of its leader (see Note 7), but other *ch'ib'als*, or patronym groups—including the Kowoj—seem to have been aligned with the Tutul Xiw. One wonders, then, if these different lineages, participating in various cabals and intrigues over the centuries of the Postclassic period, might have co-opted certain calendrical beliefs and practices as their charters for action. Along these lines, I suspect that two of the supposedly Xiw-allied books of the *chilam b'alams*, *Chumayel* and *Maní*, for example, are products of two different Xiw families—the *Maní* more likely associated with the Tutul Xiw and the *Chumayel* with a group of Xiw aligned with a faction of Itza (or Itza allied with Xiw).

Xiw-Itza disagreements about initial versus terminal naming and K'atun 8 Ajaw versus K'atun 11 Ajaw cycling simmered throughout the Postclassic period. A conference in 1539 resulted in a new "Mayapán calendar," which represented compromises on several issues. According to Edmonson, the Xiw (or certain factions of them) agreed to abandon the practice of counting months beginning with 0 and terminating cycles with K'atuns 8 Ajaw, and the Itza (or factions) accepted the Xiw pattern of initial dating of the *k'atun* and *may* (but still used terminal dates for the *winal, tun,* and *b'ak'tun*). Thus, the new Mayapán calendar used a count of 1 to 20 for days of the month, *k'atuns* and the *may* were counted forward and named for their first day, and a new *may* cycle was seated beginning on 11 Ajaw 7 Wo (Edmonson 1988: 127, 202). In addition, "new" yearbearers were adopted—K'an, Muluk, Ix, and Kawak. Hofling (Chapter 4, this volume) notes that Ix (or Hix) appears forty-six times in the *Tizimin* and only two in the *Chumayel*. About a century after the Mayapán calendar was adopted, the Christianized Xiw abandoned *k'atun* seating, and presumably its politico-economic entailments, following the K'atun 1 Ajaw of 1638–1658.

Colonial-period sources in Yucatán record that the Maya celebrated the completion of *k'atuns, mays,* and *b'ak'tuns* with extravagant ceremonies. Edmonson (1985, 1986: 21–29, chapters 12 and 29) describes these as historico-mythological "dramas" in multiple "acts" performed over several days and including processions of masked and costumed actors, banquets, speeches and recitations, sacrifice, recognition of ranks and titles, and other activities. In 1618 the Xiw celebration of the ending of the twelfth *b'ak'tun* (of 400 *tuns,* or 394 solar years) in Mérida, in their home province of Maní, consisted of 20 acts (recall 20 *k'atuns* in a *b'ak'tun*); the earlier turning of the *may* in 1539 in Mérida paralleled that of the *b'ak'tun* except that it took place in 13 acts (13 *k'atuns* in a *may*).

Despite the initiation of the Mayapán compromise calendar, calendrical disputes continued to fester. In the Valladolid calendar proposed in 1752, Itzá priests maneuvered to establish 24-year *k'atuns,* thus allowing them to rule longer (Edmonson 1988: 263; cf. Milbrath and Peraza Lope 2003). This calendar ceased active usage in 1848 (Edmonson 1982: 11), as by then most of the Maya populace followed the Julian and, later, the Gregorian calendars with 365-day years.

These fundamental and long-simmering internal ideological conflicts could only have been exacerbated by the tensions of dealing with the Spaniards and their demands for conversion to Catholicism and abolition of the Maya's idolatrous ways. From their heartland in Sotuta province, however, the Kokom/Itza and the people of the other eastern provinces of Yucatán (Cupul, Cochuah, Sotuta, Chetumal, Tases), plus the Itza occupying the Petén lakes area of Guatemala, remained hostile to the Spaniards and vigorously opposed the idea of conversion.

Ethno-Political Groups in Petén: The Itza and Kowoj

The Petén Itza

Sparse but critical evidence reveals centuries of close connections between the Itzaj speakers of Petén and the Itza of Yucatán, and the Postclassic Itza likely had their original home in central Petén in the Classic period. Epigraphic studies (e.g., Boot 1995, 1997, 2005; Schele, Grube, and Boot 1995; Schele and Mathews 1998) reveal that the name or title Kan Ek' appears on Seibal Stelae 10 and 11 (A.D. 849) and on Yaxchilán Stela 10 (766). This name/title is the same one used by the ruler of the Petén Itza capital of Taiza/Nojpeten in 1525, 1618–1619, and 1697 — the last claiming descent from Chich'en Itza; and the name/title Kan Ek' also appears in inscriptions in the Great Ballcourt at Chich'en Itza. The title K'ul Itza Ajaw ("divine Itza lord") appears on Late Classic Stela 1 from Motul de San José, on the northwest shore of Lake Petén Itzá, raising the possibility that "Itza" was a toponym (e.g., Voss 1999: *itz' ja* 'watery place'). In addition, a text on a looted Classic polychrome vessel identifies its owner as a *yune Itza ahaw* 'child of the Itza lord' (Schele and Mathews

1998: 203). Because the name/title Kan Ek' and the Itza Ajaw title appear in Chich'en Itza inscriptions, this group was likely part of an Itza migration from Petén to that city around A.D. 672 to 692 (Boot 1995: 337; Schele and Mathews 1998: 187–203).

Erik Boot (1995: 337) proposed "an Itsa heartland in the Central Petén . . . [bounded by] Tikal in the north, to the southwest at Lake Peten and Motul de San Jose, to the south in which Dos Pilas and Seibal are situated, further to the southeast to Naj Tunich, up to the northeast to Ucanal." Boot's reconstruction is supported by the Terminal Classic introduction of architectural forms that later dominated in the Postclassic and Colonial periods in the lakes region (D. Rice 1986), regardless of the social identity and settlement history of whoever constructed the buildings. Although these forms have not been found in association with glyphic references to the Itza or to Kan Ek', their earlier occurrence in the Petexbatun-Pasión region (Demarest 2004, pers. com. 2003), plus the presence of Pasión-related ceramics in the western lakes region in the Terminal Classic period (Rice 1987a: 63–89), support this zone as a source for these innovations.

Linguistic evidence lends additional credence to the idea of Itza origins in Petén. The Contact-period Itza in Petén spoke Itzaj Maya, a dialect of Yukatekan that may have begun to differentiate as early as ca. A.D. 1000 (Hofling 2002, 2006a, Chapter 4, this volume). Fray Avendaño y Loyola observed that the dialect of the Itzaj in Petén was different from, and more conservative than, that of the Itza in northern Yucatán (Avendaño y Loyola 1987: 44; Jones 1998: 427; Schwartz 1990: 61). It is indeed the case that Itzaj shares a number of features of verbal morphology with early Colonial Yukateko that were lost by later northern Yukateko speakers. Nonetheless, modern Petén Itzaj ethnobotanical terms are Yukatekan (Atran 1993).

The outline of Itza history in the *Tizimin* recounts, albeit with some dating imprecision, a series of migrations apparently ending in Petén (Boot 2005; Edmonson 1982). According to this chronicle, the Itza established Chich'en Itza as their "capital" city, or *may* seat, in a K'atun 8 Ajaw in the late seventh century. They ruled there for 256 years until they were overthrown by the Xiw and the site was ritually terminated. At that point, some Itza fled to Chak'an Putun, apparently an existing Itza settlement in the south, where they ruled for another 256 years. Considerable disagreement exists about the location of Chak'an Putun, and it is frequently thought to be the location of modern Champotón on the southwestern coast of Campeche. Given the possibility of a Classic-period Itza "heartland" in the Petén lakes region, however, this toponym may refer to the large savanna area (*chak'an* 'savanna') south of Lake Petén Itzá or to the smaller patches of grassland on that lake's north shore. This latter location is of interest in light of late factionalism in central Petén: it suggests an early Itza occupation of the Chak'an Itza community known in the seventeenth century as the home of an Itza faction allied with the Kowoj against Ajaw Kan Ek', who was of the Chich'en Itza faction of Itza (Jones 1998: 430n18). Wherever the location of Chak'an Itza, this early in-migration likely resulted in the seating of a *may* cycle in Petén.

In the early thirteenth century Chak'an Putun was ritually destroyed, and the Itza there claim to have returned to Chich'en Itza. According to the *Chumayel*, however, Chich'en Itza was again overthrown (in a K'atun 8 Ajaw) by Xiw from Mayapán, and the Itza were forced to flee once more. This time they went to the heart of the forest, to Tan Xuluk Mul, the precise location of which is not known. Literally translated — *tan* 'first', *xuluk* 'remnant', *mul* 'mound' — it might mean "first (or front) ? mound." The *Diccionario Maya* identifies Xulukmul as a toponym in Cehpech province, but it does not appear on Roys's (1957: 40) map. The "heart of the forest" and Tan Xuluk Mul are traditionally viewed as being in the Lake Petén Itzá region. Friar Avendaño y Loyola identified a pond named Tanxulukmul "not far north of the western end of Lago Petén Itzá" (cited in Jones 1998: 10), thus raising the possibility that it lies near an old trail that eventually became the north-south road between Campeche and Petén. Edmonson (1982: 104n2698) suggested it might refer to a place "in the middle of the water," such as the Tayasal peninsula in Lake Petén Itzá. Support for such an interpretation comes from Arlen Chase's (1990) summary of the population history of the Tayasal-Paxcamán zone, which suggests a large population increase sometime after 1200. The Itza of Petén identified themselves as the *Xuluk*, "the remnant of the Itza" (Edmonson 1986: 38), suggesting that Tan Xuluk Mul might mean "first Itza mound/town." Tan Xuluk Mul was recorded as a Late Postclassic *k'atun* seat in the *Chumayel* in 1441 and 1461 (Edmonson 1986: 275–276), indicating that it was a relatively important town.

As recounted earlier, in the early to mid-thirteenth century some group of Kokom/Itza joined with the Xiw in "founding" Mayapán and ruling it jointly until another K'atun 8 Ajaw, 1441–1461, when Xiw leaders overthrew the Itza. Some Itza fled south to the Petén lakes area, where they became known as the Petén Itza and established (or perhaps reestablished) their capital on the "great island" of Nojpeten. Here they became powerful politico-religious leaders, with Tayasal a *may* seat in 1480 (Edmonson 1979: 16).

The first references to and descriptions of the Itza of Petén come from Hernán Cortés, who stopped briefly among them in spring of 1525. His guides from Acalan told him the province was called Tayça, and its capital was on a small island in a "very large lake which seemed to be an arm of the sea" (Cortés 1986: 373). Bernal Díaz, writing long after the actual journey, referred to the island capital as Tayasal (cited in Jones 1998: 429n9). Both are apparently hispanicizations of *ta* (or *ti-aj*) *itza* 'at the place of the Itza' (ibid.). We are not told what the people called themselves, their capital city, or their territory. In 1698 the Itza ruler referred to their capital as Nojpeten (ibid.: 7), and the Spaniards provided descriptions of the city, which included reference to between nine and twenty-one houses of idolatry. The principal temple, described as a *castillo*, was square in plan, about 16.5 meters on a side, with nine tiers and facing north (ibid.: 74, 99),[8] thus making it almost a replica of the Castillos at Chich'en Itza and Mayapán. Itza territory was called Suyuja Peten Itza, "whirlpool of the province of the sacred-substance water" (ibid.: 7, 427–429n8), which seems to be a ritual name or title, perhaps designating its status as a *may* seat. It might be more appropriate to refer to these "Lake Petén Maya" (Thompson 1977) and their territory as the Kan Ek', in the same way the Tutul Xiw and their territory seem to have been identified by the name of their founding lineage leader (Blom 1928: 254).[9]

Jones's (1998: 60–107) reconstruction of the seventeenth-century geopolitical organization of the Kan Ek' conforms closely to the *may* model I have proposed for the Classic Maya (Rice 2004a). That is, the island capital seated the *may* for the kingdom, which was divided into four quarters. Ajaw Kan Ek' and other senior elites governed alongside a ruling council of thirteen members, each with the title Ach Kat, who were the heads of the thirteen *k'atun* seats in the Itza territory and also military captains. This dual role of the Itza Ach Kats clarifies the dual meaning of the word *k'atun* itself, which refers both to a twenty-year calendrical interval and to war or warrior.

As Jones (Chapter 3, this volume) comments, the "maturity" of this geopolitical organization suggests that the "Itza" had been in the area for a long time, a point echoed by Hofling (Chapter 4, this volume) in discussing the background of the Itzaj language. These observations support the scant epigraphic data that suggest a background for Itza/Kan Ek' in the Petén lakes region. Given this long history, plus the frequent in-migrations of various Itza-related (and other) groups from the northern lowlands, it is not surprising that by the late seventeenth century numerous factions were pursuing different, often contradictory interests in the face of the threats to political and religious autonomy posed by the invading Spaniards.

For example, the Petén "Itza" acted aggressively to thwart development of alliances between their neighbors and the Spaniards, and they were renowned for their ferocity in dealing with enemies, Maya and Spaniard. In the 1630s (note that 1633 was a Calendar Round completion) they promoted rebellion among the Maya living in Franciscan mission towns in central Belize, uprooting them and forcing them to resettle in a single town, Tipu, "which became in essence an Itza colony" (Jones 1998: 58, also 1989). Similarly, in 1694, as the Spanish arrival in the Petén lakes area was imminent, the Petén Itza raided Kan Itzam, a *reducción* (settlement congregation) founded by Franciscan missionaries in 1671 in the area of Tenosique, Tabasco.

The Petén Itza fiercely resisted conversion to Catholicism. Although the first Xiw to convert did so in 1542, the first Petén Itza lord to adopt Catholicism, Cap Wah of Tayasal, did not convert until 1611 (Edmonson 1982: xviii). This did not play well back home:

> Then there was the enslavement of Cap Uah of Tayasal, causing dissension, and the priests ended the ceremony by inaugurating Uuc Het in 1611. Back in exile with a Spanish saint to protect the lake, abandoned by the Maya lords, Cap Uah spread the new religion and new calendar and customs, destroying the wooden idols of 11 Ajaw and destroying even the metal idols, because of two days' drinking and a riot. And when they got back to the towns and villages the respected nobles were seized and beaten. The return of the Itza was a disaster. They suffered penance in fulfillment of the oath of office but also at the desire of the villages. (Edmonson 1982: 104–105)

In the late 1690s, Ajaw Kan Ek' contemplated capitulation to the Spaniards' unremitting demands for conversion, but his advisers strongly pressured him against such action (see Jones, Chapter 3, this volume). Significantly, Ajaw Kan Ek''s most violent opponents, the Kowoj, were relatives: Kan Ek''s nephew — the son of his older sister in Chich'en Itza — was married to the daughter of Aj Kowoj. In addition, K'in Kante, Kan Ek''s uncle and ruler of Chak'an Itza on the northwestern lake shore, was an ally of Aj Kowoj. These internal disagreements and vacillations at the highest levels ultimately contributed to the final conquest of the Itza.

The Kowoj

We are aware of the existence of a people known as Kowoj in Petén primarily from Spanish writings of the seventeenth and later centuries, but what are their origins? Surprisingly little is known archaeologically or historically about the Kowoj in Yucatán. Part of the reason for the lack of historical understanding of the Kowoj may be the inconsistent orthography of early Spanish writers and Spanish-language transcriptions of indigenous literature, in which the Kowoj were referenced as Couoh, Co Uoh, Cohuoj, Covoh, Cobox, Coboje, and perhaps also Col Ox, Colox, and Colah. *Co uoh* has been translated as "beak glyph" (Edmonson 1986: 287); *uoh/woj* is "glyph," but *coh* or *cooh* may be "puma." The most common translation of *couoh* (Yuk.) is "spider, tarantula;" in Ch'olan, "tarantula" is *chiwo*.[10]

Sir J. Eric Thompson, in his proposal to constitute a "Chan Maya subgroup" in Petén, raised several interesting possibilities about the origins of the Kowoj. One is that they were an aboriginal group in Petén "conquered by the immigrant Itza rulers" (Thompson 1977: 24). He also suggested that "Couoh was a Chan name which may have been introduced to Yucatán by immigrants" from Petén (ibid.: 24–25). It is possible that the Kowoj had origins in the Classic period in Petén, as did the Itzá; recall, for example, the claim in *The Chilam Balam of Maní* that the Xiw came into Yucatán after spending 500 years in Petén (Craine and Reindorp 1979). Although I know of no Classic texts in Petén attesting a "Kowoj" glyphic collocation, it is possible that the Kowoj only came to be strongly differentiated by that *ch'ib'al* patronymic identifier during the Postclassic period or later, in the same way the Kokom came to be distinguished.[11]

The Kowoj are mentioned three times in the *Chumayel*: (1) as guardian of Mayapán's East Gate at the end of a K'atun 11 Ajaw; (2) as one of four *jolpops* (*jol* 'head,' *pop* 'mat') of the south in a ceremony of the *ja'ab'*, the 365-day year; and (3) in the context of bemoaning the internal conspiracies among various Maya groups (Edmonson 1986: 81, 106, 109). These references are of interest because the Kowoj cannot be clearly identified with any of the allied provinces whose rulers resided at Mayapán. Nonetheless, multiple lines of evidence suggest that they were affiliated with the Xiw in sixteenth-century (and earlier) Yucatán. One comes from the account of the Itza massacre of Xiw rain priests at Otzmal in 1536. *The Chilam Balam of Oxcutzcab* states that "[t]he year 1537 [sic], 8 Cauac on the first of Pop (current), the water throwers died there at Otzmal. They account for the Head of the Toltec Xiu and Ah Ziyah, Na Puc Chi and Na May Che and Na May Tun and the curer Euan Ha . . . people there at Maní who were rain pilgrims to Chichen Itza. There escaped Na Ahau Pech and Na Pot Couoh exactly on 10 Zip" (in Edmonson 1988: 73, citing Morley 1920). The general conclusion has been that everyone in the Xiw party was killed, but this passage suggests two individuals survived, one having a Kowoj (Couoh) patronym. He may have gathered family members and others and fled to Petén or to another sympathetic territory.

Although the Kowoj were one of the major families in sixteenth-century Ebtun, in the southern Cupul province east of Chich'en Itza (see Roys 1939), the southwestern peninsula seems to have had the most significant historical relations with the Kowoj. This is particularly true of the provinces of Champotón and Campeche, which remained independent of the Late Postclassic Mayapán confederacy, and adjacent Acalan-Tixchel. In 1517 the Spanish explorer Francisco Hernández de Córdoba left the new Spanish settlement on Cuba and sailed around the northern and western coasts of the Yucatán peninsula, where he encountered the "great town" of Champotón and its ruler named Mochcovoh (Moch Kowoj) (Tozzer 1941: 9–13). The Spaniards needed to take on fresh water for drinking, but Moch Kowoj would not let them do so, and a battle ensued. Despite the ostensible advantage of the Spaniards' metal weapons, Córdoba and his forces were defeated by the Kowoj. The following year an expedition led by Juan de Grijalva sailed around the western coast of the Yucatán peninsula and attempted to land at Champotón, but they too were fiercely opposed by the Kowoj.

A small sixteenth-century settlement in the Acalan-Tixchel region is called Chiuoha (Benavides and Mirambell 1991: 103), possibly Chiwo-ha 'water/lake of the Chiwo/Kowoj.' It is described as a small *aldea* of Chontal speakers who were not catechized (ibid.), lying on the boundary between Maya and Chontal speakers and perhaps east of the Río Mamantel (ibid.: 107). In central Petén a late community south of Lake Sacnab is given as Chinoha (Jones 1998: 65, 368–370), possibly a mistranscription of Chiuoha. In southern Campeche, one Na Pol Kowoj was a cacique, or chief, of a village west of Isla Pac, just north of Kejach territory (Thompson 1977: 24, citing Scholes and Roys 1968: 505). Kowoj is also a surname among the Lacandon (Thompson 1977: 18).

Later commentary suggests a linguistic distinction: Tozzer (1941: 17n95) quotes Ciudad Real, who wrote in 1588, in noting that the inhabitants of Yucatán spoke "a language called *Mayathan* or *Maya* language, except those of *Campeche* who differ in some words and call their language *Campechthan* or language of *Campeche*." The latter might indicate that a modern Yukateko dialect in the southwestern peninsula around Campeche (see Hofling, Chapter 4, this volume) may be linked to Xiw/Kowoj ancestry.

It is not clear to what extent the Kowoj of Petén and the Kowoj of Champotón/Campeche and elsewhere in Yucatán were in contact with each other, although it seems reasonable to surmise that there was considerable interaction. In the seventeenth century the Kowoj of Campeche were still recognized as one of the most important ruling lineages in Yucatán (Benavides and Mirambell 1991: 68–69), and a Spanish Mercedarian priest in Petén noted that it was "the refuge of trouble-making Christian Indians from the province of Campeche" (cited in Jones 1998: 333). This is of no little interest, given that so many Spanish expeditions directed toward pacification of the Maya in Petén embarked from Campeche. There were doubtless factions of Kowoj: those in Campeche who had voluntarily or by force submitted to Christianity, and those in Petén who strongly opposed conversion.

The reference in the *Chumayel* to the Kowoj being a guardian (*kanul*) of one of Mayapán's gates in a K'atun 11 Ajaw raises the question whether it was the *k'atun* ending in 1303 or in 1539. Edmonson (1986) appears to believe it references the latter, but I argue the former for two reasons. First, Tecoh Red-on-buff pottery at Mayapán displays painted banded and curvilinear decoration remarkably similar to that on Chompoxté Red-on-cream: Chompoxté variety, common in the Postclassic deposits at the Topoxté Islands in Lake Yaxhá and their settlement by Xiw-related Kowoj. Second, as discussed, recent excavations at Mayapán Structure Y-45a, an elite residence in the south part of the site near the city wall, revealed unusually large quantities of this pottery. This structure, which appears to have been abandoned at the time of the K'atun 1 Ajaw revolt, not only seems to have been an area of possible Kowoj occupation but may support the statement that the Kowoj were *jolpops* of the south. Finally, small but significant quantities of Tecoh Red-on-buff pottery were found in excavations at civic-ceremonial structures at the epicenter of Mayapán (pers. obs.). This suggests that the Kowoj had some degree of prestige and longevity in northern Yucatán as opposed to being mere arrivistes.

The *Chumayel* also relates that in a K'atun 4 Ajaw, perhaps 1224–1244 (Edmonson 1986: 57–58), "there occurred the overthrow of Chichen of the Itzas" in Yucatán, and four new capitals (*may* seats) were named:

Four Parts [*tzuk*] they raised:
Four-Part Country was their name.
Arising in the east, Kin Colah Peten
Became one part.
Arising in the north, Na Cocob appeared
As one part.
And then there appeared one part
At Hol Tun Zuyua
In the west.
There appeared one part
At Can Hek Uitz:
Bolon Te Uitz was the name of that land.
4 Ahau
Was the *katun* period
When there occurred
Their separating into four parts. (Edmonson 1986: 57–58)

I read this passage as a description of the early-thirteenth-century establishment (or, more correctly, renewal) of Maya quadripartite political organization based on the cardinal or inter-cardinal directions and an indication that two of the four capitals were to be in Petén.[12] In the east, the capital and its ritual leader, or *k'in* ("sun priest; daykeeper"), was K'in Colah (Kowoj?) Peten. This corresponds to the distribution of key archaeological indicators of Kowoj identity — temple assemblages and Clemencia Cream Paste (Chompoxté Red-on-cream) ware pottery — in the eastern lakes region and at Tipu in Belize. In counterclockwise order, the capital in the north is Na Cocob, or "house of Kokom," established at Mayapán. In the west, the capital was Hol Tun Zuyua, which Edmonson (1988: 234) translates as "gate of bloody water"; Thompson (1970: 23) translates *holtun* as "harbor" and suggests it might refer to the Campeche region. And although it is not specified as the southern capital, Can Hek Uitz in the land of Bolon Te Uitz[13] can be inferred to be such from the context, as Kan Ek' Witz, or Kan Ek''s Mountain. Tayasal Structure T-65, an extremely tall mound on the western tip of the peninsula, retains the toponym "Cerro Kan Ek'" and is visited regularly by tourists who want a sweeping vista of the lake basin. I see this passage as indicating that by the early thirteenth century(?) there was a recognized geopolitical unit identified with the Kowoj (and also the Itza) in Petén.

One *may* cycle later, in the early sixteenth century, two *k'atun* seats likely to have been in Petén were identified in the *Chumayel* (Edmonson 1986: 275): Kin Colah Peten (in 1500 and 1539) and Colox Peten in 1539. I suggest that Colox and Colah are different orthographies indicating the group known as the Kowoj. A passage in the *Chumayel* relates that in "11 Ahau, the new base year, Col Ox Peten got its *tun* period." Edmonson (1986: 63) interprets this "new base year" as referring to the year 1539, when the compromise calendar of the Xiw and Itza began. I agree, but I add that this year in the early mid-sixteenth century was when the Kowoj (or Col Ox) of Petén came into power by "getting its *tun* period," that is, seating the *may* (see also ibid.: 276). This relates to the Kowoj claim of "arriving" in Petén in the early mid-sixteenth century, which likely refers to their arrival "in power" or their re-seating of the *may* (see Note 3). In sum, I suggest that Topoxté and Zacpetén were the *k'atun* seats Kin Colah Peten and/or Colox Peten in 1500 and 1539. Further, I propose that two capitals identified in the prophetic histories were in Petén: one was a Kowoj-related capital in the east, and the other was an Itza-related capital (Nojpeten/Tayasal) in the west.

Given these speculations based on scant historical records for the Postclassic period in Petén, the origins of the Kowoj can be more confidently investigated from a different perspective, that of material culture. The Xiw/Kowoj appear to have introduced Mayapán-style temple assemblages in the eastern part of the lakes region, because all evidence available to us thus far suggests that such architectural complexes do not exist in Itza territory in western Petén. If my reading of the *Chumayel* is correct and "Kin Colah Peten" became a *may* seat and geopolitical capital in the early thirteenth century, and if Topoxté is Kin Colah Peten, then that means the first construction phase of its temple assemblage would have begun then.

A slight variant of this scenario is based on the hypothesis that *k'atun* and *may* seats were selected at the half period before they actually came into power (Rice 2004a: 111–115). Thus, if a *may* seat came into power in 1204, it would have been elected into this role half a *may*, or 128 years, earlier. It is possible that the *Chumayel* passage refers not to the seating of the *may* itself but rather to the election of four new *may* seats that were to take office around 128 years later. In this particular case, because the naming of the new capitals occurred five *k'atuns* early (or perhaps eight *k'atuns* late?) in a K'atun 4 Ajaw instead of the traditional mid-*may* K'atun 7 Ajaw, this might be a way of explaining the earlier initiation of temple assemblages at Mayapán and their mimesis in Petén.

Regardless, it is evident from Mayapán that the Postclassic Maya in Yucatán refurbished temple floors every *k'atun* within a *may* cycle, as there are thirteen plastering events in the plaza in front of the Castillo at that city (Note 4). Similarly, they seem to have constructed and then later reconstructed the structures: the Castillos at Chich'en Itza and Mayapán appear to have had two major phases of construction (Milbrath and Peraza Lope 2003), as do the temple assemblages at Topoxté (Wurster 2000) and at Zacpetén (Pugh 2001; Pugh and Rice, Chapter 7, this volume). I expect that these were constructed initially to commemorate their cities' respective *may* seatings and then were reconstructed and refurbished at the half-*may* as a rededication to the principles of cosmic cycling.

In sum, the late-seventeenth-century occupants of eastern Petén known as Kowoj have poorly understood origins. People with the surname Kowoj were known in various places in Colonial-period Yucatán, particularly in the Champotón-Campeche region lying outside the Mayapán confederacy. Some Kowoj were present at Mayapán, and we conclude that the Kowoj represented one of several lineages affiliated with the Xiw in the northern peninsula, in growing enmity toward the Itza. In 1699 a Kowoj informant told Spanish captain Marcos de Abalos y Fuentes that they had migrated from Mayapán at the time of the conquest, meaning sometime in the first several decades of the sixteenth century. We suspect, however, that these might have been one of the last of a group of Kowoj-Xiw–related migrants to Petén and that these movements had occurred at least since the late fourteenth century. In particular, the occupants of Mayapán Structure Y-45a likely had some affiliations with the Kowoj/Xiw lineages of Petén, on the basis of ceramic stylistic similarities, and they might even have been of the Kowoj lineage. This structure was abandoned during late-fourteenth-century rebellion (in K'atun 1 Ajaw, 1382–1401), and it is not unlikely that the inhabitants and others fled to Petén. In this regard, it is significant that the mass grave at Zacpetén (see Duncan, Chapter 15, this volume) has a radiocarbon date of 1389–1437 (1-sigma) from a charcoal stratum underlying the human remains, and the perimortem violence evident on the bones signals conflict between the residents and the newcomers.

Notes

1. Each quarter had an associated color: east, red; north, white; west, black; south, yellow; and center, blue-green.

2. Similarly, the Itza *Tizimin* says Chich'en Itza was established by the Itza in a K'atun 8 Ajaw, but the supposedly Xiw *Chumayel* claims the Itza arrived in the next *k'atun*, a K'atun 6 Ajaw. The "founding" of Mayapán is placed in a K'atun 2 Ajaw by the *Tizimin* but in the next *k'atun*, K'atun 13 Ajaw, according to the *Chumayel*. The discrepancy between the *Chumayel* and *Tizimin* dating has not been satisfactorily explained, but two factors may have been at work. One is the use of different calendars: the Itza and *Tizimin* may have dated events by the *k'atun* termination date (the ending of a K'atun 8 Ajaw), as in the traditional Classic calendar, and the Xiw and *Chumayel* by the beginning of the next *k'atun* (K'atun 6 Ajaw), as in the Campeche calendars, because the ending of one *k'atun* and the beginning of the next occur on sequential days. However, this is the reverse of Edmonson's reconstruction of naming practices (see Table 2.3, columns C and D). Second, the conflicts created by the use of these different calendars were putatively resolved in 1539 with the adoption of a compromise system, the Mayapán calendar, which featured elements of both. But there may have been differences in when and where the new calendar was accepted and differences or errors as manuscripts were recopied and "corrected," and these plus other factors (e.g., tradition, factionalism) could have resulted in the variations.

3. For the Maya, the verb "arrive" (*hul-*) means more than simple physical entry ("come"); it is used euphemistically to refer to achieving political power and dynastic founding.

4. If these thirteen plaza floorings can be linked to specific *k'atun* dates, I suggest that the first began with the construction of the earliest Castillo in a K'atun 6 Ajaw, 1204 to 1224 (Milbrath and Peraza Lope 2003). This was also the *k'atun* of a Calendar Round ending in 1217, and the *k'atun* ending date in 1224 also marked the turning of *b'ak'tun* 10 to 11 (11.0.0.0.0) The four associated floor surfaces would have been in 1204, 1224, 1244, and 1263 if they were done at *k'atun* endings or in 1217, 1237, 1257, and 1277 if they were done at twenty-year celebrations of the first construction at a Calendar Round. The next Calendar Round after 1217 occurred in 1269 in a K'atun 13 Ajaw, which was the *k'atun* of the "founding" of Mayapán, or its establishment as a *may* seat, according to the *Chumayel*. Following this line of reasoning, the second construction of the Mayapán Castillo would have occurred sometime between 1263 and 1283, perhaps in 1269. The next nine floor resurfacings would have occurred in 1283, 1303, 1323, 1343, 1362, 1382, 1402, 1422, and 1441 if they coincided with *k'atun* endings, or at nine twenty-year anniversaries of the 1269 Calendar Round; a Calendar Round was completed in 1425 in the K'atun 10 Ajaw of 1422–1441.

5. In this regard, it may be telling that Farriss (1984: 122–123) notes that these are also the only areas said to have had "markets" — or entrepôts — in the Colonial period.

6. One of the questions, however, references a horse and stirrups, suggesting that the K'atun 3 Ajaw in question fell in the seventeenth century (Milbrath and Peraza Lope 2003: 37), although this could have been a late addition to the manuscript. Because of the difficulties of correlating Maya *k'atuns* with the Gregorian (or earlier Julian) calendar, it is unclear whether the "Interrogation of the Chiefs" occurred at the end of a K'atun 3 Ajaw in 1125, 1382, or 1618. Related information does not clarify matters. The last date, 1618, would have occurred when the Xiw were closely allied with the Spaniards in Mérida rather than at Mayapán, and it also marks the end of B'ak'tun 11, raising the possibility that the questioning was part of *b'ak'tun*-ending ceremonies.

7. Hunak Keel seems to appear in two episodes, raising the possibility that the events are conflated. Alternatively, Hunak Keel might not be an individual name but

instead a chiefly title held by the ruler of Izamal province. Such is the case with the name/title Tutul Xiw, which, as Frans Blom (1928: 254) noted, occurs in the literature for a century (from 1450 to 1541), suggesting that it is both the name of a province and the title of its leader. The same longevity of the name/title is true for the "Itza" leader Kan Ek' in Petén.

8. Although it is not clear if this temple at Nojpeten is a "radial" (four-stairway) structure, its description, as Jones (1998: 74) notes, suggests a structure similar to the Castillo of Mayapán (Str. Q-162) but about half its size. The Mayapán Castillo, in turn, with its four stairways and nine tiers, is about half the size of the Castillo at Chich'en Itza. All three *castillos* face north. These similarities suggest that nine-tiered, north-facing, radial structures are architectonic signatures of the Itza/Kokom, in the same way that temple assemblages are indicative of the Xiw/Kowoj; these radial structures do not occur in Kowoj territory in eastern Petén. The quadripartite footprint of radial temples resembles the Maya glyph marking completion of calendrical intervals, and these structures might be associated with celebration of Wayeb' rites (Carlson 1981: 181; Fox 1987: 129) and the turning of *k'atuns* (see also Note 4), as in the twin-pyramid complexes of Tikal (see Rice 2004a: 121–126).

9. An important difference here, however, is that Kan Ek' is a compound matronym (Kan)-patronym (Ek') appellative rather than a patronymic alone.

10. Yukatekan *kowoj* can be translated as "tarantula" or, more generally, "spider." Tarantulas are large, spider-like creatures with eight hairy, segmented legs and two-part (cephalothorax and abdomen) hairy bodies. Many genera and species are found in Mesoamerica, often with limited geographic ranges, as they seem to be highly sensitive to variations in temperature, moisture, and ground cover. The tarantula referenced as *kowoj* (*chiwoj*) is likely one of two species in the terrestrial genus *Brachypelma*. A tarantula specific to arid northern Yucatán, *B. epicureanum* (Chamberlin 1925), closely resembles one found widely in humid Guatemala, Belize, and El Salvador, *B. vagans* (Ausserer 1875), but theraposodists (experts in the study of tarantulas) are uncertain if these are really two distinct species (R. C. West, pers. com., June 2004). Both species are crepuscular, emerging from their deep underground burrows at dusk to feed on insects. Their similarities are highlighted by their common names: *B. epicureanum* is the "Yucatán Rust-rump" and *B. vagans* the "Mexican Red-rump (or "black velvet").

11. The collocation "K'ul Kokum," however, has been identified on a frieze on the Casa Colorada at Chich'en Itza (Schele and Freidel 1990: figure 9.2).

12. Boot (2005: 95–106) interprets this passage as indicating the *origins* of the four groups that "discovered" Chich'en Itza, putting the K'atun 4 Ajaw in A.D. 978–997.

13. Bolon Te Witz is a common toponym in hilly regions of the Maya area, highlands and lowlands.

Appendix 2.I. Concordance of Named K'atuns with Gregorian Dates and Other Important Calendrical Intervals in the Postclassic Period.

K'atun Ajaw*	Gregorian Year	Other Calendrical
	1717	
8		
	1697	March 13, 1697: final conquest of the Petén Itzá Maya
10		1685 Calendar Round
	1677	
12		
	1658	End of Xiw practice of seating *k'atuns*
1		1633 Calendar Round
	1638	
3		
	1618	1618: new *b'ak'tun*, 12.0.0.0.0
5		
	1599	
7		1581 Calendar Round
	1579	
9		
	1559	
11		
	1539*	1539: end of *may* cycle; beginning of Mayapán calendar
13		1529 Calendar Round
	1520	
2		
	1500	
4		
	1480	
6		1477 Calendar Round
	1461	
8		Collapse of Mayapán
	1441	
10		1425 Calendar Round
	1422	
12		
	1402	
1		
	1382	
3		1373 Calendar Round First appearance of Chen Mul Modeled censers at Mayapán
	1362	
5		
	1343	
7		
	1323	
9		1321 Calendar Round
	1303	

K'atun Ajaw*	Gregorian Year	Other Calendrical
11		
	1283	1283: end of *may* cycle
13		1269 Calendar Round
	1263	
2		
	1244	
4		
	1224	1224: end of *b'ak'tun*, 11.0.0.0.0
6		1217 Calendar Round
	1204	
8		
	1185	
10		
	1165	1165 Calendar Round
12		
	1145	
1		
	1125	
3		1113 Calendar Round
	1106	
5		
	1086	
7		
	1066	
9		
	1047	
11		
	1027	1027: end of *may* cycle
13		
	1007	
2		
	987	
4		
	968	
6		
	948	
8		
	928	
10		
	909	
12		
	889	
1		

continued on next page

Appendix 2.I — *continued*

K'atun Ajaw*	Gregorian Year	Other Calendrical
	869	
3		
	849	
5		
	830	*b'ak'tun* ending 10.0.0.0.0
7		
	810	
9		
	790	
11		
	771	771: end of *may* cycle
13		
	751	
2		
	731	
4		
	711	
6		
	692	
8		

*K'atuns are counted by their ending date before 1539, by their beginning date thereafter.

The KOWOJ in
ETHNOHISTORICAL PERSPECTIVE

—— Grant D. Jones ————————————————————————

The Yukatekan-speaking Kowoj Maya of central Petén, Guatemala, were virtually unknown until about a decade ago. Primary-source documentary research in Spanish archives, however, coupled with intensive archaeological research in areas known to have been occupied by the Kowoj, has rescued this significant Colonial-period polity from oblivion. This research has demonstrated that, in addition to the better-known kingdom of the Itza and more scattered populations of Mopan Maya speakers, the Kowoj—named for their principal patrilineage, or *ch'ib'al*—represented a major force in Petén history. This was especially true during the final years of the seventeenth century and the early years of the eighteenth century, when these native societies suffered the devastating effects of Spanish invasion, occupation, and colonization. The Kowoj were the most effective anti-Spanish force in the region during these years, although they ultimately suffered severe population loss and became Colonial subjects along with their other native neighbors.

Because I first became aware of the significance of the Kowoj through a study of the Spanish documentary record, I present here a summary of what we know of them from an analysis of these sources. The context for these sources is unusual. The Kowoj and their immediate neighbors and enemies, the militarily more powerful and better-known Itza, came to the wider world's attention as a result of the late "conquest" of the two groups by Spanish forces from Yucatán in 1697. Spanish attempts to control the Kowoj during campaigns beginning that year are much less well-known than are the Spaniards' invasion and occupation of the Itza capital town of Nojpeten (now Flores, Petén), often taken as the event marking European conquest of that "last Maya kingdom" (Jones 1998).

The Kowoj, named for their powerful ruling lineage, specified that their ancestors had migrated from Tankaj (referring to Mayapán) at the time of the conquest of Yucatán, that is, in the early sixteenth century. In 1697 the Kowoj controlled the northern shore and the eastern port area of Lake Petén Itzá, as well as a significant amount of inland territory north and northeast of the lake toward Tikal (Jones 1998: map 3; see Rice and Rice, Chapter 1: Map 1.3, this volume). Although the Kowoj appear to have been culturally and linguistically similar to the Itza (who stated that their ancestors had migrated from Chich'en Itza at the time of the mid-fifteenth-century collapse of Mayapán), Spanish sources consistently distinguish between the two as political and territorial groups. In fact, they did represent, as I maintain in this chapter, fundamentally different types of sociopolitical organization, a conclusion that would confirm their significantly different historical backgrounds.

Issues of Ethnohistorical Methodology

Prior to the initiation of my documentary research into the historical Yukatekan-speaking populations of Petén, knowledge of the identities, history, and geographic distribution of the region's ethnic polities was sketchy at best. The principal published source of knowledge about these groups around the time of the 1697 Spanish occupation was the Spanish chronicler Juan de Villagutierre Soto-Mayor's detailed volume, written at the time as a defense of Spanish actions (1701, 1933, 1983, 1985). Although Villagutierre consulted the same documents that are now accessible in the Archivo General de Indias in Seville, Spain, modern historical methods as well as the substantial accumulation of knowledge about the Maya since the era of his writing have rendered his work relatively obsolete and unreliable (Jones 1998: xxii). Other Colonial-period sources (e.g., Avendaño y Loyola 1696, 1987; López de Cogolludo 1688, 1971; Vayhinger-Scheer 1997) offer much important information, but they take on full meaning only when read and interpreted in light of the vast assemblage of Spanish-language primary sources, especially those of the late seventeenth and early eighteenth centuries.

The quantity of documentation for the preparation, execution, and after-effects of the 1697 Spanish occupation of Nojpeten is vast, and the contents of these sources vary in every way imaginable: in authorship and authorial intent, political perspective, accuracy and reliability, and content, to name only a few. Although the quantity of sources is large, the authors—mostly military men, missionaries, and government officials—were generally ignorant of the Maya populations whom they were meeting for the first time. In reading the corpus of documentation in chronological order, one sees emerging, in a gradual fashion, the writers' growing but often frustratingly incomplete understanding of the peoples with whom they increasingly interacted, sometimes in relatively peaceful situations but even more frequently in conditions of mutual hostility.

Prior to the 1697 occupation, the Spaniards understood little more than the fact that a kingdom known as Itza dominated central Petén and that other Yukatekan-speaking Maya known as Mopan lived to their south and east under a shadow of Itza domination and military superiority. They comprehended almost nothing of the complex political system and internal divisions that characterized and sometimes divided the Itza polity, and they knew virtually nothing about the people called Kowoj, save through an important but sketchy description by the Franciscan missionary Fray Andrés de Avendaño y Loyola, who had visited Nojpeten in early 1696 and had met with Itza and Kowoj authorities (Avendaño y Loyola 1696, 1987; Vayhinger-Scheer 1997). The negative impact of the 1697 Spanish occupation on the indigenous political order was so great, however, resulting in intense internecine conflict and massive population movements among Maya groups, that later Spanish eyewitnesses found themselves confused and unable to reconstruct accurately the native political systems that were already collapsing and reconstituting themselves in new alliances and social formations.

Weaknesses and inconsistencies in Spanish knowledge and reportage pose major challenges to the ethnohistorian who tries to make sense of indigenous politics and population distribution. Added to these challenges is the absence of any documents written by the Maya themselves. Although a few documents in the Spanish language do report on what Maya witnesses are said to have told Spanish recorders and officials, most of these were written under political circumstances that compromise much of the potential value they might have as genuine native documents.

Despite these potent challenges to ethnohistorical study, when the body of documentation is analyzed as a whole, a picture of the ethno-politics of pre-occupation central Petén does eventually emerge. During 1988–1989 I transcribed and produced a detailed index (including general topics, events, and names of people and places) of nearly all the available documentation in Spain and a small amount from the Archivo General de Centroamérica in Guatemala City. During subsequent years I focused not only on creating a chronology of events related to the occupation but also on piecing together all the evidence related to ethno-politics, including lineage associations with major groups, the identities of principal leaders, and the distribution of populations in relation to local and regional political affiliations.

It was during this later stage of research that the identity of the Kowoj finally began to emerge clearly. While I had known for some time of a group of people whom Spanish observers called by this name and that they were led by high-ranking officials who bore the surname Kowoj, it eventually became clear that they were not only a group distinct from the Itza but that they were also the Itza king's principal enemies and a significant threat to the Itza rulership. Knowing this, pieces of the larger geopolitical and pre-occupation historical puzzle of central Petén at last began to come together. The Kowoj were clearly an autonomous polity with the ability to form alliances with factions of the Itza ruling council against the king Ajaw Kan Ek' and his loyal internal allies, as well as against the threatening Spanish intruders. Although the Itza ruling council and the Kowoj shared many cultural features, including assumptions concerning the historical contingency of *k'atun* prophecies, their political aims conflicted deeply, and these conflicts had major ramifications for the political outcome of the Spanish aggression against the Itza kingdom.

My first preliminary presentation of an Itza-Kowoj structural opposition appeared in a tentative model that integrated these ethnographic findings with a prospectus for future joint archaeological-ethnohistorical research on the political geography of central Petén (Rice, Rice, and Jones 1993). Archaeological research designed to explore this model began in 1994 (Rice, Rice, and Pugh 1998; Rice et al. 1995, 1996) and has recently been continued in Itza territory on the western shore of Lake Petén Itzá. While details of the ethnohistorical model changed slightly over subsequent years (see Jones 1998) as a result of revised documentary analysis and consultations with the archaeological investigators, its essential form has remained much the same, and its major components have been consistently validated through archaeological analysis.

Background: The Spanish Invasion and Its Impact

Nearly all our knowledge of the Itza and Kowoj in Petén emerges from the archival record concerning the preparations for and execution of the Spanish invasion and occupation of the Itza island capital of Nojpeten, as well as that detailing the aftermath of this event. The brief summary that follows provides a skeletal outline of these events; for a much more detailed description, consult my book-length study (Jones 1998).

In 1693 the Spanish crown authorized Martín de Ursúa y Arismendi, a Basque bureaucrat and governor-designate of Yucatán, and the president of the Audiencia of Guatemala to open jointly a new road that would connect Yucatán and Guatemala (the highlands). While "pacification" of the Itzas was not specified in official orders, Ursúa quickly made that his principal goal. As troops began to advance toward Itza territory in 1695, rumors began to circulate about Maya *k'atun* prophecies predicting a new age when the Itza would surrender peacefully to Spanish civil and religious authorities. In Mérida these rumors were reinforced by the arrival of Aj Chan, son of the Itza ruler's sister, as the king's ambassador. Aj Chan repeated a recent offer by Ajaw Kan Ek' to submit peacefully to Spanish colonization. Both he and Ajaw Kan Ek' directly referred to a prophecy that the turning of K'atun 8 Ajaw signified the inevitability of the Itza's acceptance of Christianity and Spanish rule.

The Franciscan Avendaño y Loyola spent several days at Nojpeten in early 1696 with the Itza king, other Itza officials, and their enemy—the principal Kowoj leader, who paid a visit in full war regalia. They discussed the prophecies and argued about their timing and meaning. For Ajaw Kan Ek' they signified the inevitability of surrender to the Spaniards, but for Aj Kowoj the prophecies meant resistance on his part to Itza complicity with the Spaniards and to Spanish designs to conquer and colonize the region. The Itza king's enemies, in particular Aj Kowoj and an Itza faction with whom he was allied, forced Avendaño to leave Nojpeten. The Itza soon captured and murdered Yucatecan and Guatemalan soldiers and missionaries arriving separately at the lake.

In February 1697 Ursúa and his troops from Campeche reached the western port of the lake, where they built and launched a sizable oar-driven, heavily armed attack boat (*galeota*). The Spanish water-based attack on Nojpeten on March 13 was brief, but it caused significant—probably massive—loss of Maya life. The Itza put up a fierce but futile resistance and were forced to abandon the island under heavy Spanish firepower; many Itza lost their lives while attempting to swim to the mainland shore while under attack. The occupiers found a nearly deserted island but soon captured Ajaw Kan Ek', other high-ranking Itza, Aj Kowoj, and their families. Ursúa returned to Campeche, leaving a small garrison isolated on the fortified island to cope with declining food supplies and a sea of hostile Itza and Kowoj on the mainland. The invaders established a garrison on Nojpeten, naming the new presidio Nuestra Señora de los Remedios y San Pablo, Laguna del Itza.

A military rescue mission, accompanied by *ladino* (persons of mixed Spanish-indigenous descent) civilians who were to form their own community at the presidio, arrived with supplies and reinforcements from Guatemala in 1699. They were joined by Ursúa, who returned for the first time from Campeche. The Guatemalans stayed only three months, during which conditions deteriorated even further. They had brought with them a devastating epidemic that killed many of the troops and settlers from Guatemala and severely ravaged the native population. When the troops left, they took with them—in shackles—Ajaw Kan Ek', his son, and two cousins, including the high priest. Only the king and his son survived the long journey to Santiago de Guatemala (now Antigua), where they spent the rest of their lives under house arrest.

During 1702–1703, priests from Yucatán established a series of mission towns around Lake Petén Itzá, populating them with surviving Itza and Kowoj whom they could cajole into resettling or, more often, whom they could capture by force (Map 3.1). In 1704 Maya leaders residing in the new missions, primarily Kowoj and their Itza factional allies, carried out a well-planned but brief rebellion that resulted in the execution of its accused leaders and the permanent abandonment of most of the mission towns. Additional missions were later established in the region as Spaniards captured and relocated other fugitive Mayas. From a native central Petén population of at least 60,000 persons in 1697, only about 6,000 remained by 1708 (Jones 1998: 68, 407–408). The

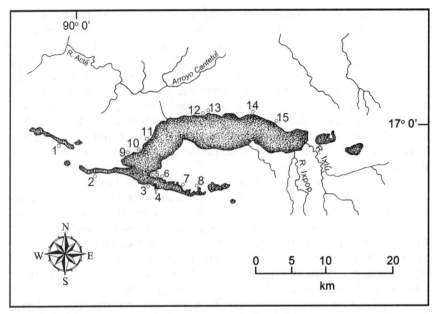

Map 3.1. Early-eighteenth-century missions in the vicinity of Lake Petén Itzá (after Jones 1998: map 10): (1) Nuestra Señora de Guadalupe; (2) Nuestra Señora de la Candelaria; (3) San José (original); (4) Nuestra Señora de los Remedios; (5) San Bernabé; (6) San Miguel; (7) Jesús María; (8) San Pedro; (9) San Jerónimo; (10) San Andrés; (11) San José Nuevo; (12) San Antonio; (13) San Martín; (14) San Francisco; (15) San Juan Bautista.

primary cause of the decline was a series of European-introduced epidemic diseases, but many had lost their lives as a result of forced Spanish roundups and intense internecine indigenous warfare.

Kowoj History Prior to the 1697 Spanish Occupation

The history of the Kowoj from the time of their migration from Yucatán until the Spanish invasion is only sketchily documented for the earlier years. During the fourteen months preceding March 1697, however, sources provide significant details about their leadership and their hostilities toward the Itza and the Spaniards. In this section I summarize this period of Kowoj history, which is extended to the post-occupation years in the section that follows.

Migration from Yucatán

Unidentified Kowoj leaders in Petén told the Spanish occupiers that their ancestors had migrated from Mayapán at the time of the conquest of Yucatán (Archivo General de Indias [AGI], Escribanía de Cámara, legajo 339B, no. 18, f.

54v; Jones 1998: 11). Because of the protracted nature of Spanish efforts to control resistance to their conquest aims in Yucatán, the Kowoj migration could presumably have occurred at any time(s) between the first Spanish expedition to the peninsula in 1511 and the 1546 bloody Spanish repression of Maya resistance in eastern Yucatán, which Matthew Restall (1998: 13–14) has called the "eastern war." Mayapán was then part of the native province of Maní, which had been ruled by the Xiws ever since the mid-fifteenth-century collapse of the Mayapán confederation. Various sources attribute Mayapán's collapse to the murder and expulsion of members of the ruling Kokom family by the Xiw and their allies at Mayapán. Xiw-Kokom enmity continued for many years after the collapse and reached a climax in 1536 when the Kokom, then in control of Sotuta province on the eastern boundary of Maní, murdered a group of Xiw dignitaries to whom they had promised safe passage across Sotuta for a pilgrimage to Chich'en Itza. Up to that time the Xiw had been neutral toward the Spanish conquest, which had begun in two unsuccessful phases, in 1527–1528 and 1531–1535, respectively. After the 1536 massacre, however, the Xiw actively supported the Spaniards, whereas the Itza of Sotuta violently opposed them for many years (Edmonson 1982: 47–48; Roys 1957: 63–66, 1962: 47–48; Tozzer 1941: 54–56).

Although I have found no confirmation from northern Yucatecan sources that noble Maya named Kowoj held positions of importance or formed a *b'atab'il* (political group governed by a *b'atab'*) within the Xiw-controlled Maní *kuchkab'al* (province), a Kowoj was identified at Mayapán in the native chronicles (Roys 1967: 69). It is plausible that such a group, which I suggest later was by then an independent *b'atab'il*, migrated to Petén following the 1536 massacre of the Xiw. In light of archaeological evidence that Zacpetén may have experienced a major reconstruction event about 1400, during the final decline of Mayapán, the sixteenth-century migration may have been a later wave in a series of Kowoj migrations to Petén. Whatever the timing or the reasons for their departure from Mayapán, when the Kowoj first come to light in documents of the 1690s they are the enemies of a still-ruling Itza king, Ajaw Kan Ek'.

Kowoj Expulsion by Itza from the Yalain region, 1630s–1660s

I have previously hypothesized that the Kowoj migration took them to the area of Petén east of Lake Petén Itzá. Documentary evidence indicates that beginning in the 1630s the Itza pursued an aggressive military campaign designed to control a wide corridor of territory between Lake Petén Itzá and west-central Belize (see Jones 1998: 52–58 for more detailed discussion). Their ultimate goal appears to have been to gain complete control over a riverine route the Spaniards might use in the future to introduce occupying forces by way of the New and Belize rivers and from there overland via Lakes Sacnab and Yaxhá. Prior to the 1630s, the area encompassing the region around Lakes Macanché, Sacnab, and Yaxhá (which I call the Yalain region after its principal town of that name following Itza occupation) was almost certainly the principal territory of the Kowoj (AGI, Guatemala 151B, no. 2, f. 10r; Jones 1998: 280). Following their migration to the area in the sixteenth century, the Kowoj may in turn have displaced or incorporated resident Mopan populations who controlled this territory at that time. Beginning in the 1630s and apparently continuing into the 1660s, the Itza military engaged the Kowoj in a series of battles that forced some of the latter to relocate to less desirable lands along the steep northern shore of the main lake, where the Itza exerted little influence.

Itza-Kowoj hostilities were extremely active around the time of Spanish invasion, although the existence of noble intermarriages between the two groups indicates that efforts had occasionally been made to reach a peaceful settlement. Until shortly before the 1697 Spanish invasion, however, the Itza controlled Yalain and the eastern lakes, under the local rulership of Aj Chan, the Itza king's nephew (his sister's son). The eastern end of the main lake, including Saklemakal (the archaeological site of Ixlú) and Zacpetén, remained contested territory between the Itza and Kowoj until after the 1697 occupation, when the Kowoj apparently gained full control over the area for at least a few years.

Hostilities and Alliances on the Eve of Spanish Occupation

When Fray Andrés de Avendaño y Loyola visited Nojpeten in January 1696, he discovered that nine principal temples on the island had recently been destroyed by fire and subsequently been reconstructed (Avendaño y Loyola 1696, ff. 33r–v; Jones 1998: 197). Later testimony taken after the occupation by Martín de Ursúa y Arismendi, while he had the imprisoned Ajaw Kan Ek' and the principal Kowoj leader Aj Kowoj (a.k.a. Captain Kowoj) in the same room, affirmed that as a result of the Itza king's positive overtures to the Spaniards before Avendaño's visit, Aj Kowoj had attacked the island capital and set fire to it, destroying many houses (AGI, Guatemala 151, no. 5, ff. 44, 45, 93; Jones 1998: 326). Another Spaniard later confirmed this information, saying he had seen Aj Kowoj's scars from arrow wounds he had received during the attack (AGI, Guatemala 151, no. 5, f. 93; Jones 1998: 326).

This conflict must have occurred two or three months before Avendaño's trip to Nojpeten. In all probability, Aj Kowoj attacked Nojpeten as soon as he heard rumors that Ajaw Kan Ek' had made contact with pro-Spanish representatives from Tipu during August or September. He was also probably aware of an earlier "secret" trip by Aj Chan to Mérida in September 1695, preceding his better-known December mission that year, as Aj Kowoj's daughter was Aj Chan's wife; their marriage clearly represented an inter-group alliance at a high level of leadership (see Jones 1998: 467n3 for numerous AGI citations). There is ample evidence that Aj Kowoj had been in league with Ajaw B'atab' Aj K'in Kante, ruler of the north and uncle of Ajaw Kan Ek', in his strong opposition to the Itza ruler's pro-Spanish stance (for example, Jones 1998: 213–215, 310–311).

Avendaño's report of his visit to Nojpeten includes a detailed eyewitness description of Spanish and Itza interaction with Aj Kowoj prior to the Spanish invasion. On his fifth and last day there (January 19, 1696) he witnessed the arrival of a military-diplomatic party of men who, given information that follows, were members of the alliance between the Kowoj and the Itza sub-ruler Ajaw B'atab' Aj K'in Kante from Chak'an Itza. They came "navigating across the lake, with their war officers and their standards. . . . I went out to receive them as a matter of courtesy, but the Indians of that peten went out only out of curiosity" (Avendaño y Loyola 1696, f. 34r). Two leaders in the visiting party stood out from the rest. One was an old man with a double-blade machete as his standard. The other was a younger man who carried a stone knife. They were "painted for war; their faces were as hideous as the evil purpose that they had in their hearts" (ibid., f. 34v). The older man was Aj Kowoj; the younger one was probably his son, later known to the Spaniards as Kulut Kowoj.

The conversations and speeches that followed the party's arrival concerned Avendaño's insistence that the time was at hand for the Itza to surrender to the Spaniards, as K'atun 8 Ajaw had long since begun. Avendaño did not acknowledge, however, that Aj Kowoj did not represent the Itza or that an agreement reached during the meeting with the Itza "priests and teachers" — that "all the adults would receive baptism" at the turning of the *k'atun* four months later — might have been acceptable to some of the Itza representatives and to Ajaw Kan Ek' but certainly not to Aj Kowoj. The latter angrily denounced the agreement, saying, "What does it matter that the time when we would be Christians is found to be completed, if the sharp point of my stone lance has not been worn out?" (Avendaño y Loyola 1696, f. 36v). While most contemporary scholars calculate a 1697 date for the turning of K'atun 8 Ajaw, Avendaño and his Maya hosts agreed that the calendrical event would occur in 1696.

Avendaño learned that Aj Kowoj and his Chak'an Itza allies (on the northwest corner of the lake) were plotting to kill him and his companions as they returned through Chak'an Itza territory, through which they had come on their way to Nojpeten. He also heard that Ajaw Kan Ek' had said that "if they [the Spaniards] would decapitate his enemy the cacique Couoh [Kowoj], with all of his followers (who in all would be between sixty and seventy), he would hand over the petens that are in his charge" (ibid., ff. 44r–v). That night Ajaw Kan Ek' and his relatives accompanied the friar and his companions across the length of Lake Petén Itzá, enabling them to escape ill fate at the hands of the Kowoj and their Chak'an Itza allies (ibid., ff. 46v–49r). The principal port area of the eastern end of the lake, at Saklemakal/Chaltunja, was under Itza control at the time.

This summary presents only a small amount of the evidence of Kowoj collusion against the already crumbling Itza rulership. Violence against Spanish visitors to Nojpeten over the following weeks and months was clearly orchestrated by increasing opposition to the Itza king's weakness in the face of a growing Spanish military threat. Aj Kowoj may well have seen the *k'atun* prophecies as indicating an internal collapse of the Itza kingdom, thus empowering him to assume future Itza rulership. This never occurred, but his role in ensuring violent military encounters with the Spaniards, as opposed to an agreement of surrender, demonstrated the strength of the Kowoj as a military and diplomatic power in the region.

Kowoj Sociopolitical Organization

Although documentation concerning the sociopolitical organization of the Itza is extensive (Jones 1998: 60–107), much less specific information addresses that of the Kowoj. Pre-occupation Spanish contact with the Itza was relatively intense, and Fray Avendaño y Loyola's eyewitness accounts as well as interviews with Aj Chan gave the Spaniards considerable information concerning the organization of the Itza kingdom. Equally detailed documentation for the Kowoj does not exist, primarily because the Spaniards had only slight contact with them before the occupation of Nojpeten. Following that event, the Kowoj polity was severely disrupted by the Spanish capture of Kowoj leaders, the execution of Aj Kowoj, a series of major military incursions across Kowoj territory, and the forced resettlement of many of its people to the northern shore of the main lake.

In this section I primarily address information about the Kowoj provided by military and other observers during the years immediately following the Spanish occupation of Nojpeten. While few Spaniards observed the Kowoj polity before its disruption (the principal exception being Avendaño y Loyola), Kowoj political and military actions in face of Spanish aggression provide some evidence of its character. I conclude that Kowoj organizational principles may have strongly resembled those of *centralized* political-territorial groups in northern Yucatán during the early Colonial period (*kuchkab'aloob'*, using the *-ob'* Yukateko plural), in contrast to the highly *decentralized* formal organization of the (Petén) Itza kingdom, which appears to differ significantly from such groups described in Yucatán.

A central question in addressing the political organization of the Kowoj is its possible relationship to the dynamic model of the *kuchkab'al,* as proposed by Sergio Quezada and T. Okoshi Harada for Yucatán at the time of Spanish contact (Okoshi Harada 1995, 1999; Quezada 1993; Quezada and Okoshi Harada 1988). In his original discussion of this entity, Quezada (1993: 36) translated it as *"el espacio territorial gobernado por un poder que reside en un lugar determinado que denominaré capital"* ("the territorial space governed by an authority who resides in a specific location to which I will give the name capital"). Quezada thus emphasized that the *kuchkab'al* always had a central capital that, in addition to carrying out mercantile and religious activities, also functioned as a political center. At the head of the *kuchkab'al* was the principal ruler, the *jalach winik*. Below him were a number of *b'atab'ob'*, each of whom governed a *b'atab'il* comprising several *kuchteelob'*, or groups of extended families (Quezada 1993: 38), most of whom would have lived in towns or smaller settlements (*kajob'*) (Restall 1997: 24–29). Following the collapse of Mayapán, itself a *kuchkab'al,* for a time numerous *b'atab'oob'* remained independent from any *kuchkab'al*; some of these were annexed to or conquered by existing *kuchkab'aloob'*, whereas others remained autonomous units up to the time of Spanish occupation. Most important, during periods of warfare and reorganization, the process of political reconstitution was flexible, resulting in a variety of sociopolitical formations that involved changing alliances and frequently contested boundaries (Quezada 1993: 37–38).

Although the specific history of the Petén Itza remains murky, the mature complexity of their political organization suggests to me that their existence in Petén long predated the collapse of Mayapán, which oral histories designated as the beginning of their existence as a diaspora polity. Petén Itza political organization does in some ways resemble the *kuchkab'aloob'* of Yucatán, but it also differs in ways that hint of deep historical roots in Petén, some of them perhaps continuities of the political organization of Chich'en Itza itself. On the other hand, Kowoj political organization suggests that this group was in fact one of the many *b'atab'oob'* displaced as a result of the collapse of Mayapán, notwithstanding Kowoj claims that their migration occurred during the Spanish conquest of Yucatán. There may be no contradiction in this assertion, as the Kowoj may have been a *b'atab'il* that was annexed to the Maní *kuchkab'al* in the early sixteenth century but that migrated southward in the face of Spanish occupation.

Whether the Kowoj had a central capital that functioned with a central governing council, as at Itza Nojpeten, is not immediately obvious in the Spanish sources. Given the absence of such information and indications that Kowoj sociopolitical organization differed significantly from that of the Itza, it seems possible that neither a capital of the Itza type (in which all the sub-rulers as well as the principal ruling pair resided) nor a complex ruling council like those of the Itza characterized the Kowoj. This conclusion, however, may be only partially correct. If, as seems likely from archaeological evidence, Zacpetén had been a major Kowoj center prior to Itza occupation during the early 1600s, that community was probably the Kowoj capital. Structure 719 of Zacpetén, a tandem room construction, had eleven seats built into its interior wall, suggesting that it was likely a council house or *popol naj* ("mat house") (see Pugh, Rice, and Cecil, Chapter 9, this volume). As I suggest later, however, the actual structures of the Itza and Kowoj polities may have differed significantly.

In 1697 both the highest-ranking Kowoj authority, known as Aj Kowoj or Captain Kowoj to the Spaniards, and his junior authority, Kulut Kowoj, probably made their residences at Ketz on the northern shore of the main lake (see Chapter 1, Map 1.4, this volume) (for AGI citations, see Jones 1998: 443n14). Ketz may have been a fairly recently established headquarters following the early-seventeenth-century Itza military capture of Zacpetén and its environs. The title "captain" may or may not have been an interpretation of the common Yucatecan title *b'atab'*, but it is significant that the Spaniards used this designation for both the elder Kowoj and his ultimate successor, Kulut Kowoj, implying that the title was inherited. *B'atab'* is simply the most likely of the possible titles they might have held. While *nakom*, a Yukatek and Itza term for military leader (Jones 1998: 45, 49), could have been another possible title, it is not recorded for the Kowoj.

Little is known about Ketz, and archaeological surveys in the area where it was located have not revealed architecture on the scale of that of Nojpeten (or of Zacpetén or Topoxté). Ketz, with a population said to be about 1,000 (Jones 1998: 325), was reportedly the headquarters of the two principal Kowoj leaders in 1697, when it was first visited by Spaniards, yet the name of the town was that of another *ch'ib'al*, Ketz, which also resided there. On the other hand, we know that by 1699, following the Spaniards' execution of Captain Kowoj, the junior ruler Kulut Kowoj was residing in the area east of Saklemakal (Jones 1998: 443n14). The most likely candidate for a central Kowoj headquarters at this later date, by which time most of the northern lakeshore towns had been abandoned, is the site of Zacpetén on Lake Salpetén. This comes as no surprise, given the long history of Postclassic construction and occupation at that site, as reported extensively in this volume. Whereas the ethnohistorical evidence strongly suggests that Zacpetén and its immediate environs were controlled by the Itza during much of the seventeenth century, up to about 1697, the Kowoj reoccupation of Zacpetén indicates that the site had remained the actual capital of the Kowoj polity. Ketz, then, had been the Kowoj "capital in exile."

Extensive cultivable land along the northern shore of Lake Petén Itzá had to be reached by climbing to the flatter areas above the escarpment that reaches to the lakeshore in this area. The Kowoj towns located along the northern shoreline were apparently supported agriculturally by numerous extended-family hamlets in these higher areas, although there were also extensive cultivations in the Ixlú-Zacpetén region, probably tended by allies of the Itza. Spaniards who visited these and other lakeshore towns in 1697 stated that there were twelve in all. Six or seven of the towns were on the northern shore (from west to east): Chak'an Itza, Xililchi, B'oj (and Aj B'ojom, possibly the same place), Uspeten, Ketz, and Yaxtenay. These towns were Kowoj-controlled except for Chak'an Itza, near the western end of the lake, which was actually an Itza town in alliance with the Kowoj. On the eastern end of the lake were Saklemakal and Chaltunja, probably one extensive community that was under Itza control during much of the seventeenth century but in earlier times was likely a Kowoj settlement area. Pop (or Poop) was on the southern shore near the eastern end of the lake. The locations of Sojkol and Tz'ola are not known.

Kowoj populations also occupied interior regions well north and northeast of the lake, possibly having established towns of some size away from the lakeshore. Little is known of these towns, although two, not identified by name but probably constructed as defenses against the Spaniards, had large wooden stockades (Jones 1998: 385). A small number of Kowoj apparently also occupied several towns and hamlets around Lake Yaxhá, in proximity to Itza-controlled (?) communities on and around Lake Sacnab. This cluster of eastern settlements apparently grew considerably after the 1697 occupation as a result of migrations there from the northern shore of Lake Petén Itzá. The area west of the lake remained dominantly Itza until the forced Spanish resettlement of most Itza to the lakeshore during the early 1700s.

We do not know the exact relationship between the senior ruler, Aj Kowoj or Captain Kowoj, and his junior ruler, Kulut Kowoj. The latter was also known as Captain Kowoj after the former was executed in July 1697, accused of being the head of a plot to massacre Spaniards (on his execution, see Jones 1998: 336–337). This continuity of title (again, probably a translation of *b'atab'* or possibly *nakom*) suggests that Kulut Kowoj had inherited authority over the *b'atab'il*. The relationship of Captain Kowoj (senior) and Kulut Kowoj was likely that of father and son, as Avendaño noted that one was older than the other. It is unlikely, however, that theirs was a joint rulership of the sort practiced by the Itza, in which the principal ruler, Ajaw Kan Ek', shared authority with his patrilateral cousin, K'in Kan Ek' (ibid.: 94–95). Succession among the Itza was determined by matrilineal as well as patrilineal descent, such that the new ruler must be the son of a woman of the Kan matriline and the Ek' patriline (ibid.: 80–81). Such a successor could be a brother, cousin, or nephew of the former king but probably not a son (ibid.: 94–95). Because Kowoj rulers did not use double surnames, it is more likely that inheritance of office went to a younger brother or, more ideally, a son. The fact that Spaniards searching for Kulut Kowoj in 1699 failed to find him and thus captured his son may suggest that they considered the son his probable successor or second in command (ibid.: 372).

Among the Itza in Petén, central power was shared between the dual rulership (king and high priest) and a sub-rulership consisting of four senior-junior ruler pairs whose territorial authority was aligned along a quadripartite geographic framework (Jones 1998: 94–101). Complicating this system further was the presence of a council of thirteen men bearing the title Ach Kat, whom I have suggested were military chiefs and possibly *k'atun* priests representing outlying towns or territories. No such complex system appears to have characterized the Kowoj, and it appears more likely that men of the Kowoj *ch'ib'al* would have constituted the principal leadership of the polity. If this interpretation is correct, Structure 719 of Zacpetén, noted earlier, might have served as the meeting place (*popol naj*) of the *ch'ib'al*. Such a system, far simpler than the elaborate governing system of the Itza, is similar to that found in areas of post-Mayapán northern Yucatán, in which a dominant *ch'ib'al* extended its influence over a number of (but not always all) contiguous towns in a *b'atab'il*.

In 1702 Ajaw Kan Ek' and other Itza held under house arrest in Santiago de Guatemala dictated to Fray Diego de Rivas an extensive list of central Petén towns and settlements, specifying the relative sizes and principal surnames associated with each (Jones 1998: 62–64, table 3.1). The towns in the Itza-dominated areas exhibit no significant pattern of domination by particular *ch'ib'alob'*, suggesting that such a system had been discouraged by a long-standing, complex system of centralized governance among the Itza. On the other hand, in the area around Lake Yaxhá, where by this time most of the Kowoj were living, of the six towns listed there, five were associated with the Kowoj *ch'ib'al*. I suspect that a census of pre-occupation Kowoj towns along the northern shore of the main lake would have demonstrated a similar pattern, indicating strong Kowoj domination. Although contemporary people in

San Andrés claim that many people named Kowoj lived in Sakpuy (west of the main lake) in historic times (Norman Schwartz, pers. com. to P. Rice, 2003), that town was under strong Itza control during the late 1600s. One Spanish observer claimed it was in this area where the last Itza ruler was crowned, possibly in 1699 (Jones 1998: 384).

Few other *ch'ib'al* names in the Kowoj region have been identified, primarily because their population dispersed rapidly following the 1697 occupation and Spanish military forays into displaced Kowoj towns resulted in little reporting of the names of individuals and families. In a table of names sorted by political region (Jones 1998: 4–25, table 1.1), I identified only four names besides Kowoj: Kab', Kamal, Kawich, and Ketz (sometimes K'etz). None of these names is identified in any of the neighboring ethnic or political regions, suggesting a high degree of *ch'ib'al* distinctiveness and possibly some endogamy among the Kowoj. The occurrence of the name Kowoj itself among the Itza is a result of the late-seventeenth-century alliance of the Kowoj with Itza leaders residing in the Chak'an Itza area along the northwestern shore of the main lake (ibid.: 63–64, table 3.1).

Several Kowoj-area names were omitted from this table of surnames, as *ch'ib'al* names were not included for families placed in the first missions during 1702–1703. Those known to have been moved from the Kowoj region include Kitis, K'ixab'on, and Tz'ib'. Kitis was recorded as a settlement name, but it also appeared as a surname in the core Itza area. When transferred to the new mission town (San José, on the southern arm of the main lake, not to be confused with the later mission San José Nuevo, the present-day San José), members of the Kitis *ch'ib'al* found themselves under attack by allies of Kulut Kowoj for having accepted Spanish overtures (Jones 1998: 391). Another report from 1710, however, identified a Kitis as a Kowoj leader (ibid.: 516n60). K'ixab'on and Tz'ib' were names also found among Itza, but those brought from the Kowoj area were probably allies of the Kowoj (ibid.: 392–93).

Following the abortive anti-Spanish rebellion in 1704, several men identified as the principal organizers were sentenced to death by shooting. They included one Kitam Kowoj from San José, his principal co-conspirator Pedro Tzin (also an Itza surname), and a man named K'ixab'on (Jones 1998: 402). I have suggested that the organization of the rebellion, all of whose leaders then lived in the mission settlements, represented the continuation of a pre-occupation alliance between the Kowoj and an anti–Ajaw Kan Ek', anti-Spanish northern Itza faction. This would explain why people with Itza surnames were identified with Kowoj territory and political activities (ibid.).

Final Observations

There is little doubt that flexibility of group membership was an essential aspect of all these Petén Maya ethno-political entities, especially during times of dislocation and warfare. The Petén Itza regularly incorporated individuals from far-flung locations into their political order, including Mopan and, in the case of their expansion into Belize during the 1630s, members of Yukatekan-speaking towns in that region. The proposed Itza Ach Kat military council, which combined territorial incorporation of "foreign" leadership with a system of *k'atun* seating places among newly incorporated populations, was a highly formalized mechanism that institutionalized such fluidity. Whether this system could have been derived from the one practiced at Chich'en Itza is a possibility worth exploring. Kowoj incorporation of Itza leaders and their families and followers, following the dislocations that accompanied post-occupation Spanish military operations in their territory, was, in contrast, an informal system that probably more closely resembled the fluid nature of population movements in Colonial-period northern Yucatán—what Nancy Farriss (1984: 200) has called "drift," although that term fails to capture the political dynamics that frequently determined such movements.

Such complexity and fluidity of human movement underscore the significance of the dynamic model of post-Mayapán collapse political reconstruction and reconstitution proposed by Quezada, as noted earlier. This process simply continued on in central Petén, abetted by internal warfare, the politics of expansion of indigenous polities, and, ultimately, the devastating impact of European invasion and occupation.

Acknowledgments

The board of managers, administration, and staff of the School of American Research in Santa Fe, New Mexico, provided a stimulating work environment during a fellowship year and three subsequent summers I spent there working on the larger project of which this chapter is a part. The administration of Davidson College provided financial assistance and personal support throughout the history of this project. The National Endowment for the Humanities provided major support for the research and writing of the book by means of a resident fellowship at the School of American Research, a sabbatical fellowship for college teachers and independent scholars in residence at Davidson College, and a summer research fellowship for work at the Archivo General de Centroamérica in Guatemala City. My earlier work at the Archivo General de Indias, whose staff's assistance is gratefully acknowledged, was supported by a fellowship from the American Council of Learned Societies and assistance from Hamilton College. The National Science Foundation has generously supported the continuing archaeological research of Proyecto Maya Colonial.

Many individuals contributed to ideas and interpretations as the larger project unfolded. In particular, I express appreciation for the intense and productive assistance of Don S. Rice and Prudence M. Rice in the interpretation of archaeological and ethnohistorical evidence for the Kowoj and their Petén neighbors. Charles Andrew Hofling spent many hours generously assisting me on issues of orthography and how best to represent and interpret Colonial-period Itza place names, personal names, titles, and other terms. His colleague Fernando Tesucún provided valuable assistance in identifying contemporary Itzaj place names. Timothy Pugh made valuable suggestions for revisions to this article. Charles Houck composed the original figures.

The LINGUISTIC CONTEXT of the KOWOJ

—— Charles Andrew Hofling ————————————————————————

The task of analyzing the linguistic context of the Kowoj in Petén can be accomplished only indirectly because we have very little textual data from Petén from the Terminal Classic through the eighteenth century. However, a variety of sources of evidence allow us to make inferences about the languages spoken in central Petén. The Kowoj were a Yukatekan-speaking group that likely migrated from Mayapán in northwestern Yucatán sometime between that site's fall in the mid-fifteenth century, if not earlier,[1] and the mid-sixteenth century (Jones 1998: 17–19). In Petén they encountered the Itza, who are reported to have migrated from Chich'en Itza in the thirteenth or fifteenth century (Jones 1998: 8–17, 430n17; Schele and Matthews 1998: 204, 363n31). Yukatekans reckoned history in k'atuns, periods of 20 tuns (360-day periods), or approximately 20 years. The uncertainty about the dates of the migrations results from differing interpretations of dates given in the k'atun histories in the Yucatecan books of chilam b'alam (see Rice, Chapter 2, this volume). Both Kowoj and Itza were clearly speakers of the Yukatekan branch of the Mayan language family, and I have previously provided linguistic evidence

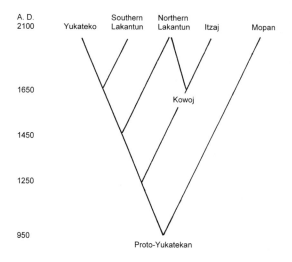

A. D.

Figure 4.1. Chronological diversification of Yukatekan language family.

for the genetic relationships indicated in Figure 4.1 (Hofling 2002, 2004, 2006a, 2006b).[2] As shown, the Itza and Kowoj dialects are fairly close genetically, and the speakers were in close contact in Petén as well.

Several scholars have recently argued that the Itza had a long history in Petén and repeatedly migrated from Petén to the north and back again (Boot 2005; Hofling 1991: 1, 2002, 2004; Rice, Rice, and Pugh 1998; Schele and Mathews 1998; Schele, Grube, and Boot 1995). These arguments are based on archaeological and hieroglyphic evidence, as well as indigenous accounts recorded in the books of *chilam b'alam* in Yukateko Mayan using the Spanish alphabet from the sixteenth to the nineteenth centuries. The *chilam b'alams* suggest periodic Itza migrations timed to *k'atun* endings in the thirteen-*k'atun may* cycle, that is, every ~256 years (Rice 2004a). According to Nikolai Grube, the title Itza Ajaw is recorded hieroglyphically not only at Chichén Itzá in Yucatán but also at Motul de San José, a Classic site on the northwest shore of Lake Petén Itzá (cited in Schele, Grube, and Boot 1995: 10; Schele and Mathews 1998: 203ff., 362n28). The name of the Itza king Kan Ek', well-known from Colonial sources, also appears in Classic hieroglyphic inscriptions at Seibal in western Petén and at Chich'en Itza during the Late Classic period (Schele and Mathews 1998: 186–187, 244–245ff.). Similarly, the toponym Mopan was recorded in the region of Naj Tunich in southeastern Petén during the Classic period (MacLeod and Stone 1995: 156), an area occupied by Mopan-speaking Maya in Colonial times (Jones 1998: 5). Some Itza may well have been present in Petén continuously, and the Mopan almost certainly were an ancient Petén population. Modern Itzaj ethnobotanical terms, like those in other Yukatekan varieties, are overwhelmingly Yukatekan, suggesting that the Itza were long-time residents of Petén or that they had merged with an existing population of Yukatekan speakers rather than being recent immigrants who borrowed terms from earlier Ch'olan-speaking inhabitants (Atran, Lois, and Ucan Ek' 2004; Hofling 2004; Hofling and Tesucún 1997).

From the Preclassic period on, the Maya lowlands were occupied by Yukatekan and Ch'olan speakers, who were in such intense and prolonged contact that the lowlands constitute a distinct linguistic area (Justeson et al. 1985: 9–11, 17–20). Yukatekan evidences a significant number of lexical borrowings, especially in religious and ritual vocabulary, likely a result of contact with Ch'olan-based ritual language reflected in hieroglyphic texts (Hofling 2004; Vail 2000a). Linguistic data confirm ethnohistoric evidence that the Mopan were in especially intense contact with Ch'olan groups to the south after the Yukatekan family began to diversify, that is, by the Postclassic period. A significant number of lexical borrowings occurred not only in Mopan but also in Itza, perhaps filtered through Mopan (Cano 1984; Hofling 2004; Jones 1998: 5). For example, Mopan and Itzaj borrowed the word *t'ot'* 'snail' from a Ch'olan source, while Yukateko did not (with *úul* 'snail'). Itzaj and Mopan independent pronouns also reflect Ch'olan contact (Hofling 2002), unlike Yukateko proper.

Most linguists and anthropologists who study Yukatekan languages stress their similarities (e.g., Bruce 1975: 2; Edmonson 1986: 2; Hofling 2002; Schumann 2000), expressing the view that what variation existed was dialectal and that the regional varieties were not separate languages. My current view is that this was the case until fairly recently, and today only Mopan might be considered a separate language (Hofling 2006a). On the other hand, it appears most likely that dialect variation is a very old phenomenon in the Yukatekan area. Considering that Yukatekan speakers have been in the Mayan lowlands continuously since approximately 1000 B.C. (Kaufman 1976: 107), regional differences must certainly have arisen. Classic-period archaeological zones such as Río Bec, Chenes, and Puuc are very likely associated with Yukateko dialect regions, and the inhabitants of these areas speak different dialects to this day. A Yukateko dictionary published by the Academia de la Lengua Maya (2002) distinguishes five dialect regions (Map 4.1): (1) the henequen area around Mérida (northwestern Yucatán), (2) the Camino Real (western Yucatán), (3) northeastern Yucatán, centered at Valladolid, (4) southeastern Yucatán, including Quintana Roo, and (5) the Chenes region. Barbara Blaha Pfeiler and Hofling (2006) report similar dialectal variation in modern Yukateko.

Colonial sources also provide support for similar regional differences. The *Book of Chilam Balam of Chumayel* (hereafter *Chumayel*) and the *Book of Chilam Balam of Tizimin* (*Tizimin*) reveal that a basic division existed between the eastern and western halves of the peninsula, with the Itza in control of the eastern half and the Tutul Xiw in control of the western half (Edmonson 1982: x, xvi, 1986: 2). The *Chumayel* is generally interpreted as reflecting the point of view of the Tutul Xiw, with whom the Kowoj were allied, while the *Tizimin* reflects the point of view of the Itza. Munro Edmonson (1986: 2) states that there are dialect differences between them, but he is vague about the nature of those differences.

To investigate dialect differences more systematically, I applied a dialect survey of several hundred items prepared for modern Yukateko to both

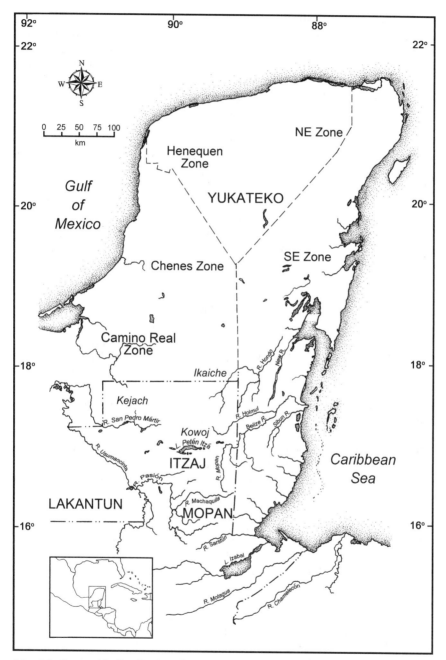

Map 4.1. Geographic distribution of Yukatekan languages in the peninsula and various ethno-political groups in Petén.

documents using Victoria Bricker's (1990a, 1990b) concordances, as well as directly comparing the concordances. As these documents were recorded over a period of nearly three centuries and early portions were likely copied from hieroglyphic codices, some of the differences are doubtless the result of change over time rather than spatially based variation.

In interpreting this survey, caution should be taken in considering counts of linguistic features because the books are not the same length. Bricker's transcriptions have 3,294 lines for the *Chumayel* and 3,126 lines for the *Tizimin*, making the latter about 95 percent as long as the *Chumayel*. However, the lines in the *Tizimin* may be a bit shorter, as the concordance for the *Chumayel* is 589 pages compared to 438 (74 percent) for the *Tizimin*. Similarly, Bricker's morpheme counts list 31,639 for the *Chumayel* (1990b: 589) but 24,225 (77 percent) for the *Tizimin* (1990a: 446). Therefore, unless the difference in frequencies is dramatic, it may be a result of sample size. In citing examples from the books of *chilam balam*, I use the adapted Colonial orthography employed by Bricker but generally conflate *y* with *i* when it is used to represent the same high-front vowel.

Phonology

Although one would expect phonological differences to be present, as in modern dialects, the orthography used by Colonial scribes did not record phonetic details that would reveal them. We know on the basis of modern dialects that syllables may be of form CVC,[3] CVVC (low tone), CVVC (high tone), or CV'VC (glottalized vowel). The books of *chilam b'alam* never record glottal stops and inconsistently record vowel length. For example, modern *hum-p'éel* 'one inanimate thing' (with a long high-tone vowel) appears as *hun-p'el* or *hum-p'el* in the *Tizimin* and always as *hun-p'el* in the *Chumayel*. It is unclear if the assimilation of the nasal consonant in the *Tizimin* reflects dialect variation, change over time, or simply a difference in scribal tradition. Sometimes long high-tone vowels are recorded as both long and short, as in *kéeh* 'deer' appearing as *ceeh* or *ceh* in both, with the *Tizimin* recording a long vowel more frequently. V'V roots also appear as either long or short in both; for example, *ya'ax* 'green' is recorded as either *yax* or *yaax* in both books. Word-final glottal stops are often indicated by doubling the vowel; for example, *ha'* 'water' appears as *haa* in both manuscripts, a convention inherited from hieroglyphic scribal traditions (Bricker 1989: 43). Although the *Motul Dictionary* of Colonial Yukateko distinguishes between *h simple* (the glottal fricative [h]) and *h rezia* (the velar fricative [ɣ]) (Martínez Hernández 1969: 358), a distinction that has been lost word-initially in modern Yukateko (Kaufman 1991; Orie and Bricker 2000), both are written with *h* in the books of *chilam b'alam*, when they are recorded. Although there is evidence that they were in contrast in both the *Tizimin* and the *Chumayel*, no difference was noted between the two. In short, the orthography used is not sufficiently accurate to confidently speak of phonological differences between eastern (Itza) and western (Xiw/Kowoj) Yukateko.

Table 4.1. Lexical differences (frequencies) between the *Tizimin* and the *Chumayel*.

	Tizimin	Chumayel
(1a)	(0)	*bix* 'how' (6)
(1b)	(0)	*nohoch* 'big' (10)
(1c)	*u-ti-al* 'for' (12)	(8)
(1d)	(0)	*tij* 'for' (27)
(1e)	*u-hel* 'other' (18)	(4)
(1f)	(0)	*u-lak* 'other' (14)
(1g)	*manan* 'neg. exist' (22)	(6)
(1h)	(0)	*minan* 'neg. exist' (57)
(1i)	*hi(i)x*, thirteenth day (48)	*hix*, thirteenth day (1)
(1j)	*y-ok-ol cab* 'on earth' (3)	(18)
(1k)	(0)	*tulis* 'whole' (10)
(1l)	*p'ix-ich* 'stay awake' (9)	(1)
(1m)	*amay-te* 'square' (8)	(0)
(1n)	*cit* 'father' (5)	(33)
(1o)	*cul* 'sit' (36)	(34)
(1p)	*cum* 'sit' (14)	(34)
(1q)	*chun* 'base' (9)	(62)
(1r)	*hul* 'arrive here' (2)	(19)
(1s)	*kuch* 'arrive' (28)	(102)
(1t)	*icnal* 'with' (2)	(16)
(1u)	*ah-bobat* 'prophet' (8)	(0)
(1v)	*bacab*, title of office (8)	(1)

Lexicon

A comparison of lexicons in both books did reveal some interesting differences, summarized in Table 4.1.

Some difference are absolute, such as the absence of (1a) *b'ix* 'how,' (1b) *nohoch* 'big,' and (1d) *tij* 'for' in the *Tizimin*, but more often we see different preferences, such as a higher frequency of *cit* 'father' (1n) and *hul* (1r) in the *Chumayel* than in the *Tizimin*. The difference between frequencies of the 260-day calendar day sign Hi(i)x (or Ix) (1i) results from a difference in the calendars and yearbearers employed in the two books (Edmonson 1982: 197, 1986: 10–11). Yearbearers are the four days in the sacred (*tzolk'in*) calendar that may coincide with the beginning of the solar (*ha'ab'*) calendar. Hix is a yearbearer in the colonial Mayapán calendar, reflected in the *Tizimin* but not in other calendars.

There also appear to be differences in the use of deictic demonstratives and locatives between the regions, as shown in Table 4.2. These presumably reflect differences in local discourse practices or styles (cf. Hanks 1990).

Not surprisingly, there is also a difference in references to places, people, lineages, and ethnic groups, as shown in Table 4.3. It is interesting that the Xiw *Chumayel* mentions the Itza more than the Itza *Tizimin* does, but the *Chumayel* does so in disparaging ways—criticizing their speech and customs and referring to then as *aj nunob'* 'stutterers, crude speakers' (Edmonson 1982:

Table 4.2. Differences (frequencies) between deictic demonstratives and locatives in the *Tizimin* and the *Chumayel*.

	Tizimin	*Chumayel*
(2a)	*te-la* 'there close' (7)	(1)
(2b)	(0)	*hel-e-la-e* 'this' (10)
(2c)	*la* 'that' (73)	(246)
(2d)	*lai* 'he/she/it' (107)	*lay* 'he/she/it' (326)
(2e)	*lei* 'the' (21)	*le* 'the' (14)

Table 4.3. Proper nouns in the *Tizimin* and the *Chumayel*.

	Tizimin	*Chumayel*
(3a)	(0)	*Couoh* (3)
(3b)	*Can Ek'* (1)	(0)
(3c)	*Xiu* (4)	(12)
(3d)	*Itza* (8), *Ytza* (33)	*Ytza* (58)
(3e)	(0)	*maya* 'maya language,' 'maya (people)' (29)
(3g)	(0)	*Suyua* 'Suyua language' (26)
(3f)	*Mayapan* (18)	(11)
(3g)	*Chi-chen Itza* (6)	*Chi-ch'een Itza* (14)

3, 221 lines 5155–5156), apparently referring to dialect differences. Itza and Ytza are apparently orthographic equivalents, with Ytza the more frequent spelling in both books. In the Itza *Tizimin* there is no mention of the Kowoj, the Maya (except in the name Mayapán), or the sacred ritual language "Suyua" and little mention of the Xiw.

Morphology

Verbal morphology also differs in some respects (Table 4.4). The patterns evident in the *Chumayel* have since spread to most Yukatekan dialects as a result of the prestige and power associated with the western dialect since Spanish contact. The newly catechized Xiw became willing allies of the Spaniards, whose capital was Mérida (formerly Tihoo) in northwestern Yucatán, and frequently criticized their pagan neighbors to the east. As a result of this contact, the *Chumayel* has many more words of Spanish and Latin origin than the *Tizimin* does (Edmonson 1986: 3). For example, the Spanish-borrowing *dios*, God, appears sixty-four times in the *Chumayel* (Bricker 1990b: 580) but only three times in the *Tizimin* (Bricker 1990a: 441). The aspectual prefixes, such as *t-* "completive" (4a) and the *k-* "incompletive" (4b), are now ubiquitous. The *-om* perfect suffix (4e) has since disappeared.[4]

Nominal morphology also shows some differences in numeral classifiers, locational expressions, and the reverential suffix *-b'il* (Table 4.5).

Table 4.4. Aspectual prefixes in the *Tizimin* and the *Chumayel*.

	Tizimin	*Chumayel*
(4a)	*t-u-Vb-ah*, COM TRAN (9)	*t-u-Vb-ah*, COM TRAN (25)
(4b)	*c-u-Vb-ik*, INC TRAN (2)	*c-u-Vb-ik*, INC TRAN (8)
(4c)	*tun*, third-person DUR (1?)	*tun*, third-person DUR (6)
(4d)	*tac*, desiderative aspect (1)?	*tac*, desiderative aspect (5)
(4e)	*-om*, PERF (250+)	*-om*, PERF (120)
(4f)	*-l-ah-om*, PERF POS (17)	*-l-ah-om*, PERF POS (2)
(4g)	*-p-ah-om*, PERF agentless (PAS (9)	*-p-ah-om*, PERF agentless (PAS (1)
(4h)	*uch-om* 'has happened' (49)	(0)
(4i)	*uch-c(-i)* 'has happened' (19)	*uch-c(-i)* 'has happened' (56)
(4j)	*-b-il*, PAS PART (6)	*-b-il*, PAS PART (24)

Note. Abbreviations are A—Set A person marker, COM—completive, DUR—durative aspect, INC—incompletive aspect, PART—participle, PAS—passive, PERF—perfect, POS—positional, TRAN—transitive verb, Vb—verb stem.

Table 4.5. Nominal morphology in the *Tizimin* and the *Chumayel*.

	Tizimin	*Chumayel*
(5a)	*hun-te Pop* 'one Pop' (19)	*hun-te Yaxkin* 'one Yaxk'in' (1)
(5b)	*hun-tul*, one animate (3)	*hun-tul*, one animate (11)
(5c)	*hun-p'el*, one inanimate (3)	*hun-p'el*, one inanimate (17)
(5d)	*ti y-actun-il* 'in its cave' (16)	*actun* 'cave' (3)
(5e)	*t-u-ch'en-il* 'in its well' (10)	*u-ch'een-il* 'its cave' (1)
(5f)	(0)	*-bil*, reverential (40)

Syntax

As seen in Table 4.6, syntactic patterns are also somewhat different in auxiliary constructions (6a)–(6c), past intransitive constructions (6d), and discourse markers (6e)–(6f).

Concluding Remarks

To summarize, there appear to be dialectal differences in the language of the *Book of Chilam Balam of Tizimin* compared with that of the *Book of Chilam Balam of Chumayel* associated with the Itza and Xiw, respectively. Such differences were likely present at least from the Terminal Classic onward. These differences are clearly dialectal and relatively slight, and there is no question that both dialects were mutually intelligible. Thus, rather slight linguistic differences indexed very different sociopolitical identities. Because the language style recorded in these books is rather formal, reflecting ritual speech, it is likely somewhat more conservative than other spoken genres, and less formal spoken varieties might have differed somewhat more.

As Grant Jones describes (1998: 7–28), several distinct ethno-political groups lived in the Petén region prior to the conquest, including the Kejach,

Table 4.6. Syntactic patterns in the *Tizimin* and the *Chumayel*.

	Tizimin	*Chumayel*
(6a)	*b'in-el u-kah*, future (5)	(0)
(6b)	*uch-k-i*, A-Vb-INC status (3)	*uch-k-i*, A-Vb-INC status, distant past (33)
(6c)	*hop'-i*, A-Vb-INC status 'begin to X' (3)	*hop'-i*, Vb-INC status (25)
(6d)	*ti tal-i* 'then s/he came' (34)	(13)
(6e)	*wal-e* 'then' (?) (89)	(2)
(6f)	*he-x* 'and that' (13)	(72)

Mopan, Itza, and Kowoj (see Map 4.1). Language differences among them were likely of the magnitude noted earlier between the language of the *Tizimin* and the *Chumayel*, which is to say that there were no strong linguistic barriers to communication. On the other hand, it is equally clear that these named groups were often enemies and controlled local territories.

As mentioned, the Mopan speakers were the farthest south and the most different of the Yukatekan language groups. It is possible that a dialect continuum extended from northern Yucatán to southern Petén and that the various groups occupying the lowland region were in virtually continuous contact with one another. Fray Andrés de Avendaño y Loyola's account of the trips he made from Mérida to Petén in 1695 includes interesting observations about sociopolitical groups in the region, including the Itza and their enemies, the Kowoj. He also observes that the dialect of the Itza in Petén was different from, and more conservative than, that of the Itza in northern Yucatán (Avendaño y Loyola 1987: 44; Jones 1998: 427; Schwartz 1990: 61). It is indeed the case that modern Itzaj shares a number of features of verbal morphology with early Colonial Yukateko that were lost by later northern Yukateko speakers (Hofling 2004, 2006a). Avendaño writes that he made a special effort to learn Itza by studying old documents. The Itza in Petén were so impressed with Avendaño's linguistic abilities that they called him *Chomach Ajaw*, 'Senior male lord,' and *Cit can*, 'Father of heaven,' titles no longer used in the north (cf. 4.1n, above).[5]

Analysis of the language history of the Yukatekan groups (Hofling 2002, 2004, 2006a, 2006b) indicates that although Mopan forms the first branch of the family tree, significant contact occurred between Ch'olan speakers and Mopan and between Mopan and Itza, which is reflected by borrowings. Fray Agustín Cano (1984: 8–9), who made a trip into Petén from the south in 1695–1696, mentions encountering Mopan who were bilingual in Mopan and Chol and subordinate to the Itza king Kan Ek'.

Ch'olan speakers occupying the Lacandon forest were resettled in the highlands in the sixteenth century (Boremanse 1998: 3). After the Itza conquest in 1697, the Kejach likely took refuge in the Lacandon forest, as did Kowoj and Itza, who, along with later Yukatekan immigrants, became the modern Yukatekan Lakantun (Hofling 2002, 2004; Pugh 2000, Chapter 16, this volume). The Ikaiche in southern Quintana Roo may have merged with eastern Yukatekan-speaking populations in modern Quintana Roo and Belize. In the Petén lakes region, the Itza and Kowoj were forcibly settled together in mission towns around Lake Petén Itzá in the early eighteenth century (Jones 1998: 390; Schwartz 1990). In San José, on the northwestern shore of the lake, where the last surviving Itzaj Maya speakers live, Kowoj (Cohuoj) is a surname but no longer reflects an ethnic identity distinct from the Itzaj. Nonetheless, San Joseños have had a turbulent relationship with nearby neighbors in San Andrés, which had a strong identification with the Kowoj (N. Schwartz, pers. com., August 25, 2003), and modern conflicts between these towns may indeed reflect the ancient enmity between the Itza and the Kowoj.

Notes

1. Susan Milbrath and Carlos Peraza Lope (2003: 3–4) recently suggested that the *k'atun* chronologies in the books of *chilam b'alam* may have been based on a twenty-four-year *k'atun* rather than a twenty-year *k'atun,* which would push chronologies back somewhat but not enough to make a significant difference in considerations of linguistic relatedness.

2. I follow the Academia de Lenguas Mayas de Guatemala and the Mayan linguists of Oxlajuuj Keej Maya' Ajtz'iib' in using the modern language names Yukatek(o), Lakantun, and Itzaj instead of Yucatec, Lacandon, and Itzá, respectively, but I retain Itza to refer to the Contact/Colonial- and Postclassic-period people because the final consonant is uncertain.

3. C = consonant, V = vowel.

4. See Bricker, Po'ot Yah, and Dzul de Po'ot (1998), Hofling (2006a), and Smailus (1989) for further explanation of the grammatical details.

5. The first vowel of *chomach* is also distinctly Itza. The Colonial Yukateko equivalent of *chomach* was *chamach*.

PART III

THE ARCHAEOLOGY OF THE KOWOJ
Settlement and Architecture at Zacpetén

Prudence M. Rice

We estimated, on the basis of Proyecto Lacustre's initial mapping and excavations, that the Late Postclassic occupation of Zacpetén, with an area of 0.23 square kilometers, was 546 persons (Rice and Rice 1990: table 6.5). Our estimates for the Lake Salpetén basin as a whole, based on our transect surveys, were 1,256 persons using an average of 5.4 persons per household and 2,324 using a 10-person household as a basis for the calculations (ibid.: table 6.6). These totals should be revised upward following Proyecto Maya Colonial's remapping of additional structures on the peninsula: the 137 residential groups at Zacpetén might have housed between 750 and 1,400 persons if they were all contemporaneously occupied.

Late Postclassic settlement throughout the central Petén lakes area exhibits a distinct focus on occupation of the many small islands and peninsulas in those lacustrine basins, a focus we believe represents a defensive posture. Such occupational siting appears to have begun in the Terminal Classic period, as indicated by chronologies at the Topoxté Islands in Lake Yaxhá and Macanché Island. At Zacpetén this is evident not only through its peninsular location but also, as discussed in Chapter 6, by the construction of a large wall-and-moat defensive system where the peninsula joins the northern mainland.

The Kowoj-dominated occupation of the eastern lakes basins is distinguished by the prominence of a specific architectural complex that does not appear in the Itza-dominated west. This complex is the "temple assemblage," long known from Late Postclassic Mayapán in northern Yucatán. The presence of these civic-ceremonial assemblages in eastern Petén supports the Kowoj's late-seventeenth-century claim that they migrated from that city, but it also suggests that such migrations of Kowoj or Kowoj ancestors — likely allied with the Xiw in the north — began centuries before that Spanish report.

The chapters in Part III deal with dating the construction, occupation, and use activities of these assemblages, as well as some of the residential areas of the site. As discussed in Chapters 5 and 7, it is interesting that Zacpetén's two temple assemblages, Group A and Group C, had two phases of Postclassic construction, as did the Castillo at Mayapán and Structure E on Topoxté Island. In Petén, these phases might correlate with episodes of major in-migration, with calendrical rituals, or both. Group A is particularly salient, having Late and Terminal Classic construction — a Plaza Plan 2 or a twin-pyramid group — raised over a large Middle Preclassic platform. Postclassic construction began with a "basic ceremonial group," also known from Mayapán (Proskouriakoff 1962a) and Chich'en Itza, that was later modified into a temple assemblage. The Group A assemblage was renovated still later. In contrast, Group C shows no evidence of earlier construction; it was built as a temple assemblage and renovated once.

We suggest that the initial construction of the basic ceremonial group at Zacpetén probably occurred around A.D. 1200. In the Maya calendar this is a K'atun 8 Ajaw (A.D. 1184–1204), which marked the turning of the 256-year *may* cycle. It coincides with a population influx in the Lake Petén Itzá basin to the west (Chase 1990) and the first constructions at Topoxté Island in Lake Yaxhá to the east after a 400-year abandonment (Hermes 2000a: 294). Our radiocarbon dates suggest that construction of the temple assemblages occurred in the very late fourteenth or early fifteenth centuries, which might reflect two events. One is a K'atun 1 Ajaw revolt in Mayapán around 1390, prompting the emigration of Xiw/Kowoj groups from that city, perhaps to Petén; the other might be the completion of a 52-year Calendar Round in 1425. The final remodeling might have occurred a little more than a century later, perhaps coinciding with the reseating of the *may* cycle in 1539 (or completion of another Calendar Round in 1529).

One of the most intriguing aspects of these temple assemblages is their mirror symmetry, which suggests complementary oppositions and a complex dual/ternary social organization at Zacpetén. We suggest that the three open halls in these groups represent three lineages. Group A features a complete and larger temple assemblage on the east side, representing the primary or most powerful of the immigrant Xiw/Kowoj group(s). This group — perhaps with deep ancestral ties to the area — appropriated the power of the past and the ancient (Classic-period) occupants of this specific locus by maintaining constructional continuities and incorporating stelae and altars into the building facades. Elements of another assemblage on the west side of the Group A plaza apparently represent another lineage and the second part of a moiety. The Group C temple assemblage, built on bedrock, displays mirror symmetry to the east side of Group A, representing a later and complementary opposition to the Group A moiety. As discussed in Chapter 7, different patterns of breakage and disposal of ritual artifact refuse in the two assemblages suggest virtually identical but complementary functions as well.

Excavations at the temple assemblages as well as in five domestic groups provided insights into both the daily activities carried out by Zacpetén's inhabitants and the settlement's abandonment. Some of the residential structures appear to have been long unoccupied, as indicated by the absence of primary and de facto refuse on their upper floors, but others — like the structures in the civic-ceremonial assemblages — appear to have been abandoned rather suddenly. Pottery vessels, incense burners, chipped stone tools and debris, and other artifacts are strewn about the floors of Structures 719, 732, and 747, as on the floors of temples, as if the residents fled hastily, leaving their possessions behind.

Structure 719 is of special interest, as discussed in Chapter 9, because it appears to be a semi-hybrid structure, part residential and part civic-ceremonial. Large quantities of refuse in the back room suggest that a variety of likely elite activities were carried out there, and evidence of late remodeling suggests that Structure 719 was modified to be a *popol naj*, or council house. We believe it was very likely the residence of the Kowoj lineage leadership at the moment of conquest. Its sudden abandonment may have been a result of visits to Zacpetén by Spaniards in the very early eighteenth century, perhaps to round up the Maya into new mission settlements known as *reducciónes*, as several European artifacts were found in Group A.

ZACPETÉN AND THE KOWOJ
Field Methods and Chronologies

—— Timothy W. Pugh and Prudence M. Rice ————————————————

The archaeological site of Zacpetén (historical Sakpeten), a late Kowoj ceremonial and residential center, occupies a cedilla-shaped peninsula extending southward from the northeastern edge of Lake Salpetén, Petén, Guatemala
(Maps 5.1 and 5.2). Its occupational history extends from the Middle Preclassic
period (ca. 800/700–300 B.C.) until just after the Spanish conquest (ca. A.D.
1697), but it was most densely populated during the Late Postclassic and
Contact periods, beginning around A.D. 1400 (Rice and Rice 1990). This occupation history, with Postclassic settlement mapping over Middle Preclassic
occupation, is a distinctive characteristic of the Petén lakes region.

Zacpetén was first discovered, mapped, and tested in 1980 as part of
Proyecto Lacustre. The site later became a focus of Proyecto Maya Colonial's
survey, mapping, and excavations between 1994 and 1997 (Pugh 2001) and
again in 2002 (Duncan 2005a, 2005b). This later research sought to refine the
site's chronological affiliations, illuminate Postclassic- to Colonial-period
architectural styles, and reconstruct ceremonial and domestic activities at the
site.

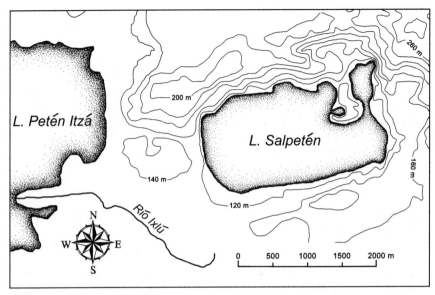

Map 5.1. The basin of Lake Salpetén, Petén, Guatemala, showing location of the Zacpetén peninsula. The site of Ixlú (Saklemakal?) occupies the low elevated area between the two lakes, and we suspect that the two basins might at one time have been joined by an east-west canal just north of this low rise.

Excavation Goals and Methods

The foremost goal of Proyecto Maya Colonial at Zacpetén was to understand the site's chronological development. For this purpose, sixty-six test units were placed in buildings and plazas, and seven looters' trenches were also cleaned, recorded, and filled during the 1994 through 1997 field seasons. Excavated by means of cultural and natural levels until bedrock was reached, these test units revealed that the structure groupings at Zacpetén had varied construction histories.

The second major goal of the field research at Zacpetén was to record Late Postclassic– to Contact-period architecture and activity areas. This objective was accomplished by means of a strategy of extensive horizontal clearing of structure surfaces, with special concern for spatial control of artifacts and their relationships to architecture. Given our focus on reconstructing the political geography of sixteenth- and seventeenth-century Petén, we directed our attention to loci we believed would reveal ethno-specific behaviors, including both ceremonial areas (following Connerton 1989: 43; Lefebvre 1991: 222–225) and domestic groups (following Bourdieu 1977).

Buildings were selected for excavation (Table 5.1) on the basis of various judgmental criteria rather than through a randomized or probabilistic sampling strategy. For example, in the ceremonial complexes, Groups A and C, nearly all structures were cleared; we also uncovered large areas of plaza, sometimes

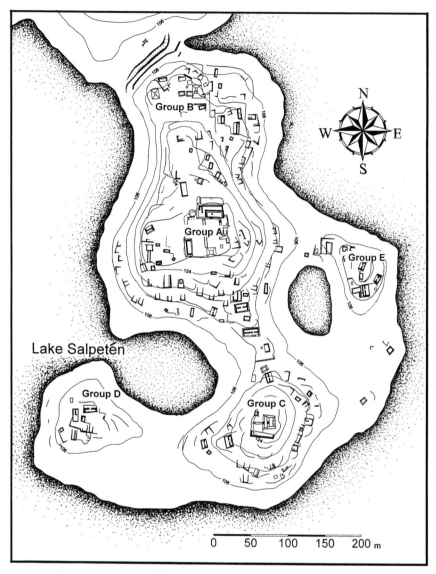

Map 5.2. The peninsular site of Zacpetén, showing major architectural groups.

by means of broad area excavations and sometimes through linear traverses. Area excavations were placed where midden deposits were expected: primarily directly in front of, and also behind, structures. Linear excavations were positioned to sample areas of open plaza. Residential groups were selected on the basis of the size of the residence, location of the group, and variety of associated buildings. Size was important because we expected this variable to be

Table 5.1. Excavated structures at Zacpetén, Petén, Guatemala.

Structure No.	Temple Assmbl.	Temple	Oratorio	Open Hall	Shrine Statue	Shrine Raised	Other	Residence
601	A					X		
602	A	X						
603	A						X	
605	A		X					
606	A			X				
607	A				X			
614	A		X					
615	A			X				
764	C	X						
765	C					X		
766	C				X			
767	C			X				
1002	C		X					
719				X				?
720					X			
721			X					
664				X				X
732				X				X
747/748				X				X
758				X				X

correlated with social status (Pugh 2004: 363–364; Rice 1988: 233). Associated buildings such as shrines, oratorios, and additional residences were also considered, as work at Mayapán revealed that elite residences boasted a large number of ancillary structures (Smith 1962: 218).

The in situ positioning of artifacts in primary contexts and de facto refuse (materials with functional value remaining at a site that was abandoned quickly; Schiffer 1987: 89) was of paramount concern in trying to reconstruct ritual practices, and for this reason excavations were carried out using a grid with a resolution of one meter. To assure the accuracy of the grid, a transit was used to lay several transects in each group from which the rest of the grid was constructed through triangulation and measurement between points. In areas where the latter method was not precise, such as extreme slopes, the transit method was used for the entire grid. Vertical control was established through an arbitrary vertical datum plane. Several datum stakes on each building were tied into the datum plane with the transit, thereby allowing accurate and comparable elevation measures. In the end, a total of 4,685 one-by-one-meter units were excavated at Zacpetén in the 1995, 1996, and 1997 field seasons. Of these, 1,466 units tested domestic areas, with the remainder investigating public areas such as central plazas and ceremonial buildings.

In general, a humus layer covered a layer of building collapse, which in turn rested above Late Postclassic– and Contact-period floors and walls. The latest in situ deposits usually lay under approximately twenty to fifty centimeters of humus and collapse. Excavations were conducted with trowels and small hand picks, as in situ deposits were often fairly shallow. All burials were excavated with wood sculpting tools. Artifacts and other materials (e.g., bone) lying directly upon floors, benches, and other surfaces were drawn and photographed in situ, then removed, bagged, and tagged by one-by-one-meter horizontal units and according to cultural and natural strata. Soil was passed through ⅛-inch hardware cloth screens to recover small artifacts such as mosaic mirror fragments, divination crystals, and small lithics.

In addition to artifact distributions, activities were also indicated by special features such as burials and caches. Because test units revealed both construction chronologies and these special deposits, we placed some units in areas where we expected to encounter caches and burials largely on the basis of the locations of such features at Mayapán (Pollock et al. 1962). Although this method worked well with caches, our burial sample is small, indicating that the occupants of Zacpetén had different burial practices than those known from excavated parts of Mayapán.

One of the most important tasks was the recording of architectural plans and profiles. Field drawings were created at a scale of 1:10. In architectural clearings, all exposed surfaces were drawn, while in test units two profiles were sketched and only one wall of each looter's trench was recorded.

Each bag of artifacts was washed and then sorted into categories such as pottery, lithics, and so on. Many artifact types such as faunal bone and unworked shell were "rough sorted" into general categories and will be examined by specialists in the future. Ceramics, human bone, and lithics (especially tools as opposed to debitage) have been examined more thoroughly. Following the artifact sorting, data were entered into a spreadsheet, and the Surfer® Surface Mapping System was used to create the plans of artifact distribution patterns that appear here and in other publications. Data derived from the artifact analyses and mapping efforts are presented in subsequent chapters.

Petén Postclassic Ceramic Chronologies

Dating the Postclassic in Petén is not an easy task. Ceramics change slowly; there are no carved and dated inscriptions; plaster floors are thin, closely superposed, or nonexistent (see Hermes 2000a: 296). Datable carbon samples are rare given the near-surface deposits, and radiocarbon dates must be fitted to a calibration curve that yields bimodal two-sigma ranges (see also Peraza Lope et al. 2006). Written records comparable to the indigenous *k'atun* histories of Yucatán, however disputed they may be, are lacking. Even a starting point—the end of the Terminal Classic and beginning of the Postclassic—is difficult to pin down (see Demarest, Rice, and Rice 2004). A reliable chronology for the Petén Postclassic, one that integrates construction stages and ceramic change such as that for Mayapán (Milbrath and Peraza Lope 2003), has been more difficult to achieve than one might imagine. This is not for lack of trying, however.

Existing Chronologies

At least five ceramic chronologies have been proposed for the Petén Postclassic, but they were created primarily on the basis of work at the eastern and western extremes of the lakes chain, which, we know now, had different Postclassic histories. Zacpetén, in the middle, partakes of both histories but is not definitively aligned with either.

Perhaps the first effort to construct a ceramic chronology is that of William R. Bullard Jr., on the basis of his 1958–1960 excavations at Topoxté (1970) and Macanché (1973: 228–232). He proposed a "Central Petén Postclassic Tradition" on the basis of what he saw as a distinctive and conservative "tradition" of three largely sequential red-slipped ceramic groups (for detailed descriptions of these ceramic wares, groups, types, and varieties, see Cecil, Chapter 10, and Rice and Cecil, Chapter 11, this volume). These groups fell into four chronological intervals in his scheme. Period I, A.D. 900–1100, which slightly overlapped the end of the Terminal Classic, was characterized by the manufacture and use of pottery of the Augustine ceramic group. Period II, 1100–1250, was characterized by the manufacture and use of Paxcamán group pottery. Period III dated from 1250 to 1450 and was characterized by the continued presence of Paxcamán pottery as well as the manufacture and use of Topoxté group pottery, characteristic of the Topoxté Islands in Lake Yaxhá. It was also at this point that effigy censers began to be used (Rice, Chapter 12, this volume). Period IV began around 1450 and was the period of the Itza in Lake Petén Itzá; Topoxté group pottery ceased to be used, and Paxcamán pottery disappeared by 1500.

In 1979 Prudence Rice published an analysis of pottery from the Central Petén Historical Ecology Project's 1974 excavations on Canté Island, one of the small islands in a cluster known collectively as the Topoxté Islands in Lake Yaxhá. Rice concluded that pottery of the Topoxté ceramic group (manufactured of Clemencia Cream Paste ware) was produced and used throughout the Postclassic period—that is, in both Early and Late facets of the Postclassic Isla ceramic complex—in contrast to Bullard's proposal. This analysis (Rice 1979, 1986: 273–278) indicated the presence of Topoxté pottery in deposits differentiated as A and B; above both A and B lay deposit C, which contained pottery with distinctive curvilinear decoration (Chompoxté Red-on-cream: Chompoxté variety) that was not present in A or B. This chronology was subsequently reiterated following Proyecto Lacustre excavations on Macanché Island in Lake Macanché, where Topoxté pottery was found only in the upper levels of midden and not in construction fills (Rice 1987a; see Rice 1979: 73–76 for a critique of misreadings of Bullard's 1973 chronology as it applies to Macanché). The occurrence of distinctive late wares prompted creation of a provisional "Protohistoric" Ayer complex/phase, dating after A.D. 1450 (Rice 1987a: 43).

The dating of late occupation at the Topoxté Islands has subsequently been revised by Bernard Hermes on the basis of pottery recovered in a joint German-Guatemalan project. According to Hermes (2000a: 294), the main island of the Topoxté Islands was unoccupied for about 400 years, from roughly A.D. 800 to 1200, while occupation continued on the smaller nearby islands of Canté and Paxté. Then, around 1200, in what he calls the Middle Postclassic, there was a flurry of construction and occupation activity on the main island, which accounts for the manufacture and use of the Postclassic Topoxté ceramic group. This scheme is basically a return to that initially proposed by Bullard and has the islands abandoned around 1450. In this chapter we question this chronology on the basis of calibrated radiocarbon dates.

A different Postclassic chronology emerged from Arlen Chase's analysis of pottery from the University of Pennsylvania's Tayasal Project on the Tayasal peninsula on the western end of Lake Petén Itzá, supplemented by other surveys and excavations (Chase 1983; Chase and Chase 1983). Chase divided the region's ceramic phases into Early, Middle, and Late Postclassic, noting the difficulty of determining the end of the Terminal Classic Hobo phase and the beginning of the Early Postclassic Chilcob phase. Clearly, because of the known Itza presence in the Lake Petén Itzá basin at the time of Spanish contact and conquest, a Late Postclassic (or Contact-period) phase is warranted; its presence was often difficult to justify in the other central Petén lake basins, however.

These Petén Postclassic chronological schemes, as well as the one utilized herein, were created primarily on the basis of stratigraphy—which is typically poor—and to a far lesser degree on chronometric dates. In these chronologies it is evident that major breaks between ceramic complexes/phases have been set at roughly 250-year intervals: around 900–950, 1200, and 1450. These intervals seem to reflect archaeologists' explicit or implicit assumptions that major periods of change in Petén corresponded to events attested in the indigenous histories of northern Yucatán. That is, the temporal transitions in Petén chronologies appear to coincide with the "*k'atun* of change," K'atun 8 Ajaw, which recur at intervals of approximately 256 years. Because of the difficulties in precisely dating the construction and occupation of these sites, however, it is unclear whether such coincident periodizations are real or illusory.

Problems in the Zacpetén Ceramic Chronology

It has been difficult for us to pin down dates for the transitions from Late Classic to Terminal Classic to Early Postclassic to Middle Postclassic at Zacpetén, in part because we lack radiocarbon dates but also because we lack clear stratigraphy to isolate ceramic changes. The problem is particularly acute with respect to the Terminal Classic to Early Postclassic transition, where the materials generally occur in the upper forty centimeters or so of an excavation and are not separated by plaster floors. This is in contrast to the situation at nearby Macanché Island, where the changes from Terminal Classic to Early Postclassic pottery types were clearly associated with different soil matrices, although not by floors (Rice 1987a). In addition, at all sites Classic polychromes are heavily eroded, making it difficult to identify types, and forms and paste have been employed as diagnostics. Finally, as frequently noted (P. Rice 1986:

282–285, 1994), basin-to-basin regionalization of ceramic complexes in the Terminal Classic, evidenced in the overlap of three ceramic spheres in the lakes area—Eznab (Tikal and Uaxactun), Spanish Lookout (western Belize), and Boca (Pasión area)—makes it difficult to apply the apparent transitional traits of one basin to another.

Continuity in occupation in the Salpetén basin is evident through the Terminal Classic period and demonstrates ties to the Tikal region. Zacpetén (and Ixlú) stelae are in the style of the Tikal realm (Rice 2004a: 158–165), and Zacpetén appears to have a twin-pyramid group (as does Ixlú). Furthermore, Postclassic buildings are closely aligned with Late Classic buildings, their foundations nearly directly atop the earlier walls. One wonders, therefore, if the Early Postclassic occupants could be direct descendants of the Late Classic residents and in particular if they could be related to the later Xiw/Kowoj who occupied the site.

Pottery changes occurred gradually at Zacpetén, with a slow diminution of Terminal Classic types and forms (e.g., Jato Black-on-Gray; large incurved-rim bowls), while Early Postclassic types, forms, and wares seemed to slide in. Most specifically, snail-inclusion pastes began to be used for red-slipped wares, but the clay was sometimes tempered with volcanic ash, in a blending of Classic and Postclassic technological traits.

In addition, in our excavations at Zacpetén we have not been able to confidently isolate a Middle Postclassic ceramic complex by quantitative or typological diagnostics, nor do we have radiocarbon dates for an interval comparable to what is called Middle Postclassic elsewhere in the region. Nonetheless, we speak here of a Middle Postclassic in terms of construction episodes and deposits that appear to lack both Early and Late Postclassic indicators.

Pottery is also of interest with regard to the relations between the Kowoj of Mayapán and those of Petén. It recently became apparent that the major class of pottery we associate with the Kowoj in Petén, Chompoxté Red-on-cream: Chompoxté variety, with distinctive red-painted curvilinear designs, is virtually identical to certain examples of Tecoh Red-on-buff type at Mayapán, which occurs in relatively small quantities at isolated locations and only in Late Postclassic contexts (Peraza Lope et al. 2006: 169), that is, postdating A.D. 1300. We believe Chompoxté Red-on-cream: Akalché variety (with spare, banded, red-painted decoration) at Topoxté begins earlier than Tecoh at Mayapán (Rice 1979), although again we are unable to date it precisely. Chompoxté is a clear "late" marker—probably 1300 or later—when found at other sites in Petén and at Tipu, however. As discussed by Leslie Cecil (Chapters 10, 11, this volume), we believe its distinctive decoration, along with some examples of Macanché Red-on-paste, represents a strong assertion of Xiw/Kowoj identity in Petén; the related decoration on Tecoh Red-on-buff, found in unusual quantities at Structure Y-45a at Mayapán (Peraza Lope et al. 2006), may also distinguish the Kowoj at that site from other ethno-lineal groups, including perhaps their allies the Xiw.

Dating the Kowoj Arrival in Petén

One of the chief problems we face in setting forth the history of Postclassic- and Contact-period occupation in the central Petén lakes region is the lack of a clear understanding of when the Kowoj arrived in the region (a similar situation exists with respect to the origins of the Itza, of course). A major issue is determining whether "Kowoj" refers to a collective comprising multiple lineages (as does "Itza") or if it references only a single patrilineage, or *ch'ib'al*, with the Kowoj appellative.

Historical knowledge of the Kowoj in Petén begins with the Spanish capitán don Marcos de Abalos y Fuentes, who reported that a Kowoj infor- mant told him the Kowoj migrated from Mayapán to Petén, fleeing the initial wave of Spanish conquest, between 1520 and 1543 (cited in Jones 1998: 11, 16, 430n24). A migration of Kowoj into Petén around this same time also might relate to the Kokom/Itza massacre of Xiw rain priests in Yucatán in 1536 (Jones 1998: 19). According to this story, the priests undertook a pilgrim- age to the rain deities at Chich'en Itza, having asked the Kokom ruler for safe passage through his territory. However, the Kokom, seeking to avenge their defeat at Mayapán at the hands of the Xiw, entertained their guests and then killed them. Two individuals, one of whom was named Na Pot Couoh (Kowoj) — also referred to as Na Pot Xiw — escaped. If he fled to Petén, which cannot be proven, this would be another explanation for a sixteenth-century entry into the lakes region. Both circumstances reference the Kowoj only by their patronym.

Although such a late entry of the Kowoj into Petén is supported by docu- mentary sources, it is difficult to accept from an archaeological viewpoint. On the basis of many lines of evidence, including radiocarbon dates, the number of Kowoj sites in central Petén, and the time we consider necessary for Kowoj populations to have achieved their known distribution, we feel they entered Petén considerably earlier. This possibility requires that we reject the idea that all material manifestations we currently consider "Kowoj" — for exam- ple, temple assemblages and certain ceramics — are strictly tied to that patro- nym. Instead, we must consider the possibility that this attested late arrival of people with a Kowoj patrilineage joined allies — who may or may not have been named Kowoj — already in Petén. Such allies could have been Mopans, peoples originally in the eastern lakes area (in the Terminal Classic period, for example), who were later pushed southward and eastward by the expansion- ist Itza (see Hofling, Chapter 4, this volume).

A more likely possibility is that groups allied with the Xiw in Yucatán moved into Petén at some point during the Postclassic. Like the Itza, the group(s) that eventually became known as the Xiw might have earlier ori- gins in Petén, arriving in Yucatán by way of the Gulf coast. We know from a variety of Colonial sources that the Kowoj were allied with or a constituent lineage of the Xiw, so a return to a Petén homeland might not be too farfetched a concept.

As one alternative to a sixteenth-century migration, the Kowoj/Xiw might have come to Petén as part of the diaspora following the Mayapán collapse.

Their flight from Yucatán would have been a consequence of the Xiw over-throw of the Itza at Mayapán in a K'atun 8 Ajaw, A.D. 1441–1461: some of the Xiw returned to their capital at Maní in the western peninsula, but others — perhaps the instigating lineage(s) — might have fled to the remote Petén lakes area. Another possibility is an uprising occurring in a K'atun 1 Ajaw (A.D. 1382–1401), which may have coincided with the abandonment of Structure Y-45 and its Topoxté-like pottery. Still earlier, flight from northern Yucatán might have been prompted by the "collapse" and abandonment of Chich'en Itza. The in-migration of presumed Itza refugees from that or a related event is attested by marked population increase around Lake Petén Itzá after 1200; it is not inconceivable that the eastern lakes also experienced a concomitant influx of migrants.

These various possibilities gain credence from radiocarbon dates from contexts we evaluate as Kowoj. For example, two of the three Topoxté Islands in Lake Yaxhá — Canté and Paxté — appear to have been occupied continuously from the Late Classic through the Postclassic, and their ceramic assemblage is characterized by the distinctive Postclassic Clemencia Cream Paste ware we identify as Kowoj (Rice 1979; Hermes 2000b). We also note the similarity between one variety of Topoxté pottery, Chompoxté variety of Chompoxté Red-on-cream type, with Tecoh Red-on-buff at Mayapán, suggesting contemporaneity of the two sites. Topoxté Island, the largest of the islands, displayed a "sudden" burst of architecture, including temple assemblage construction, in the Postclassic (see Hermes 2000c: 60–61). Such an abrupt influx of population and new construction in Petén might reasonably be expected to correlate with the abandonment of either Chich'en Itza or Mayapán in the north. However, radiocarbon dates from structural collapse of a temple at Topoxté suggest abandonment of that site around 1450–1475 (Wurster and Hermes 2000: 249). Although we believe these dates have been misinterpreted in terms of site abandonment, as discussed later, for purposes of the present discussion these dates make it extremely unlikely that the Kowoj (in the sense of a broader collective of Xiw-related allies) first came to Petén around either 1450 or 1530. They do, however, suggest a parallel to the population influx in the Lake Petén Itzá area around 1200.

In the end, we cannot assert a firm date for entry of the Kowoj in Petén. We propose that some group(s) of people related to the later Xiw in Yucatán, and perhaps having deep ancestry in Petén, moved into the lakes area in or around a K'atun 8 Ajaw — around 1200 — following the termination of the Chich'en Itza polity. They were joined by later migrants, who seemed to share a mutual and growing antipathy for the Itza/Kokom in both Yucatán and Petén. The Kowoj per se — an elite lineage with the patronym Kowoj — may have been a very late entry into this group of émigrés and dissidents in the eastern Petén lakes area and may have forged an alliance with a faction of Itza. In the absence of data to the contrary, we refer to this entire collective as "Kowoj."

Construction History of Zacpetén: Radiocarbon Dates

Although the construction histories of the various architectural groups at Zacpetén differed, the constructions of Group A and Group C were complementary during the Postclassic and Contact periods, and, as seen in Chapter 7, the activities of these ceremonial areas were also nearly identical. Furthermore, the construction histories of Groups A and C at Zacpetén correspond to that of Topoxté Island, and new construction episodes at the two sites may attest to the incursions of migrants into Petén.

Construction History of Group A

The earliest cultural deposit underlying Group A was a thin layer of very dark brown soil overlying an outcrop of limestone (Figure 5.1). This level, likely a buried A horizon, contained Tzek 1 (Middle Preclassic) ceramics (Rice et al. 1996: 47). Above it was the fill of a very large Middle Preclassic platform, up to three meters deep/high in some excavation units, which covered virtually the entire northern and eastern sectors of what later became Postclassic Group A.

An early excavation that created the later Postclassic mass grave (Operation 1000), on the northwest corner of Group A, disturbed this platform. This was originally a pit measuring approximately four meters in diameter and half a meter deep excavated into bedrock. The base of the pit was filled with *mezcla*, a mixture of collapsed fill including cut stone but lacking pottery to date it. A shallow hole was excavated into the collapse of the platform on the southern side of the pit, into which was placed a large Middle Preclassic dichrome plate—red on the interior and black on the exterior—with its rim and sides missing (Figure 5.2b). Other Middle Preclassic pottery, including a semi-reconstructible Juventud Red cuspidor (Figure 5.2a) on the north side of the pit under the collapse of overhanging bedrock, reinforces the initial creation of this pit in the Middle Preclassic period, perhaps in connection with the construction of the large platform. Above the *mezcla* and extending over bedrock to the north was a thin layer containing very small, eroded sherds that had obviously been exposed to weathering and recycling in other fills before being deposited in this pit.

In the area of Structure 606, a pit containing a cache intruded this Middle Preclassic plaza floor: the cache included an inverted Desprecio Incised (Middle Preclassic) jar covering an obsidian blade. A larger drywall masonry structure was also built upon the plaza surface. We are uncertain whether the cache preceded the masonry construction, but if it did, it dedicated the structure. Test units encountered traces of only one building from this period, a faint foundation deep beneath Structure 606.

Structure 605 had a construction history similar to that of Structure 606: the earliest plaster surface was forty centimeters lower than the surfacing underlying Structure 606, but the two likely formed the same plaza. Below Structure 605, this plaster surfacing capped a more substantial Middle Preclassic fill,

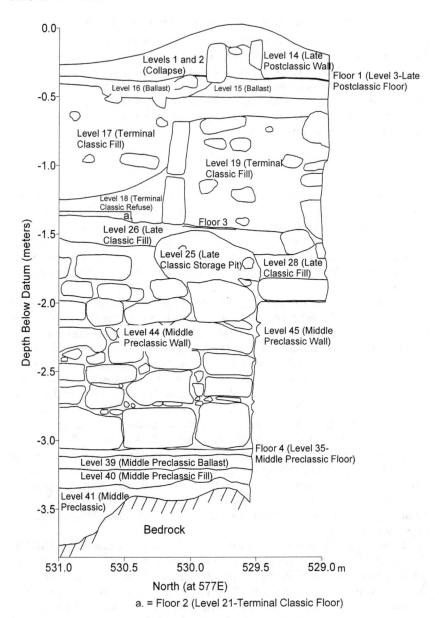

Figure 5.1. Zacpetén Group A, test unit N531/E577, east profile.

as it was built upon a slope. The first building encountered under Structure 605 sat directly on this plaza surface, following the pattern observed below Structure 606. We were not able to define all of the early buildings associated

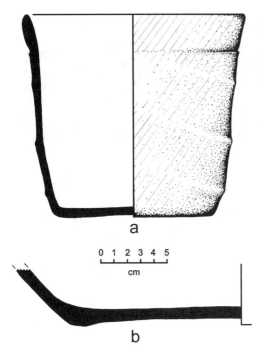

a

b

Figure 5.2. Middle Preclassic pottery from Operation 1000, Group
A: (a) Juventud Red cuspidor,
broken but complete, with broad,
shallow diagonal fluting; (b)
unnamed red-and-black dichrome
(red interior, black exterior) platter
with rim and sides removed; exterior base shows heavy use-wear.

0 1 2 3 4 5

cm

with the earliest (Middle Preclassic) plaza, as Structures 601 and 602 could not
be deeply tested because of instability caused by looters' tunnels.

We did not identify Early Classic constructions in Group A, although
some sherds of that date were recovered from Operation 1000 (the mass
grave), but the Late to Terminal Classic period saw a plethora of construction that defined the essential shape of the group. These constructions were
composed of dressed and mortared soft-limestone masonry veneer covering
a rubble core (Figure 5.3). A range structure lay on the north side of the plaza,
directly beneath Structure 606A, with fragments of Late Classic censer stands
in front of it. Buildings also existed on the east and south sides of the plaza
beneath Structures 601 and 602. A fourth Late to Terminal Classic building
was positioned in the area of Operation 1001, on the west side of the plaza, but
it had been dismantled (Map 5.3), leaving only its rubble core and a burial. No
grave goods were encountered with the burial and the remains were crushed,
but several preserved teeth had been drilled and filled with round serpentine inlays. An AMS analysis (AA-35234) of carbon from the fill of Operation
1001 indicated a conventional age of 880 ± 40, calibrated to A.D. 1030–1260
(two-sigma).

During the Terminal Classic to Early Postclassic period, then, Group A
may have been laid out as a Plaza Plan 2 (Becker 1971: 178–193), with a range
structure, an eastern structure, and two other buildings. However, the group
included plain stelae and a carved altar and stela typical of twin-pyramid

Figure 5.3. Comparison of Late Classic and Late Postclassic masonry styles, Structure 606, Zacpetén.

complexes (Becker 1971: 183; Coggins 1980: 732; Guillemin 1968: 19–25; Jones 1969: 13–14), raising the possibility that the objects may have been moved from Group B (the twin-pyramid complex to the north) or that Group A may once have been such a complex as well. The latter seems most likely, as a carved stela was also recovered in Group B and twin-pyramid complexes generally contain one carved stela.

The complex stratigraphy in the mass grave, Operation 1000, on the northwest corner of Group A, reveals that the Middle Preclassic platform collapse was (re)excavated at some point during the Terminal Classic or Early Postclassic. Pottery was a mixture of Late Classic, Terminal Classic, and Early Postclassic types, the latter including types in the Paxcamán and Topoxté ceramic groups as well as censer fragments. Sherds were frequently small and eroded, indicating that they represented already weathered refuse deposits — perhaps refuse that had accumulated in the pit after its original excavation.

Feature 3, in the southwest corner of Operation 1000 and extending under Structure 614 (Duncan 2005a: 119–121, Chapter 15, this volume), was an eroded excavation filled with fine gray fire ash and capped with plaster and small stones. It contained an almost pure Terminal Classic deposit with many polychrome sherds, including some that looked like precursors to Ixpop Polychrome, a ceramic tube burned on the outside, and a possible pregnant human figurine. In addition, Feature 3 included human remains — an adult and a juvenile — although the skeletons were not complete, and some of the bones indicated burning. Two large rims of unslipped jars (Figure 5.4) were set into the pit and appear to have had something burned in and around

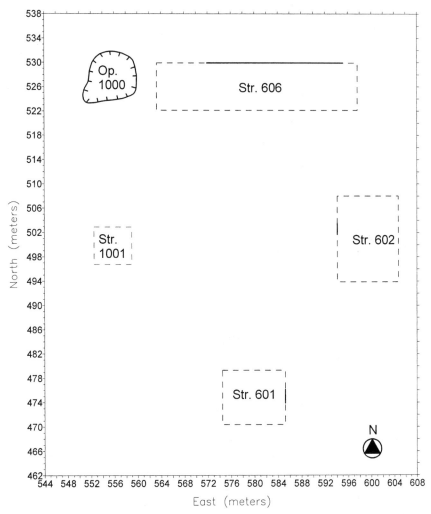

Map 5.3. Zacpetén Group A, reconstruction of how it might have appeared in the Terminal Classic period.

them. Duncan (2005a: 121) concluded that Feature 3 "was excavated during the Terminal Classic, and two large potstands were placed on the floor of the deposit; some material was burned in situ, with other ceramics and bones being deposited after the burning had stopped but before it was completely cool."

Terminal Classic pottery found in this feature as well as in other levels of Operation 1000 included the types Harina Cream, Jato Black-on-Gray, and a dull orange-brown ware — all common at Macanché Island (Rice 1987a). There were also unusual amounts of pottery closely resembling the Terminal Classic

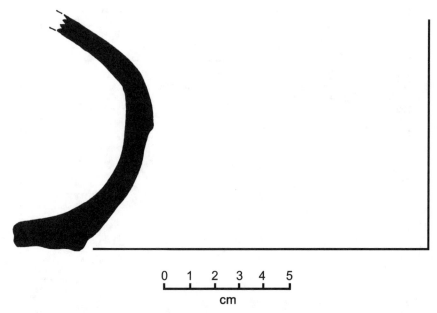

0   1   2   3   4   5
cm

Figure 5.4. Large Cambio Unslipped jar rim or potstand, one of two found in Terminal Classic Feature 3 in the southwest corner of Operation 1000. The lower exterior is ashy gray and appears to have been buried in ash; the upper interior is fire-blackened.

Tolobojo assemblage from Yaxhá to the east (Rice, pers. obs.), including forms and pastes of Tinaja Red, Zacatal Cream Polychrome, Sahcaba Molded-carved, and distinctive piecrust-rim Cambio Unslipped jars. A small, partially reconstructible Tinaja Red tripod dish with inslanting sides was found on bedrock, representing a primary deposit (Figure 5.5). The quantities of Terminal Classic material in Operation 1000 suggest a construction episode of this date in the vicinity that eroded into the pit (see also Figure 5.1).

Above this mixed and eroded stratum, in the central-northeastern portion of the pit, we encountered the remains of a ritual event that had three components: (1) a pile of ash and hardwood charcoal AMS dated (Beta-112318) with a conventional radiocarbon age of 540 + 30 years B.P., calibrated to A.D. 1310–1360 and 1380–1440 (two-sigma); (2) a large sherd of a Chompoxté Red-on-Cream: Akalché variety tecomate/cache vessel (Figure 5.6) resting atop the ash, probably terminated as part of the rites; and (3) a deposit of largely disarticulated human remains (Duncan 2005a, Chapter 15, this volume). On the basis of the lack of intervening erosional sediments among these three deposits in the pit, we conclude that they were placed in relatively quick succession, perhaps within a month (Pugh 2001: 286–287). Pottery fragments commingled with the human remains were small and eroded and from a wide variety of time periods, perhaps representing the same excavated material as that below the ash and charcoal layer. The bones were then carefully covered by a forty-

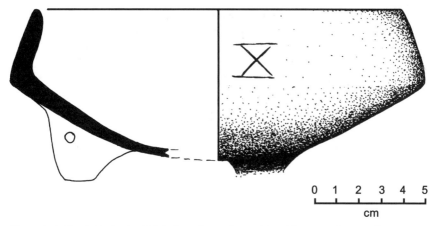

Figure 5.5. Tinaja Red tripod dish from Operation 1000, with a post-slip, pre-fire X incised on the exterior. Interior surface is completely eroded.

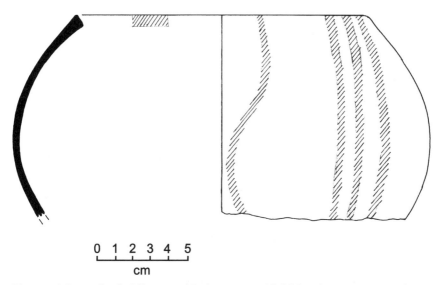

Figure 5.6. Large sherd of Chompoxté Red-on-cream: Akalché variety tecomate *cache vessel found in Operation 1000 atop a deposit with radiocarbon-dated material and directly below the mass grave.*

to seventy-centimeter–thick layer of medium to large rocks; few artifacts were incorporated, but sherds indicate a Late Postclassic date. Around these rocks, the edges of the pit evidenced a series of strata composed of collapsed bedrock and further eroded deposits of the Middle Preclassic platform.

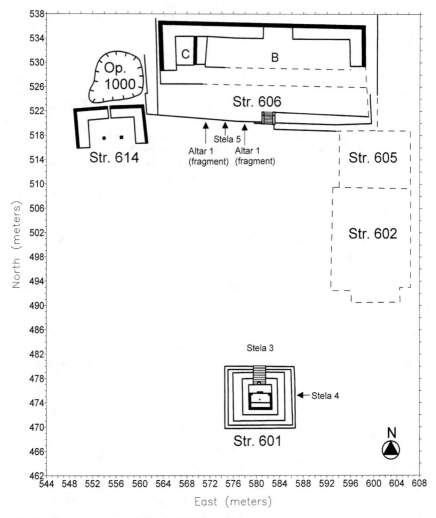

Map 5.4. Zacpetén Group A, Early/Middle Postclassic periods.

During the Early (or Middle) Postclassic period, Group A experienced a substantial reconstruction (Map 5.4), using masonry of random limestone rubble rather than cut stone. Structure 606B was transformed from a range structure to a large, 38.9-meter-wide open hall, which stood 2.4 meters above the adjacent plaza on the rear of its platform. This first hall appears to have been centered upon Structure 601 to the south, a raised shrine. Later, an additional perpendicular extension was added in the western portion of the hall, forming a small end room (606C). The central feature of the hall was a niche centered upon the interior space defined by the eastern arm of the hall and the added western partitioning wall; thus, the niche was likely added after and contemporary with the end room. Structure 614 may have been built at this time as well. If so, the arrangement of Structures 601, 606, and 614 formed a "basic ceremonial group" known at Mayapán. Basic ceremonial groups include a raised shrine facing into an open hall and an oratorio in varied positions (Proskouriakoff 1962a: 91).

Structure 602 and possibly Structure 605 also underwent some rebuilding during this period, although our test units revealed little concerning their shapes. In addition to construction, the occupants of Zacpetén dismantled the structure standing in the area of Operation 1001 and used its stones as building materials. Furthermore, two halves of a carved altar, a carved stela, and a plain stela — all presumed Terminal Classic–period monuments — were incorporated into the south wall of Structure 606 and the east wall of Structure 601.

Group A was reconstructed in the late fourteenth or, more likely, the early fifteenth century, creating a "temple assemblage" on the eastern side of the plaza (Pugh and Rice, Chapter 7, this volume). Temple assemblages were originally defined at Mayapán (Proskouriakoff 1962a: 91), but they have possible roots at Chich'en Itza and Ek Balam (Ringle and Bey 2001: 280). They are generally focused on a temple, typically the tallest building in the group. Temples usually face west, but some face east and others south. To the "right" (north, if the temple faces west) of the temple stands an oratorio. Oratorios are poorly understood, but they appear to have been small temples. An open hall stands orthogonal to the temple and oratorio (Proskouriakoff 1962a: 91). At Mayapán, a raised shrine sits directly in front of and facing into the temple. Between the raised shrine and the temple is a statue shrine, a small rectangular platform that, at Mayapán, housed stuccoed deity effigies (Proskouriakoff 1962a: 91, 136).

As at Mayapán, the focus of the Zacpetén Group A temple assemblage is a temple (Structure 602) with a statue shrine (Structure 607A) to its west and a small rectangular altar (Structure 607B) at its end. Immediately north of the temple lies an oratorio (Structure 605), and an open hall (Structure 606) stands at a right angle to the temple and oratorio. A smaller hall (Structure 606A) was added to the front of the earlier hall (Structure 606B) during the Late Postclassic period. A raised shrine (Structure 601) stands on the south side of the plaza facing north into the westernmost room of the open hall (Structure 606C) with the small masonry platforms.

Temple assemblages are found at other sites in the eastern lakes region, including Topoxté Island in Lake Yaxhá and Muralla de León in the Lake Macanché basin, and they exhibit some variations on the Mayapán pattern. Temples sit on the east side of the plaza, facing west, and they house multiple ceramic effigy censers (Pugh and Rice, Chapter 7, this volume); they are the spaces most closely connected with these ritual vessels (Pugh 2001: 146). Oratorios in Petén generally housed a single effigy censer (perhaps the "lord of the *k'atun*" or the "idol" associated with the new year) instead of the multiple effigies seen in temples. Perpendicular to the temple and oratorio stands an open hall, a long building with a C-shaped bench and often colonnaded; it likely served as a council house (Carmack 1981: 192; Rice 1988: 240–241). The raised shrine is on the south side of the assemblage instead of on the west side of the plaza, in line with and facing into the temple, as at Mayapán.

The Late Postclassic ceremonial buildings on the east side of Group A (see Chapter 7, Map 7.1, this volume) were constructed primarily of hard, unshaped rubble, with larger stones at the base (Figure 5.3). With the exception of the statue shrine, all the buildings on the east side of the plaza were superimposed on Early and/or Middle Postclassic structures, which, in turn, had been built over Late to Terminal Classic constructions. A small *sakbe* (raised causeway; Structure 603) marked the western edge of the temple assemblage and divided Group A into eastern and western halves. The western side of the group included a second open hall (Structure 615) and a second oratorio (Structure 614).

Although we did not recover datable materials directly from the earliest construction of the temple assemblage, we obtained a sample of copal resin inside an effigy censer in a deposit of ritual refuse at the base of the southwest corner of Structure 602. An AMS analysis (Beta-112316) of the resin indicated a conventional age of 500 ± 50, calibrated to A.D. 1300–1370 and 1380–1490 (two-sigma). This temporal range corresponds to the other dated deposit in Group A, the mass grave of dismembered individuals (Operation 1000) in the northwest corner of the group. Structure 614, an oratorio adjacent to the borrow pit, appears to have been constructed in association with deposition of the remains; however, its use was temporary, as it was subsequently partially dismantled. The deposition of the remains likely accompanied and may have dedicated the newly constructed ceremonial group.

Most of the Late Postclassic buildings of Group A, including the *sakbe*, experienced at least one major renovation. The cache in the temple was removed and replaced, and this event corresponded with the burning of the building and its reconstruction. Both halls feature low masonry platforms, one of which was built at the time of the initial construction and the other added later. The superstructure of the eastern oratorio (Structure 605) was completely rebuilt, but the western oratorio was abandoned and its facing stones were removed. Both the statue shrine and the rectangular altar to its west were widened after their initial construction. The southern raised shrine experienced a renovation, although we are uncertain whether this event correlated with the renovation of the other buildings of the group. The *sakbe* was completely reconstructed along with a new plaza surface.

At the time of the renovation of the plaza and *sakbe* (and presumably the other buildings of Group A), several caches (a cranium, seven mandibles, and other human bones) were placed west of the *sakbe* in a deposit we called Operation 1001. Whether these were the remains of sacrificial victims, trophies collected from fallen warriors, or relics amassed from burials, their deposition just prior to the renovation of the groups likely rededicated the newly reconstructed plaza. Late Postclassic pottery fragments adjacent to the mandibles indicate a late deposit.

Our work in Group A recovered three pieces of iron and part of a white clay pipe stem. One of the pieces of iron and the pipe stem were found behind

Structure 615, the open hall in the southwestern corner of Group A. In addition, an unusual, angular pottery handle was found that must have been part of a European-style pitcher, but it was manufactured of local Snail-Inclusion Paste ware with a characteristically late, dark reddish-purple slip (see Figure 12.10b). Debris behind (northwest of) the building included sherds from about a dozen censers, composite and effigy, but the latter were represented almost entirely by fragments of the receptacles; components of the effigies— for example, arms, legs, costumes—were missing except for one head. This raises the possibility that Spaniards occupied this structure at some time and destroyed the most obvious evidence of "idolatry."

Construction History of Group B

The most prominent construction in Group B was a crude twin-pyramid complex or related form, which could date to either the Late or Terminal Classic. Twin-pyramid complexes were defined at Tikal (Jones 1969) by two identical radial (four-stairway) pyramids facing each other on the east and west sides of a plaza, but at Zacpetén the temples varied in size, and both were less than four meters high. The groups generally featured a carved stela inside a roofless enclosure on the north side of the plaza, plain stelae in front (west) of the eastern temple, and a nine-doorway structure to the south. In Group B at Zacpetén, a plain stela stood to the west of the eastern temple, and a carved stela was found buried near one of the temples in earlier investigations by Proyecto Lacustre (D. Rice 1986: 323). Structures vaguely suggesting the north and south components of twin-pyramid complexes were present in Group B, but they were asymmetrically aligned.

Excavations in Group B consisted only of test units rather than clearing operations, and these units did not reveal substantial stratified deposits. In many areas bedrock lay only thirty centimeters beneath the surface. Several Late Postclassic effigy incense burner sherds encountered in the plaza suggest that the use of this group extended beyond the Terminal Classic period.

Construction History of Group C

Unlike the Group A temple assemblage, the area of Group C does not appear to have been used by Middle Preclassic occupants of Zacpetén. Test units indicated that prior to the building of the Postclassic plaza and temple assemblage, most of Group C was an exposed outcrop of bedrock that had been burned in several areas, perhaps by dedication fires or milpa clearing. The bedrock on the south side of the plaza of Group C (underlying Structure 767) was initially much lower than the rest of the plaza (Figure 5.7). This lower terrace was capped by a plaster surface and was then built up about 1.5 meters, leveling the entire plaza with the exception of areas with protruding bedrock. Strata with Terminal Classic ceramic diagnostics were encountered in the base of some test units, but this material may have been brought in as fill from elsewhere. Plaster plaza surfaces encountered in the test units were relatively

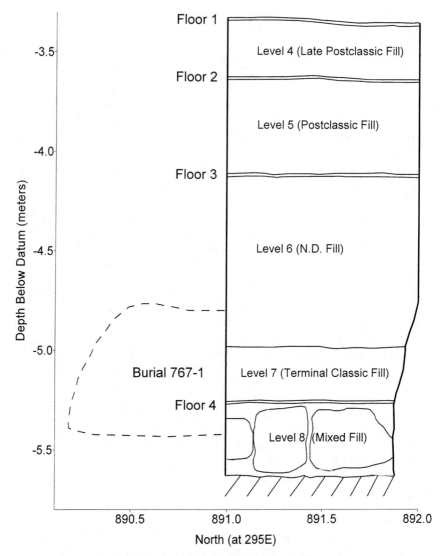

Figure 5.7. Zacpetén Group C, test unit N892/E296, east profile.

thin, and at Zacpetén thin floors generally dated to the Late Postclassic and thick floors to the Classic or Preclassic periods.

An early version of Structure 764, likely the temple of the temple assemblage, was built on the east side of the plaza (Map 5.5). In front (west) of the temple stairway were two small altars or shrines and a circular, tiered altar (Figure 5.8). Similar structures are depicted in the Codex Dresden holding human sacrifices (Villacorta and Villacorta 1930: 78–95). To the east of the cir-

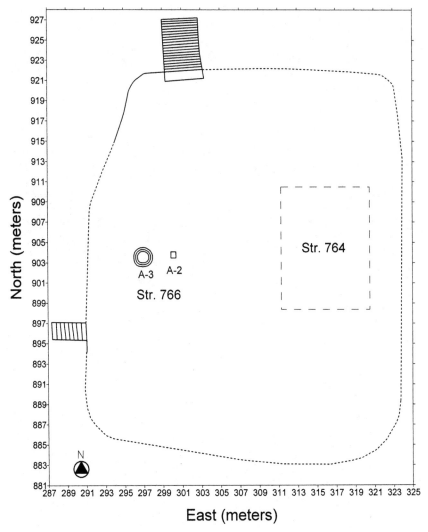

Map 5.5. Zacpetén Group C, Early/Middle Postclassic periods.

cular altar was a small rectangular altar. While we have no dates for this early version of the temple and its two associated shrines, they were likely built during the Early or Middle Postclassic period.

The final version of Structure 764 was a five-doorway temple built during the Late Postclassic period. An AMS-dated sample (AA-35235) of wood charcoal found in collapsed building material had a conventional age of 585 ± 45 B.P., calibrated to A.D. 1290–1430 (two-sigma). The other elements of a temple assemblage were constructed at the same time: a hall (Structure 767), a raised shrine (Structure 765), and a statue shrine (Structure 766). Interestingly,

Figure 5.8. Structure 766A, Group C, Zacpetén.

the layout of this group exhibits mirror symmetry to the eastern side of Group A: as in Group A, the temple faced to the west toward the statue shrine, but in Group C the raised shrine stood on the north side of the plaza and faced south into the open hall.

As with Group A, all buildings of Group C appear to have been renovated once after their initial construction (Pugh 2001: 391). For example, the original central cache of the temple, Structure 764, was terminated and then reactivated with a new vessel and contents, indicating that the building had been renovated, both materially and spiritually. The open hall, Structure 766, was originally constructed with a medial niche as the central feature. This niche was filled in, and at least one of the masonry rectangles in the western side of the building was added during the later renovation.

The statue shrine, Structure 766, a low, narrow platform abutting the earlier circular shrine and covering the rectangular altar/shrine, was widened slightly in a subsequent reconstruction. Upon this platform stood two rectangular altars, the western of which rested almost directly above the earlier rectangular altar, suggesting continuity in practice. These altars appear to have been initially associated with the primary construction of the long platform. Just to the west of the circular altar was another rectangular altar, the elevation of which suggests it was contemporary with the construction of the long platform. Like the platform, it appears that this rectangular altar was widened after originally being built.

We are uncertain of the temporal interval between the initial construction of the temple assemblage and its renovation. The assemblage was used for at least 200 years, as demonstrated by the radiocarbon date of construction material in Structure 764 and the finding of a lead musket ball adjacent to Structure 766. Thus, the latest use of the group postdated the arrival of Spanish goods into Maya trade networks.

Construction Histories of Domestic Groups

All excavated domestic groups had Late Postclassic– to Contact-period components; however, only Structure 719 and Structure 747 had evidence of earlier construction stages. The three other tested groups (Structures 732, 664, and 758) had construction levels with earlier diagnostics, but this fill was likely brought from other portions of the site to build their platforms. One wonders about the locations of the homes of the site's Preclassic- and Classic-period inhabitants because we did not find evidence that they substantially leveled the sloping terrain. The use of uneven terrain appears to have been a Late Postclassic innovation or necessity at Zacpetén.

As mentioned in Chapters 8 and 9 of this volume and elsewhere (Pugh 2004), three of the excavated domestic groups (Groups 719, 732, and 747) had substantial de facto refuse, including in situ ceramic vessels containing organic remains. Structure 719 (see Pugh, Rice, and Cecil, Chapter 9, this volume) had a ceramic jar holding maize kernels dated with AMS (Beta-107791), indicating a conventional age of 200 ± 40 B.P., calibrated to A.D. 1640–1700, 1720–1820, 1830–1880, and 1910–1960 (two-sigma). The dates between A.D. 1830 and 1960 have low relative probabilities (19.3 percent), and the lack of iron artifacts in the building does not support them. Nevertheless, as mentioned in Chapter 9, a cow mandible was encountered in this residence, indicating that it was in use during the Contact period and probably at conquest. Structure 719 was preceded by an earlier Late Postclassic construction, built over an even earlier structure with Early Classic ceramic diagnostics in its fill.

In Structure 732, a ceramic incense burner containing preserved copal (*Protium copal; pom*) resin sat on an "altar." AMS dating (AA-35236) indicated that the resin has a conventional age of 426 ± 30 B.P., calibrated to A.D. 1420–1520 (91.7 percent probability) and 1600–1620 (3.7 percent probability) (two-sigma). Test units excavated into Structure 732 did not encounter evidence for earlier constructions.

A smashed jar on the floor of Structure 747 contained numerous net weights and a fragment of wood (Beta-112317) with a conventional age of 370 ± 30 B.P., calibrated to A.D. 1440–1530 and 1550–1640 (two-sigma). Group 747 was superimposed upon a Terminal Classic or Early Postclassic construction.

Radiocarbon Dates in Comparative Context

All seven radiocarbon assays (Table 5.2) from Zacpetén date to the Postclassic or the Contact period. The selection of probable late samples was purposeful, representing the focus of Proyecto Maya Colonial. In addition to dating various Postclassic constructions, the analyzed materials tie Zacpetén to radiocarbon

Table 5.2. Radiocarbon Dates from Zacpetén.

Sample #	Context	δ13C	C14 Age	Calib. Range (95.4%) A.D.‡	Probability	Material
AA35234	Op. 1001, fill layer	-14.9	880 ± 40	1030–1260	95.4%	charcoal/burned clay
AA35235	Building collapse, Str. 764, Group C	-25.3	585 ± 45	1290–1430	95.4%	wood charcoal
Beta-112318	Burning event, Op. 1000, Group A	-27.9	540 ± 30	1310–1360	26.5%	wood charcoal
				1380–1440	68.9%	
Beta-112316	Ritual refuse pit, Str. 602, Group A	-27.4	500 ± 50	1300–1370	15.3%	copal resin
				1380–1490	80.1%	
AA35236	Copal inside in situ censer, Str. 732	-27.1	426 ± 30	1420–1520	91.7%	copal resin
				1600–1620	3.7%	
Beta-112317	Wood inside in situ vessel, Str. 747	*	370 ± 30	1440–1530	52.4%	wood charcoal
				1550–1640	43.0%	
Beta-107791	Maize inside in situ vessel, Str. 719	-13.3	200 ± 40	1640–1700	25.3%	maize
				1720–1820	50.8%	
				1830–1880	4.9%	
				1910–1960	14.4%	

‡ Calibrated with OXCAL.
* Not available.

Table 5.3. Two-sigma calibrated radiocarbon date ranges (and percentage probabilities) from Topoxté Structure E-2.

Sample Number	Calibrated Ranges	
Bln-4741A	1430–1530 (57.1%)	1540–1640 (38.3%)
Bln-4742	1430–1530 (74.4%)	1560–1630 (20.7%)
Bln-4743	1420–1530 (72%)	1560–1640 (23.4%)

Source: Wurster and Hermes 2000.

dates obtained from other sites in Petén and the larger Maya world (Appendix 5.I). It is not possible to determine which events occurred at precisely the same time. Nevertheless, probable chronological ranges can be compared to reveal relative contemporaneities.

Relations with the Topoxté Islands

The relationship between Zacpetén and Topoxté is critical, as the latter has the most elaborately constructed temple assemblage in central Petén and is the only such assemblage with beam and mortar roofs in some buildings. The group may have been constructed by early Kowoj or their ancestors (Xiw) who migrated from Yucatán. Three dates taken from Structure E-2 at Topoxté have the same problem with bimodal distributions as the Zacpetén dates do (Table 5.3).

Both Structure E (E-2) and its immediate predecessor (E-1) were part of a temple assemblage (Hermes 2000c: 61), although Structure E-2 was an oratorio and Structure E-1 a shrine. Structure E-1 appears to have been part of a sudden construction event that occurred around A.D. 1200 after the main island had been abandoned for about four centuries (Hermes 2000a: 295). This event marked the initial construction of temple assemblages at Topoxté and in Petén (and possibly also at Zacpetén).

Wolfgang Wurster and Bernard Hermes (2000: 249) have argued, on the basis of these radiocarbon results, that Topoxté was abandoned between A.D. 1450 and 1475. Unfortunately, their Late Postclassic samples were all derived from the same ceremonial building (Structure E) and could hardly date the abandonment of the site. The samples might date the final use of Structure E, but even this possibility seems unlikely, as they were obtained from debris on the floor with the assumption that these carbonized remains were contemporary with incense burners lying on the same floor (Wurster and Hermes 2000: 249). The roof of Structure E, which crushed the in situ censers when it collapsed, was composed of wooden beams and mortar (Hermes et al. 2000: 42). If the samples were derived from roofing materials, then they date the building's final construction phase rather than its abandonment. Finally, even if the samples did correspond to the site's abandonment, they do not indicate a range of A.D. 1450 to 1475 but rather ranges from 1420 to 1530 and 1540 to 1640 (combined 95 percent probabilities).

Topoxté was very likely abandoned before Zacpetén, as the former lacks Colonial artifacts, but the precise time of that abandonment is unknown. Sherds of Ídolos Modeled effigy censers, manufactured at Topoxté of Clemencia Cream Paste ware, were never found in primary refuse at Zacpetén. Those censers were copied in a late-occurring local coarse orange-brown carbonate paste (Uapake Carbonate Paste ware) and were classified as Kulut Modeled (see Rice, Chapter 12, Appendix 12.I, this volume). We interpret this as indicating that the Kowoj continued to create effigy censers featuring what appears to be their unique deity image but ceased doing so using the distinctive cream-colored clay of the Lake Yaxhá area.

Furthermore, the earlier Postclassic construction phases were not dated at Topoxté by the German-Guatemalan team. Interestingly, the construction sequence of the central ceremonial group at Topoxté Island closely matches that of Zacpetén's Group A and Group C. The Early/Middle Postclassic stages in Groups A and C at Zacpetén correspond to Topoxté's *Estadio* (construction stage) 8, the Late Postclassic reconstruction of the ceremonial groups into temple assemblages at Zacpetén with Topoxté's *Estadio* 9, and the renovation of Zacpetén's assemblages with *Estadio* 10 of Topoxté (see Hermes 2000c: 60–61).

Furthermore, the main ceremonial structures at Topoxté, Zacpetén, and Mayapán all appear to have experienced two episodes of Late Postclassic construction: the original building of the assemblage and a later renovation. One possibility is that these construction and reconstruction events might have been timed to the same calendrical celebration; however, the dates of construction and renovation of the Mayapán Castillo may have been timed to a K'atun 6 Ajaw, 1204–1224, perhaps more specifically to the Calendar Round ending in 1217 or the turning of the *b'ak'tun* in 1224 (see Rice, Chapter 2, Note 4, this volume). The reconstruction of the Castillo may have occurred in a K'atun 13 Ajaw, A.D. 1263–1283. These dates appear linked to Itza/Kokom histories, however, and may be specifically tied to Calendar Round celebrations.

Xiw/Kowoj histories in Petén appear to begin with some Xiw-related groups that migrated to the lakes region as a result of the K'atun 8 Ajaw (1185–1204) through 4 Ajaw (1224–1244) conflict between the Xiw, Itza/Kokom, and possibly others. This conflict coincided approximately with the end of Chich'en Itza as a *may* seat and the beginning of Mayapán's prominence in that role. This early group of immigrants, together with any remnant populations in the area—perhaps Mopan—would have created the basic ceremonial groups at Zacpetén, which resemble those at Chich'en Itza. The incorporation of Late or Terminal Classic monuments into the facades of these structures, and their exact alignments with earlier buildings at Zacpetén, strongly suggests that the newcomers identified closely with the site and its late Tikal-allied ruling family and sought to proclaim this association very publicly.

The construction of the first temple assemblages appears to be related to the revolt of the Xiw against the Kokom at Mayapán in a K'atun 1 Ajaw (1382–1402), after which some Xiw lineages—which we suspect bore the Kowoj patronym—fled. Some settled in Petén, where they appear to have joined the earlier immigrant Xiw-affiliated groups. The subsequent reconstruction or refurbishment of the temple assemblages might coincide with the collapse of Mayapán in the next K'atun 8 Ajaw, 1441–1461, or, perhaps more likely, with the later Calendar Round completion in 1529 and the *may* completion in 1539. The last (or nearly last) important influx of Xiw-related lineages into the area may have been that of the 1530s, when a group self-identifying as Kowoj is reported to have entered.

Temple assemblages or variants were constructed at Topoxté Island (and apparently earlier at the other islands in Lake Yaxhá), at Tipu in Belize, and at Muralla de León in the Lake Macanché basin; two were also built at Zacpetén.[1] Problems of imprecise dating make them all appear approximately coeval. What does this apparent contemporaneity of five to seven temple assemblages in the eastern Petén lakes area mean ethno-politically, particularly at Zacpetén, which had two? One suggestion is that they corresponded to different Xiw-affiliated lineages in Petén, each of which had the responsibility for creating and recreating its identity through these distinctive ritual complexes. Mayapán also had at least five temple assemblages, and these groups may also have been linked to lineages (Pugh 2003b).

Zacpetén Dates in Broader Context

In the 200 years prior to the earliest radiocarbon date at Zacpetén, major Late- and Terminal Classic–period centers such as Caracol, Copán, Quiriguá, Xunantunich, Chich'en Itza, Uxmal, Tikal, Seibal, and Isla Cerritos were on the decline. Nevertheless, radiocarbon dates indicate at least the possibility of later occupations at these sites (Appendix 5.I; see also Demarest, Rice, and Rice 2004). Many of the earlier monuments of the former Maya states found new uses, as in the case of Stela 26 at Tikal, which was broken and used as an altar with associated burning (Sample P-278) (Ralph and Stuckenrath 1962: 156). This reveals that the smashing and resetting of monuments in Group A at Zacpetén was not an isolated event (see also Hammond and Bobo 1994; Satterthwaite 1958). In addition, a great deal of ritual activity is evident in caves such as Balankanche in Yucatán (Andrews and Andrews 1980: table 4) and Meyehal Xheton in Belize (Prufer 2002: table 9.2). In northern Yucatán, a small town emerged in the area that later became Mayapán (Peraza Lope et al. 2006). As seen in Appendix 5.I, the burned material (AA-35234) from Operation 1001 in Group A at Zacpetén was contemporary with renovation events and effigy censer use at Cuello (Hammond, Housley, and Law 1991: 73); the deaths of individuals at Copán, Seibal, and Nebaj; and construction at Tulum, Santa Rita Corozal, and Muyil, which stands south of Tulum.

We have no radiocarbon assays testifying to Middle Postclassic construction events at Zacpetén that occurred between the date obtained from the burned Early Postclassic material and the Late Postclassic reconstructions of Group A and Group C, but ceremonial architecture dating to this period was encountered in both groups. The Maya world outside Zacpetén was also fairly active. Mayapán (Milbrath and Peraza Lope 2003; Peraza Lope et al. 2006), Santa Rita Corozal, and Caye Coco experienced numerous construction and depositional activities, and the last known pre-Hispanic Copanero was laid to rest (although one wonders who interred the individual). The Codex Grolier may also have been produced at this time. Mayapán experienced a massive growth spurt, including the initial construction of its Castillo in imitation of the Castillo at Chich'en Itza (Appendix 5.I).

Sometime between the late thirteenth and late fifteenth centuries, Groups A and C of Zacpetén were reconfigured into temple assemblages. Two dates at Mayapán are consistent with numerous samples obtained by more recent work, suggesting that the site was largely abandoned by the mid-fifteenth century. Structure Y-45 was abandoned at this time, and a large number of "butchered and burned human remains" were placed in a mass grave in the southwest corner of the Itzmal Chen Group (Peraza Lope et al. 2006: 161). Construction events in Zacpetén Group C and dedicatory events and the use of effigy censers in Group A correspond with the K'atun 1 Ajaw revolt — perhaps supporting notions of population movements to Petén from that northern city. Corresponding to the events at Zacpetén were construction and caching activities at Santa Rita Corozal and Topoxté, the construction of a stucco mask at Naco, the accumulation of midden at Caye Coco and Naco, and the placement of burials in sites and offerings in caves in southern Belize (Appendix 5.I).

The construction or final use of Structure E at Topoxté matches nicely with in situ (final use) materials encountered in Structures 732 and 747 at Zacpetén. These dates also correspond to wood from a sediment sample from Lake Salpetén (CAMS-62939). At this time, the percentage of organic carbon deposited on the lake bed was high, suggesting that a population decline had occurred slightly earlier (Rosenmeier et al. 2002: 188). Whereas inhabitants seem to have abandoned most of the shoreline of Lake Salpetén (Rice and Rice 1980), those behind the walls of Zacpetén were fairly stable — at least until the abandonment of Structures 732 and 747.

An elaborate cache at Santa Rita Corozal (Appendix 5.I) has slightly later ranges than most samples collected from Zacpetén, with the exception of the maize samples from Structure 719, which place terminal occupation at the site after A.D. 1640. The cow mandible in this building and other European artifacts in Groups A and C support the late date of the maize kernels. Because it is unlikely that the elites of Structure 719 were the only occupants of Zacpetén, the absence of additional late dates was likely the result of an inadequate sample. The ranges of the maize sample from Structure 719 correspond well with those of wood (CAMS-62943) from another sediment sample from Lake Salpetén. At this time, the percentage of organic carbon in the lake was at its maximum (Rosenmeier et al. 2002: figure 3), perhaps reflecting that the final "hangers-on" at Zacpetén had vacated. The large amount of de facto refuse in Structure 719 and the presence of small but valued copper alloy objects indicate that the building was rapidly abandoned (Inomata and Webb 2003: 3; Stevenson 1982: 241–246). The range of the latest date from Zacpetén slightly predates those obtained from European ships wrecked off the coast of Honduras.

Zacpetén had a long occupational history—nearly as long as the Maya occupation of Petén. Our research focused on Zacpetén's Postclassic developments, but the site also possesses substantial Preclassic and Late to Terminal Classic deposits. The precise date of the Xiw/Kowoj arrival at the site is uncertain. It is clear from documentary sources that Kowoj lived there during the Contact period, and, archaeologically, this latest occupation melded seamlessly from the Late Postclassic period. New ceremonial assemblages and ceramic styles that appeared at the beginning of the Late Postclassic suggest some sort of break with what occurred before. However, it is possible that these changes resulted from return migrations of relatives who lived in Yucatán during the Mayapán hegemony. As discussed in Chapter 6, these new ceremonial assemblages were patterned after the temple assemblages of Yucatán and were the locations of most central Kowoj ritual performances.

Note

1. Other sites with temple assemblages include Ek Balam in Yucatán (Ringle and Bey 2001: 279–280), Isla Cilvituk in Campeche (Alexander and Canché Manzanero 1998), and Cozumel (Freidel and Sabloff 1984: 97) in the lowlands and Kawinal, Iximché, and Utatlán in the Guatemalan highlands (Arnauld 1997: 122–123; Carmack 1981: 385; Ichon et al. 1981: 194).

Appendix 5.I. Select Radiocarbon Assays Falling within the Postclassic Range

Lab Number	Context	C-14 Age	Calibrated Range (A.D.)	Prob.	Source
P-2533	Quiriguá, test unit	1150 ± 50	770–1000	95.4%	Fishman and Lawn 1978
P-278	Tikal, Room 3, Cache 19	1150 ± 47	770–1000	95.4%	Ralph and Stuckenrath 1962
LJ-87	Chichen Itza, Las Monjas	1140 ± 200	500–1300	95.4%	Andrews and Andrews 1980
Y-626	Chichen Itza, Castillo lintel	1140 ± 100	660–1040	95.4%	Andrews and Andrews 1980
UCLA-1985BC	Cuello, test unit	1140 ± 100	660–1040	95.4%	Hammond et al. 1976
P-2534	Quiriguá, Str. 2C3-3	1140 ± 50	770–1000	95.4%	Fishman and Lawn 1978
P-2535	Quiriguá, test unit	1130 ± 180	600–1300	95.4%	Fishman and Lawn 1978
AA40691	Saki Tzul, burial	1127 ± 35	780–1000	95.4%	Prufer 2002
P-1200	Tikal, Temple IV	1125 ± 46	780–1000	95.4%	Sidrys and Berger 1979
SI-281	Bilboa, last phase of ballcourt	1110 ± 80	690–750	3.6%	Long and Mielke 1967
			960–1040	90.7%	
			1090–1120	1.1%	
UM-1891	Macanché, fill, test unit 6	1105 ± 90	680–1070	90.8%	Rice 1987a
			1080–1160	4.6%	
P-2538	Quiriguá, test unit	1100 ± 170	600–1300	95.4%	Fishman and Lawn 1978
UCLA-1640F	Seibal, Mass Burial 4	1100 ± 100	680–1160	95.4%	Berger et al. 1974
WIS-144	Sayil, Palace beam	1100 ± 70	770–1040	95.4%	Bender, Bryson, and Baerreis 1967
Beta-139616	Copán, Str. 11L-141	1100 ± 40	870–1030	95.4%	Manahan 2003
X-9372	Xunantunich, Str. A-24	1095 ± 75	780–790	1.3%	LeCount et al. 2002
			770–1050	90.6%	
			1080–1160	3.5%	
LJ-272	Balankanche, urn contents	1090 ± 200	400–1250	95.4%	Hubbs, Bien, and Suess 1962
LJ-273	Balankanche, hearth	1090 ± 200	400–1250	95.4%	Hubbs, Bien, and Suess 1962
P-1132	Balankanche, cave shrine	1072 ± 51	810–1040	95.4%	Andrews and Andrews 1980
Beta-139614	Copán, Str. 11L-137	1070 ± 40	890–1030	95.4%	Manahan 2003
GrN-613	Uxmal, Monjas lintel	1065 ± 120	650–1250	95.4%	Andrews and Andrews 1980
AA40683	Meyehal Xheton, cave offering	1062 ± 42	890–1030	95.4%	Prufer 2002

Lab no.	Provenience	Date (BP)	Calibrated range (AD)	%	Reference
UCLA-1992C	La Canteada, Str. 5	1050 ± 220	550–1400	95.4%	Sidrys and Berger 1979
Y-1289	Lake Petenxil II, core (91 cm b.s.)	1040 ± 200	600–1400	95.4%	Stuiver and Deevey 1961
Beta-139615	Copán, Str. 11L-141	1030 ± 40	890–930 / 940–1050 / 1090–1160	8.4% / 78.3% / 8.7%	Manahan 2003
P-1133	Balankanche, cave shrine	1028 ± 42	890–1050 / 1080–1160	84.1% / 11.3%	Andrews and Andrews 1980
UCLA-1938F	Aventura	1025 ± 80	860–1220	95.4%	Berger and Sidrys 1983
UM-122	San Jose, Belize	1010 ± 50	890–930 / 950–1170	4.8% / 90.6%	Fishman and Lawn 1978
UCLA-1640A	Seibal, Burial 12	1000 ± 65	890–1210	95.4%	Berger et al. 1974
AA45744	Ek Xux, Str. 70	998 ± 39	970–1160	95.4%	
AA45652	Ek Xux, Str. 70	995 ± 44	970–1170	95.4%	
UCLA-1617	Chinkultic, tomb	990 ± 70	890–930 / 940–1220	4.0% / 91.4%	Sidrys and Berger 1979
Beta-139617	Copán, Str. 11L-141	980 ± 40	980–1170	95.4%	Manahan 2003
A-12785	Mayapán, Q-95?	960 ± 40	990–1170	95.4%	Peraza Lope et al. 2006
A-12778	Mayapán, Str. Q-97, pit features	955 ± 40	990–1180	95.4%	Peraza Lope et al. 2006
UCLA-1640B	Seibal, Burial 13	940 ± 70	980–1250	95.4%	Berger et al. 1974
Beta-18079	Santa Rita Corozal, Str. 77	930 ± 110	890–1290	95.4%	Chase and Chase 1988
UCLA-1985F	Cuello, test unit	930 ± 85	970–1280	95.4%	Hammond et al. 1976
A-12793	Mayapán, Str. Q-162a, "sub-Castillo"	930 ± 30	1020–1170	95.4%	Peraza Lope et al. 2006
BM-37	Las Cuevas	920 ± 150	750–1400	95.4%	Barker and Mackey 1959
Beta-139612	Copán, Str. 11L-137	920 ± 40	1020–1220	95.4%	Manahan 2003
A-12782	Mayapán, Str. Q-82, "early plaza floors"	905 ± 45	1020–1220	95.4%	Peraza Lope et al. 2006
OxA-1809	Cuello, Str. 35 addition	900 ± 120	890–1310	95.4%	Hammond, Housley, and Law 1991
Penn-3076	Santa Rita Corozal, Str. 77	880 ± 190	700–1450	95.4%	Chase and Chase 1988
OxA-1808	Cuello, Str. 35 addition	880 ± 110	960–1310	95.4%	Hammond, Housley, and Law 1991

continued on next page

Appendix 5.1 – *continued*

Lab Number	Context	C-14 Age	Calibrated Range (A.D.)	Prob.	Source
Y-393	Tulum, Str. 21, lintel	880 ± 60	1020–1260	95.4%	Deevey, Gralenski, and Hoffren 1959
A-12777	Mayapán, Str. Q-59a, burial in shrine	845 ± 40	1040–1090	9.8%	Peraza Lope et al. 2006
			1120–1270	85.6%	
A-12781	Mayapán, Str. Q-77, "middle plaza floors"	820 ± 55	1040–1100	8.8%	Peraza Lope et al. 2006
			1110–1290	86.0%	
Y-392	Tikal, Str. 60, beam	800 ± 50	1060–1090	1.7%	Deevey, Gralenski, and Hoffren 1959
			1120–1140	1.7%	
			1150–1300	92.0%	
Beta-18068	Santa Rita Corozal, Str. 7	780 ± 70	1030–1100	6.9%	Chase and Chase 1988
			1110–1320	84.5%	
			1350–1390	4.0%	
UCLA-1935A	Tiger Bay Cave, torch	780 ± 60	1040–1090	3.6%	Sidrys and Berger 1979
			1120–1140	2.0%	
			1150–1310	88.1%	
			1360–1390	1.7%	
Beta-139613	Copán, Str. 11L-137	780 ± 40	1180–1300	95.4%	Manahan 2003
Y-369	Nebaj, tomb lintel	770 ± 60	1060–1090	1.6%	Deevey, Gralenski, and Hoffren 1959
			1120–1140	1.3%	
			1150–1310	88.7%	
			1350–1390	3.8%	
CAMS-63094	Caye Coco, midden	770 ± 40	1190–1300	95.4%	Rosenswig and Masson 2002
UCLA-1938C	Patchchacan, burial	760 ± 110	1030–1410	95.4%	Berger and Sidrys 1983
A-12804	Mayapán, Str. Q-72	760 ± 35	1210–1290	95.4%	Peraza Lope et al. 2006
A-12799	Mayapán, Str. Q-88a	750 ± 50	1170–1310	91.3%	Peraza Lope et al. 2006
			1360–1390	4.1%	

Lab No.	Provenience	Radiocarbon age	Calibrated range	Percentage	Reference
A-12803	Mayapán, Str. Q-70	750 ± 45	1180–1310	92.7%	Peraza Lope et al. 2006
			1360–1390	2.7%	
Penn-3073	Santa Rita Corozal, Str. 81	740 ± 50	1190–1320	86.7%	Chase and Chase 1988
			1350–1390	8.7%	
AA-64972	Mayapán, Ossuary near Str. Q-79a	733 ± 47	1200–1320	86.1%	Peraza Lope et al. 2006
			1350–1390	9.3%	
Beta-18082	Santa Rita Corozal, Str. 81	730 ± 70	1160–1410	95.4%	Chase and Chase 1988
Teledyne 1-6107	Codex Grolier	720 ± 130	1030–1440	95.4%	Coe 1973
A-12807	Mayapán, Str. Q-98	715 ± 30	1220–1310	87.1%	Peraza Lope et al. 2006
			1360–1390	8.3%	
Beta-18083	Santa Rita Corozal, Str. 81	710 ± 70	1180–1410	95.4%	Chase and Chase 1988
AA45755	Muklebal Tzul, Str. 7 tomb	710 ± 41	1220–1330	73.2%	Prufer 2002
			1340–1400	22.2%	
GrN-452	Mayapán, trench near Castillo	700 ± 115	1040–1100	4.8%	Ringle, Gallareta Negrón, and Bey 1998
			1110–1440	90.6%	Ringle, Gallareta Negrón, and Bey 1998
Penn-3075	Santa Rita Corozal, Str. 81	700 ± 50	1220–1330	63.1%	Chase and Chase 1988
			1340–1400	32.3%	
CAMS-64541	Caye Coco, midden	700 ± 40	1240–1330	65.1%	Rosenswig and Masson 2002
			1340–1400	30.3%	
A-12784	Mayapán, Str. Q-95	690 ± 45	1240–1400	95.4%	Peraza Lope et al. 2006
UCLA-1938E	Aventura, Str. 15	680 ± 80	1210–1430	95.4%	Berger and Sidrys 1983
AA40686	Zecklebal Kaab Pek, cave altar	673 ± 35	1270–1330	47.6%	Prufer 2002
			1340–1400	47.8%	
CAMS-64544	Caye Coco, midden	670 ± 50	1260–1410	95.4%	Rosenswig and Masson 2002
A-64974	Mayapán, Itzmal Chen, Ossuary	679 ± 50	1250–1400	95.4%	Peraza Lope et al. 2006
A-12780	Mayapán, Sector Q	665 ± 45	1260–1400	95.4%	Peraza Lope et al. 2006
Beta-18081	Santa Rita Corozal, Str. 81	660 ± 80	1220–1430	95.4%	Chase and Chase 1988
A-12787	Mayapán, Str. Q-127?	660 ± 40	1270–1400	95.4%	Peraza Lope et al. 2006

continued on next page

Appendix 5.I – *continued*

Lab Number	Context	C-14 Age	Calibrated Range (A.D.)	Prob.	Source
A-12798	Mayapán, Str. Q-88a	660 ± 40	1270–1400	95.4%	Peraza Lope et al. 2006
A-12795	Mayapán, Str. Q-87a	660 ± 35	1270–1330	47.5%	Peraza Lope et al. 2006
			1340–1400	47.9%	
A-12788	Mayapán, Str. 152, midden	655 ± 40	1270–1400	95.4%	Peraza Lope et al. 2006
A-12791	Mayapán, Q-152c	655 ± 35	1270–1330	45.7%	Peraza Lope et al. 2006
			1340–1400	49.7%	
A-13862	Mayapán, Str. Y45a	655 ± 30	1270–1330	45.4%	Peraza Lope et al. 2006
			1340–1400	50.0%	
A-12783	Mayapán, Str. Q-84, burial cist	650+100/-95	1180–1450	95.4%	Peraza Lope et al. 2006
Penn-3074	Santa Rita Corozal, Str. 77	650 ± 40	1280–1400	95.4%	Chase and Chase 1988
A-12794	Mayapán, Str. Q-83	650 ± 40	1280–1400	95.4%	Peraza Lope et al. 2006
GrN-1166	Mayapán, Str. R-87, beam	640 ± 55	1280–1410	95.4%	Ringle, Gallareta Negrón, and Bey 1998
Y-987	Lake Petenxil, Core (92 cm b.s.)	635 ± 140	1000–1650	95.4%	Stuiver and Deevey 1961
A-12790	Mayapán, Str. Q-151	615 ± 45	1280–1410	95.4%	Peraza Lope et al. 2006
Beta-18078	Santa Rita Corozal, Str. 77	610 ± 60	1280–1430	95.4%	Chase and Chase 1988
A-12806	Mayapán, Str. Q-64	605 ± 35	1290–1410	95.4%	Peraza Lope et al. 2006
AA55949	Pine Torch Rockshelter, pine torch	604 ± 36	1295–1414	95.4%	Peterson 2006
A-12779	Mayapán, Str. Q-214	595 ± 40	1290–1420	95.4%	Peraza Lope et al. 2006
AA45746	Muklebal Tzul, Str. 1 tomb	591 ± 38	1290–1420	95.4%	Prufer 2002
A-12789	Mayapán, Q-152, "floor at base"	585 ± 40	1290–1420	95.4%	Peraza Lope et al. 2006
A-64973	Mayapán, burial	570 ± 46	1290–1440	95.4%	Peraza Lope et al. 2006
A-12800	Mayapán, Str. Q-88a	565 ± 40	1290–1370	54.5%	Peraza Lope et al. 2006
			1380–1440	41.0%	
Beta-18076	Santa Rita Corozal, Str. 58 cache	530 ± 60	1290–1470	95.4%	Chase and Chase 1988
A-12797	Mayapán, Str. Q-88	520 ± 60	1290–1470	95.4%	Peraza Lope et al. 2006

TBN-315-2	Bilboa, test unit	503 ± 70	1290–1520	92.5%	Chandler, Kinningham, and Massey 1963
AA44452	Chabil Ukal, cave shrine	499 ± 39	1590–1630 1320–1350 1390–1470	2.9% 7.1% 88.3%	Prufer 2002
Beta-18080	Santa Rita Corozal, Str. 77	490 ± 100	1290–1640	95.4%	Chase and Chase 1988
M-719B	San Gervasio, Str. 3, beam	480 ± 200	1150–2000	95.4%	Andrews and Andrews 1980
UCLA-1921A	Santa Rita Corozal, midden	475 ± 50	1320–1350 1390–1520 1590–1620	4.8% 88.2% 2.5%	Berger and Sidrys 1983
A-13861	Mayapán, lime production quarry	430 ± 110	1290–1700 1750–1800	94.4% 1.0%	Peraza Lope et al. 2006
A-12776	Mayapán, Str. Q-59a, burial in shrine	425 ± 45	1420–1500 1550–1620	76.5% 18.9%	Peraza Lope et al. 2006
Bln-4742	Topoxté, Str. E	407 ± 37	1430–1530 1560–1630	74.7% 20.7%	Wurster and Hermes 2000
Bln-4743	Topoxté, Str. E	406 ± 39	1420–1530 1560–1640	72.0% 23.4%	Wurster and Hermes 2000
CAMS-62939	Lake Salpeten sediments (59 cm b.s.)	400 ± 40	1430–1530 1550–1640	67.3% 28.1%	Rosenmeier et al. 2002
Bln 4741A	Topoxté, Str. E, debris on final floor	384 ± 41	1430–1530 1540–1640	57.1% 38.3%	Wurster and Hermes 2000
A-12786	Mayapán, Q-95	365 ± 45	1440–1640	95.4%	Peraza Lope et al. 2006
P-2140	San Jeronimo, Guatemala, Burial 6	360 ± 40	1440–1640	95.4%	Fishman, Forbes, and Lawn 1977
GrN-450	Mayapán, Str. 21?, beam	355 ± 130	1300–2000	95.4%	Ringle, Gallareta Negrón, and Bey 1998
Beta-18087	Santa Rita Corozal, Str. 183 cache	330 ± 70	1400–1700 1750–1800	93.5% 1.9%	Chase and Chase 1988
P-1930	Port Royal, Honduras, Shipwreck PR-1	310 ± 40	1480–1660	95.4%	Lawn 1974

continued on next page

Appendix 5.I – continued

Lab Number	Context	C-14 Age	Calibrated Range (A.D.)	Prob.	Source
A-12801	Mayapán, Ossuary near Str. Q-69	280 ± 30	1490–1670	93.1%	Peraza Lope et al. 2006
UM-636	Port Royal, Honduras, Shipwreck PR-1	260 ± 60	1460–1700	70.4%	Stipp, Eldridge, and Cadwell 1976
			1720–1820	19.9%	
			1910–1960	5.1%	
UM-625	Port Royal, Honduras, Shipwreck PR-1	230 ± 70	1480–1890	85.9%	Stipp, Eldridge, and Cadwell 1976
P-1799	Port Royal, Honduras, Shipwreck PR-1	230 ± 40	1910–1960	9.5%	Stipp, Eldridge, and Cadwell 1976
			1520–1580	7.3%	
			1620–1690	38.4%	
			1720–1820	40.3%	
			1930–1950	9.4%	
M-719A	San Gervasio, Str. 3, beam	200 ± 200	1428–1950	95.4%	Andrews and Andrews 1980
CAMS 62943	Lake Salpetén sediments (24 cm b.s.)	180 ± 50	1640–1890	80.3%	Rosenmeier et al. 2002
			1910–1960	15.1%	
A-12796	Mayapán, Str. 87a	170 ± 40	1650–1890	77.9%	Peraza Lope et al. 2006
			1910–1960	17.5%	
A-12792	Mayapán, Str. 162f	150 ± 35	1660–1960	95.4%	Peraza Lope et al. 2006
AA45723	Ek Xux, Str. 91	148 ± 45	1660–1960	95.4%	Prufer 2002
UM-622	Port Royal, Honduras, Shipwreck PR-4	130 ± 60	1660–1960	95.4%	Stipp, Eldridge, and Cadwell 1976

DEFENSIVE ARCHITECTURE AND THE CONTEXT OF WARFARE AT ZACPETÉN

—— Prudence M. Rice, Don S. Rice, Timothy W. Pugh,——————————————
and Rómulo Sánchez Polo

A rchival data indicate that the Itza and Kowoj and their allies engaged in intermittent warfare during the seventeenth century. Conflicts in the form of skirmishes, raids, and major combat between the Itza and Kowoj are recorded in ethnohistoric accounts, as are hostilities between the Maya and Spaniards (Avendaño y Loyola 1987; Cortés 1986; Díaz del Castillo 1973; Jones 1989, 1998; López de Cogolludo 1957; Scholes and Roys 1968; Villagutierre Soto-Mayor 1983; Ximénez 1929–1931). Aggression is also attested in the archaeological record by the remains of defensive systems, human victims, and weaponry.

Such conflicts undoubtedly existed for centuries before being documented by the Spaniards; indeed, various kinds, causes, and degrees of warfare in the Classic period are attested both epigraphically and archaeologically. In the central Petén lakes region, the consequences of warfare were dramatically underscored by a shift in settlement to the islands and peninsulas in the lake basins in the Terminal Classic period, and this settlement focus was maintained throughout the Postclassic and Contact periods. This chapter reviews evidence for intra-Maya warfare and Maya-Spanish hostilities in central Petén, especially among the Kowoj and as evidenced at Zacpetén's defensive system.

Warfare and the Maya

Although words such as aggression, conflict, hostility, violence, and warfare are often synonyms and used interchangeably, "warfare" has consistent connotations. The term implies the presence of organized groups of combatants, offensive and defensive strategies, specialized weaponry and tactics, and destruction of capital and human resources (or the intent to destroy them). Identification of warfare can be made difficult, however, by the varied social expressions in which conflict is made manifest (Fried 1967). As a result, definitions of warfare, as analytical constructs, are often debated. Issues of scale can also confuse efforts to distinguish between more informal modes of aggression and highly organized hostile activities. This variability in expression and scale, in turn, can make determination of causes and outcomes of warfare problematic.

William Tulio Divale and Marvin Harris (1976: 521, emphasis in original) define warfare broadly to include "all organized forms of *intergroup* homicide involving combat teams of two or more persons, including feuding and raiding." Within this broad reach, warfare may involve small- and large-scale expressions of violence, including individual and group killing, mutilation, physical destruction, and psychological acts such as humiliation. David Webster (1998: 313) defines warfare as "planned confrontations between groups of people who conceive of themselves as members of separate political communities." Political groups define and maintain internal interests, and they are prepared to defend those interests through the exercise of aggression. However, the definition of political groups is often inextricably entwined with definitions of ethnicity, and in many circumstances the term "warfare" encompasses conflicts among groups of similar ethnic identity, as well as between different ethnic communities (Cohen 1978).

Ethnic similarities and dissimilarities are basic to Karl F. Otterbein's (1968, 1973) distinctions between internal and external warfare. Internal warfare is defined as occurring "between political communities within the same cultural unit," where political communities are characterized as sharing a common territory but having separate decision-making leaders (Otterbein 1968: 277). Conventions of warfare may be implemented during internal conflicts, with opposed forces agreeing to follow these mutual agreements. External warfare, on the other hand, occurs between culturally dissimilar groups whose identities and values are not shared or respected. Disagreements over group history, membership, and norms influence external conflict, with warfare trespassing cultural barriers and territories.

Arthur Demarest (1978) recast Otterbein's distinctions into a model of Classic Maya warfare that identifies two patterns. One is conflict that primarily involved elites. Reflected mostly in art and inscriptions, this type of warfare occurred when conflicting groups were ethnically similar. Conflict among similar ethnic groups is considered more ritualized and characterized by cultural restrictions. Moreover, combat of this kind does not deteriorate as it does in "total war." Cultural agreements in this phase of warfare are seen as restricting the scale of warfare; consequently, war among these groups appears limited and, despite genuine aggression, has relatively low-level impact on local populations.

The second pattern, more extensive and deadly, is indicated archaeologically principally by the appearance of defensive systems. In this form of aggression dissimilar, opposed factions do not share these mutual cultural warfare "standards," and their antagonisms largely reflect ethnic differences. Warfare between two different ethnic groups is described as the last phase of "unlimited" or "total" war. In this type of warfare, no limits or restrictions in conducting war can be detected archaeologically. Although Demarest's model of Maya war suggests the possibility of large-scale warfare, it still assumes that Maya conflict was highly ritualized.

Ross Hassig (1992), however, in his study of warfare in Mesoamerica, argues that all warfare should be considered ritualized to some degree (see also Webster 1998: 337–339). In situations where identities and values are shared, as in internal warfare, there can be a high degree of ritualization. But even between very dissimilar groups, common weaponry and tactics and common philosophies of conflict can ritualize organized aggression, where ritual is understood as action that has symbolic value as prescribed by a religion or by traditions of a group.

Many Mayanists agree that warfare in the Late Classic period was largely ritualized, as evidenced by the choreographed events narrated in inscriptions and depicted in sculpture, and that there may have been specific rules and goals that guided participants (Brown and Garber 2003). Scholars do not fully understand many of the fundamental aspects of Late Classic Maya conflict, however, such as how it was organized, directed, and carried out. Nor are they in agreement about the causes of Maya warfare—status rivalry, securing political or religious power, fulfilling supernatural mandates, control of capital resources, boundary maintenance, and so on. Most, however, espouse that Late Classic combat was mainly an elite activity, with a broadly shared elite "culture" structuring the nature and goals of conflict (Demarest 1997, 2004; Demarest, Rice, and Rice 2004; Fash 2001; Freidel 1986a; Rice 2004a, 2007b; Schele and Freidel 1990; Webster 1977, 1998). As primarily an elite activity, Late Classic warfare can be considered to have been largely internal conflict (as defined earlier) characterized by small scale, close-quarter engagement, low technological investment, and low impact with regard to consequences for commoner populations.

Archaeologists tend to consider conflicts in the Postclassic period to be culturally and symbolically different from the wars of the Classic period, with the transformation occurring during the eighth to eleventh centuries. This period of transition and the later Postclassic period are often characterized by the dissolution of governance by dynastic kings, population pressure on local capital resources, demographic shifts and increased internal migration, in-migration of non-Maya peoples (e.g., central Mexican and Gulf coast groups), incorporation of Maya populations into broader Mesoamerican economic and political spheres, and the rise and fall of large, centralized hegemonies in the northern Maya lowlands. These changes did not occur without conflict, and warfare is thought to have changed substantially so as to involve elite and non-elite participants, internal and external conflict, larger scale, engagement at greater distances, more technological investment, and higher impact on Maya populations.

Reasons for conflict in the Postclassic and Colonial periods included territorial boundaries but also acquisition of slaves, disputes over access to salt, resolution of debts, familial or lineage brawls, revenge for ill treatment of vassals, and the rights to obtain contracts with other towns (C.D.I. 1898; Repetto Tio 1985; Roys 1943: 65–70). We find it difficult to believe that Classic-period conflicts did not arise over similar issues, but that is not the topic of our discussion. We think it important to note, however, that although warfare in the Postclassic period has often been characterized as concerned with more secular issues than was warfare in Classic times, ritual issues and structure remained.

In particular, warfare is known to have occurred over and been structured by calendrical issues, which, in turn, had implications for definition of territorial boundaries, rights to resources, and so on (Edmonson 1982, 1986; Rice 2004a). Rivalry over calendrical matters led to antagonisms and wars among political entities involved in an extended competition for the prestige and practical advantages of seating twenty-year *k'atuns* and the *may* in the Postclassic and Colonial periods.

The connection between religion and combat is evident in the titles and duties of war leaders. For example, the Postclassic *nakom* was a war leader — reported as a kind of "captain" by the Spanish — and also had administrative as well as ritual functions in organizing wars (Roys 1943: 66). Bishop Diego de Landa (in Tozzer 1941: 122) reported that the *nakom* was treated as if he were a god during the time of his duties, remaining in sexual abstinence and ruling over the Mayan month of Pax.

Some sources suggest that war leaders were also priests. Father Diego López de Cogolludo (1957: 547) referred to a Maya group commanded by a captain "Aj K'in P'ol," who was reported to be a priest or a "priest of their idols" (*k'in* usually refers to priests with calendrical duties; *k'in* 'day, sun, time'). He was also known as Aj Chata P'ol and Nakom P'ol, names that suggest his function as a priest and a military leader. This individual was also known as the Itza territorial leader Aj K'in P'ol (Jones 1998: 48–49).

One of the governing bodies among the Itza in Petén was a group of thirteen individuals known as Ach Kat, who also appear to have had combined military and religious responsibilities (Jones 1998: 61). In particular, the existence of thirteen of these persons suggests connections to the thirteen twenty-year *k'atuns* in a *may* cycle and the likelihood that the Ach Kat represented the thirteen towns that were rotating *k'atun* seats within the *may*. This position clarifies the otherwise bewildering dual meanings of the word *k'atun* as both a twenty-year period of time and also war(rior) or battle: the Postclassic *k'atun* wars (*u k'atun k'atunob'*) were waged over competing calendars (Edmonson 1982: xvi–xvii) as well as the seating of the *k'atuns*. "Seatings" of the *may* occurred at periods of 260 *tuns* (approximately 256 years), with transitions probably occurring at the middle of the *may* (Rice 2004a: 111–115). Thus, the *may* model suggests that the midpoint of the cycle—a K'atun 7 Ajaw—would have been a period of competition, struggle, and possible warfare associated with selection of a new cycle seat (Rice 2007b: 172).

Spanish References to Warfare and Weaponry

Fortifications and Fortified Villages

When Hernán Cortés and his entourage passed through Kehach territory, northwest of Lake Petén Itzá, he reported finding a number of fortified towns. The first such town was located on a "high rock" near a lake and a river that debouches into it and was surrounded by a deep moat and a wooden palisade (Cortés 1986: 371). Another town, Tiac—said to be at war with the first—was larger, with earthworks, walls, watchtowers, and three separately fortified residential districts inside (ibid.: 372). Both towns had recently been abandoned.

Perhaps the most informative commentary on Kowoj warriors comes from Franciscan Friar Andrés de Avendaño y Loyola, who described an encounter with a group of Maya warriors on a trip to the Itza island capital of Nojpeten in 1696. The encounter involved Aj Kowoj and a party of Kowoj political and military leaders and attendants, who arrived from the northern shore of Lake Petén Itzá:

> I found myself thus occupied [in baptizing and catechizing children] when on the said day some of the governors, captains, and heads of the other *petens*, began to come, navigating across the lake, with their war officers and their standards, such as lances and stone knives a little less than a quarter of a vara (21 cm) long. Instead of ribbons the lances were decorated with feathers of many colors, very showy and all hanging down. I went out to receive them as a matter of courtesy, but the Indians of that *peten* [Nojpeten] went out only out of curiosity to see them arrive, painted and feathered, in war dress, their faces painted black. (Avendaño y Loyola 1987: 38)

Avendaño described two of the Kowoj visitors to Petén as appearing to be high-ranking military leaders—an old man who carried a standard, accompanied by a younger man. These standards presumably consisted of lances—wooden poles topped with large stone knives and decorated with feathers—and suggest similarities to colorfully decorated lances or spears in northern Yucatán, sometimes called *nabte* (C.D.I. 1898). The two individuals were probably the leaders of the Kowoj territory, one known as Cacique or Aj Kowoj and the other as Captain (or Kulut) Kowoj. This political and military leadership pairing resembles both the Itza arrangement and dual military/

political partnerships known in northern Yucatán during the Postclassic and Colonial periods (see Roys 1943: 62, 66–67). Grant Jones (1998: 326) has suggested that Captain Kowoj was the individual who attacked Nojpetén prior to Avendaño y Loyola's 1696 visit and who was later executed by the Spaniards after the conquest of Nojpetén.

Avendaño's description mentions the use of black face painting by the Kowoj during their visit to Nojpetén, describing them as ferocious looking. Other references to body painting come from López de Cogolludo (1957), who stated that when Franciscan fathers Bartolomé de Fuensalida and Juan de Orbita left Nojpetén after their first visit in 1618, their departure was blemished by threats from armed and blackened warriors in canoes who warned them never to return. Black paint was also the most common body painting used by ordinary warriors in northern Yucatán, although red paint was used as well (Repetto Tio 1985; Roys 1943: 66; Tozzer 1941: 89n378). Individuals using tattoos or paint were probably persons of high status. One individual described by Fray Agustín Cano (1942) had tattoos on his face, chest, and thighs. This person appears to have been a warrior who knew something about Spanish weapons: he indicated that he was familiar with the muskets, asked for a machete, and inquired about a wide sword a Spanish soldier carried.

Later Spaniards remarked on abandoned fortifications in the eastern lakes region in what would have been Kowoj territory. In 1698 Pedro de Zubiaur reported one of wood northeast of Lake Petén Itzá, which was said to be capable of resisting even artillery (cited in Jones 1998: 385). Another abandoned fortified town in the Kowoj area was observed when the Spaniards opened a new road from Chanchanjá to Lake Petén Itzá. In 1702 they occupied this fortification—located about three leagues northeast of the eastern port of Saklemakal (ibid.)—which they described as very strong, made of thin stakes in the shape of an O, with well-planned entrances and exits. The stockade is described as capable of holding 500 men; however, Jones (ibid.: 511n120) suggested that the residences in this Kowoj town were outside the boundary of the stockade, which served as a refuge in time of war. The roads that linked the fortified town with Lake Petén Itzá were apparently closed or camouflaged for a distance of two leagues. Jones (ibid.: 385) suggested that the stockade was probably used as defense against native attacks, not against the armaments of the Spaniards. The location suggests the fortified site of Muralla de León, on the northern edge of Lake Macanché (Rice and Rice 1981).

The priest José Francisco Martínez de Mora and his companions, in search of food provisions, discovered an additional fortification on the north shore of Lake Petén Itzá (quoted in Jones 1998: 348): "Disembarking at the abandoned settlements, they climbed to the top of the hill and found a fort, industriously constructed in such manner, they say, that they not were able to deal with it, even with artillery. But they found it abandoned (to the) northeast and north. From there they went directly north to the settlements of the Couohs, which they found completely burned." Jones (ibid.) acknowledged that the location of the fortification could have been anywhere north of Lake Petén Itzá, where initial Kowoj settlements were founded then abandoned as the Kowoj moved closer to the Lake Petén Itzá basin.

The use of defensive walls at Nojpeten is also likely. Aj Chan, Aj Kan Ek"'s nephew, told Martín de Ursúa y Arizmendi that the Itza were prepared to defend themselves against any invasion. The description referred to defensive preparations made on the large "*peten*" (Nojpeten) and other "*petenes*" (islands).[1] These defenses appear to have been built on low ground, and none were noted on high levels of the island (Jones 1998: 279). There are some indications that these defenses were made quickly by the Itza, probably fearing attacks from the Spaniards and other Maya enemies.

Weaponry

For archaeological purposes, some of the most interesting elements of Spanish descriptions concern weaponry. López de Cogolludo (in Tozzer 1941: 49n240) said of the Maya who ambushed Spaniards near Ake, "They appeared with all the arms which they use in the wars, quivers of arrows, poles (pointed) by fire, lances ending in sharp-pointed flints, two-handed swords of very strong wood (set with) obsidian, whistles and beating the shells of large turtles with deer horns, blasts of great sea snail shells."

Maya weapons were made primarily of stone and wood, but raw materials varied depending on the implement; they included bone and marine cartilage and teeth (Roys 1943: 65). These materials, particularly lithics, distinguished themselves by their quantity, quality, and ease of reduction to functional implements. They were fashioned into diverse offensive weaponry, including spears, knife-spears and knives, a variety of bladed and unbladed clubs, spearthrowers or atlatls, and bows and arrows. Many of these weapons were used in earlier Classic times as well as through the Postclassic and Colonial periods, however, and therefore are not diagnostic of late warfare.

Atlatls. The atlatl or spearthrower is a stick with a handle on one end and a hook or socket that engages a light spear or dart on the other. The spear or dart is thrown by the action of the upper arm and wrist in conjunction with a shift of balance of the body, with the flipping motion of the atlatl providing leverage in propelling a projectile faster and farther than it could be thrown by the hand alone. An atlatl can cast a well-made dart to ranges greater than 100 meters. Bishop Landa (in Tozzer 1941: 32) described the atlatl as "a piece of wood about three fingers thick, pierced to about the third of its length, and six palms long." The Maya used this stick with a string. It is difficult to distinguish the stone points tipping darts from those on arrows and spears.[2]

No Spanish descriptions of combat implicate the atlatl as a major weapon, and the degree to which Maya used the atlatl has been the subject of debate (Follett 1932; Hassig 1992; Robicsek 1990). Their use may have been largely restricted to the Late Classic and Early Postclassic of northern Yucatán. The few depictions of atlatls, which are limited to public monuments, as well as rare recovery of dart points suggest that this weapon played little significance in Classic-period Maya warfare (Hassig 1992). Hassig (ibid.: 97) suggested that their use among the Maya was as a status marker.

Short sword or broadsword. The elder of the two Kowoj leaders visiting Nojpeten carried what Avendaño y Loyola referred to as a "double-bladed machete."[3] What Spaniards called a double-bladed machete was probably the short sword called *hadzab* in northern Yucatán; the Maya word *hadzab* literally means "that with which one strikes a blow" (Roys 1943: 66). Interestingly, the Spanish soldiers referred to it using the word *macana*, probably a derivation of the previously learned Nahuatl word *macuahuitl* (ibid.).

It is not clear whether the Maya broadsword was introduced from central Mexico (Hassig 1992: 160) or was an elaboration of bladed clubs used in the Terminal Classic period, for example at Seibal (ibid.: 96). Comprising a thin, wide wooden shaft, with small obsidian or chert blades set in narrow length-wise channels (Hassig 1992; López de Cogolludo 1957), these weapons are variously described as made of a strong, dark wood called *chulul* (*Apoplanesia paniculata*, a flowering tree in southern Mesoamerica; Roys 1943: 65). They measure three to five *palmos* (palm of the hand) long (up to eighty cm) and three fingers wide (ibid.: 66; C.D.I. 1898). The descriptions suggest a weapon that relied on large cutting surfaces for effect.

Bow and arrow. The bow and arrow was widely used throughout Meso-america prior to the Spanish conquest; however, no consensus exists about its time of arrival in the Maya area. The traditional view is that the bow and arrow, and tactics associated with its use, were brought to northern Yucatán from central Mexico and the Gulf coast by the Tutul (Toltec) Xiw or people with strong connections to the Xiw (Tozzer 1941: 35, 121n550). Afterward, the technological achievement of the bow and arrow spread through the rest of the Maya lowlands and continued to be used during the Colonial period (Hassig 1992; Jones 1989, 1998; Robicsek 1990).

Revision of this traditional scenario comes from Kazuo Aoyama's recent analyses of lithic artifacts from Aguateca and Copán. Small, narrow chert points and obsidian prismatic blade points measuring approximately 2.5 to 4 centimeters in length—that is, arrow points—appear to have been in use by the end of the Late Classic period at Aguateca and during the Early and Late Classic periods at Copán (Aoyama 2005: 294, 300, figures 3 and 4).[4] In Petén, these points have been found in Terminal Classic contexts at Seibal (Willey 1978: 127) and Macanché Island, and at Colha, Belize, they are known from contexts dating to A.D. 900–1050 (Rice 1987a: 215).

In the northern lowlands in the Colonial period the weapon was described as a bow of medium length to almost the height of a man, strung with a hen-equen cord and accompanied by quivers of reed arrows with flint or bone points and feathers (Roys 1943: 65; Tozzer 1941: 121). Bows were constructed of *chulul* wood, the same used for spears (C.D.I. 1898; Roys 1943: 65), and the *Relación de Campocolche y Chochola* refers to the bow itself as *chuhul* (in C.D.I. 1898). The arrow is described as made of long, slender reeds found near lakes, with a thin piece of wood fastened to them. The chert or flint point was placed into the end of the wood, but occasionally the tip was made from fish "teeth" (Roys 1943: 65; Tozzer 1941: 121). Although some researchers claim that bows were poorly developed among the Maya and were used primarily for hunting (Follett 1932), Landa (in Tozzer 1941: 31) stated that the Maya used only traps and snares, rather than bows and arrows, for hunting.

Knives and spears. Stone knives were used from Classic times onward (Hassig 1992; Robicsek 1990), both in warfare and in household activities. Described as "short daggers" (Roys 1943: 66), these knives consisted of a short, strong knife-spear characterized by an elongated, flaked blade of chert or obsidian inserted into a piece of wood that served as a handle. At Motul, Yucatán, knives were made of stone and *chulul* wood and measured one *jeme*, or approximately twenty centimeters, in length (C.D.I. 1898). As military weapons, they were undoubtedly used in hand-to-hand combat.

Spears or *nabte* (*Relación de Campocolche y Chocola*, in C.D.I. 1898) are known as Classic-period weapons from the appearance of points throughout the Maya lowlands; they are illustrated as personal arms on ceramic vessels, in graffiti, and in murals (Kerr 1989; Miller 1986; Reents-Budet 1994; Robicsek 1990). Maya spears, sometimes stone-tipped and other times fire-hardened wooden shafts, were used primarily to thrust and cut, but all spears are thought to have functioned to some degree as javelins as well. Chipped stone blades inserted into the upper shaft made spears more efficient, but the larger the point, the more likely the weapon's primary use was thrusting rather than being thrown (Hassig 1992).

Bernal Díaz del Castillo (1973) referred to spears as big as those used by the Spaniards, but he distinguished various sizes. Size variability implies dissimilar uses: Beatríz Repetto Tio (1985) suggested the use of smaller implements as throwing spears, while bigger ones may have been used as crash spears during combat. Distinctions between knife and spear points of chipped stone are difficult to discern when these objects are recovered in excavations because they could have had either use.

Other weaponry. Other implements of aggression—such as clubs, axes, slings, knuckle-dusters, and blowguns—are less common than spears, knives, and bows and arrows in the archaeological and artistic records. As depicted in the Bonampak murals and Uaxactun Stela 5 (Hassig 1992: 218n27), clubs had large single or multiple stone blades embedded in a wooden handle (ibid.: 96), lashed to the sides (Robicsek 1990), or both. Clubs were used to beat and tear an opponent; those topped with stones were most likely "maces" (Parsons, Carlson, and Joralemon 1988), emphasizing a stronger "crushing" function than that of clubs with blades.

Axes are shown in Classic Maya art being used to decapitate prisoners or in sacrifices (Freidel 1986a), and it seems probable that they could have been used in warfare in Postclassic times. Most axes were made of wood and stone, but metal—probably a copper alloy (Tozzer 1941: 121)—was also used for ax heads in the Postclassic. In the process of making copper axes, the Maya appear to have used the traditional technique of beating the edge for sharpening (ibid.).

The use of slings for tossing projectiles is difficult to document for the Classic Maya, but they are mentioned in descriptions of Colonial-period combat, and their use may go back as far as 900 B.C. in association with the Olmecs (Hassig 1992: 28–29). Slings (*yumtun* or *yuuntun*; Roys 1943: 66) were used by the Maya of Yucatán. Although Landa did not mention the use of slings, he described how the Maya of Champotón threw stones without a sling, very hard and accurately, using the left arm and index finger.

Shields and Armor

Conquest- and Colonial-period accounts from Yucatán suggest that important warriors often went to battle wearing armor (C.D.I. 1898; Tozzer 1941: 121). According to Roys (1943: 66; also Tozzer 1941: 35, 121), protective coverings consisted of short cotton jackets packed with rock salt and tight bindings of leather or cloth on forearms and legs.The *Relación de la Ciudad de Mérida* reported the use of armor that consisted of a long, narrow piece of cotton tied to the trunk of the body, generally without a sleeve (in C.D.I. 1898). The *Relación de Campocolche y Chochola* described a kind of twisted wrapper made of rolled cotton worn all over the body that was so strong arrows could not penetrate it (in C.D.I. 1898). Cotton armor was occasionally festooned with various decorations and frequently edged with featherwork. While elite soldiers or "captains" were clad in such elaborate garb, perhaps including helmets (Tozzer 1941: 122), commoners wore little more than loincloths and body paint (López de Cogolludo 1954; Roys 1943: 66; Villagutierre Soto-Mayor 1983). Shields carried by Maya warriors were faced with deerhide over two covers of wooden bars placed at right angles to each other or woven with split reeds (Landa in Tozzer 1941: 121; Roys 1943: 66).

Zacpetén's Wall-and-Ditch Defensive System

The settlement of Zacpetén was physically and symbolically set apart from the northern shore of Lake Salpetén by a defensive system located at the northern end of the peninsula, where it joins the mainland. This defensive system appears to date from the Terminal Classic period and is composed, from north (the lowest elevation) to south (highest elevation), of (1) a canal, (2) a parapet-ditch-parapet complex, (3) a low, possibly perishable wall, (4) a large wall (Wall 1) with side extensions, and (5) a wall (Wall 2) constructed in a deep ditch. The major components of the system stretch 80 to 90 meters in length, east-west, and approximately 40 meters north-south.

This complex was tested archaeologically by two trenches, T-1 and T-2 (Pugh 1995). Trench T-1 was an excavation unit 30 meters long by 1 meter wide, rising in elevation from north to south (Figure 6.1). It was excavated as a series of eight units of variable size, numbered (from north to south) as Units

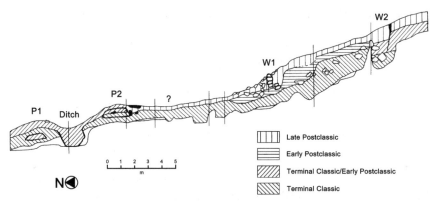

Figure 6.1. Composite profile of the east wall of trench T-1 cross-cutting defensive works at the northern end of the Zacpetén peninsula: "P1-Ditch-P2" on the north (left) is the parapet-and-ditch complex; "?" is the possible shallow trench for a perishable wall; "W1" indicates Wall 1 of well-dressed stone, possibly the northern boundary of a broad parapet; "W2" is the location of another wall of large stones set in a deep trench dug into bedrock, the possible northern facing of the proposed broad parapet.

11, 10, 9, 8, 12, 7, 14, and 13. Trench T-2, measuring 5 meters by 1 meter, was excavated to the northwest of T-1 in order to examine the canal. Both trenches were excavated to sterile soil, which consisted of a natural deposit of soft, white marl, or *tierra blanca,* lacking artifacts.

At the lowest elevation, at the narrow neck of land between the peninsula and the mainland, a canal had been cut into sterile clay (not bedrock), making Zacpetén an artificial island. As revealed in Trench T-2, the deepest part of the canal measured 2.9 meters below ground surface. Although its width was not exposed in the excavation unit, it is estimated on the basis of surface contours that the canal was approximately 4 meters wide. Directly above the base of the canal cut were 1.4 meters of layered clay sediments deposited by the waters of Lake Salpetén, above which were 1.2 meters of layers of sand. This sandy deposit contained freshwater snail shells, indicating deposition by shallow water, as well as large limestone rocks probably resulting from erosional processes.

Immediately south of this canal was a system of two parapets separated by a ditch, exposed in Units 10 and 11 of Trench T-1 (Figure 6.1). This complex was approximately 80 to 90 meters in length, east to west. The ditch was created by cutting into marly bedrock, with the cut 1.05 meters deep and 1.8 meters wide. The marl from the excavation was used to build the parapets on either side, with various additional layers of gray to gray-brown clay added above the marl to raise the structures' height. Large limestone rocks on the northern parapet and in the ditch probably represent stone facing or a wall that collapsed. The northern parapet, 3 meters wide, stood 1 meter above ground level; the southern parapet, built on a higher ground level, was approximately 50 centimeters high and 2.5 meters wide. Considering the depth of the ditch between them, the parapets probably stood about 2 meters above the base of the ditch.

A short distance beyond (south) and uphill from the parapet-ditch complex, in Unit 8 of T-1, a small feature 35 centimeters wide and 30 centimeters deep was encountered (labeled "?" on Figure 6.1). We did not excavate it sufficiently to determine its function, but it might have been the remains of a footing trench for a wall of perishable materials, which appears to stretch east-west.

Farther to the south and uphill, in Unit 7 we encountered the base of a wall (Wall 1) constructed of large, mostly dressed stones. Approximately 85 meters long east-west, the excavated remains of the wall were only 1.7 meters high, but the amount of collapse suggests that it might originally have stood as high as 3 or 4 meters (W1 on Figure 6.1). To the east of this large wall were two smaller walls about 80 centimeters in height. The closest of these was 20 meters long; the other, about 20 meters east of Wall 1, was 10 meters long. These walls could have provided additional protection for the northeastern portion of the peninsula, which lacks the steeper natural inclines of the northwestern part.

Finally, the southernmost and highest portion of the defensive complex was located in Unit 13 (W2 on Figure 6.1). This was a trench a meter or more deep that appeared to have had a wall (Wall 2) constructed against its northern face. Large (up to 50 centimeters) dressed stones in the trench and on the slope north of the wall/trench suggest that this wall construction must have been substantial.

There are several possible interpretations of Wall 2. One is that it also might have served in part as a retaining wall that partially supported the basal fill of the Group B platform immediately to its south, but its defensive function is clearly indicated by the fact that its edges curve to the southeast and southwest. The wall's presence accentuated the steep gradient that must be climbed to reach Group B, thus making access to the residential and ceremonial areas of the site more difficult. Another possibility is that Wall 1 and Wall 2, 8 meters apart, were facing walls of a single structure, a broad parapet constructed across the north slope of the peninsula.

Pottery sherds from the excavations indicate that the entire north-facing slope covered by the defensive works was underlain by a thick deposit of Terminal Classic debris. Wall 2, the southernmost and highest wall-and-trench arrangement, appears to be the earliest component of this complex, as the lowest levels of fill in the trench contained only Terminal Classic pottery. Similarly, Wall 1 seems to have been constructed directly on top of the Terminal Classic debris. The 8-meter space between the two walls was largely filled (primarily in the south half) with a single thick layer of Terminal Classic fill, mixed with substantial quantities of rocks—including some very large ones—presumably collapse from Wall 2. This raises the possibility that, as noted previously, the two walls were part of a single, large, parapet-like structure.

At the lower, northern end of the defensive system, the ditch-and-parapet arrangement appears to have been constructed in the poorly defined Terminal

Classic to Early Postclassic transition. These mixed materials filled the ditch, were incorporated into construction of the parapets, and surmounted them.

Early Postclassic materials per se were recovered in the area between Walls 1 and 2. Between the walls, in the southern half of the area, this deposit was a thin layer overlying the Terminal Classic fill, but it was much thicker and deeper toward Wall 1. This further supports the possibility that Walls 1 and 2 demarcated an early platform/parapet construction that was modified and elevated during the Early Postclassic. At some point Wall 1 shifted off its foundations, moving about 30 centimeters to the north but retaining the vertical alignment of the stones. The uppermost stones toppled northward and were embedded in a small Early Postclassic deposit below Wall 1 on its north side.

Late Postclassic deposits were found in the upper 10 to 30 centimeters of T-1, from the southernmost edge northward to the southern parapet. These late deposits were defined by the presence of Topoxté ceramic group pottery, including Topoxté Red and small (ca. 22 centimeters diameter) tripod plates of Chompoxté Red-on-cream: Akalché variety. Late Postclassic materials were also recovered in the gap between the south edge of the transposed Wall 1 and the Early Postclassic fill, along with small to medium stone collapse. Larger stones collapsed into Late Postclassic debris layers above the Early Postclassic deposit at the base of the wall, indicating that the wall actually maintained appreciable height before its final collapse. This may indicate that some time passed between the shifting of the wall and Late Postclassic activity in the area or that the wall was partially reconstructed in Late Postclassic times.

Not surprisingly, artifacts found in association with the Zacpetén defensive system included projectile points, such as knives and lance points of chert—often broken—and small projectile points. Preservation in this area is not such that wooden clubs or the handles and shafts of these weapons would have survived. One large chert point found between Wall 1 and the southern parapet was 16 centimeters long and 8 centimeters wide. Unfortunately, these weapons do not inform on the dates of the fortifications or the specific engagements that occurred there.

Implications for the Nature of Postclassic Warfare

Classic Maya warfare, especially weaponry, was transformed during the Terminal Classic period. Classic Maya offensive weaponry during the Classic period is thought to have consisted primarily of spears, knives, and clubs (Hassig 1992; Robicsek 1990), limiting combatants to the use of these personal weapons primarily in close-range, hand-to-hand combat. In the northern Yucatán peninsula, the transformations appear to have occurred through the acceptance of central Mexican implements and paraphernalia for protection (Hassig 1992; Tozzer 1941: 35, 121n550) and the tactics they imply. These changes are best illustrated at Chich'en Itza, in that site's murals and in the atlatls and darts recovered from the Sacred Cenote. Use of the atlatl in the southern lowlands is unclear, but this weapon suggests increased distance between combatants. Atlatls have been deemed ineffective in forest situations and where raids were surprise assaults with limited combat time. If one assumes the existence of forest or heavy vegetation in the Classic through Colonial periods in the southern lowlands, Maya warriors there would have had difficulty efficiently amassing concentrations of atlatl darts because of obstructions to the darts' flight. In addition, atlatl users would not have had enough time to throw a significant number of darts at a sufficient distance from the enemy to assure safety.

Spanish observations on Maya warfare and weapons also shed light on the practices. There is some indication that access to and use of specific weapons was confined to particular social classes. It appears that most commoners used bows and, to a lesser degree, slings. However, certain arms such as spears, atlatls, and swords appear to have been used more by elites (Repetto Tio 1985). Atlatls, spears, and swords are less commonly mentioned in ethnohistoric accounts; their use might have been socially restricted to nobles and professionals who had access to the necessary training and thus possibly manifested status and social prestige (Hassig 1992). On the other hand, fewer accounts of the use of these implements may simply indicate fewer occasions of close-range combat.

The best explanation for changes between Classic and Postclassic warfare in the central Petén lakes area appears to be the widespread incorporation of the bow and arrow into the Maya's military arsenal, as this has wide-ranging ramifications for the disposition of Maya communities and for military strategy. The main difference is that the bow and arrow permits significant distance between attackers and defenders, as compared to weapons used in hand-to-hand combat such as clubs, broadswords, and spears. In the Petén lakes, for example, the introduction of the bow and arrow appears to coincide with a major settlement shift in the Terminal Classic, from mainland locations to easily defended occupation on the lakes' many islands and peninsulas. This shift was accompanied at some locations, such as Zacpetén, by the construction of substantial fortifications to protect inhabitants. By the time the Spaniards arrived, many towns had constructed, reconstructed, and enlarged these structures.

Strategically and tactically, archery provides a number of other advantages. Bows and arrows are considered area weapons, which are more effective than individual weapons because they allow massive fire by great numbers of participants (Hassig 1992: 156). The bow and arrow is easier to operate and with greater accuracy than weapons such as the atlatl, allowing for greater numbers of lesser-trained participants in conflict (ibid.). Bows and arrows are light in weight, which brings the advantage of high mobility during military campaigns. Use of bows and arrows also allows for more concentrated fire, resulting in greater damage (ibid.). Moreover, arrows are faster than previous weapons used by the Maya, and they cause damage by penetration, which results in more life-threatening injuries. Another benefit is the ability to collect and reuse spent arrows; arrowheads are practical to produce and do not require a specialist manufacturer. Aoyama (2005: 294, 300), however, believes that one objective in warfare was to leave the arrow point behind in the body of the enemy; this, he notes, explains both the relative lack of recovery of arrowheads in archaeological contexts and the relative careless-ness of manufacture of these artifacts. Because of the damage that could be inflicted by the wider arsenal of weapons used in Postclassic times, the use of body protection—including quilted cotton armor—appears to have been more widespread than during the Classic period.

Another implication of the introduction of the bow and arrow is the spe-cialization of warriors. Repetto Tio (1985) has suggested that Maya armies had two classes of combatants: archers and storm troops, who wielded swords or spears with shields. Warriors were able to fire with bow and arrows initially and later engage in individual combat. According to her (ibid.), linguistic evidence may suggest such specialization. The Motul Dictionary (Martínez-Hernández 1969) gives the titles *aj to ox* and *aj tul* for a Maya archer, *aj hul te* and *aj nab te* for the men who carry and fight with a spear, and *aj pul chimal* for warriors who carry a shield.

Why Were the Kowoj and the Itza at War?

The Xiw-related Kowoj and the Itza in Petén had a history of quarrels and factionalism going back centuries to their ancestors in northern Yucatán. Although the roots might lie in conflicts developed in the years of Chich'en Itza's hegemony, their existence becomes much more evident in the books of the *chilam b'alams*. The notable events in their conflictive history include a rebellion at Mayapán in a K'atun 1 Ajaw (ca. 1390), the overthrow of the Mayapán confederacy in a K'atun 8 Ajaw (ca. 1450), and the massacre at Otzmal in 1536. These disagreements were only exaggerated by the presence of the Spaniards, a third faction for each to play against the other in their unceasing struggle for geopolitical dominance against the tide of diseases, taxes, overwork, demands for conversion, extirpation, punishment, and more. Their battleground stretched southward into Petén as the arguments swelled and grew with each perceived threat or slight as the *k'atuns* rolled on.

The Maya of Petén, particularly the Itza, had firsthand contact with the Spaniards on their home turf beginning in 1525 when Cortés and his army vis-ited the Itza capital of Nojpeten. Sporadic *entradas* of missionaries and military men occurred over the next 175 years, with the Spaniards becoming more and more intently focused on forcing both the submission of this last kingdom of independent Maya to the Spanish crown and their conversion to the Catholic faith. But the Maya of the Petén lakes region lacked a unified vision of how to respond to these pressures.

One particular concept may have played a critical role in Maya-Spanish interactions: prophetic history. In particular, the "prophetic history of the *k'atuns*" may have been of increasing importance during the final decades of interrelations between central Petén Maya and the Spaniards (Edmonson 1982, 1986). The Spaniards were apparently introduced to the notion of "prophetic history" during the visits of friars Fuensalida and Orbita at the beginning of the seventeenth century. According to ethnohistoric accounts, the Ajaw Kan Ek' whom Fuensalida met during his visit to Nojpeten discussed the prophecies of the *k'atun*. Ajaw Kan Ek' is said to have declared that "the time had not arrived in which their ancient priest had prophesied that they would have to give up their worship of their gods . . . and the one that had been indicated to them was not approaching soon" (quoted in López de Cogolludo 1957: xx).

According to Jones (1998: 159, 172, 174), this prophecy colored not only Maya-Spanish relations but also the Spanish understanding of Maya political and religious behavior. Spanish clergy were convinced that the Itza prophecies had strong connections to the ultimate conversion of the Maya to Christianity. In their understanding, the K'atun 8 Ajaw was the most important of the repeating *k'atun* intervals in Itza history (see Rice, Chapter 4, this volume), and it therefore had to play a major role in the Itza vision and transformation of their world (Avendaño y Loyola 1987; López de Cogolludo 1957). Furthermore, the end of this Maya era in 1697 represented the timing by which the Itza would surrender to Spanish rule (Jones 1998).

Irrespective of Spanish perceptions, internal Maya disagreements about this critical *k'atun* coalesced by the end of the seventeenth century. Ajaw Kan Ek', the Itza, and more recent immigrant Maya groups resident in the region may have begun to apprehend connections between increased Spanish activities and *k'atun* prophecies. The association between the "turning" of the *k'atun*, particularly the beginning of a K'atun 8 Ajaw — the *k'atun* of change — which was to occur in July 1697, and the turning or initiation of a new sacred/reverential period based on Christianity may have been interpreted negatively by certain factions of the Itza and the Kowoj.

An indication of the level of disagreement between the Itza and the Kowoj about the exact date of the *k'atun* turning and accompanying religious conversion, and the Spanish missionaries' misunderstanding of the conflict, emerged only shortly before the conquest. The Franciscans were of a millennial bent, and Maya calendrical prophecies played into what they wanted to hear, supporting the likelihood of passive conversion rather than military conquest. A missive sent from a priest in the Kejach town of Chuntuki on the new *camino real* the Spaniards were constructing in Itza territory, the priest reported to his superior that the Itza who came to Kejach territory told the Kejach "not to run away from the Spaniards when they came, because they knew that the time to establish friendship with them had arrived" (quoted in Jones 1998: 159). Not long thereafter, Fray Avendaño y Loyola visited Lake Petén Itzá and spent several days at Nojpeten with Kan Ek'. On his last day there, Aj Kowoj and his retinue came to the island, and a vigorous discussion ensued about calendrical prophecy among the Itza and Kowoj leaders and Avendaño y Loyola. It was finally determined that these groups would become Christians four months hence, at the beginning of the K'atun 8 Ajaw. Aj Kowoj nonetheless denounced the agreement in terms that suggested he would prefer to fight the Spaniards and that he did not agree with the Itza about the date of the end of the *k'atun* (Jones 1998: 207). The depth of hostility between the groups at this time, on this and perhaps other issues, was made clear to Avendaño y Loyola when the Itza told him the island had been attacked and burned by the Kowoj shortly before his visit.

Underlying this debate may have been differing views on how to manage the Spaniards, but it also appears that the Kowoj (and their allied Itza faction on the north shore of the lake) had a very different understanding of the implications of the turning of the *k'atun* and a very different political agenda. As noted, calendrical matters could lead to antagonisms and wars among political groups because of competition over the prestige and practical advantages of seating *k'atuns* and the *may* (Edmonson 1979: 11, 1982: xvi, 1986: 4–5; Rice 2004a). The Kowoj, who might have already seated the *k'atun* at Topoxté and Zacpetén in 1500 and 1539 (Rice, Chapter 2, this volume), may have intended to (re)seat not only the new *k'atun* but also the *may* and to assume a dominant role in geopolitico issues in the region. The Itza's apparent acquiescence to the Spaniards may have been a ploy on their part to create an alliance that would stifle Kowoj ambitions and keep the Itza in power.

If such a scenario is correct, the Spaniards were unwitting participants in this game. Jones's (1998) analysis of historical documents suggests strongly that the Spaniards were hopelessly ignorant of the ethnic and political diversity of central Petén in the seventeenth century. Following the model of monarchy and state from their homeland, they assumed the Ajaw Kan Ek' was the ruler of a region, perhaps not a unified region but one that had no other legitimate king. Such a view explains the uncertain Spanish assessments of Ajaw Kan Ek' as contact between the Itza and the Spaniards intensified in the late seventeenth century. Intimations of duplicity arose from some parties of Spaniards having been welcomed at Nojpeten and then attacked as they attempted to leave the region and from the slaughter of others as they approached Lake Petén Itzá.

A cogent explanation for these seemingly contrary actions is that at least some attacks on the Spaniards were orchestrated by the Kowoj, who were settled in zones traversed by the routes of Spanish *entradas* from the missionized areas of Belize. To be sure, the Itza inflicted direct casualties on the Spaniards as a result of perceived aggression or cultural violations, but those hostilities that occurred as Spanish groups moved into or out of the region, from or to the north and east of Lake Petén Itzá, were likely not the product of Itza aggression alone in the late seventeenth century. As Jones has noted (1998: 323–327, Chapter 3, this volume), the Kowoj were playing a duplicitous game, endeavoring to appear to be friendly allies of both the Spaniards and the Itza (or at least their northern faction) while at the same time maneuvering to thwart Ajaw Kan Ek's capitulation to the yoke of domination in order to overthrow the Spanish usurpers.

Notes

1. An impressive defensive moat-and-wall structure exists at the large site of Nixtun-Ch'ich', at the base of the Candelaria peninsula on the western edge of Lake

Petén Itzá. Although it appears to have been constructed well before the Postclassic period, it doubtless continued to function through the conquest.

2. It has been suggested by discriminant function analysis that dart points can be differentiated by maximum width (Thomas 1978: 470) or by being stemmed and bifacially flaked (Rovner and Lewenstein 1997: 27–28), but there is considerable overlap of functions within these characteristics (Aoyama 2005: 297).

3. The term "machete" was used by the Spaniards particularly during their *entradas* and in Colonial times in Petén (Robicsek 1990). The Spanish machete of metal was very valuable and attractive to the Maya, possibly because they saw it as more effective and durable for both war and other tasks.

4. Aoyama (2005: 294) concluded from the low percentage of occurrence of these points that the bow and arrow was not a major weapon in Classic Maya warfare.

KOWOJ RITUAL PERFORMANCE AND SOCIETAL REPRESENTATIONS AT ZACPETÉN

———Timothy W. Pugh and Prudence M. Rice————————————————

The Kowoj in Petén grounded their social reality in claims of ancestry from Mayapán, a major Late Postclassic city in Yucatán dating approximately A.D. 1200–1450 (Milbrath and Peraza Lope 2003). Mayapán, along with the earlier Chich'en Itza, were powerful landmarks in the historical consciousness of the Colonial-period lowland Maya (Tozzer 1941: 25; Edmonson 1986: 51–113). This chapter examines Zacpetén's ritual spaces relative to the social climate of the Late Postclassic and Contact periods in Petén. Material evidence in the two major ceremonial assemblages at Zacpetén, Groups A and C, demonstrates stereotypical traits of ritual including repetition, order, tradition, and discreteness. Such structured practices reveal precise social diacritics, and, in the case of Zacpetén, they are Kowoj-specific performances.

Ritual Performance and Identity

Ritual performances exist in all societies; however, they resist definition because they vary cross-culturally (Williams and Boyd 1993: 1–2). Nevertheless, certain characteristics remain sufficiently consistent to classify various behaviors as ritual. Rituals are symbolically laden performances that tend to be formal, ordered, traditional, and repetitive; they are distinct from everyday activities by virtue of their special spatio-temporal contexts and deviation from typical behaviors (Bell 1997: 138–164; Tambiah 1979: 116–118). This is not to say that rituals do not occur in domestic contexts, as they certainly cross-cut the continuum of public and private domains. This chapter focuses on the former pole of this continuum.

Ritual symbols are noted for their paradoxical qualities. The contradictions within many such symbols iconically represent the "liminality" or marginality of the ritual events themselves (Turner 1967: 93–110). This liminality in turn reflects the symbols' role in mediating between discrete phenomena, especially social categories. Ritual symbolism is not reducible to literal analysis, as it lies somewhere between a statement and an action (Bloch 1986: 245). Ritual communication is more akin to musical than literary discourse, and ritual performances are essentially "orchestras of symbols" (Leach 1976: 43–45; Turner 1967: 48). Ritual is experienced unconsciously, at an emotional level, and it can evoke feelings such as group solidarity or estrangement from outsiders, fear, and hatred (Turner 1967: 27–30). Such emotional responses are intentional results of performances and an important component of political power (Kertzer 1988: 174–184).

Rituals and their symbols represent and act as models for society (Geertz 1973: 93). Social rituals and their key symbols — including anthems, flags, and other icons — represent society and its core values. Ritual events condense a broad range of social phenomena into a limited number of social emblems (Turner 1967: 28–32). Through these symbols, group members can identify themselves in relation to other groups. Rites and their associated monuments help members of a society to collectively remember (Connerton 1989) and forget (Forty 2001: 9–10). Some rites meld the social categorization scheme with the worldview, thereby venerating society itself (Durkheim 1915: 424–429). Political rites often project an official model of the social reality and its place in the cosmos (Connerton 1989: 50).

Because rituals tend to be ordered, repetitive, formal, and traditional behaviors that differ from everyday life, they can be expected to dramatically pattern the archaeological record. In addition, if ritual events are intentional "models for and models of" social realities (Geertz 1973: 93–95), then their material remains should have much to say about former societies. Performance of rituals according to a specific order can proclaim a "summarizing symbol" (see Ortner 1973: 1340) that signifies the group and its internal relationships (Turner 1969: 166–168). If these behaviors are performative anthems of specific social groups, then their overt patterning should correlate with the distribution of those groups.

The Setting for Ritual Performance: Architectural Correlates of the Kowoj

The Mayapán polity of northern Yucatán heavily influenced Late Postclassic social groups in central Petén. Mayapán was the capital of the Middle to Late

Postclassic *mul tepal*, which Susan Kepecs and Marilyn Masson (2003: 41) have characterized as a "voluntary confederation." The nature of its "influence" is poorly understood, as we know little about Mayapán's political weight in the Petén communities. Nevertheless, this polity dominated the interior of the northern Yucatán peninsula. Elites from provinces controlled by Mayapán lived in the capital (Tozzer 1941: 37), but following the collapse of the *mul tepal* around 1441–1461, they returned to their home territories carrying codices and constructing "temples" when they arrived (ibid.: 39). Descent from the city was prestigious and a matter of public record (ibid.: 98). Of particular interest here is the transmission of ritual knowledge from Mayapán to Petén communities, as the Kowoj claimed to have migrated from Mayapán (Jones 1998: 16).

Apart from its civic-ceremonial core comprising a radial temple or "Castillo" and a "Caracol," mimicking features at Chich'en Itza, Mayapán has two primary types of ceremonial architecture: basic ceremonial groups and temple assemblages (Proskouriakoff 1962a: 91). Basic ceremonial groups are formed of three structures: an open hall, a shrine, and an oratorio. Open halls were spaces of lineage rituals such as marriages and councils (Carmack 1981: 287–290; Rice 1988: 240–241). Buildings referred to as shrines likely had a number of uses such as burial, ancestor veneration, and deity worship (Leventhal 1983: 74–75; Pugh 2003a: 946). Although not all shrines house human remains, those that do may be the lowland equivalents of highland *warabal ja*, houses where the ancestors sleep (Carmack 1981: 161; McAnany 1995: 28–29). The exact functions of oratorios are uncertain and perhaps also varied. Whereas they appear to be simply smaller temples, these buildings are occasionally found in domestic groups and contain internal features that suggest they should be classified differently from temples (Proskouriakoff 1962a: 91). Nevertheless, in form, oratorios are more similar to temples than to other structure types. In basic ceremonial groups, both oratorio and shrine are often centered on and face into the open hall, with the shrine between the hall and the oratorio (ibid.). Open halls are obviously the central buildings of basic ceremonial groups; therefore, the groups may be focused on lineage or "house" (see Gillespie 2000) rituals.

Mayapán's temple assemblages (Map 7.1) include the three buildings that compose the basic ceremonial group, but they also have a temple, or "god house," as their central feature. The god house is a "house" where deity representations "lived" and were venerated. Facing and centered on the temple is a raised shrine, and a low platform for statues often sits between them. An open hall stands at a right angle to the temple. An oratorio sits to the right of and facing the same direction as the temple.

Variants of temple assemblages exist outside of Mayapán (see Pugh and Rice, Chapter 5, Note 1, this volume). In Petén, variants are known at Topoxté, Canté, and Paxté islands in Lake Yaxhá (Johnson 1985: 163); Muralla de León on Lake Macanché; and Zacpetén (Rice 1988: 241; D. Rice and P. Rice 1981: 278–279; P. Rice and D. Rice 1985: 177–179) and possibly Tipu in adjacent western Belize (Map 7.2). The similarities between the assemblages at these

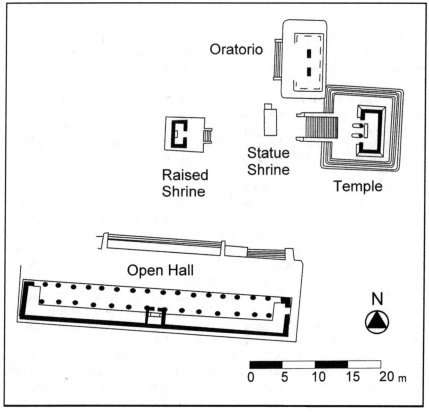

Map 7.1 Temple assemblage at Mayapán. Redrawn from Proskouriakoff 1957.

sites and at Mayapán could have been the result of migrations from Mayapán (Pugh and Rice 1997), elite pilgrimages to the city (Arnauld 1997: 124), trade relations and political alliances with Mayapán (Masson 2000: 265–276), or some combination. The five known temple assemblages in Petén are found where defensive systems, natural boundaries, or both limit spatial access to the site (Rice and Rice 1985: 182): on the Paxté, Canté, and Topoxté islands, which are naturally defendable features; and, in the case of Muralla de León, on high ground surrounded by water on three sides with a system of defensive walls (Rice and Rice 1981: 274–275). As discussed in Chapter 6 of this volume, Zacpetén's peninsular location has a complex defensive system on its narrow northern connection to the north-shore mainland.

The temple assemblages in eastern Petén were most likely built and used by late immigrants who observed ritual practices different from those in the western (Itza) portion of the lakes region (Bullard 1973: 231–241). The defensive posture of the settlements matches that described historically for the Petén Kowoj (Jones 1998: 324–325), which overlaps the distribution of temple

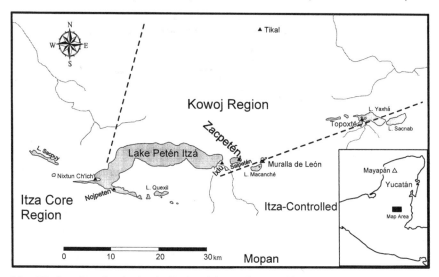

Map 7.2. Late Postclassic sites in Petén with temple assemblages.

assemblages, defensive settlements, and pottery of the Topoxté ceramic group. These overlapping phenomena, along with the Kowoj claim to have been late migrants from Mayapán, support the interpretation that temple assemblages are material indicators of the Kowoj (Cecil 2001a; Pugh 2001, 2003b: 425). The archaeological evidence of ritual practices at Zacpetén is discussed here to illuminate how Xiw/Kowoj–specific ritual spaces were utilized.

The Group A Temple Assemblage and Its Ritual Deposits

In the early fifteenth century, the Group A basic ceremonial group was reconstructed as a temple assemblage similar to those of Mayapán (Map 7.3; Pugh 2001). The presence of two oratorios and two open halls makes Group A nearly identical to the assemblage focused on Structure Q-143 at Mayapán (Pugh 2003b: 423). The east side of Zacpetén Group A has the five essential buildings of temple assemblages: a temple (Structure 602), an oratorio (Structure 605), an open hall (Structure 606), a statue shrine (Structure 607), and a raised shrine (Structure 601). Several other buildings stand on the west side of the group, including another open hall (Structure 615), a small *sakbe* ('white road'; ceremonial way) (Structure 603), a second oratorio (Structure 614), and three low platforms south of Structure 602. Most of the buildings were constructed with a combination of hard unmodified limestone and soft dressed limestone borrowed from earlier constructions. The builders concentrated the latter material in the facades.

Although it presently stands only 3.7 meters high, the Group A temple, Structure 602, is its tallest building. The superstructure, which rests on a substructure with two terraces, faces west and has two rectangular columns

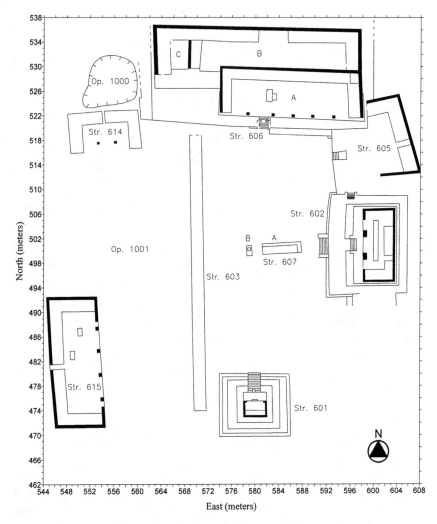

Map 7.3. Zacpetén Group A, Late Postclassic/Contact periods.

forming three doorways. A medial altar stands on the east side, and an L-shaped bench lines the southeast portion of the structure. The floor of the building was constructed twice: the original superstructure was burned as part of a termination rite, resulting in a severely burned plaster flooring that was subsequently resurfaced. The occupants also removed the pottery cache associated with the first burned floor, but the vessel's lid remained adjacent to the in situ cache, which was placed after the temple renovation. It is possible that the earlier cache lid remained as a symbol of continuity between the old and new dedications. The temple renovation also included construction of an interior rectangular masonry altar, extending north to south. Another cache

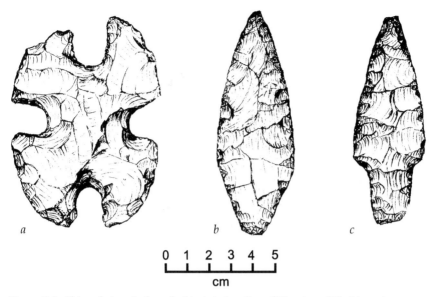

Figure 7.1. Chipped stone tools cached in interior altar of Structure 602: (a) semi-translucent eccentric; (b) possible dart point of brown Colha chert; (c) spear or lance point.

lay in this altar and included three chert objects, two of which are projectile points or knives—one with a tapered base and the other with a stemmed base—and the third of which is a white chert eccentric likely recovered from a Classic-period context (Figure 7.1).

Incensarios—various kinds of pottery vessels used for burning incense (see Rice, Chapter 12, this volume, for type and form descriptions)—are the most common ritual ware used in the Late Postclassic period throughout the Maya area, along with cache bowls, drums, ladles, cups, and other vessels. The greatest quantity of incensario fragments in Group A was recovered from the temple Structure 602, occurring as primary refuse on the surface of the substructure in front of the temple proper and as secondary refuse swept off the platform to the north, just east of the stairway joining this structure to the oratorio platform of Structure 605. A total of at least twelve partially reconstructible anthropomorphic effigy censers was found in association with Structure 602, along with nineteen composite censers. In addition, three Canoas Red cache-type vessels, a drum, ladles, and five miniature cups were noted in and around the structure. One Canoas Red cache vessel was found in the altar's renovated cache and had a lid similar to that of the cache it replaced. This vessel (Figure 7.10c) contained various worked stone, greenstone, copper, bone, and shell objects. A small ceramic cup buried with the cache vessel may have played a part in the ritual placement of the vessel and the activation of the temple.

Effigy incensarios were found primarily in or near the temple structure proper (see Map 7.4), evidently smashed in situ when the roof collapsed.

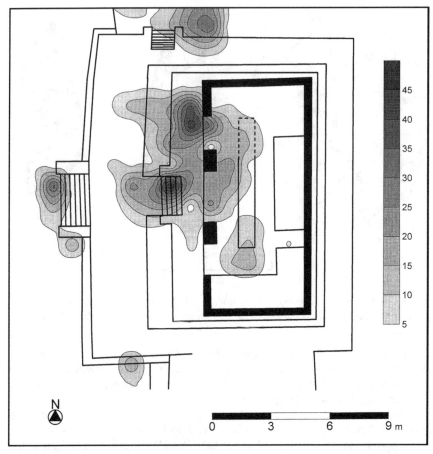

Map 7.4. Distribution of Patojo Modeled effigy censer sherds, Structure 602, Zacpetén.

Fragments of a pair of partially reconstructible Patojo Modeled: Patojo variety censers were recovered from a deposit between two of the front columns, and they may represent a male and a female. Just to the north was a pair of partially reconstructible censers of Patojo Modeled: Moza variety; they appear to represent Chaak and perhaps God D or Itzamna. Inside the temple was another pair of Patojo Modeled: Patojo variety censers, one of which wears a serpent effigy helmet and might be another representation of Itzamna (Figure 7.2), but the face of the other effigy was not recovered. Fragments of effigy arms indicate that at least three other incensarios might have stood in the temple. Several beads — green, red, and black — overlapped the distribution of censers. The Northern Lacandon used the same colored beads to awaken their god pots (Davis 1978: 77); thus, the beads and censer pairing in Structure 602 may indicate a similar awakening rite. The pairing of censers (typically of the same

Figure 7.2. Reconstructed Patojo Modeled: Patojo variety effigy incensario probably representing Itzamna, one of a pair recovered from the interior of Structure 602 in Group A. Note the reptile helmet, braided breastplate, and grotesque proportions of arms relative to body.

ceramic type and, sometimes, variety) in Structure 602 may indicate k'atun rites in which one "idol" replaced another (Chase 1985a: 119–120; Chase and Chase 1988: 72). It also recalls the Spanish soldiers' comments about paired "idols" after they conquered the Itza capital of Nojpeten.

Partially reconstructible composite censers were found outside the temple structure and included two Extranjeras Composite, four La Justa, two Fíjate (in front of the platform south of the main stair, along with a Kulut Modeled effigy censer), and four Mumúl/Zaklak censers. Ladles included four of La Justa Composite and one of Mumúl. All these sherds were scattered over the lower platform, and some were recovered in secondary refuse. Several small shotglass-like offering cups also rested on the west side of the structure (see Chapter 12, Figure 12.10c, d, this volume). The recovered incense burners of Structure 602 were apparently ritually "alive" because they had not been "killed" by smash-and scatter activity.

At the base of the southeast corner of Structure 602, excavations encountered a pit containing ceremonial refuse such as charred incense, ash, portions of a Patojo Modeled effigy censer, composite censers, and a nearly complete Sacá Polychrome tripod vessel (Figure 7.3). A sample of burned incense had a conventional age of 500 ± 50 B.P., with 2-sigma calibrated results of A.D. 1300 to 1370 (15.3 percent probability) and 1380 to 1490 (80.1 percent probability) (Beta-112316). This date indicates that the activity represented by the primary remains in and around the temple superstructure postdates this secondary deposit.

Structure 605, an oratorio or smaller temple, is located to the right (north) of the main temple and faces west. It was completely rebuilt once after its initial construction. The superstructure's orientation is skewed slightly south of the rest of the ceremonial group, but the reason for the skew is uncertain. The superstructure stands at the rear of the platform, leaving a relatively large "open" platform space. This building has a C-shaped wall and an L-shaped bench with a medial niche that, like a medial altar, was a central focus of ceremonial activity along the back wall of the structure. Such niches may represent doorways that accessed virtual back rooms (Pugh 2002: 313). A broken Kulut Modeled effigy censer stood in situ in the medial niche of Structure 605. This vessel is smaller than the incense burners of Structure 602, and the effigy represents a deity not found in the larger god house: it has a sunken face, ear spools, a reptilian headdress, pointed teeth, and round bolt-like objects in its mouth and likely represents Itzamna (God D). Composite censers were largely absent from Structure 605.

The space between Structures 602 and 605 contained secondary refuse deposits that included fragments of partially reconstructible incensarios of Patojo, Ídolos, Kulut, and Pitufo (the latter a diving god/God E; Chapter 12, Figure 12.6, this volume) types. The Kulut Modeled vessel had been terminated, with sherds spread about the superstructure, and was likely the predecessor of the in situ vessel in the medial niche. A similar pattern was described at Santa Rita where one censer of each pair was slightly less complete (Chase and Chase 1988: 72). Fragments of a nearly complete Topoxté Red drum (Figure 7.4) lay in this deposit as well as inside the Temple 602 superstructure north of the medial altar, indicating that it had been smashed in the temple and then most of the fragments were removed. Other pottery included fragments of two Macanché Red-on-paste dishes with notched flange (Figure 7.5) and a quincunx cup of Tirso Rojo-Modelado (Mayapán Red?) (Figure 7.6). Fragments of a similar cup were found in the superstructure, but they could not be conjoined with those in the refuse deposit. Non-ceramic artifacts included two small squares of gold foil, several side-notched projectile points, and numerous fragments of turtle carapaces, which could have been the remnants of drums, offering containers, sacrifice, or feasting.

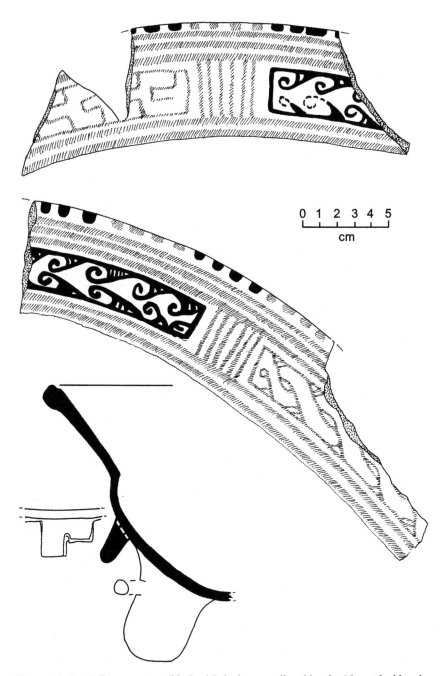

Figure 7.3. Partially reconstructible Sacá Polychrome collared bowl with notched basal flange, from a pit containing ceremonial refuse at the base of the southeast corner of Structure 602.

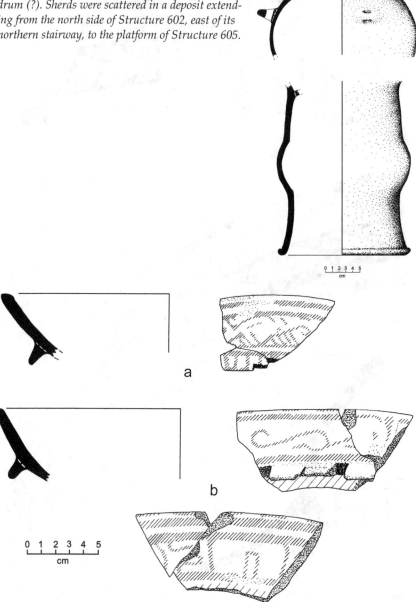

Figure 7.4. Partially reconstructible Topoxté Red drum (?). Sherds were scattered in a deposit extending from the north side of Structure 602, east of its northern stairway, to the platform of Structure 605.

a

b

0 1 2 3 4 5
cm

Figure 7.5. Two Macanché Red-on-paste dishes with notched flanges, from the same deposit as the Topoxté Red drum between Structures 602 and 605: (a) exterior banded decoration; interior features "allover" decoration; (b) exterior and interior (lower center) banded decoration; the upper right corner of the exterior features a small patch of Maya Blue pigment.

Figure 7.6. Semi-reconstructible quincunx cup or chalice from the same deposit as Figures 7.4 and 7.5. The interiors of the cups are unslipped; the exterior is slipped red. Note face on cup on the lower left.

The colonnaded hall, Structure 606, is a complex construction, initially a platform upon which the occupants built a large, 35.3-meter-long (east-west) open hall with a C-shaped wall and bench with a medial niche. The building was later reduced to a 29.3-meter-long hall (Structure 606B) with an end room (606C). Eventually, a 24.3 meter-long hall, Structure 606A, was added in front of Structure 606B, partially constructed of stones from that earlier structure's bench. Unfortunately, the temporal span of this construction sequence could not be ascertained. Structure 606A has a C-shaped wall and bench but lacks a medial niche. In the west side of Structure 606A are two low masonry altars. A test unit placed over the north wall of Structure 606A revealed deep stratigraphy, with major constructions during the Middle Preclassic, Late to Terminal Classic, and Late Postclassic periods.

The Late Postclassic occupants of Group A reset a plain stela (Stela 5) and a carved altar, Altar 1 (Stuart, Chapter 13, this volume), into the south platform wall of Structure 606. Altar 1 was broken in half, and each half was incorporated such that the carved surface faced outward into the plaza. Fragments of Late Classic Jaguar God of the Underworld (JGU) censer stand(s), made

153

of characteristic ash-tempered paste, were found in a deposit at the base of Structure 606 in front of the altar, suggesting that these vessels may have been (re)placed in veneration (see also discussion of Structure 603).

Structure 606 had a pair of partially reconstructible Kulut Modeled effigy incensarios; a deep, open basin of Mumúl Composite: Dark paste variety in the medial niche of Structure 606B; miscellaneous sherds of Patojo Modeled: Patojo variety and Pitufo Modeled; and a vessel of Tirso Rojo-Modelado/ Mayapán Red. Partially reconstructible composite censers included thirteen Extranjeras/La Justa vase censers, two Zaklak censers, and some sherds of Fíjate Composite. Structure 606 also yielded great quantities of Paxcamán Red slipped serving wares, a Canoas Red cache vessel, a ladle, and two pregnant female figurine fragments. Eleven small quartz crystals were found on the floor. Crystals are still used by Maya ritual practitioners for divination (Brady and Prufer 1999: 130–133).

Structure 607, an elongated shrine, sits 3.1 meters west of the west stairway of Structure 602 and slightly south of its medial axis. It consists of a long, low platform (Structure 607A) with a small masonry altar (Structure 607B) at its west end, both having been constructed twice. In 1995 we identified several low masonry altars on Structure 607A, similar to those of Structure 766A in Group C, described later. These altars were not discernible in the excavation of the structure, which occurred in 1997, and were likely disturbed by foot traffic during the intervening years. Artifacts were concentrated south of the structure, indicating the sweeping of artifacts in that direction and away from the medial axis extending from Structure 602. Patojo Modeled effigy censer sherds were concentrated at the east end of Structure 607A. Between Structures 607A and 607B lay a cluster of La Justa/Extranjeras Composite censer sherds. To the south of Structure 607B was a scatter of human bone and teeth. Excavations tracing the plaza surface associated with the first construction of Structure 607 indicated that its activity areas matched those of the second construction. Hence, the earlier building staged rituals similar to those of the later one.

Structure 601, a raised shrine on the south side of the plaza, consists of a small superstructure on a relatively high (3.6 m) platform with four terraces. The superstructure includes a small bench/altar in front of which is a small circular pedestal. The platform masonry of Structure 601 included at least two Late to Terminal Classic monuments. Stela 3, a plain monument, was found in fragments in front of the stairway, which had been destroyed by a looter's trench; the stela was either incorporated into the north platform wall or mounted at the top of the stairway. Examination of the looter's trench revealed a Late to Terminal Classic construction beneath Structure 601. Stela 4, built into the east wall with the carved side facing outward, depicted a regionally typical Terminal Classic image: a ruler scattering with a "cloud rider" above, also scattering. The largely effaced date had an 8 prefix, which we tentatively read as the *lajuntun* (half a *k'atun*) of 9.19.10.0.0, May 6, A.D. 820. As with Altar 1 in the wall of Structure 606, large quantities of ceremonial refuse had been deposited near Stela 4, including both effigy and composite censers and a stingray spine (Pugh 2001: 229).

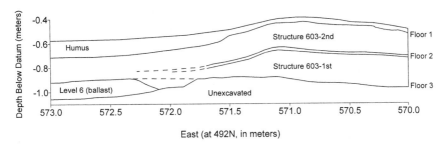

Figure 7.7. Profile of Structure 603, Zacpetén (facing south).

At least two Patojo Modeled: Patojo effigy censers stood outside the superstructure. Fragments of a pair of Gotas Composite censers were recovered inside the front of the superstructure, along with an apparently curated Late Classic Benque Viejo Polychrome bowl recycled as an offering vessel. A fragment of a colander-like perforated sherd might be part of a locally made European-style thurible of the sort found at Tipu (Pendergast 1993: 127; cf. also Topoxté, Wurster 2000: lámina 2). Fragments of an Extranjeras/La Justa Composite censer were found on the plaza level on the east side of the structure, just below the inset Stela 4.

Structure 603 is a low, forty-five-meter-long *sakbe* dividing the Group A plaza into eastern and western halves. Because of its small size, this structure is more a symbolic representation of a *sakbe*, although it likely staged ritual processions. It is similar to a small north-south *sakbe* proposed by Linda Schele and Peter Mathews (1998: 286) at Uxmal and may correspond to the northern *sakbe* of Chich'en Itza. Similar small intra-group *sakbes* exist at Cozumel (Freidel and Sabloff 1984: 83). Like most buildings in Group A, Structure 603 had been constructed then reconstructed once (Figure 7.7).

Structure 603 was relatively clean of debris, but concentrations of artifacts lay adjacent to the north end and at its center where it bisected the plaza's medial axis extending from Structure 602. These concentrations were either ritual refuse deposits or primary refuse composed of offering containers fashioned from vessel fragments. The northern concentration incorporated Late Classic JGU censer fragments against Altar 1 in the wall of Structure 606, as well as fragments of Postclassic censers including Ídolos and Patojo and a Pitufo Modeled diving god/God E censer. Composite incense burners were apparently not used in this area. The medial concentration included miscellaneous sherds of Patojo and Kulut Modeled and Fíjate and Gotas Composite censer types; other pottery included Chipotle Red, two partially reconstructible Gotas Composite ladles, a Picú Incised: Thub variety drum, an unusually deep Paxcamán Red bowl with a stepped flange and atypical paste, and a Macanché Red-on-paste tripod dish with one support modeled as a human head. These objects, plus miscellaneous bone and a single greenstone ax, were clustered near the western edge of the structure, as if they had been swept off.

Structure 614 stands at the south side of a large borrow pit (Operation 1000; see Duncan, Chapter 15, this volume) in the northwest corner of Group A. It is a small C-shaped building with a bench and a medial niche similar to typical oratorios at Mayapán. The use of Structure 614 seems to have been brief, and, as with Structure 606B, most of the facing stones in the bench had been robbed for use in other constructions. Structure 614 was largely devoid of artifacts, but numerous small projectile points littered its surface. A light scatter of human bone lay in the eastern half of the structure.

A second open hall, Structure 615, in the southwest corner of Group A, has a C-shaped wall and bench broken by a medial niche and two low masonry altars like those of Structure 606A in the northern half of the building. As with most buildings in Group A, Structure 615 was renovated once. It may have been occupied or used very late in the history of Zacpetén, judging from the presence of European artifacts in heavy refuse deposits behind the building: a piece of iron, the stem of a white clay pipe, and a vertical right-angle handle (Figure 12.10b) — resembling the handle of a European-style pitcher — made of local purplish-red–slipped Snail-Inclusion Paste ware. Fragments of perhaps as many as eight composite incensarios included two large La Justa vases with quadripartite spike/disk appliqués, at least one (possibly two) Gotas censers, and perhaps one Fíjate vessel. Effigy censers include fragments of one Ídolos and one Pitufo, the latter having a goggle-eyed headdress and a beaded flap. Although some Patojo vase sherds were noted, no effigy figures were recovered — perhaps a consequence of a late Spanish occupant having destroyed them. A miniature cup of Topoxté Red and a grater fragment were noted at this structure, but there were no drums or Canoas cache vessels. Other artifacts included small crystals, hematite mirror fragments, and speleothems in or adjacent to the building. The Maya employed hematite mirrors as well as crystals in divination (Brady and Prufer 1999: 130–139).

Operation 1000 is a borrow pit originally created in Middle Preclassic times, judging from pottery recovered in excavations by William Duncan in 2002 (Duncan 2005a, Chapter 15, this volume). A layer of crushed limestone rested on the bedrock of the nearly circular pit, likely deposited as it was excavated. Above, a layer of charred wood and ash suggests a fire was burned directly on the pulverized limestone. Radiocarbon dating (Beta-112318) of the burned wood yielded a conventional age of 540 ± 30 B.P., with 2-sigma calibrated results of A.D. 1310 to 1360 (26 percent probability) and 1380 to 1440 (68.9 percent probability). This range corresponds nicely with that of the deposit adjacent to Structure 602, mentioned earlier, and may date a dedication rite.

Operation 1001, on the western line of the medial axis extending from the eastern temple stairway, revealed the base of a building — likely Terminal Classic in date — that was dismantled for Late Postclassic construction fill. East of this former building was an area of plaza fill contemporary with the second construction of Structure 603. At the base of this fill were several human mandibles with articulated cervical vertebrae, a skull, a bundle of long bones, several quartz crystals, chert bifaces, and sparse (n=43) Late Postclassic censer sherds.

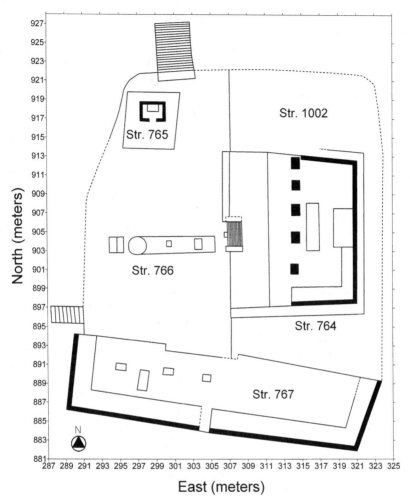

Map 7.5. Zacpetén Group C, Late Postclassic/Contact periods.

The deposit likely dedicated the second construction of the plaza and the other buildings of Group A, although we do not have an absolute date for this event. A carbon sample from the area (AA-35234) dated an earlier construction.

The Group C Temple Assemblage and Its Ritual Deposits

The latest construction phase of Group C has the five essential components of a temple assemblage (Map 7.5): a temple, Structure 764; an oratorio, Structure 1002; an open hall, Structure 767; a statue shrine, Structure 766; and a raised shrine, Structure 765. All buildings in Group C were excavated, but Structure

1002 was only partially uncovered. The activity areas of Group C match those of Group A, and its masonry also included both unmodified hard rubble and dressed soft limestone.

With the exception of its five-doorway entrance, the temple of Group C, Structure 764, is nearly identical in form and activities to Structure 602 in Group A: it faces west and rests on a substructure with two terraces. The superstructure features a medial altar, an L-shaped bench, and an interior altar bisecting the chamber. Carbonized wood recovered from the collapsed masonry of Structure 764 had a conventional age of 585 ± 45 B.P., with two-sigma calibrated results of A.D. 1290–1430 (AA-35235). The wood was likely construction material and hence predated the final activities in the building. This temple was initially constructed, then renovated once; as in Structure 602 in Group A, the medial cache also appears to have been terminated and subsequently replaced. Like its parallel in Structure 602, the extant cache of Structure 764 was a lidded globular vessel buried west of the medial altar; however, the cache vessel of Structure 764 was unslipped. It contained green-stone and red shell beads, coral, shell, and copper foil (Figure 7.10b).

As with the Group A temple (Structure 602), temple Structure 764 in Group C had the largest quantity and variety of incense burners in this assemblage; it also had the largest quantity and variety of slipped and decorated serving wares (see Rice and Cecil, Chapter 11, this volume). Effigy incensarios included sherds of fourteen Patojo Modeled: Patojo variety censers (see Map 7.6), plus fragments of Pitufo and Ídolos. The Patojo censers were slightly larger than those of Group A and were found west (in front) of the interior altar. Pairing was not as clearly evident here as it was in Group A. Of these vessels, there were several probable Chaak effigies and two faces with zig-zag appliqués ("lightning bolts") on the cheeks (Chapter 12, Figure 12.4c, this volume), plus one female figure. The latter was missing a head and arms, but the fragmentary upper body was depicted wearing a *huipil* (loose blouse), with a long skirt covering the legs (Chapter 12, Figure 12.3, this volume). The most likely interpretation of the identity of this female effigy figure is Ixchel, goddess of the moon, weaving, and pregnancy. Fragments of two pregnant figurines were also found behind Structure 764.

Besides the fourteen effigy incensarios, fragments of at least fourteen composite censers were found around the columns at the front of the Structure 764 temple superstructure, including seven Gotas (Figure 7.8a), six Mumúl/Zaklak, and one Fíjate, plus fragments of Extranjeras/La Justa. Fragments of grater bowls and Chipotle Red bowls were recovered in or around the temple. Sherds of a possible Tirso/Mayapán Red ware drum with a stepped flange and a cross-shaped cutout in the base lay on the east side of the medial altar, along the medial axis; a fragment of a whistle/flute lay near the drum. In addition, fragments of a Tirso Red quincunx chalice were found east of the interior altar, and several sherds from a second cup were spread around the interior of the superstructure.

The apparent presence of fourteen image/effigy and fourteen composite censers raises the possibility that each effigy censer, or "god pot," may have

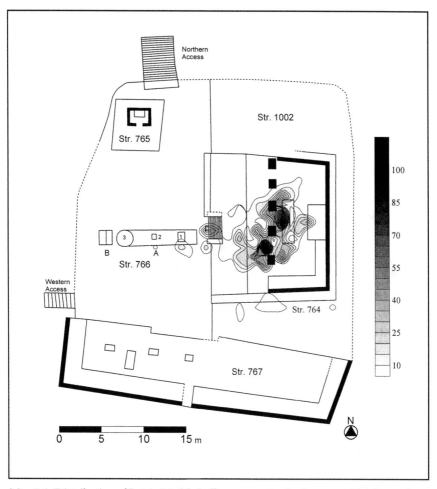

Map 7.6. Distribution of Patojo Modeled effigy censer sherds, Structure 764, Zacpetén.

had its own offering vessel (composite censer). Unfortunately, the effigy censers were smashed and their fragments mixed in two large piles, making it impossible to determine whether they were once paired with each other or with the composite censers. The distribution of censer fragments and the lack of evident pairing of censers indicate smash-and-scatter termination activity.

A long, low elongated shrine, Structure 766A, with a rectangular masonry altar at its end (Structure 766B), lies 1.4 meters west of the temple, just south of its medial axis as in Group A Structure 607. The west end of Structure 766A was built against an earlier, tiered, "wedding cake"–shaped, circular altar (see Chapter 5, Figure 5.8, this volume). Two masonry rectangles rested upon Structure 766A, one of which was built over an earlier rectangular altar

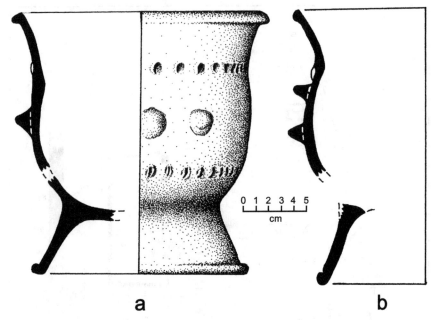

a **b**

Figure 7.8. Gotas Composite censers from the Group C temple assemblage: (a) Structure 764; (b) Structure 765.

contemporaneous with the circular altar. Structure 766A was built and then later widened, with the earlier construction associated with a buried plaza surface. Artifact distributions associated with the original version of Structure 766 matched those of its second construction, indicating similar ritual practices through time.

Structure 766A contained four caches that included a miniature Chilo Unslipped jar, a Chompoxté Red-on-cream: Akalché variety tripod dish (Figure 7.9), a Canoas Red cache vessel containing beads and a stingray spine (Figure 7.10a), and a large, modeled Tlaloc/Chaak face on an open-mouthed jar of possible Mayapán Red ware (Figure 7.11). Deity masks—specifically those of God C—have been identified in Maya codices (Vail 2000b: 128). Incense burners were associated with the Structure 766B altar, which had fragments of at least four Patojo Modeled: Patojo and Rojo varieties, plus a Mayapán Red (?) censer and a ladle. As with Structure 607, the statue shrine in Group A, no composite censers were found with this shrine. Most artifact distributions were heavily skewed to the south and were likely swept there. Again like Structure 607, a sparse scatter of human remains lay near Structure 766B and the northern end of Structure 766A.

Structure 767, the open hall of Group C, features a C-shaped bench with a medial niche that was later filled. Four low masonry altar features, similar to those in Structures 615 and 606A, lie in the northern half of the building. A human burial lay deep beneath the westernmost of the four altars, but it

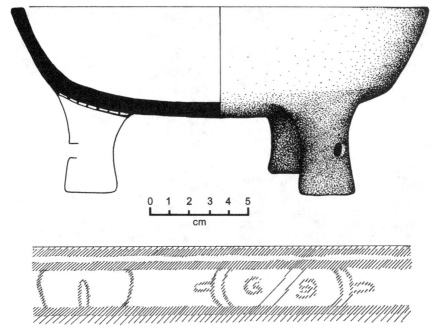

Figure 7.9. Partially reconstructible Chompoxté Red-on-cream: Akalché variety tripod dish, recovered upside-down in a cache in Structure 766A. The decoration on the interior wall (not to scale) features a band of alternating motifs bounded by "parenthesis" cartouche-like elements, creating four informally defined panels. The interior base is red-slipped, as is the exterior. The underside of the foot shows use-wear.

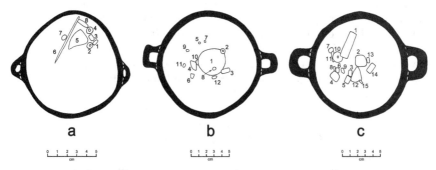

Figure 7.10. Cache vessels and contents: (a) Cache 2, Structure 766, Group C: 1, 2, 7, greenstone bead; 3, 8, red stone bead; 4, black stone bead; 6, stingray spine, plus tiny bone fragments; (b) Cache 2, Structure 764, Group C: 1, 2, 5, 7, 9, greenstone beads or fragments; 3, 8, red stone/shell bead; 4, coral fragment; 6, 10, marine shell; 11, copper foil; 12, shell; (c) Cache 4, Structure 602, Group A: 1, 3, 5, 8, 14, tubular greenstone beads; 2, 4, 10, 12, 15, other greenstone; 6, tubular stone bead; 7 tubular bone bead; 9, 11, copper foil; 13, tubular red/orange stone bead; quartz crystal and shell fragments not shown.

Figure 7.11. Chaak/Tlaloc "mask" (the side of an urn-like semi-effigy vessel, possibly Mayapán Red ware) cached in an altar in Structure 766.

is unknown if burials lie under the other altars because they were not investigated. At least one masonry altar was built as part of a renovation event, constructed directly upon a section of plaster floor with a deep red wash absent elsewhere. The surface of Structure 767 was relatively clean and therefore largely uninformative as to patterns of censer usage. Fragments of a wide variety of effigy and composite incensarios—Ídolos, Patojo, Pitufo, Kulut, Extranjeras/La Justa, Mumúl/Zaklak—were found with graters and drums, but there were no evident patterns of distribution. Other artifacts included a limestone phallus and many small objects including six quartz crystals, a hematite mirror fragment, and three spindle whorls. Spindle whorls, used to make thread, have also been linked to divination (Brown 2000: 330).

Structure 765, the raised shrine of Group C, faces south toward the masonry altars in Structure 767. The small superstructure was built upon a low platform, and its small medial altar was a later addition, indicating that the shrine had been renovated at least once. An oval-shaped offering dish recycled from a sherd of a large Chilo Unslipped jar lay west of the altar. On the edge of the platform to the west of Structure 765, a bundle burial contained long bones of at least one human adult and one child.

Two smashed Gotas Composite incense burners lay inside the front of the superstructure of the shrine, one with fragments spread throughout the interior and the other concentrated above a burned spot on the plaster floor in the southeastern corner (Figure 7.8b). At least two Mumúl/Zaklak Composite censers and some Extranjeras/La Justas sherds were also found in the shrine structure, but in no discernible patterns. The Gotas censers appear to represent the latest use of the shrine and likely replaced the fragmented Mumúl Composite censers. The change of censer types may represent shifts in ritual sponsorship. Fragments of effigy censers—including Patojo, Ídolos, and Pitufo Modeled types—were recovered, along with sherds of Chipotle Red and Mayapán Red, but they were in low frequency and patterns of placement or use could not be identified.

Unlike Group A, which began its Postclassic existence as a basic ceremonial group constructed over Late/Terminal Classic constructions, Group C originally began with a temple and two altars to its west. It was rebuilt as a temple assemblage in the late fourteenth or early fifteenth century. "Extra" buildings did not accompany the formal temple assemblage arrangements as they did in Group A. Nevertheless, the activity areas of the structures in the Group C temple assemblage were remarkably similar to those of Group A.

Kowoj Civic-Ceremonial Activity Areas and Ritual Performance

Both Zacpetén Groups A and C underwent massive construction during the early fifteenth century, when temple assemblages were raised in each group. This construction likely signaled the migration of a group of Xiw/Kowoj from Mayapán (Pugh 2003b: 423) (perhaps accompanying the 1390 K'atun 1 Ajaw revolt; see Rice, Chapter 2, this volume) and distinctive Xiw/Kowoj ritual performances. The timing of the final (re)constructions of Groups A and C is problematic. Although we have roughly corresponding dates from the two assemblages, it is unlikely that these samples specifically date construction events. Furthermore, even if they did represent construction events, the precision of carbon dating does not allow us to determine the specifics, such as the order of or interval between constructions.

The Zacpetén temple assemblages suggest that the Petén Kowoj had strong ties to one of Mayapan's prominent lineage groups: the Xiw. Group A at Zacpetén is the most similar in layout to the Ch'en Mul Group at Mayapán (Pugh 2003b: 416–417), both of which include temple assemblages with cave-like features in their northwest corners and two open halls. Structure Q-151, "the Hall of Chaak Masks" in the Ch'en Mul Group, includes masonry masks apparently imported from a Puuc (Xiw) site (Milbrath and Peraza Lope 2003: 33; Ringle and Bey 2001: 286). This double-hall assemblage includes the eastern serpent temple in the site's ceremonial core (Pugh 2001: 255). The Itzmal Ch'en Group of Mayapán also resembles Group A of Zacpetén and is located adjacent to one of Mayapán's eastern gates, said to be guarded by a Kowoj noble (Edmonson 1986: 81). Either or both of these groups at Mayapán could have been associated with the Kowoj (Pugh 2003b: 417).

We know that Mayapán endured as a foundation of Kowoj historical consciousness. How was this history remembered and perpetuated? When the Xiw/Kowoj left Mayapán in the late fourteenth century, they would have held a memory of the city in which they dwelled. However, "the city" for the Kowoj was not a two-dimensional rendering (Jones 1952) but rather a series of three-dimensional spaces enclosed by a wall. The most familiar spaces were residential, but those that most powerfully communicated "Mayapán" were public—specifically, the temple assemblages replicated within the city's walls.

Thus, the Xiw/Kowoj invoked Mayapán each time they inscribed the Petén landscape with these assemblages, and within these architectonic quotations they conducted their most critical social and religious rites. Consequently, the nearly simultaneous construction of two temple assemblages at Zacpetén is important for several reasons. First, it reiterates the importance of this spatial template and, therefore, the referenced city, Mayapán. Second, it makes this city available for commemoration: the past was brought into the present. Third, the recreated space endows Mayapán with a role in contemporary ceremonials, which not only empowers the rituals but allows the city itself to be remembered as a homeland.

Each temple assemblage was composed of various buildings. The rituals in each structure indicate that they played divergent yet interconnected roles that reflected the religious and political realities of the Xiw/Kowoj in Petén. The temples of Group A (Structure 602) and Group C (Structure 764) occupied medial positions on the east side of the plaza and had nearly identical forms except for the number of doorways. The contrast between three and five doorways is common in Classic Maya ceremonial buildings and can be seen at Yaxchilán, Palenque, and other sites. However, its significance in respect to the activities within the temples is uncertain. Activity areas in the temples at Zacpetén were otherwise very similar. In both temples, ritual paraphernalia such as red-slipped pottery drums and quincunx cups was concentrated to the east, suggesting that this was the location of the primary human participants. Fragments of deity effigy censers lay in the western half of the temples, indicating that this was the location of supernatural participants. In the southeast portion of both buildings is a bench upon which the primary ritual practitioners probably sat. Both structures can be interpreted in terms of Lacandon "god houses" in which participants interacted with and made offerings to deities (see Pugh, Chapter 16, this volume). There was also some correspondence in the deities represented by censers left as de facto refuse in the public temples. Each temple contained one female deity, but in neither case could we match a head to the female body. Each temple also contained a deity with zigzag appliqués on each cheek. The remaining images appear to have represented Chaak, although some heads appear to have been removed and placed elsewhere.

Despite the many examples of ritual repetition, some differences existed in the activities of Group A versus Group C. Within the temple superstructures, the effigy censers of Structure 602 were recovered in pairs, but the greater numbers of effigy and composite incensarios in Structure 764 were smashed and mixed together. This suggests that those of Structure 764 were terminated, whereas those of Structure 602 were still in use or perhaps in the process of being activated. Furthermore, the ritual practitioners using Group C disposed of their refuse differently than those in Group A did: excavations around Structure 602 and other buildings in Group A revealed considerable quantities of terminated censer sherds (both effigy and composite), but only sparse effigy censer fragments lay to the south of Structure 764. This differential deposition of ceremonial refuse is no small matter, as the disposal was also a ritual event (see Davis 1978: 76; McGee 1998: 46). Significantly, in Group A the effigy censers rested in situ, in pairs, while the ritual paraphernalia had been terminated. In Group C the ritual paraphernalia was largely intact, but the effigy censers had been terminated. The two temples with nearly identical ritual objects were obviously involved in two very different ritual performances.

In addition, the platform of Structure 764 was littered with human and animal teeth, which were absent from the superstructure; Structure 602 did not demonstrate this pattern. However, concentrations of teeth were found in Structure 721, the oratorio of the Structure 719 elite residential group. Tooth caches have been described at other archaeological sites such as Yakalche (Pendergast, Bartley, and Armelagos 1968: 637–638) and Lubaantun (Saul and Hammond 1974: 124). This practice is not described in ethnohistoric documents, but it occurred from the Classic to the Contact periods. The precise significance of teeth is uncertain, but a riddle in the *Chilam B'alam of Chumayel* suggests that teeth were the "hearts of stones" (Edmonson 1986: 202) — an obvious metaphor referring to their shape and hardness. Tooth removal could be a form of auto-sacrifice, but it is possible that teeth lost naturally were saved and cached adjacent to temples.

We were also able to illuminate some of the roles of open halls. The interiors of halls were very clean of typical refuse such as sherds, animal bone, and shell; but small quartz crystals were found in all three halls at Zacpetén. Crystals were recovered in other buildings at the site, but they were always found in relatively high frequencies in halls. Halls also often contained sparse fragments of polychrome ceramics and tripod supports. Open halls differed in the presence of other artifacts, however. For example, speleothems were found only in Structure 615, and several spindle whorls were found in Structure 767. These objects were likely linked to divination, but the variations suggest differences in the performance of divinatory rites. Two halls, Structures 615 and 767, contained small phalli carved of limestone. A similar phallus was encountered at Nixtun-Ch'ich' Structure 188 on the western edge of Lake Petén Itzá. The cleanliness of halls is likely evidence of ritual activities, as sweeping was a ritual performance in certain contexts such as new year's rituals (Tozzer 1941: 103). Cleaning and ritual sweeping define social space (Hanks 1990: 337–364), and so such activity in halls may have defined the space of the social group that occupied the halls — whether lineages or "houses" relative to the other spaces in the ceremonial assemblages.

Open halls seem strongly related to residences. They were constructed in the same form as the front room of tandem-shaped houses, and many halls had vestigial doorways dividing the bench but ending when they met the back wall (Pugh 2002: 313). The association between halls and houses may extend to directionality. The three halls at Zacpetén face south, east, and north, leaving only the west unrepresented. Residences at Zacpetén were also strongly structured against western directionality. This apparent rule differentiates houses and halls from temples and oratorios, which all faced toward the west. The pattern at Zacpetén matches that described in Colonial documents (Tozzer 1941: 25), but the documents do not mention halls. It is unlikely that open halls were used as residences, as occupants generally slept in the back rooms of houses except in the heat of summer (Smith 1962: 180). Because the front rooms of houses were social areas (Tozzer 1941: 86), halls can be seen as a sort of architectural quotation referring to social interactions of the lineage or "house."

The two statue shrines, Structures 607 and 766, had artifacts concentrated on their south sides, with effigy censer sherds primarily in the east end and sparse human remains on the west end. The southern skew of the artifacts likely resulted from cleaning the shrines, with debris swept away from the primary path leading to the central temple stair. The opposing effigy censers and human remains on the eastern and western ends, respectively, of the statue shrines match a larger pattern evident in Group A, where deity images and celestial symbolism dominated the eastern side of the group and human remains and Underworld imagery dominated the west side (Pugh 2003b: 423). Ritual activity areas associated with the first constructions of both Structures 607 and 766 corresponded to those of their latest constructions. The raised shrines in both ceremonial groups held Gotas Composite censers (Map 7.7) and offering containers. In both cases the offering containers had been recycled, one from a Classic-period context and the other reshaped from a sherd of a large Chilo Unslipped jar. The significance of the recycling is uncertain, but it may indicate an attempt to establish connections with the past.

Only one of the two public oratorios, Structure 605 in Group A, contained de facto refuse. It held a single deity effigy censer (Kulut Modeled) portraying Itzamna (see Chapter 9, Figure 9.1, this volume), who was not represented on the numerous censers included as de facto refuse in either public temple. This vessel is also smaller than the temple god pots, corresponding to the smaller size of the oratorio.

Zacpetén's ritual activity areas are nearly identical to those evident in the temple and other structures at Topoxté Island in Lake Yaxhá, approximately twenty-eight kilometers northeast of Zacpetén and the largest known settlement in the Kowoj region. Topoxté has a temple assemblage (Johnson 1985: 163), and Late Postclassic radiocarbon dates from the ceremonial groups of the two sites are roughly contemporaneous. The activity areas in the temple (Structure C) of Topoxté included the use of effigy censers in the anteroom and smashed red-slipped (Topoxté Red type) vessels in the inner chamber (Bullard 1970: 295). Although the forms of the red-slipped vessels were not specified, drum sherds were present. The front/west area was the space of the god pots, and the back/east area was the space for ritual participants and paraphernalia for offerings.

Topoxté also has an oratorio (Structure E), with activity areas similar to those of Structure 605 at Zacpetén. Structure E of Topoxté contained a single in situ effigy censer, matching the pattern in Structure 605 at Zacpetén; however, Structure E also included numerous in situ composite censers (Hermes 2000d: figures 67, 68), which were absent from the latter. Structure E contained a carved limestone turtle with a human head emerging from its mouth and decorated with stucco and paint (ibid.: figure 63), a sculpture that can be

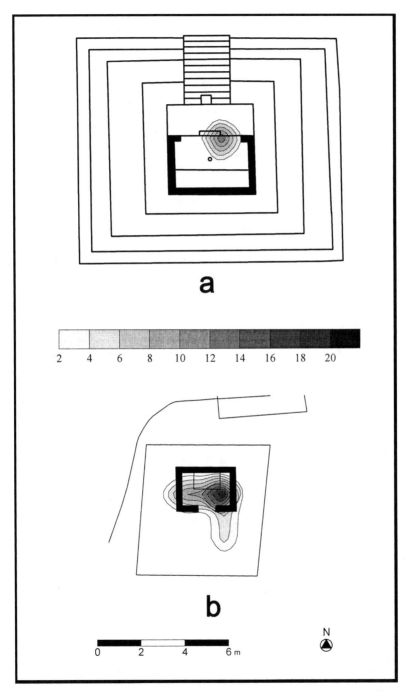

Map 7.7. Distribution of Gotas Composite censer sherds in raised shrines, Zacpetén: (a) Group A, Structure 601; (b) Group C, Structure 765.

compared to the large quantities of turtle shell encountered in Structure 605 at Zacpetén. Sculpted limestone turtles were frequently found in oratorios at Mayapán (Masson 2000: 215).

Finally, the contents and position of the ossuary of dismembered humans, Operation 1000, in the northwest corner of Group A at Zacpetén, correspond to an ossuary with similar contents (Structure L) northwest of the temple of the Topoxté assemblage (Bullard 1970: 267; Pugh 1998). Both deposits include dismembered human remains. Although a complete picture of ritual activities at Topoxté has yet to be painted, many of the behaviors that occurred in its central temple assemblage mirrored those at Zacpetén. Both sites lie within the Kowoj region of Petén, and the similarities suggest Kowoj-specific practices.

One cannot be completely sure which practices are Xiw/Kowoj–specific without examining ritual performance in the Itza-controlled western region of Petén. Temple assemblages have not been encountered in this part of the lakes area, where civic-ceremonial architecture appears primarily composed of basic ceremonial groups (Rice 1988: 245). An open hall at Nixtun-Ch'ich' on the western end of Lake Petén Itzá, Structure 188 (Pugh 1996: 216–221), differs considerably from those of Zacpetén but is similar to some halls at Mayapán in having round columns, a medial shrine, and a carved limestone altar turtle similar to the sculpture in Structure E at Topoxté. Although altar turtles are common at Late Postclassic sites, none were encountered at Zacpetén. At the same time, however, Structure 188 is similar to the halls at Zacpetén because it had a C-shaped bench and was about the same size as the smaller halls at Zacpetén. It also contained quartz crystals, hematite mirror fragments, and a limestone phallus, as did the halls of Zacpetén. Crystals were also found in Structure T99b of Tayasal (F. Castellano, pers. com., 1997), but Structure 188 at Nixtun-Ch'ich' and Structure T99b of Tayasal differed from halls at Zacpetén, as the former contained in situ deity image and composite censers. On the basis of this minimal sample, it seems that open halls in the Itza region incorporated various ritual practices that were housed in distinct structures in the Kowoj region. On the other hand, some continuities exist between halls in the two regions, as evidenced by the presence of divination objects and limestone phalli.

Activity areas in the two civic-ceremonial groups at Zacpetén present the material remains of rituals performed in the groups. The performances in the two temple assemblages at Zacpetén are nearly identical and are similar to the central temple assemblage of the other excavated Xiw/Kowoj site in Petén, Topoxté. Furthermore, the spatial patterning of artifact concentrations in temple assemblages in the Kowoj area appears to differ from that encountered in basic ceremonial groups of the Itza region. The performances defined in the temple assemblages at Zacpetén and Topoxté are Xiw/Kowoj–specific. They also occurred within the context of an architectural metonym of the Kowoj homeland—Mayapán.

Rituals in Zacpetén temple assemblages were formalized. The range of variation of in situ artifact types was narrower in Group A and Group C than in domestic groups, suggesting behavior restrictions and a clear focus on specific actions. Evidence of activities other than those involved in making offerings, communicating with deities, divination, activation, termination, and ensouling is scarce.

Formality is also evident in the traditionalism of the temple assemblages. Temple assemblages at Zacpetén were built with the same buildings and basic layout as those of Mayapán; hence, their construction was traditional. As with traditionalism in many cultural groups (Bell 1997: 145), that of Zacpetén evoked legitimacy through precisely repeating forms of the past. Because the Kowoj claimed to have migrated from Mayapán, the appeal to tradition through these ritual places was critical (Pugh 2002). This mimesis of that city's ritual places would have created a symbolic tie between Zacpetén and Mayapán and implied the continuity of its esteemed ritual knowledge. Furthermore, most buildings in the temple assemblages of Groups A and C incorporated Classic-period dressed stone and monuments into their facades, thereby appealing to tradition, as they cloaked the faces of the buildings in masks of the past. This practice was also encountered at Mayapán (Proskouriakoff 1962a: 95).

Rituals conducted in most domestic settings differed strongly from those in the two civic-ceremonial groups. Effigy censers, dismembered human remains, and multiple quartz crystals were not found in situ in most domestic groups (see Pugh, Chapter 8, this volume), and domestic areas were not found in the civic-ceremonial groups. Furthermore, the layout of domestic groups clearly differed from that of temple assemblages. The one exception to most of these rules is Group 719, a late elite residential group that was also constructed as a temple assemblage (Pugh 2002; Pugh, Rice, and Cecil, Chapter 9, this volume). This group was likely the final manifestation of the temple assemblage at Zacpetén, but its activities were combined with those of a domestic arrangement.

Colonial-period ritual practices were highly ordered according to specific rules and followed strict formats. Nevertheless, at times within these structured performances some variation was allowed. For example, commemorations and predictions varied from rite to rite (Edmonson 1986: 20–29). It is nearly impossible to recreate the temporal order of acts in ritual performances at Zacpetén, but horizontal patterning of activity areas indicates spatial order in temple assemblages. Because structures were combined into architectural groups incorporating interrelated ritual settings, most rituals would likely have involved all the buildings; therefore, procedures were spatially divided and ordered by the various divisions in ritual space. The major buildings in the assemblages represented distinct cultural categories: ancestors (shrines), councils (open halls), and gods (temples). Although Bishop Diego de Landa (in Tozzer 1941: 139–141) did not describe rituals in Petén, he did note that those in Yucatán involved a series of interrelated ritual settings. It is likely that all buildings in Zacpetén's temple assemblages were involved in most large-scale ritual performances. Each building would have housed particular rites that were organized into a set of temporally ordered performances similar to those described by Landa.

Ritual Performance and Social Structural Representations

The temple assemblages of Group A and Group C are mirror images of each other. Reversing the placement and orientation of the halls and the raised shrines brought about their reflective symmetry; the positions of the temples, oratorios, and statue shrines remained constant. These constants suggest that the spatial transformation permitted some level of symbolic differentiation while maintaining continuity in ritual performance. Open halls likely defined the orientation of raised shrines, as the shrines at Zacpetén face the small masonry altars in the halls. Thus, open halls appear to have been the key to the differential orientation. Nonetheless, the activity areas in the temple assemblages of the eastern sides of Group A and Group C were nearly identical, and both temple assemblages were constructed and then reconstructed later. The correspondence of ritual performances between Group A and Group C suggests a high degree of ritual repetition, repetition that appears to extend beyond Zacpetén to other sites in the Kowoj region.

As mentioned, rituals often project politically sanctioned representations of society. Because open halls were loci of councils that ruled either lineages or "houses," the distinctions created by facing the main hall of Group A to the south and that of Group C to the north suggest structural opposition. Opposing tensions might have existed between the mirrored groups, illuminating divisions in the social reality of Zacpetén. The differing orientations of the open halls suggest that, on a gross level, Zacpetén likely had social segments whose relationship paralleled north and south. If each architectural group were constructed by a faction within the larger community, then these two factions constructed their ceremonial cores to complement each other. Whereas the temple of Group A appears to have been involved in a new god pot ceremony, that of Group C held terminated god pots. Thus, some of the ceremonial responsibilities of one group were ending, while those of the other had been renewed.

A particularly intriguing separation exists within Group A, the northern segment of this opposition, where a ceremonial *sakbe* divided the arrangement into east and west divisions, each of which included an open hall. This has suggested a moiety organization among the builders and users of Group A (Pugh 2003b: 424–425). More specifically, Plaza A and its moiety are associated with east-west divisions and thus solar movements, the eastern half with sunrise and birth and the western half with the setting sun and death. In the case of the western side, this is immediately apparent in the presence of the mass grave, Operation 1000, in the northwestern corner of Group A, and other human remains (mandibles) in Operation 1001. The supremacy of the eastern faction is evident not only in its greater height vis-à-vis the western half but also in the striking incorporation of Classic monuments into the facades of Postclassic civic-ceremonial buildings. As seen in David Stuart's analysis of Zacpetén Altar 1 (Chapter 13, this volume), the inscribed text refers to the mythological rebirth of a historical personage — perhaps a ruler of Zacpetén — as the sun on the winter solstice. This Terminal Classic monument and its placement in Postclassic Structure 606 of Group A, along with the ritual re-interments in Operation 1000, are testimony to the celebration of an event of cyclical renewal that was of immense importance to the Zacpetén Kowoj moiety associated with Group A.

The relationship between the east and west sides of Group A seems much more complementary than that observed between the east sides of Group A and Group C. Group C, in this model, is associated with south (against Group A's north) and is likely also the Underworld (see Pugh 2003b: 425). The two assemblages, however, are distanced and functionally identical. The two sides of Group A lie adjacent to one another and, with the exception of the behaviors within the open halls, have dissimilar activities with converse symbolism.

Despite the opposing symbolism of the east and west sides of Group A, both sides of the assemblage included an oratorio and an open hall. The oratorios seem to have served auxiliary roles: Structure 605 accompanied the eastern temple, and Structure 614 complemented the western earthly penetration. The two opposing halls in Group A were analogous to complementary social relationships, and Structure 767 in Group C seated a third lineage or "house," but the three were not equal. Structure 606, the eastern hall of Group A, was "opposed" to Structure 767, as the two halls belong to mirrored temple assemblages. Thus, the faction seated in Structure 606 was pivotal, as it complemented the other two factions whose social relations were not architecturally represented. In other words, Structure 606 opposes Structures 615 and 767, but the latter two do not oppose each other. Structure 606 was of a higher structural order (sensu Turner 1977: 58) and was therefore central. This higher, pivotal order is also reflected in the literal height of the building—Structure 606 is the most monumental hall at the site—as well as its antiquity: Structure 606 was built upon an earlier hall, thereby appropriating the ancestral leadership. Structure 606 likely seated Zacpetén's ruling council.

Beyond interpretations extrapolated from the open halls at Zacpetén, the site's social organization is elusive. Group A incorporated two complementarily opposed halls—it housed a moiety. However, Group C had only one hall. The fact that Group A and Group C were involved in some sort of opposition suggests dualism at another level. This additional opposition was not superficial because Groups A and C coexisted at the site for a few hundred years. The Structure 606 faction was most closely allied with that of Structure 615, as they were symbolically paralleled as the rising and setting sun. Nevertheless, politics at Zacpetén were likely dominated by the tension between Structure 606 and Structure 767 or, perhaps better, Structures 606/615 versus Structure 767. Moieties are often combined into larger relationships, often ternary (Lévi-Strauss 1963: 154–162). In this case, however, the tripartite structure is less likely the result of some sort of "deep structure" than an idealized Maya form. In the Itza capital, three nobles—Ajaw Kan Ek', Aj K'in Kan Ek', and Aj Tut—retained the central ceremonial structures (Villagutierre Soto-Mayor 1983: 314–315). Because Ajaw Kan Ek' and Aj K'in Kan Ek' were likely two aspects of a "single political persona" (Jones 1998: 94), this structure of ceremonial responsibilities might parallel the binary/ternary pattern at Zacpetén. A similar binary/ternary arrangement may underlie the temple assemblages or variants at Topoxté, Canté, and Paxté islands in Lake Yaxhá.

Although temple assemblages were "imported" from Mayapán, Zacpetén's past was not completely silenced. In fact, it was literally built into the Late Postclassic architecture. Group A incorporated several monuments into the platforms of two buildings, with the inscribed sides facing outward. The masonry of Groups A and C incorporated soft dressed limestone along with the hard rubble, typical of most Late Postclassic buildings at the site. A similar pattern was seen in Group 719, an elite residential group/public ritual area (Pugh, Rice, and Cecil, Chapter 9, this volume). Dressed stones were borrowed from Classic-period constructions and placed in the facades of Late Postclassic constructions; they were meant to be seen.[1] Because no Classic-period constructions were identified in Group C, these stones were not included simply through the convenience of proximity; the builders intentionally incorporated them. Thus, the Xiw/Kowoj immigrants appropriated the sacred power of the earlier Classic groups to symbolically integrate themselves into Zacpetén and its past.

Ritual performances reflect and archetypically represent society. Although we lack an interpretive bridge to fully illuminate the meaning of the performances in Kowoj temple assemblages, we do know that they included interaction with deities, death and probably sacrificial rites, and lineage rituals, which included marriage and divination rites and phallic imagery. While this assortment of performances occurred in many other areas of the Late Postclassic Maya lowlands, the specific manner in which the elements were architecturally composed at Zacpetén was spatially restricted to the Kowoj region of Petén. It is unknown if similar practices existed in the assemblages of the Kowoj homeland, Mayapán, because early excavations in the temple assemblages were not conducted in such a way as to illuminate activity areas (Pugh 2001: 571). Despite the harmony between Group A and Group C, slight variation existed, especially the reversing of the hall and raised shrine. Variations also existed between performances at Zacpetén and those of Topoxté. Hence, Kowoj symbolism was manifest in a fugue-like orchestration between Group A and Group C or between Zacpetén and the other Kowoj centers. Temple assemblages in Petén manifested Kowoj-specific performances, but each did so with its own voice, illuminating social differences within the whole.

Note

1. The incorporation of older architectural elements into publicly visible portions of new structures seems particularly associated with the Puuc, for example at Sayil (Carmean 2008) and Mayapán (Milbrath and Peraza Lope 2003; Proskouriakoff 1962a: 95).

RESIDENTIAL AND
DOMESTIC CONTEXTS AT ZACPETÉN

—— Timothy W. Pugh ——————————————————————————————

A total of 137 residential groups have been mapped on the Zacpetén peninsula; most, if not all, of them had Late Postclassic– to Contact-period
components (Rice 1988: 236–238; Rice and Rice 1980), which we associate
with Xiw-affiliated groups and the Kowoj. In 1996 Proyecto Maya Colonial
excavated five residences, associated architecture, and plaza areas (Map 8.1).
These excavations revealed substantial quantities of primary (in situ) and de
facto refuse (Schiffer 1987: 89) on the latest floors. As in the civic-ceremonial
structures, primary and de facto refuse provided a great deal of information
about Postclassic life, domestic activity patterns, social inequality, and residential construction styles at Zacpetén.

All of the residences excavated at Zacpetén were constructed as "tandem
structures"; that is, they have two rooms, front and back (Map 8.2). No other
known structures at the site have this pattern. The tandem domestic pattern at
Zacpetén is not unique, as it was depicted in Maya imagery, described in historical accounts, and seen in archaeological investigations at Terminal Classic
through Late Postclassic sites in Yucatán. For example, residences with the

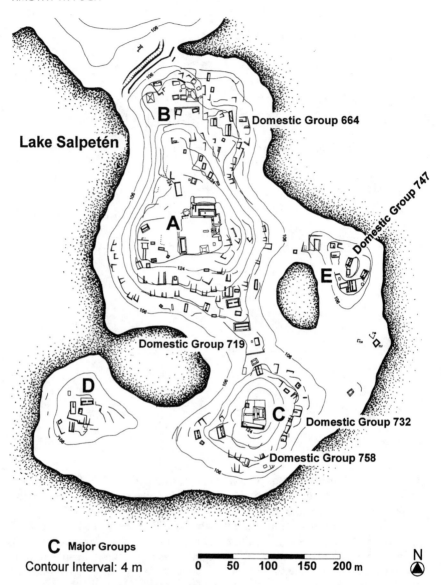

Map 8.1. Excavated residences at Zacpetén.

tandem plan are depicted on frescoes in the Temple of the Jaguars and the Temple of the Warriors at Chich'en Itza (Wauchope 1938: 14, 100); these buildings were constructed on low platforms and had open front rooms and enclosed back rooms. Similar structures are depicted in graffiti at Uaxactún and in architectural decoration at Chich'en Itza (Smith 1950: 27, 1962: 176–177).

Map 8.2. Tandem residence at Mayapán.

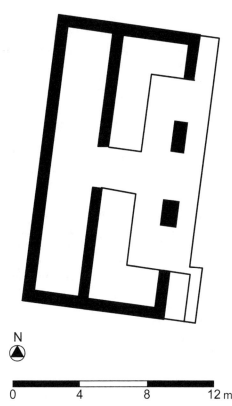

N

0   4   8   12 m

Domestic Structures in Postclassic Yucatán

In the sixteenth century, Bishop Diego de Landa (in Tozzer 1941: 85–87) described residences in Yucatán as having thatched roofs and being divided by an interior wall on the long axis. An opening in the wall allowed access between the front and back rooms. The front room was open, with its floor and features covered with plaster. The back room was closed, accessed by the opening in the divider wall and sometimes by a back door. The front room was a social area and a place where guests slept, while the occupants slept in the back room most of the year (ibid.: 86). A similar pattern characterized the house of the Petén Itza Ajaw Kan Ek', who received guests in a plastered front room (Jones 1998: 71). Residences in Colonial Yucatán tended to face toward the east, but they occasionally faced north or south; few were oriented toward the west (Tozzer 1941: 86; Smith 1962: 182). The houses of elites were well constructed, and the plaster in their front rooms was painted with elaborate designs. These residences were built by the "common people," and the nobility conducted political and religious activities in them (Tozzer 1941: 86–87).

The majority of the approximately 2,100 houses at Mayapán were tandem structures (Freidel 1981: 315–316; Smith 1962: 217), a surprising conformity given that the city included multiple ethnic groups (Freidel and Sabloff 1984: 182; Roys 1972: 12). Some variation in residences at the site suggests social differences (Smith 1962: 217–219); the largest and most elaborate dwellings have back rooms completely enclosed by masonry walls and occasionally partitioned, accessed by one or several openings from the front room. The front rooms of large houses are colonnaded and vestibular, with C-shaped benches against the walls, interrupted only by the entrances to the back room. The smallest residences at Mayapán had straight or L-shaped benches, also broken by an entrance between the front and back rooms. These structures lacked standing masonry enclosing the back room, and it is assumed that the walls of the structures were perishable (ibid.: 217). Domestic structures at Mayapán existed in a range of sizes.

Residences at Mayapán typically existed in structural groupings, many with two tandem dwellings (32 percent) and a few (4 percent) with more than two. In multi-residence groups, one of the residences was larger and better constructed than the others and was likely occupied by the head of the household; the multiple dwellings may represent an extended family (Smith 1962: 206). Residential groups at Mayapán apparently accommodated not only lodging but also food-related activities, production, and religious or ritual functions, as evidenced by the presence of kitchen houses, shrines, and oratorios.

Kitchen houses, or k'oben, are commonly found in the residential groups of the modern Maya of Yucatán and are spaces associated with women (Hanks 1990: 329–332). In addition to cooking implements, k'oben often house a three-stone cooking hearth, which can also be found inside some residences rather than in a separate building (Wauchope 1938: 117, 134). At Mayapán, only two three-stone hearths were encountered, both in the same building. Although A. Ledyard Smith (1962: 199, 219) has suggested that this structure was likely a kitchen house, three-stone hearths are not confined to kitchen houses; they are also found in temples and hunting sites among the modern Maya (Pugh, pers. obs.). Furthermore, even in known domestic contexts, Maya hearths are difficult to discern in the archaeological record (Pyburn 1989: 333–335). Hence, in most cases, archaeologists must use other forms of data to define kitchen spaces.

Shrines were constructed within residences as an interior shrine in the back room or in a special room attached to the rear of the back room, typically along the structure's medial axis. Residential groups also included freestanding shrines and oratorios. Shrines were usually "centered on and faced" the primary residence (Smith 1962: 222); oratorios were small temples, usually with an altar against the back wall, columns, and a C-shaped bench (ibid.: 220–221). Most oratorios held burials, and some contained large quantities of deity effigy censers (Pugh 2003a: 945).

Of particular interest to us is the Y-45 residential group in the south-central portion of Mayapán (Peraza Lope et al. 2006: figure 4), where unusual quantities of Tecoh Red-on-buff pottery — stylistically similar to Chompoxté Red-on-cream pottery from the Petén lakes — were noted. This group consisted of four structures: a relatively large (ca. twenty meter) tandem structure (Structure Y-

45a) on the south side of a plaza, facing north; a nearly square structure on the east side (Structure Y-45b); and two small structures on the north (Y-45c and d), opposite the hall. Structure Y-45a appears to have multiple altars, shrines, and small spaces in and around the back room. The two northern structures are probably small shrines, and the eastern structure might be an oratory.

At Cozumel, off the east coast of Yucatán, residential groups differed from those of Mayapán. There, most domestic groups had only a single dwelling structure, which were single-room rather than tandem structures (Freidel 1981: 315; Freidel and Sabloff 1984: 38, 111). The few residences that followed the Mayapán style belonged to the social elite, and this emulation may represent an effort by these individuals to associate themselves with the inland city (Freidel and Sabloff 1984: 38). A similar pattern was observed at Tulum and Ichpaatun (Freidel 1981: 317).

Domestic Structures at Zacpetén

Most residences at Zacpetén were clustered on the sloping terrain of the peninsula around two elite residential groups (D and E) and three ceremonial groups — A, B, and C (Rice 1988: 236) (Map 8.1). Shorelines were avoided, perhaps reflecting knowledge of shifting lake levels, and the area adjacent to the defensive system had sparse settlement as well. No known domestic structure at Zacpetén faced west. Other than this, the orientations of residences largely appeared to be adaptations to the slopes upon which they were constructed (ibid.).

Group 664

The structures of Domestic Group 664 (Pugh 2001: 425–429) sit on a low platform east of Group B, between that group and the lakeshore. Group 664 was uncovered in its entirety through a 224-square-meter excavation block (Map 8.3). The excavation penetrated thick Terminal Classic fill below the fill of the Late Postclassic platform. A residence (Structure 664) on the north side of the platform faces south toward a small rectangular structure (Structure 799), perhaps an altar or shrine, aligned with Structure 664's stairway. The group's plaza, which did not have an extant plaster surface, was accessed by an eastern stairway leading to the lakeshore.

Structure 664 is a small tandem residence with no remaining plaster surfaces. A single-course wall foundation defined the northern edge of the back room, and between this feature and a small stair on the southern edge of the basal platform were a bench and an irregularly shaped low platform. To the west of the bench, under an adjacent platform, was a partially flexed human burial, facing west with the skull to the north (Pugh 2001: 428, figure 9.5); no diagnostic artifacts accompanied the burial. The building had no standing walls lining the edges of the back room, and it is assumed that such walls were perishable. On the basis of the placement of the stairway and back wall, we assume that the area south of the bench was the front room.

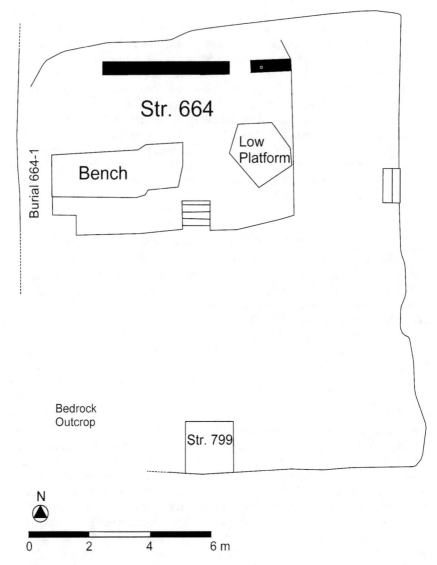

Map 8.3. Domestic Group 664, Zacpetén.

The front room of Structure 664 was fairly clean, but the back room had high frequencies of bone, chert and obsidian blades and flakes, and manos. Artifacts found around the structure included chert and obsidian side-notched points and human and animal teeth. A small refuse deposit outside the residence at its southwest corner included human teeth, pottery, obsidian points and blades, chert flakes, animal bone, and shell; animal bone was also found to the east of the platform. Many of the artifacts in the western part of Group 664 were secondary refuse from a higher platform to the west and included animal bone, shell, ceramic fragments, chert and obsidian flakes and blades, net weights, hammerstones, metate fragments, and animal teeth. Ceramics included sherds of the red-slipped Paxcamán and Topoxté ceramic groups, the latter in relatively large quantities and with a tan paste variant. Fragments of a variety of composite censer types were also recovered, including Fíjate, La Justa/Extranjeras, Zaklak, and Mumúl. A fragment of a pregnant female figurine was found in the patio.

Group 719

Domestic Group 719, discussed in detail in Chapter 9 (see also Pugh 2001: 429–443, figures 9.9–9.29), was centered between temple assemblage Groups A and C and between an *aguada* (waterhole, pond) and a small "bay" of Lake Salpetén (Map 8.1). Excavations focused on the group's three buildings (Chapter 9, Map 9.1, this volume), including a tandem building (Structure 719) on the north side of a small plaza and an oratorio (Structure 721) on the east, with a statue shrine (Structure 720) in front.

Structure 719, a possible residence, had a plastered front room with an L-shaped bench and an earth-floor back room. A 1-by-1-meter test excavation into the center of the long (northern) portion of the bench extended 1.55 meters to bedrock. Early Classic fill overlay bedrock and was topped with a floor, the whole apparently representing a structure or plaza roughly 65 centimeters high (Pugh 2001: figure 9.13). Above that was approximately 20 centimeters of Early Postclassic fill topped by a floor, upon which was the Late Postclassic fill of the final bench structure. Approximately 2 meters west of Structure 719, a test unit encountered a burial just below the ground surface. Only the lower portion of the deceased was encountered; the upper portion had eroded away (Pugh 2001: 431). No offerings were recovered with the interment.

Artifacts indicate that different activities were carried out in the front and back rooms of Structure 719. The back room was full of patterned refuse and in situ artifacts, including lithics, net weights, manos and metates, animal bone, shell, and pottery; the same kinds of artifacts were also found in relatively high frequencies behind the residence. The front room of Structure 719 was relatively clean except for ritual objects, including an extensive deposit of composite censers on the east side.

The group's oratorio (Structure 721) had no earlier construction stages. Against the east wall was the medial altar, and in the center of the room was an "interior" altar; both lacked caches. In front (west) of Structure 721 lay a low statue shrine (Structure 720). It is evident from the fire blackening of the plaster surface and construction stone of Structure 721 that it and Structure 720 were destroyed by fire, perhaps in ritual termination. Large numbers of sherds representing composite and effigy incensarios were intermingled in, on, and around these structures.

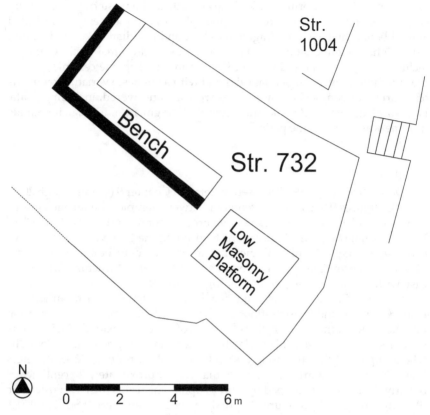

Map 8.4. Domestic Group 732, Zacpetén.

Domestic Group 732

Group 732 (Pugh 2001: 443–446) stands east of the temple of Group C at the base of the steep hill on which that assemblage was constructed. The platform of Group 732 was accessed by an eastern stairway leading toward the lake, about sixty meters to the east (Map 8.1). This group (Map 8.4) included a tandem residence (Structure 732) facing an associated building (Structure 1004) that was relatively clean of refuse, except for seven net weights; thus, its functions are unknown. Unlike the other four excavated residences, Structure 732 lacks an entry stairway on its front (northeast) side. Excavations revealed no construction levels earlier than the single Late Postclassic episode of building this group. A tightly flexed burial of a child lay off the eastern edge of the patio; no grave goods were in the interment (ibid.: 445).

The front and back rooms of Structure 732 are separated by a standing wall. The front room has an L-shaped bench with a small ad hoc shrine at its southeastern end. This room has a two-centimeter-thick coat of plaster, thicker than that on most Late Postclassic constructions at Zacpetén, and the plaster of

Figure 8.1. Mold for producing censer faces from Structure 732: (a) cast of the face formed from the mold; (b) the mold.

the shrine and the "elbow" of the bench have charred patches indicating burning. A low masonry platform stands southeast of the bench, overlapping the centerline, but the opening between the platform and the bench allows movement from the front room to the back room. The back (southwest) room has an earthen floor and is not enclosed by standing masonry walls, although a single-course foundation defines its rear edge. The back room of Structure 732 appears to have been a storage and production area in addition to its assumed use as living quarters. It held a large amount of de facto refuse, including chert flakes, cores, and hammerstones; obsidian flakes, side-notched points, and a core; net weights, animal bone, shell, mano and metate fragments (eight: four of limestone and four of basalt), and pieces of gypsum.

Except for the area of the shrine at the southeastern end of the bench, the plaster surface of the residence's front room was relatively clean of artifacts. The shrine held an in situ Zaklak Composite spiked censer and a spindle whorl, and charred areas of plaster within the shrine suggest the burning of offerings. Other censer types include Mumúl Composite, La Justa, and Extranjeras. Spindle whorls are used to produce yarn or thread, although they may be recycled as divination tools (Brown 2000: 330). The location of the whorl in a shrine indicates that it may have been last used in ritual practices rather than cloth production, although a bone needle was also found in the structure.

Quantities of red-slipped and decorated pottery were found during the clearing of Structure 732—including fragments of Paxcamán, Trapeche, and Topoxté slipped groups, Sacá Polychrome, and Macanché Red-on-paste—

181

particularly adjacent to the interior wall. Effigy censers were probably not used in Group 732, as only two sherds of such vessels were recovered. Nevertheless, they may have been produced by the occupants, as indicated by the recovery of a mold for a small effigy censer face (Figure 8.1), probably of Kulut Modeled type, immediately northeast of the shrine; two animal claws were near the censer mold. An in situ Zaklak Composite spiked censer sat on the north corner of the low platform opposite the one on the shrine, forming a pair. A sample of the resin inside the incensario was submitted for AMS analysis (AA-35236) and produced a conventional age of 426 ± 30 years, with two-sigma ranges of A.D. 1420–1520 (91.7 percent probability) and 1600–1620 (3.7 percent probability). The paired censers likely defined sacred space within the residence and ritualized the opening between the front and back rooms.

Several concentrations of refuse were found outside the structure, both on and off the platform. One lay immediately north of the northwest corner of the bench and included a heavy deposit of large ceramic sherds (especially Paxcamán jars), five human teeth, three animal teeth, a chert lance or knife, animal bone, net weights, shell, and obsidian flakes. A ritual refuse deposit immediately southwest of the low platform included two quartz crystals, a small greenstone ax (a Postclassic artifact type common at Topoxté), two chert side-notched points, a lithic biface, high frequencies of shell and pottery sherds, and relatively large amounts of animal bone, chert flakes, obsidian blades, and non-effigy censer sherds. Another possible ritual refuse area lay outside the house, approximately two meters south of the low platform; it contained a shark's tooth, a chert lance or knife point and a biface, miscellaneous pieces of greenstone, two obsidian side-notched points, four obsidian blades, animal bone, shell, chert flakes, net weights, and non-effigy censer sherds. A fourth major refuse deposit lay off the platform and did not appear to have been specific to ritual objects; it contained ceramics; obsidian blades; animal bone; shell; chert flakes, cores, and points; net weights; and human and animal teeth.

Group 747

Domestic Group 747 (Pugh 2001: 446–452) occupies the epicenter of Group E on a hill 4 meters higher than the surrounding, artificially leveled prominence of the easternmost portion of the peninsula (Map 8.1). The group includes an east-facing Late Postclassic tandem residence (Structure 747) and a slightly earlier building (Structure 748) 3.3 meters to the south (Map 8.5). These structures sit upon a plaza with an area of approximately 390 square meters. Although Structure 747 is sizable, an even larger domestic structure (Structure 741) sits immediately to the south of Domestic Group 747 at a lower elevation. The prominence was likely too small to hold this residence and its associated buildings and activities.

Group 747 was investigated by means of a 193-square-meter excavation block focused on the two buildings and areas of adjacent plaza. A test unit in

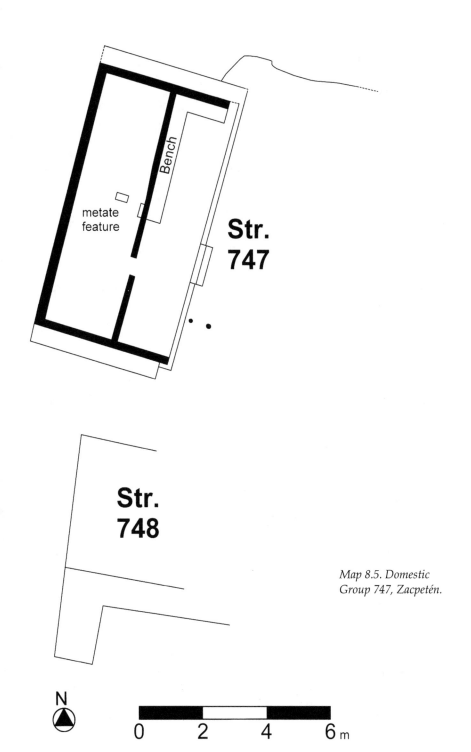

Bench

metate
feature

**Str.
747**

**Str.
748**

*Map 8.5. Domestic
Group 747, Zacpetén.*

N

0   2   4   6 m

the northern part of the front room of Structure 747 was excavated to bedrock and revealed two levels of Terminal Classic fills, each approximately 35 centimeters thick, with the uppermost covered by a plaster floor. The foundation of a Terminal Classic masonry structure was found on this floor. This was covered by about 35 centimeters of Late Postclassic structural fill and another floor, creating a platform 1.05–1.10 meters above bedrock, upon which the latest version of Structure 747 — facing east — was built.

Structure 748, a low platform south of Structure 747, had much of the facing on its north side dismantled, perhaps as construction material for Structure 747. No evidence of a superstructure was encountered on this platform, and it also may have been removed for construction. Testing of Structure 748 revealed the same or a similar Terminal Classic fill and floor over bedrock as found in Structure 747, but this one included large dressed blocks and was covered by Early Postclassic fill. This Early Postclassic fill was topped by a very thin floor at about 1.5 meters above bedrock, which was then covered with the fill of an early Late Postclassic structure.

Late Postclassic Structure 747 is the second largest of the excavated residences at Zacpetén and has a total area of 95.2 square meters. The layout of this building is similar to that of Structure 719. Its back room — except for much of the west side, which had eroded downhill — is enclosed by a wall and accessed by an opening on its east side. The floor in the back room is earthen except for a small patch of partially charred plaster in the southeast corner. In the center of the back room, two metates (Feature 747-1) embedded in the floor formed a "table" or perhaps an altar. A small pedestal of unknown function rests against the medial wall near the metate feature. An L-shaped bench in the northern portion of the front room is covered by a thin layer of plaster, as is the floor. A small stairway exists on the east side of the building, and two postholes were discerned in nearby shallowly buried bedrock. Additional postholes for roof support likely existed but could not be identified in the dark soil.

Structure 747 contained quantities of de facto refuse, but not as much as that in Groups 719 and 732. A reconstructible Pozo Unslipped utilitarian jar holding forty-five net weights or line sinkers and wood fragments was found in the back room, northwest of the metate feature. The wood was submitted for AMS analysis and produced two-sigma ranges of A.D. 1440–1530 and 1550–1640 (Chapter 5, Table 5.2, this volume). It has been identified as *Piscidia erythina*, commonly used throughout the Americas as a fish poison (Lee Newsom, pers. com., 2003). Thus, the jar held a fishing tool kit. Three smooth cobbles were found in the southwest corner of the back room; their function is unknown, but similar objects in Structure 719 were used to grind pigments. Additional artifacts in the back room included obsidian blades, side-notched points, and a core; two chert bifaces (one of Colha chert) and a uniface; animal bone, shell, ceramic fragments, net weights, and a small stone ax with use-wear polish on the tip. Immediately behind (west of) Structure 747 were two obsidian cores and two ceramic figurine sherds; five quartz crystals were found near the building's southwest corner, and at the southeast and northeast corners were deposits of large ceramic sherds.

The front room was relatively clean, like those of the other residences, but it contained puzzling concentrations of lithics and other artifacts. Sixteen obsidian flakes and debitage, an obsidian core, a chert ax, and a concentration of animal bone and shell were found on the southernmost meter of the bench. Associated with these objects was a deposit of pottery sherds on the bench and nearby floor, perhaps representing a vessel that had held the artifacts. Another concentration immediately west of the stairway into the front room consisted of various chert objects including two blades, six cores, sixty-six flakes and debitage, a lance/knife, and a side-notched point, plus twelve pieces of miscellaneous shell. Because it might be unusual for the primary access point into the structure to double as a lithics production area, it is possible that these objects were once held in a perishable container (such as a basket or net bag) that hung from the building's rafters. Alternatively, but less likely, these materials may have been deposited after the residence was abandoned.

Numerous censers were associated with Structure 747, including one Patojo Modeled, three Extranjeras Composite, and miscellaneous sherds of both Gotas and Zaklak Composite types. Among the slipped vessels were at least two Paxcamán Red jars and some grater bowls.

Structure 748, by contrast, contained no de facto refuse. As mentioned, the superstructure and much of the platform facing had been removed from the Early Postclassic building for later constructions. Secondary refuse against the north and west walls of Structure 748 included animal bones, freshwater shell, charcoal, pottery sherds, and metate fragments. This material was likely refuse discarded from Structure 747.

Group 758

Domestic Group 758 (Pugh 2001: 452–454), approximately 40 meters south of Group C (Map 8.1), included the smallest and least substantial of the five excavated residences and one of the smallest at Zacpetén. The platform of Group 758 leveled the steeply sloping natural terrain such that it blended into the slope on its north side but descended sharply 4.5 meters on its south side. The only discernible structure on the platform was Structure 758, and excavations were restricted to this building and its immediate surroundings (Map 8.6).

A 71-square-meter excavation block exposed most of Structure 758. This simple east-facing tandem residence had a straight masonry bench on a low basal platform that separated the front and back rooms. Relatively poorly constructed, the structure sat on a platform with Early Postclassic fill and was probably built primarily of perishable materials. A stairway accessed the partially plastered east side of the basal platform, and a back wall composed of a single-course foundation west of the bench indicates that the building faced toward the open patio to its east. A low rectangular platform lay to the northeast of the stairway, off the basal platform, but it is probable that the residence's thatch roof once covered this feature.

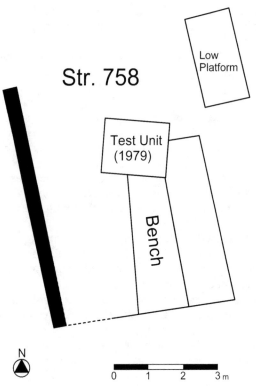

Map 8.6. Domestic Group 758, Zacpetén.

Structure 758 had few in situ artifact deposits, but the patterns that could be discerned reinforced those noted in the other excavated structures. The most obvious pattern was the dichotomy between the clean front room and the relatively high frequency of artifacts in the back room, as the latter included greater numbers of pottery sherds (especially against the bench), net weights, lithic flakes, and mano and metate fragments. As with Structure 732, no effigy censers were found in Structure 758, but a clay mold for making a censer face was found in the back room; a skull was incised into the back of the mold. Although no artifact concentrations lay in the front room, several light deposits were found near the low rectangular platform. Between the platform and bench was a light deposit of Gotas and Extranjeras Composite censer sherds—the only concentration of censer sherds in the entire building. On top of the low platform was a quartz crystal, and to its west were several animal teeth and a human tooth. Immediately south of the platform was a chert core and a scatter of chert flakes, which contrast with the general focus of ritual objects around the platform. Relatively high frequencies of shell, obsidian blades, and bone were encountered on the south end of the bench. This "concentration" was likely the result of the bench eroding off the edge of the platform and exposing artifacts contained in construction fill. Slipped pottery included sherds of types in the Paxcamán and Topoxté ceramic groups, but in small quantities.

Discussion

The five tested residences at Zacpetén varied slightly in construction, and these variations, along with building size and artifact content, reveal disparity in the occupants' social statuses (Pugh 2004: 364–365). All excavated residences were tandem structures on basal platforms, all of which, except that of Structure 732, were accessed by stairways. Except for Structure 664, the front rooms were coated with plaster and the back rooms were largely devoid of plaster surfacing. Each residence had a bench in its front room.

The two smallest buildings of those studied had straight (I-shaped) benches. The three smallest buildings had low masonry platforms at the intersection of the front and back rooms. These small residences likely had perishable interior walls and enclosing walls. In contrast, the larger structures had more substantial construction features. For example, the three largest structures were bisected by interior masonry walls that firmly defined front and back rooms, with L-shaped benches against the interior wall in the front room. The two largest residences lacked the low platforms found in the smaller residences. Instead, the interior masonry wall bisected the entire structure — with the exception of the doorway to the back room. In addition, the back rooms of the two largest structures were completely enclosed by masonry walls, and the extended side walls created vestibule-like front rooms. Metates were embedded in the floors of the back rooms of the two largest structures, forming features of unknown significance.

Only the largest excavated residence, Structure 719, had an elaborately painted bench and Classic-period cut soft limestone embedded in the facade. This limestone removed from Classic-period constructions appears to have been viewed as valued, alienable property because it was appropriated for use in public structures. A similar pattern was described at Mayapán, where the houses of wealthy families incorporated stones borrowed from Classic-period Puuc-style buildings (Smith 1962: 218).

The plan of the residences at Zacpetén differed from most of those of early-twentieth-century Yucatán and of the Northern Lacandon, which did not have covered front rooms/porches (Wauchope 1938: 98). Nevertheless, such structures were found at Late Postclassic Mayapán, Tulum, and Cozumel. One house at Valladolid had an uncovered plastered porch with benches, and residences in the Maya highlands had tandem plans with vestibule entrances, some with paving (Wauchope 1938: 15–16, plate 5a).

Although both Mayapán and Zacpetén had tandem residences, their plans differed slightly. Most of the residences of Mayapán had C-shaped benches, but this form was not discerned in residences at Zacpetén, although it was seen in open halls. I- and L-shaped benches, which were characteristic of Zacpetén, were observed at Mayapán, but in relatively low frequencies. In addition, a doorway between the front and back rooms interrupted the bench in even the poorest residences at Mayapán. At Zacpetén, the bench terminated at the opening and did not continue on the other side. Shrines in residences at Zacpetén were placed in the front room rather than the back room. Finally, columns or roof supports in Zacpetén's residences appear to have been perishable. These minor differences in construction may have been the result of gradual stylistic changes in residences. Cozumel also differed from Zacpetén because its elites occupied tandem residences, whereas the domiciles of most commoners were single-roomed. If David Freidel and Jeremy Sabloff's (1984: 38) suggestion that Mayapán-style residences at Cozumel represented a conscious affiliation with Mayapán holds true at Zacpetén, then the entire population of this site—not just the social elite—may have linked themselves with that city.

Two differences between Mayapán and Zacpetén that cannot be ascribed to gradual stylistic change are the inclusion, at Mayapán, of more than one residence in a given patio group and the masonry walls surrounding residential groups. As at Cozumel (Freidel and Sabloff 1984: 111), few, if any, groups at Zacpetén included multiple residences (Rice 1988: 242). It may be that it is simply easier to discern associated residences at Mayapán because the groups are surrounded by walls and the residents did not have to cope with uneven terrain. Nevertheless, the absence of multiple dwellings at Zacpetén suggests that this site had a different residential pattern than many residential groups at Mayapán. Zacpetén and some of the single-dwelling groups at multi-ethnic Mayapán might represent a neo-local residential system. The walls bounding domestic groups at Mayapán occasionally surrounded multiple domestic groups, suggesting that they integrated social entities within the larger community (Brown 1999: 583). The absence of such walls at Zacpetén suggests that this means of integration did not exist or was not needed. Zacpetén's residences tended to cluster around the site's high-elevation points occupied by Groups A, B, C, D, and E; and it is possible that the town was divided into five barrios, although it seems just as likely a function of there being five elevated areas on the peninsula. The most prominent divisions evident at Zacpetén are its two temple assemblages, which suggest some sort of internal social duality (Pugh 2003b; Pugh and Rice, Chapter 7, this volume).

Although the plan of the Late Postclassic Petén residences differs from that of twentieth-century houses in Yucatán, in both areas residences were constructed on platforms. Robert Wauchope (1938: 15) asked, "When and why was the practice [of building on platforms] temporarily discarded after the end of the stela epoch?" The present data do not speak to the Early Postclassic period, but one can clearly observe that during the Late Postclassic and Contact periods at Zacpetén and at Late Postclassic Mayapán, residences were built on low platforms. Thus, Wauchope (1938: 15) is incorrect in placing this transformation at the end of the Classic period; it seems more likely to have been an aftereffect of conquest.

As at Mayapán, residences and residential groups at Zacpetén were constructed in a range of sizes, which we interpret as indicating a range of social statuses. Residence size symbolized a family's status and wealth, although much less labor was invested in Late Postclassic habitations than in domiciles of earlier periods (Rice 1988: 233). In addition, occupants of larger domestic structures had greater access to nonlocal goods and more storage space (Pugh 2004: 363–364). Only the largest, presumably elite, residential groups at Zacpetén included elaborate ceremonial buildings; similarly, at Mayapán, only approximately 5 percent of the residential groups had masonry oratorios. Elite homes were constructed by the community, which explains their size, extensive walls, decoration, and numerous features. In this light, Structure 719 can be considered a manifestation of idealized residential space. Members of the community who built but did not occupy the house or its associated buildings internalized social inequality through their participation in the construction of a house very different from their own in size and form. In other words, social inequality was partially constructed by those who suffered from it most.

The Maya of Colonial Yucatán did not face their houses to the west (Tozzer 1941: 86), and such appears to have been the rule at Zacpetén as well. Structures 664 and 719 faced south, Structure 747 faced southeast, Structure 758 faced east, and Structure 732 faced northeast. None of the excavated residences faced west, and the unexcavated structures also appeared to conform—largely, if not universally—to this rule. The open halls at Zacpetén also followed this stricture, although at other Postclassic sites such as Mayapán some halls faced west. Temples and oratorios at Zacpetén that held deity effigy censers did face west, however (Pugh and Rice, Chapter 7, this volume). This contrast is important, as these structures were the houses of the deities. It is probably not important that temples faced to the west; what seems critical is that participants faced east as they entered the structures with doorways on their west sides. Among many modern Maya groups, the east is the location of the most powerful divine beings (Hanks 1990: 305–373; McGee 2002: 129–138). We do not know why human residences were constructed in opposition to divine residences, although it was probably meant to emphasize the difference between human and divine space. Alternatively, deities may have seen the world in its reverse form, as described for the Lacandon (Davis 1978: 24–25).

Zacpetén residences also displayed a status-related continuum in regard to exotic goods (Pugh 2004: 363–364). All cleared residences except the smallest (Structure 758) had greenstone or serpentine artifacts, and the three largest structures, especially Structure 719, yielded obsidian cores. Only the largest residence, Structure 719, yielded copper artifacts and had parts of its facade composed of soft cut limestone removed from Classic-period constructions. In addition, this structure held thirty-six mano and metate fragments, more than the combined total of the other four excavated residences. As suggested in Chapter 9, the occupants of Structure 719 were likely Kowoj nobility, and those of the other domestic groups represented a continuum of social statuses.

One feature completely lacking in the clearing of domestic groups at Zacpetén is hearths. Their absence appears to result from our failure to identify and excavate kitchen houses, whether domestic or ceremonial. Such buildings were likely composed of perishable materials, and hearth features may not necessarily have been placed on residential platforms. Apparently, cooking did not occur inside the residence unless the hearth was constructed on a perishable table. Many Maya domiciles in early-twentieth-century Guatemala created cooking hearths on wood tables with an insulating layer of gravel and clay (Wauchope 1938: 117; also in rural Petén through the 1970s, P. Rice, pers. obs.); however, no ash or burned clay was encountered in the back rooms at Zacpetén. Evidence of extensive burning was detected behind Structure 719, but no kitchen house or hearth was noted. In practice, hearths are not well described in the archaeological record of the Maya, and it is possible that occupants reused hearth stones (Pyburn 1989: 333–335; Wauchope 1938: 117). Defining kitchens is also difficult because three-stone hearths are found in other contexts.

Although hearths were not identified in residential contexts at Zacpetén, excavations revealed features composed of metates standing on end and partially buried in the floors of the back rooms of two residences. In both cases the feature stood roughly in the medial portion of the back room. No artifacts in the vicinity of the features revealed how they might have been used. Nevertheless, in Yucatán, altars used in New House ceremonies were set up in the middle of the residence (Redfield and Villa Rojas 1934: 146), similar to the positioning of these embedded metate features.

The most generally repeated patterns of artifact deposition are seen in the dichotomies between front and back rooms of tandem structures. The front rooms were relatively clean, and, except for lithic scatters in Structure 747, they displayed ritual objects such as censers. Given that chert and obsidian cores were associated with scatters in Structure 747, these resources were likely held in containers suspended from the rafters. Censer use in the front rooms tended to focus on the areas around the passage to the back rooms.

Shrines in residences in early-twentieth-century Yucatán were often located near their entrances, although these were not tandem structures. The burning of incense protected the houses from bad spirits (Wauchope 1938: 143); thus, in addition to providing a place for offerings to deities and ancestors, the household shrines may have protected the residences' open doorways. Incense burners in residences at Zacpetén were almost exclusively non-effigy censers, the main exception a Kulut Modeled effigy censer in the interior shrine of Structure 719. Bishop Landa (in Tozzer 1941: 108–144) indicated that nobles and other high-status individuals possessed "idols" (deity effigies), and their houses played critical roles in Wayeb' rites, in which some effigies were renewed. In this regard, it is interesting that the only censer face molds at Zacpetén were found in mid- and small-sized residences near Group C. Although the residents of these structures did not use effigy censers in their dwellings, they appear to have made them there.

The back rooms of all residences were cluttered with pottery fragments, lithics of various sorts, animal bone, shell, net weights, and mano and metate fragments. Many of these objects were likely originally stored on tables, in "attic" rooms, or in nets, baskets, or cloth containers suspended from the rafters or walls (following Wauchope 1938: 124). Non-censer ceramic sherds and sometimes in situ vessels were concentrated in the back rooms against the interior walls. This pattern was not limited to Zacpetén, as Wauchope (1938: 120, figure 44a, plate 32c) found that ceramic vessels tended to be placed on tables against walls at Chan Kom, Yucatán. The two pottery vessels embedded in the floor of Structure 719 seem anomalous, although they probably represent "built-in" storage for staples.

Most residences had large amounts of secondary refuse behind their back rooms. Refuse was also deposited adjacent to unused buildings within some groups. In the case of Group 664, for example, much of the trash on its west side was contributed by the higher group to its west. Three residences had small concentrations of primary refuse consisting of large ceramic sherds, bone, shell, and lithics immediately off their basal platforms at one or both exterior corners of the front room. These deposits were buried after disposal, differentiating them from more typical refuse disposal, and two of the three dwellings included human teeth in these deposits. These characteristics suggest that they represented a combination of refuse disposal and caching, such as used items being broken and discarded after a ritual.

The excavated residences reveal a great deal about domestic activities and social inequality at Zacpetén, as well as about depositional processes. Unfortunately, not all residences contained large amounts of de facto refuse. Structure 719, discussed in detail in Chapter 9, was rapidly abandoned and its occupants appear to have lost all of their possessions, while the occupants of Structure 664 left little, if anything, behind. The other residences are somewhere along the continuum defined by these extremes, indicating that the final experiences of particular families at Zacpetén varied significantly. It is unlikely that all these residences were contemporary, but most were occupied during the Contact period—and some likely through conquest. It was in this milieu that the Kowoj families struggled with the decision to remain at Zacpetén or to move to other settlements: some chose or were forced to join Spanish *reducciones,* and others fled into the forest.

ZACPETÉN GROUP 719,
THE LAST NOBLE RESIDENCE

—— Timothy W. Pugh, Prudence M. Rice, and Leslie G. Cecil ——————

Zacpetén's Group 719 consists of three masonry structures—a tandem open hall (Structure 719), a temple (Structure 721), and a shrine (Structure 720)—on a platform roughly 1200 square meters in area (Map 9.1). The complex is situated between the two temple assemblages, Group A and Group C, on a low ridge that provides the easiest path between the two ceremonial complexes. It is also in one of the most desirable living areas of the site—on terrain that is not flood-prone or a dramatic slope—and between two *aguadas* (waterholes), one of which connects to Lake Salpetén. Thus, the occupants had optimal access to water while being sheltered from possible attacks launched from the open lake.

Excavations in this group were concentrated in the three visible buildings; the plaza was not intensively probed. However, fourteen test units excavated into Structure 719 and adjacent areas revealed that this building had been constructed atop an earlier Late Postclassic structure, which in turn had been built on a structure with Early Classic pottery in its fill (Pugh, Chapter 8, this volume). The final occupation of this complex—represented by primary

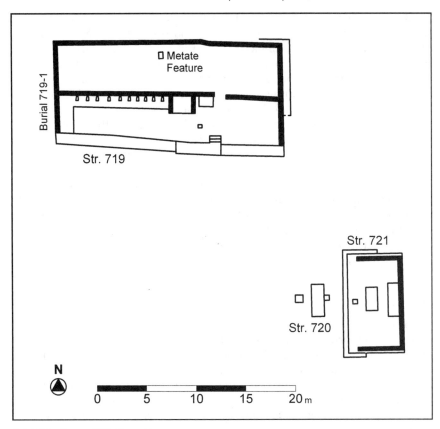

Map 9.1. Group 719, Zacpetén.

or de facto refuse deposits on the floor surfaces of the structures — occurred very late in the Contact period, likely just before and after conquest, and over-lapped with Spanish accounts of the region. Moreover, the group's occupants were among the site's latest ruling elite and probably members of the Kowoj social group, if not carrying the actual patronym "Kowoj."

Structure 719 appears to have been rapidly abandoned because the occu-pants left behind a large quantity of de facto refuse, including small valuable items (following Inomata and Webb 2003: 3; Stevenson 1982: 241–246). The large amount of refuse allowed documentation of specific behaviors in and around the structure. They included a variety of production activities as well as ceremonial remains not seen in the other four excavated residences.

Structure 719

Structure 719 is the largest building of the group, measuring approximately 24 meters east-west by 11.5 meters north-south, and it is possibly the largest residential structure at Zacpetén. It faces south and has a typical tandem form, divided into front (south) and back (north) rooms by a long interior masonry wall broken by a single door east of center. The structure exhibits marked asymmetry in several respects, including architecture and artifact distributions. In particular, the eastern third of the structure was offset from the western two-thirds by a different angle of the rear, interior, and front walls. Thus, at some point Structure 719 was remodeled on the east side, perhaps by removing part of an existing structure and replacing it with the part that is now visible along with a small sub-platform bounding the eastern edge and northeast corner. We were not able to discern the eastern edge of the earlier construction, however.

The final occupation of the structure was tested by 532 square meters of excavation that uncovered the entire building and adjacent areas, particularly behind (north of) the structure. Its two rooms were very different, both from front to back and side to side: the front room was plastered and the rear room had an earthen floor, and each displayed distinct architecture and artifact assemblages and distributions.

The Front Room

The western half of the front room is dominated by an L-shaped bench with a medial shrine at its east end. This shrine is bounded by three walls and open on the south side. East of the shrine is a rectangular altar; an opening east of the altar leads to the back room. In front of the altar is a small rectangular masonry feature (forty by forty centimeters), possibly a miniature altar, which matches a similar feature in Structure 721. The front room was relatively clean of refuse, particularly in the western half, as compared to the back room — perhaps reflecting practice in Colonial Yucatán, where houses were cleaned and renovated to purify them during certain rituals (Tozzer 1941: 86, 151). A thin layer of plaster covers most of the front room; on the edge of the bench the plaster was painted with red curvilinear designs, a hallmark of Kowoj pottery (Cecil 2001a; also Rice and Cecil, Chapter 11, this volume). Relatively unfaded red stains on the floor in front of the bench and altar suggest a painting event or the offering of red pigment not long before abandonment. The front rooms of elite residences in Yucatán were painted during the Colonial period, and on a mural at Mayapán (and in Mixtec codices) decoration on images of temples represents particular places, officials, and possibly social groups (Pohl and Byland 1990: 113–116; Proskouriakoff 1962a: 137; Pugh 2001: 254–255; Smith 1962: 172–175). Thus, the decorated bench of Structure 719 likewise may have represented the occupants and possibly a larger social unit. The painted stucco lay in fragments against the front edge of the bench and appears to have been intentionally destroyed.

The L-shaped bench in Structure 719 is unique in that it has ten slabs of cut soft limestone, unplastered and embedded in the fill along the long side of the "L". They divide the bench into eleven niches, which we interpret as seats (see Carmack 1981: 288 for bench seating arrangements). As discussed elsewhere (Pugh and Rice, Chapter 7, this volume), cut stones from Classic-period constructions were used as decorative facing in the two ceremonial groups and in Group 719. Relatively few artifacts were found in this portion of the front room, and the long east-west arm of the bench was virtually devoid of material. Those items that were recovered, largely lithics and net weights, were found primarily on the floor in front of the bench or on its shorter west arm.

The medial shrine yielded several ceremonial items, including a complete Kulut Modeled effigy incense burner (Figure 9.1; Chapter 12, Figure 12.5, this volume). The effigy — which bears traced of red, black, and blue pigments — depicts an elderly male with pigtails, filed teeth, two bolt-like objects at the corners of his mouth, ear spools, and a monster headdress. Censers with this figure usually occurred alone at Zacpetén; none were found among the temple deities (Pugh 2002: 311–316). The effigy may depict Itzamna or another aged deity or even an ancestor. The censer receptacle was heavily burned and held a small ceramic cup, probably used to offer ceremonial drink to the deity. Similar cups were found in temples at Zacpetén, often near larger deity censers. Adjacent to the Kulut Modeled censer was the central portion of the left mandible of a cow, heavily worn on both distal and proximal ends as if ground, used for smoothing, or both (Figure 9.2; Susan DeFrance, pers. com., July 2006). Alfred Tozzer (1907: 115) noted that the Lacandon kept animal mandibles in the ceilings of ceremonial buildings as evidence of sacrificial offerings.

At the base of the shrine and on the edge of the platform, directly south of the altar, were sherds representing a portion (less than 25 percent) of a Patojo Modeled: Patojo variety effigy censer. At Zacpetén, in situ deposits of Patojo censers rarely occurred outside of temples, and this seems to be a discard — likely from Structure 721, although its presence in Structure 719 is puzzling. Possibly, this incensario was paired with the one resting on the medial shrine.

The altar was relatively clean of artifacts, and excavations into the interior of this feature uncovered the bases of paired Extranjeras/La Justa composite censers just below the surface. The bases seem to have settled into the altar as it deteriorated. Portions of a plaster figure, perhaps disassembled statuary, lay near the altar. These fragments exhibited multiple layers of whitewashing and painting with black-and-red designs, also characteristic of Kowoj pottery. It appears, then, that the altar had elaborate decoration that was destroyed at the structure's termination. Below the censer bases was cached a small Chilo Unslipped bowl with loop/ring handles, covered by a lid with a loop handle (similar to those in Figure 12.12 [Chapter 12, this volume]). The bowl held a greenstone bead, two red shell beads, and a flat greenstone rectangle. This cache probably activated or renewed the structure and helped protect it from evil winds (adapting Stuart 1998: 395; Redfield and Villa Rojas 1934: 146). It seems strange that this vessel was not removed as part of what might have been the termination of the group, but it is possible that its presence was forgotten.

Figure 9.1. Kulut Modeled effigy figure incense burner, reconstructed from fragments found on medial altar of the front room in Structure 719.

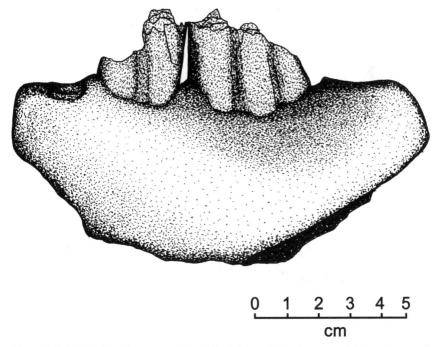

Figure 9.2. Labial side of center portion of the left mandible of a cow, retaining its second and third molars, found on medial altar of the front room of Structure 719 (identification by Susan deFrance). Both proximal (right) and distal (left) ends, as well as the lower left edge, are smoothed (but not polished) as a result of some kind of use.

Reconstructible or partially reconstructible polychrome vessels included a Macanché Red-on-paste collared bowl, a Macanché Red-on-paste plate (Figure 9.3), and four Ixpop Polychrome plates (for type descriptions, see Cecil, Chapter 10, this volume). Outside (south) of the front room, directly in front of the bench, was a trash pit with quantities of freshwater shell, animal bone, and sherds from two Chompoxté Red-on-cream: Akalché variety plates. This deposit was likely refuse from feasting and other ritual activities. In addition, sherds of several censer types were scattered in front of Structure 719, including a semi-reconstructible vessel of Gotas Composite and rare sherds of a Fíjate Composite censer, as well as an Ídolos Modeled sherd.

The Back Room

The rear room of Structure 719 had no built-in architectural features, other than two metates embedded in the dirt floor near the back wall. The room contained large quantities of de facto refuse—particularly pottery, stone, and bone, as well as more unusual items—scattered over the floor and indicating

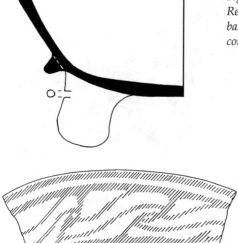

Figure 9.3. Large sherd of Macanché Red-on-paste tripod dish with notched basal flange. The interior decoration is completely eroded and looks burned.

0 1 2 3 4 5
cm

a variety of activities. No evidence of intentional desecration was discerned in the back room.

Pottery was distributed mostly against the interior wall and included several complete or nearly complete domestic vessels. Two large, wide-mouthed utilitarian Chilo Unslipped jars were embedded in the dirt floor just north of the shrine and appear to have been semipermanent storage features. Both held carbonized remains, including maize kernels. An AMS-dated sample (Beta-107791) had a conventional age of 200 ± 40 B.P., calibrated to A.D. 1640–1700, 1720–1820, 1830–1880, and 1910–1960 (two-sigma) (see Chapter 5, Table 5.2, this volume).

In addition to the two jars, large portions of a Picú Incised: Picú variety plate and two Macanché Red-on-paste plates were found adjacent to and two meters south of the back (northeast) wall, and a Chompoxté Red-on-cream: Akalché variety plate was also found nearby. Large quantities of miscellaneous non-conjoinable ceramic sherds represent the majority of the Postclassic slipped pottery types. Zoomorphic figurines concentrated in the western portion of the room could have been used as decoration, toys, or ritual objects.

In the eastern portion of Structure 719, on the floors of both the front and back rooms, sherds of at least eleven and possibly as many as fifteen partially reconstructible composite incense burners were found on either side of the interior wall beneath collapse (see Map 9.2). These censers were highly variable: they were generally small and asymmetrical, with forms varying from

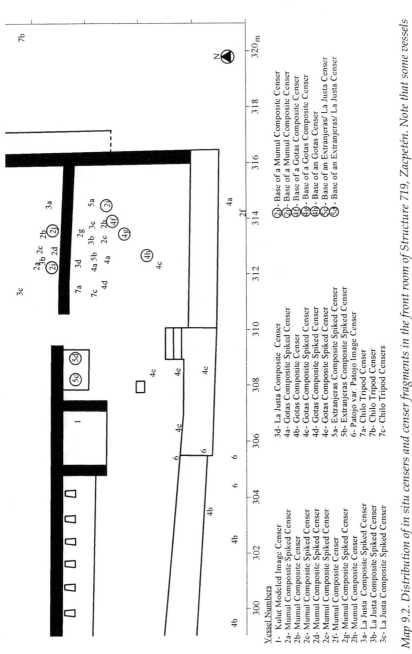

Vessel Numbers

1- Kulut Modeled Image Censer
2a- Mumul Composite Spiked Censer
2b- Mumul Composite Censer
2c- Mumul Composite Spiked Censer
2d- Mumul Composite Spiked Censer
2e- Mumul Composite Spiked Censer
2f- Mumul Composite Censer
2g- Mumul Composite Spiked Censer
2h- Mumul Composite Censer
3a- La Justa Composite Spiked Censer
3b- La Justa Composite Spiked Censer
3c- La Justa Composite Spiked Censer

3d- La Justa Composite Censer
4a- Gotas Composite Spiked Censer
4b- Gotas Composite Censer
4c- Gotas Composite Spiked Censer
4d- Gotas Composite Spiked Censer
4e- Gotas Composite Spiked Censer
5a- Extranjeras Composite Spiked Censer
5b- Extranjeras Composite Spiked Censer
6- Patojo var. Patojo Image Censer
7a- Chilo Tripod Censer
7b- Chilo Tripod Censer
7c- Chilo Tripod Censers

⑥a - Base of a Mumul Composite Censer
⑥b - Base of a Mumul Composite Censer
⑥c - Base of a Gotas Composite Censer
⑥d - Base of a Gotas Composite Censer
⑥e - Base of an Gotas Censer
⑥f - Base of an Extranjeras/ La Justa Censer
⑥g - Base of an Extranjeras/ La Justa Censer

Map 9.2. Distribution of in situ censers and censer fragments in the front room of Structure 719, Zacpetén. Note that some vessels originally typed as Mumul have since been reclassified as Zaklak Composite (see Appendix 12.1).

cups to larger vases, some with ring or pedestal bases and others with tripod feet. Most interiors showed evidence of burning. Types represented were La Justa/Extranjeras (Chapter 12, Figure 12.8a, f, this volume), Zaklak (Map 9.3), and Gotas (Figure 9.4); it may be significant that these types were comparatively rare in deposits outside the structure. Reconstruction of the vessels revealed that in several cases sherds from the same censer were encountered on both sides of the wall. It seems likely, therefore, that these vessels were resting atop the interior wall when the perishable roof collapsed, smashing the pots and scattering their sherds to either side. Later, the upper portion of the wall itself collapsed on top of the sherds. Nearly half of a small Sacá Polychrome collared jar (Figure 9.5), three small Chilo Unslipped tripods, a quartz crystal, and part of a copper ax head also lay on the floor of the front room with the incensarios.

Besides pottery, enormous quantities of chipped obsidian and chert were recovered in the back room, suggesting production of stone tools. Structure 719 had more obsidian cores (eight) than any other structure at Zacpetén, indicating that viable obsidian trade networks still existed at the time of conquest (see Rice and Cecil, Chapter 14, this volume). It is possible that the embedded metates were used as anvil stones in making blades from the obsidian cores, as a concentration of blades was found adjacent to this feature. Forty-four manos or mano fragments were also found in the back room, and the entire building had eighty-five such objects of limestone, basalt, and granite—more than all the other excavated Zacpetén residences combined. Several tiny pieces of worn gravel near the interior wall appear to be gizzard stones, indicating the butchering of birds. In addition, net weights and miscellaneous bone and shell (including a few pieces of marine shell) were recovered in the back room.

Red paint was produced in the back room of Structure 719 as indicated by the presence of three deep-red stones, one more than thirty centimeters in size. A field test produced water-soluble pigment from these stones, and LA-ICP-MS analysis suggests that the red pigment is chemically similar to the Postclassic red slips (Cecil and Neff 2006). Two small limestone mortars with finely shaped hemispherical bowls were embedded in the western portion of the room, and four smooth crystalline cobble pestles—two of which had red stains in their fracture lines, suggesting pressure contact with pigment—were found in the area. Two pieces of gypsum lay near one of the four cobbles, and a few meters south of the gypsum lay a piece of fired gypsum. Gypsum, found naturally in some areas of the Lake Salpetén basin, becomes plaster of paris when heated and, crushed into a powder, could have been used as a base for pigment. The red pigment produced in the back room of Structure 719 might have been used in the bright red designs on the face of the front-room bench.

Two copper bells were found within two meters of one another: one inside the back room, and the other outside the structure in association with three shell beads. Other than this deposit, bells were only encountered in the civic-ceremonial groups at Zacpetén. It is possible, although decidedly speculative, that these items were part of a decorative element located on the wall behind the metate feature. Bells were affixed to the back door of residences in other

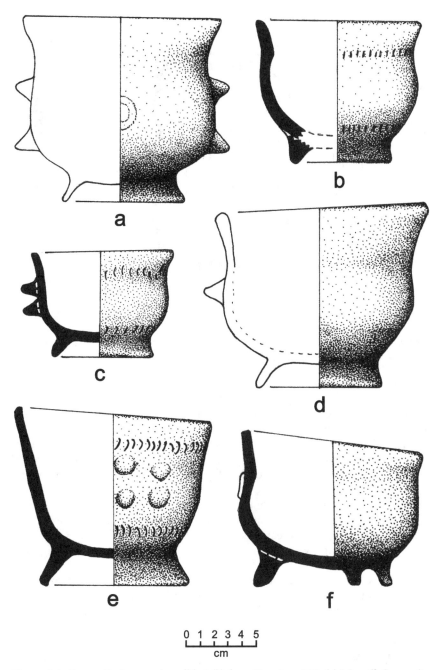

Figure 9.4. Composite incensarios, all but (b) from Structure 719: (a) Mumúl Composite; (b) Zaklak Composite, Structure 721; (c) Extranjeras Impressed/Composite; (d–e) Zaklak Composite; (f) Mumúl Composite.

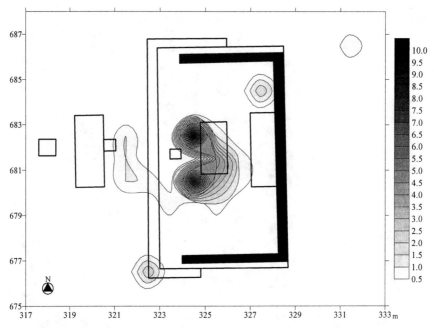

Map 9.3. Distribution of Zaklak Composite censer sherds, Structure 721, Zacpetén.

parts of Mesoamerica to indicate when someone passed through that entrance (Tozzer 1941: 86). Although the back room of Structure 719 appears to have been enclosed, it is possible that a doorway or window-like opening existed in the area of the bells.

The distribution of these large quantities of artifacts was relatively continuous over the floor of the rear room. However, an overlay of the artifact distribution maps, which plot each category of artifact by one-by-one-meter excavation units, indicates three small areas in the western two-thirds of the back room—little more than one to two square meters in area and spaced three to four meters apart—that were devoid of artifacts. It is unclear what these clean spaces might mean. Perhaps they were covered with mats people sat on while working with the lithics and other materials, demarcating individual activity areas.

Outside (north of) the back room of Structure 719, excavations revealed large concentrations of materials next to the exterior (north) wall that appeared to be secondary deposits of refuse. These deposits included pottery sherds, net weights, and lithics, but especially large amounts of bone and shell. Also outside the back room was a deposit that included a Sacá Polychrome plate, a Mengano Incised collared jar, and a Chompoxté Red-on-cream: Akalché variety plate. It appears that trash from inside the structure was tossed outside over the low rear wall. These concentrations only occurred behind the western two-thirds of the back wall and were not present in conspicuous quanti-

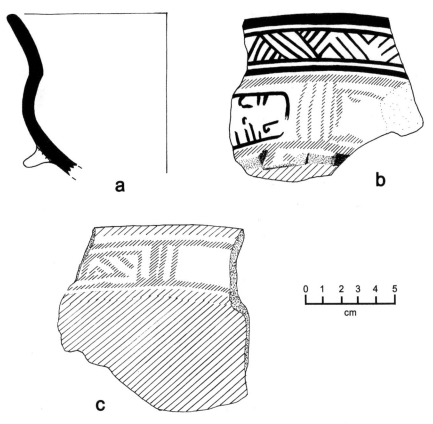

Figure 9.5. Fragments of small Sacá Polychrome collared jar with notched basal flange, found in the front room of Structure 719: (a) profile; (b) exterior decoration; (c) interior red-on-paste decoration on collar and red slip on body.

ties behind the eastern third, the portion of the structure that appears to be a later remodeling.

Structures 720 and 721

Group 719 includes a small temple, Structure 721, with a small shrine, Structure 720, in front of it. Both buildings were partially composed of cut soft limestone removed from Classic-period constructions. Although such structures were referred to as "oratorios" at Mayapán (Smith 1962), their use at Zacpetén more closely followed that of the temples of Group A and especially Group C. Structures 720 and 721 were exposed by an excavated area of 168 square meters.

West-facing Structure 721 lies twelve meters southeast of Structure 719 on a low platform possibly painted with red curving lines, with a low apron wrapped around the front of the structure. The back (east) of Structure 721 is a C-shaped wall, but an interior bench is lacking. Three altars lie on an east-west centerline: a large medial altar against the back wall, a smaller central altar bisecting the interior space, and an even smaller rectangular masonry outside feature that appears to be a miniature altar similar to that in front of the altar in Structure 719. This miniature "altar" may have been a pedestal or a base to display a standard. Structure 721 differs most conspicuously from other temples at Zacpetén by its lack of masonry columns and a substantial platform; the miniature altar is also anomalous. The plaster inside Structure 721 was gray-colored and charred in places, indicating burning, but patches of paint on the floor indicated that it had once been painted red or held offerings of red pigment that spilled.

Structure 720, in front (west) of Structure 721, is a small rectangular shrine oriented parallel to the north-south axis of Structure 721. Corresponding to the "statue shrines" described at Mayapán (Proskouriakoff 1962a: 90), it stands about twenty centimeters high and has two smaller ancillary structures east and west. Public temples have similar altar platforms, but with a different orientation. Although Structure 720 stands outside and in front of Structure 721, it is actually best considered an extension of the temple, as considerable activity occurred in the space between the two structures. Its size corresponds to that of the large medial altar inside Structure 721, and these two constructions may define the eastern and western boundaries of this particular ritual space.

Because Structure 720 seems to be an extension of Structure 721, the artifacts found in refuse deposits in the two buildings are discussed together here. The primary activities in the area involved the use of incensarios, both effigy and non-effigy. The vast majority of the censer sherds lay between the western edge of the central altar of Structure 721 (particularly its southwestern corner) and the eastern edge of Structure 720, and almost all ritual activities occurred between the latter and the western edge of the medial (rear) altar of Structure 721. A total of 822 censer sherds was recovered in the excavations, most of which had been burned; 34 percent were burned to the point that they could not be sorted by type. The burning of the sherds corresponds to the burning of the plaster surface and stones of the walls of Structure 721, all of which indicates that the building was destroyed by fire.

Analysis and reconstruction of the composite censer sherds suggested that there were originally eleven incense burners in, on, or near the structure: three Fíjate, four Zaklak, two La Justa, and two Gotas. At least five of these were found near the central altar: a pair of Zaklak Composite censers to the west and paired La Justa and Gotas Composite censers between the medial altar and interior altar; another La Justa/Extranjeras censer was part of the concentration at the southwest corner of the central interior altar. Outside the structure, on the first step, three sherds of a type we named Tirso Rojo-Modelado — although possibly an import from Mayapán (Mama Red type) — were found, along with a concentration of sherds of a Fíjate Composite censer near the southeast corner of Structure 720. The sherds of six additional censers, two of them heavily burned on the interior, were scattered between Structure 720 and 721.

Analysis and reconstruction of the effigy censer sherds suggested the presence of at least twelve vessels in Structure 721. Two (possibly three) of these were Kulut Modeled, the small and crudely made censers specific to Kowoj sites. Most of the Kulut Modeled sherds were from one vessel located in the concentration of non-effigy censers at the southwest corner of the interior shrine, suggesting that both vessel types were utilized or disposed of similarly. A second partial Kulut Modeled vessel lay on the front step with fragments of a possible third Kulut vessel and a Fíjate Composite censer. We did not recover effigies with the Kulut Modeled censers in this structure. Four Ídolos Modeled sherds were also found in Structure 721.

Nine incensarios were the larger Patojo Modeled type, widespread in the Petén lakes area, and two—presumably a pair—were the darker-fired Moza variety. The distribution of the 299 Patojo Modeled censer fragments is puzzling. Concentrations were found north of the medial (rear) altar, west of the interior (central) altar, and on the front of Structure 721 on the step adjacent to the southern half of the east side of Structure 720 (Map 9.4). Some of this distribution overlaps that of the composite censer sherds. Nevertheless, close examination of the distribution of the Patojo Modeled sherds does not allow one to simply conclude that they were used in the same activities, usually as pairs, as the composite incensarios were. Instead, each concentration represented not a single vessel but several; stated differently, sherds representing individual Patojo vessels did not remain in situ after breakage but were scattered around and in front of the building. Moreover, sherds of each vessel were dispersed between the interior altar of Structure 721 and Structure 720. The composite censer fragments were less jumbled than the effigy censer sherds.

In the southeast corner of Structure 721, several offering dishes were found. Two were ceramic, one a shallow saucer and the other a large modified sherd in the same form. Similar recycled sherd dishes were recovered in Late Classic contexts at Aguateca (Inomata et al. 2002: 316–317). Quantities of turtle carapace fragments lay near the pottery dishes, suggesting that the carapaces also likely served as offering containers.

A scatter of sherds representing Canoas Red cache pots and lids was found north of the interior altar of Structure 721 and in greater abundance outside the southeastern edge of the structure. These sherds appear to represent two vessels similar to those in the central cache of Structure 602. Excavations into the platform fill of Structure 721 did not reveal any caches, however, so these Canoas sherds may have resulted from the termination of an altar cache. Evidence for a similar rite was encountered in Cache 2 of Structure 602, but in that case the cache, and hence the building, were rededicated (Pugh and Rice, Chapter 7, this volume). In Structure 721 the rite was terminal, as evidenced by the subsequent burning of the building.

In contrast to Structure 719, slipped Postclassic pottery from Structures 720 and 721 was dispersed throughout and around the structures and was

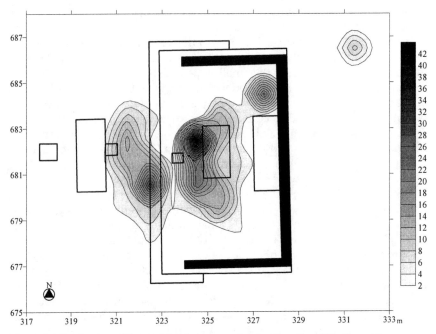

Map 9.4. Distribution of Patojo Modeled censer sherds, Structure 721, Zacpetén.

not clearly associated with distinct ceremonial refuse or other trash deposits. The relative quantities of decorated pottery also differed, with much less in Structures 720 and 721; the decorated pottery that was found there was of inferior design execution compared to Structure 719. However, the quantity of Clemencia Cream Paste-ware pottery — pottery indicating Xiw/Kowoj identity (Cecil 2001a, Chapter 10, this volume) — surpassed that of the other slipped Postclassic wares and groups.

Structures 721 and 720 yielded a variety of non-ceramic artifacts and other materials similar to those of Structure 719 but in much smaller quantities. Most were found behind Structure 721 or in association with collapsed wall fill and therefore did not represent de facto refuse. Numerous chipped obsidian and chert artifacts were found in Structure 721 — primarily cores and finished tools such as points, blades, and knives — with far less of the production debitage and flakes that characterized Structure 719. These structures also yielded net weights, manos and metates or fragments thereof, miscellaneous shell, and a greenstone ax.

Structure 721 had two major concentrations of animal bone in addition to the turtle carapace fragments noted earlier. One lay on the west edge of the building along the structure's medial axis. Although the majority of these remains have not yet been identified, they included a bird's cranium. Outside, along the northern edge of the building, were four animal teeth and one human tooth, which may have been offerings as well. A similar concentration was encountered adjacent to the temple in Group C.

Structure and Function: Interpreting Group 719

It has been argued that Structure 719 was an elite dwelling (Pugh 2002, 2004). Structure 719 is among the three largest tandem/domestic structures at Zacpetén and the largest of five residences excavated at the site. The building is structurally similar to the other dwellings, especially Structure 747: it is divided into a front room and a back room, the former plastered, painted, relatively clean, and containing ceremonial artifacts. The use of the front room as a public ritual area is understandable, as the front rooms of all residential structures at Zacpetén were likely social areas — being generally open and paved with stucco — and also sites of ritual performances (Pugh 2004: 363). The rituals conducted in the front room of Structure 719, however, were probably the most elaborate of those in the presumed residential structures excavated.

Group 719 appears to have been constructed to resemble the temple assemblages associated with Mayapán and to have been built and maintained in the Xiw/Kowoj region of eastern Petén from the early Late Postclassic through the Contact periods. The layout of Group 719 — the temple (Structure 721), statue shrine (Structure 720), and the front room of Structure 719 — is similar to Groups A and C at Zacpetén (Pugh and Rice, Chapter 7, this volume). This is not merely a case of superficial imitation, as activities occurring in Group 719 were comparable to the activities found in temple assemblages (Pugh 2002). Except for Group 628, another likely elite domestic context, the layout of Group 719 differs significantly from the rest of the domestic groups at Zacpetén in having an associated temple structure. In addition, Group 719 yielded copper objects, which were not found in any of the other domestic groups but were recovered in the civic-ceremonial complexes. Given the anomalous artifact assemblage and ancillary buildings, one must ask whether Group 719 — particularly Structure 719 — was a domestic compound, whether it had primarily ceremonial functions, or whether it was some combination of both.

Incense Burners

The use of incense burners in Group 719 was much more intense than in other domestic groups (Table 9.1). Two effigy censers, Kulut and Patojo, were present in Structure 719, plus a few sherds of two other modeled types, and twelve effigy incensarios were found in the Structure 721 temple; in addition, thirty-four to thirty-seven composite censers were found in the group. At least eleven of the composite incense burners, and perhaps as many as fifteen, were found in fragments near the interior wall on the east side of Structure 719. This abundance of incensarios contrasts with the other four excavated residential structures at Zacpetén, where sherd distributions suggested the presence of only one or two composite censers and no effigy censers were found in situ.

Table 9.1. Minimum numbers of censers in Group 719, by type (x = a few sherds present).

	Structure 719	Structure 721
Composite type		
Mumúl	5	—
Zaklak	5	4
La Justa/Extranjeras	7–8	2
Gotas	6–8	2
Fíjate	x*	3
Modeled type		
Patojo: Patojo var.	1*	7
Patojo: Moza var.	—	2
Kulut	1*	3
Ídolos	x*	x
Pitufo	x*	—

* Found in the front room of the structure.

The composite incense burners found on either side of the eastern medial wall of Structure 719 merit further discussion. From the breakage patterns, it appears that these vessels sat upon the wall and were smashed when the roof collapsed. They are highly variable in size, form, and paste/type, suggesting that they represent different producing groups. Their usage was subjectively and informally assessed by the relative degree of smoke blackening and charring on the interior, which resulted from burning incense; this was noted as heavy, moderate ("burned"), and light ("some burning"). Interior burning could not always be recorded because frequently only rims and upper-body fragments of incensarios were recovered.

Three vessels found together in the back room of Structure 719 were Zaklak Composite. The interior of one vessel was heavily burned, probably from repeated episodes of burning incense; another had a moderately burned interior; and the third had a lightly burned interior, suggesting it might have been used only once. Fragments of three (possibly four?) La Justa/Extranjeras Composite censers were found on both sides of the interior wall; one was heavily burned on the interior, another was moderately burned, and degree of burning was not noted for the third. Three Gotas censers were found on the south side (front room) of the interior wall; one was heavily burned on the interior, one was lightly burned, and burning could not be determined on the other. Two Zaklak censers were found in the front room; both had lightly burned interiors, suggesting little usage.

The three Zaklak Composite censers in the back room, the three La Justa incensarios, and two of the three Gotas censers are of particular interest because each set exhibits heavy, moderate, and light burning, indicating different degrees of usage. These patterns might be interpretable in light of Ralph Roys's interpretation of Bishop Diego de Landa's description of the rotation of "k'atun idols," which were likely incensarios—including non-effigy censers — in early Colonial Yucatán (in Tozzer 1941: 168n885). Each "idol" or censer was active for a total of thirty years, or one and a half *k'atuns*. A new one was brought in as a "guest" (B) of the reigning *k'atun* idol (A) for ten years (a *lajuntun*, or half a *k'atun*), absorbing the power of A, which was correspondingly losing power. B then acted as the sole ruling lord of the *k'atun* for the next decade/*lajuntun*, accepting sacrifices and issuing auguries. Then, during the last ten-year period B lost power as a new guest idol (C) was put into position to assume power and eventually rule.

If this model can be applied to the reconstructed composite censers in the eastern half of Structure 719, then the heavily burned Zaklak, La Justa/Extranjeras, and Gotas censers would have been close to serving out their full thirty-year terms and retiring from power. The moderately burned Zaklak and La Justa censers (and perhaps one of the lightly burned Gotas censers) had probably just finished their "rule" as *k'atun* lord and were about to begin their third-term decline from power as the lightly burned (or unburned) censers came in as "guests." Three Zaklak and two (perhaps three) La Justa censers in these deposits appeared lightly burned, suggesting that perhaps these were the new guests brought in to join the ruling idols, but the latter had not yet been fully activated by additional burning of incense to darken them further.

Along these same lines, in temple Structure 721 there appear to have been two Kulut Modeled censers. The Kulut censer in Structure 719, with a heavily burned interior, was found on the medial shrine of the front room facing west. The Northern Lacandon face their censers to the west only during rituals in which the vessels "die" and are replaced (Tozzer 1907: 110–112). Thus, the vessel in Structure 719 might have been dead or in the process of "dying" at the time of the building's abandonment, losing its power during its third period of the cycle as the guest *k'atun* lord came in. Parts of a second vessel, with only light burning, were concentrated on the front step of Structure 721, as were fragments of a third Kulut censer, the degree of burning of which could not be ascertained. It is tempting to suggest that the two on the exterior of the temple were the incoming and reigning *k'atun* idols. Two of the eight reconstructible Patojo Modeled incensarios exhibited heavy burning, two had light burning, and two others had none. Because the fragments of these censers were so extensively scattered and commingled inside and in front of the building, it was impossible to determine their original position in the structure. Nonetheless, the distribution of Patojo sherds in Structure 721 was nearly identical to that of the temple (Structure 764) in Group C, which likewise had terminated effigy censers (Pugh 2001: 531). With respect to composite censers in Structure 721, two Zaklak Composite vessels stood in situ northwest and southwest of the interior altar; the one to the southwest was heavily burned.

This interpretation combines elements of Landa's discussion of *k'atun* rituals and their three-term cycles with his observations on new year's ceremonies, particularly for yearbearers (in Tozzer 1941: 138–169). In the latter, the idols of the year were moved, with much ceremony and feasting, between heaps of stone lying at the four entrances to the town and the house of the chief, or *principal*. It is not unlikely that the rituals of the Kowoj in late-seventeenth-century Petén had evolved in a considerably different direction from those of mid-sixteenth-century Yucatán (a direction more like that of the Northern Lacandon). Moreover, it is interesting that censers and censer sherds occurred only in the remodeled eastern part of Structure 719 and on its central shrine and altar, with other fragments scattered in front of but outside the structure. Aside from these few fragments in the front, there were no censers in the western part of the structure or in the back room except for those that fell off the wall. This hints that the remodeling of the eastern part might have been done specifically to transform a former elite residence into a civic-ceremonial structure: a god house.

In addition, post-conquest censuses in Yucatán indicate that families lived together in larger extended household units than in pre-conquest times.[1] Given that Structure 719 is very late, it is possible that its remodeling (and enlargement?), its ambiguous residential/ceremonial character, and its unusual kinds and quantities of artifacts could reflect a similar response to the stresses of decades of war and final Spanish domination. The multiple kinds of incense burners might have resulted from the need to house the god pots of several families. Bringing them to a single location might have made it easier to protect them if Spanish visitors came to the site.

Non-Censer Artifacts

The sheer volume of artifacts and debris, both raw material and finished goods—especially lithics, bone, and shell (Tables 9.2, 9.3)—littering the dirt floor of the back room of Structure 719 suggests that it was oriented toward production activities involving obsidian and chert, pigments, animal remains, and so on. It is evident that certain artifact types were focused in specific areas. Nevertheless, it is very unlikely that the objects were lying where suddenly dropped by occupants at the time of the structure's abandonment. In early-twentieth-century Maya houses, ceramic vessels and other objects were kept on tables; items also hung in perishable containers from the rafters, and many houses had attics for storage (Wauchope 1938: 120–124). Thus, many of the distribution patterns indicate where the items were stored, not the precise spot where they were regularly used—as seen in the composite censers on the east side of Structure 719.

At Zacpetén, there was a strong linear correlation between the size of excavated residences and the number of obsidian cores (r=.92, p=.03) and exotic stones (r=.91; p=.03) recovered (Pugh 2004: table 2). These data suggest that higher-status individuals and households enjoyed greater access to nonlocal goods. Structure 719, one of the largest tandem/residence structures at the site, had substantial investment in masonry, with cut soft limestone blocks, a shrine, and an altar. It had eight obsidian cores—more than any other building at the site—and more metates and manos, greenstone, and serpentine than any other excavated residential group, plus copper bells and an ax head. Slipped and decorated sherds from Structure 719 represent the highest quality of artistic execution found at Zacpetén. This may suggest that the occupants of the structure were the upper echelon of the elite class, that the pottery was created for important rituals, or both.

The combination of usually discrete domestic and civic-ceremonial elements indicates that the occupants of Group 719 were living in a ceremonial area. They lived and "produced" under the public eye and in a largely performative context. Yet an equally persuasive argument can be made that Structure 719 was not residential but rather had civic-ceremonial functions. It has been noted that, except for the back room of Structure 719, Group 719 appears to have been a temple assemblage. The occupants of Group 719 possessed objects generally restricted to these ceremonial groups and exotic goods that were less common, or absent entirely, in other residences, such as marine shell and copper artifacts. Similarly, cut soft limestone blocks were used in Structure 719 and in ceremonial groups but not in the other residential structures, and they may have been a means of appropriating the past and conspicuously incorporating it into the present (Pugh 2002: 317–319). The occupants of the elite Group 719 thus had special access to powerful ritual objects. Given the size, amount of masonry, and nonlocal artifacts in and around the structure, we conclude that this structural complex was occupied by a (probably extended) family of elite status who had considerable access to labor and resources.

A *Popol Naj*

Structure 719 might have been a communal structure such as a council house, or *popol naj* (*popol* 'council,' *naj* 'house'), a public building used for administrative meetings of rulers and their subsidiary lords and for receptions or feasting. It was headed — or used — by an official(s) known as a *jolpop* (*jol* 'head,' *pop* 'mat'), the mat a long-standing symbol of a seat of authority. At Copán, Structure 10L-22A, a Classic-period *popol naj*, was decorated with mat symbols and glyphs apparently representing the names of the towns whose officials were part of the council (Fash et al. 1992). Dennis Tedlock (1985: 345), in referring to *jolpops* among the K'iche' of highland Guatemala, noted that the mat is both metonym and metaphor, referring to a council whose members sat on mats and also serving "to interweave those whom they represented." Because *jolpop* could also mean the "head" or beginning of the month of Pop, it might also refer to the *jolpop* seated on the first day of the Maya new year (Thompson 1999: 243). The Kowoj were identified as one of four *jolpops* of the south at Mayapán in the *Book of Chilam Balam of Chumayel* (Edmonson 1986: 106), and perhaps this office was hereditary within certain family lines.

The eleven marked "seats" on the bench in the front room of Structure 719 suggest a meeting place with formal seating, and perhaps the eleven individuals seated there were responsible for the eleven composite censers found in Structure 721. The quantities of bone, shell, and decorated pottery in and outside of the back room might represent the remains of feasts, perhaps those accompanying ceremonies associated with the new year or period endings. In support of this thesis, Postclassic slipped pottery in Structure 719 commonly

Table 9.2. Chipped stone artifacts in Group 719.

	Structure 719*		Structures 721/720[†]	
	Obsidian	Chert	Obsidian	Chert
Points	32	41	5	11
Lance/knife	1	5	–	1
Cores	8	13	1	2
Blades	263	49	50	5
Debitage/flakes	134	1,891	11	270
Scraper	–	1	–	–
Bifaces	–	16	–	2
Unifaces	–	2	–	1
Awls	–	–	–	1
Hammerstones	–	7	–	–

* Primarily from the back room of Structure 719 or immediately exterior to it.
† Primarily in or around Structure 720.

Table 9.3. Miscellaneous artifacts in Group 719.

	Structure 719*	Structure 720/721[†]
Manos/fragments[‡]	30	3
Metates/fragments	55	4
Greenstone	4	1
Net weights	147	25
Misc. bone	4,938	658
Misc. shell	7,153	315
Marine or worked shell	5	–
Gizzard stone?	6	–

* Primarily from the back room of Structure 719 or immediately exterior to it.
† Primarily in or around Structure 720.
‡ Includes various pounders and pestles.

displays red-painted mat (*pop*) motifs (roughly three times as many as in other structures), and these vessels may have been used during feasts to mark the new year month of Pop. The great number and variety of censers, both effigy and composite, in Structure 719's de facto refuse appear to represent different producing units because the vessels were produced from at least eight distinct pastes and vary appreciably in form and size.

A "House"

Group 719 mixes domestic and ceremonial architecture and activities in a way not seen in any of the other excavated groups. Although such inter-mingling of civic-ceremonialism and elite domestic architecture appears to be "spatial chaos" (Lefebvre 1991: 223), it is not uncommon for the everyday lives of elite individuals to be celebrated and institutionalized. The fact that the late Kowoj in Petén were identified by the name of their ruling family is indicative of such institutionalization, as is the housing of the elite in central palaces. In the case of Structure 719, the living quarters of the elite ultimately seem to have been combined with a *popol naj*. Furthermore, this council house was grouped with other buildings to form a temple assemblage.

Robert Carmack (1981: 192) described similar agglomerations of elite residences and council houses known as *nimja*, or "big house," of the Late Postclassic K'iche'. *Nimja* and the naming of social groups after the family names of ruling elite may be indicative of "house societies" (Braswell 2001: 327; Gillespie 2000: 477). In such societies, in addition to governing, the ruling house becomes the most fundamental symbol of the social system and a source of solidarity (sensu Lévi-Strauss 1982: 163–187; Carsten and Hugh-Jones 1995: 20; Gillespie 2000: 475–478). Because the Kowoj in seventeenth-century Petén were identified by their ruling family, they too might rightfully be designated a house society (Pugh 2003b: 413).

One possible problem with this interpretation is that the historical descriptions may be tainted because the Spaniards themselves existed in a house society. In addition, the name Kowoj was used by the Northern Lacandon in connection with a social formation that does not fit descriptions of house societies (see Tozzer 1907: 40; McGee 1990: 32–33). Other evidence suggests that many Contact-period Maya communities were named after the most common patronym (De Vos 1980: 229).

Elsewhere, we have suggested that temple assemblages were core symbols of Xiw/Kowoj identity (Pugh 2003b). The juxtaposition of the nobility with a core symbol by virtue of their living in it poses a strong independent case for a noble "house." If Structure 719 were the "house" centering a "house society," one wonders about the impact of its abandonment for the Kowoj at large and their sense of social self: it would have been highly symbolic in the context of conquest.

The End of Group 719: Abandonment or Termination?

Test pits excavated in Structure 719 revealed that it was built over an earlier Late Postclassic structure. Radiocarbon dates on carbonized remains from storage jars in the back room of Structure 719 indicate late occupation and use dates of this building, between A.D. 1639 and 1818, which we extend to the entire group. The duration of occupation and the date of remodeling of the eastern portion of the structure are unknown, although the patterns of burning on the censers suggest at least thirty years of use of the vessels prior to the inhabitants' departure. The presence of European artifacts—a pipe stem, musket ball, and pieces of iron—in the temple assemblages at Zacpetén and the cow mandible in Structure 719 further indicate late occupation, and it is possible that the site was visited by Spaniards at some point. It is not clear, however, when such contact might have taken place. We favor occupation dates in the early-middle part of the radiocarbon interval, say, in the 1680s through the first decade of the 1700s.

The end of occupation and use of the 719 Group is of considerable interest in light of the enormous quantities of ceremonial and nonceremonial refuse apparently in situ on the floors and interior altars of Structures 719 and 721. This debris suggests that the structures were rapidly abandoned (Cameron and Tomka 1993; Inomata and Webb 2003: 3; Stevenson 1982: 241–246), ritually terminated, or both. How might we distinguish among these alternatives?

With respect to rapid abandonment, we can consider the refuse deposits, particularly those in the back room of Structure 719. What do these deposits actually represent in terms of behavior? Do the concentrations of pottery and lithic artifacts represent primary refuse (discard at the site of use) as opposed to trash, for example, the quantities of bone and shell tossed into an already abandoned space (secondary refuse)? Do they represent "abandonment refuse" resulting from the relaxation of normal housekeeping standards (assuming one knows what was "normal") in the face of gradual site abandonment (Schiffer 1987: 25)? We believe the deposits constitute either primary refuse or de facto refuse (deposits of usable materials), in part because important possessions — including incense burners and possible heirlooms such as copper artifacts and the cow mandible — were left in situ on the medial wall, and censers remained in the cache in the interior altar. In addition, numerous usable artifacts in the back room of Structure 719, particularly chipped stone tools (points, blades), manos and metates, and decorated pottery, lay scattered about the floor and were not carefully cached as might be expected if the occupants were planning to return. Although they were found on the floor when excavated, most of these artifacts likely originally sat on tables or hung from the rafters at the time of abandonment. The fact that they were not scavenged by later occupants of Zacpetén (if there were any) further suggests very late occupation of Group 719. We believe, in fact, that this structural complex might have been the latest group occupied at Zacpetén, that its abandonment was sudden, and that it marks the complete abandonment of the site.

If the inhabitants departed in haste, why might they have done so? Two reasons come to mind. One relates to the fact that the various inhabitants of central Petén, especially in the lakes region, were in a state of civil war in the late seventeenth century. In particular, Itza and Kowoj conflict was escalating — note the seventy-three projectile points in Structure 719 (Table 9.2) — and it is possible that the Itza could have attacked the Kowoj at Zacpetén in this group in retaliation for the Kowoj burning of Nojpeten in 1695 (Jones 1998: 326). The smashing of incense burners and the burning of temple Structure 721 might reflect such an attack, with symbolic demolishment of the very symbols of Kowoj identity.

On the other hand, in the aftermath of the 1697 Spanish conquest of the Itza capital of Nojpeten (modern Flores Island) in Lake Petén Itzá, soldiers traveled around the countryside in 1702 and 1703 to round up the scattered native populace and try to bring them under control. It is not unlikely that they visited Zacpetén as part of these efforts and forced the Kowoj to leave Group 719. The smashing of "idols" in Structure 719 and the burning of Structure 721 could easily be understood as part of such an event: the occupants were forcibly moved to a new location, and transportation of most possessions was not feasible; therefore, many items were left. It is possible, then, that the destruction of Group 719 was brought about by Spaniards and the destination of its residents was a mission settlement—perhaps part of the Spanish reductions into newly established mission towns—where the use of deity imagery other than Jesus and the saints was forbidden. Alternatively, the Kowoj could have suddenly abandoned their home in advance of such unwelcome contact.

Another, and different, interpretation is possible: the inhabitants of Group 719 may not have abandoned the buildings in extreme haste, perhaps under attack, but rather their departure may have been deliberate and planned. In such a case, the destruction of structures and ceremonially important artifacts would indicate ritual termination. Desecration is a common means of ritual termination in Mesoamerica (Grove 1981; Freidel and Schele 1989: 237–240; Grove 1981; McGee 1998; Mock 1998b; Sugiyama 1998), and it is well-known that the Maya, from Late Preclassic times onward, celebrated the ending of various calendrical intervals through the ritual destruction—"termination"—of civic-ceremonial buildings. Indeed, this behavior may go back to the Middle Preclassic, with the destruction of carved monuments at Olmec sites in the Gulf coast region (Grove 1981; Rice 2007a: 99–100). In Postclassic and early Colonial Yucatán, it is said that the major civic-ceremonial buildings of cities that seated the 20-year *k'atuns* and the 256-year *may* were ritually destroyed and the site was "abandoned" (although this abandonment might simply have been the departure of the ruling lineage) when the period ended (Edmonson 1982: xvi, 1986: 4–5). The ending of a *may* cycle was to occur on July 25, 1697, within the radiocarbon date range of our sample from Structure 719 and only a few months after the Spanish attack on Nojpetén, and this might have been "celebrated" by the occupants of Group 719 by termination of the complex.

Such termination activity can be recognized in various ways in Group 719. The fresh painting of the bench of Structure 719 was likely carried out in preparation for a ritual, perhaps the cycling of the *may* and subsequent termination proceedings and perhaps indicating the presence of additional participants and an audience. The Lacandon painted their ceremonial buildings and objects red prior to rituals to set them apart from everyday activities (Davis 1978: 169–177). In Structure 719, censers fell or were swept off the medial wall and part of the wall itself was knocked down; the effigy censer on the shrine in the front room was turned to the west, indicating its death; and the recently painted portion of the bench was chiseled away. Structure 721 was burned and its censers were smashed and scattered, both activities representing termination of ritually powerful objects and spaces. In this interpretation, then, the burning of Structure 721 and the smashing of its censers plus those in Structure 719 would have been conducted by the occupants of Zacpetén rather than by enemies such as the Itza or Spaniards. The patterning of terminated censers in Structure 721 was nearly identical to that of Structure 764 in Group C, indicating that this was not haphazard destruction but an orderly event: ritualized termination (Pugh 2003c). Because effigy censers were personified and their mistreatment — in the form of abandonment — could bring about the anger of the supernaturals, they were terminated, as was their "house."

Alternatively, we might draw an analogy with Contact-period Utatlán, where the palaces of K'iche' lords were whitewashed and painted upon their deaths because K'iche' palaces materialized "the wealth and power" of the nobility (Carmack 1981: 194–195). In this light, the renovation of Structure 719 prior to the termination of the temple and abandonment of the group may signify the death of a Kowoj lord — perhaps the execution of Aj Kowoj or his son Kulut Kowoj after the 1697 conquest — or the deaths of Kowojs in the 1704 rebellion (see Jones, Chapter 3, this volume. One is reminded of the simple burial our excavations recovered to the west of Structure 719 and just below the surface. Could this be a recent death?). Although Grant Jones (ibid.) believes Aj Kowoj and his son, known to the Spaniards as Kulut Kowoj, resided at a place called Ketz on the north shore, we think it more likely that they lived at Zacpetén. It is not impossible that the elite Group 719 complex itself was occupied by Aj Kowoj or Kulut Kowoj because it is known that the latter lived east of the eastern end of Lake Petén Itzá in 1699 (Jones 1998: 443n14).

Regardless of the veracity of any of these scenarios, after the Spanish conquest of the Itza the Kowoj were, however briefly, the dominant native group in the lakes area. And regardless of the specific causes of the abandonment of Group 719 at Zacpetén, the fact that its residents were occupying a civic-ceremonial group reflects that this was the final vestige of independent indigenous nobility in Petén.

Note

1. A small post-conquest Kowoj settlement west of Yaxhá, Ix Tus, resembled a refugee camp, with twenty-five adults and children living in a single house (Jones 1998: 368).

PART IV

THE ARCHAEOLOGY OF THE KOWOJ
Pottery and Identity

Prudence M. Rice

The three chapters in Part IV attempt to answer the question "Who were the Kowoj?" through examination of various kinds of pottery they made and used in their daily lives and on ritual occasions. It has long been realized that pottery, because of the multitude of variables involved in its production — variables of its composition, form, surface finishing — provides valuable insights into its makers and users. Pottery is formed and *in*formed. In creating a vessel, potters constantly make decisions and choices about what clay to use; whether to "temper" it and, if so, with what; what shape to make; how big it should be; how to decorate it, and so on. Many of these decisions are unconscious, a result of tradition and custom. When ethnographers asked Fulani potters in Bé, Cameroon, why they made pottery a certain way (David and Hennig 1972: 27), they responded with a mix of irrefutable logic and ill-concealed incredulity: "because that is how pots are made at Bé." Indeed.

Similarly, Kowoj potters in the eastern Petén lakes made their pottery a certain way "because that is how pots are made in the eastern Petén lakes." Unlike in Bé, however, where the question was about a particular ethnographic moment, in the case of the Kowoj we are dealing with several centuries of pottery making. And although pottery making is a rather conservative technology (Rice 1984a, 1987b: 449–468), changes inevitably occur over a period of centuries. Our interest here is in determining the underlying decisions and choices Kowoj potters made and repeated over many generations, which inform us about Kowoj identity and identification.

The serving ware pottery we identify with the Kowoj is characterized by use of a cream-colored marly clay (Clemencia Cream Paste) from the Topoxté area that is slipped red and painted with a darker red pigment. This red-on-paste decoration was copied, late in the Postclassic sequence, on vessels made of gray-fired Snail-Inclusion Paste, using organic lacustrine clay from an unknown source or sources. We believe the small quantity of red-and-black-painted pottery in this paste (Sacá Polychrome) is also a Kowoj identifier.

Chapter 10 makes the key point that, with respect to pottery, the Kowoj in Petén cannot be identified solely by decorative style and traditional analytical approaches to that style. Instead, the Kowoj identified themselves by — and are best studied through — what may be called "technological styles," the choices potters made about the clay "recipes" used for making slipped and decorated Postclassic vessels. Using a battery of physicochemical analyses as well as "low-tech" observations to characterize these fabrics mineralogically and chemically, Leslie Cecil identified seven technological styles among the three major ceramic paste wares. Three of these are distinctly Kowoj, representing decorated pottery of Clemencia Cream Paste ware; the groups vary compositionally but also in terms of the forms and decoration of the pottery in each.

Such technological differentiation is bolstered by study of the decorative style and motifs, mostly painted, on this pottery. Postclassic pottery, both Kowoj and non-Kowoj, exhibits considerable continuity with Classic wares in design structure (the use of decorative bands), slipping technology, and motifs. Many of the motifs on the Postclassic vessels are those found in Classic-period skybands, but they are simplified and isolated. In the Late Postclassic, Kowoj potters began a new decorative program, still using their signature dark red paint, but instead of the restrained banded designs they painted exuberant curves and swirls and plumes and dots all over the interiors of their bowls. They also used a combination of red and black pigment to decorate their wares. There is an obvious but chronologically imprecise relationship between this decoration and a red-painted type at Mayapán, Tecoh Red-on-buff, which underscores connections explored previously between the Kowoj in Petén and the Xiw in western Yucatán.

In addition, Kowoj potters seem to have selectively incorporated into their pottery decoration elements of the Postclassic "international style" and symbol sets, best known from the "Mixteca-Puebla" style of south-central Mexico. These elements are evident in shared Early Postclassic design layouts and Late Postclassic motifs, suggesting complex and long-term interregional interactions. A major point of difference — both stylistic and functional — is that the Kowoj painted their decoration primarily on vessel interiors rather than exteriors. This prompts questions about precisely what, if any, affiliational "meanings" were understood or being conveyed by these motifs.

Many Kowoj motifs resemble graphemes (hieroglyphic signs), particularly day-names, and at least three of them appear to be "yearbearer" days Ak'b'al, Lamat, and Etz'nab'. No single one of these motifs occurs as more than a few examples at most, but one unusual feature of their occurrence is that Ak'b'al seems associated with the Group C temple assemblage. The color and directional associations of the Ak'b'al yearbearer are red and east, respectively, and at the end of the seventeenth century the years ended in the Gregorian month of June. This means, for example, that just before and after the conquest, the years that Ak'b'al "bore" were:

Maya Date		Gregorian Date	
Tzolk'in	Ja'ab'	Beginning	Ending
8 Ak'b'al	1 Pop	June 19, 1693	June 18, 1694
12 Ak'b'al	1 Pop	June 18, 1697	June 17, 1698
3 Ak'b'al	1 Pop	June 18, 1701	June 17, 1702

As discussed in Chapter 7, Group C appears to be a relatively late construction (in comparison to Group A). If principles of moiety-like complementary oppositions guided the socio-structural arrangements at Zacpetén, then perhaps the social segment "in charge of" Group C was responsible for year-bearer rituals at the start of Ak'b'al years.

While it is possible to read too much into the comparatively sparse distribution of these calendrical signs, it may bear noting that Ak'b'al, Lamat, and Etz'nab' are yearbearers in the so-called Campeche calendar, known from Late and Terminal Classic dates in the Puuc region (Edmonson 1988: 148). This would add support to our interpretation that the Kowoj were allied with Xiw lineages (the Xiw's homeland was in the Puuc region of western Yucatán).

Related information about Kowoj identity comes from analysis of the fragments of pottery incense burners and other ritual ceramics, as discussed in Chapter 12. The Xiw/Kowoj in Petén, like Late Postclassic peoples throughout the lowlands, burned incense in two general categories of pottery vessels—one distinguished by attached anthropomorphic or zoomorphic "effigy" elements and the other characterized by the presence of "composite" decoration of appliquéd spikes, disks, and fillets. Both kinds exhibited similar patterns of use in the two temple assemblages, with effigy censers in pairs inside structures and composite censers on and around the substructural platforms. As at Santa Rita Corozal (Chase 1985a), the archaeological findings at Zacpetén substantiate Bishop Diego de Landa's (in Tozzer 1941) sixteenth-century account of the use of "idols" during new year's and k'atun ending ceremonies. The Xiw/Kowoj of Zacpetén used effigy incensarios made of five paste wares, suggesting multiple loci of production. They also represented numerous deities including Chaak/Tlaloc, a diving god, and, most distinctively, a small Itzamna-like deity formed of the same clay used to make the broader repertoire of ritual pottery, including composite censers and cache vessels. Despite Colonial efforts to extirpate these "idols" in the north, they continued to be made and used in remote areas of Petén until the moment of conquest and perhaps until the Kowoj of Zacpetén were physically removed from their peninsular home.

Chapter 10

TECHNOLOGICAL STYLES OF
SLIPPED POTTERY AND KOWOJ IDENTITY
— Leslie G. Cecil —

According to ethnohistorical documents and confirmed by archaeological excavations, ethno-political groups in seventeenth-century Petén, primarily the Itza and Kowoj, contested socio-political boundaries and were at war (Jones 1998, Chapter 3, this volume). Under such unstable conditions, a sense of group identity is often important: Maya potters as well as other members of Maya society might have continuously, but perhaps unconsciously, constructed and reconstructed their identity by creating and recreating their social structures through daily activities such as pottery manufacture (Giddens 1984: 17).

Potters make choices about resources (such as clay and pigment colors) and decoration when manufacturing vessels, and these choices are made within a social structure that embodies their social identity. The existence of differences in resources and decoration allows the archaeologist to study material such as clay and mineral inclusions, and categories of pottery such as vessel form and decoration, as patterned social behavior. Patterns of manufacture are not merely "'added on' in order to signal group identity," but they

221

represent choices made by the potter "by which a sense of group identity is formed and transformed as being coeval with and identical to the process by which a sense of technique is formed and transformed" (Dietler and Herbich 1998: 247).

As a day-to-day activity, pottery making becomes a social activity when the choices made during the production process are examined as social phenomena. Patterns of manufacture may be reproduced without the potter being fully cognizant of an established set of "rules" or operations; they may simply be *costumbre*. For example, a clay source may be used continually without question because a particular social group does not have access to clays in another territory, because it is customary to use that source, or for other reasons. As a result, clusters of technological and stylistic traits (technological styles) reflect the culture that produced the pottery.

To test the possibility that technological decisions reflect identity, I undertook a study of technological styles of Postclassic slipped pottery from the sites of Nixtun-Ch'ich', Tayasal, and Flores Island/Nojpeten (all Itza sites) and Ixlú, Zacpetén, Macanché Island, Topoxté Island, and Tipu. Results support the proposition that the Xiw/Kowoj produced and reproduced pottery technological styles as part of their social identities during the Postclassic and Contact periods.

Technological Style

Despite different approaches to style in material culture (Adams 1973; Arnold 1983; Brainerd 1942; Braun 1985; Deetz 1965; Hill 1970; Hodder 1977, 1978, 1982; Longacre 1970; Sackett 1982, 1986; Whallon 1968; Wiessner 1983, 1985; Wobst 1977, among many others), none are sufficient in and of themselves to differentiate Xiw/Kowoj identity from that of other Petén groups because none of these approaches conjoins technology and surface decoration to define a style. The one "theory" of style that accounts for both technological and stylistic[1] characteristics is that of technological style (Lechtman 1977, 1979, 1981, 1984a, 1984b, 1988, 1993, 1994; Lemonnier 1986, 1989, 1992, 1993; Stark 1998; Wright 1985).

Technological and decorative variability results from the relationships between decorative elements and the observable patterning people produce through various repeated behaviors. When creating material objects, the producer may have many choices (operational sequences)[2] that reflect social and cultural constructs underlying and directing her or his actions, and subtle differences in choices (e.g., of matter, energy, motor patterns) can influence the social representation of material culture (Lechtman 1977: 6; Lemonnier 1992: 23, 1993: 9). Therefore, both the material and the process of manufacture contribute to an object's style as much as surface decoration does because technological acts are embedded in a symbolic system that reflects social reality and indigenous knowledge. It is the combination of choices "defined by these relationships that is stylistic in nature" (Lechtman 1977: 6). Thus, the integration of behavioral events at each level of manufacture defines technological style, which is "recognizable by virtue of its repetition which allows us to see the underlying similarities in the formal arrangements of the patterns of [manufacturing] events" (ibid.: 7).

An object's technological style reflects technological acts that are also embedded in a symbolic system embodying social reality and indigenous knowledge, all of which are "translated by, among other things, implicit or explicit classification of the materials treated, of the processes brought into play, of the means and tools employed, and of the results obtained, without speaking of the presentation of the actor's roles" (Lemonnier 1986: 160). Thus, style is a technological aspect of social production and mental schemes that need not carry directly observable meaning and can be learned and transmitted from generation to generation (Lechtman 1977: 6, 1993; Lemonnier 1993: 3).

By studying the options available from the technological and stylistic realms, archaeologists can better understand "emic behavior based upon primarily etic phenomena of nature" (Lechtman 1977: 7). This type of analysis is possible because the social representations behind the technological style presented on material culture are the perspectives of the producer toward the raw materials used, "the attitudes of cultural communities towards the nature of the technological events themselves," and the attitudes of the community toward the end product (ibid.: 10, 1988: 369). However, to fully understand the technological and stylistic realms, one must conduct a synchronic and diachronic analysis of the design elements and the transformation and social representations that permeate beyond the material world (Lemonnier 1992: 3).

Different technological styles may be developed and may operate synchronically, but they will not be perpetuated unless the technological style is compatible "with the natural environment and with the state of technological systems at the time of creation" (Lemonnier 1993: 12). Because choices are arbitrary from a technological point of view, technological styles are a result of accommodation rather than alteration. As such, the new style has to fit into an already existing structure of social meaning and practices, and the object needs to be interpretable by those within the social group as well as those from "competing" social groups to be perpetuated in a culture (Lemonnier 1992: 18, 1993: 14). As a result of a new technology having to fit into an already existing system, some choices will impinge on the transformation of technological systems. A technology may also not appear in society because it is not "in fashion" or does not look like something that already exists (Lemonnier 1989: 166). If this happens, some innovations will not be reproduced and will never be seen by the cultural group at large because selective pressures at the individual and community levels always exist that decide what will represent social structures, such as power, ancestry, and identity (Lemonnier 1993: 15). On the other hand, it is possible to have many different stylistic schema representing the same social group because there is "no necessary or unique correspondence between the expression of a 'socially' defined 'technical' aim . . . and the physical objects and actions that a given culture uses to perform its function" (ibid.: 16). Therefore, the resulting technological style of an object is the "source of precise information about the history of its own manufacture" (Lechtman 1994: 5).

The technological style approach is appropriate for analyzing the slipped and decorated pottery of the Postclassic Petén lakes region because similarities in formal arrangements of technological and stylistic patterns contribute to the assessment of the socio-ethnic identities and histories of different social groups in Postclassic- and Contact-period Petén. In particular, known differences in fabrics or pastes relate to resource variability, and different decorative motifs reflect various themes specific to the Kowoj (Rice and Cecil, Chapter 11, this volume). By identifying distinct technological styles associated with different ceramic groups or archaeological sites, it is possible to refine our understanding of the settlement and socio-political relations of the Kowoj in Petén.

Methods of Analysis

To identify patterns defining technological styles of the Kowoj, several types of analysis of the five Petén Postclassic slipped pottery groups (Paxcamán, Fulano, Trapeche, Augustine, and Topoxté—described later) were conducted to obtain technological and stylistic information: type-variety analysis, "low-tech" observations, petrography, X-ray diffraction, scanning electron microscopy, energy dispersive X-ray spectroscopy, and acid-digestion laser ablation inductively coupled plasma spectroscopy (for detailed descriptions of analytical procedures, see Cecil 2001a; Cecil and Neff 2006). After each step, preliminary technological style groups were defined and redefined, and by combining data from all levels of analysis it was possible to define Kowoj slipped pottery technological styles.

The first level of study consisted of a typological analysis using the type-variety system (Smith, Willey, and Gifford 1960). This hierarchical system uses a series of categories — ware, group, type, and variety, in descending inclusiveness—to organize levels of variability in archaeological pottery. Postclassic slipped sherds from Nixtun-Ch'ich', Tayasal, Flores Island (Nojpeten), Ixlú, Zacpetén, Macanché Island, Topoxté Island, and Tipu were classified as to ware, ceramic group, type, and, where possible, variety. For purposes of studying technological styles, it is particularly useful to consider pottery at the ware and group levels because these levels of classification convey information about geographic location, time period, decoration, and function (Rice 1982: 50). Three paste-based (as opposed to slip-based) wares had been identified in previous studies of these materials: Snail-Inclusion, Vitzil Orange-Red, and Clemencia Cream (Chase 1983; Rice 1979). These distinctive wares were used in producing the five slipped Postclassic ceramic groups included in the analysis of technological styles: Paxcamán, Fulano, and Trapeche in Snail-Inclusion Paste ware, Augustine in Vitzil Orange-Red Paste ware, and Topoxté in Clemencia Cream Paste ware.

After typological analysis, two provisional macro-typological technological style groups were defined. The first macro-group reflected distinctions in paste-ware categories: the sherds were grouped according to differences that indicated selection of clays by the potters. The second macro-group reflected differences in decorative modes: four painting modes (unpainted [monochrome slipped], red-on-paste, black-on-paste, and red-and-black) and two incising modes (fine-line and groove). These decorative modes occur in virtually all the ware categories and reflect stylistic choices made by Postclassic Maya potters.

The second level of examination, "low-tech" observational analysis, included slip and clay paste color measurements, degree of dark coring, hardness measurements, surface treatment and decoration sequence identification, vessel form measurements, and refiring experiments. A stratified random sample of 551 sherds was selected to represent the diversity present in the total sample to be used in the subsequent analyses. After conducting the typological analysis, I determined the variability present (in pottery pastes, decoration, and excavated structures represented) and chose a smaller proportional allocation with the goal of selecting 50 decorated sherds from each ceramic group and archaeological site. In cases where 50 decorated sherds were not available, I selected monochrome slipped sherds by stratified random sampling. First, I placed all decorated sherds from one site on a table grouped according to the structure from which they were recovered. Second, I ascertained the number of pottery types and varieties represented at each structure. The number of sherds per type and variety and per structure determined the number to be randomly selected, and the number selected varied depending on the structure, so that buildings with more decorated types were sampled more heavily. Third, each lot number was recorded on a piece of paper and placed in a container according to the structure, type, and variety. The predetermined number of sherds to be selected for each structure established how many lot numbers were drawn for inclusion in the sample. This selection process continued until all categories were sampled.

As a result of differences in paste and surface characteristics, three general and preliminary technological styles were defined that correlate with differences in the three ceramic wares of this study. These groups reflect differences in diversity indexes of slipped surfaces, slipped surface characteristics such as double slipping and "waxy" surface finishes, and firing technologies. Technological style groups based on observations at this level of analysis suggest that Kowoj potters made choices based on matter (clay and slip), energy (surface finish and decoration), and specific knowledge (know-how, such as firing technology and surface finishes).

Mineralogical analysis—the third level of analysis of this pottery—identified the clay minerals, non-plastic inclusions, minerals, and rock fragments in the clay pastes as well as slips on the vessel surface. To gather these data, petrographic analyses were conducted on 273 sherds along with X-ray diffraction (XRD) analysis of 18 sherds and 4 raw clay samples collected at Zacpetén and Yaxhá. Petrography permits the identification of minerals by their unique optical properties and provides qualitative (shape and sorting) and quantitative (size and frequency) data for comparison at the ware level. Because petrographic analysis does not reveal the full mineralogical composition of a clay or pottery sample, it was combined with XRD analysis to identify clay minerals (montmorillonite and halloysite) by their crystalline structure in unfired clay samples. XRD also provided data on the presence of other minerals, such as gypsum and feldspar.

The results of these three levels of analysis provided full descriptive characterizations of the five ceramic groups and three paste wares of the Postclassic pottery of central Petén, as well as major components of data for characterizing technological styles. Before discussing the technological styles themselves, I present the ceramic group descriptions.

The *Paxcamán ceramic group* (Snail-Inclusion Paste ware) is characterized by variable paste colors throughout the Petén lakes region, including dark gray to light gray (10YR 5/2, 2.5YR 6/1), tan (10YR 6/3), and reddish-brown (5YR 5/6). Pastes of this ceramic group can have calcite (euhedral, polycrystalline, cryptocrystalline, or some combination), quartz, freshwater snail shell, hematite, biotite, chert, and chalcedony inclusions. In addition to a distinctive paste, the Paxcamán ceramic group is defined by a red to red-orange (10R 4/6 to 2.5YR 4/8) monochrome slip. Many slips have a low luster, but the majority have a matte finish. Decoration occurs as black (Ixpop Polychrome), red (Macanché Red-on-paste), or red-and-black (Sacá Polychrome) painting and post-fire fine-line and pre-fire groove incising (Picú Incised: Picú variety and Picú Incised: Thub variety, respectively).

Pottery representing the *Fulano ceramic group* (Snail-Inclusion Paste ware) has a similar paste; however, the majority of sherds have grayish-brown (10YR 5/2) and gray (5YR 6/1) colors. Unlike the Paxcamán ceramic group pastes, those of the Fulano ceramic group do not demonstrate wide color and texture variability. Fulano pastes include calcite (euhedral and polycrystalline), freshwater shell, hematite, quartz, and biotite. Slips are black (7.5YR 3/1 to 2.5Y 2.5/1) and can have a low luster. Occasionally, the black slip exhibits red mottling, suggesting that the color resulted from firing an iron-based slip in a reducing atmosphere (also indicated through experimental refiring procedures). Decoration appears as red (Sotano Red-on-paste) painting and post-fire fine-line and pre-fire grooved incising (Mengano Incised: Mengano variety and Mengano Incised: Bobo variety, respectively).

The *Trapeche ceramic group* (Snail-Inclusion Paste ware) resembles general trends of the Paxcamán and Fulano ceramic groups. Pastes are dark gray (2.5Y 4/1, GLEY 14/N), gray (10YR 6/1), brown (10YR 6/2), and light brown (10YR 8/3). The clay matrix contains calcite (euhedral, polycrystalline, and cryptocrystalline), freshwater shell, quartz, hematite, biotite, and chert in various quantities. Slip colors range from red (2.5YR 5/6) to yellowish red (5YR 5/6) to light brown (7.5YR 6/4) to light brownish-gray (10YR 6/2). The majority of sherds are double slipped: the primary slip near the sherd surface is red or brown, and it is covered by a thin, translucent, tan-to-cream secondary slip with a "waxy" feel. Decoration appears as black (Mul Polychrome) or red (Picté Red-on-paste) painting and as post-fire fine-line incising (Xuluc Incised).

Augustine ceramic group (Vitzil Orange-Red Paste ware) pottery has distinctive red (2.5YR 5/6–2.5YR 5/8), pale red (10YR 7/4), and yellowish-red

(5YR 5/6–8) carbonate pastes with inclusions of calcite (euhedral and poly-crystalline), quartz, hematite, biotite, chert, volcanic ash, or combinations thereof.[3] Red (2.5YR 4/6, 2.5YR 5/8, 10R 4/6) to pale red (10R 6/4) slips occur with matte, low-luster, and occasionally glossy (common at Tipu) finishes. Black or tan fireclouding is common on the exterior of vessels and the interior of tripod plates. Decoration occurs as black (Pek Polychrome) or red-and-black (Graciela Polychrome) painting and as post-fire fine-line and pre-fire groove incising (Hobonmo Incised: Ramsey variety and Hobonmo Incised: Hobonmo variety, respectively).

The fifth ceramic group, the *Topoxté ceramic group* (Clemencia Cream Paste ware), is characterized by white (2.5YR 8/1), pale brown (10YR 8/2-3, 10YR 7/3-4), and light gray (10YR 7/1, 2.5Y 7/1) fine, marly pastes. Calcite (euhedral, polycrystalline, and cryptocrystalline), quartz, hematite, biotite, chert, and chalcedony occur in varying frequencies in the paste. Pottery from this group is slipped red (10R 5-4/6, 2.5YR 5-4/8) to yellowish red (5YR 5/6). Most slips have a matte finish, but some exhibit a low luster that may be the result of double slipping (red and creamy white) or deposition. Black (Pastel Polychrome), red (Chompoxté Red-on-cream), and red-and-black (Canté Polychrome) painting as well as post-fire fine-line and pre-fire groove incising (Dulces Incised: Dulces variety and Dulces Incised: Bebeto variety, respectively) typify the types of decoration common in the Topoxté ceramic group.

Concerning technological styles, four groups were developed at the mineralogical level of analysis, and they reflect different paste characteristics, mineral suites, or both of the clay pastes: (1) pastes dominated by volcanic ash; (2) pastes dominated by cryptocrystalline calcite; (3) pastes with quartz, chert, chalcedony, hematite, and calcite inclusions; and (4) pastes with quartz, chert, chalcedony, hematite, calcite, and biotite inclusions. These provisional technological style groups suggested that potters made choices based on matter (such as tempers or clays with different mineral suites) that may have been influenced by the socio-political milieu of contested boundaries during the Postclassic period.

The final level of study—chemical analysis—involved scanning electron microscopy (SEM), energy-dispersive X-ray spectroscopy (EDS), and laser-ablated inductively coupled plasma mass spectroscopy (LA-ICP-MA: strong-acid digestion for ceramic pastes and laser ablation for slips and paints). These analyses were carried out on 100 fragments that represented the diversity in the larger sample. A proportional stratified random sample of sherds (as described earlier for the initial selection) from each ceramic group was selected from the petrographic results. Selection procedures ensured that all types and varieties and paste variations within each type were included.

Chemical analyses provide information on the elemental composition of the clay paste that, when combined with the other levels of analysis, creates a powerful tool for interpretation. SEM and EDS analyses were employed because XRD analysis is not able to detect clay minerals fired above 450°C as a consequence of changed crystalline structures. EDS analysis produced clay groups based on various intensity peaks of the most common elements in the clay pastes. SEM analysis provided comparable images that further grounded the EDS clay groups. LA-ICP-MA analysis was conducted to determine the elemental and composition groupings of the clay pastes that resulted from different clay resource choices during manufacturing. The analysis resulted in seven chemical compositional groups that represent different pottery wares and mineral suites. In addition to paste chemical compositions, red and black pigments used for painted decoration were analyzed by LA-ICP-MA. The elemental differences of the pastes and the decorative paint pigments demonstrate choices in clay and mineral resources and possibly knowledge of the clays and minerals used by Kowoj potters.

When data from the four levels of analysis were examined together, seven technological style groups were identified that reflect differences in decisions made at the technological and decorative levels. The seven technological style groups demonstrate within-group homogeneity and between-group heterogeneity when typological, low-tech, mineralogical, and chemical characteristics were examined together. (For decorative styles, see Rice and Cecil, Chapter 11, this volume).

Technological Style Groups

Technological Style Group 1

Group 1 includes sherds of the Topoxté ceramic group from Ixlú, Macanché Island, and Tipu. Petrographically, this group is dominated by volcanic ash (60–80 percent) in a light greenish-gray (1 GLEY 7/1) to very pale brown (10YR 8-7/1-4) montmorillonite clay paste. A few quartz, dolomite, and gypsum inclusions are present, but they do not occur in any significant quantity (less than 1 percent). LA-ICP-MA analysis suggests that the group is distinctive because of its moderate concentrations of iron (Fe) and titanium (Ti) and low concentrations of calcium (Ca) and zinc (Zn). The body sherds of this group are thin (approximately two mm) and exteriorly slipped, with no decoration. These sherds may represent incensario fragments.

Technological Style Group 2

Augustine ceramic group sherds from Nixtun-Ch'ich', Tayasal, Ixlú, Zacpetén, and Macanché Island comprise Group 2. Petrographically, volcanic ash dominates the montmorillonite clay paste. Small amounts (less than 1 percent) of quartz, calcite, and hematite are also present in the dark red to yellowish-red paste (2.5YR 5/8–5YR 5/6). LA-ICP-MA analysis distinguishes this group from Technological Style Group 3, also an Augustine ceramic group, because of its low concentrations of calcium (Ca). The majority of sherds in this group lack decoration (Augustine Red), although three sherds have either black-line painted decoration (Pek Polychrome) or incising (Hobonmo Incised). Plates, collared jars, restricted orifice bowls, and drums are the pottery forms represented in this group.

Technological Style Group 3

Group 3 also represents Augustine ceramic group sherds from Nixtun-Ch'ich', Tayasal, Flores Island (Nojpeten), Ixlú, Zacpetén, Macanché Island, and Tipu. Euhedral and polycrystalline calcite and quartz inclusions dominate the red (10R 4/6) to reddish-yellow (5YR 5/6) montmorillonite clay paste. Lesser amounts of hematite and gypsum also occur in the sherds from this group. LA-ICP-MA analysis separates Group 3 from Group 2 by its high concentration of calcium (Ca).

Jar, tripod plate, flanged tripod plate, collared jar, and drum sherds are decorated by incising (Hobonmo Incised), black (Pek Polychrome), or red-and-black decoration (Graciela Polychrome). Pek Polychrome decorative motifs include hooks, plumes, curvilinear lines, and mats. Graciela Polychrome sherds most likely had decorated panels, but because of the fragmentary and eroded nature of the sherds, motifs are not detectable. Hobonmo Incised: Ramsey variety decorations occur as *ilhuitl* (reverse scroll signifying "festival, sky") glyphs, mat motifs, and plumes. Hobonmo Incised: Hobonmo variety drum sherds from Tipu have a series of grouped vertical incised lines (four per group) and red slip applied below the incising.

Technological Style Group 4

Technological Style Group 4 is composed of pottery that represents the Paxcamán, Trapeche, and Fulano ceramic groups from Nixtun-Ch'ich', Tayasal, Flores Island (Nojpeten), Ixlú, Zacpetén, Macanché Island, Topoxté Island, and Tipu. Sherds from this group are characterized by a calcite-rich light and pale brown (7.5YR 6/4, 10YR 5-7/3) to gray (2.5Y 5/1) montmorillonite clay paste. In addition to euhedral, polycrystalline, and cryptocrystalline calcite, the pastes also include biotite, chalcedony, chert, quartz, hematite, and freshwater snail shell. LA-ICP-MA analysis distinguishes this group from Group 5 (also composed of Paxcamán, Fulano, and Trapeche group sherds) because of lower concentrations of beryllium (Be), cadmium (Cd), and manganese (Mn) in Group 4.

Group 4 consists of tripod plates, collared jars, flanged plates and jars, grater bowls, and drums—in other words, the majority of the Postclassic forms. Two-thirds of the sherds in the group are decorated with incising (Picú Incised), black (Ixpop Polychrome), red (Macanché Red-on-paste), or red-and-black (Sacá Polychrome) decorative motifs. Typical black decorative motifs include hooks, plumes, stepped pyramids, circles with connecting lines, possible reptilian motifs, and variations of the Lamat (Venus) glyph. Black-and-red decorative elements include hooks, plumes, and embedded triangles, as well as other eroded geometric shapes. Red decoration typically appears as circles, hooks, curvilinear mat motifs, birds painted in negative relief (the background is red), stepped pyramids, and *ilhuitl* glyphs. Incised decorative elements include the *ilhuitl* glyph, embedded triangles, hooks, plumes, circular elements, mat motifs, birds, and a possible reptile eye (RE) glyph (Rice 1983: figure 2b). The remaining sherds are slipped, without decoration.

Technological Style Group 5

Technological Style Group 5 has Paxcamán, Fulano, and Trapeche ceramic group sherds from Nixtun-Ch'ich', Tayasal, Flores Island (Nojpeten), Ixlú, Zacpetén, Macanché Island, and Tipu. Petrographically, Groups 4 and 5 differ because Group 5's montmorillonite clay pastes are dominated by cryptocrystalline calcite.

A variety of forms—including plates, flanged tripod plates, collared jars, grater bowls, tecomates, and jar forms—are present in this group. The majority of sherds in the group (68 percent) are slipped but undecorated (Paxcamán Red, Fulano Black, and Trapeche Pink). Thirty-two percent of the sherds are decorated with black (Ixpop Polychrome), red (Macanché Red-on-paste), red-and-black (Sacá Polychrome), or incised (Picú Incised and Mengano Incised) decoration. The majority of the decorated sherds (79 percent) have black-painted decoration with hook, stepped pyramid, and other eroded decorative motifs. The three Sacá Polychrome sherds are fragmentary and eroded, with only circumferential bands demarcating a decorative area. Macanché Red-on-paste decorative motifs consist of hooks, and Picú Incised: Picú variety and Mengano Incised decorations occur as circumferential bands of repeated mat motifs.

Technological Style Group 6

This style group represents Topoxté ceramic group sherds from Tayasal, Zacpetén, Macanché Island, Topoxté Island, and Tipu. Petrographically, cryptocrystalline calcite dominates the group's very pale brown (10YR 8/2) to white (10YR 8/1) montmorillonite clay pastes. In addition to cryptocrystalline calcite, small quantities (less than 3 percent) of euhedral and polycrystalline calcite, quartz, hematite, and biotite occur in the pastes. LA-ICP-MA analysis distinguishes this group from Groups 1 and 7 (also the Topoxté ceramic group) because of its slightly higher concentrations of iron (Fe) and titanium (Ti). Vessel forms represented in this group include bowls, tripod plates, drums, and narrow-neck jars. The sherds are either slipped with no decoration or decorated with red paint that is darker than the slip color (Chompoxté Red-on-cream). Curvilinear lines, parentheses, and ajaw glyphs comprise the decorative motifs of the group.

Technological Style Group 7

Like Style Group 6, this grouping includes Topoxté ceramic group sherds from Zacpetén, Macanché Island, Topoxté Island, and Tipu. The white, pink, and very pale brown (7.5YR 8-7/3, 10YR 8-7/1-3) montmorillonite clay pastes of this group contain euhedral and polycrystalline calcite, hematite, quartz, biotite, chalcedony, gypsum, and chert inclusions. LA-ICP-MA analysis separates this group from Groups 1 and 6 because of lower relative concentrations of aluminum (Al), iron (Fe), and titanium (Ti).

Tripod plate, bowl, restricted orifice bowl, narrow-neck jar, collared jar, and drum vessel forms occur in this group. Eighty-five percent of the sherds in this group are decorated with red- (Chompoxté Red-on-cream), black- (Pastel Polychrome), or red-and-black– (Canté Polychrome) painted decoration. This group also contains Dulces Incised type. Black decoration typically occurs as hooks and parentheses motifs. Although most red-and-black–painted decorations are eroded, one sherd has a black curvilinear decoration surrounded by red dots. Unlike black- and red-and-black–painted decorations, red-painted motifs appear in positive and negative painting and include stepped pyramids, stepped pyramids encircled by small red dots, circles, birds, plumes, mats, and possible aquatic creatures.

Discussion

As discussed by Timothy Pugh and Prudence Rice (Chapter 7, this volume), by the Middle Postclassic or early Late Postclassic period, the Xiw/Kowoj may have displaced the Itza, Yalain, and/or Mopan social groups at Topoxté Island and Zacpetén. Bernard Hermes and Raúl Noriega (1997: 757–758) have stated that the Topoxté Islands were occupied at this time by a group that built civic-ceremonial architecture similar to that at Mayapán. Around this same time, Clemencia Cream Paste-ware pottery, especially Chompoxté Red-on-cream and Canté Polychrome, appeared at sites in the eastern portion of the Petén lakes region and Tipu. During the Late Postclassic period, one or more migrations of Xiw/Kowoj may have arrived at the Topoxté Islands and other areas within what later became Kowoj territory. This population continued to create pottery with local clays reflective of its ethno-political identity, and that pottery appears to have been traded among the Kowoj, with only small quantities of sherds occurring outside its territory. Given this reconstruction, by comparing the technological style group data with architectural, burial, and additional pottery stylistic characteristics, it appears that the Kowoj did indeed construct and reconstruct their social identity through mundane activities such as pottery manufacture.

The "hallmark" signature of the Kowoj in Petén was red-on-paste decoration that first appears in the Topoxté ceramic group (Clemencia Cream Paste ware) with the florescence of Chompoxté Red-on-cream pottery. Topoxté group pottery is made from marly clays with very little iron content and is believed to have been produced at and traded from the Xiw/Kowoj site of Topoxté from the Early Postclassic through Contact periods. On the basis of data from the 1973–1974 Central Petén Historical Ecology Project excavations at Topoxté, it was concluded that "the Topoxté Islands do not share in the other Petén Postclassic ceramic traditions. No Trapeche group sherds, for example, were found at Topoxté, and no Chilo Unslipped; only one sherd was tentatively classified as Augustine, and only three sherds were identified as being of probable Yucatecan manufacture. The inhabitants of the Topoxté Islands, in short, seem to have sent some of their pottery throughout a relatively broad territory in Petén [and elsewhere], but to have brought in very little in return" (P. Rice 1986: 278).

Petrographic and X-ray diffraction examination of clays from the Yaxhá area and sherds of the cream-colored marly clay paste revealed that Clemencia Cream Paste-ware pottery was made from local clays near Yaxhá (Cecil 1999). Pottery made from this clay or clays is found primarily at sites in the eastern portion of the central Petén lakes region: Zacpetén, Macanché Island, Topoxté Island, and Tipu in western Belize. According to Grant Jones (1998: maps 5 and 6), ethnohistoric data suggest that the Kowoj occupied the eastern portion of the Petén lakes region in the Contact period. Clearly, then, the cream-colored marly clay source existed in Kowoj territory, pottery made from that clay was traded mainly within that territory, and Technological Style Groups 1, 6, and 7 reflect Kowoj social and ethno-political identity.

Xiw/Kowoj traditions/customs began at the Topoxté Islands around the Terminal Classic–Early Postclassic transition and continued at Zacpetén throughout the Postclassic period. The Kowoj recreated and/or imported pottery with the red decoration of Chompoxté Red-on-cream type made with different clays that fired to gray, rather than cream, to reinforce their socio-ethnic identity. Macanché Red-on-paste pottery (Snail-Inclusion Paste ware), found in the eastern lakes almost exclusively at Zacpetén, is a very Late Postclassic– and Contact-period type and as such may reflect the practice of expressing Kowoj ethno-political identity with red-on-paste decoration as they moved westward and used different clays (see Jones, Chapter 3, this volume). In addition to its presence at Zacpetén, a small quantity of Macanché Red-on-paste sherds (40) was identified at Macanché Island, Flores Island (Nojpeten), and Tayasal. George Cowgill (1963) also noted a large quantity of what he called Tachis pottery (similar to Macanché Red-on-paste pottery but with "purplish" painted decoration instead of red) at Flores Island (Nojpeten), which suggests trade with or inspiration from the Kowoj. Nevertheless, red-on-[gray] paste pottery (present in Technological Style Groups 4 and 5) is rare outside Zacpetén and is indicative of Kowoj affiliation.

In addition to red-on-paste decoration, red-and-black–painted decoration indicates Kowoj social identity for the same reasons stated earlier. Sacá Polychrome pottery of Technological Style Group 4 (Paxcamán, Fulano, and Trapeche ceramic groups; Snail-Inclusion Paste ware) and Graciela Polychrome of Technological Style Group 3 (Augustine ceramic group) may have been attempts to recreate Canté Polychrome pottery (Topoxté ceramic group). Canté Polychrome was most prevalent at Topoxté Island but also occurred at Zacpetén and Tipu (2 sherds). However, Sacá Polychrome pottery was found almost exclusively at Zacpetén (127 fragments; 18 fragments were found at Macanché Island, 2 at Tayasal, and 14 at Flores Island). Again, this type of pottery may exist at the three sites because of trade or socio-political alliances or both in the early 1600s.

Chemical analysis of the red and black pigments used to decorate slipped Postclassic pottery further suggests that the Kowoj selected varied resources for different purposes. For example, the red pigments used to decorate Chompoxté Red-on-paste and Macanché Red-on-paste pottery differ chemically from the red pigments used in conjunction with black decoration (Sacá Polychrome and Canté Polychrome) (Cecil and Neff 2006: 1490). In addition, the black pigments used to decorate Kowoj-specific pottery (Sacá Polychrome, Pastel Polychrome, and Canté Polychrome) are also compositionally different from those of Itza-specific black decorations (Ixpop Polychrome). It also appears that different black pigments were used depending on the motifs being painted (hooks versus other motifs) in black-painted and black-and-red–painted types (Figure 10.1).

In northern Yucatán, Late Postclassic red-and-black–painted decoration is found almost exclusively (although in very small frequencies) at Mayapán — the Kowoj's ancestral home—as compared to Chich'en Itza, Uxmal, and Kabah (Smith 1971). Therefore, red-and-black decorated pottery appears to indicate Kowoj or Kowoj-related Xiw social identity both in northern Yucatán and in Petén, where it reinforced socio-ethnic ties with their homeland during a time of social and political unrest. Similarities in decorative motifs also exist between Kowoj and Mayapán (Smith 1971) slipped pottery. These motifs include the ajaw glyph (e.g., Masson and Peraza Lope 2005: figure 5), embedded triangles, terraces/stepped pyramids, and the *ilhuitl* glyph (see Rice and Cecil, Chapter 11, this volume, for more extensive discussion of iconographic motifs.) Motif similarities demonstrate choices made by the potters and a possible desire to refer to their ancestral ties and thus their socio-ethnic identity.

Technological Style Groups 1, 6, and 7, red-and-black decoration from Technological Style Groups 3 and 4, and red-on-paste decoration from Technological Style Groups 4 and 5 are all read as indicating Kowoj identity in Petén. To judge from pottery type counts in published ceramic reports (Bullard 1970; Cowgill 1963), these technological styles are most common at Zacpetén, Macanché Island, and Topoxté Island; they occur less frequently at Ixlú and Tipu and are rare at Tayasal (preliminary data from Nixtun-Ch'ich' in Itza territory suggest that they are rare there, too). In addition to their site location, some correlations with intra-site proveniences can also be noted. These Kowoj technological styles are concentrated most heavily in temples, open halls in temple assemblages, oratorios, shrines, and elite residences. This suggests that the pottery that is most important in displaying social identity is related to ritual functions.

In contrast to Kowoj technological styles in the eastern Petén lakes region, Technological Style Groups 2 and 3 and the black-line decoration of Technological Style Groups 4 and 5 may represent Itza identity in the west, in part because of the presence of reptilian (*kan* or *caan*) motifs that may reflect the ruling Kan Ek' lineage of the Petén Itza. These characteristics are abundant in the technological style groups at Nixtun-Ch'ich', Tayasal, and Tipu but are nearly absent at Zacpetén, Macanché Island, and Topoxté Island (Technological

Style Groups 2 and 3 only). Sherds that represent these technological style groups occur in all types of excavated buildings except oratorios.

Unfortunately, at this time the majority of sherds that represent Technological Style Groups 4 and 5 cannot be assigned to a social group. Excavations of Itza, Yalain, and Mopan archaeological sites in the future may aid in the differentiation of technological style groups and the social groups that produced that pottery.

Conclusions

Analysis of technological and stylistic attributes of five Petén Postclassic slipped pottery groups resulted in the definition of seven technological style groups that reflect the socio-ethno-political identity of the people who produced the pottery. In addition to these identity representations, analysis of Petén Postclassic slipped pottery demonstrates that technological and stylistic attributes have a social context as products of producers who are active agents within a social structure (Dietler and Herbich 1998; Lemonnier 1992). The operational sequences (choices) that resulted in the different Postclassic Petén technological styles reflected the social context of the culture because the pottery was created from interrelated choices of matter, energy, and specific knowledge learned in social settings that "guide the perception of an acceptable range of variation and choice" (Dietler and Herbich 1998: 250; Lemonnier 1992). Because potters are part of a larger social group and social structure, they "understand" the group ideologies that are structured and systematic of their social/ethnic group. Thus, through practice, potters display, form, and transform the social context of technological and stylistic choices.

Technological and stylistic choices are also embedded in a social context because they are social reproductions of Petén Postclassic society. The seven technological styles described in this chapter reflect the social and political changes that differentiate Postclassic Maya socio-political groups. These technological styles in the Petén lakes region are associated with at least two distinct socio-political groups distinguished by different origin and migration myths and histories. The Petén Itza and Kowoj appear to have selected specific symbols, colors, and pottery pastes that allowed differentiation of seven technological styles of pottery. As described in other chapters in this volume, the differences between these two groups and between Postclassic and earlier cultural periods are also reflected in other elements of material culture, such as ritual pottery and civic-ceremonial architecture. Because the mental construction of being a member of Petén Postclassic Maya society—and, more specifically, a member of the Itza or Kowoj socio-political group—appears in multiple lines of material culture, the technological styles of Postclassic slipped pottery serve as symbols of socio-ethnic identity.

The presence of distinctive technological styles in the Petén lakes region also demonstrates that technology affects style because technologies are the result of human behavior and "styles are the symbols through which communication occurs. The relationships among the formal elements of the tech-

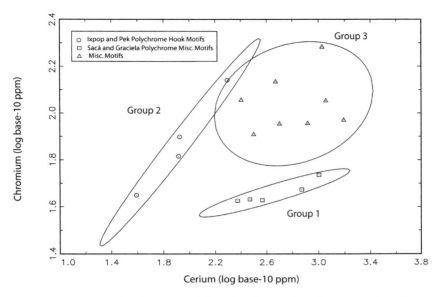

Figure 10.1 Bivariate plot of cerium and chromium base-10 logged concentrations show-ing separation of black-painted decoration on certain types and motifs of Late Postclassic slipped and decorated pottery. Ellipses represent 90 percent confidence level for member-ship in the three groups.

nology establish its style, which in turn becomes the basis of a message on a larger scale" (Lechtman 1977: 13). Technologies also affect styles because the resulting product is a reflection of the attitude of the producer toward the product and the attitude of the community toward both the technology and the product (ibid.: 10). Although a multitude of technological alterna-tives for the production of an object exist, cultures tend to select a technology compatible with and perhaps restricted by its social and physical environ-ment (Sackett 1982: 72–73). As such, the chosen technology is a behavioral performance that results in a style and a cultural message (Lechtman 1977: 12). Technological behaviors not only mediate "between society and the natu-ral world" but also act "as an important vehicle for creating and maintaining a symbolically meaningful environment" (ibid.: 17).

Finally, the technological style approach demonstrates that compat-ible choices reinforced the existing technology and social ideology of Petén Postclassic society. Because potters are agents acting in a specific social milieu, their products may reflect social, political, and economic structures particular to the potter's culture that may also occur in other forms of material culture (Shanks and Tilley 1987: 148). These reflections of Petén Postclassic technology and social ideology are most notable in the differences in clay sources, deco-ration colors, design motifs, and forms previously discussed. Technological and stylistic choices illuminate the Kowoj social structure and social practice because social structure and potter agency are mediated through the practice of pottery production, making it a social activity through which compatible choices are reinforced (Dietler and Herbich 1998: 238).

In sum, examination of the technological styles of Petén Postclassic pottery demonstrates that (1) technological and stylistic choices have a social context, (2) technology and style are social reproductions of Postclassic society, (3) some technological and stylistic choices were more compatible than others within Postclassic Maya society, (4) technology affects style, and (5) these compatible choices reinforced the existing technology and social ideology. Technological style groups interrelate choices made by potters and demonstrate that the Kowoj made decisions about technology and style in the manufacturing of pottery that reflected their distinct social identity. Similarities of formal arrangements of technological and stylistic patterns contribute to the assessment of the social/ethnic identities and histories of different ethnopolitical groups in Postclassic- and Contact-period Petén.

Acknowledgments

This chapter is the result of archaeological research conducted by Proyecto Maya Colonial under the direction of Don S. Rice, Prudence M. Rice, Grant D. Jones, and Rómulo Sánchez Polo from 1994 to 1999. Additional funding was provided by the National Science Foundation (Dissertation Improvement Grant SBR-9816325), Sigma Xi Grants-in-Aid of Research, and Southern Illinois University Carbondale (SIUC) in the form of a University Fellowship and a Dissertation Research Award. Dr. Steve Schmitt and Dee Gates of the Micro-Imaging and Analysis Center conducted SEM and EDS analyses at SIUC. Strong acid-extraction LA-ICP-MA analysis was conducted under the guidance of Dr. Bradley Paul of the Department of Mining Engineering at SIUC. Petrographic and X-ray diffraction analysis was conducted under the guidance of Dr. Richard Fifarek of the Department of Geology at SIUC. Comparative studies of excavated pottery samples from additional archaeological sites in the Petén lakes region were possible thanks to the assistance of Dr. Gloria Greis at the Peabody Museum at Harvard University (Topoxté Island — William R. Bullard's excavations), Ann Cordell at the Florida Museum of Natural History at the University of Florida (Macanché Island), Arlen Chase at the University of Central Florida (Tayasal), and Bernard Hermes at Yaxhá, Guatemala (Topoxté Island).

Many individuals have contributed to the present work through their research and inspiration. I would like to thank Prudence Rice and Don Rice for their support and invaluable guidance. Grant Jones's work provided ethnohistorical background for the Postclassic social groups. Tim Pugh excavated Zacpetén and provided field notes and comments. Rómulo Sánchez Polo excavated Ixlú and helped with field data and endless hours of assistance in Guatemala. I express my sincere thanks to Tim Pugh, Prudence Rice, and Marilyn Masson for their valuable suggestions on this manuscript.

Notes

1. "Technology" is seen here as the operational sequence of choices of manufacture that includes decisions concerning matter (clay), energy or labor (the forces that move and transform matter), objects (artifacts), human gestures (the movement of raw materials involved in manufacture), and specific knowledge (the know-how that produces the end product that is a result of all possibilities and choices for technological action or social representations) (Lemonnier 1992: 5–6). "Style" refers to the "visual representations, specific to particular contexts of time and place, that at the least transmit information about the identity of the society that produced the style and about the situation or location where it appears" (Rice 1987b: 244). The visual representation can be painted, incised, appliquéd, or modeled.

2. Choices made by potters and how those choices contribute to a vessel's "style" have been noted by many authors (esp. Sackett 1986; Wiessner 1985). The role of choices in technological style studies differs from that in isochrestic and emblemic styles because technological style (as defined by Lechtman 1977) employs the sequence of operations as an *active* aspect of style rather than merely a place where style resides, a method by which primary material is brought from its natural state to a fabricated state, or functions. Technological style also attempts to understand the artisan's attitude through the choices made during the manufacturing process. Therefore, to understand how people define themselves through their material culture, it is best to envision people using style actively.

3. When Augustine and Topoxté ceramic group sherds of Technological Style Groups 1 and 2 were examined with a petrographic microscope, the sherd paste appeared to be dominated by irregularly shaped and angular voids. They were point counted and recorded as voids because they remained in extinction under crossed nicols. However, when the same sherds were evaluated with LA-ICP-MS analyses, Pb and Th appeared in frequencies consistent with volcanic ash. Therefore, the voids may represent volcanic ash or more likely a combination of voids and volcanic ash.

THE ICONOGRAPHY AND DECORATIVE PROGRAMS OF KOWOJ POTTERY

—— Prudence M. Rice and Leslie G. Cecil ———————————————————

Symbols have the capacity not only to express and communicate, but also to guide and effect action (Braithwaite 1982: 80).

Material culture is rarely neutral in its meaning. People who share a common identity and culture will have and display similar symbols of that identity, and these symbols are apparent in their material culture repertoire (Darish 1989; Pollard 1994). Promulgating a common identity through material culture may also establish social boundaries that are maintained by the manipulation and display of symbols having political, economic, or religious importance (McGuire 1982). It is no wonder, then, that the conflict-ridden socio-political groups in the Petén lakes region during the Late Postclassic and Contact periods asserted distinct identities in the decorative programs on their slipped pottery—programs that included Kowoj-specific motifs, colors, and layouts.

Any discussion of Kowoj identity as displayed on pottery demands its consideration in the broader context of Petén Postclassic pottery decorative styles, and that context, in turn, must be set against the still wider field of Postclassic pottery in Mesoamerica. Late Postclassic Mesoamerican art — including pottery, sculpture, codices, and murals — is often described in terms of an "international style" (Robertson 1970) stretching from central and southern Mexico into the Maya area. A central component of this style is labeled "Mixteca-Puebla" (Nicholson 1960) for the region in south-central Mexico where it seems most abundant, and it is manifest, particularly in pottery, as far south as Costa Rica (Day 1994; Stone 1982). The Mixteca-Puebla style is best known through its exuberant polychrome pottery painted in vivid shades of glossy red, orange, yellow, black, and brown, beginning about A.D. 1300.

Recent discussions of Postclassic art styles (Boone and Smith 2003: 189–193; Masson 2003; Pohl 2003) have indicated that the "Mixteca-Puebla style" is a slightly later (post-1300) subset of a more general "Postclassic international style" dating after ~1200, which can be divided into two "international symbol sets." The "Early Postclassic international symbol set" includes step-fret designs and serpent heads, often with plumes, appearing in horizontal bands around bowl exteriors and associated with Fine Orange and Plumbate pottery (Boone and Smith 2003: 189; Ringle, Gallareta Negrón, and Bey 1998). The "Late Postclassic international symbol set" includes a large vocabulary of specifically Mexican referents (Boone and Smith 2003: 189–192).

Although the Mixteca-Puebla/Postclassic international style can be seen in the murals of Santa Rita Corozal in northern Belize (Masson 2003; Quirarte 1982), there has been little discussion about its presence in the Petén lakes region. Potters in the lakes region shared some Early Postclassic stylistic conventions and symbol sets that preceded the Mixteca-Puebla/international style in various areas of central Mexico, including the Early Aztec (Basin of Mexico) and Cholula styles in Puebla (McCafferty 1994, 1996, 2001). The broad spread of these Postclassic styles throughout Mesoamerica and in Petén presents challenges for identifying the Kowoj ceramically as well as their deployment of the Postclassic international style, but we believe we are able to do so.

Petén Postclassic Pottery Typological Units and Styles

The decorative programs of Petén Postclassic slipped and decorated pottery in the lakes region exhibit striking similarities (P. Rice 1983, 1986, 1989), resulting in an extraordinarily coherent "classificatory structure" within the type-variety typological system used by many Mayanists (Table 11.1; see Smith, Willey, and Gifford 1960). The pottery occurs primarily in three distinctive local *paste wares* (P. Rice 1976): coarse red-orange carbonate (Vitzil Orange-Red Paste ware), silty gray-to-brown with snail inclusions (Snail-Inclusion Paste ware), and marly "white" or cream (Clemencia Cream Paste ware). We interpret these as (minimally) three nodes of production, although variability within Snail-Inclusion Paste ware makes it probable that multiple production centers used these lacustrine clays (Cecil 2004).

These paste wares were used to manufacture the three most common Postclassic red-slipped ceramic *groups*: Augustine (Vitzil Orange-Red Paste

Table 11.1. Classificatory structure of Postclassic Petén slipped and decorated
ceramic wares, groups, types, and varieties

PASTE WARE	Snail-Inclusion	Snail-Inclusion	Snail-Inclusion
CERAMIC GROUP	Paxcamán	Fulano	Trapeche
TYPES:VARIETIES			
Monochr. Slip	Paxcamán Red	Fulano Black	Trapeche Pink
	Paxcamán var.	Fulano var.	Trapeche var.
w/ Black lip cache vessel	Escalinata var.		Tramite var.
Black-painted dec.	Ixpop Polychr.	Yamero Polychr.	Mul Polychr.
Red-painted dec.	Macanché Red-on-paste	Sotano Red-on-paste	Picté Red-on-paste
banded dec.		Sotano var.	Picté var.
curvilin. dec.	Macanché var.		
geom. dec.	Ivo variety		
Red-and-black pt.	Sacá Polychr.		
	Sacá var.		
	Doble var.		
Paint & Incising	Doña Esperanza		
Incised dec.	Picú Incised	Mengano Inc.	Xuluk Incised
Fine-line	Picú var.	Mengano var.	Xuluk var.
Groove-inc.	Thub var.	Bobo var.	Tzalam var.
			Ain var.
Modeled			
Non-censer	Chamán		
Censer	Pitufo		

ware), Paxcamán (Snail-Inclusion Paste ware), and Topoxté (Clemencia Cream
Paste ware). These groups were originally thought to be temporally sequential (Bullard 1973) but are now known to overlap considerably (see Pugh and
Rice, Chapter 5, this volume). Each red- (or, rarely, other color, such as black-)
slipped ceramic group includes these decorative *types*: monochrome, black-
painted, red-painted, red-and-black painted, incised, modeled, and so on.
Each of these types may, in turn, include one or more *varieties* (e.g., fine- or
groove-incised).

There is also a striking uniformity of design layout. In the early part of the
Postclassic period, regardless of paste ware/production unit, painted decoration was applied on an unslipped circumferential band on the interior wall
of dishes or the exterior body of jars, bordered above and below with two or
more lines (see Chapter 7, Figure 7.9, this volume). This decorative band was
often divided by vertical lines to create two or four panels, each featuring a

ail-Inclusion	Vitzil Orange-Red	Clemencia Cream	Uapake Carbonate
acchiato	Augustine	Topoxté	Chipotle
acchiato Brown acchiato var.	Augustine Red Augustine var. Cafetoso var.	Topoxté Red Topoxté var.	Chipotle Red Chipotle var.
			Canoas Red
icharrín	Pek Polychr.	Pastel Polychr.	
		Chompoxté Red-on-paste Akalché var. Chompoxté var. Kayukos var.	Saqueo Red-on-paste Saqueo var.
	Graciela Poly.	Canté Polychr.	Sangria Poly.
	Hobonmo Inc. Ramsey var. Hobonmo var.	Dulces Incised Dulces var. Bebeto var.	

motif that often appeared to be a greatly simplified glyphic sign, such as an X, a curl, a wavy line, or a similar sign.

The coherence of this Early Postclassic scheme is neither perfect nor exhaustive: for example, Snail-Inclusion Paste (hereafter SIP) ware includes not only the red-slipped Paxcamán ceramic group but also a "pink"-slipped Trapeche group and a black-slipped Fulano group. The point is that Early Postclassic potters across the Petén lakes area had a uniform and widely shared set of ideas about what constituted proper pottery decorative schemes no matter what their clay and temper resources. They adhered to a set of rules — a decorative canon — for design structure, layout, colors, and (although to a lesser extent) motifs. Vessel forms and proportions varied slightly from ware to ware and settlement to settlement, but the principles that structured how and what kinds of decoration were to be applied were observed for generations throughout the entire region.

Variations in this structurally ordered scheme occurred in the Late Post-classic period. While the basic classificatory structure continued to exist in the lakes region, at least at the ware and group levels, innovations occurred at the type and variety levels. In particular, instead of red- *or* black-painted decoration, there began to be red-*and*-black–painted decoration. Moreover, Clemencia Cream Paste (hereafter CCP) ware pottery (Topoxté ceramic group; Chompoxté Red-on-cream type) boasted elaborate decoration covering the entire interior of tripod dishes (Figure 11.1) rather than being restrained to a band around the walls. We think it was likely also at this later point that ophidian/saurian symbolism entered the repertoire of decorative motifs. Still more decorative freedom is evident by the very Late Postclassic and Contact periods, as greater variability and combinations of possible choices came into use: both painting *and* incising or interior *and* exterior decoration (e.g., Chapter 9, Figure 9.5, this volume), a flange of stepped frets (Chapter 7, Figure 7.3, this volume), squared spirals with dark purplish-red paint and slip. We propose that this increase in decorative variety and freedom, plus some new forms, coincides with the increase in hostilities among the Petén populations and with the assertion of distinct ethno-political or social identities, Kowoj versus Itza, in such a regional climate.

The Kowoj Decorative Program

Clemencia Cream Paste Ware

Decorated pottery made and used by the Xiw/Kowoj in Petén is techno-logically distinctive, as elucidated by Leslie Cecil (2001a, 2001b, 2004, Chapter 10, this volume), on the basis of two characteristics: its cream-colored paste and almost exclusive use of red-painted decoration. The fabric, CCP ware (Rice 1979), is a marly cream-colored clay very low in organic matter. Two clay deposits sampled during the Historical Ecology Project are very similar, chemically and mineralogically, to this pottery (Cecil 1997). One was from the archaeological site of Yaxhá (on Brecha 4 at Mound S12, 100–110 centi-meters below surface) and the other from a cut near the intersection of the roads to Yaxhá and Melchor de Mencos (kilometer marker 64–65). The red slip applied over this "white" clay typically has a clear, bright, orange-red color (10R 4–5/8). We believe this pottery was produced at or near the Topoxté Islands in Lake Yaxhá, where it was virtually the only "kind" (e.g., type, ware) of Postclassic pottery recovered archaeologically (Bullard 1970; Rice 1979; Hermes 2000b), and it circulated among other sites primarily within Kowoj territory (i.e., in the eastern lakes region and Tipu).

The decoration on Topoxté group pottery, primarily executed in red paint, has been classified as Chompoxté Red-on-cream type. Bernard Hermes (2000b: 195), who analyzed large quantities of this pottery from excavations and recon-struction at the Topoxté Islands, encountered more decorative variability than we found in our test-pitting and elevated the term Chompoxté to designate a ceramic group. His Chompoxté group incorporates Pastel Polychrome, Canté Polychrome (with a "fine-line" painted variety), and a new "simple designs"

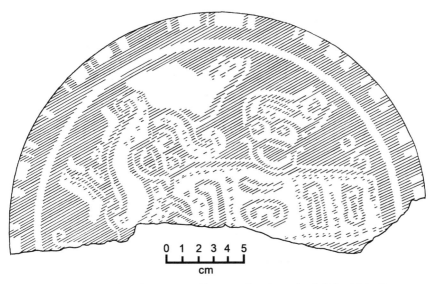

Figure 11.1. Chompoxté Red-on-cream: Chompoxté variety tripod dish with bulbous supports, showing "allover" interior decoration featuring an open-jawed reptilian creature. Note feathers, plumes, U-shapes, circles, lines of dots, and similar features. Recovered from Cache 38 on Canté Island in Lake Yaxhá. Redrawn from Hermes 2000b: figure 151.3.

variety in the Chompoxté Red-on-cream type proper. We do not oppose his more fine-grained schema, but we feel comfortable retaining Chompoxté as a type name within the Topoxté ceramic group.

The Chompoxté red-painted decoration is usually, but not always, markedly darker (at 10R 3/6) than the red of the slip. Much of the pottery exhibits the circumferential banding characteristic of the other Petén decorated wares, groups, and types. These bands, often divided vertically into four panels, typically occur on the interior walls of tripod plates/dishes and collared bowls; on necked jars and incurving-rim bowls, they occur on the exterior. The motifs in the panels occur in other Postclassic wares and types, as discussed presently. Simple, banded decoration in the Chompoxté type is designated Akalché variety.

Non-banded, red-painted pottery has two identified varieties. One features curvilinear decoration over the entire interior surface of tripod dishes (its occurrence on jars cannot be determined easily because of the fragmentary nature of the remains), and its motifs are very difficult to identify and label. Pottery with this allover curvilinear decoration is classified as Chompoxté Red-on-cream type: Chompoxté variety (Figures 11.1, 11.2a). A "geometric" variant featuring angular decorations, triangles, chevrons, and stepped pyramids on both interiors and exteriors of the vessels has been designated as Kayukos variety.

Although the vast majority of decorated CCP ware pottery in the Topoxté ceramic group was painted with red pigment (estimated ~80 percent of the sherds), black was also used and followed the general Petén Postclassic canon in classificatory structure, layout, and motifs. Rare (~ 8 percent) black-painted decoration is typed as Pastel Polychrome and red-and-black painting (~10 percent) as Canté Polychrome. Besides painted decoration, pre-fire incising, classified as Dulces Incised type, also occurs in still lower amounts (~2 percent) in this ware category.

Snail-Inclusion Paste Ware

In the Late Postclassic period, important changes occurred in pottery decoration in SIP ware and in the Paxcamán ceramic group. SIP ware is characterized by the use of highly organic lacustrine clays containing tiny fragments of freshwater snails (Rice 1987a: 105), but the specific lake source(s) of the clays is/are not known at present. Early decoration in SIP was primarily black-painted (Ixpop Polychrome; similar to Peto Cream in northern Yucatán), with some incising (Picú Incised); in the Late Postclassic period red-and-black–painted decoration appeared and is classified as Sacá Polychrome. Dark red-on-paste painted decoration also began to appear very late in the Paxcamán group in both banded and non-banded (curvilinear and geometric) modes, replicating that on Chompoxté and Kayukos varieties of Chompoxté Red-on-cream; it often occurs on both the interior and exterior of vessels and introduces new motifs. Typically, the vessels are poorly fired, with the result that the background paste color is grayish-brown (7.5YR 4–8/6, 10YR 7/4) and the red paint is dark purplish-red (7.5R 4/6). Typologically, this new pottery is classified, depending in part on the decoration or as Macanché Red-on-paste, as George Cowgill's (1963) Tachis type.

The appearance of the Xiw/Kowoj's "signature" red-painted decoration on SIP pottery appears to accompany their westward expansion out of the Yaxhá region. If this movement represents abandonment of Topoxté, potters may have lost access to their clean white clay source and have had to use unfamiliar, highly organic clays from around the lakes' margins. The new pottery is typically poorly fired; perhaps the potters were unable to create the oxidizing firing conditions that would remove organics to develop clear colors. We do not know the sources of the clay or the areas of production, but some of this dark red-on-paste pottery may have been produced by potters on the northern or northwestern shore of Lake Petén Itzá, who were part of the Chak'an Itza faction of Itza allied with the Kowoj (Jones, Chapter 3, this volume).

Xiw/Kowoj Decorative Motifs

As described earlier, identifiable decorative icons on Petén Postclassic pottery typically occur in clearly defined bands on the interiors or exteriors of vessels (Cecil 2002). Many, if not most, of these motifs resemble simplified glyphic signs or graphemes, an interpretation enhanced by flanking single or double "parentheses" that give the appearance of a cartouche. They do not occur sequentially as in a text or phrase but rather are isolated in two to four panels around the decorative band. These motifs are of interest in light of John Pohl's (2003: 201; Pohl and Byland 1994: 197) comments about Mixteca-Puebla pottery, which bears simple glyph-like icons that conveyed concepts or words and facilitated international elite communication among groups speaking a dozen different languages.

Decorative motifs are grouped into five categories: calendrical glyphs, glyph semblants, geometric icons, naturalistic motifs, and abstract-cursive motifs. The calendrical glyphs and glyph semblants emphasize day signs in the Maya 260-day calendar, or *tzolk'in*; "head variants" were not noted. Day signs are common in the Late Postclassic "international symbol set" (Boone and Smith 2003: 190, 192) and suggest elements of Classic-period skyband iconography (Carlson and Landis 1985). Motifs identified as "geometric" also frequently have glyphic referents and may have functioned the same way, as signs conveying abstract meanings and facilitating communication.

Here we describe these motifs on the pottery of Zacpetén and Topoxté, other significant occurrences, and their possible "meanings." Icons resembling graphemes are indicated by the three-digit alphanumeric coding in the system developed by Martha J. Macri and Matthew G. Looper (2003; hereafter "ML" plus page number) and their "T-number" in J. Eric S. Thompson's (1962) catalog. For example, the exterior line of the double "parenthesis" is sometimes embellished with one or two protuberances, the latter read as *te'/che'*, a sign for wood or tree in Classic iconography (XGC, YG2/T013; ML: 187, 204).

Calendrical Glyphs

Ajaw. Ajaw signifies both the title of a ruler ("lord") and a day-name in the 260-day calendar; *k'atun* periods are typically designated by their Ajaw ending day (e.g., K'atun 8 Ajaw) in the Terminal Classic and Postclassic "short count." The ajaw glyph AM1/T0533 (ML: 65) occurs frequently during the Late Classic period on lowland pottery in eastern Petén (especially Codex-style pottery) and is abundant in date phrases on other forms of material culture such as stelae, altars, and lintels.

In the Postclassic period, the ajaw sign is rare and has been found only on red-painted pottery (Chompoxté Red-on-cream: Kayukos variety; CCP ware; Figure 11.2a) at Zacpetén. Similar ajaw representations appear on a vessel from northern Yucatán (Kerr 1990: figure 3199c) and at least two in Tecoh Red-on-buff at Mayapán, one from the Structure Y-45 group (Masson and Peraza Lope 2005: figure 5; see Smith 1971: 66). Ajaws commonly appear in the *Chilam Balam of Chumayel* (Craine and Reindorp 1979) and in Postclassic Maya codices.

Ak'b'al. Ak'b'al (XH9/T0504; ML: 194), a day-name in the *tzolk'in*, was identified on pottery from Zacpetén as both red-painted and black-painted

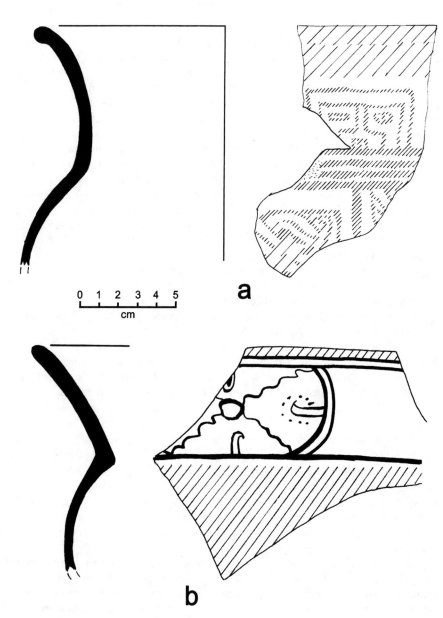

0 1 2 3 4 5
cm

a

b

Figure 11.2. Calendrical signs on Petén Postclassic pottery: (a) Ajaw (above) on partially reconstructible Chompoxté Red-on-cream: Kayukos variety wide-mouth jar from Structure 767; note mat motif on body; (b) elaborate Etz'nab' sign on Ixpop Polychrome collared bowl from Structure 734.

motifs. Ak'b'al is a yearbearer in the so-called Campeche calendar introduced in A.D. 672 (Edmonson 1988: 148) and in the Paris and Dresden codices, appearing on new year's page 27 in the latter (Schele and Grube 1997: 161); it was not a yearbearer in the Madrid Codex. In Ch'olan and Yukatekan, ak'b'al means "night" or "darkness" and is associated with jaguars and the Underworld (Carlson and Landis 1985: 126). Ak'b'al glyphs co-occur with the sun sign to complete the day/night dyad (Willson 1924).

Ak'b'al glyphs appear on Late Classic polychrome pottery as part of a bench with a seated ruler (Kerr 1994: figure 4689). The simplified ak'b'al glyph on Postclassic pottery resembles what John Carlson and Linda Landis (1985: 137) called the "codex" form, characterized by two hooks separated by a "V" (Figure 11.3c). In the Paris Codex the ak'b'al glyph occurs in skybands where Pawahtuns (quadripartite gods who hold up the sky) sit, on the Ak'b'al yearbearer page as a vertical column, and in skybands and thrones throughout the codex (Love 1994: 71, 83, 89; Miller 1982: 93).

The ak'b'al skyband element might also represent an insect or reptile: two eyes with hook motifs for pupils, a triangular nose, and an undulating body of a serpent or dragon (Carlson and Landis 1985: 126). Postclassic pottery motifs often consist of only the eye elements that resemble scroll eyes in other reptile depictions. It differs from the hooks discussed later because those of the ak'b'al glyph occur in pairs rather than singly.

Lamat. Lamat is a day in the 260-day *tzolk'in* and a yearbearer in the Campeche calendar. The glyph (also read *ek'* 'star') displays a + cross (*k'an* 'cross') or an X with dots in the "corners" (ZQD/T510a, b; ML: 229–230) and appears on an Ixpop Polychrome (SIP ware) tripod plate from Ixlú (Figure 11.3a, b). One wonders if the glyph might be read "K'an Ek'" (B. Myers, pers. com.). The lamat glyph also occurs on Late Classic pottery as part of a bench on which the Moon Goddess sits (Kerr 1997: figure K504), as a glyph in the skyband (Kerr 1989: figure 1898, 1994: figure 5007), and in an underwater scene with fish (Kerr 1992: figure 3134). Lamat glyphs are common in the Postclassic Paris, Dresden, and Madrid codices. Lamat is associated with 1 Ajaw in the Tancah cave, suggesting Venus as morning star during the five Wayeb' days (Miller 1982: 87; see also Carlson and Landis 1985; Thompson 1970: 220).

Etz'nab'. Like Ak'b'al and Lamat, Etz'nab' is a day in the 260-day *tzolk'in* and a yearbearer in the Campeche calendar. The glyph for etz'nab' (XQ8/T0527; ML: 199) is characterized by a wavy X, interpreted as "flint." A highly elaborated Etz'nab' day sign appears on the interior rim band of a large Ixpop Polychrome collared bowl recovered in residential Structure 734 at Zacpetén (Figure 11.2b). Macri and Looper (2003: 199) noted an interpretation by Yuri Knorozov of *etz'nab'* as *hetz'* ('seat'), perhaps relating to the seating of the *k'atun* or *may*.

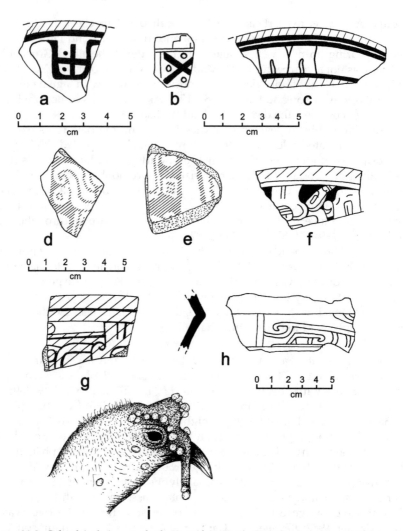

Figure 11.3. *Calendrical signs and other motifs on Petén Postclassic pottery: (a)* k'an *cross version of Lamat sign on interior of Ixpop Polychrome tripod dish, Ixlú Structure 2023; (b) Lamat sign, Ixpop Polychrome (Ixlú); (c) Ak'b'al sign on interior of Ixpop Polychrome tripod dish (Structure ???); d–g, God M eye motif: (d) Chompoxté Red-on-cream: Chompoxté variety jar exterior, Structure 747; (e) Chompoxté Red-on-cream: Chompoxté variety tripod dish interior, Structure 732; (f) Picú Incised: Black Label variety, incising on a black band on interior of a collared bowl, Structure 764; (g) Picú Incised: Picú variety collared bowl, Structure 735; (h) ilhuitl sign on Hobonmo Incised: Ramsey variety (Augustine ceramic group) jar; (i) head and neck of ocellated turkey* (Meleagris ocellata) *showing the "snood" draped over the beak and nodular growths (yellow-orange to red) around the eye and on a small crest. The head and neck are blue (Maya Blue?), and the skin surrounding the eye is red-brown. Drawn from photograph at http://www.taxidermy.net/reference/bird/ocellated/70a/html.*

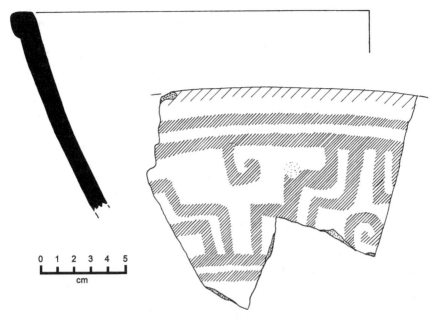

Figure 11.4. Stepped-terrace and hook motifs on fragment of large bowl of Tecoh Red-on-buff pottery from Mayapán Structure Q-162 (the Castillo). This sherd represents one of four large open bowls of Tecoh with dark red decoration on a cream background on the exterior and a Chompoxté-like glossy red-orange slip on the interior and over the rim. The other three are from Structure Q-80, a north-facing temple in the northern part of the ceremonial core. All four bowls have thirty-four-centimeter mouth diameters.

Glyph Semblants

Hook or curl. The hook or curl (hereafter hook) is so widespread that it cannot be described as Kowoj-specific or even Maya-specific, as it also occurs on Mixteca-Puebla pottery (Nicholson and Quiñones Keber 1994). Hooks are often simply vertical elements with the distal curve removed (Chapter 7, Figure 7.9, this volume); these may be feathers. Hooks (including the simplified vertical) are the most common and simplest decorative motif on Petén Postclassic slipped pottery, Kowoj and non-Kowoj, appearing as single painted elements in two or four "cartouches" of the decorative bands; these could be simplifications of the 819-day count Glyph Y (SSG/T0739; ML: 214) or *mu* (YSA/T0019; ML: 213).

The hook may be a simplified version of more elaborate scrolls, spirals, and volutes — appearing in moderate to abundant quantities on pottery of northern Yucatán, including Tecoh Red-on-buff (Figure 11.4; Smith 1971, 1: 58–60; pers. obs.). Hooks/curls have many interpretations: curled plumes or feathers, shells (a watery Underworld), monkey tails (Mock 1997), a butterfly proboscis (Headrick 2003), a speech or breath scroll (Taube 2001), rubber or incense (ZUQ/T0576, T0577; ML: 245), water (ZUP/T0578, ZUN/T0856; ibid.: 244–245), or, if dotted, as Glyph 33A/T0044 "to burn" (ibid.: 299, see also 213).

Hooks also appear as lines of diagonally oriented curls with supports (Chapter 7, Figure 7.3, 7.5a, this volume). Another related motif — the *ilhuitl*, or reversed volutes — is the Aztec sign for day, sun, or festival; it appears in Maya skybands (Carlson and Landis 1985: 127–128). An *ilhuitl*-like motif occurs on Chompoxte Red-on-cream: Akalché variety and on Hobonmo Incised: Ramsey variety (Figure 11.3h).

The hook icon appears on Early Classic–period pottery and continues through the Late Postclassic period. In the Classic period, hooks and curls occur in three contexts: commonly in the eyes of snakes, gods, and particularly reptiles or water monsters in Underworld scenes (Hellmuth 1987: figure 5, p. 156; Kerr 1989: figures 1834, 1119; 1990: figure 2713; 1992: figure 3622; 1994: figures 4926, 4957); as round stone seats (altars) or rests made of hook elements (Kerr 1989: figure 1398, 1992: figures 3422, 3007, 3198); and in conch shell trumpets (Kerr 1989: figure 808). In the Terminal Classic and Postclassic periods, the hook is common in murals and codices as well as on pottery (Sanders 1960: figures 4, 5; Smith 1971, 2: figure 47). At Tulum, hooks co-occur with Underworld scenes and with representations of Chaak (Miller 1982: 91). Bruce Love (1994: 44) noted that God C/K sits on hooks in the Dresden and Paris codices. The hook is depicted in the Dresden Codex on food offerings — probably tamales (Taube 1989a) — given during new year ceremonies. This review suggests complex associations with eyes, the Underworld, and seats. The last two might be explained as punning on the Yukateko Mayan words *hok'*, meaning "hook" (including fishhook), and *hok*, meaning "rest or recline" (*Diccionario Maya-Español*).

Mat and braid. Mat motifs appear on Kowoj Postclassic slipped pottery in two variants: multistrand woven mats (Figure 11.2a) and two-strand twists, plaits, or braids (Chapters 7 and 9, Figures 7.3, 9.3). They appear as early as Middle Preclassic (Mamom) pottery in Petén (Smith 1955: 64) and are common on various Classic wares. Mats may be painted or incised, often as panels alternating with some other motif (Brainerd 1958: figure 80bb; Hermes 2000b: figure 152.4; Sanders 1960: figure 7c; Smith 1955: 64, 1971, 1: 48). Single twists/braids occur horizontally or vertically, also frequently as panel or design dividers. Mats and braids on Late Classic polychromes separate glyph bands from main design areas, divide round reptile faces, and demarcate the lip/rim area from the body of a vessel (Kerr 1989: figure 1117, 1994: figures 4628, 4629).

Pop is also the name of the first month in the Maya 365-day calendar (*ja'ab'*), and its glyph has an infixed braid (ZQ8/T0615; ML: 228). The mat (*pop* in Yukateko Mayan) is a metaphor for a ruler's "seat of power." Thus, mats represent not only the throne or seat for kings but also the "seating" of the new year in the month Pop. The mat was synonymous with rulership by the Late Classic period, if not earlier, and appears widely on carved stela and pottery (Robicsek 1975): rulers hold bicephalic monster bars with mat motifs on the body, sit on mats or thrones with the braided design, and wear mats as part of their accessories and headdresses. At Zacpetén the relative frequency of mat motifs in Structure 719 might coincide with new year ceremonies, as well as the possibility that the structure represented a *popol naj*.

In northern Yucatán, braids, plaits, and twists are common, particularly as encircling bands on slateware pottery (Sanders 1960: figure 11; Smith 1971, 2: figures 7, 8, 21, 47i, o), but multistrand mats are rare on pottery at Mayapán (Smith 1971, 1: 54; pers. obs.). Mats and braids are common as architectural embellishments, however. At least some of the braids/twists may represent the body of a serpent, as seen at Chich'en Itza on the Tomb of the High Priest and the Casa Colorada (among other buildings). Mat motifs appear on Postclassic structures at Tulum, on serpents and in skybands (Masson 2000: figure 6.10), and may indicate elite lineages or lineage celebrations. In the mural in Tulum Structure 16, figures stand above woven mats that separate them from an Underworld scene, and Arthur Miller (1982: 91, plate 37) suggested that the twisted braids symbolize the "mythical umbilical cord" in the Kusansum Myth (ibid.: 94) or the path of the sun (Milbrath 1999: 74). Similar umbilical cords appear on murals at Chich'en Itza and in Postclassic codices from highland Mexico that may represent the Late Postclassic international style (Miller 1982).

A related icon is the double reverse spiral or reverse S-curve, perhaps a simplified *muyal* (cloud) glyph (usually appearing in a dotted oval; XGK/ T0632; ML: 189); it may be painted (Chapter 7, Figure 7.5b, this volume) or incised. Like the braid, the S-curve occurs early on slatewares in the Puuc region (Brainerd 1958: figures 18je, 50i3, 57d, 61b, 61e, 77b). Smith (1971, 1: 48–49) indicated that this motif occurs in northern Yucatán from the Early Classic to Late Postclassic periods but more frequently in the Postclassic.

Mat motifs appear to have three distinct meanings—serpents, umbilical cords, and symbols of kingship—and together they suggest themes of royal birth, descent, and rulership. Also, as Prudence Rice (1989: 316) earlier noted, in its "usage as a divider and also in its occurrence as a circumferential band around pottery vessels or as a framing mechanism on murals, the mat or twist may be considered to function as a 'mediational' device, literally as well as figuratively establishing boundaries and/or structural oppositions between the divine and powerful versus the secular or profane."

RE glyph. The RE, or "reptile eye," glyph (von Winning 1961), long associated with central Mexico and particularly Teotihuacan, displays the profiled head of a serpent with curling plumes in front of and above the eye. It occurs widely throughout Mesoamerica (see Ringle, Gallareta Negrón, and Bey 1998: 209–210) but has been found only in painted decoration in the Petén lakes region and almost exclusively in SIP ware (Rice 1983, 1989). The RE glyph is part of a more extended repertoire of ophidian/saurian symbols on Petén Postclassic pottery. In highland Mexico, the RE sign is one of the day-names in the 260-day calendar, and the glyph may represent fire rather than the eye of a reptile (Miller and Taube 1993: 143).

God M eye. The version of the Petén Postclassic reptile previously described as a "split-representational" depiction (Rice 1983, 1989), for lack of a better term, may be better characterized as an eye. A simple version is a "jaguar cruller eye" (ST7; ML: 176) or the "God M name glyph" (T0680). Macri and Looper (2003: 177) described it as substituting for God 7 as the patron of the month Wo. The God M glyph consists of "an eye within a U-shaped element" (Taube 1992: 88), with a crenelated eyebrow and two round elements at the lower "corners" of the U (Figure 11.3d–g); these elements share some resemblance to the eye of the ocellated turkey (Figure 11.3i). God M, usually depicted with black skin, is associated with Ek Chuah, a merchant god, and with cacao (Taube 1992: 88–92).

A similar eye-like motif appears on pottery of highland Mexico. In the Zapotec area it resembles what Alfonso Caso (1928) called "Glyph C" and a "jaguar mouth," which is common in the headdresses of deities — particularly that of the rain god Cocijo — on modeled effigy urns (Rice 1983: 871–872). It also appears painted in black-on-orange Aztec 1 pottery (Rice 1983: figure 5).

This U-shaped dotted half-cartouche commonly appears as the eye (or "goggle eye") of other gods (e.g., God K on the body of a snake in the Madrid Codex). The Postclassic Maya of Petén had numerous uses for the God M eye glyph, which appears as (1) the eye (?) of a "split representation" snake; (2) on the reptilian headdress of Kowoj effigy censers (Chapters 7 and 12, Figures 7.2, 12.6, this volume) and also at Mayapán on censers (Smith 1971, 2: figure 32k, Itzamna) and as the eye on sculptured snake heads (Proskouriakoff 1962a: figure 7a, f, g, h, i); (3) incised on SIP pottery from Zacpetén; and (4) as the eye, and also on the back, of a reptilian creature in Chompoxté Red-on-cream (Figure 11.1). Although it is a bit of a stretch, this motif might be seen as a curvilinear version of the rectilinear stone mosaic Chaak faces.

Zip monster. In the central Petén lakes area, this motif may be red-painted or incised. The Zip monster is the patron of the third month (Zip) of the 365-day calendar; recall that a day 10 Zip was the day on which a Kowoj "rain priest" escaped the Kokom massacre of Xiw priests on their pilgrimage to Chich'en Itza. The Zip monster is often identified as the "Mars Beast" because of its appearance with the four Mars Beasts in the Dresden Codex (Milbrath 1999: 219–223). Its angular S-shape in skybands may represent the Zip monster in its most abstract form (Carlson and Landis 1985). The Zip monster takes many glyphic forms, but the one painted on Postclassic slipped pottery has its origin in the Olmec dragon (or God I) (Lowe 1982: 42). The motif is common on Late and Terminal Classic pottery (Coe 1973, 1978; Sabloff 1975: 205; Smith 1955: 74).

Zip monsters occur on pottery and skybands at Las Monjas at Chich'en Itza (Brainerd 1958: figure 83b16, 17, 18) and on incised pottery in Quintana Roo (Sanders 1960: figures 4, 5) and at Mayapán (Smith 1971, 2: figure 48). It also appears as an element in a throne, as a rooftop skyband with the death god seated on top on the Lamat yearbearer page, and in constellation pages of the Paris Codex (Love 1994: 11, 71, 89). The Mexican Codex Mendoza Folio

70r depicts a scribe with a box that has the Zip monster symbol on the outside (Berdan and Anawalt 1997: 231). It may also be associated with the Aztec *ilhuitl* sign for day, sun, or festival (Carlson and Landis 1985: 127–128).

"*Ladder.*" A few examples of a ladder- or step-like motif appear in CCP ware on sherds of Chompoxté Red-on-cream: Akalché variety (Figure 11.5d), Canté Polychrome, and Dulces Incised pottery. This might relate to occasional depictions of similar elements in glyphs: the conjunction "and then" and the Posterior Date Indicator (YM1/T0679; ML: 207–208), the "shine" or "reflection" marks in a mirror (1M2/T0617; ML: 274), or the steps of a pyramid (ZH4/T0685; ML: 224). The ladder motif is rare in Early Postclassic Yucatán (Smith 1971, 1: 54).

Venus. The exterior bounding lines of an unusual "abstract-cursive" paneled motif exhibit the eye-like glyph for Venus; also *ek'* 'star, planet' (ZQD/T0002; ML: 230). This motif is very rare and was only noted on an incurved-rim bowl from Topoxté.

Geometric Icons

Circles. Circles, like hooks, are extremely common and occur on Xiw/Kowoj pottery in several variants—single, concentric, and dotted (Figure 11.5c)—as well as on Late Classic polychromes. Circles with interior dots, circles ringed with dots, and "feathered circles" are elements of Mixteca-Puebla style pottery (Lind 1994; McCafferty 2001) and the "Late Postclassic international symbol set" (Boone and Smith 2003: figure 24.9). At Mayapán, circles may be concentric or they may occur with bars, dots, squiggles, and in chains (Smith 1971, 1: 49–50, 53). In the Late Postclassic, circles appear on jars of Pele Polychrome and Tecoh Red-on-buff (pers. obs.) and appliquéd on effigy censers.

Circles might have hieroglyphic references, as they abound in graphemes on Classic texts. One set is calendrical: (1) *pet,* "round, circular, island; dayname Muluk" (nested circles without dots; XG1/T0511; ML: 183; Montgomery 2002: 206) or (2) with dots, month name Mol (BP5/T0582; ML: 93–94). Other variations include (3) concentric circles with dots or small circlets around the exterior, "make, build, sculpt" (2G4/T0079; ML: 285); or *pat,* a "general 'dedication' verb" (Montgomery 2002: 203); and (4) concentric circles with dots or circlets (and cross-hatched U-shape below; 2G2/T0603, T0634; ML: 284): *ch'a,* "incense, droplet" (or *pom*). Aside from glyphs, circles are often interpreted as something precious, as, for example, *chalchihuitl,* or jade.

Recent examination of Tecoh Red-on-buff pottery in the Mayapán ceramic lab in Telchaquillo, Mexico, revealed the use of concentric circles to depict the abdomen of a descending spider or tarantula. Although the image (Figure 11.5a) is incomplete owing to breakage, it clearly shows the chelicerae, "palps," and multiple eyes on the cephalothorax. The image appears on the exterior body of a jar from Structure Q-98, a shrine structure facing into an

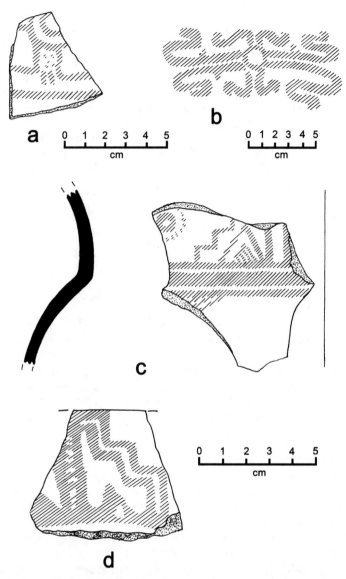

Figure 11.5. Miscellaneous decorative motifs: (a) sherd of Tecoh Red-on-buff jar from Structure Q-98 at Mayapán, showing a descending spider or tarantula; (b) exterior spider/flower decoration on Late Classic Zacatal Cream Polychrome semi-spherical bowl from Topoxté (redrawn from Hermes 2000b: figure 140.12); (c) exterior decoration on large, wide-mouthed jar of Chompoxté Red-on-cream: Kayukos variety, showing dotted circle, stepped-terrace, and nested-and-embedded triangle motifs, Zacpetén Structure 732; (d) Chompoxté Red-on-cream: Akalché variety decoration on interior of tripod dish, showing ladder motif and stepped terrace with interior triangle, from Topoxté (redrawn from Hermes 2000b: figure 152.10).

open hall on the eastern edge of the Mayapán civic-ceremonial core, northeast of the "observatory" Structure Q-152. A possible Late Classic antecedent to the spider motif is evident on a Zacatal Cream Polychrome bowl from Topoxté (Figure 11.5b), although the paired lines radiating out from a circle also resemble the sign (XQ2/T0646; ML: 196) for the plumeria flower (*nikte'*).

Triangles, embedded and nested. Triangles with cross-hatching are common in the Classic period and are commonly interpreted as "serpent segments." In Postclassic Kowoj territory triangles are rarely, if ever, cross-hatched, instead being simplified by embedding or nesting and painted red or red-and-black (Chapter 9, Figures 9.5, 9.6, this volume; Figure 11.5c). Triangles are a common motif in the Maya lowlands, with painted and incised examples increasing in frequency from Preclassic through Early and Late Classic pottery in Petén and adjacent regions (Gifford 1976: figure 72c; Sabloff 1975: 113; Smith 1955: 68, 1971: 61; Willey et al. 1994: figures 34, 108a), including nested triangles at Topoxté (Hermes 2000b: figure 140.11). Grapheme 33G/T0143, a line of three horizontally hatched triangles, is read as water (ML: 301–302). The triangles may be part of various central figures' thrones (Kerr 1994: figure 4929, 1997: figure 744) or serpent segments in Classic-period skybands (Carlson and Landis 1985: 126). Embedded and nested triangles are common on Early Postclassic incised pottery from Colha (Valdez 1987: figure 57d), on painted pottery from Uxmal, and in several incised and painted Postclassic variants at Mayapán (Smith 1971, 1: 61–62; pers. obs.). The designs on Petén and northern Yucatán pottery are almost identical.

Step-frets and terraces. Several similar icons on pottery from Mayapán and related sites may be called steps, step-frets (*grecas*), terraces, split terraces, and terraces with various infixes such as a hook or a U (Smith 1971: 60–61). The motif may represent steps of a temple or an abstract mat motif; it also resembles the glyph *hoy/joy* (T843) 'bless, ascend' (ML: 252), and abstract serpent imagery (Sharp 1978). A related *tau*, or T motif—an inverted stepped terrace—may "represent the Ik glyph for wind that is internationally also associated with Quezalcoatl/Kulkulkan" (Masson 2000: 234). Step-fret and stepped-terrace designs are characteristic of the symbol sets of both the Early Postclassic and Late Postclassic periods in Mexico (Boone and Smith 2003) and the Maya area, including Tecoh Red-on-buff pottery from Mayapán (Figures 11.4, 11.5c, d).

Step-fret and stepped-terrace motifs are common on Classic polychromes (Gifford 1976: figures 72, 96, 126; Sabloff 1975: 140). At Uaxactún (Smith 1955: 61) and Terminal Classic Seibal (Sabloff 1975: 188), the interior motif of terraces is U-shaped; at Barton Ramie, an interior circle (Gifford 1976: figure 114–115); and at Altar de Sacrificios, a hook (Adams 1971: figure 44b). Step-frets also appear on slatewares from northern Yucatán (Brainerd 1958: figure 24f 2, 4; Smith 1971, 2: figure 7).

On Postclassic pottery of northern Yucatán, step-frets are "abundant" and T-shapes "moderate" in occurrence, but the other related motifs are "rare"

(Smith 1971, 1: 60–61, figure 22). On Postclassic pottery from the eastern Petén lakes, step-frets appear as incised and red-painted motifs; stepped pyramid (or "terrace") motifs also occur on pottery from Zacpetén (red) and Topoxté Island (red-and-black). The stepped pyramid typically has an interior element that may be a U-shape, triangles, or a hook (Figures 11.4, 11.5c, d). Central Mexican cultures used the stepped pyramid and step-frets, which appear in bands on the necks of jars or on dishes (Nicholson and Quiñones Keber 1994). The Codex Nuttall (1975) and the Mixtec codices (Pohl 1994) incorporated the stepped pyramid as part of toponyms (e.g., Tollan), design panels, skybands, thrones, and pyramids. In the Maya highlands, step-frets may have been serpent motifs (Fox 1987: 67).

The location of these stepped motifs is of some interest. On Mixteca-Puebla pottery, step-frets appear around the necks of jars (Nicholson and Quiñones Keber 1994); similarly, a Late Classic polychrome scene shows the step-fret motif on a jar neck (Kerr 1992: figure 4339). On another Late Classic vase (Kerr 1994: figures 4550, 4661), stepped pyramids appear as a panel divider that serves as a wall behind a seated scribe and as a motif above a serpent scene. Painted step-frets on the mural in Structure 5 at Tulum alternate with woven mat symbols (Masson 2003: 197). On Postclassic Petén pottery, the junctions of walls and bases of tripod dishes and other vessels are emphasized by notched flanges representing steps or stepped terraces. All this suggests that these stepped elements constituted mediational devices of long standing, playing a role similar to that of mats/braids.

U-shapes. U-shapes are not common on Petén Postclassic pottery, but they occur as single and nested elements. They are described as "abundant" at Mayapán (Smith 1971: 62), occurring on one Tecoh Red-on-buff vessel (pers. obs.) with three to five vertical lines in the hollow "combs" (ibid.: 66). At Topoxté, they occur singly or nested (Figure 11.1). U-shapes are common in sculptural art from the Middle Preclassic through the Early Classic throughout eastern and isthmian Mesoamerica. In Classic glyphs, they may indicate spikes on an incensario (ZD2/T0595, ZD4; ML: 220); the moon sign; the sign for twenty, which has three dots in the center (ZU1/T0683b; ML: 237); or, less likely, the sign *hul*, "arrive" (ZU2/T0683a; ML: 238). Nested U-shapes abound in the upper register of the mural in Tulum Structure 5, along with solar-ray V-scrolls.

Chevrons. Chevrons, repeated horizontal or vertical V-shaped elements, are part of the Maya Late Postclassic symbol set and are most commonly painted. They occur fairly widely on Classic pottery (Sabloff 1975: figure 392; Smith 1955: 62) and are perhaps best known as a narrow encircling band of black chevrons above the scenes on the famous Chamá polychrome funeral pottery (Miller 1982: 91). In Late Postclassic Petén, red-painted chevrons often decorate the lips of dishes or collared bowls or, on very late pottery, are nested around the exterior of tripod dishes (e.g., Macanché Red-on-paste: Tachis variety; Chompoxté Red-on-cream: Kayukos variety). They also appear in black paint on Pele Polychrome dishes at Mayapán (pers. obs.). Depending on the context, chevrons may be an angular convention for indicating woven, braided, or rope-like materials. Their location suggests that they often played a role in demarcating boundaries, much as twists/ropes and stepped terraces/frets did.[1]

Squared spirals. The squared spiral, seen on Early and Late Classic pottery of Uaxactún (Smith 1955: 66) and Seibal (Sabloff 1975: 205), is also a very late motif painted in red on Petén Postclassic slipped pottery at Zacpetén. Squared spirals occur on late pottery with banded decorative panels and as a single element occurring twice in each panel. In Macanché Red-on-paste and Tachis Red-on-paste (SIP ware), this motif frequently alternates with chevrons, either in a band or on the interior vs. exterior of decorated bowls; it also appears on Chompoxté Red-on-cream: Kayukos variety (CCP ware). Squared spirals are also found on Mixteca-Puebla pottery from Cholula (McCafferty 2001: figure 4.45) and on Tecoh Red-on-buff pottery at Mayapán, where they are called angular scrolls (Smith 1971: 58).

Naturalistic Motifs

Naturalistic motifs are of interest because previous studies of Petén Postclassic pottery (Rice 1983, 1987a, 1989) appeared to indicate that reptile motifs, common on SIP ware pottery, were absent in CCP ware decoration. With the considerable volume of Chompoxté Red-on-cream: Chompoxté variety pottery from more recent excavations at the Topoxté Islands (Hermes 2000b), we now believe some of these puzzling curvilinear motifs may indeed represent reptiles (Figures 11.1, 11.6), and some might even be related to tarantulas, reflecting the *kowoj* ("tarantula") patronym.[2]

One of the most common, if confusing, suites of motifs on Petén Postclassic pottery consists of sinuous, feathery, reptilian-ophidian creatures that are not clearly snakes, crocodiles, or birds but instead combine elements of any two or all three. Our recent work at Zacpetén, plus that of Guatemalan and German archaeologists at the Topoxté Islands and Yaxhá in the Lake Yaxhá basin to the east, has greatly expanded the database of these images beyond those studied earlier (P. Rice 1983, 1986, 1989). In addition, given that the name or word Kowoj means "tarantula" in Yukatekan Maya, it might be expected that these motifs could be interpreted as arachnids or, more specifically, the red, black, and cream-colored tarantula *Brachypelma vagans* found in this area (see Note 2). We have found little to substantiate this possibility, however.

Plumes and feathers. Representations of plumes or feathers, sometimes as elaborate hook motifs, are common on Petén Postclassic pottery. At Zacpetén, plumes and feathers occur as red-painted motifs with the distinctive "allover" decoration; at Topoxté Island, they are more common and occur in all the painted types and varieties of CCP ware. Similar motifs occur on Tecoh Red-on-buff pottery from Mayapán (Smith 1971, 2: figure 53; pers. obs.).

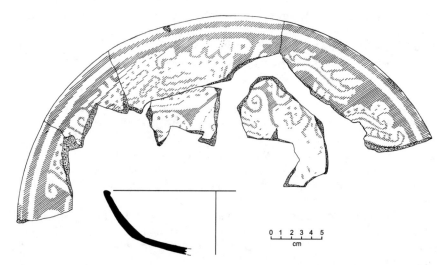

Figure 11.6. Partially reconstructible Chompoxté Red-on-cream: Chompoxté variety dish, probably tripod, from other project excavations at residential Structure 760 near Group C. About three-quarters of the vessel was found in pieces, suggesting primary breakage.

In the Classic period, feathers are common, most conspicuously and naturalistically in rulers' headdresses. A characteristic motif of Late Classic polychrome pottery in the Tikal region, the "dress shirt" motif, may be a turkey tail feather, painted in black-and-white bands on red-slipped pottery.

Various birds are depicted on numerous categories of pottery, too many to review here, throughout the history of the Maya: macaws, water birds (particularly cormorants; Reents-Budet 1994: 244–248), and turkeys (ibid.: figure 6.22). Birds are also depicted on the codices, and avians — including vultures, macaws, falcons, and owls — play a central role in the *Popol Vuh* myth. The "Celestial Bird" or "Principal Bird Deity" reflects this importance, having been killed (as Seven Macaw) by Hunahpu/Hun Ajaw (Benson 1997: 91–92; Milbrath 1999: 274). The Principal Bird Deity is also associated with Itzamna (Milbrath 1999: 295) and with the skyband of the Cosmic Monster, suggesting astronomical associations such as Venus (ibid.: 285, 288; Taube 1989b: 9; Thompson 1970: 228–229).

In addition, the co-occurrence of birds/feathers and snakes/reptiles inevitably suggests reference to the plumed serpent, Kukulcan or Quetzalcoatl, raising the likelihood that the Petén lakes region participated in the Quetzalcoatl cult or "world religion" characteristic of much of "Epiclassic" Mesoamerica (Ringle, Gallareta Negrón, and Bey 1998), with its liberal displays of ophidian iconography. In Petén, however, feather elements are particularly associated with Late Postclassic pottery, suggesting that this "cult," if such it was, entered the region very late.

Profiled reptile. The most straightforward representation of a reptilian-saurian creature is presented in profile, sometimes showing only the head and other times depicting its body. The head is carefully elaborated, with a round eye and open mouth with upturned snout, sharp maxillary teeth, and a reverse curving element at the corner. The body may be that of a snake or a broader-bodied reptilian creature in Chompoxté Red-on-cream: Chompoxté variety (Figure 11.1), but in the latter case the legs, if any, are not evident owing to breakage of the vessel. The creature typically displays heavy plumage on the head, body, and tail, but the feathers are stylized: the head and body have large, curving plumes like that of the RE glyph, while on the tail they are angular, individual feathers, much like the Late Classic "dress shirt" motif.

The complete profiled reptile is never common but appears primarily in SIP ware; one example occurs on a Xuluc Incised: Ain Variety collared bowl from a Late Postclassic context at Macanché Island (Rice 1987a: figure 51). Reptile heads are painted in Ixpop Polychrome. Variations in details might relate to the heads of two intertwined serpents in Tulum Murals 2, 4, 5, and 6 of Structure 16, where one has a God K head (also seen in the Madrid Codex) and the other has a Chaak head (Masson 2003: 199). The depictions at Tulum may have associations with ascent to rulership, divine rulership, rituals and relations between different lineages, lineage heritage, ancestors, or some combination thereof (Masson 2000: 211–248; Miller 1974; Schele and Matthews 1998: 218–219).

Profiled reptiles are not common in CCP ware, although the jaw can be recognized on a Chompoxté Red-on-cream: Chompoxté variety tripod plate recovered from Nakum (P. Rice, pers. obs.); in this example, the rest of the design probably represents the creature's body. Another example at Topoxté (Hermes 2000b: figure 152.4) occurs in an unnamed incised bichrome type. Plumed profile reptile heads appear as far away as the Greater Nicoya region of Costa Rica and Nicaragua in the Late Postclassic period (Day 1994).

Some icons may represent a conflation of reptiles and turkeys. The Late Classic "dress shirt" motif may represent the tail feathers of the ocellated turkey (*Meleagris ocellata*), which have a prominent blue-green "eye" at the ends. The nose of the profile reptile often has a looping element, not clearly a feather, reminiscent of the prominent nose element ("snood") on male turkeys. In addition, the reptile head is frequently embellished with circles or concentric circles, resembling the characteristic small nodules on the heads of male ocellated turkeys (Figure 11.3i).

Abstract-Cursive Motifs

An unusual abstract-curvilinear decoration, embellished with plumes, dots, ticks, and circles, is a distinctive element of Kowoj pottery, occurring on CCP ware at Topoxté (Rice 1979) and Zacpetén and later copied on SIP ware as Macanché Red-on-paste type. It may relate to the "scroll, meander" motif in the earlier Sotuta complex (Smith 1971, 1: 59). Overall, the style or set of motifs on this pottery is extremely abstract, although the decoration appears to be in positive rather than in negative. Determining exactly what is portrayed is not easy, especially in the case of tripod dishes, in which the entire interior is covered with this stylized painting. As a result, it is hard to describe, let alone label, these motifs.

A tripod dish from a chultun on Canté Island clearly shows the profiled head and body of a snake or saurian "monster" with open jaws and plumes on the snout (Figure 11.1; Hermes 2000b: figure 151.3), which suggests that other examples of this decorative style/motif may also be reptiles. Another vessel with a similar depiction was recovered at Nakum (pers. obs.).

In the banded decoration of Chompoxté Red-on-cream: Akalché variety, a similar motif occurs on the exterior of neckless jars (*tecomates*) (Hermes 2000b: figure 152.16, 152.19). This may be some variant of the RE glyph or what was earlier (Rice 1983, 1989) termed the "split representation" serpent motif. A Topoxté example may have Zip monsters on the sides. One possible identification of this motif is through some connection to the "bearded sky," "bearded dragon," or "beard and scroll" motif or to the "cursive eye" motif found on skybands (Carlson and Landis 1985). Alternatively, it might be a version of the "maize foliage" on either side of an ajaw head on some Late Classic Codex-style pottery (e.g., Fields 1994: 314–315). These motifs frequently incorporate lines of dots outlining or paralleling the major areas of dark red. These dots may parallel the dots or drops in Classic art as well as in the glyph and phonetic sign *k'u*, 'sacred, divine,' but ticks and dots are also devices to indicate hair or fur on an animal, and we wonder if these motifs might represent tarantulas' hairy appearance. However, little in these motifs suggests unambiguous identification of a tarantula—for example, eight legs—compared to the profiled reptilian head.

Finally, still other examples of Chompoxté Red-on-cream: Akalché variety exhibit abstract but vaguely serpentine motifs that seem to be in this same general category but occur in fairly large panels (Figure 11.7). The closest parallels to these motifs are found on certain examples of Mixteca-Puebla types from Cholula (Lind 1994: 98; McCafferty 2001: 70, figure 4.28b, e).

Spatial Contexts of Iconography at Zacpetén

Many decorative motifs on Xiw/Kowoj–related Postclassic pottery are found throughout Late Postclassic Mesoamerica as part of the so-called international style: stepped pyramid, step-fret, squared spiral, RE glyph, hooks, God M eye, and abstract-cursive motifs. This pottery was particularly found in the oratorios of the temple assemblages at both Zacpetén (especially Group A) and Topoxté. At Topoxté Island, resemblances between Kowoj and Mixteca-Puebla (or Cholula) pottery are most evident in the CCP ware from Structure E, the oratorio of the temple assemblage (pers. obs.; see also Hermes 2000b).[3] Although one might expect temples to yield abundant pottery with elaborate decoration, it may not be found there because the pottery used in various rituals was often broken and discarded after use. Oratorios, however, were

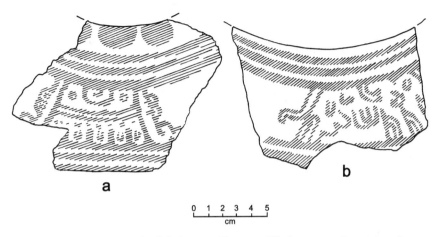

Figure 11.7. *"Abstract-cursive" designs on Chompoxté Red-on-cream incurving-rim bowls from Topoxté: (a) note Venus/star symbols on external panel borders. Redrawn from Hermes 2000b: figure 152.16. (b) Redrawn from Hermes 2000b: figure 152.19.*

suggested to have been "used by male members of the family for retirement purposes before important ceremonies" (Proskouriakoff 1962a: 90), and there is no mention of cleaning them before or after rituals. Thus, elaborately decorated pottery used for pre-ritual preparations may have been allowed to accumulate or may have been reused in these structures. In addition to different discard rates between oratorios and temples, pottery intended for use in temples may have had a prescribed or restricted decorative program, whereas that for oratorio use might not have been restricted.

In Petén, international style motifs occur on pottery excavated from both ceremonial complexes and domestic groups at Zacpetén and the Topoxté Islands. Zacpetén has two main loci of ritual activity, Groups A and C, which may represent different social units within the Kowoj group; five different sites of residential architecture were excavated (Pugh 2001, Chapters 7, 8, and 9, this volume).

In Group A, Postclassic slipped plates bearing the decorative motifs described previously were excavated from Structures 602/605 (temple and oratorio), 603 (*sakbe*), and 606 and 615 (colonnaded halls) (Table 11.2). The majority of the decorated sherds are Macanché Red-on-paste (SIP ware) and Chompoxté Red-on-cream: Akalché variety (CCP ware). These vessels are decorated with red paint, have banded decorative zones, and include a wide variety of decorative motifs. Pottery from the two colonnaded halls also includes the allover red-on-paste decoration of Chompoxté Red-on-cream: Chompoxté variety and Macanché Red-on-paste. For the most part, decorated pottery in Group A is from primary refuse pits, ceremonial refuse deposits, or both (Pugh 2001: 264). These sherds also include numerous image and non-

Table 11.2. Decorative motifs in Group A at Zacpetén.

	Str. 603 Sakbe	Between Str. 602 & 605	Str. 605 Oratorio	Str. 606 Colonn. Hall	Str. 615 Open Hall
Hook/curl	–	M	M	–	M
Mat motif	–	M	–	M	M
Embedded triangles	–	–	–	CA, M	–
Ajaw glyph	–	–	–	–	–
Ak'b'al glyph	–	M	CA, M	–	–
Zip monster	–	–	M	–	–
Bird or feathered serpent	–	–	–	M	–
Banded	S, CA	–	M, CA	CA	CA
Decoration but no banding	–	–	–	M	CC
Circles	–	–	–	–	–

Key: CA = Chompoxté Red-on-cream: Akalché variety
CC = Chompoxté Red-on-cream: Chompoxté variety
M = Macanché Red-on-paste: Macanché variety
S = Sacá Polychrome: Sacá variety

image censer fragments, bone, shell, gold foil, a smashed Topoxté Red drum, and quincunx cups (ibid.: 243–244).

At Group C, the smaller temple assemblage at Zacpetén, Postclassic slipped pottery with discernible Kowoj decorative motifs occurs in or around all of the structures except Structure 766 (the elongated shrine) in this group. This pottery exhibits several differences from that of Group A (Table 11.3). First, more types are present, with the addition of Canté Polychrome (red-and-black paint) and Pastel Polychrome (black paint) in CCP ware; these types are found primarily at the Topoxté Islands and are rare elsewhere. Second, with the exception of Macanché Red-on-paste and two Sacá Polychrome sherds, decorated pottery of SIP ware is not common. Finally, in addition to hook, mat, and Ak'b'al motifs, one vessel in Group C has a representation of the ajaw glyph.

Although most of the pottery bearing motifs associated with Kowoj identity was recovered from ceremonial refuse deposits in Group C, the temple (Structure 764) had three unique depositional loci that may relate directly to ritual activities: inside the temple, on the northwest side, and outside the southern wall. Inside Structure 764, fourteen incensarios were terminated through smash-and-scatter activity, and fragments of five plates were recovered between the altar and the columns of the facade; decoration on the pottery included hook and Ak'b'al motifs. At the northwest corner, two Chompoxté Red-on-cream: Akalché variety plates were found, with a band of mat and hook motifs; two spindle whorls and an animal claw/talon were also in this deposit (Pugh 2001: 373). The third deposit, against the south wall, included

Table 11.3. Decorative motifs in Group C at Zacpetén.

	Str. 764 Temple	*Str. 765*	*Str. 767*
Hook/curl	CA	CA, M	–
Mat motif	CA, M	CA, CC	CA
Embedded triangles	–	–	–
Ajaw glyph	–	–	CA
Ak'b'al glyph	CA, M	M	–
Zip monster	–	–	–
Bird or feathered serpent	–	–	–
Banded	M, P, S, CA	CA, M, P, S	C, CA, P
Decoration but no banding	CC	–	–
Circles	–	–	–

Key: C = Canté Polychrome: Canté variety
CA = Chompoxté Red-on-cream: Akalché variety
CC = Chompoxté Red-on-cream: Chompoxté variety
M = Macanché Red-on-paste: Macanché variety
P = Pastel Polychrome: Pastel variety
S = Sacá Polychrome: Sacá variety

one Chompoxté Red-on-cream: Akalché variety plate with an Ak'b'al motif. This deposit—which contained bone, shell, cache vessels, censers, human teeth, obsidian, and chert notched points—represents a concentration of ceremonial refuse that may have resulted from sweeping activities at the beginning of rituals such as new year's ceremonies (Pugh 2001: 370).

In addition to the two ceremonial groups (A and C), decorated plates were also recovered from three domestic groups: Structures 732, 747/748, and 719. Structure 732, a domestic structure downhill from temple Structure 764, had a deposit on its southeast side that included Chompoxté Red-on-cream and Macanché Red-on-paste vessels. The plates and collared bowls had hook, embedded triangle, Ak'b'al, and circle motifs. South of Structure 748, two Sacá Polychrome (SIP ware) plates and one Chompoxté Red-on-cream plate were recovered in a secondary refuse deposit (Pugh 2001: 453). The motifs of the Sacá plates included embedded triangles and hooks, and the Chompoxté plate motif was a hook. Compared to all other structures at Zacpetén with decorated pottery, Structure 719's pottery displays the greatest variety of decorative programs and decorative motifs, particularly mats (Table 11.4).

Discussion: Some Comparisons

From the previous survey, it is evident that the decoration on the Petén Postclassic pottery that we believe indicates Xiw/Kowoj identity demonstrates strong continuities with lowland Maya pottery of the Late Classic period (Table 11.5). It is also evident that these decorative styles and iconography show similarities with contemporaneous pottery elsewhere in Mesoamerica, as close as the northern Maya lowlands and as distant as south-central Mexico.

Table 11.4. Occurrence of decorative motifs at domestic structures at Zacpetén

	Str. 719	Str. 720	Str. 721	Str. 732	Str.747/748
Hook/curl	P, S, CA	–	–	CA	CA, S
Mat motif	CC, CA, M	–	–	–	–
Embedded triangles	M, S	S	–	CA	S
Ajaw glyph	–	–	–	–	–
Ak'b'al glyph	CA, P	–	–	CA	–
Zip monster	CA	–	–	–	–
Bird or feathered serpent	–	–	–	–	–
Banded	C, CA, P, S	–	CA, M	CA, M	CA, M
Decoration but no banding	CC	–	–	CC	CC
Circles	M	–	–	CA	–

Key: C = Canté Polychrome: Canté variety
CA = Chompoxté Red-on-cream: Akalché variety
CC = Chompoxté Red-on-cream: Chompoxté variety
M = Macanché Red-on-paste: Macanché variety
P = Pastel Polychrome: Pastel variety
S = Sacá Polychrome: Sacá variety

Classic Maya Pottery

The Postclassic Maya seemed to "recycle" traits of earlier pottery into their own late vessels (Masson 2003: 197), a practice also evident in the incorporation of carved Classic monuments and dressed stone blocks into Postclassic buildings at Zacpetén. This is not simply casual, ad hoc copying but rather deliberate maintenance of cultural continuities and identification with, and appropriation of, the past and ancestors. Postclassic Petén pottery, particularly Xiw/Kowoj pottery, demonstrates numerous continuities with that of the Classic Maya in technology, decorative motifs, and layouts.

Background colors. Studies of Late Classic Petén pottery have noted distinct differences between eastern and western regions. Robert Rands (1973) distinguished two elite traditions, polychrome and fine paste wares, in the east and west, respectively. Within the polychrome tradition, Antonia Foias (1996: 572) noted differences in background colors, with orange polychromes more common in the Pasión and western areas and cream polychromes more prevalent in central-eastern Petén and Belize.

The pottery of the Xiw/Kowoj in Petén seems to represent a continuation of the cream polychrome tradition, in that its hallmark is red paint on the cream background of CCP ware. The use of a cream underslip is common in several Late Classic Petén polychromes, chiefly Zacatal and Julecki Cream Polychromes, and also some orange polychromes such as Saxche and Palmar. There do not appear to be direct continuities between Kowoj pottery and any

Table 11.5. Occurrence of motifs on Petén Postclassic pottery, comparing decorated Clemencia Cream Paste-ware types to Snail-Inclusion Paste-ware types, Classic skybands, and some central Mexican Postclassic pottery.

	Clemencia Cream Paste Ware				Snail-Inclusion Paste Ware			Classic	Central
	Chom	Akal	Pastel	Top I^	Sacá	MacRp	Pax*	Skyband	Mexico**
GLYPHIC									
Hook (*mu, yi*)		X	X	X	X	X	X		X
Mat/braid (*pop*)		X		X	X	X	X	X	
Ajaw		X							
Ak'b'al		X	X			X	X	X	X
Zip		X				X	X	X	X
Lamat/Venus							X	X	X
K'in					?				X
Kan cross									X
Etz'nab'									X
GEOMETRIC									
Emb. triang.#		X		X	X	X	X	X	X
Chevrons		X		X		X	?		X
Squared spiral		X				X	X		X
Crossed bands								X	
Step-fret^^		X		X		X			X
Stepped pyramids		X		X			X		X
Circles##	X	X		X			X	X	X
Mirror/shield						X			
NATURALISTIC									
Feathers	?	?				X	X	X	X
Serpent							X		X
Segment#								X	

continued on next page

Table 11.5—continued

| | Clemencia Cream Paste Ware | | | | Snail-Inclusion Paste Ware | | | Classic | Central |
	Chom	Akal	Pastel	Top I^	Sacá	MacRp	Pax*	Skyband	Mexico**
RE									
Jaws				X			X		X
Bones								X	X
ABSTRACT									
Unknown	X			X		X			
Illuitl (beard and scroll)				X			X	X	X
"Cursive eye"				?			X	X	X
GODS									X
God M									X

^ At the Topoxté Islands themselves (recent excavations; pers. obs.; Hermes 2000b).

^^ Sharp (1978) relates step-frets to serpent imagery (see Ringle, Gallareta Negrón, and Bey 1998: 195).

* All types and varieties in Paxcamán except Macanché Red-on-paste and Sacá Polychrome.

** As noted in sources and figures cited in text only.

Embedded triangles may be "serpent segments" (see Carlson and Landis 1985: 126).

These typically have a smaller circle in the center and are variously described as eyes, jade symbols, stars, and similar elements. There is also the "two eyes" symbol that resembles the Venus glyph.

of the seven Classic-period painting "styles" identified by Dorie Reents-Budet (1994), although similarities in color palette to the Holmul style can be suggested. This style combines orange and red paints on a whitish background and was apparently manufactured around Holmul, Naranjo, and western Belize (Reents-Budet 1994: 179–185).

Polychromes in gray to brown SIP ware frequently exhibit a cream underslip on the decorative band. Painted lines created the circumferential bands, with motifs painted in the bands in black as in Ixpop Polychrome (less commonly in red or red-and-black paint), and then the red slip was applied. The slip was often carelessly applied, such that it overlapped the decorative bands—often appearing as a thin, translucent orange slip (similar to the "gloss ware" overslips of Classic polychromes).[4] Alternatively, the black-painted decoration may appear directly on the tan/orangey color of well-fired (oxidized) paste; this seems to be a later trait and is also noted in Pek Polychrome of the Augustine group. Ixpop Polychrome (and SIP ware pottery in general) is common in the central and western Petén lakes, including Zacpetén in Lake Salpetén, and we consider it, along with Augustine group pottery, an Itza identifier.[5] SIP pottery is not found at Topoxté in Lake Yaxhá, where Clemencia Cream Paste ware appears to have been manufactured.

The Classic cream background remained important through the Postclassic period in the eastern lakes area, whereas in the western lakes region the Classic orange background remained important through the Postclassic.

Banded decoration. Banded decoration, with one or two encircling lines defining the top and bottom of the band, was long used in the Maya area. It is also associated with the Early Postclassic international symbol set (Boone and Smith 2003: 189), although usually on bowl exteriors rather than interiors, as in Petén Postclassic pottery. As discussed, the elements in bands on Kowoj pottery can be compared with those of the Maya skyband, well-known from Classic-period art and iconography (particularly sculptural rather than ceramic) as well as Postclassic codices. Skybands represent the body of the bicephalic dragon or monster, which embodies both celestial and terrestrial realms of the Maya world (Carlson and Landis 1985). Classic skybands may incorporate any of thirteen main signs or elements: *k'in* (sun or day), Ak'b'al, lunar symbol, Venus/Lamat, paired circles or "two-eyes," *kan* cross, serpent segment, sun deity, "mirror/shield" pendant, and four elements described as closely associated with the bicephalic creature itself: Zip monster, crossed bands (the most common element in skybands), "bearded sky," and "beard and scrolls." Other elements, infrequent in occurrence, include God C head, Kab'an, Imix, Kawak, Etz'nab, shell, bones or crossed bones, and single-twist mat elements, which may conflate with crossed bands.

Many elements in Classic skybands have origins in Olmec (Middle Preclassic) art and iconography (Carlson and Landis 1985), revealing their deep roots in Mesoamerican cosmology. The skyband signs or motifs can be reduced into three primary themes: celestial phenomena, days in the 260-day *tzolk'in* calendar, and reptilians/saurians—particularly Itzamna, the creature(s) personified by the skyband itself. At least two of these themes, day glyphs and reptilian/saurian signs, continue in the decorative bands of Postclassic Maya pottery in Petén.

Differences. A hallmark of elite Late Classic painted pottery—the depiction of human figures, deity impersonators, and elite ritual scenes—is conspicuously absent in Petén Postclassic pottery, in contrast to northern Yucatán (Smith 1971, 1: 64–65). One Chompoxté Red-on-cream sherd from Topoxté shows a human head (Hermes 2000b: figure 152-17).

Differences between Petén Classic and Postclassic slipped and decorated pottery are also evident in forms: Postclassic vessel assemblages lack the cylindrical beaker-like vases (cacao-drinking vessels) common in the Late Classic period; Kowoj tripod plates are smaller, often considerably so, than Classic forms;[6] and decorated jars are common in the Postclassic. The significance of these differences probably relates to the kinds of foods served, whether the context is domestic or ritual, and whether the serving style is for individuals or communal. Vessels at the Itza capital of Tayasal (Flores Island) are markedly larger, as are plates and jars from Mayapán in Yucatán (pers. obs.), suggesting that their communal feasts involved different consumption patterns from those accompanying Xiw/Kowoj rituals.

Highland Mexican Pottery

Antecedents to the Late Postclassic Mixteca-Puebla style bear striking similarities to Late Classic Maya polychrome pottery, leading to the conclusion that "Mixteca-Puebla polychromes may have been derived, with modification," from Maya styles (Lind 1994: 98). At Cholula, early hemispherical bowls of Cristina Polychrome, dating ca. A.D. 1000–1200 and commonly considered a Gulf coast product, display the Maya *k'in* sign and reptile eye (RE) (Plunket Nagoya 1995: 104–106, figure 2). Marta and Estela Polychrome types, ca. 950–1150, also resemble Maya polychromes, particularly those with a cream background (Lind 1994: 98; see also Pohl 2003: 322n2).

Classic Maya polychrome influences are evident in certain motifs on Cocoyotla Black on Natural, Banded Elegante subtype; Cuaxiloa Matte Polychrome; Ocotlán Red Rim, Banded Elegante and Elegante subtypes; and Torre Red and Orange on White Polychrome, especially in the use of herringbones and squared spirals on the latter (McCafferty 2001: figures 4.28b, e, 4.30a, 4.36c, d, and 4.45b, c, respectively). These types date between 900 and 1300, just preceding development of the Mixteca-Puebla style. Some Kowoj designs, particularly the abstract-cursive (reptile?) motifs, are closely related to these Mexican types—particularly Ocotlán Red Rim type, subtype Elegante (McCafferty 2001: figures 4.36b, 4.37; Lind's Estela Polychrome), the earliest polychrome type at Cholula, ca. 1000–1200 (McCafferty 2001: 70). There are also similarities to Cholula's Cocoyotla Black on Natural type, Banded Elegante subtype (McCafferty 2001: figure 4.28b, e; also known as Xicotenco

Black-on-orange [Lind 1994] and Aztec 1). The date for this pottery corresponds to the early part of Ocotlán Red Rim, roughly 1000–1150.

It is also of interest that in Yucatán, central Mexico, and central Petén, Early Postclassic pottery features conspicuous black-painted, banded decoration in tripod dishes. In the southern basin of Mexico this is known as Culhuacan Black-on-orange, in Yucatán it is Peto Cream, and in Petén it is Ixpop Polychrome in SIP ware, with minuscule quantities as Pastel Polychrome in CCP ware. Motifs on Culhuacan Black-on-orange are "floral and so-called glyph-like motifs, including the *caracol* or spiral motif, and representations of serpent jaws and reptile eyes" (Minc, Hodge, and Blackman 1994: 144, figure 6.4) as well as a motif similar to the God M name glyph. Whether common factors underlie this widespread decorative style cannot be determined at present, although vessels with black line painting in Late Classic Petén were well-known as the Codex style. Additional comparisons can be drawn between Petén Postclassic pottery decoration and the red-on brown and red-on-white pottery Laurette Séjourné called Paste Group 8 at Teotihuacan, the former especially common in the Yayahuala residential compound (Séjourné 1966: figures 174, 176, 179, 180, 184, 191).

A study of the Late Postclassic Mixteca-Puebla "horizon" style itself (Ramsey 1982: 33, citing Nicholson 1960: 614) identified a broad range of motifs and symbols central to that style, including deities and their insignia, day signs in the Mexican 260-day calendar, and zoomorphic signs (e.g., serpent, jaguar, deer, rabbit, spider) but also solar, lunar, and jade disks; celestial and terrestrial bands; Venus; human body parts (skull, skeleton, heart, eye); water and fire motifs; shields, arrows, banners; mountains, feather balls, flowers, stepped frets, and shells.

Importantly, the international style in Mexico incorporates regional and ethnic variations (Pohl 2003): for example, Eastern Nahua decoration displays motifs such as skulls and crossed bones, suggesting a theme of human sacrifice; Mixtec and Zapotec variants share other motifs, but Mixtec pottery has narrative scenes that Zapotec vessels lack. A detailed analysis and tabulation of motifs on two Mixteca-Puebla pottery styles (Lind 1994) included those we identified on Postclassic Kowoj pottery: step-frets, feathers, dots, circles with dots, spots with dots, hooks, *ilhuitls,* and so on. These elements typically appear in secondary design contexts on Mexican polychromes—that is, on the rim and basal bands—while on Petén pottery these bands are generally the primary decoration.

A smaller group of motifs seems to have been common to Mixtec, as opposed to Mixteca-Puebla, art: the "celestial band," comprising the butterfly, flower, S-curve (resembling the Maya *muyal*), and *ilhuitl*; and hands, skull, crosses, and crossbones (Ramsey 1982: 33). These may be signifiers of Mixtec identity, in the same way we find elements diagnostic of Xiw/Kowoj identity within the overall Petén style. Petén decorated pottery lacks the Mixtec hand, skull, and cross constellation; we might speculate that perhaps hands did not appear because they were common Maya glyphs and could be too literally read.

Compared with Epiclassic and Postclassic pottery elsewhere in Meso-america, for example, south-central Mexico, the Petén Postclassic motif reper-toire is relatively limited and the decoration more sparingly used.

Postclassic Yucatán Pottery

The closest similarities to Kowoj pottery in Petén can be found in San Joaquin Buff ware and Mayapán Red ware pottery (pers. obs.). Mayapán Red ware (Smith 1971, 1: 23) is characterized by a cream-colored carbonate paste that is visually nearly identical to that of Clemencia Cream Paste ware. The primary differences between the two are that Topoxté pottery is finer in tex-ture and has thinner walls; Mayapán Red ware (Mamá Red type) is distinctly coarser or sandier, vessels have thicker walls, and the general impression is one of greater size and weight.

Of particular interest here is Tecoh Red-on-buff type in San Joaquin Buff ware (basically identical to Mayapán Red ware). Tecoh Red-on-buff has two varieties, Tecoh and outline-incised; with respect to the latter, Hermes (2000b: figure 152.4) illustrated an unnamed "incised bichrome" type in his Chompoxté ceramic group. Our own examination of Tecoh Red-on-buff sherds from Mayapán revealed considerably more variation than originally suggested by Smith's (1971, 1: 29, 231–232) description. Importantly, much of the decoration is painted in the distinctive curvilinear style of Chompoxté Red-on-cream: Chompoxté variety (CCP ware) and Macanché Red-on-paste (SIP ware) (Rice 1979: 40–41).

Tecoh occurred only in the Tases phase (1300–1450) at Acanceh, Chich'en Itza, Maní, and Mayapán and had "no immediate Yucatán predecessor" (Smith 1971, 1: 29, 231). Thus, Late Postclassic potters in Xiw territory in west-ern Yucatán were making pottery exhibiting the same decorative style we associate with the Mayapán-derived Xiw/Kowoj peoples in the eastern Petén lakes region. It is not yet possible for us to assign temporal priority of one over the other. Traditional arguments based on the Kowoj's late flight from Mayapán would suggest that Chompoxté is a later copy of Tecoh, with the Xiw/Kowoj of Petén copying the Tecoh pottery of their homeland. We sus-pect, however, on the basis of earlier project excavations at Canté and Topoxté islands and the lack of stylistic precursors in Yucatán, that the curvilinear design of Chompoxté Red-on-cream: Chompoxté variety is earlier than Tecoh Red-on-buff. Macanché Red-on-paste is a late local copy of Chompoxté Red-on-cream: Chompoxté variety using different clay resources.

Conclusions

The Xiw/Kowoj in the eastern Petén lake basins followed the same decora-tive canon as Postclassic potters throughout the lakes region and incorporated iconography widely shared throughout Mesoamerica in the so-called inter-national style. By the Late Postclassic and Contact periods, a time of political strife and contested boundaries, their repertoire of technological and stylistic choices had evolved into an ethno-politically distinct decorative program. Its elements include:

- The use of a cream-colored marly clay (Clemencia Cream Paste ware).

- A design layout covering the entire interior of plates, along with the banded arrangement.

- Dark red– (Chompoxté Red-on-cream and Macanché Red-on-paste) and red-and-black– (Canté Polychrome and Sacá Polychrome) painted decoration. Although black paint was also used alone (Pastel Polychrome) and incising appears (Dulces Incised), these variants are rare.

- Glyph-like motifs (especially day signs in the 260-day calendar), hooks, feathers, mats/braids, and stepped terraces.

- Very late additions include use of SIP paste, purplish slip, squared spirals, nested chevrons, decoration on interior and exterior, use of stepped flanges, and a deemphasis of banding. These additions may roughly coincide with the appearance of Kulut Modeled censers.

The ethno-political style of Xiw/Kowoj slipped and decorated pottery in eastern Petén, then, combines choices about paste, decoration placement, colors, and motifs.

This distinctive style appears on a suite of vessel forms found throughout the lakes area and broadly in the Maya lowlands: footed tripod plates, bowls, and necked and neckless jars. Secondary form characteristics vary from region to region, such as details of necks and rims, supports (primarily bulbous or short cylinders), and dish bases (slightly rounded rather than flat). It is of interest, however, that although the Early Postclassic international symbol set typically occurred "in horizontal bands around the exteriors of ceramic bowls" (Boone and Smith 2003: 189), Postclassic Petén decoration—banded and non-banded, Kowoj and non-Kowoj—was primarily placed on the interiors of dishes and collared bowls. This placement suggests that the decorative motifs on these vessels were not deployed to send messages of identity affiliation to external groups or to boast of participation in whatever was signaled by the international symbol set. Instead, these vessels seemingly were used in Xiw/Kowoj–only contexts, or the motifs (especially the allover decoration) were highly related to Kowoj-specific ritual use. Necked and neckless jars have their decoration on the exteriors, a placement dictated at least in part by morphology, so little can be inferred as to function. It is only as part of the very late stylistic developments of Xiw/Kowoj pottery that decoration came to appear on the exteriors of dishes.

To evaluate this proposition, however, it is necessary to differentiate the styles of the Xiw/Kowoj from those of their enemies, the Itza, in Postclassic- and Contact-period Petén. We believe we have some preliminary bases for doing so, but these propositions—which emerged around twenty years ago—must be tested by excavations in Itza territory in the western Petén. Rice (1989: 315) suggested that Late Postclassic Petén lakes decorated pottery can be described and categorized through a series of oppositions: (1) decorative medium: painting *or* incising; (2) if painted, colors: red *or* black; (3) if incised, type: fine *or* groove; (4) location of the decoration: interior *or* exterior; (5) layouts: non-banded *or* banded; and (6) motifs. We can now see that the Xiw/ Kowoj decorative program represents the first listed of some of these — painting, red color, and non-banded layout — but also a late combination of modes: red *and* black painting, interior *and* exterior decoration.

The alternatives in this scheme — black painting, incising, and banded decoration — are likely to represent Itza ethno-political style. Snail-Inclusion Paste ware itself may be associated with the Itza, although its complex patterns of broad spatial and long temporal distribution in central Petén suggest that this may be too simplistic an identifier. The ware is traditionally linked to the western lakes, especially Lake Petén Itzá, although substantial quantities of SIP ware were recovered at Zacpetén, Macanché, and Tipu; virtually none has been found at the Topoxté islands. At Zacpetén and Macanché, unusual combinations of attributes, such as pastes similar to SIP in Terminal Classic vessel forms and volcanic ash in Early Postclassic forms, suggest that potters were exploring different combinations of resources and new forms during this transitional interval.

Black-painted decoration is common on other wares, groups, and types of Postclassic pottery, on which it begins early and lasts late. Black decoration, of which Ixpop Polychrome (SIP) is the best-known example in Petén, might have ultimate ties to the Late Classic Codex-style vessels, the production of which was possibly controlled by Calakmul. Also, Ixpop and other decorated SIP-ware types exhibit technological continuities with certain Late and Terminal Classic polychromes in central Petén. Ixpop Polychrome and Picú Incised commonly display reptilian motifs (P. Rice 1983, 1986, 1989) — either painted profiled snakes with open jaws or the RE glyph — and incised braids, suggesting links to the Quetzalcoatl cult widespread in Mesoamerica during the Epiclassic period. In particular, black-painted decoration on Petén pottery might be related to Peto Cream ware of Chich'en Itza (see Milbrath and Peraza Lope 2003; Ringle, Gallaretta Negrón, and Bey 1998: 189–192), as part of what Ringle, Gallareta Negrón, and Bey (1998: 185) have called an "Early International style."

If these proposed affiliations are correct — that SIP ware and black-painted decoration are Itza markers and CCP ware and red-painted decoration are Xiw/Kowoj identifiers — then the late combination of modes on CCP ware suggests a melding of the two. That is, the combined red *and* black painting and interior *and* exterior decoration on Xiw/Kowoj pottery may reflect the late alliance between the Kowoj and the Chak'an Itza faction on the northwestern shore of Lake Petén Itzá. Information on matri- vs. patri-locality of residence would likely shed needed light on this complex issue.

It is also important to consider the function of these vessels. At Zacpetén, pottery in the Xiw/Kowoj–related style was found in both temple assemblages and domestic structures. Because of their frequent recovery in temples and oratorios, and because some of the pottery is decorated with glyphs that represent *tzolk'in* calendar days (Ak'b'al and Ajaw; also Lamat at Ixlú) or relate to the cycling of the *ja'ab'* (Pop), we believe it is likely that these vessels were used in calendrical ceremonies.

With respect to the 260-day calendar, the Codices Dresden and Madrid depict two types of vessels on their yearbearer pages: composite censers and footed bowls holding various types of offerings, such as tamales. Ak'b'al and Lamat are yearbearers in the "Campeche calendar," introduced to southwestern Yucatán in the Late Classic period, and although this calendar is considered the predecessor of the Contact-period Mayapán calendar, the latter employed a different set of yearbearers. Ak'b'al motifs were particularly common in Group C at Zacpetén, and these vessels may have been used in rituals and feasts as part of yearbearer ceremonies every four years.[7]

In the case of the 365-day calendar, three categories of rituals were observed in Yucatán—monthly, new year, and *k'atun*-ending—and these rituals were likely celebrated in Petén as well. Certain ceremonies were dedicated to the gods of various months (see Landa in Tozzer 1941: 151–166), accompanied by the burning of incense and feasting. Associated serving vessels might have been reused repeatedly and kept in the residences of the elites who sponsored such events. According to Bishop Landa, elaborate celebrations were associated with the five Wayeb' days at the end of a year and the first four days of Pop (which coincided with the arrival of the new yearbearer)—the first month of the new year—involving food, drink, and incense offered to "idols" as well as participants (ibid.: 151–153; also Bill, Hernandez, and Bricker 2000: table 2). On the first day of Pop/new year, houses (and perhaps temples) were swept and old utensils such as plates and jars were thrown away as part of a renewal process to purify the area (Landa in Tozzer 1941: 103), which might account for the deposits of ritual refuse in the Zacpetén temple assemblages. It is possible that plates were made anew and decorated to reflect these special days as well as the new year. The Ajaw and Pop mat/braid glyphs on Xiw/Kowoj pottery may be associated with these new year's or other calendrical ceremonies. Ajaw glyphs might more specifically indicate *k'atun*-cycling ceremonies, perhaps signifying the "plate of the *k'atun*," because *k'atuns* are counted by Ajaw ending days.

The "Kowoj style" might be further differentiated by archaeological sites. For example, CCP ware pottery at Topoxté has more design variability and complexity—in types and varieties as well as in motifs, especially unbanded decoration—than seen at other Kowoj sites. This may be explained by the Topoxté Xiw/Kowoj producing and trading out CCP ware with simplified key identity markers (e.g., motifs, color) and keeping the more elaborately decorated pieces for themselves. In addition, day glyph signs were not noted on CCP ware at Topoxté Island, but they are present at Zacpetén in both Groups A and C (Ajaw and Ak'b'al), reinforcing our suggestion that these vessels were used in calendrical rituals at Zacpetén.

The Postclassic period in Mesoamerica was one in which many societies produced material culture that reflected their socio-ethnic or regional identities as well as their participation in a larger "international" network of stylistic interaction that facilitated communication, commercial exchanges, and cultural integration (Smith and Berdan 2003b: 8). We see the decorative style and iconography of Kowoj pottery as one of many local expressions within this network. It is less flamboyant than the Mixteca-Puebla style of pottery in south-central Mexico, but nonetheless it shares features of layout (banded and paneled zones) and motifs (e.g., hooks, feathers, chevrons) with that larger style. To these features the Xiw/Kowoj added day signs and mats and introduced red- and red-and-black–painted decoration, as well as the "all-over" decoration of feathers, swirls, and dots of Chompoxté Red-on-cream: Chompoxté variety and Macanché Red-on-paste.

This last, what might be called the "signature" Kowoj decorative program, has no clear parallels either locally or in the Postclassic international style and its symbol sets. This suggests that the Xiw/Kowoj of Petén and a Kowoj faction of their Xiw allies at Mayapán (makers and users of Tecoh Red-on-buff) wished to set themselves apart from such an identification. By conspicuously rejecting the widespread and long-standing restrained, banded decorative layout—especially executed in black paint—that had dominated Petén pottery throughout the lakes area since the Early Postclassic period, it appears that the Kowoj were not only displaying their own distinctive identity but were also proclaiming their resistance against the aggressive Itza and their stance vis-à-vis the Spaniards.

Acknowledgments

The authors express their appreciation to Susan Milbrath for facilitating access to Mayapán ceramic collections in the INAH Ceramoteca in Mérida, Yucatán, in July 2004. Susan introduced us to Silviane Bouchet and Carlos Peraza Lope of INAH, who opened their ceramic collections for us to study; we are grateful to them for their time, interest, and stimulating intellectual exchange.

Subsequently, with the generous cooperation of Marilyn Masson and Carlos Peraza Lope, we returned to the Mayapán ceramic lab in Telchaquillo in March 2008 for Leslie to take samples of slipped Postclassic for NSF-supported petrographic and INAA analyses. We were able to study further the Tecoh pottery recovered from the site, and we are again indebted, particularly to Carlos, for facilitating our studies.

Notes

1. Late Xiw/Kowoj decorated pottery employed various icons identified as boundary markers in the international style—chevrons, mats/twists, frets/terraces—as primary decorative motifs. Stepped terraces, for example, were not only primary painted motifs in bands but also modeled flanges at the angled join of vessel walls to the base. Their significance, symbolic or use-related, cannot be determined.

2. The two species of tarantula found throughout the Yucatán peninsula are similar in appearance, as highlighted by their common names—*Brachypelma epicureanum*, the "Yucatán Rust-rump," and *B. vagans*, the "Mexican Red-rump" (also "Mexican black velvet")—so named because reddish hairs cover the abdomens of their otherwise black bodies. Their overall coloring includes black, red, and cream, as the round carapace

of their cephalothorax is ringed with white or cream color and features thin radiating lines; sometimes it takes on a pinkish color. The adjoining two small proximal sections of the legs also may be cream-colored. According to theraposodist Rick C. West (pers. com., May 2004), the black-and-red coloration is brightest right after molting, then fades to a duller brown or reddish brown. The molt takes place at the beginning of the rainy season. It is tempting to suggest a "watery Underworld" association for these tarantulas, given that they burrow in the earth, emerge at dusk, and molt at the beginning of the rainy season.

3. In William Bullard's (1970) earlier excavations into the temple assemblage on Topoxté Island, he recovered most of the slipped pottery of Topoxté Red near the temple, Structure C; between the temple and Structure D; and in the open hall, Structure F. Decoration included hooks, plumes/feathers, circles with dots, squared spiral, stepped pyramid, and abstract-cursive motifs.

4. Another Postclassic ceramic group, the Trapeche group in SIP ware, is often completely double slipped, with a red to reddish-brown slip covered with a waxy, translucent overslip.

5. These traits of Itza Postclassic polychromes represent continuities with Classic-period practices for creating surfaces upon which to paint decoration. That is, the two Late and Terminal Classic orange polychrome types common in central Petén, Palmar and Saxche, had a white underslip painted over the generally light brown paste surface, much in the same way codices and modern painters' canvases are sized with lime or gesso to create a smooth white surface for painting. Paint was applied over this underslip, then a thin, glossy, translucent orange coating was applied. In Saxche Orange Polychrome, this coating covered the entire painted area; in Palmar Orange Polychrome, the underslip was not completely covered, leaving the "cream" background color in negative as part of the design (P. Culbert, pers. com., June 16, 2005).

6. In contrast, Early Postclassic Paxcamán Red and Ixpop Polychrome tripod dishes (SIP ware) are often fairly large in diameter, with disproportionately tall, trumpet-shaped supports.

7. In the very late seventeenth century, the new years began in mid-June, such that Ak'b'al years were from mid-1693 to mid-1694, 1697–1698, and 1701–1702, for example. Ak'b'al (associated with East and red) years were followed by Lamat (North, white) years, then B'en (West, black), and Etz'nab' (South, yellow).

INCENSE BURNERS AND
OTHER RITUAL CERAMICS

—— Prudence M. Rice ——————————————————————

During the Postclassic period, as in earlier Preclassic and Classic times, Maya public and private rituals incorporated specialized containers to hold, transport, or process various substances essential to the proceedings. Of these, the most common were pottery vessels for the burning of resins, particularly *pom* incense (the sap of the copal tree, *Protium copal*), which archaeologists refer to as incense burners, censers, and incensarios (or sometimes braziers/*braseros*). The Spaniards decried these vessels, which continued to be made and used clandestinely well after conquest, as "idols," and missionaries and clergy considered them irrefutable evidence that the Maya were "heathens," "pagans," and "idolaters." The Spaniards "were not always precise in their own verbal distinctions" on the subject of idolatry (Farriss 1984: 209), however, carried away by their zeal to extirpate these abominations; as a result, it is difficult to specify the material cultural remains associated with these practices. Nancy Farriss (1984: 290) considers idolatry to refer to "any kind of ritual involving idols," particularly those performed publicly in temples and plazas that "represented the Maya's collective bond with the

276

supernatural." As for the "idols" themselves, they seem to be among the various objects of clay, wood, stone, or metal also referred to as images, statues, braziers, and even "demons."

The sheer quantities of these objects appalled the Spaniards. Franciscan Bishop Diego de Landa noted that the sixteenth-century Maya of northern Yucatán had "such a great quantity of idols that even those of their gods were not enough; for there was not an animal or insect of which they did not make a statue, and they made all these in the images of the gods and goddesses . . . it was the custom that each idol should have its little brazier in which they should burn their incense to it" (in Tozzer 1941: 161). At Tipu (Belize) in 1619, decades after the establishment of a mission church, Franciscan friars Bartolomé de Fuensalida and Juan de Orbita were shown "a great multitude of idols, so many that Father Fuensalida says they could not be counted. . . . The Father destroyed all that they found and threw them into the deepest part of the [Macal] river" (Jones 1989: 149, citing Diego López de Cogolludo). Similarly, at Nojpeten, the Itza island capital and center of resistance in Lake Petén Itzá, Spanish officers and soldiers culminated their brutal attack and defeat of the Itza in 1697 by spending "the entire remaining part of the day . . . accomplishing nothing more than the breaking of idols, some of which they found *arranged in pairs on top of small benches*" (Jones 1998: 302, emphasis added).

The Petén Postclassic Incensario Subcomplex

The great variety of pottery censer forms from the Middle Preclassic through Colonial periods can be generally differentiated into two broad categories, which I call image and composite (or non-image). Image censers have attached anthropomorphic or zoomorphic elements in varying degrees of elaboration; composite (or non-image) censers may have applied or impressed decoration, the most enduring of which consists of spikes. Each period of Maya (pre-)history features its own variations of these two basic kinds of incense burners, accompanied by other pottery forms for caches, drinking cups, drums, figurines, and so on, and recovered in their own temporally specific contexts of use or disposal.

In the category of image censers, the most distinctive vessels in the Late Postclassic lowland ritual subcomplexes are large vases adorned with full-figure effigies of various deities or humans (rarely animals). They are best known from Mayapán and are frequently referred to simply as "Mayapán-style effigy censers." Classified as Chen Mul Modeled type, they consist of two parts—a tall vase and an attached full-figure human or deity effigy: "The vessel form is cylindrical with a high pedestal base. The figure, partly modeled and partly moldmade, is usually created independently in full round and attached to the vessel" (Smith 1971, 1: 74). These effigies are typically "stylized, out of proportion, and rather frozen. . . . The overall effect is similar in general to the representations of gods in the Mixteca-Puebla or international style, as portrayed in the Maya codices and Late Postclassic codex-style murals" (Brown 1999: 322).

These and other styles of Postclassic incense burners and associated ritual ceramics have great potential to illuminate relations among lowland polities, considering their complex iconography displayed via modeled, molded, and painted elements. Although some of these elements are generalized and widely shared, others can be more narrowly tied to particular times, regions, or social groups. Thus, censer form, iconography, typology, and context of recovery provide a material basis for establishing the social and ethno-political identity of the Kowoj and their ancestors in Petén.

Excavations at Zacpetén yielded greater quantities of Postclassic censers than have been recovered at most of the other sites investigated in the region. This is in part the result of an excavation design focused on ritual architecture and ritual behavior (Pugh 2001; Pugh and Rice, Chapter 5, this volume), but it also appears that the site did not experience early visits by Spanish clerics, who typically smashed the "idols" and dumped them in the lakes. Incense burners are described here as a ceramic "subcomplex," a component of a larger ceramic complex that includes the utilitarian wares, serving pieces, trade items, mortuary offerings, and so on that characterize a particular period.

Methods of Analysis

Petén Postclassic incensarios exhibit considerable variation in size, proportion, elaboration, and paste composition. Study of the Zacpetén censers involved organizing this morpho-technological variability, beginning with the clay–temper pastes used in their manufacture. Systematic patterns of technological variability within broad form categories are more useful than form alone in shedding light on production and use, which were of primary interest. Consequently, all incensarios and other pottery from ritual contexts and deposits (frequently accompanying censers) were classified according to the principles of the type-variety system, beginning with paste-ware identification (P. Rice 1976; see Appendix 12.I for ware and type descriptions).

Stylistically, I categorized the Zacpetén incensarios by a combination of embellishment and form into image and non-image, or composite, censers. Postclassic image censers are vases (Figures 12.1, 12.2) with anthropomorphic effigies, either modeled, full-figure attached effigies (Chapters 7 and 9, Figures 7.2, 9.1, this volume) or appliquéd "semi"-effigies. Postclassic composite (non-image) censers occur in two forms. One is a vase, cylindrical to urn-shaped, with a pedestal base and applied or impressed ("composite") decoration, or both (Chapter 7, Figure 7.8, this volume; Figures 12.7, 12.8). This category incorporates form variants often distinguished as biconical, hourglass, or pedestal-based "jars" and "bowls" because I found substantial continuities in contours among them, at least in the Petén samples. A second non-image censer form is a small open bowl or cup with a ring or low pedestal base and composite decoration (Chapter 9, Figure 9.4, this volume). Ladle "censers," noted at Mayapán and elsewhere, are present but not common and show no sign of interior darkening to suggest their actual use in burning incense.

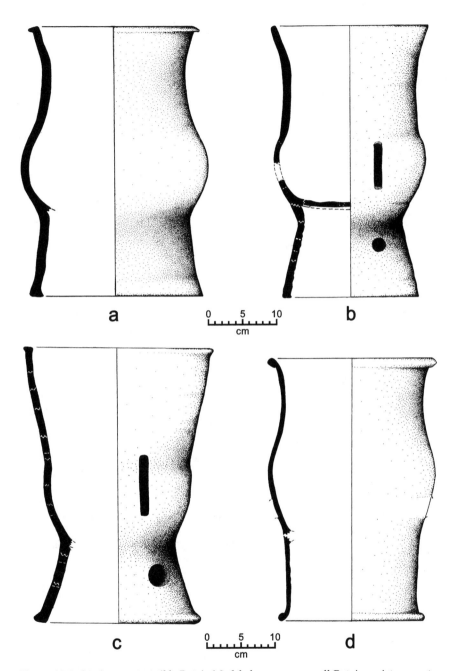

Figure 12.1. Semi-reconstructible Patojo Modeled censer vases, all Patojo variety except (a), showing variations in rim, vase, and base form: (a) Moza variety, Structure 607; (b–c) Structure 764; (d) Structure 602.

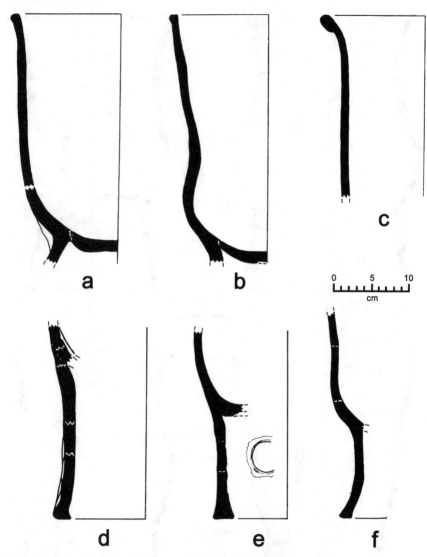

Figure 12.2. Portions of semi-reconstructible Patojo Modeled censer vases and bases:
(a–b) Structure 602; (c) Structure 747/748; (d–f) Structure 764.

A specific objective was to conjoin fragments to establish minimum numbers of individual vessels (MNV) of incensarios in any particular context. In the case of effigies, this process was furthered because, as in human osteology, the human/deity effigies had only one head, two arms, two legs, one breastplate, and so on; limbs could be paired by matching styles of wristbands, sandals, anklets, and other ornamentation. For the vases and the composite censers, I estimated MNV by first separating sherds by paste and then subdividing on the basis of differences in size, form elaboration, and other details of rim and base fragments (using counts but not weights). "Adornos"—small appliqué elements from the costume or vase (e.g., braided pectorals, fingers, spikes, disks)—were abundant, but only rarely could they be used as part of MNV determinations. They did, however, help identify spatial concentrations of incensarios and censer-based ritual activity.

Most vessels were only partially reconstructible, but Timothy Pugh and I feel our estimates of MNV are conservative. We were cautious in naming specific deities represented by the figures because characteristic features indicated by post-fire painted colors were generally missing owing to erosion, but we felt reasonably successful in distinguishing individual effigies. This level of close examination, coupled with mapping of individual censer sherds and concentrations on structure floors at Zacpetén (Pugh 2001), provided an unparalleled opportunity to investigate the role of these vessels in Late Postclassic— and Contact-period ritual at a Xiw/Kowoj–occupied site.

Many Zacpetén censers had been smashed on the floors of the temples and shrines or swept into refuse piles near the substructures (see Pugh and Rice, Chapter 7, this volume). Examination of the interiors of the receptacles revealed that virtually all were blackened and many had layers, sometimes thick and sometimes multiple, of burned resin in the bottom and on the sides. The sooty blackening in the interior frequently appeared in horizontal streaks, suggesting that the incensarios were used repeatedly and the streaks represented careless scraping to remove soot and ash, but thorough cleaning was not deemed necessary.

Image Censers: Full and Semi-Effigy Censer Wares and Types

In Petén, effigy incensarios were first described archaeologically from excavations in Itza-controlled territory around Lake Petén Itzá, including Flores Island and the Tayasal peninsula (Cowgill 1963; also Chase 1983). At these sites censers were comparatively rare, doubtless a consequence of the Spaniards having purged the "idols" immediately after the conquest. To the east in Kowoj territory, effigy censer fragments have been recovered from the Topoxté Islands (Bullard 1970; Hermes 2000b: 196; Rice 1979) and Macanché Island (Rice 1987a: 184–190, 194–197), but the contexts, methods of recovery (lack of piece-plotting), levels of analysis (lack of paste-ware identifications), and small quantities were not conducive to providing special insights into their usage.

The most common full-figure effigy censers at Zacpetén are classified as Patojo Modeled type: Patojo variety, although three other varieties—likely firing variants—have also been identified. Effigies, fairly crude and often grotesquely proportioned (Chapter 7, Figure 7.2, this volume), were created by separately modeled elements. Rare traces of stucco and paint on these figures suggest that such surface treatments originally existed and better preservation would have improved identification of the individual deities represented. One effigy represents a female, probably Ixchel or Chakchel? (Figure 12.3); another

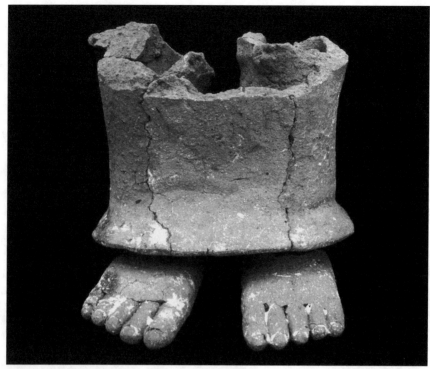

Figure 12.3. Semi-reconstructible Patojo Modeled: Patojo variety female effigy, probably Ixchel/Chakchel or Goddess I/O, from Structure 764 in Group C.

may be the merchant god Ek Chuah/God M. On the basis of photographs, Susan Milbrath and Silviane Bouchet (pers. com., July 21, 2004) indicated that several of the censer faces (as well as the pottery "mask"; Chapter 7, Figure 7.11, this volume) display a combination of traits of Chaak and Tlaloc, the former a long nose and sunken cheeks and the latter goggles or underlined eyes and fang-like teeth (see also Milbrath 2007). Combined Chaak/Tlaloc faces are characteristic of sculptured masks in the Puuc and Champotón regions (ibid.), supporting our position that the Kowoj were closely related to the Xiw of western Yucatán. One partial censer face with a long nose may be an import from Mayapán (Figure 12.4a). In addition, at least one censer shows an old face with a headdress reminiscent of the Mexican Fire God[1] with a brazier on his head (Figure 12.4b).

Effigy incense burners were made of two other paste wares commonly used for slipped and decorated serving items or utilitarian pieces. Ídolos Modeled: Ídolos variety censers were made with cream-colored Clemencia Cream Paste ware, associated with the Topoxté Islands (Bullard 1970; Hermes 2000b: 196; Rice 1979). These censers feature relatively small and well-made effigies of a deity we tentatively identified as Itzamna/God D. Ídolos Modeled

Figure 12.4. Patojo Modeled: Patojo variety effigy censer heads from Zacpetén. (a) is a long-nosed censer head stylistically similar to those from Mayapán.

sherds occur in low frequency at Zacpetén and never in primary refuse (Pugh 2001: 200). In fact, this type is found in low frequencies everywhere, including Topoxté.

Kulut Modeled: Kulut variety effigy censers were made in Uapake Carbonate Paste ware, but the figures and faces are virtually identical to those of Ídolos. Probably representing Itzamna/God D, the faces (Chapter 9, Figure 9.1, this volume; Figure 12.5) feature a grimacing mouth with bolt-like fangs in the corners and a prominent nose, often with a bead above. Figures wear a reptilian headdress with the characteristic eyes having a dotted scroll beneath; Milbrath and Bouchet (pers. com., July 21, 2004; see also Taube 1992: figure 14) suggest that this headdress might be the Pax monster, which lacks a lower jaw. The figure wears a tunic with a braided pectoral or necklace and bells on the hem.

Image censers with "semi-effigy" figures applied onto the exterior walls of vase receptacles were relatively uncommon in the central Petén lakes compared to other lowland regions. For example, I would call Diane Chase's (1988) Santa Unslipped modeled tripod jar censer from Santa Rita a semi-effigy form and Mayapán's Hoal Modeled incensarios, which preceded the Chen Mul

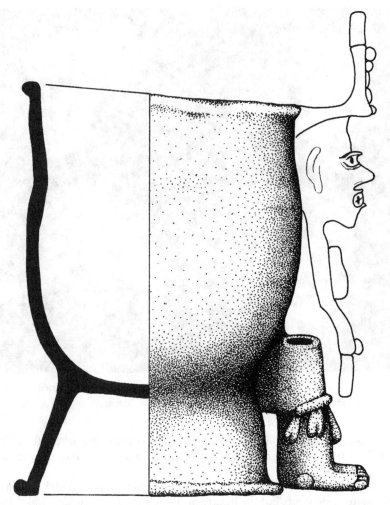

Figure 12.5. Profile of the partially reconstructible Kulut Modeled incensario shown in Figure 9.1. Note the separately formed and attached upper body and legs.

Modeled full-figure effigies, semi-effigy forms. One vase from Zacpetén consisted of the head (from Structure 602; Figure 12.6) and legs (from Structure 605) of a diving god applied onto the vase, fragments of which were primarily found on Structure 602. Diving figures seem particularly common along the east coast of Yucatán and may represent conjured ancestors (Masson 2000: 225–229), the Maize God/God E (Peraza Lope, Masson, and Russell 2005; Taube 1992: 41), or Kukulcan (Masson 2000: 231–234). Slipped red and decorated with red and blue paint, this Zacpetén vessel was classified as Pitufo Modeled: Pitufo variety in Snail-Inclusion Paste ware. Censers of this type/paste ware were rare: only nine sherds, including an effigy head and a ladle

Figure 12.6. Head of diving god/God E from broken Pitufo Modeled semi-effigy censer, fragments of which were scattered over Structures 602 and 605 in Group A.

censer handle modeled as a human head, were recovered at Macanché Island (Rice 1987a: 184, 187, figure 61), and no Pitufo sherds were found in primary refuse at Zacpetén (Pugh 2001: 200).

A large fragment of an open-mouthed jar or urn-shaped vessel had a Chaak/Tlaloc face appliquéd on the side (Chapter 7, Figure 7.11, this volume). This sherd had no evidence of burning on the interior. We originally classified it as Tirso Rojo-Modelado type, within Clemencia Cream Paste ware, but we are now inclined to view this type as possibly Mayapán Red ware. The facial features and beads of the headband resemble a censer from Structure 1 at Champotón (see Milbrath 2006: figure 5).

Composite Censer Wares and Types

"Composite" incensarios are non-image/non-effigy incense-burning vessels resembling early Late Postclassic Cehac-Hunacti Composite (appliqué, painted, or both) type from Chich'en Itza and Mayapán and the rare later type

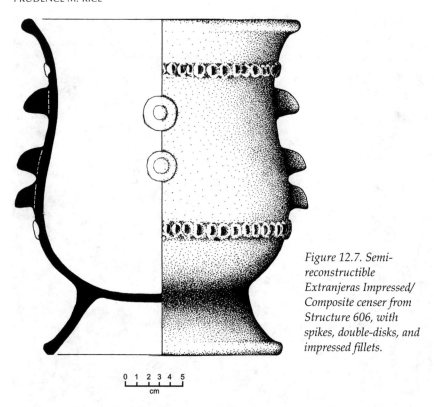

Figure 12.7. Semi-reconstructible Extranjeras Impressed/ Composite censer from Structure 606, with spikes, double-disks, and impressed fillets.

```
0 1 2 3 4 5
└─┴─┴─┴─┴─┘
     cm
```

Acansip-Thul Composite. Cehac-Hunacti Composite censers began to appear sometime before 1200 at Mayapán, perhaps representing developments out of Chich'en Itza's hourglass censers, and they occur in two forms: a pedestal-based vase or urn and a small bowl or cup with a ring base (rarely tripod supports). The composite decoration of Petén examples does not include painting (or it has not survived) but consists of impressed or appliqué elements or both, including appliquéd spikes (conical, pinched, or down-curving), single- or double-disks, buttons, and impressions of fingers, fingertips, or fingernails on vessel walls or appliquéd fillets—and typically some combination of the above. Spiked vessels are particularly common, occurring throughout the lowlands in various forms and depicted in codices. Vessels often display traces of a white stucco coating, which originally might have been painted.

The most common composite censers in the Petén lakes area are Extranjeras Impressed and La Justa Composite types, the latter often having distinctive paired or quadripartite arrangements, or both, of spike and disk appliqués (Figures 12.7, 12.8). La Justa includes large vase, cup, and ladle censer forms. Other types of composite censers (see also Appendix 12.I) include (1) Mumúl Composite: Dark Paste variety large, shallow basins or bowls, often stuccoed (Figure 12.9a–c); (2) small cups or bowls of Zaklak Composite with pedestal

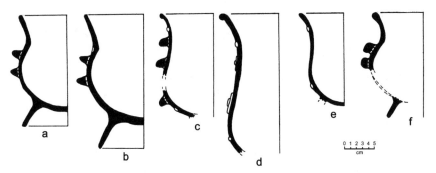

Figure 12.8. Semi-reconstructible composite censers with spikes and double-disks: (a, b, d, f) La Justa Composite: (a) Structure 719; (b) Structure 721; (c) La Justa/Extranjeras, Structure 601; (d) Structure 615; (e) Extranjeras Impressed, Structure 606; (f) Structure 719.

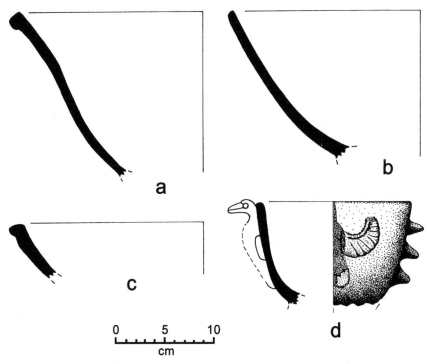

Figure 12.9. Fragments of composite censers: (a–c) Mumúl Composite: Dark Paste variety: (a) Structure 606; (b) Structure 721; (c) Structure 605; (d) Zaklak Composite with bird adorno and spikes, Structure 719.

or rare tripod bases, sometimes stuccoed (Chapter 9, Figure 9.4b, d, e, this volume)—note also bird (cormorant?) modeled on Figure 12.9d; (3) Fíjate Impressed/Composite, rather large and thin-walled vases (Figure 12.10a); and (4) fairly small vases and cups of Gotas Composite type (Chapter 7, Figure 7.8, this volume), made of Uapake Carbonate paste. Among these last four, all except Gotas Composite are relatively uncommon; Gotas and Fíjate seem very late in date.

Other Ritual Ceramics

In addition to incense burners, several other kinds of pottery were found either in caches or in the same deposits that included reconstructible censers and are thus interpreted as having ritual functions. They include ladle censers, quincunx cups, cache vessels, drums, and pregnant female figurines.

Ladle "censers" are small, shallow dishes with cylindrical handles. They are not common at Xiw/Kowoj sites (see also Hermes 2000b: 196) and show little to no evidence of burning, suggesting that by the Late Postclassic in Petén they had ceased to be used to burn incense, if that was ever their actual or intended function. Elizabeth Graham (1987: 85, figure 5f), in discussing Lamanai incensarios, refers to them as "frying pan" censers, while noting that the orientation of the effigy head on the handle of one of these ladles suggests it was a lid. At Zacpetén, the lack of evidence for burning suggests that these ladles had other uses, perhaps to hold and transport incense into the burner receptacles or perhaps something altogether different, such as ladling food or beverages during feasts. Ladle censers seem particularly associated with Chich'en Itza and late Sotuta-affiliated ceramic complexes in Yucatán (Cobos Palma 2004; see Ringle, Gallareta Negrón, and Bey 1998: 216–217).

A rare and unusual vessel at Zacpetén was a red-slipped quincunx cup or chalice (see Chapter 7, Figure 7.6, this volume; Figure 12.11): four small cups arranged around, and open to, a central cup, creating a quincunx shape. One cup was modeled as a human head. Similar vessels were recovered at Mayapán (Smith 1971, 2: figures 37a, c, 75c), where they were called "cluster bowls" or "candlestick clusters." We originally classified this vessel, which was a coarser, gray-cored cream paste, as Tirso Rojo-Modelado, considering it a variant of Clemencia Cream Paste ware. After studying the Mayapán collections in Mérida, however, we are now inclined to see this vessel as Mayapán Red ware. A possible example of one of the exterior cups was found at Topoxté (Hermes 2000e: figure 156D5). The quincunx is a long-standing Maya symbol of completion (Coggins 1980), and, given the apparent year-ending/beginning ceremonies represented in Zacpetén's temple assemblage deposits, their presence is not unexpected. Quincunx arrangements are also used in modern rituals and divination (Tate 2001: 155): for example, modern Mixe (highland Maya) rituals for personal and village protection, marriage, and maize-seed divination include digging five holes into the ground in a quincunx arrangement; in protection rituals, chickens are sacrificed and their feathers and blood are placed in the holes as offerings.

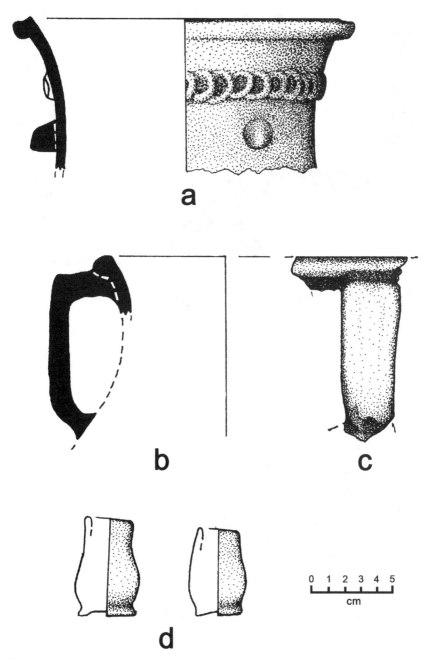

Figure 12.10. Examples of very late pottery at Zacpetén: (a) rim of Fíjate Composite censer; (b) unusual European-style handle (of a pitcher?) made of Snail Inclusion Paste ware with a dark purplish-red slip, Structure 615; (c–d) small shotglass-like cups of Paxcamán Red: (c) Structure 603; (d) Structure 602.

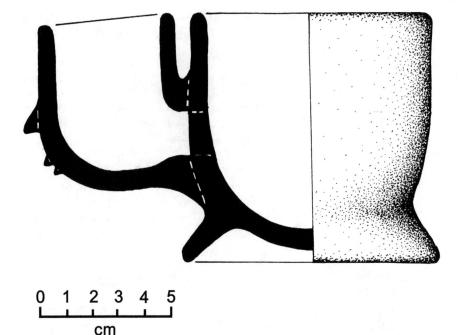

0 1 2 3 4 5

cm

Figure 12.11. Profile of quincunx cup or chalice, one of two recovered from Structure 764, the temple in Group C (see also Figure 7.6).

Cache vessels are small, semi-spherical, lidded bowls used in special deposits. With a maximum diameter of ca. 13–14 centimeters, these bowls (Figure 12.12) may be unslipped (Chilo Unslipped) or with red (sometimes specular hematite) slips and two horizontal loop handles on the sides (Canoas Red); lids have a vertical loop handle. They appear to have held offerings of copal or other resin into which were set small beads of jade and shell. Chipotle Red slipped cache vessels were manufactured in Uapake Carbonate ware. In Chompoxté Red-on-cream (Clemencia Cream Paste ware) a tecomate-shaped bowl has a red lip stripe and multiple narrow red lines down the unslipped exterior (Chapter 5, Figure 5.6, this volume). Identical vessels were recovered from Topoxté Island, some slipped and some unslipped (Hermes 2000b: figures 150, 151).

Some cache vessels feature attached human or animal heads, appendages, or both. Uncommon at Zacpetén, these bowls resemble the zoomorphic cache vessels of clay (Smith 1971, 2) and "altar figures" of stone (Proskouriakoff 1962b: figures 1, 5e) that were common at Mayapán, at sites in Belize — particularly Santa Rita (Chase 1985a, 1985b) and Lamanai (Pendergast 1993) — and at Topoxté (Wurster 2000: laminas 2 and 3). At Zacpetén, one was found during 1980 fieldwork (P. Rice 1986: 266–267) on the back bench or low wall of an open hall structure west-southwest of Group C. The bowl was made of a paste similar to Uapake Carbonate Paste ware, and exterior surfaces retained stucco

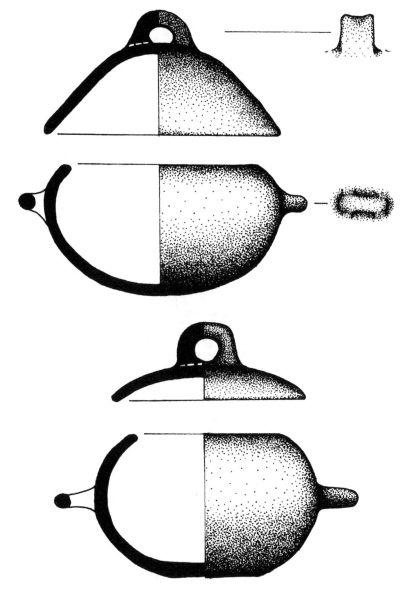

Figure 12.12. Chipotle Red cache vessels: (a) Structure 766a; (b) Structure 602.

coating. Appliqué strips on the sides formed the limbs and tail of an uniden-
tifiable animal, perhaps an anthropomorphic turtle (T. Pugh, pers. com.,
February 26, 2002), while the head was a (probably) mold-made Kulut-like
deity with fangs, earplugs, and nose ornamentation. Inside the vessel were a
tubular jade bead and a flat disk bead of *Spondylus*. These bowls with appliqués

resemble, and are perhaps precursors of, "Lacandon" "god pots" (Thompson 1977; Chapter 16, Figure 16.1, this volume): small cup- or bowl-like incense burners "animated" by the presence of small stones or beads placed in the receptacle, which also assist communication with the gods (McGee 1998: 43).

Small "shotglass"-like cups were found in some deposits containing incense burners. These cups, ca. 5 to 6.5 centimeters tall, are pyriform to cylindrical in shape, with small pedestal bases (Figure 12.10c, d). They are poorly made and asymmetrical, and the slip is typically the unpolished dark purple-red color known from late decorated types such as Macanché Red-on-paste (see Cecil, Chapter 10, this volume). Identical miniature cups were found at Topoxté (Hermes 2000e: figure 156c) and also at Mayapán (M. Masson, pers. com., July 2006).

Hand-held pottery drum fragments, or perhaps rattles (see Figure 12.13), usually red-slipped Snail-Inclusion Paste or Clemencia Cream Paste wares, were often found with censers. They typically have groups of gouge-incised vertical lines at the rim of the cylindrical "handle" and then flare out to a larger, semi-globular mouth that was presumably covered with animal skin. The Maya also used freshwater turtle carapaces as drums, and fragments of these were recovered with ritual pottery at Zacpetén. They suggest that music, singing, and dancing accompanied the ritual burning of incense. Some of the turtle remains were from very large animals, and Susan de France (pers. com., July 2006) raised the possibility that turtles were raised in pens around the lakes.[2]

Other ceramic artifacts found in these deposits at Zacpetén include notched sherds or clay pellets commonly thought to be either weights for textile looms or fishing nets/lines, or gaming pieces for playing patolli. Supporting the former interpretation is the occasional recovery of spindle whorls; whorls have been found in deposits associated with Aztec New Fire ceremonies (Elson and Smith 2001), but they may also be used in divination (Brown 2000: 330).

Pregnant Female Figurines

About a dozen small, hollow female figurine fragments were recovered at Zacpetén and also at Ixlú (Rice 2004b). They generally wear a skirt and a short, triangular covering (*quechquemitl*) over the shoulders and upper chest, leaving the breasts uncovered. Some wear earspools and necklaces, such as a pendant conch shell. One depicts a squatting female with hands and arms holding widespread knees and an open, grimacing mouth, as if in childbirth (Figure 12.14a), or they are legless with arms extended downward, protectively clasping an obviously pregnant abdomen (Figure 12.14b). None shows evidence of an infant actually being born, although the basal portion of these figurines — which could have shown details of both feet and birthing baby — were generally missing. The heads were also frequently missing, a detail that recalls the two lunar goddesses in Aztec myth, Coyolxauhqui and Cihuacoatl, who are depicted as decapitated. Possible pregnant female figurines, also headless, were found at Mayapán (Masson and Peraza Lope 2006; Peraza Lope, Masson, and Russell 2005).

Figure 12.13. "Drum and rattle of the k'atun," both presumably made of pottery, on mural on the west wall of Structure 1 at Santa Rita Corozal, Belize, one of the few southern lowland examples of the "international style" (redrawn from Roys 1967: figure 4, after Gann 1900). The drummer/dancer has been identified as an impersonator of the Old Coyote God (Huehuecoyotl), the Aztec god of dance and music (Miller and Taube 1993: 92; Quirarte 1982). The drum, standing on stepped-fret supports and appearing to be tied with rope, has a skeletal deity face with God M–like eyes applied to its side, which suggests a "semi-effigy"-type vessel. Note the use of dotted circles, U-shapes, and "grape clusters" of the Kawak day sign embellishing the drum, the latter probably referring to the sound of thunder. The rattle, held aloft by the drummer, is embellished by sound scrolls (?) on its upper surface and by feathers below its handle. A seven Ajaw glyph, not drawn here, appears to the lower left of the figure.

Where it was possible to classify them, the figurines were identified as Chamán Modeled type (Paxcamán ceramic group), as they seemed to be made primarily of Snail-Inclusion Paste ware. On most, the front detailing was mold-

Figure 12.14. Female figurines, Chamán Modeled type, both surface finds at Ixlú.

made and red or purple-red slipped, occasionally with black paint, although some were crudely modeled. The back was usually missing but was smooth where present. Judging from perforations, most were intended to be hung on a cord like an amulet; some were clearly whistles. Details varied, suggesting multiple molds.

Although these figurines were not common in the Zacpetén temple assemblages, several observations can be made about their occurrence or, rather, where they did *not* occur: in primary contexts on floors, altars, niches, or caches; inside the temples; and in direct association with incense burners. Instead, the fragments were recovered in secondary deposits of non-ritual paraphernalia, swept out of the temples and the upper terraces and deposited around the perimeters and on substructures. This indicates that pregnant female figurines were components of some kind of ritual that took place on or around temple structures, but because they occurred in secondary — hence, earlier — contexts, they were not part of the final rituals evidenced by the in situ deposits recovered on the inner temple floors or altars.

Figurine fragments were also found in four domestic or residential structures. In Structure 758 the figurine, not obviously pregnant, was an entire whistle recovered from Early Postclassic fill below a floor. In Structure 719 (see Pugh, Rice, and Cecil, Chapter 9, this volume), which we believe was an important semi-residential "council house" type building, two figurine fragments were incorporated into a floor that separated Early Postclassic structural fill from Late Postclassic fill above.

Excavations at Topoxté yielded two female figurines that might be whistles (Hermes 2000d: figure 62). Both are broken and missing the lower portion that would have shown legs or feet. One has a necklace or covering over the upper chest similar to the Zacpetén examples, with the left arm slightly curved over a not clearly pregnant abdomen. The other figurine has hands clasped over what is obviously a swollen, pregnant belly. While these objects resemble the Zacpetén Postclassic figurines, the Topoxté examples are identified in the figure caption as Late and Terminal Classic. A mold-made female figurine from Macanché Island (Rice 1987a: figure 68) has a long skirt, necklace, and triangular shoulder covering with a circular pendant. Arms are held loosely at the sides. Made of the same Snail-Inclusion Paste as the Zacpetén examples, this figurine is slightly larger, thicker, and not hollow or as whistle-like as those of Zacpetén. A similar figurine was recovered at Tipu (Graham 1991: figure 15-2d).

At Mayapán, Postclassic ceramic artifacts included whistles and hollow mold-made human figurines, mostly female, classified as Chen Mul Modeled (Smith 1971, 2: 56, figure 35a1–17, 98, figure 65a–c, e). Most had painted decoration, and some may have been whistles. They were found in "middle and late lots," including a burial, at the site. However, none were clearly pregnant, nor were the hands, legs, or knees in the same position (but see ibid.: figure 35a16–17); in addition, most were found in residential contexts. It may be significant, however, that a pregnant female modeled in stucco was recovered from a colonnaded hall near the Mayapán Castillo (Milbrath and Peraza Lope 2003: 26, figure 21a).

The evidence seems to suggest that at Zacpetén, pregnant female figurines were made and used primarily in the very late Early Postclassic and early Late Postclassic periods, perhaps from ca. 1100/1200 to ca. 1400/1500. Their fragmentary and worn condition may indicate that some were curated heirlooms, perhaps passed down from mother to daughter to ensure successful pregnancy. They recall the practice described by Bishop Landa (in Tozzer 1941: 129) in sixteenth-century Yucatán, who reported that "[f]or their childbirths they had recourse to the sorceresses . . . and put under their beds an idol of a goddess called Ix Chel whom they said was the goddess of making children." This "idol" may have been analogous to the pregnant female figurines recovered at Zacpetén. Landa (in Tozzer 1941: 154) also reported that in the month of Sip, "the physicians and the sorcerers . . . opened the bundles of their medicine, in which they kept many little trifles and, each having his own, little idols of the goddess of medicine, whom they called Ix Chel."

Female deities and female censer figurines were prominent on the east coast of Yucatán, where there was a deeply revered shrine to Ixchel on Cozumel Island. In addition, female torsos occurred in high frequency among the effigy censers recovered at Postclassic sites in Quintana Roo (Fry 1987: 119). One wonders if this eastern emphasis on female deities and pregnancy is connected to the importance of descent and naming through the female line in Yucatán, as evidenced by the use of double naming (matronym preceding patronym) and the *na* matronymic prefix (Jones 1998: 79–81; Roys 1972: 37–38). Double naming was used by the Itza in Petén, but *na* was not.

Comparisons: Incense Burners at Other Late Postclassic Sites

At Zacpetén, incense burners were recovered from contexts that also included slipped and decorated pottery (jars, dishes, drums, graters), projectile points, net/line weights, spindle whorls, crystals, and metates, plus a great variety of fauna (thus far unidentified). The variety and quantities of artifacts suggest the kind of ritual feasting described by Landa on the occasion of calendrical celebrations. Moreover, the volume of artifacts does not appear atypical, judging from other Postclassic sites. Most of what we know contextually about Postclassic Maya incensarios comes from the northern lowlands, particularly from excavations at Mayapán (Milbrath 2006; Peraza Lope, Masson, and Russell 2005; Smith 1971, 2; Thompson 1957) and at Santa Rita Corozal in northern Belize (Chase 1985a, 1985b, 1988). Other data come from Tulum (Masson 2000: 216–226), Caye Muerto (Progresso Lagoon; Masson 1999a), and Laguna de On (Masson 1999b).

Mayapán, Yucatán

At Mayapán, the earliest effigy censers were classified as Hoal Modeled and are associated with the Hocabá ceramic complex (A.D. 1200–1300). They are described as what I would call semi-effigy censers, having "low-relief modeling on the cylinder wall embellished with some applique ornaments"; one displayed a diving god (Smith 1971, 1: 196). Slightly later censers with full-figure attached anthropomorphic effigies are Chen Mul Modeled type.

Insights into the functions and uses of "ceremonial" pottery at Mayapán come from two analyses of their contexts of recovery. The earliest of these, by Robert E. Smith (1971, 2), identified five contexts based on structure types, burials, and caches. The distribution of ritual pottery was significantly non-random, with the highest percentages (of sherd counts) recovered from architecture with presumed civic-ceremonial functions: temples (especially those with serpent columns) and colonnaded halls (ibid.: Tables 8–22). In general, ritual pottery was less common in dwellings, although the amounts varied by structure size. A more recent study by Carlos Peraza Lope, Marilyn Masson, and Bradley Russell (2005; see also Masson 2000: 198–216), based on data from their own plus earlier Carnegie Institution excavations, identified specific deities represented by effigies (including non-censer materials) distributed around the site. They found that most structures had multiple deities represented and no structure had only a single deity censer, suggesting that the differential distribution of deities may reveal a kind of "ceremonial specialization" relating to different kinds of rituals, supernaturals venerated, or both.

Censer use at Mayapán is important because the Kowoj claimed to have migrated to Petén from that city. Unfortunately, the existing tabulations of ceremonial pottery/effigies by frequency and percentage do not always clearly separate pottery incense burners from other categories of effigies. Nonetheless, Zacpetén appears to share the same general pattern, with censers found primarily in temples and colonnaded halls. Certain categories of ritual vessels identified at Mayapán were absent or nearly so at Zacpetén, including tripod jar censers, pedestal-based non-censers, toys and whistles, and masks. However, the large cached Chaak/Tlaloc face sherd (Chapter 7, Figure 7.11, this volume) in Structure 766A might be construed as a mask, and the female figurines might represent the Mayapán category of "small personal idols." The other forms might be associated with non–Xiw/Kowoj lineage practices.

Santa Rita Corozal, Belize

The Late Postclassic site of Santa Rita Corozal, a probable *may* seat in northern Belize, had no apparent relations with the Kowoj, but Diane Chase's (1985a, 1985b, 1988) painstaking analysis of a series of ritual vessel types — most of which showed parallels with those at Mayapán — is revealing in terms of censer use. As at Mayapán, the spatial distribution of ceremonial vessels was significantly nonrandom. Kol Modeled effigy censers were usually found smashed in pairs on abandoned buildings, including Structure 81, a large multi-room structure with an interior shrine. Pum Modeled censers (bowls or basins with ring bases) and other ritual vessels had more limited distributions. Chase interpreted the distribution of paired, smashed effigy censers and dedicatory caches in terms of calendrical ritual described by Landa in sixteenth-century Yucatán: the paired inensarios are analogous to the pairs of *k'atun* idols that resulted from the cyclical transfer of authority over yearly and twenty-year periods, marking the recovery contexts as loci of Wayeb' and *k'atun* rites.

Tipu, Belize

The site of Negroman-Tipu, in western Belize, has a large, elevated platform in its southeastern corner that appears to be a variant of the Petén and Yucatán temple assemblages we associate with the Kowoj. Censers and caches at Tipu were recovered primarily in the two-room superstructure of Structure 2, the larger of two buildings on the east side of this complex. Analysis of 151 effigy censer fragments recovered from excavations in this structure (Foor 1994) suggested that at least 8 vessels had been smashed in and around it: 3 inside the structure (24 sherds of Pitufo Modeled, 45 of coarse gray ware, and 73 Patojo Modeled: Rojo variety); 2 Patojo Modeled: Rojo variety near the altar in the rear room; 1 Pitufo effigy face west of the altar; 1 coarse gray ware near the door; and 1 Patojo: Rojo sherd in the doorway. Outside the structure at the rear, or east, wall, fragments of 3 effigy vessels were found: 2 of Pitufo and a braided breastplate of Patojo Modeled: Rojo variety. Fifty sherds of non-effigy censers were recovered from Structure 2, but their widely scattered distribution precluded inferences concerning behavior related to their disposition. A censer with a diving figure was recovered along with a "Lacandon-type" censer face in a very late intrusive feature in Structure 3 of the Postclassic assemblage, probably representing a pilgrimage deposit.

Two subfloor caches came from the rear room of Structure 2. One (Offering 6), placed in a cut through the lowermost of two floors north of the altar, consisted of 2 probable Augustine Red jars, 1 of which contained more than 300 jade and *Spondylus* beads; a copper turtle effigy accompanied the cache. A second cache consisted of a ceramic disk with a spike handle, a plaque with appliqué braids, and a funnel-like tube.

Topoxté Island

William Bullard's excavations of Structure C, the large temple in Topoxté Island's temple assemblage, recovered effigy censer fragments on the interior floor of the superstructure; they included one partly restorable censer of Ídolos Modeled and two of coarse gray paste. About 10 percent of the censer sherds were lighter in color and weight (Bullard 1970: 281), characteristics typical of Ídolos Modeled type.

More recent excavations in Structure E, an oratorio, recovered eighteen partially reconstructible censers, primarily composite but also one effigy (not Ídolos) in the south end of the room (Hermes 2000d: 85, figures 67–70; Hermes et al. 2000: 42). Fragments have copal not only in the interior but also in the fractures and the exterior, suggesting the vessels broke while in use. They do not appear to have been placed in pairs (Hermes 2000d: figure 70), however, and they appear to be an accumulation from periodically repeated activities. In these excavations, only 2 percent of slipped sherds were of the Ídolos group (Hermes 2000b: 194). Excavations also recovered numerous examples of small, lidded, semi-effigy bowls with an anthro- or zoomorphic effigy, mostly turtle effigies with a human face emerging from the animal's mouth (Hermes 2000d: figure 64). Composite censers were represented by Extranjeras Impressed and La Justa Composite types; ladles were present but not common.

Lake Macanché

Macanché Island, twenty-five kilometers southwest of Topoxté in Lake Macanché, was also a site of Xiw/Kowoj occupation. Small quantities of Ídolos Modeled were recovered in excavations of the main platform and structure on the island, but only in the upper levels (Rice 1987a: 197); effigy censer sherds in lower Postclassic levels were of Patojo Modeled and Pitufo Modeled. No Kulut Modeled censers were noted. Composite censer types included Gotas and La Justa; no sherds of Fíjate or Extranjeras were identified, and ladles were rare.

Discussion: Sources of Information on Censer
and Ritual Pottery Use and Function

The great variety of incense burner forms and the multi-millennia of their use suggest that while censers' immediate "use" may have been simply to burn incense, rubber, or other resins, their broader "functions" were well differentiated and varied through time and also ethno-regionally. Interpreting Late Postclassic incensario use and function is made problematic by the Spaniards' lumping a variety of containers into the category of "idols," making it difficult to extract ethnohistoric data to supplement archaeological contexts of recovery. A similar ambiguity can be seen in the Yukatekan terms for "incensario" and "to burn incense": *yum k'ak'* (lord fire) or *yum pom* (lord copal) (Krochock and Freidel 1994: 363, 365, citing pers. com. from Brian Stross). These terms suggest the personification of censers (as deities or "idols") as well as a lack of distinction among the vessel, the material burned, and the person who handles both.

Postclassic Codices

Ceramic incensarios—especially composite censers, virtually identical to those recovered archaeologically at Mayapán and throughout the lowlands—appear in the codices, particularly in the yearbearer almanacs. These are tables of the first day-names or "bearers" of the years in the 260-day calendar, and they appear on pages 25–28 in the Codex Dresden (Paxton 1991; Villacorta and Villacorta 1930) and pages 34–37 in the Codex Madrid (Graff 1997; Graff and Vail 2001: 68–73; Vail 1996). Each codex references a different calendar by presenting different sets of yearbearers (Edmonson 1988: 5–11; Sharer 1994: chapter 11).[3] The yearbearer pages of both codices depict vase-shaped, pedestal-based, composite censers with appliquéd spikes, disks, buttons, and other elements.

Other almanacs in the codices show composite incensarios with all decorative elements except appliquéd disks, which may be very late adornments (Graff 1997: 166). Among them are 260-day almanacs, divided into five 52-day runs of four *trecenas*, or 13-day intervals. For example, pages 59a and 60a of the Madrid Codex identify four intervals, each showing a deity seated next to a composite censer with different kinds of incense: *pom* (copal), God R with rubber (scroll glyph), God A with *chahalte* (wood), and God E with *sacaj* (maize) (ibid.: 147). Madrid page 61a shows two almanacs in five 52-day runs (260 days total) having days beginning with 2 Muluk, Imix, B'en, Chikchan, and Kab'an and spiked censers with captions labeling the four directions (ibid.: 147–148). Similar composite censers are shown on numerous other pages (ibid.: 164).

In contrast to composite censers, image/effigy incensarios rarely appear in the codices. One possibility is Madrid Codex pages 63c and 64c: they show five 52-day runs of 260 days, beginning on a day 6 Ajaw. Six figures—Itzamna, Aj Kimil, God N?, an Ak'b'al-headed deity, God R/N, and Itzamna (Graff 1997: 162)—sit with their backs against vases in the manner of attached effigy censers. The vases are post-fire painted with black on blue vertical panels (ibid.: 166). In addition, objects in the Borgia and Nuttall codices resemble modeled vessels from Santa Rita (Chase 1985a: 122–123), and the rectangular breastplates or necklaces worn by effigy figures appear on Late Postclassic murals (Paxton 1991, 2004).

The differential appearance of composite versus effigy censers in the codices might give a clue as to their different uses. The Late Postclassic codices treat astronomical and calendrical topics, particularly yearbearers and other matters of the *tzolk'in*, or 260-day calendar, and depict composite censers on these pages. Composite censers with appliqué spikes, impressed fillets, and other ornamentation are recovered in the Maya archaeological record beginning in Middle Preclassic times, indicating their use in rituals of deep and abiding significance—perhaps those involving the cycling of the *tzolk'in*. Their directional associations, as given on Madrid page 61a, raise the possibility that they represent Pawahtuns, quadripartite skybearers (Miller and Taube 1993: 132); Pawahtuns may appear as God N and are often represented within or wearing a turtle shell (ibid.).[4] Effigy censers appear only rarely, if at all, in the codices, hinting that their functions lie in another realm.

Ethnohistoric Accounts

Evidence of incensario use derived from ethnohistoric accounts is necessarily based on assumptions of equivalence between the ubiquitous "idols" that so infuriated the Spaniards and the pottery effigy incense burners known archaeologically. Bishop Landa's observations of Maya ritual in sixteenth-century Yucatán called attention to the role of these idols in calendrical cycling and a host of feasting activities associated with monthly rituals. A recent analysis of his comments isolated forty-two different contexts for twenty-nine rituals; these contexts were primarily residences (especially elite, as is also known archaeologically), temples, oratories, and stone piles at the entrances to towns (Russell 2000: tables 7a–d).

Community-wide feasts and processions of idols were sponsored by a lord or lineage head of a particular town during these ceremonies. The patron idols of the incoming yearbearer along with that of the appropriate Wayeb' period—probably composite incensarios—were moved from their directionally associated entrances to the town into the lord's home, where they stayed during the five Wayeb' days. After this, the patron idol of the new year was moved into the public temple and the Wayeb' idol was moved to the new, directionally appropriate entrance to the town. If various misfortunes occurred during the year, the priests could order more idols made to one or more deities to remedy the situation.

In addition to these events, the Maya celebrated the new year's day associated with the fifty-two-year Calendar Round, perhaps with a "New Fire ceremony" similar to that of the Aztecs. These celebrations entailed the destruction of household goods prior to the production of replacements (Elson and Smith 2001). The ritual debris behind or beside structures at Zacpetén suggests that civic-ceremonial areas were ritually swept between celebratory events.

Bishop Landa (in Tozzer 1941: 166–169; see Chase 1985a) also discussed ceremonies involving "*k'atun* idols," deities presiding over periods of approximately twenty Gregorian years known as *k'atuns*. A *k'atun* idol first entered the temple to begin rule as "guest" (B) of the ruling idol (A) for ten years. The ruling idol (A) was then removed and the newcomer (B) ruled alone in the temple for ten years, after which another new idol (C) was brought in as guest of (B), and so on. The result was that each idol served for thirty years (see discussion of burning patterns in incensarios in Structure 719; Pugh, Rice, and Cecil, Chapter 9, this volume). Landa's description appears to explain the pairing of effigy censers in Postclassic temples, and the possibility of multiple deities associated with new year's ceremonies could account in part for the multiple pairs of incensarios found in temples at Zacpetén. Along these lines, distributional patterns of effigy censer fragments in these structures might represent the "termination" of the replaced "idol" (see Pugh and Rice, Chapter 7, this volume). For example, in Group A, the Structure 605 oratorio had a broken, in situ effigy censer of Kulut Modeled type—lord of the *k'atun*? yearbearer?—in its medial niche, but judging from sherd distributions, the presumed other member of the pair had been smashed and scattered over the surface of the structure. Similarly, in Group C the fragmentary remains of various composite censers in Structure 765 (raised shrine) might represent earlier, terminated vessels that were replaced by more nearly complete Gotas Composite censers.

As interpreted by Munro Edmonson (1985, 1986), rituals commemorating the end of *k'atuns* (and other calendrical intervals, such as the *b'ak'tun* in 1618) were accompanied by music, dancing, feasting, and other celebratory activities. For example, the Colonial-period books of *chilam b'alam* make reference to utensils of clay and other materials, such as the plate, cup, drum, and rattle of the *k'atun* (Figure 12.13). These musical and feasting activities might be represented in the Zacpetén temple assemblages through the decorated ceramic plates, cups, graters, drums, and turtle carapaces recovered alongside incense burners.

If the Xiw/Kowoj of Zacpetén celebrated the same regular calendrical rituals that were observed in Yucatán, including those dedicated to gods of various months (see Landa in Tozzer 1941: 151–166), the incensarios found in temples might have been accumulated over a period of a year or multiples of years. In Yucatán, idols were taken to the houses of the lords who sponsored these monthly events and associated feasting, a practice that could explain the presence of (composite) censers in large/elite residential complexes.

Ethnographic Analogy: The Lacandon

The multiple incense burners at Zacpetén might be functionally analogous to the Lacandon god pots in their temples or god houses (Boremanse 1998; McGee 1990, 1998; Pugh, Chapter 16, this volume). The Lacandon lived in a non-ranked acephalous society that lacked chiefs and priests, although there seem to have been rough equivalents to "big men" who had large families and enjoyed some prestige among the group. Part of the prestige with which these individuals were regarded was accrued through "their ability as diviners and mediators: that is, their ability to communicate with the gods through the incense burners" (Boremanse 1998: xix). Their censers more closely resembled the small, globular cache pots of the Postclassic period and would be classed as semi-effigy forms. They played an important role in the welfare of individuals, families, and the larger group, as they were consulted, fed, and prayed to in the event of illness, pregnancy, misfortune, bad feelings between individuals, or curses (ibid.).

All married males were expected to have a collection of god pots, each of which held small stones or other relics from a place sacred to the god the censer represented. Men who did not make their own censer sets had to use those of their fathers or fathers-in-law: "Thus, a set of incense burners could be a factor of cohesion among the members of a cluster of households, since there was a bond of ritual dependency" (Boremanse 1998: xix). When a man died, he customarily left his censers to his eldest son, who was expected to let his younger brothers and his brothers-in-law also use them (ibid.: 98).

Effigy Censers: The Problem of Origins

The distinctive Late Postclassic anthropomorphic effigy incense burners have no immediately apparent antecedents in the Maya lowlands, and questions about their origins have been posed for decades. On the one hand, "image censers" — incense burners or supports adorned with anthropomorphic or zoomorphic figures — are known from virtually all periods of Maya occupation in the lowlands (see Note 1), especially from the Early Classic period onward. Classic-period cylindrical censer stands were distinguished by modeled Jaguar God (of the Underworld; JGII) faces and other ornamentation and seem to have primary associations (that is, archaeological contexts) with kingly mortuary ritual. In such usage, they presumably signified the deceased divine king, or k'ul ajaw, often attired in jaguar regalia, in his new role as Lord of the Underworld (Rice 1999). Postclassic-period political organization was no longer dominated by divine kings, and Postclassic censers bear them no reference; instead, the attached, modeled semi- or full-effigy figures celebrate deities or perhaps deified ancestors (see Masson 2000: 221–241). Thus, it is difficult to discern formal and functional analogies between Preclassic and Classic modeled censers and stands and Postclassic effigy incensarios (beyond simply burning resins), and the question of origins really concerns the proximate stimulus for the latter's production.

Part of the problem is that the date of initial manufacture and use of these effigy censers is uncertain. At Xcaret, an effigy in Puuc Slate ware occurs as early as Cehpech times, A.D. 800–1000 (Smith 1971, 1: 255), and Hoal Modeled semi-effigy censers can be dated between 1000/1050 and 1100/1200 at Mayapán (ibid., 2: 104, figure 68a). At Mayapán, full-figure effigies were associated with "middle" or transitional (Hocabá-Tases) contexts dating ca. 1300 and later, with Smith suggesting that "the idolatrous practice of worshipping stone- and pottery-made idols may reflect the Cocom taking over at Mayapán after a revolution . . . about 1382" (ibid., 1: 255–256). Elizabeth Graham (1987: 82) indicated that Late Postclassic effigy censers might have precursors in the Middle Postclassic (ca. 1050–1350?) effigy censers found at Lamanai, Belize (see also Terminal Classic censer stands at Caracol; Chase and Chase 2004b: 353). Marilyn Masson (2000: 241, 2003: 197, following Sidrys 1983: 139) proposed possible origins in Gulf coast or Zapotec traditions. Meredith Paxton (1986: 612–622, 1991: 307) suggested that effigy censers developed from Tohil Plumbate vessels with appliquéd human and animal effigy heads and limbs and originated ca. 1150/1250.

Considering the similarities in painted motifs between Postclassic Maya lowland slipped and decorated pottery and the Mixteca-Puebla "international style" (see Rice and Cecil, Chapter 11, this volume), it seems reasonable to turn to south-central Mexico in search of stimuli for effigy censers. Most discussions of this style emphasize the painted polychromes rather than ritual vessels, but several possibilities assert themselves. For example, Geoffrey McCafferty (2001: 32–33) described *braseros* (incense burners) of Cerro Zapotecas Sandy Plain type: biconical vases with attached full-figure anthropomorphic effigies that may be stuccoed and painted blue, green, or black. They date to the "Epiclassic" and Early Postclassic periods, between roughly A.D. 700 and 1050 (ibid.: 14). Some of these are polychrome-painted *xantiles* ("incense burner covers modeled as human figures," found particularly in the Tehuacan Valley; Ramsey 1982: 34, 39, figure 13), which sit upon bases decorated with spikes. James Ramsey (ibid.: 39) dated these to 1100–1300. Other related vessels include an "annular-base urn with modeled face" from Zaachila, Oaxaca (ibid.: figure 14), which I would describe as a semi-effigy form, and a "tripod urn with attached figure" from Miahuitlan, Oaxaca (ibid.: figure 15), which is a full-figure human effigy.

Some Spanish records report that, according to their Maya informants, the practice of idolatry was brought to Yucatán by Mexicans and a "captain" or "prince" known in Yukateko as Kukulcan (Nahuatl: Quetzalcoatl, 'feathered serpent'; see discussions by Landa and Tozzer in Tozzer 1941: 21–26; Ringle, Gallareta Negrón, and Bey 1998). It was he who is said to have taught them idolatry. These accounts convey some confusion as to whether Kukulcan established Chich'en Itza or Mayapán or both, thus making it difficult to know when these practices began. According to Tozzer (1941: 23–24n129), the Kokoms considered themselves descendants of Kukulcan. Depending on these dates, the arrival of Kukulcan might also account for the presence of elements of the "Early Postclassic international symbol set" or the late one, the latter associated with the Mixteca-Puebla style (see Rice and Cecil, Chapter 11, this volume).

Conclusions

Four categories of incense burners were used in Postclassic ritual throughout the lowlands: effigy, semi-effigy, composite, and ladle incensarios. Among the Kowoj, the most common were the image censer with full-figure effigy appliqués and the composite censer; the semi-effigy was less common, and fragments of ladles do not show evidence of burning. The two major forms had closely related yet distinct contexts of occurrence, with composite censers found around the exteriors of temples and in residences whereas effigy censers were rare outside structures and more commonly found inside temple superstructures.

Effigy censers depict a large number of individuals or deities in full-figure form. At Zacpetén, as at many other sites (see Masson 2000: 239–241), specific deities were difficult to identify because of the fragmentary nature of the censer remains (particularly the frequent absence of heads) and the lack of surviving painted decoration. Nonetheless, we believe that, minimally, we have representations of Chaak/Tlaloc, Itzamna/God D, possibly a merchant deity (Ek Chuah/God M?), and a female deity (Ixchel/Goddess I or O?). At Mayapán a large effigy-figure censer depicted a female, possibly with a broken V-neck collar or necklace like those on the Zacpetén figurines. This image, probably the goddess Ixchel, was not pregnant (Smith 1971, 1: 104, 2, figure 68b1). The multiple representations of Itzamna in Ídolos Modeled and Kulut Modeled types suggest that the residents of Zacpetén had a special affinity for this deity. Itzamna is described as "one of the most important and perhaps *the* major god of the Classic and Post-Classic Maya" (Taube 1992: 31, emphasis in original). He is referenced as an elderly high priest, a sky god as well as an earth god; and he has broad associations with writing (its invention), world trees, caimans, fire, divination, and curing, with his probable consort Ixchel (ibid.: 31–41; Miller and Taube 1993: 99–100). Itzamna is also patron of the day Ajaw, the last day of a *k'atun,* and the presence of this deity on effigy censers in temples at Zacpetén may indicate *k'atun*-ending ceremonies.

Although some of these characteristics are general and widely shared, others can be more narrowly tied to particular times, regions, or social groups. Thus, the form, iconography, typology, and context of recovery of incense burners and other ritual ceramics provide a material basis for establishing the social and ethno-political identity of the Xiw/Kowoj and their ancestors in Petén. Characteristics of the ritual subcomplex that are Xiw/Kowoj ethnospecific include the small size of the effigies and particular characteristics of the eyes and feet (as compared to Mayapán); representations of Itzamna, Chaak/Tlaloc, a diving god, and distinctive headdresses; use of these objects in temple assemblages; presence of pregnant female figurines; near absence of ladles; and distinctive local pastes.

Three interrelated features of censer occurrence and distribution are of particular interest at Zacpetén and have not been adequately explored elsewhere to date: pairing of vessels, use of multiple pastes, and organization of manufacture. At Zacpetén, pairing of censers was evident in a pattern similar to that at Santa Rita Corozal (Chase 1985a, 1985b), with effigy censers paired inside or in front of temples and paired composite censers outside temples on structural platforms or near stairways. Typically, although not invariably, at Zacpetén both censers of a pair were manufactured of the same paste and could be classified into the same type and variety in the type-variety classificatory system.

Five distinct paste wares were used to make the effigy censers found in the Kowoj region: Snail-Inclusion, Patojo Coarse, Uapake Carbonate, Clemencia Cream, and an unnamed coarse gray (not noted at Zacpetén). Three of these (Snail-Inclusion, Uapake, Clemencia) were also used to make slipped serving and unslipped utility wares of varying ubiquity at sites in the region. The use of multiple pastes for effigy censer manufacture was common throughout the Petén lakes area and also to the northeast in Quintana Roo, where Robert Fry (1987: 119; see also Sanders 1960) noted "significant differences in pastes." The use of five pastes at Kowoj sites in Petén and adjacent Tipu suggests that censer (and other pottery) production was noncentralized and nonstandardized,[5] perhaps the responsibility of individual communities or kin groups with their own local clay sources.

The fact that three of the five pastes used for effigy censers were also used to make the major slipped serving and unslipped utility wares provides unambiguous evidence of local (lakes region) manufacture rather than the vessels having been imported from elsewhere (such as Mayapán). Although we cannot specify precise locations of manufacture, fragments of the molds for effigy faces were recovered in domestic contexts at Macanché (Rice 1987a: 204) and Zacpetén (Chapter 8, Figure 8.1, this volume).[6] These fragments indicate that effigy censers were produced in residential areas, but we did not find any fired effigy censer fragments in the refuse of either structure.

In addition, the fact that pairs of effigy censers were often of the same pastes suggests that different producing units (perhaps lineages or wards or entire communities) had the responsibility of making pairs of incensarios for yearbearer/new year's ceremonies as part of their civic duties. It also hints at the existence of four or five production units in the Kowoj area, at least one associated with each of the five paste wares, although temporal variation must be considered. This might also reflect the overarching quadripartite community organization and cosmovision so well-known in Classic-, Postclassic-, and Colonial-period Maya communities (see M. Coe 1965; Jones 1998; Paxton 2001).

With the introduction of (semi-)effigy censers in the lowlands by A.D. 1150–1300 and perhaps earlier, a sharp distinction seems to have developed between the two categories of incense burners, image and non-image, and the contexts of their use. Non-image or composite incensarios are widespread throughout the lowlands in the Postclassic period—with spiked censers dating back to the Middle Preclassic in Petén—and evidence points to their use in varied calendrical rituals. Human/deity effigy censers are widespread through the Late Postclassic lowlands; that, plus their distinctiveness, led to the suggestion that they represent "an over-all unity in religious concepts and ritualistic techniques" in the Late Postclassic period (Sanders 1960: 245). This viewpoint has recently been restated by Masson (2001: 98) as "local participation in a revivalist religious cult sponsored by Mayapán." Although it is not readily apparent what concepts and techniques are being revived or the principles of such a "cult" involving effigy censers, several suggestions have been made. Diane and Arlen Chase (2004: 21) discussed the religious "meaning" of Postclassic incensarios and pointed to "privatized or individualized worship" of multiple gods and use of household shrines. Similarly, others (Andrews 1993: 59; Sabloff and Rathje 1975b) have interpreted the widespread distribution of censers in terms of a decentralization of religious practices in the Postclassic period.

I suggest that the new principles accompany the return to more traditional—that is, Classic-period—practices of k'atun-ending celebrations and may-based geopolitical organization (Rice 2004a) at Mayapán. The evidence for such a return is the renewed practice of erecting carved stelae at 20-year k'atun intervals at Mayapán (according to Landa), following abandonment of the ritual during the 256-year period of Chich'en Itza domination.

More important, perhaps, ethnohistoric and archaeological evidence makes it clear that the Postclassic effigy censer "cult" endured in the southern lowlands well beyond the collapse of Mayapán (Chuchiak in press; Roys 1967: 201–203). In 1619, when Franciscan fathers Bartolomé de Fuensalida and Juan de Orbita visited the mission site of Tipu, they discovered to their horror "great idolatry" and threw the idols into the river. Slightly later, at Lamanai to the north, the Maya buried a composite censer in the floor of the chancel of the second church sometime after 1641 (Graham 1987: 91). By the seventeenth century, the remoteness of the Petén lakes region conferred its status as a center of survival of indigenous ritual for the lowland Maya, and doubtless the effigy censers manufactured there were covertly traded outward to neighboring areas suffering more continuous surveillance by Spanish missionaries (Jones 1998: 40).

Acknowledgments

I thank Tim Pugh and Leslie Cecil for stimulating conversations in the field, for freely sharing their data with me, and for reading and commenting on early drafts of this chapter. The identification of the deities represented on these vessels was greatly aided by a conversation with Susan Milbrath and Silviane Bouchet in the INAH Ceramoteca in Mérida in late July 2004, and I am particularly grateful to them for sharing their insights and experience. In addition, I thank Merideth Paxton for sharing her views on the Dresden and Madrid codices and her suggestions for clarifying various points in this chapter.

Notes

1. Representations of the Old Fire God may be of great antiquity in central Petén. A face modeled onto the side of a flat-based bowl (a censer?) resembles this deity and was recovered in Middle Preclassic fill at Nixtun-Ch'ich' in the western Lake Petén Itzá basin.

2. Joseph Ball (1979: 34) commented on what he sees as "a shared emphasis among the Puuc centers and at Mayapan on the tortoise and tortoise-related motifs. There is some reason for suspecting the latter to have represented a tutelary or totemic being to

the Xiu lineage of Uxmal." "Tortoise" can be a synonym for "turtle," but it is commonly used to distinguish a land reptile from a freshwater turtle, and it is unclear from Ball's remarks if he intended this distinction.

3. One interpretation of the Dresden yearbearers favors the set Eb', Kab'an, Ik', and Manik', which were also yearbearers during the Classic period. Another interpretation posits a forward movement of one day to B'en, Etz'nab', Ak'b'al, and Lamat (Edmonson 1988: 36; Paxton 1986), which are those of the Late Classic–introduced Campeche calendar in the southwestern Yucatán peninsula. Several of these day glyphs can be found as icons on Kowoj pottery (Rice and Cecil, Chapter 11, this volume). The dates and iconography of the Dresden suggest it was a Late Postclassic document created in the Puuc area or around Chich'en Itza (Paxton 1991). One wonders if the two calendars represented on its yearbearer pages were actually a formal correlation of the two. The Madrid Codex presents a third set of yearbearers: Kawak, Kan, Muluk, and Ix, the same set used in the post-1539 Mayapán compromise calendar. Recent studies have revived the possibility that it might have been created in Petén rather than in the northern lowlands (Coe and Kerr 1998: 181; Schuster 1999; cf. Paxton 2004). Stylistically, it resembles the murals at east coast sites such as Tancah and Tulum (Miller 1982), although the censers in this region tend to have less emphasis on spiked decoration (but cf. Tancah Structure 12, Terminal Classic/Early Postclassic mural; Miller 1982: plate 6).

4. The appearance of Pawahtuns/God N in turtle shells explains the many modeled pottery vessels of turtles with human heads emerging from their mouths at Postclassic sites. They are common at Santa Rita, for example, and at least one was found at Topoxté Island (Hermes 2000d: figure 64), along with a large stuccoed and painted carved stone image (ibid.: 85–86, figure 63). These turtle cache vessels were not recovered at Zacpetén, suggesting that the Kowoj group at this site did not share the belief system underlying these representations. Other vessels, such as composite censers, may have served in this role.

5. It has been suggested that only one paste was used to make incensarios at Mayapán, the same one used to make the preponderance of slipped and unslipped wares at the site (Brown 1999). This could be interpreted as reflecting a centralized and possibly controlled and specialized socioeconomic organization of pottery production at that city, one that would appear to bear out Smith's (1971, 1: 74) inference of "an assembly line, mass production technique." In my own cursory review of effigy censers recovered in the epicenter, however, I found that at least three pastes were used: sandy light gray-tan, coarse red-brown, and coarse gray-brown.

6. A face mold was also found at Barton Ramie (Willey et al. 1965: 398–401).

Appendix 12.1

Paste-Ware and Type-Variety Classification of Postclassic Incensarios from Zacpetén

The most common full-figure effigy incense burners in Petén are classified as Patojo Modeled type, with four varieties: Patojo, Moza, Rojo, and Light. Patojo Modeled censers were manufactured from Patojo Coarse Paste ware, a coarse-textured, reddish-brown, calcite-inclusion fabric used almost exclusively for censers and effigy cache vessels and atypical of other kinds of pottery in the lakes area. Patojo Modeled: Patojo variety censers fit this description; other varieties likely represent firing differences (although other sources of variability should not be excluded). Moza variety is darker brown (less well oxidized) in color and fireclouded. Rojo variety is generally well oxidized throughout (2.5YR 5/6 "red," but more a clear pinkish-brown); the paste has abundant coarse white and gray calcite and a somewhat crumbly texture resulting from the reduced organic content. Light variety is a lighter orange-red color.

All Patojo Modeled censers, regardless of variety, are large, heavy, and thick-walled. Vases were constructed by coiling, as evidenced by coil fractures in intervals of 2.5 to 4.5 cm. From examination of breakage patterns and other evidence, it appears they were made in three parts or stages. The upper receptacle was formed with a slightly incurving lower section, but it was not closed; the pedestal base was formed as a separate cylinder, sometimes with an internal "lip" thickening the foot. The receptacle was then placed over the base and joined to it by means of another coil; and a small, relatively thin disk, apparently perforated, was inserted as the interior base. The join of the upper receptacle and lower pedestal stand was reinforced and smoothed over with more clay on the exterior and also smoothed on the interior; the underside of the basal joint was reinforced with lumps of clay that were not smoothed. The interior bases were almost always missing from reconstructible vessels, probably disintegrating easily as a result of repeated burnings, and the method of making these vessels might have been intended to allow bases to be replaced as necessary over time.

Overall vessel form varies from an open, rather straight-walled urn shape to a more sinuous, hourglass or slightly pyriform shape with a "waist" and gently out-slanting rim, generally exhibiting some asymmetry. There may be a slight tendency for vessels of Moza variety to be more pyriform. Wall thickness varies from unusually thin 7 mm (an unusually well-made vessel from Structure 602) to 12 mm. Mouth diameters measured on eleven vessels varied from 17 to 30 cm, with nine in the range of 24–30 cm. The lip is usually direct, although occasionally slightly bolstered or folded. The receptacle varies from 26–31 cm high and sits on a high pedestal base measuring 12–14 cm in height and 1.5–1.6 cm in thickness. Typically, 2–4 vertical vents are cut in the receptacle, paired with 2–4 circular vents directly below in the base. Total vessel height is difficult to measure because of breakage, but four nearly reconstructible vases measured 40–46 cm in height. Vases are sometimes stuccoed (the frequency of visibility doubtless a consequence of preservation) and typically have either opposing vertical flanges on either side or large curving flanges behind the effigies.

The hollow effigy figures attached to Patojo Modeled vases, fairly crudely modeled and often grotesquely proportioned, were created by separately modeled components. Faces were formed in molds, with added clay to form the full head. Headdresses were formed by separately modeled and appliquéd elements. Arms and legs were formed with hollow cylinders of clay, with hands and feet added on; finger- and toenails were indicated by incising or appliquéd pellets, and other appliquéd elements were added to indicate sandals, anklets, bracelets, and other ornamentation. Unlike the feet of Mayapán effigies, which were slightly convex to show the arch, Patojo feet were flat slabs. The torso was formed by building up bands of clay and smoothing the surface to form the tunic, with a braided breastplate, bells, and other decoration. Although the exteriors were reasonably well smoothed, the interiors preserved signs of the original strips and dabs of clay used like tape to secure the careless construction. Rare surviving traces of stucco coating and paint on these figures suggest that such surface treatments would have hidden the shoddy production and also, if painted, aided in identification of the individual deities represented.

Patojo Coarse Paste ware was rarely used to produce other kinds of Postclassic pottery and not in any quantity (at least at Zacpetén). Nonetheless, a few unslipped dish fragments have been identified in this paste, along with rare examples of vase and cup censer forms. It is possible that the Moza variety of Patojo bears some relation to the dark paste of Mumúl Composite.

The Patojo type name was originally applied to a small collection of incensario sherds of various pastes recovered from Macanché Island (Rice 1987a: 184–192). Now, after study of the much larger collection of effigy censers from subsequent excavations in the Petén lakes region, it is evident that most of those fragments should be reclassified.

Ídolos Modeled

Some effigy censers were manufactured in the distinctive cream-colored paste of Clemencia Cream Paste ware, best known through the abundant red-on-cream polychrome serving wares in Xiw/Kowoj territory of eastern Petén (see Rice 1979; Cecil, Chapter 10, this volume). These censers, classified as Ídolos Modeled: Ídolos variety, are of a light-colored marly paste that may vary slightly to very pale orange or very light gray. Fragments are thin and often unusually light in weight, which initially suggested leaching of the calcite inclusions, but Leslie Cecil's recent technological analyses suggest that potters appear to have incorporated volcanic ash into the paste.

Ídolos Modeled effigy figures are relatively small and well made and are duplicated almost exactly (except in quality) by Kulut Modeled (discussed in the next section). Faces have a punched hole for the pupil of the eye (also seen in eastern Yucatán and Belize; Smith 1971, 1: 212), and the teeth are indicated individually. Fingernails and toenails are created by appliqué pellets, as are anklets and details of clothing; figures often wear braided breastplates. Deities portrayed may include Itzamna and a miniature Chaak. Ídolos Modeled censers are surprisingly rare, even at Topoxté, perhaps a consequence of breakage of the thick-walled vessels.

Clemencia Cream Paste ware was not used to manufacture composite censers.

Kulut Modeled

Kulut Modeled: Kulut variety censers were made in Uapake Carbonate Paste ware (originally Uapake Unslipped ware), widely used to make a variety of very late vessel forms and types in the Petén lakes region: Gotas Composite censers, Chipotle Red cache vessels, and Chilo Unslipped utilitarian jars (see Rice 1987a: 179–184). Vessels are characterized by a dull, light orange-tan to grayish orange-tan color (5YR 5–6/5–6 to 10YR 7/1–2), relatively coarse calcite paste, and relatively thin walls with dark cores; surfaces may have a thin, faint red "wash" or slip. Vessels are poorly made, as evidenced by marked asymmetry, unevenly thinned walls, poor surface finishing, and frequent fireclouding.

Kulut Modeled censers exhibit these same characteristics in both the incense receptacle and the attached effigy figure. Vases are small and squat (total height 18–19 cm; internal mouth diameter ca. 11 cm), poorly made, and poorly proportioned, with rolled rims and a thin, unpolished light red wash or slip. Effigy figures and faces look like those of Ídolos, except they were made with less skill (and different clay). Heads typically feature braided hair, pointed teeth, large earspools, and a reptile or Pax monster headdress. They appear to represent Itzamna, but in a distinctive style that copies Ídolos Modeled censers, and they occur only in the Kowoj area of eastern Petén. Unlike Patojo Modeled censers, the legs of the effigy are not attached to the body but are made separately and attached separately to the vase. Kulut Modeled incensarios occur only at Zacpetén and are usually semi-reconstructible in primary contexts.

Pitufo Modeled

Pitufo Modeled incensarios are manufactured of the most common paste composition of the Postclassic period in the lakes region: Snail-Inclusion Paste ware. Snail-Inclusion Paste is made from a fine, silty, organic clay, probably obtained from the lake margins as it contains—as the name suggests—tiny fragments of lacustrine snails occurring naturally in these sediments (for details, see Rice 1987a: 105–107; also Cecil, Chapter 10, this volume). This paste, which varies in color from reddish-brown to tan to light gray to almost black, depending on firing and depositional conditions, was used to make the ubiquitous red-slipped (and sometimes incised or polychrome-painted) plates, bowls, jars, and other serving vessels of the Paxcamán ceramic group. In addition, serving vessels with "pink" (Trapeche group) and sometimes tan/brown (Macchiato) or black (Fulano) slips were made of this paste.

Pitufo Modeled censers are found in the Petén lakes region, at Zacpetén and Macanché Island, and also at Tipu, but they are nowhere common. They seem particularly associated with semi-effigies of a diving god.

Composite Censers

Composite incense burners include large vase and cup forms and perhaps "ladles" and are described as "composite" because their decoration may include both appliquéd elements and impressions in the form of fillets, spikes, disks, and so on. They were typically made of the same pastes used for utilitarian wares. Vessels were often covered with stucco on the exterior and interior, but at Zacpetén and other sites in the lakes region, the stucco was usually eroded. Types include Extranjeras Impressed and various composite types: La Justa, Mumúl, Zaklak, Gotas, and Fíjate.

The most common types of composite censers in the eastern Petén lakes region were initially classified as Extranjeras Impressed and La Justa Composite on the basis of pottery from the Topoxté and Macanché islands (Rice 1979, 1987a: 176–179). Both were made of the same or very similar gray to light brown, moderately coarse, calcite paste, classified as Montículo Unslipped ware, which was also used for Pozo Unslipped utilitarian jars. Excavations at Zacpetén yielded larger quantities of composite censers as well as larger fragments exhibiting combinations of decorative modes, making it difficult to consistently differentiate Extranjeras (defined by impressed decoration) and La Justa types.

Ultimately, I concluded that most of the Zacpetén incensarios should be classified as La Justa Composite type, also distinguishable from Extranjeras by shape and proportion: La Justa Composite censers are more open and globular, while Extranjeras vessels are more narrow and vase-shaped. La Justa composite censers, in other words, are intermediate in proportion between those of Puxteal Composite from the Tayasal area in the west (Chase 1983), which are broad and urn-shaped, and those of Extranjeras Impressed to the east at Yaxhá, which are more typically tall, narrow, and vase-shaped (but cf. Hermes 2000d: figure 68). These differences in shape and proportion might be related to differences in incense burners used at Chich'en Itza and Mayapán: censers at Chich'en Itza were more open and globular (see Brainerd 1958: figure 97c), whereas those at Mayapán were taller and vase-shaped. La Justa Composite censers at Zacpetén often displayed paired or quadripartite arrangements of appliqués as, for example, columns of spikes on opposite sides of the vase or double-disks arranged in a square on opposite sides between the spikes. Because many fragments of these censers do not display these diagnostic characteristics of form or embellishment, however, they are called Extranjeras/La Justa.

Mumúl Composite type became confusing, as my initial field sortings, based on the definition of Mumúl at Macanché (Rice 1987a: 192–193), incorporated excessive paste variability. At Zacpetén, Mumúl came to be a quasi-residual category with two varieties: light and dark paste. With the accumulation of more and more material, I realized that these were not simply firing variants but two distinct paste wares and, hence, types. Mumúl Composite: Dark Paste variety most closely fits the original type at Macanché. Relatively uncommon, it has a dark brown and fairly coarse paste (possibly related to Moza variety of Patojo Modeled). Vessels include large shallow basins or bowls, often stuccoed, with a thick appliqué fillet and a pedestal base. They are not always clearly censers; some look like receptacles used with Late Classic censer stands, whereas others may lack appliqués. Some are nearly identical to Diane Chase's (1988) Pum Modeled pedestal bowl censers. It is not possible to satisfactorily date these vessels. There may be some relation to Late and Terminal Classic Miseria Appliqué type.

I subsequently renamed the "light paste variety" of Mumúl as Zaklak Composite. Zaklak Composite most commonly occurs as small, often crudely made and asymmetrical cups or open bowls with appliquéd spikes and fingernail impressions. The base can be described as either a low pedestal or a high ring base; rare examples have tripod feet. The paste is light yellowish-tan to grayish (typically 10YR 8/2–3), soft, and fine; I have not given it a pasteware designation. Vessels are often relatively thick-walled, given their size.

Gotas Composite censers are manufactured of the orange-brown and poorly finished Uapake Carbonate Paste ware (Rice 1987a: 181–183). At Zacpetén, Gotas Composite censers sometimes had only fingernail impressions in the exterior wall (i.e., not true composite treatment) and frequently displayed rolled rims. Gotas censers are late.

Fíjate Impressed/Composite censers are uncommon and very late. They are typically dark red-orange on the exterior and black on the interior, with very thin walls. Decoration consists of broad, shallow fingertip impressions on a fillet or directly into the wall; spikes are sometimes present.

ADDITIONAL PERSPECTIVES ON THE KOWOJ

────── Prudence M. Rice ──────────────────────────────

The four relatively short chapters in Part V contribute to the answer to our question, Who were the Kowoj, by adding various perspectives, chrono-logical and behavioral. These perspectives do not so much add new ways to identify the Kowoj archaeologically as they do inform us on their strategies for negotiating relations with their pasts and with the increasingly bitter cir-cumstances of their present realities.

Chapters 13 and 16 provide temporal anchors to the Kowoj story in Petén. Chapter 13 is an elucidation of the text and imagery of Zacpetén Altar 1, which we found broken and reset into the plaza-facing southern facade of Structure 606, a large open hall on the north side of Group A. The unusual text and layout, as discussed by David Stuart, provide ties to Late and Terminal Classic mythology relating to solar — and thus kingly — (re)birth on the morn-ing of the winter solstice. Both its presence in the Late Postclassic structural facade and its message make Altar 1 of unusual import. First, it supports our proposition that the Postclassic Xiw/Kowoj settlement of Zacpetén represents a return to a homeland: the Late and Terminal Classic residents of the penin-sula or the Lake Salpetén basin were ancestral to the Postclassic occupants, who deliberately and meaningfully appropriated that past into a highly vis-ible civic-ceremonial structure. Second, it supports the concept, articulated in Chapter 7 but also earlier (Pugh 2003b), that the buildings on the higher east side of the Group A plaza represented a higher social unit as well: the dominant half of a moiety. In Maya cosmovision, east is the primary and most powerful direction, the direction of sunrise. Thus, the incorporation of this early sunrise-referring text into the east side of a centuries-later architectural complex speaks volumes about social, physical, and mythic continuities from the Classic period, through the "collapse," to the Late Postclassic in the southern lowlands.

Chapter 16 refers to the later years of the temporal scale, addressing the ethnogenesis of the Northern Lacandon Maya and the role of the Kowoj in this process. Throughout the Yucatán peninsula after the early sixteenth century, the widespread response of the Maya to their new Spanish overlords was to emigrate from settled areas to those relatively empty and isolated. Timothy Pugh proposes that this was the Kowoj response to the 1697 conquest of the Itza and Spanish attempts to round up the Maya in the lakes area. The increasingly common presence of the Kowoj surname in eastern Chiapas suggests that the Kowoj fled there, where they mingled with refugees from Yucatán and became known as the Lacandon Maya. His proposal is strongly supported by continuities in ritual structures and layouts, particularly between the oratorios and temples of the temple assemblages at Zacpetén and the Lacandon god houses. The social structure of the Northern Lacandon in the "ethnographic present" emphasizes a totem-like entity called *onen*, pairs of which may share a ceremonial name. Kowoj is one of the ceremonial names and includes two *onen* identified with different species of peccary, making one wonder if the two sides of the Group A temple assemblage—which we suggest in Chapter 7 represents a moiety—could represent two *onen*. In any case, the lack of direct reference to tarantulas (Kowoj = *chiwo* = tarantula) is of interest.

Anchored by these temporal bookends, Chapters 14 and 15 discuss two very different aspects of Late Postclassic life in Petén as lived by the Kowoj. Chapter 14 is an examination of long-distance trade in the Postclassic world through the lens of the obsidian artifacts from Zacpetén. It is evident from Bishop Diego de Landa's (in Tozzer 1941) account, and others, that during Colonial times the Maya maintained circulation of a variety of indigenous valuable goods such as obsidian but also marine shell and jade that would not have entered the formal economy of the Spaniards and the Euro-centered world system. This trade probably also included officially unsanctioned goods used in their "heathen" rituals, such as copal incense and the pottery or wooden "idols" in which the incense was burned. This underground system of production and exchange, which continued to operate for about 200 years of Colonial rule, might be called a "gray" economy or market (or perhaps "black market," in the case of incensarios), a parallel system of unauthorized circulation of goods that is not uncommon in the modern economy. Within this sector of the dual economy, the Petén lakes area—distant, isolated, and far from the vigilant eyes of Spanish colonial authorities—became in effect a core area, where Itza-dominated production and exchange of key indigenous commodities flourished. One line of support for this idea is a previous suggestion that obsidian was more widely available in the lakes area in the Postclassic than in earlier periods, as it was no longer found primarily in special deposits. Another is the region's sustained access to multiple obsidian sources.

Chapter 15 examines one specific point on the Zacpetén sacred landscape: the Operation 1000 mass grave in the northwest corner of the Group A temple assemblage, immediately west of Structure 606. The pattern of multiple burials in the northwest corner of plazas is found at Mayapán in Yucatán and also at Topoxté, suggesting that their creation is a Kowoj-specific behavior. William Duncan argues that Operation 1000 was created by exhuming previously interred individuals (possible "enemy ancestors") at Zacpetén and reburying them in an act that represented ritual violence: the remains were dumped in the center of the pit, with select elements missing, and they lacked grave goods. He proposes that the presence and timing of the creation of the mass graves at Zacpetén and Topoxté suggest that they were part of the Kowoj's early migration to, and emergence as a political force in, the Petén lakes region.

Duncan's analysis is of interest in terms of the text on Altar 1, reset into Structure 606, which refers to a mythological birth occurring in a "hole" or cavity of some sort. One wonders if this hole might refer to the pit of the mass grave just west of that structure, which seems to have been excavated early in the history of occupation of the Zacpetén peninsula. Perhaps this early pit in some way marked the location of the setting sun on the winter solstice, for example, as viewed from an earlier structure under Structure 602. The Kowoj mass grave there may represent a reappropriation of this long-taboo space, reviving its sacrality and rededicating it through ritual mass reburial.

THE SYMBOLISM OF ZACPETÉN ALTAR 1

—— David Stuart ———————————————————————————

In 1996 a remarkable disc-shaped stone sculpture was found at the site of Zacpetén, located in the central lake district of Petén in northern Guatemala. The stone no doubt once served as an altar, probably placed before an upright stela, but the two large pieces were found reused in later construction. In this chapter I focus on the interpretation of the hieroglyphic texts and iconography of the monument and in doing so reveal that the altar is important to our understanding of Classic Maya cosmology and political ideology.

The visual design of Zacpetén Altar 1 (as it is designated) is unusual in many ways, but it is also revealing in its symbolism (Figure 13.1). Four large mat designs are arranged around the outside of the circular layout, each separated by a square frame of four glyphs. Obviously, the mats are oriented in some way to the four world directions, and one might hazard a guess that they were designed here as mat-thrones for effigy figures. A circle of twenty glyphs appears inside the four glyph blocks, for a total of thirty-six glyphs. Inside this circle is another circle with a large, glyph-like head—damaged, it seems, by intentional burning—but enough of the carving exists to show

Figure 13.1. Altar 1, Zacpetén. Drawing by David Stuart.

a profile zoomorphic face adorned with a *k'an* (cross) element, and the entire head has a "seven" prefix. This is known from other artworks and texts to be a hieroglyph for a supernatural or mythical location, one of a pair of vaguely understood places having some cosmological importance. Evidently, the altar was conceived as a representation of a cosmic locale and served as a base for ritual burning of fire and incense. More will be said of this in the subsequent discussion.

The circular text and the four radiating text panels constitute one continuous inscription, and the arrangement is unlike any other (Figure 13.2). The inscription begins with the four glyphs in the square panel at upper left, read left-to-right and top-to-bottom (A1, B1, A2, B2), and then it runs down to the circular text, to C. The inscription then runs clockwise for five blocks to glyph G before moving up to H1 in the square panel at the upper right. The reading then proceeds down to J and K and passes to L, M, and N, and so forth. The full sequence of blocks is: A1, B2, A2, B2, C, D, E, F, G, H1, I1, H2, I2, J, K, L, M, N, O1, P1, O2, P2, Q, R, S, T, U, V1, W1, V2, W2, X, Y, Z, A', B'. This sequence reproduces a clockwise motion, with intermittent passages through "stations"

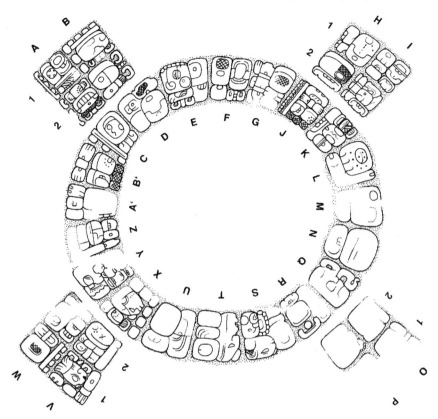

Figure 13.2. Reading order of glyphic text of Altar 1, Zacpetén. Drawing by David Stuart.

between each of the four cardinal or inter-cardinal directions. The replication of the movement of a ritual procession is striking and no doubt intentional.

The Text

The inscription begins in the outer square at the upper left (at B1-A2) with a Distance Number interval of 2.0.9.3, a span of just over forty solar years. No base date for the time calculation is provided, but the end point of the reckoning into the past is given in the first two blocks of the inner ring text (C and D) as 8 Kab'an, the Seating of Kumk'u. Only one placement of this date in the Long Count seems possible — 9.18.19.8.17 — because the 2.0.9.3 Distance Number nicely connects to the K'atun 5 Ajaw ending 10.1.0.0.0. I suspect the *k'atun* ending was recorded on a stela, now lost, that accompanied Altar 1. This 10.1.0.0.0 placement is very late, but it makes it contemporary with several other monuments at nearby Ixlú and Jimbal (Table 13.1). In the

Table 13.1. Cycle Ten dates* on monuments in central Petén.

Monument	Long Count	Gregorian Year
Uaxactun Stela 13	10.0.0.0.0	830
Flores Stela 3	10.0.0.0.0	830
Ucanal Stela 3	10.0.10.0.0?	840
Zacpetén Altar 1	10.1.0.0.0	849
Ucanal Stela 4	10.1.0.0.0	849
Seibal Stelae 8–11	10.1.0.0.0	849
Flores Stela 2	10.1.0.0.0	849
Ixlú Stela 1	10.1.10.0.0	859
Tikal Stela 11	10.2.0.0.0	869
Flores Stela 1	10.2.0.0.0	869
Ixlú Altar 1	10.2.10.0.0	879
Jimbal Stela 1	10.2.10.0.0	879
Jimbal Stela 2	10.3.0.0.0	889
Uaxactun Stela 12	10.3.0.0.0	889

* Because many of these dates are given only by the "Short Count" (day-names in both calendars), the Long Count dates are reconstructions.

widely accepted calendar correlation (the so-called GMT), the *k'atun* ending falls on November 30, A.D. 849, around which time the altar must have been dedicated. But "8 Kab'an Seating of Kumk'u" is the featured date of the altar inscription—a day that had long since passed four decades previously, on December 23, 809. This came just two days after the winter solstice, a connection that proves important to the interpretation of the altar and the text overall.

The event recorded in block E is "was born," spelled here in the somewhat unusual grouping **SIJ?-ji-ya-ja**. The presence of the sequence **-ji-ya-ja** after the upturned head seems to provide a more complete phonetic spelling of the verb than found elsewhere. Usually, after this event glyph we would expect to find a personal name, but in block F we come across something very different. It looks to be a place reference, based on the so-called hole or maw sign, widely agreed to refer to earthly cavities, caves, or wells. As an iconographic element this sign is identical to the skeletal-looking jaws of the centipede, often depicted in Maya art as a "portal" of the Underworld (Carrasco and Hull 2002; Taube 2003). Here it takes a **-ya** suffix, as is often the case in other examples, probably as a phonetic complement. (The phonetic value of the main sign is thought to be **WAY**, but this is still difficult to confirm on epigraphic evidence.) The prefix in glyph F is a still undeciphered term that works in other inscriptions as a preposition or relational noun of some kind, usually prefixed before words for locations or physical spaces. In the inscriptions of Chich'en Itza, it is replaced in one text by the syllabic grouping **i-chi-la**, suggesting that there it may have carried the value *ich* or *ichil*, meaning "within." In the southern inscriptions it surely would have had a Ch'olan pronunciation, probably *wuut-il*, "within." In any event, the overall sense of the glyph is to specify a location in connection with the birth described in the previous glyph. We can understand the two together (E and F) to mean "he is born within the hole/cavity," or something similar. As we will see, this looks to be a mythical event.

The birth phrase in E and F is followed by the more specific place name that is damaged in places. We nevertheless see the **K'INICH-** prefix before *pa* and one or two effaced elements. Moving to the next glyph at H1, we find clearly spelled **wi-tzi**, for *witz*, "hill, mountain" (Stuart 1987). *K'inich Pa . . . Witz*, 'the Great Sun ? Mountain,' is probably named here as the location of the "hole" and of the birth in general. The mountain name is incomplete, yet the honorific prefix K'inich shows that it names some important aspect or entity identified with the divine sun, K'inich Ajaw. Another component of the place name seems to be written in the first half of block I1, but it is difficult to discern. Finally, at I1b and H2 we read that the entire episode is said to have taken place in "the cosmos," here referred to by the couplet noun *chan ch'een*, or "in the sky and in the caves." This two-part phrase is common in many inscriptions, but to my knowledge it only accompanies records of ritual or mythological activities—never more mundane historical events. I revisit this issue after reviewing the forms and readings of the individual glyphs around the stone altar.

The name of the protagonist finally comes in the next several blocks, beginning at I2 and running along the interior band, from J through N and perhaps beyond. The glyph at I2 shows again the honorific prefix K'inich-, now before an unusual assortment of elements that include, in part, **TAHN-na**. Two personal references come next (at J and K), confirming that this portion of the text names our subject. The first of these is **AJ-YAAX-KALOMTE'-ma**, *Aj Yaax Kalomte'* 'He, the Green Kalomte'.' Although *kalomte'* is a common title for Classic Maya kings, the *yaax* prefix is odd. A similar title appears in the late inscriptions of Seibal—roughly contemporary with the texts here—where it seems to work as a personal name. It may have had the same role here, in conjunction with the preceding block.

The next glyph, at K, is a war-related title based on the noun *b'aak*, meaning "captive." Its full sense is unclear because the middle element is an unreadable logogram, but it may be closely related to the "count of captives" title found in inscriptions of several sites (Stuart 1985). The exact same honorific appears in a few examples in the text of Yaxchilán. At the least, it can be said to be a term referring to captive taking and militaristic prowess.

The next several glyphs are severely eroded. Context would suggest that many, if not all, of them, leading to block N and up to columns O and P, contain more titles and references to the historical protagonist of the opening birth statement. This is also strongly suggested by the glyph at block R, which, to anticipate, is a common "child-of-mother" term that introduces a parentage statement; a child's name must necessarily precede it. Of the eight name or title glyphs in L through Q, very little can be said. L may read **ma-le-[le]**, and N looks to have the form of **CHAN-na**. The final glyph of the passage (Q) is clearly **K'AWIL**, a deity name encountered a bit later as a part of another royal name.

From this point forward the inscription contains nothing but an extended parentage statement, naming the mother and father of the protagonist. The mother is named in blocks T and U as Ix K'inil Ikaatz, 'Lady Sun Burden.' She carries the title at V1 **ZAK-CHAY-ya-AJAW**, *Zak Chay Ajaw*, 'White Fish Lord.' We then find the enigmatic glyph *9-pa-ta*, which possibly relates to the reckoning of units of tribute (*patan*) (Stuart 1998). A new relationship expression comes at V2 and W2, written as **U-si-hi U-CHIT-ta-CH'AB**. The words *u sih u chit ch'ab'* '(the child is) his gift, his *chit* creation,' appear in other inscriptions as a way of describing the relationship of a son to his father, and the same is true here, complementing the earlier statement naming the protagonist's mother.

The father's name phrase comes at X-B', the very end of the inscription. He carries the title **4-WINIKHAAB'?-AJAW-wa** 'the four-score years lord,' and his proper name is given in block Y. Remarkably, this name is familiar to students of Maya glyphs as that of Ruler 1 of Dos Pilas, B'ahlaj Chan K'awil (Houston 1993). The temporal distance precludes this from being the same individual, but the presence of an identical name may reflect a historical connection between the two sites. This should not be too surprising, given that the lords of Dos Pilas made use of the same Mutul emblem glyph used by rulers at Tikal and sites near Zacpetén, such as Ixlú and Jimbal.

The father may in fact carry the same emblem glyph of Mutul, but it is largely effaced. This follows a title **K'INICH-AJ-CHAK-?-TE'**, which also occurs with the name of the earlier Tikal ruler Yik'in Chan K'awil (Ruler B). The king is finally given the important but little understood title *kaloomte'* (**KALOOM-ma-TE'**) in the final glyph of the text.

In summary, the gist of the inscription is fairly simple, despite its ornate layout and presentation. The featured event is birth, but not as a historical event in a ruler's life cycle. Rather, the references to "(from) within the maw" and to a cosmological mountain strongly suggest a supernatural setting for the episode. Now that the details of the glyphs and signs have been put forward, we can consider what the mythological significance of the birth may be.

Discussion: Altars, Sacred Landscapes, and Places of Rebirth

The date of the birth event is probably a key to the overall interpretation of the altar and its inscription. As mentioned, the 9.18.19.8.17 placement corresponds to December 23, A.D. 809, very close to the winter solstice. The language of the text is not very direct, yet I believe it describes the ancient Maya understanding of the winter solstice and how it was related to other types of cyclical phenomena they perceived in the world around them. The opening event glyph shows that the Maya saw the winter solstice as the birth or rebirth of the sun—a widely attested belief still found throughout the Maya area and beyond (Girard 1962; Gossen 1986). There is a real historical name after this opening statement, suggesting that the sun is here equated with a deceased and resurrected king of the Zacpetén polity.

Support for this interpretation comes from distant Palenque, where the well-known sarcophagus lid of K'inich Janab Pakal also presents a theme of solar rebirth. The image on the lid has been studied by numerous writers (e.g., Schele and Mathews 1998: 95–132), and there is general agreement that the image represents the apotheosis of the ruler after death, or after he "enters the road." The prevailing interpretation of the image suggests that the king, shown reclining atop a "sun bowl," is falling into the open maw of the Underworld as the setting sun (Freidel, Schele, and Parker 1993: 269; Schele 1981). I disagree with this traditional view of the sarcophagus's symbolism, for several reasons. As several writers have pointed out (e.g., Taube 1994), the figure of Pakal is shown in the distinctive position of an infant, suggesting that a clear birth metaphor is at work in the design of the sarcophagus. Indeed, the "sun bowl" on which he lies corresponds to the glyphic sign **EL**, the basis of the word for "east," *el-k'in*, 'sun emerges.' *El* is also an important word associated with ritual burning, and Karl Taube (1994) is surely correct in stressing that the solar bowl on the sarcophagus is a depiction of a ceremonial incense burner. The related meanings of *el* ("rise up, burn") are a clear indication that Pakal should more correctly be understood metaphorically as the rising sun in the east. He is specifically the reborn fiery sun, resurrected after death with the cross-like tree of life and sustenance. The sarcophagus thus offers a visual parallel to what is textually described on the Zacpetén altar: the sun being born anew from the "maw" or "hole" of the earth. Interestingly, the Temple of the Inscriptions at Palenque, which holds Pakal's tomb, has been previously interpreted as having significant alignments with winter solstice sunset (Schele 1981).

As mentioned earlier, the central zoomorphic head of the Zacpetén altar is one of a pair of similar emblems that are important in Maya iconography, one with the prefix "seven" and the other with "nine" (Figure 13.3). They most often appear as glyphs, either paired or individually, or as glyphs integrated into more iconographic settings, as is the case here on Zacpetén Altar 1. The "7 and 9 Heads," as they are sometimes called, are likely names of important locations in the overall framework of Maya cosmology, although their precise meaning is difficult to ascertain (Freidel, Schele, and Parker 1993; Kubler 1985; Miller and Taube 1993: 151). The "young maize" sign (-**NAL**) above each glyph is also likely related to this toponymic function (Stuart and Houston 1994). The locational function of the 7 and 9 Heads is suggested by their common use as "pedestals" beneath standing or seated portraits. Otherwise, they are sometimes found held in people's hands, as if they are offerings or qualities those individuals in some way possess. Another important visual aspect of the 7 and 9 Heads is their skeletal appearance, strongly linking them to certain representations of animated seeds in Classic Maya art.

Although my own ideas are not well formulated at this stage, I believe the 7 and 9 Heads represent some type of dualistic aspect of cosmic regeneration and rebirth. They are specific places in the sense that they are place names and are often replicated by means of altars such as the Zacpetén stone, but they are simultaneously very general or even universal in their scope of reference. The two glyphs are routinely associated with the symbolism of growth and resurrection, often in direct association with deceased persons.

Figure 13.3. The "7 and 9 Heads," as they appear on the Temple of the Sun at Palenque (redrawn from Miller and Taube 1993: 151). Both feature a skeletal-jawed, long-nosed creature with an elaborate headdress. Left: the 7 Head, facing left, with the bar-dot number seven (shaded) on the front of the headdress. Right: the 9 Head, facing right, with the number nine (shaded) atop the headdress.

The connection to ancestors seems to rely on a conceptual linkage in Maya philosophy among rebirth after death, agricultural growth of new maize, and the rising of the eastern sun. Although I have no evidence to prove it, I have wondered if the dualism underlying the 7 and 9 Heads may be based in part on the natural partition between the winter and summer solstices.

The suggestion that the Zacpetén altar serves as a "text version" of the iconography on Pakal's sarcophagus lid at Palenque is strengthened by the imagery on Stela 3 from Tzum, Campeche. There, a king is dancing above an example of the "7 Head" place glyph, strikingly similar in form to the central emblem of the Zacpetén altar. This in turn rests atop a damaged calendar sign (possibly "12 Ajaw"). All of the stela's stacked elements—king, place glyph, and temporal indicator—emerge from the open jaws of the centipede, much in the way Pakal is depicted in his tomb. The composition suggests that the Period Ending date commemorated by this stela was a time of renewal and cosmic resurrection. At the least, the Tzum stela establishes that the "7 Head" is one location for the Underworld portal, lending weight to the interpretation of the Zacpetén altar as a commemoration and representation of this place of rebirth.

Conclusion

Numerous Maya altars had important functions as varied replications of points on the sacred landscape, and indeed this idea has had great continuity in Mesoamerica, up to the ritual *mesas* of the present day. Altar 1 of Zacpetén is a remarkable example of a Classic Maya effort to condense many important meanings into one stone monument. Like many circular altars found at Toniná, Tikal, Copán, and other sites, Zacpetén Altar 1 seems to have been a place for much ritual burning, perhaps of copal incense—so much so, in fact, that the central image was severely damaged by heat and exfoliation (see Stuart 1996). The burning of ritual fire on the altar should not seem surprising, however, for the stone's design replicates a cosmic structure, and in its center it depicts the hieroglyph of a place where resurrection took place from the earth.

Altar 1's inscription explicitly links this theme to a historical person who probably lived and died at Zacpetén in the Terminal Classic period. After his passing he was "born from the maw" as the new sun on the winter solstice, apparently fulfilling the destiny of many Maya kings and following in the perpetual cycles of regeneration that operate in both the earth and the sky.

Appendix 13.I
Transcription of Zacpetén Altar 1

A1: U-TZ'AK-AJ
B1: 3-4-WINIK-ji-ya
A2: 2-WINIKHAAB?-ya
B2: u-ti-ya

C: 8-"KABAN"
D: CHUM-HUL?-OHL
E: SIJ?-ji-ya-ja
F: ?-la-WAY?-ya
G: K'INICH-pa-?-?

wi-tzi
?-?-?-CHAN-na
CH'EEN-na
K'INICH-?-TAHN-na

AJ-YAX-KALOOM-ma-TE'
a-?-BAAK-ki
ma-le-le?
?-?-?
CHAN-na

?
?
?
?

K'AWIIL
U-BAAH-U-1-TAHN
?-IXIK-K'UH
IX-K'IN-ni?
i-ka-tzi

SAK-CHAY-ya-AJAW
9-pa-ta
U-si-hi
U-CHIT-ta?-CH'AB

4-WINIKHAAB-AJAW
BAH(LAJ)-CHAN-K'AWIIL
K'INICH-AJ-CHAK-HUH?-TE'
K'UH(UL)-MUTUL-AJAW
KALOOM-TE'

POSTCLASSIC TRADE
Sources of Obsidian at Zacpetén

—— Prudence M. Rice and Leslie G. Cecil ————————————————

The political economy of the Postclassic period in Mesoamerica is generally believed to have differed considerably from that of earlier periods. In particular, trade networks and mechanisms are believed to have been dominated by maritime rather than overland routes, with various trading ports, or entrepôts (sometimes identified as ports of trade; Chapman 1957; see Gasco and Berdan 2003; Smith and Berdan 2003a), existing along the coast of the Yucatán peninsula. Among these are Isla Cerritos (Andrews et al. 1989), Cozumel (Sabloff and Rathje 1975a), and the cayes off the Belize shoreline, such as Ambergris Caye (Guderjan 1995) and Marco González (Graham 1989; Graham and Pendergast 1989).

One interpretation is that a new "merchant class" may have arisen by or during the Postclassic period, which may have been responsible for the increase in mercantile activity (Sabloff and Rathje 1975b). Another suggestion is that the primary "currencies" of Mesoamerica had changed by the Contact period, and the demand for obsidian — a possible earlier currency — had diminished (Freidel 1986b: 418). More recently, it has been proposed that Postclassic

Mesoamerica represents a pre-capitalist "world system" characterized by a high degree of commercial exchange of goods that was not tightly tied to state institutions (Smith and Berdan 2003a). Specifically, Mesoamerica has been divided into different zones of participation in this world system: core zones, affluent production zones, resource extraction zones, exchange circuits, and style zones.

In the lowland Maya core zone of this proposed pre-capitalist world system, the Late Postclassic politico-religious capital of Mayapán in northern Yucatán was likely also its economic center, at least until that city's collapse and apparent abandonment in A.D. 1450. Affluent production zones consisted of numerous and populous polities where high levels of critical agricultural, craft, or specialized extraction activities permitted heavy participation in exchange networks (Smith and Berdan 2003c: 26–27). The central Petén lakes area has not been characterized within this scheme, but it probably constituted an affluent production zone throughout most of the Postclassic period. Postclassic Petén might be very similar to the affluent production zone of northern Belize, characterized by production of honey, wax, cotton, textiles, animal pelts, feathers, dyes, paints, vanilla, achiote, copal, and wooden canoes and paddles (ibid.: 28). Petén lacked the high-quality chert known from northern Belize, but it was a center of production of effigy incensarios, and it also may have been a source of lacustrine products such as dried fish (*blanco*: *Petenia esplendida*), freshwater snails and shells, or turtles and their carapaces.

The politico-economic situation in the northern Maya lowlands in the decades after 1450 is difficult to assess, as it is not clear which site(s), if any, replaced Mayapán as a center(s) of political and economic leadership, although Tihoo/Mérida is a strong possibility. During the first half of the sixteenth century, sometime between 1520 and 1540, most of Mesoamerica came—at least nominally—into the capitalist world system as a consequence of incorporation into the Spanish colonial empire in the Americas. The Maya lowlands, given their lack of mineral wealth as a resource extraction zone, began and remained on the periphery of this system, despite influential Spanish politico-economic and ecclesiastical capitals in Mérida and Campeche.

Nevertheless, all indications suggest that a thriving underground or gray economy operated among the Maya during Colonial times, propelled by the desire for indigenous goods that continued to be highly valued. In addition, the remote location of the central Petén lakes constituted an ideal location for ensuring that such trade could proceed uninterrupted. One such trade network focused on obsidian.

Obsidian in the Postclassic and Colonial Indigenous Economic Systems

In the proposed pre-capitalist, Postclassic world system, obsidian was considered a "key commodity" and a necessity for domestic tools (Smith 2003: 123). It was also, as discussed in other chapters, widely used in weaponry. The collapse of obsidian as a possible currency, and its commodification, is thought to have occurred near the end of the Late Classic period (Braswell

2004: 186–187; Freidel 1986b: 428), when it appears to have moved through market exchange systems rather than through redistribution. Most studies of obsidian at lowland sites in the Classic period have been conducted from the consumers' point of view: the occurrence and spatial distribution of material from different sources. Comparatively little attention has been given to the politico-economic circumstances of the supply regions, although several features of these areas are of interest (Braswell 2003: 155, 2004: 182–184). First, obsidian materials from any particular source are not distributed evenly (concentrically) around that source; rather, they are distributed in specific directions. Second, and more important, there is no clear evidence of any major politico-economic centers controlling two of the major Guatemalan sources of obsidian that reached the Maya lowlands, El Chayal and San Martín Jilotepeque (Braswell 2002). This suggests to Geoffrey Braswell that procurement of obsidian from its highland sources was managed independently by individual politico-economic centers in the lowlands, as opposed to being controlled by polities at the sources themselves. An example of this comes from Copán, Honduras, which seems to have been a regional center of procurement and distribution of obsidian from the Ixtepeque source (Aoyama 2001). According to Braswell (2003: 155), available evidence suggests that "obsidian extraction and circulation were governed more by demand than by central planning." He concluded that populations near obsidian sources may have deliberately maintained political autonomy through tribute or gift giving.

Obsidian trade in the Maya area throughout the Terminal Classic through Late Postclassic periods has been described in terms of a single, largely undifferentiated exchange sphere extending from northern Yucatán and narrowing southward to the Pacific coast. This lack of specificity of exchange routes is doubtless a consequence of the fact that, in general, source data exist for only a limited number of artifacts from a limited number of sites, and the most common source is Ixtepeque in extreme southeastern Guatemala (Braswell 2003: 154). Large quantities of obsidian are known primarily from Mayapán, which Braswell (ibid.: 155) interpreted as indicating that that city controlled circum-peninsular trade in obsidian. It was earlier hypothesized (Nelson, Sidrys, and Holmes 1978) that Chich'en Itzá, Tulum, and Cozumel also played a role as Postclassic redistribution centers.

The Sample of Zacpetén Obsidians Analyzed by X-Ray Fluorescence

To begin to understand the role of obsidian in the economy of Zacpetén, a total of 262 samples from that site, plus 19 obsidians from nearby Ixlú and one from Nixtun-Ch'ich' to the west, were analyzed by X-ray fluorescence (XRF) to determine their geological sources (Cecil, Rice, and Glascock 2008). The artifacts chosen for analysis represent a purposive or judgmental sample drawn from the total populations of Zacpetén and Ixlú excavated obsidians, rather than a probabilistic one. A major criterion for selection was the likelihood that the objects represented actual Postclassic artifacts rather than earlier materials incorporated into Postclassic construction fills along with pottery and miscellaneous debris from Classic or Preclassic deposits. The analyzed obsidians included a variety of shaped artifacts (projectile points, drills, disks), blades and blade fragments, cores, and flakes. Here we report primarily on the projectile points from Zacpetén.

Nondestructive elemental analysis was carried out by Leslie G. Cecil at the Missouri University Research Reactor facility using an ElvaX desktop energy-dispersive X-ray fluorescence (EDXRF) spectrometer.[1] Elemental concentration values were correlated with known obsidian sources in Guatemala (El Chayal, Ixtepeque, and San Martín Jilotepeque) and Mexico (Pachuca, Ucareo, Orizaba, and Zacualtípan) using the ElvaX software comparison spectra feature.[2] The interpretation of compositional data obtained from the analysis of archaeological materials has been discussed in detail elsewhere (e.g., Baxter and Buck 2000; Bieber et al. 1976; Glascock 1992; Harbottle 1976; Neff 2000). The main goal of data analysis is to identify distinct homogeneous groups within the analytical database. On the basis of the provenance postulate, different chemical groups may be assumed to represent geographically restricted sources (Weigand, Harbottle, and Sayre 1977). For obsidian, raw material samples are frequently collected from known outcrops or secondary deposits, and the compositional data obtained on the samples are used to define the source localities or boundaries. Obsidian sources tend to be more localized and compositionally homogeneous, making artifact-source comparisons straightforward. Groups are characterized by the locations of their centroids and the unique relationships (i.e., correlations) between the elements. Decisions about whether to assign a specimen to a particular compositional group are based on the overall probability that the measured concentrations for the specimen could have been obtained from that group.

All obsidian samples were scanned as unmodified samples; a spot where the X-ray would hit was wiped clean with deionized water and a kemwipe. Each sample was placed in the sample chamber with the flattest surface, having the maximum surface area facing the X-ray beam. Accuracy errors result from inaccuracies of the regression model, statistical error of the calibration spectra, inaccuracy of the intensity of the calibration curve, and the energy calibration. When the error is taken into account, the relative analytical uncertainty for this project is less than 7 percent with this portable XRF unit (Elvatech 2004).

Results

Source determinations for 262 obsidian samples from Zacpetén assigned these objects to seven different sources: three in Guatemala and four in Mexico (Table 14.1). The only sample that did not consistently plot within the 90 percent ellipse of an obsidian source was LCO004, from Zacpetén Structure 602. Although the artifact did not consistently plot within the Ixtepeque ellipse, the Ixtepeque comparative X-ray spectrum and Mahalanobis distance calculations suggest that the artifact was made from Ixtepeque obsidian. This sample was a very thin microblade.

Table 14.1. Sources of 262* obsidians from Zacpetén.

| | Guatemala | | | Mexico | | | | |
	EC	IXT*	SMJ	PCH	UCA	ZAC	ORZ	Total
N =	97	98*	50	8	7	1	1	262
% =	37.0	37.4	19.1	3.0	2.7	0.4	0.4	100

Key: EC = El Chayal, IXT−Ixtepeque, SMJ = San Martín Jilotepeque, PCH = Pachuca, UCA = Ucareo, Zac = Zacualtípan, ORZ = Orizaba.
* Two Ixtepeque obsidians from Zacpetén were fragments of a single projectile point and are counted as one artifact here, although both halves were analyzed separately.

Table 14.2. Sourced obsidian from temple assemblages and Group 719 at Zacpetén.

				Source				
Group		EC	IXT	SMJ	PCH	UCA	ORZ	Total
Group A	N	30	30	11	–	2	–	73
	%	41.1	41.1	15.1		2.7		100
Group C	N	15	20	9	3	2	–	49
	%	30.6	40.8	18.4	6.1	4.1		100
Group 719	N	17	17	11	3	1	1	50
	%	34	34	22	6	2	2	100
Total		62	67	31	6	5	1	172

It appears from these data that during the Late Postclassic period, obsidian from both the El Chayal and Ixtepeque sources were intensively utilized at these sites and the San Martín Jilotepeque source considerably less so. Data from sourcing studies of obsidian from other Late Postclassic lowland Maya sites indicate that the Ixtepeque source strongly dominated usage, and in this the Zacpetén data appear to differ. This might be a consequence of the judgmental sampling strategy in which Ixtepeque obsidians were not emphasized because of their ease of recognition. Preliminary visual sourcing of the entire Zacpetén obsidian assemblage by the senior author (admittedly not an expert), however, suggested that El Chayal obsidian was indeed the most abundant, and the highly variable physical characteristics of the material (e.g., color, sheen, inclusions) indicated that a number of El Chayal source flows were exploited.

The spatial distribution of source material at the site is of interest and can be examined through the sourced obsidians from the two temple assemblages, Group A (n=73) and Group C (n=49), and Group 719 (n=50) at Zacpetén (Table 14.2). Groups A and C appear to have slightly different patterns of distribution of obsidian, with Group C having less from El Chayal and more (10 percent of the analyzed sample) from the Mexican sources, Pachuca and Ucareo, than did Group A. Group 719 is similar to both temple assemblages, being like Group A in having an equal percentage from the two main Guatemalan sources but like Group C in having a wider distribution of Mexican sources.

Table 14.3. Sourced obsidians from residential structures at Zacpetén.

Structures		EC	IXT	SMJ	PCH	Total
				Source		
Str. 732	N	9	10	8	–	27
	%	33.3	37.0	29.6		99.9
Gen. res.	N	18	17	8	2	45
	%	40	37.8	17.8	4.4	100.0
Total		27	27	16	2	72

Table 14.4. Sourced cores, chunks, and flakes of obsidian at Zacpetén.

Form		EC	IXT	SMJ	Mexico	Total
				Source		
Cores	N	7	5	1	–	13
Chunks	N	4	5	1	–	10
Flakes	N	0	4	7	–	11
Total		11	14	9	–	34

Only small samples of obsidian from residential structures at Zacpetén (Table 14.3) were analyzed: except for twenty-seven objects from Structure 732, the number analyzed varied from two to fifteen. These distributions show little variation from the overall patterns in the temple assemblages, providing little evidence to suggest that individual households or temple groupings "controlled" access to or distribution of material from different sources. It is interesting, however, that two of the seventeen obsidians (11.8 percent) from Mexican sources were recovered in domestic contexts.

Perhaps a better view of questions of "access to" or "control of" obsidian sources comes from analysis of the sources of the cores, chunks, and flakes of obsidian reflecting primary production (Table 14.4). Although tiny debitage was not included in the sample for XRF analysis, all recovered cores and core fragments, all chunks, and many flakes (i.e., non-blades) were included. Cores, chunks, and flakes were found only from the three main Guatemalan sources and none of the Mexican sources.

It is interesting that exhausted cores were recovered only in the three main groups at the site: the two temple assemblages, Group A and Group C, and the Structure 719 group. One was an exhausted bipolar core of Ixtepeque obsidian only 2.8 centimeters in length, with both ends having ground striking platforms. This might reflect the same practice as among the Lacandon, where blades were struck from chert cores only in the temples, or perhaps the cores were put to some ceremonial use. No cores were recovered in excavations in residential structures. Chunks and flakes, however, were found in wider contexts, both civic-ceremonial and domestic, suggesting that some obsidian-knapping activities took place in these structures.

Figure 14.1. Obsidian arrow points from Zacpetén and Ixlú.

Projectile Points

Bishop Diego de Landa reported that tools of siliceous stone (flint or chert and presumably also obsidian) were made and used in Yucatán in the sixteenth century (in Tozzer 1941: 186). Colonial dictionaries give some idea of how these were made: *bah tok* can be translated as "to make lancets and knives of flints and points for arrows, getting them from some thick [piece of] flint [*tok*], which is set upright" or, more specifically, to use a hammerstone "to drive something like a punch or chisel into the flint" core, which was probably held between the feet (Roys 1972: 49–50).

The most distinctive chipped stone tools of the Postclassic period in the Maya lowlands are tiny projectile points made on obsidian and chert blades. The occurrence of these small points (Figure 14.1) is significant because it relates to the introduction of bow-and-arrow technology. In the lowlands, these points are most commonly associated with the Late Postclassic, as at Mayapán (Proskouriakoff 1962b: figure 30), Santa Rita Corozal (Chase and Chase 1988: figure 57), and Tipu (Simmons 1995). In the Petén lakes area, we have previously reported the recovery of tiny arrow points from Terminal Classic deposits at Macanché Island (Rice 1987a: 215), and a small side-notched point was also recovered in a Terminal Classic context at Seibal (Willey 1978: 127).

At Copán, however, Kazuo Aoyama reported that these small side-notched points — which he calls "prismatic blade points" (Aoyama 2001: figure 2g, 2005: figures 3g–m, 4e–i) — were produced even earlier, in the Late Classic period. Similarly, eighteen prismatic blade points were recovered at Late Classic Aguateca (Aoyama 2007: table 1). Illustrations of these points suggest that they were larger (longer) than the Late Postclassic Petén points by 0.5 to 1.0 cm, but it is not known if this might be a consequence of the tools' function (their targets: birds, medium mammals, humans) or the relative abundance

Table 14.5. Sourced obsidian projectile points at Zacpetén.

	Source				Total
	EC	IXT	SMJ	ORZ	
N	42	33	33	1	109
%	38.5	30.3	30.3	0.9	100

Table 14.6. Sourced obsidian projectile points from civic-ceremonial structures.

	Source					Total
	EC	IXT	SMJ	ORZ	PCH	
Group A structures						
601	1	–	–	–	–	1
602	2	2	3	–	–	7
605	2	2	3	–	–	7
606	1	–	–	–	–	1
607	1	–	–	–	–	1
614	2	1	–	–	–	3
1000	1	–	–	–	1	
Subtotal	9	6	6	–	–	21
Group C structures						
764	–	–	–	–	–	0
766	–	–	–	–	–	0
767	2	–	2	–	–	4
Subtotal	2	–	2	–	–	4
Group 719 structures						
719	2	–	3	–	–	5
721	2	1	2	1	1	7
Subtotal	4	1	5	1	1	12
TOTAL	15	7	13	1	1	37

of the two materials, with obsidian—an import from the highlands—used in considerably smaller tools than chert.

A sample of 109 of 130 small obsidian projectile points, generally regarded as arrow points, from Zacpetén was included in the sample analyzed by XRF. The distribution of the sources of these points is shown in Table 14.5. These data are of particular interest because although Ixtepeque is generally regarded as the most widespread, and perhaps preferred, source of obsidian in the Postclassic, it does not seem to have been preferentially used at Zacpetén for making arrow points. The broader distribution of sources in this artifact category is not a consequence of the judgmental sampling procedure used to select obsidians for XRF analysis because virtually all points were included in the sample.

Comparison of sources of the obsidian points from civic-ceremonial contexts, including Group 719 for these purposes, is revealing (Table 14.6). It must be remembered that the Kowoj made projectile points from locally or regionally available chert, but these data suggest significant differences between the two temple assemblages, Groups A and C, in the activity of making or repairing obsidian projectile points, as well as the possibility of restricted access to certain sources. The 719 Group, particularly its temple, Structure 721, seem to be a focus of activity with regard to obsidian projectile points. The relative abundance of obsidian points in the temple and oratorio structures (Structures 602, 605, 614, and 721) at Zacpetén suggests a parallel to the modern Lacandon practice, cited earlier, of striking chert blades only in temples.

Conclusions

X-ray fluorescence analysis of 262 Postclassic- and Contact-period obsidian artifacts from the site of Zacpetén greatly increases the total sample of sourced obsidians from these time periods in the central Petén lakes region. The data from the current sample suggest a broader range of sources available in this area, as compared to the dominance of the Ixtepeque source in Belize and northern Yucatán. This is evident in the total analyzed sample; in the sources evident in cores, chunks, and flakes; and in the sources used for making characteristic Postclassic arrow points.

The possibility should be considered that some of the typically small Postclassic tools at Zacpetén and Ixlú were made from blades or flakes from earlier periods. For example, Aoyama (2001: 356) noted that the Early Postclassic inhabitants of Copán appear to have "scavenged exhausted polyhedral cores, macroblades, and large flakes from earlier deposits . . . and recycled them or produced new cutting tools from them." Similarly, obsidian hydration dating of artifacts from Tipu, Belize, indicates that the residents recycled earlier tools (Simmons 1995: 141, citing Graham 1991: 324). Among the Lacandon, obsidian is the preferred material, and Lacandon hunters prize blades they find at archaeological sites. James Nations and John Clark (1983: 42) quoted one individual who explained succinctly, "Obsidian makes a wound that causes heavy bleeding. A flint point will usually kill, but an obsidian point always kills."

One way to partially address this issue is to look at the striking platform of proximal blades. It has generally been noted that during the Postclassic period obsidian knappers prepared the striking platform by grinding it or otherwise roughening the surface, which was not the practice during the Classic period. Table 14.7 shows the appearance of ground platforms on forty-nine Zacpetén proximal blades. This table shows that the striking platforms of proximal blades from all sources exhibited grinding, although this was less common on blades of the San Martín Jilotepeque source. It supports the idea that the Petén lakes area did indeed use obsidian from multiple sources during the Postclassic and later periods. Although the practice of scavenging cannot be eliminated, it does not seem to be the primary explanation for the presence of a variety of sources of Postclassic obsidian.

Returning to questions of routes of obsidian trade and transshipment points, it is useful to take a broader overview of obsidian sourcing data from

Table 14.7. Sourced Zacpetén obsidian blades exhibiting ground versus plain striking platforms.

Platform		EC	IXT	SMJ	Mexico	Total
			Source			
Ground	N	10	17	3	5	35
	%	28.5	48.6	8.6	14.3	100
Plain	N	5	2	5	2	14
	%	35.7	14.3	35.7	14.3	100
Total	N	15	19	8	7	49
	%	30.6	38.8	16.3	14.3	100

the central Petén lakes area in comparison to other lowland Maya sites. Table 14.8 presents data on sourced obsidians from several Postclassic sites in the Maya lowlands of Yucatán, Belize, and Petén. Given the wide range of numbers of artifacts from these sites (many with fewer than twenty), it seems appropriate to compare percentages rather than actual numbers. It is evident from this table that the Guatemalan sources dominate the supply, particularly the Ixtepeque source. At least six Mexican sources are represented in the sample, but they occur as very small numbers of artifacts.

The data in Table 14.8 indicate different patterns of access to and use of obsidian at Postclassic sites in the central Petén lakes region as compared to Postclassic sites in Belize and Yucatán. The most distinctive difference is that the latter sites heavily emphasized the Ixtepeque source, generally thought to have been distributed by maritime trade routes. In contrast, sites in the lakes region made extensive use of all three Guatemalan sources, as well as having access to small but varied amounts of obsidian from Mexico. Ixtepeque obsidian probably reached the lakes region by being moved upriver from coastal Belize along the Belize River to Tipu and then westward into Petén (Cecil et al. 2007). El Chayal obsidian may also have been moved as part of maritime trade, given its presence at coastal sites, although it would be interesting to know if obsidian from different flows in the El Chayal source might have been traded along different paths.

The quantity of San Martín Jilotepeque obsidian constitutes the most marked difference between the Petén lakes sites, where it was apparently widely available, and sites in Belize and Yucatán, where it was present in only very small amounts. This suggests that obsidian from this source was not moved along coastal trade routes but was transported overland — although perhaps along river systems — into central Petén. San Martín obsidian is not a particularly desirable material in comparison to that of Ixtepeque and El Chayal because of the presence of tiny crystals and bubbles that raise the possibility of errors in delicate flaking. Thus, the question arises whether obsidian from the San Martín Jilotepeque source was more widely used in the Petén lakes region because it was desired — perhaps it was somehow easier to access there than elsewhere — or because it was relatively "cheap" in comparison to the other sources as a result of its low quality, or, alternatively, if it was

Table 14.8. Percentages of previously sourced Postclassic obsidians from from the Maya lowlands and the Petén lakes area.

| | Source Areas | | | | | | | | | | |
| | Mexico | | | | | | Guatemala | | | | Total Anal. |
	PCA	PAR	PO	ZAC	UCA	ZAR	EC	IXT	SMJ	Unk	
Mayapán	<1	<1	<1			<1	11?	98	<1	<1	1,241
Isla Cerritos	Mexico	66					34				12
San Gervasio					3			97			37
Xelha	18						10	90			29
Santa Rita			9				27	45			11
Colha								100			10
Wild Cane	Mexico	5					8	85	2		74
Lag. de On							27	67	3	20	660
Tipu	1						11	79	5	4	171
Petén lakes area				<1			25.5	51	23		
Topoxté							38	45	17		47
Macanché	Mexico	8					38	46	8		26
Salpetén	Mexico	2					20	58	20		34
Zacpetén	3		0.4	0.4	2.7		37	37.4	19	262	
Quexil							29	42	29		17
Ixlú			5.3		5.3		21	37	31		19
Tr. Nosotros	3					1	29	56	11		70

Sources: Tipu, Topoxté, and Mayapán data from Braswell (2003: 149–150) (based on visual methods; see individual sources cited therein); Petén lakes data from Rice et al. (1985: table 9), including 46 from Zacpetén; Trinidad de Nosotros, Isla Cerritos, Laguna de On, Colha, and Wild Cane Caye data from Cecil et al. (2007).

Key: PCA = Pachuca, Hidalgo; PAR = Paredón, Hidalgo; PO = Pico de Orizaba, Veracruz; ZAC = Zacualtipan, Hidalgo; UCA = Ucareo, Zinapécuaro, Cruz Negra – Michoacán; ZAR = Zaragoza, Puebla; EC = El Chayal, Guatemala; IXT = Ixtepeque, Guatemala; SMJ = San Martín Jilotepeque, Guatemala.

little used outside central Petén because consumers rejected it on the basis of quality.

Earlier, the senior author concluded (Rice 1984b: 194), on the basis of obsidian sourcing data, that the Topoxté Islands participated in a different network of external interactions than other Postclassic sites with similar data. The new data from Zacpetén reinforce this observation, indicating that the Xiw/Kowoj of the eastern Petén lakes participated in Late Postclassic– and Contact-period trade networks that allowed broad access to a variety of obsidian sources.[3]

A different but perhaps complementary explanation for the extensive use of multiple obsidian sources in the lakes area is that central Petén might have emerged as a core area in the lowland Maya economic sphere after the ca. A.D. 1450 fall of Mayapán and after the 1540 Spanish conquest of the northern lowlands. Despite the continual efforts of Spanish military and ecclesiastical personnel to bring the region under the Catholic crown, these efforts were futile until the closing years of the seventeenth century (see Jones 1998). During this interval, central Petén experienced an influx of migrants from areas to the north and east, and these immigrants might have brought with them economic ties to the highlands. Yet the Spaniards had also conquered the highland Maya in the early sixteenth century, disrupting social and economic patterns there, as in the northern lowlands. In any case, it is of no little interest that exotic obsidian continued to be obtained in the Petén lakes region during the sixteenth and seventeenth centuries, revealing the existence of a thriving gray economy.

Acknowledgments

XRF analysis of the obsidian artifacts was supported in part by a grant from the U.S. Department of Energy Office of Nuclear Energy, Science and Technology Award no. DE-FG07-03ID14531 to the Midwest Nuclear Science and Engineering Consortium under the Innovations in Nuclear Infrastructure and Education program.

Notes

1. The spectrometer consists of an X-ray generator, an X-ray detector, and a multi-channel analyzer (MCA). The detector is a solid-state Si-pin-diode with an area of 30 mm^2 and a resolution of 180 eV at 5.9 keV (at 1,000 counts per second). The ElvaX does not require liquid nitrogen cooling of the solid-state detector. The output signal of the detector is formed by a time-variant time processor with pileup rejector, baseline restorer, and automatic adaptation of shaping time to the input count rate. The MCA consists of a fast-shaping amplifier and a 4K-channel spectrometric analog-to-digital converter (SADC), built as a successive approximations ADC with conversion time of 2 µs, 4,096 channels, a 32-bit per channel buffer RAM, "sliding-scale" linearization of differential nonlinearity, and dead-time correction circuit (Elvatech 2004). The X-ray tube is air cooled and low powered, with a tungsten anode and 140-µm beryllium end window. Analyses were conducted at 35 kV, with a tube current of 45 µKA and a 400-

second live time using a 0.8 mm primary aluminum filter. Ten elements were detected: titanium (Ti), manganese (Mn), iron (Fe), zinc (Zn), gallium (Ga), rubidium (Rb), strontium (Sr), yttrium (Y), zirconium (Zr), and niobium (Nb). Concentration values (in parts per million) were determined using *ElvaX Regression* — a program based on the quadratic regression model using data derived from ten reference samples (obsidian from Guatemala and Mexico) of similar composition:

$$C_i = \sum_{\substack{j=0 \\ k=0}}^{S} A_{ijk}\, I_j I_k \qquad \text{(Elvatech 2004)}$$

The quadratic regression model describes the relationship between the set of analytical intensities and analyte concentrations, where C_i is the concentration of analyte i in the sample, $I_0 = 1$, I_j and I_k are the analytical intensities of analytes j and k, respectively, and S is the number of analytes in the product. The regression coefficients $A_{ijk} = A_{ikj}$ are determined from calibration by a set of reference samples. As a rule, as their number exceeds the number of reference samples at hand, not all of the coefficients can be estimated, and only the most significant ones are taken into account (Elvatech 2004). The number of significant coefficients present in the model for each analyte i is referred to as the number of degrees of freedom of the regression model.

2. To verify matches made with the comparison spectra, elemental concentrations were transformed using base-10 logarithms, plotted, and grouped according to statistical group membership. Use of log concentrations rather than raw data compensates for differences in magnitude between the major and minor elements. Transformation to base-10 logarithms also yields a more normal distribution for many elements.

3. The degree to which this pattern differs from western Petén will not be securely known until we characterize the obsidians from Nixtun-Ch'ich', a site on the western edge of Lake Petén Itzá occupied by the Kowoj enemies, the Itza. Sourcing data on Early Postclassic obsidians from the site of Trinidad de Nosotros, a port on the northwest shore of Lake Petén Itza, appear to reveal a pattern similar to that of the eastern lakes, but it is not known if or how that might differ from the Late Postclassic in the region.

Chapter 15

THE BIOARCHAEOLOGY OF RITUAL VIOLENCE AT ZACPETÉN

—— William N. Duncan ——

In 1996, excavations carried out under the auspices of Proyecto Maya Colonial identified and partially excavated a mass grave (Operation 1000) at Zacpetén. This was the second Postclassic mass grave identified in the lakes region, the other on Topoxté Island in Lake Yaxhá (Bullard 1970). Preliminary analyses documented that the grave was created between A.D. 1389 and 1437 (Pugh 2001), likely by the peoples known as Kowoj (Duncan 2005a) or earlier Xiw-affiliated groups from the important Late Postclassic city of Mayapán in northern Yucatán (Rice, Chapter 2, this volume). This prompted four questions: How did the Xiw/Kowoj create the grave? Why did they make the grave? Whom did they place in the grave? And how does the grave inform on interaction between the Xiw/Kowoj and other ethno-political groups around the time of their movement to the Petén lakes region? In 2002 I excavated the remainder of the mass grave and analyzed the human remains in hopes of answering these and other questions. Here I present the results of those excavations and address the four questions insofar as possible.

The strongest evidence indicating the Xiw/Kowoj created the mass graves at Zacpetén and Topoxté was their occurrence in distinctive architectural arrangements known as temple assemblages. Tatiana Proskouriakoff (1962a) originally described certain complexes she called temple assemblages at the site of Mayapán, and decades later Don Rice (1986) and Timothy Pugh (2001) identified similar assemblages in the eastern lakes region at the sites of Zacpetén and Topoxté. Pugh argued that their presence constituted material evidence supporting the Kowoj claim of migration to the Petén lakes from Yucatán.

Mass graves were associated with these assemblages at Topoxté and Zacpetén. Zacpetén Operation 1000 lies on the northwest corner of Group A at Zacpetén, a Petén variant of a Mayapán-style temple assemblage. Similarly, on the northwest corner of the Group C temple assemblage, an interment contained what appear to be at least two individuals. At Topoxté Island, William R. Bullard (1970) found a mass grave in the fill of Structure L, in the northwestern area of the temple assemblage. Although not fully excavated, the grave revealed disarticulated remains of both adults and juveniles similar to the demography and level of articulation found in Operation 1000. Thus, at both Topoxté and Zacpetén, mass graves were associated with the northwest corners of temple assemblages. Ceramic evidence provided further support for these associations: Leslie Cecil (2001a) found that Clemencia Cream Paste wares and red-and-black decoration on pottery were common in what was thought to be Kowoj territory, particularly at Topoxté and Zacpetén. To date, then, the only known Postclassic mass graves in the Petén lakes region occur in conjunction with Mayapán-style temple assemblages and Xiw-/Kowoj–related ceramics, suggesting that both graves were made by these groups.

Interments from Mayapán lend peripheral support to this argument. First, a mass grave was found in the Cenote X-Coton (Smith 1953). Although the remains were only generally described, at least twelve individuals of ages ranging from adult to infant were included. It is unclear if the remains were deposited in one episode, as were those in Operation 1000, but all were disarticulated except for one set of arm bones (ibid.). It is not possible to determine whether this deposit was created by the Xiw/Kowoj, but it does establish a precedent for the creation of mass graves. Other mass graves were found at Mayapán in Structure Q-58 ("El Crematorio") on the west side of a plaza and the northern part of the site center and at Q-95, directly opposite on the east side (Shook 1954b). Also, seven individuals were dismembered and burned on the southwest edge of the Itzmal Chen platform (Peraza Lope et al. 2006). A second mortuary connection between Zacpetén and Mayapán is the recovery of human teeth with holes drilled in the roots. Structure H-18, adjacent to Itzmal Chen, also had a mass burial of four individuals in one layer under another burial of eleven individuals (Chowning 1956). These graves are particularly interesting because the skulls and mandibles had either been moved or removed from these individuals postmortem, consistent with the use of mandibles and teeth at Zacpetén, and this constitutes a second mortuary connection between the sites. Radiocarbon dating of charcoal from the stratum immediately below the human remains in Operation 1000 (Chapter 5, Table

5.1, this volume) revealed that the Zacpetén mass grave was created between 1389 and 1437, around the time of a major revolt at Mayapán (Milbrath and Peraza Lope 2003) and just before the city's fall.

Archaeology

The Operation 1000 mass grave at Zacpetén is a roughly circular depression at the northwest corner of Group A, west of and adjacent to the Middle Preclassic platform underlying Late Postclassic construction and north of and adjacent to Structure 614 (see Chapter 7, Map 7.3, this volume). The pit measures 8 meters north-south and 7 meters east-west. Its circumference slopes from east to west, so that its center is approximately 3.75 meters lower than the east edge and 1.5 meters lower than the west edge. On the basis of a test unit, it was originally thought to have been a borrow pit that may have begun in the Terminal Classic (Pugh 2001), but complete excavation revealed a much more complex history.

My excavation of the mass grave was designed to identify and record the location of individual elements, and I maintained articulated and bundled skeletal elements to produce a map of the entire grave (see Duncan 2005a for specific methods of excavation). It was also important to investigate the history and construction of this pit. The depression was covered with a one-by-one-meter grid, and excavation proceeded in natural/cultural levels, with eleven levels and three features distinguished. The chronology of the pit was difficult to discern because the stratigraphy represented erosion of adjacent cultural deposits (the Preclassic platform and Postclassic Structures 606 and 614) as well as erosion of the bedrock and sides of the pit itself, all intermingled and producing temporal palimpsests. The eastern profile on the E106 gridline is shown in Figure 15.1.

This pit was first created and used in the Middle Preclassic period, as investigated in Levels 2e, 2f, and Feature 1 in the southern part of the pit. Level 2e was a lens of loose, light brown soil with Middle Preclassic artifacts in it, and Level 2f consisted of Middle Preclassic collapse from the platform embedded in a hardened limestone matrix. Feature 1 was a semicircular hole cut out of Level 2f at the southern edge of the pit, in which the base of a Middle Preclassic red-and-black dichrome dish had been placed. This means that at some point in the Middle Preclassic the main plaza collapsed, forming Level 2f, after which Feature 1 was created.

Apparently subsequently, the northern part of what later became the mass grave was excavated, as it consisted of fist-sized chunks of limestone lying upon bedrock (Level 8). Above that was a level of small limestone pebbles and brown-gray soil, containing few sherds (Level 7). The deposit of human remains constituted Level 6, in a matrix like that of Level 7. The remains were all placed in one episode, thickest in the northeastern part of the pit and eroded to the west. In excavating these remains, each long bone, cranial fragment, and set of articulated or bundled bones was called a component, and each bone within that set was labeled as a subcomponent. Using

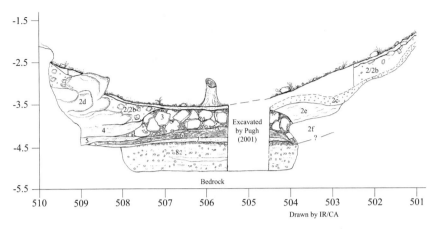

Figure 15.1. Eastern profile of Operation 1000 on the E106 gridline (after Duncan 2005a: figure 5.5).

the grid, northings, eastings, and below-datum measurements were recorded on each end of each component. Because of time constraints, it was possible to bag carpals, tarsals, metcarpals, metatarsals, phalanges, and ribs separately only when they were articulated or in bundles. No grave goods were found in association with the remains except isolated sherds.

Two deposits were placed over the human remains, identified as Level 3 and Level 5. Level 3, consisting of medium to large limestone rock, capped the center of the remains, while Level 5 was a layer of yellow limestone chipped from the edge of the pit to cover the northern and eastern edges of the bones, as suggested by Pugh (2001: 281). Above Level 5 was a Preclassic layer (Level 4) that eroded out of the eastern wall of the pit under Structure 606.

The uppermost strata, Levels 1 (humus), 2a, 2/2b, 2c, and 2d, were all layers of erosion. Level 2/2b was Postclassic collapse from Structures 614 and 606 on the south and east sides of the pit, respectively. Level 2a was Postclassic erosion without collapse, found primarily on the north and west sides of the pit. Level 2c was Terminal Classic fill that eroded in from the plaza. Level 2d was collapsed bedrock on the north and east sides.

Two features associated with the south side of the pit appear to be Terminal Classic in date. Feature 2 was a semicircular shaft, approximately 1.5 meters in diameter north-south, that had been excavated into Level 2f in antiquity. The soils and rock of Levels 1, 2, 2c, and 4 were all found in the feature. Feature 3 was a problematic deposit in the southwest corner of Operation 1000 that continued under Structure 614, but our permit precluded us from excavating further. The feature had eroded from Structure 614 into Operation 1000 three meters to the north and was filled with Level 2g, a fine gray ash with animal and human remains. This ash was eighty-four centimeters thick at its maximum, but the top 25 percent was mixed with small stones and the entire deposit was capped with plaster. The majority of the diagnostic ceramics were from the Terminal Classic, and many sherds had the gray ash stuck to them. The two largest ceramic pieces were large unslipped potstands (see Chapter 5, Figure 5.4, this volume) that were fairly level in situ, in spite of the general erosion of the deposit to the north. The pattern of the ash adhering to these ceramics suggested that they had been placed in the feature and then had something burned in and around them, accounting for all the ash.

Following these excavations, all laboratory analysis (see Duncan 2005a for methods) was completed by the author and students from the Centro Universitario del Petén (CUDEP) with the exception of the ceramic analysis, which was completed by Prudence Rice.

Osteology

Quantification

The remains of at least thirty-seven individuals in Operation 1000 (minimum number of individuals; MNI) were in the mass grave. These remains were largely disarticulated, included all ages and both sexes, and were poorly preserved. Few animal bones were present. I quantified the excavated remains by separating, compiling, and tabulating them by element, age, and side. The majority of the bones could only be classified as adult, juvenile, or infant. Sex was so rarely estimable that it was not considered for quantification purposes, and conjoining was not attempted. Temporal counts were achieved by counting the petrous portions. Ribs were quantified by counting the number of ribs with heads and necks intact; juvenile ribs were counted if the ends were present where the epiphyses for the head and neck would have fused. Long bones were quantified in multiple ways (see Duncan 2005a). Carpals, tarsals, phalanges, and patellae were quantified by counting the number of elements scored as a 1, after the methods of Jane Buikstra and Douglas Ubelaker (1994). If there was a fragment of an element from an age class that was not scored 1 but was unique because of age class (e.g., an infant bone), it was added to the table in parentheses. For juvenile carpals there were enough unsided bones to change the MNI for that element, which was also added in parentheses (Tables 15.1–15.4).

Several patterns emerged from these data. First, there are different ratios of adult and juvenile MNIs for different elements, which stems from the faster maturation of some skeletal elements than others. This discrepancy characterizes assemblages with a significant percentage of individuals in age ranges from late childhood to young adulthood (Ubelaker 1974). The second point is that smaller elements are underrepresented in the assemblage, characteristic of secondary depositions or remains left exposed for a period of time.

Third, there was a discrepancy between left and right arm and forearm bones, with the right bones relatively underrepresented. Comparing the left and right elements of the arm and forearm in a chi-square (χ^2) test demonstrates that the results are statistically significant at the 0.10 level with 5 degrees of freedom ($\chi^2 > 9.236$). There is no such discrepancy between the carpals and metacarpals (actual χ^2 tables presented in Duncan [2005a]).

Table 15.1. MNI for the temporal and ribs, Operation 1000 (reproduced from Duncan 2005a: table 5.2).

Element	Side	Adult MNI	Juvenile MNI	Infant MNI	Side	Adult MNI	Juvenile MNI	Infant MNI	Total MNI
Temporal	R	24	10	0	L	24	13	0	37
Rib 1	R	17	5	0	L	13	6	0	23
Rib 2–10	R	25	6	0	L	24	5	0	31
Rib 11–12	R	17	6	0	L	18	3	0	24

Table 15.2. MNI for carpals, metacarpals, patella, tarsals, and metatarsals, Operation 1000 (reproduced from Duncan 2005a: table 5.3).

Element	Side	Adult MNI	Juvenile MNI	Infant MNI	Side	Adult MNI	Juvenile MNI	Infant MNI	Total MNI
Carpals	R	6	1	0	L	7	1(1)	0	9
Patella	R	20	1	0	L	17	1	0	21
Tarsals	R	18	1	0	L	15	1	0	19

Table 15.3. MNI for phalanges, Operation 1000 (reproduced from Duncan 2005a: table 5.4).

Element	Adult MNI	Juvenile MNI	Infant MNI	Total MNI
Hand phalanges				
Distal	6	1	0	7
Middle	9	2	0	11
Proximal	7	3	0	10
Foot phalanges				
Distal	8	1	0	9
Middle	10	1	0	11
Proximal	21	1	1	23

Table 15.4. MNI for long bones, Operation 1000 (reproduced from Duncan 2005a: table 5.4).

Element	Side	Adult	Juvenile	Infant	Total MNI
Humerus	L	15	5	0	20
Humerus	R	7	6	0	13
Radius	L	15	7	0	22
Radius	R	10	4	0	14
Ulna	L	17	11	0	28
Ulna	R	11	3	0	14
Femur	L	33	4	0	37
Femur	R	24	10	-1	35
Tibia	L	28	5	-1	34
Tibia	R	26	4	0	30
Fibula	L	20	2	0	22

During excavations it was also clear that the teeth had been removed from occlusion postmortem. One unit contained more than seventy loose human teeth. In addition, at least two human teeth and one animal tooth had holes drilled in the roots. MNIs for permanent and deciduous tooth fields are presented in Table 15.5. These numbers are congruent with the MNIs based on skeletal remains, both in overall number and proportions of permanent and deciduous teeth. The maxillary molars were underrepresented relative to the other permanent teeth, suggesting that this tooth field was selectively omitted in the same fashion as the right arm and forearm bones.

Spatial Analysis

During excavation it became clear that the bones were not randomly distributed throughout the pit. Rather, they were piled in the northeast corner and eroded to the west in a thinning lens. It was worth considering the spatial distribution statistically, though, because it was not obvious that all the elements were distributed in the same way. To analyze the spatial distribution, I divided Operation 1000 into twenty units, labeled 1–20 in Map 15.1, for a chi-square analysis. The use of twenty units (rather than each one-by-one-meter unit) reduced the degrees of freedom (df=19) and resulted in fewer cells in the chi-square table with small frequencies. However, not all of the twenty units were the same size. Some two-by-twos were fully excavated with an area of four square meters, while others were on the edge of Operation 1000 and only had one unit excavated. Pugh's earlier three-by-one-meter test trench area also needed to be taken into account. Thus, for each two-by-two I calculated how many square meters were excavated. The total minimum number of bones per element was then summed. This allowed me to normalize the expected values for each element in each two-by-two unit by the area excavated. I considered juvenile elements when possible; however, the majority of the elements could only be considered adults. I selected elements from all parts of the body for analysis (axial skeleton, limbs, hands, and feet).

The chi-square is a rather crude method to evaluate the spatial distribution relative to other methods (cf. Herrmann 2002). A number of cells had fewer than five elements, which lowers statistical power considerably. However, it was already evident during excavation that the remains were not distributed randomly, and the results of the chi-square bear this out (Table 15.6; Duncan 2005a: appendix 2). Except for the right humerus, each element was nonrandomly distributed. The deviation of the right humerus from the pattern is likely an artifact of low sample size. The usefulness of the chi-square table is found in its potential for pattern recognition: the ability to see if different elements were clustered in individual units. It appears that they were. Units 7, 10, 11, and Pugh's trench (unit 20) consistently have the highest contribution to the chi-square for each element. Thus, it appears that all the elements were piled in the northeast portion of Operation 1000 without segregation by element, side, or apparently, age.

Table 15.5. MNI for dental classes, Operation 1000 (reproduced from Duncan 2005a: table 5.7).

	Max *RM*	*Max* *RP*	*Max* *RC*	*Max* *RI*	*Max* *LI*	*Max* *LC*	*Max* *LP*	*Max* *LM*	*Man* *LM*	*Man* *LP*	*Man* *LC*	*Man* *LI*	*Man* *RI*	*Man* *RC*	*Man* *RP*	*Man* *RM*
Permanent	6	13	12	18	18	22	11	8	21	22	19	28	25	19	23	21
Deciduous	max rm 3	max rp 2	max rc 3	max ri 6	max li 4	max lc 3	max lp 0	max lm 2	man lm 9	man lp 6	man lc 6	man li 7	man ri 5	man rc 4	man rp 6	man rm 8

Abbreviations: Max – maxillary, Man – mandibular, R – right, L – left, M – molar, P – premolar, C – canine, I – incisor.

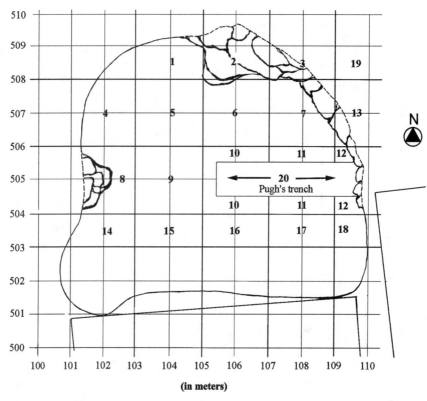

Map 15.1. Plan of Operation 1000, showing the twenty units used for spatial analysis. Modified from Duncan 2005a: figure 5.3.

Table 15.6. Chi-square results for spatial analysis, Operation 1000 (reproduced from Duncan 2005a: table 5.8).

Bone	Chi-Square Value	Significance Level
Left fused temporal	58.677	$\chi > 0.05$
Right fused temporal	61.943	$\chi > 0.05$
Left unfused temporal	39.92	$\chi > 0.05$
Right unfused temporal	50.958	$\chi > 0.05$
Adult thoracic 1–9	194.56	$\chi > 0.05$
Juvenile thoracic 1–9	152.17	$\chi > 0.05$
Adult left humerus	33.059	$\chi > 0.05$
Adult right humerus	21.116	ns
Adult left metacarpal	74.384	$\chi > 0.05$
Adult right metacarpal	53.907	$\chi > 0.05$
Adult left tibia	101.63	$\chi > 0.05$
Adult right tibia	120.19	$\chi > 0.05$
Adult left metatarsal	282.31	$\chi > 0.05$
Adult right metatarsal	327.38	$\chi > 0.05$

Table 15.7. Articulated and bundled sets of bone, Operation 1000 (reproduced from Duncan 2005a: table 5.9).

Element	Articulated	Bundled	Both
Vertebra	10	34	10
Os coxae (and sacrum and coccyx)	1	0	0
Ribs	10	10	0
Humerus/radius/ulna	2	0	0
Carpals/metacarpals/phalanges	0	4	0
Femur/patella/tibia/fibula	6	11	0
Tarsals/metatarsals/phalanges	1	22	0
Mixed	4	1	0

Articulation

The remains in Operation 1000 were largely disarticulated, suggesting that the mass grave was a secondary deposit. During excavation the remains were classified as articulated, bundled, or isolated. Identifying articulated sets of bone was fairly straightforward. A set of bones was counted as bundled if there was reason to think they were placed in the ground together, a subjective distinction (Duncan 2005a). To count the long bones as bundles, they had to be placed parallel to one another in situ and had to be in contact with one another, or almost so, which was judged on a case-by-case basis. This had the potential to underrepresent the number of bone bundles. Bundles of smaller bones were also less likely to be identified in the heart of the deposit. Small bones, such as carpals and phalanges, were more likely to fall apart from one another when placed on other bones. Thus, bone bundles were more likely to be identified around the periphery of the deposit than in the center, and almost all of the bones in the center were placed with little organization. Because there were no complete crania, I only present postcranial articulation data in Table 15.7.

Table 15.7 indicates a large number of articulated and bundled vertebrae, likely a result of four factors. First, identifying bundles was subjective. Second, only two vertebrae needed to be present to be counted as articulated or bundled; there were only two cases with more than six articulated vertebrae. Third, vertebrae are larger than, say, phalanges and are therefore less likely to fall through crevices in the stratum of bones or to be disturbed. Thus, vertebrae are more likely to stay together in situ upon placement. Fourth, vertebrae remain articulated for longer periods than other elements (Haglund 1997a). If the elevated number of articulated vertebrae can be explained by these factors, then it is apparent that very few cases of articulated bones are in the deposit. The low number of articulated bones coupled with the relatively higher number of bone bundles is consistent with this being a secondary deposit.

Table 15.8. Periosteal reactions from Operation 1000 (reproduced from Duncan 2005a: table 5.10).

Element	Minimum Number of Elements	Number of Bones with Periosteal Reaction	Percentage of MNE Affected
Humerus	33	1	3
Radius	36	1	2.7
Ulna	35	1	2.8
Femur	72	1	1.4
Tibia	64	2	3.1
Fibula	50	9	18
Rib 3–10	423	1	0.24
Metatarsal	157	1	0.63
Phalanx (prox foot)	201	1	0.5

Cultural Modification

Few of the crania in Operation 1000 could be observed for modification, although one young adult female skull exhibited tabular erect modification. Dental modification during life was similarly rare: two lower left central incisors, a lower right central incisor, and an upper right central incisor exhibited modification on both the mesial and distal edges without alteration of the labial surface. This would be classified as type 3-3, 3-2, or 3-6 under Javier Romero's (1970) classification. Dental wear has made it impossible to say for certain which of these three types were represented.

Pathology

The high level of disarticulation and the selective omission of elements in Operation 1000 generally preclude statements about aggregate health. Nonetheless, the data are worth considering because they can be used to falsify, or at least argue against, several scenarios. Description, inventory, and analytical methods for identification of pathologies followed those outlined in Buikstra and Ubelaker (1994).

Periostitis is typically a reaction to some insult, either from infection or a secondary infection stemming from trauma (Ortner 2003a). Eighteen cases of periostitis were identified in Operation 1000 (Table 15.8). Infections clearly secondary to trauma are reported later. There was only one case of osteomyelitis from Operation 1000 (Duncan 2005a: 140).

Carious lesions stem from a demineralization of enamel and dentin as a result of bacteria. Frequencies of lesions within populations may reflect a variety of dietary factors. This, coupled with greater preservation of teeth in the material record, is one reason caries has been studied extensively. Caries is most commonly examined per individual (Hillson 1996), but when the individual is not the unit of analysis lesion frequencies can be informative (Larsen 1997: 69). Caries rates for adult tooth classes in Operation 1000 are presented in Table 15.9. No permanent teeth exhibited multiple lesions, no deciduous teeth lacked lesions, and the posterior teeth had the highest frequencies of lesions. However, the elevated frequency among upper right molars is clearly an artifact of their underrepresentation in the deposit. That said, the MNI for the other tooth fields is closer to that found for the skeletal elements.

Numerous environmental circumstances may influence the growth and development of bones and teeth. Consequently, it is fairly complex to understand how stress is manifest in the skeleton and dentition and to reconstruct the health and behavior of an individual or population level from these markers. The remains from Operation 1000 exhibited only one nonspecific indicator of stress: linear enamel hypoplasias (LEH) (Table 15.10). LEHs were found in twelve teeth, 4 percent of the overall number of adult teeth; no juvenile teeth had LEHs. As with caries, the number of teeth with LEH likely slightly underestimates the total number of LEH teeth of all the individuals who eventually made their way into the pit. However, increasing the overall number of teeth would likely only reduce the percentage of teeth exhibiting LEHs.

Trauma and degenerative disease are often intertwined because injury may promote later age- and activity-based degeneration, which, in turn, may facilitate trauma. Seven examples of fractures and activity-related trauma were found in Operation 1000 (photographs in Duncan 2005a). One case was an adult rib (2–10) with a simple break on the ventral third of the body; although the break had healed, there was evidence of an old associated infection. In five cases adult middle and distal foot phalanges were fused, likely stemming from trauma. An adult radius exhibited periostitis only on the radial tuberosity, which is not a separate epiphysis and is unlikely to have been attributable just to fracture; the pathology was likely activity-induced. Other cases of perimortem trauma, found in conjunction with cutmarks, are presented later.

Vertebrae are particularly susceptible to age- and activity-related conditions. Three examples of vertebral degenerative changes were found in Operation 1000 (Table 15.11). Overall, almost one-third of the thoracic vertebrae and half of the lumbar vertebrae exhibited some form of degenerative change. It is unclear if a large percentage of these come from a small number of individuals. In most populations vertebral degenerative change is fairly common, with most adults exhibiting some change (Ortner 2003b).

Taphonomy: Environmental and Animal Processes

The remains from Operation 1000 were examined for evidence of several taphonomic processes that may be attributable to the environment, animals, and human activity. I define environmental processes as causes other than animal or human action. One such process was the draining and percolation of water through the limestone in Operation 1000, the lowest point in the Group A plaza. This drainage and percolation caused a pseudo-pathology such that portions of the bone appeared to have been eaten away. This damage undoubtedly hindered potential observation of certain phenomena on the bones, such as pot polish or some examples of animal modification or cutmarks. A second process was root action, but virtually all of the bones reflected percolation and

Table 15.9. Caries rates by tooth field, Operation 1000 (reproduced from Duncan 2005a: table 5.11).

Tooth field	Max RM	Max RP	Max RC	Max RI	Max LI	Max LC	Max LP	Max LM	Man LM	Man LP	Man LC	Man LI	Man RI	Man RC	Man RP	Man RM
Number of affected teeth	5	3	0	0	0	0	4	0	4	0	0	0	0	0	4	4
Number of teeth	6	13	12	18	18	22	11	8	21	22	19	28	25	19	23	21
Percentage of teeth affected	83	23	0	0	0	0	36	0	19	0	0	0	0	0	17	1

Abbreviations same as in Table 15.5.

Table 15.10. Hypoplastic defects, Operation 1000 (reproduced from Duncan 2005a: table 5.12).

Tooth field	Max RM	Max RP	Max RC	Max RI	Max LI	Max LC	Max LP	Max LM	Man LM	Man LP	Man LC	Man LI	Man RI	Man RC	Man RP	Man RM	
Number of affected teeth	2	0	1	1	1	0	0	0	0	0	2	2	2	0	1	0	12
Number of teeth	6	13	12	18	18	22	11	8	21	22	19	28	25	19	23	21	286
Percentage of teeth affected	33	0	8	6	6	0	0	0	0	0	11	7	8	0	4	0	4

Abbreviations same as in Table 15.5.

Table 15.11. Degenerative changes in the vertebrae from Operation 1000, Zacpetén (reproduced from Duncan 2005a: table 5.13).

Vertebrae	Minimum Number of Elements	Schmorl's Node	Centrum Osteophyte	Articular Facet Osteophyte	Syndesmophyte
Cervical 1	15	0	0	3	0
Cervical 2	14	0	1	3	1
Cervical 3–6	67	0	12	1	1
Cervical 7	9	0	2	0	0
Thoracic 1–9	72	7	20	2	3
Thoracic 10–12	26	2	8	0	0
Lumbar	40	3	20	3	1

root processes; because of time limitations, they were not recorded separately for each bone. The bones were also examined for weathering, which occurs when bones are left exposed to the elements and is manifest in a distinctive series of cracking and splintering stages (Behrensmeyer 1978; Lyman and Fox 1997). The Operation 1000 remains exhibited no definitive signs of weathering; consequently, there is no reason to think they had been exposed to the elements.

Animals generally influence skeletal remains in one of several ways: moving, trampling, chewing, or a combination of these (Haglund 1997a, 1997b). Overall, animal influence on the Operation 1000 assemblage seems to have been minimal. Movement of remains by animals tends to produce assemblages with an underrepresentation of smaller elements, which is the case here, but animals do not select certain elements for movement by side. Secondary burial, which also tends to result in underrepresentation of smaller elements as a result of movement, is more likely.

Trampling is another means by which animals may influence skeletal remains, although this seems unlikely in Operation 1000 given the dearth of large animals indigenous to the region. A variety of methods have been suggested for identifying trampling, ranging from the angle at which bones lie in the soil (Hill and Walker 1972) to the presence of spiral fractures (Myers, Voorhies, and Corner 1980). Anthony Fiorillo (1989: 62) has offered one criterion: the presence of "shallow, subparallel scratches." Only five cases could be classified as such from Operation 1000, on two ulnae and three ribs, but various other processes can cause such scratches, including percussion strikes (discussed later). The small number of such potential scratches gives no reason to suspect trampling influenced the assemblage.

Animal chewing also leaves distinct marks on bone. Rodent gnawing generally leaves marks that are not rounded (Haglund 1997b). These marks were fairly rare in the remains from Level 6 in Operation 1000, although higher strata of collapse had more bones with gnaw marks. This is unremarkable, though, because rodent burrows (and indeed one rodent) were found in the excavations. More important is the fact that there were no unequivocal signs of carnivore marks in Operation 1000. Carnivore marks may be manifest as either circular puncture marks or rounded, irregular furrows (Haglund 1997a). Carnivores tend to chew the ends of long bones, which produces assemblages with elevated numbers of midshafts relative to the proximal and distal thirds of the diaphyses. This was the case in Operation 1000 (see Duncan 2005a for inventory of element segments). Environmental conditions may have masked some evidence of carnivore influence, but if there had been significant influence on the assemblage by carnivores one would have expected some evidence of gnawmarks not masked by other taphonomic processes.

Taphonomy: Human Processes

In addition to environmental and animal influence on the remains, a variety of anthropogenic modifications of the remains in Operation 1000 were found, including cutmarks, certain break patterns, and worked bone and tooth.

Cutmarks. Cutmarks were distributed throughout the skeleton, including on all segments of the long bones (proximal, middle, and distal), although in relatively low frequency. The rationale for recording cutmarks is presented elsewhere (Duncan 2005a). Marks were identified through two stages of examination and were then classified as a cutmark, a chopmark, or random striae (White 1992). Percussion striae can produce subparallel scratches, in the same way trampling can (Hurlbut 2000; White 1992), although the former typically occur in conjunction with flake scars (Hulburt 2000). Thus, I did not classify marks as percussion striae (hammer and anvil marks) or scratches, primarily to avoid the potential of misidentifying other taphonomic processes. Chopmarks (Figure 15.2) were distinguished from cutmarks (Figure 15.3b, c) primarily by the presence of hinging on the edge of the mark or some evidence of a depressive force versus a cleaner V-shaped cross-section from a slice or cut (Buikstra and Ubelaker 1994). There were only two examples of chopmarks, and they were included in the total number of marks.

Quantifying cutmarks is difficult for a variety of reasons ranging from the experience of the person making the cuts to the experience of the person counting them (see Lyman 2005; Rautman and Fenton 2005; White 1992). I tallied the number of cutmarks (Tables 15.12, 15.13) by skeletal element and segment (e.g., anterior or posterior aspects, and proximal, middle, and distal segments of long bones). This is similar to the method described by R. Lee Lyman (2005). Most cutmarks were found on the limbs. Undoubtedly some elements, such as bones of the face and cranial vault and flatbones, are underrepresented because of preservation. The cutmarks were not restricted to the proximal and distal aspects of the long bones, though, indicating that some form of processing other than simple dismemberment occurred.

Breakage patterns. Virtually all bones in Operation 1000 were broken; however, the vast majority of the breaks were postmortem, as evidenced by the

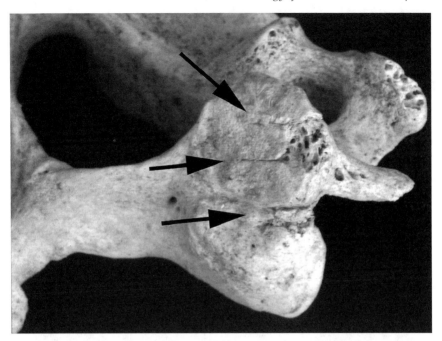

Figure 15.2. Chopmarks on right superior articular facet of cervical vertebra 3–6 from Operation 1000. Note depression fractures on edges of the cutmarks (reproduced from Duncan 2005a: figure 5.28).

perpendicular nature of the broken edge (Sauer 1998). Consequently, only breaks that were clearly perimortem trauma were recorded separately. That is to say, spiral breaks and depression fractures were recorded, of which there were four clear examples. One example was on the anterior portion of a proximal tibia (Figure 15.4a), which exhibited a depression fracture with hinging. Distal to that fracture was a spiral fracture (Figure 15.4b), likely caused by the same trauma event. A clavicle exhibited cutmarks in conjunction with a spiral fracture that was clearly perimortem and likely the product of some percussive action. No other definitive evidence of hammer-and-anvil percussion was noted in the assemblage. As with other taphonomic processes, it is possible that the number of perimortem fractures is underestimated here because of the preservation. That said, if all the remains in Operation 1000 had been processed immediately after death, one would have expected considerably more evidence of perimortem trauma.

Postmortem worked bones and teeth. Cutmarks are generally an unintentional by-product of the processing of remains (i.e., the goal is to dismember or deflesh the deceased, not to leave cutmarks on the bones). Other processes are intentional modification of bones, such as carving, grinding, drilling, and

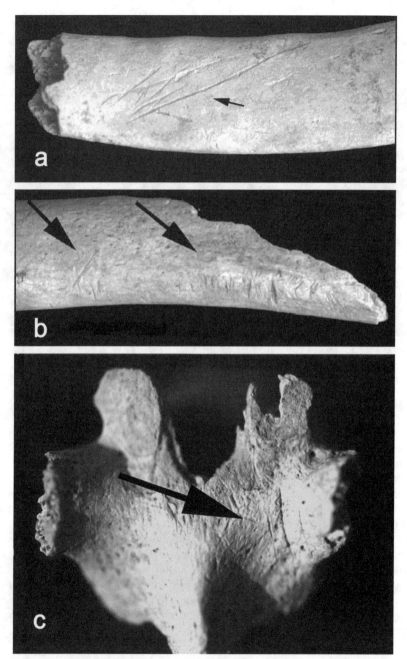

*Figure 15.3. Marks on bones from Operation 1000: (a) random striae on left rib frag-
ment; (b) cutmarks on left clavicle and associated fracture; (c) cutmark on thoracic
vertebra, posterior right aspect of neural arch. Reproduced from Duncan 2005a: figures
5.18, 5.32, and 5.19, respectively.*

Table 15.12. Cutmarks on axial skeletal elements from Operation 1000 (reproduced from Duncan 2005a: table 5.16).

Bone	Left	Middle	Right	Unsided Fragment
Cervical	na	2	na	0
Thoracic	na	2	na	0
Lumbar	na	0	na	0
Clavicle	6	na	6	0
Clavicle	0	na	0	0
Clavicle	0	na	0	1
Scapula	2	na	0	0
Rib	10	na	11	3
Oscoxae	0	na	1	0
Total	18	4	18	4

Table 15.13. Cutmarks on appendicular skeletal elements from Operation 1000 (reproduced from Duncan 2005a: table 5.17).

Bone	Side	Proximal	Middle	Distal
Humerus	L	0	0	2
Humerus	R	3	1	3
Radius	L	3	2	5
Radius	R	1	2	2
Ulna	L	1	2	3
Ulna	R	2	3	3
Femur	L	4	1	6
Femur	R	3	1	6
Femur	?	0	1	0
Tibia	L	5	5	6
Tibia	R	2	2	1
Fibula	L	7	5	6
Fibula	R	2	5	4
Fibula	?	0	2	0
Total		33	32	47

some forms of polishing. Three bones and three teeth in Operation 1000 exhibited intentional modification. The proximal third of a femoral shaft was split distally and rounded on one end, either through grinding or use as a tool. A second femoral midshaft had been ground in a similar fashion, although it was less symmetrical on the end than the first. The third example of worked bone was a needle made from animal bone. The worked bones from Operation 1000 are similar to one another in their modification: both were ground on one end and split longitudinally. Their purpose remains unclear, but Pierre Agrinier (1960) has suggested that a similar femur recovered at Chiapa de Corzo may have been used as a spout for water in rituals. Other authors (Talavera, Martín Rojas, and García 2001) have noted that human long bones

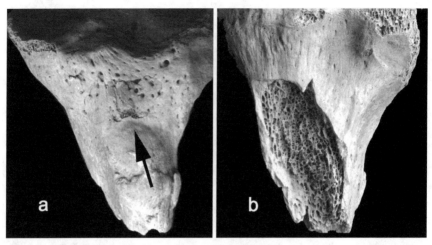

Figure 15.4. Fractures on proximal left tibia from Operation 1000: (a) depression fracture on anterior aspect; (b) spiral fracture on posterior aspect. Reproduced from Duncan 2005a: figures 5.30 and 5.31, respectively.

have been used as musical instruments or as tools to decorate ceramic vessels in Puebla, Mexico.

Two human teeth, a right maxillary molar and a mandibular incisor, and an animal canine had holes drilled in their roots. Two human tooth caches have been recovered in the lowland Maya area in Belize, at Altun Ha (Pendergast, Bartley, and Armelagos 1968) and Lubaantun (Saul and Hammond 1974); and at Zacpetén, Pugh (2001) found human mandibles cached in the plaza of Group A to the south of Operation 1000. Caches of teeth with holes drilled in the roots are even rarer. At Chau Hiix, a Postclassic site in northern Belize, a cache of dog teeth was found with holes drilled in the roots (Gabriel Wrobel, pers. com., 2004). Although there have been cases of human teeth with holes drilled in the roots from Mexico (Talavera et al. 1997), the only other cases of drilled teeth from the Maya area I have found are from Belize at Progresso (Briggs and Patt 2005; Oland and Masson 2005) and Caracol (Chase and Chase 1996) and from Mayapán. At Progresso one burial in a shrine (Structure 219) included at least fifty human and five faunal teeth exhibiting holes drilled in the roots similar to those from Zacpetén (Briggs and Patt 2005). At least six human teeth from Caracol were found in the lower tomb in Structure A34 (Chase and Chase 1996). At Mayapán a cache of thirty perforated human teeth found under the east bench in Structure J-50a consisted of eight molars, nine premolars, three canines, eight incisors, and two unidentified teeth—all of which were thought to have been in a necklace (Ruppert and Smith 1952: 57). The drilled teeth in Operation 1000 may or may not have come from the same sample as the rest of the individuals interred in Operation 1000. Nonetheless, this establishes one more connection between Zacpetén and Mayapán.

Discussion: The Four Questions

To summarize, the Operation 1000 mass grave was placed in a depression on the northwest corner of a Mayapán-style temple assemblage. Although the bones seem to have been interred between A.D. 1389 and 1437, as indicated by calibrated radiocarbon dates, on the basis of stratigraphy and the presence of smaller features around the edge of the grave it was clear that this feature had been used since the Middle Preclassic period. A minimum of thirty-seven individuals were in the pit and ranged in age from infant to adult, with both males and females represented. The remains had low levels of articulation, and certain elements (right forearm bones and maxillary molars) were significantly underrepresented relative to others. The remains were piled in the northern part of Operation 1000 and eroded from that central location. There is no evidence that certain elements or demographic classes were selected for special spatial treatment within the grave. Only limited evidence was found for cultural modification in the form of cranial and dental modification, although the former was rarely observable owing to poor preservation. No evidence suggests that the individuals in the grave were remarkable for either presence or absence of signs of disease—whether of deficiency, infection, degenerative conditions, or trauma—when compared with the most comparable graves in the region. Evidence of animal influence on the remains was minimal. Cutmarks were primarily noted on the long bones, and on all segments of them, which suggests that processing of the bones included defleshing and possibly dismemberment rather than only the latter. The remains showed evidence of intentional cultural modification in the form of ground bones and teeth with holes drilled in the roots. The low level of articulation, underrepresentation of smaller skeletal elements, and low frequency of cutmarks indicate that the grave was a secondary one and that processing was not completely responsible for the level of disarticulation (Dirkmaat et al. 2005).

We can now turn to the four questions posed at the beginning of this chapter. The first question is, how was the mass grave created? Several scenarios can be falsified using a combination of osteological and archaeological data, beginning with cannibalism. Through the work of Tim White (1992) and Christy Turner and Jacqueline Turner (1999), several minimal taphonomic criteria for cannibalism have been established in the southwestern United States. They include burning, perimortem trauma, pot polish, and missing vertebrae (Hurlbut 2000). Although it has recently been shown that not all cases of cannibalism necessarily reflect these criteria (Rautman and Fenton 2005), Turner and Turner (1999) have noted that the criteria from the southwestern United States do seem applicable to Mesoamerica. In Operation 1000, cuts were found on all parts of the long bones, indicating that the bodies were not simply dismembered or filleted. As Sandra Olsen and Pat Shipman (1994: 380; see also Rautman and Fenton 2005) have noted:

> Defleshing is usually represented by short, fine cutmarks or broader scraping over the surfaces of bones caused when a sharp tool is used to remove

soft tissue adhering to the bone. Such marks frequently appear in clusters, an indication that repeated strokes were necessary to successfully clean the bone. . . . The difference [between defleshing and filleting] is that defleshing marks can occur anywhere on the bone where skin muscles, tendons, ligaments, periosteum, or any other soft tissue attaches, whereas filleting marks are usually concentrated at the points of origin and insertion of muscles and tendons.

Thus, the placement of the marks is congruent with what Olsen and Shipman (1994) described as characteristic of defleshing. However, cannibalism seems unlikely in Operation 1000 for several reasons: lack of evidence of burning of the remains, minimal perimortem damage, and the lack of underrepresentation of vertebrae. If cannibalism were responsible for the bone deposit in Operation 1000, then, it would be manifest in a different pattern than that seen in the southwestern United States and apparently elsewhere in Mesoamerica (Turner and Turner 1999).

The next scenario that can be argued against, if not falsified, is an epidemic or health-related basis for creating the mass grave. Most diseases do not leave evidence on the skeleton, and those that do may not do so quickly, as in the case of an epidemic. Also, the disarticulation of the remains and the influence of taphonomic processes limit the reliability of statements about aggregate health in such a deposit. That said, there is nothing to indicate that the mass grave was created on the basis of the health of the deceased.

The remains did not exhibit high levels of periosteal reactions. As for evidence of deficiencies, in tooth classes other than those clearly underrepresented the percentages of teeth with caries are not inconsistent with a maize-based agricultural population (Larsen 1997). Direct comparisons must be taken with a grain of salt, but LEH and caries frequencies in Operation 1000 are no higher than those found in the mass burials at Cuello, the most similar mass graves from the Maya area with comparable data (see Duncan 2005a). Elbows and knees were the non-vertebral joints most frequently influenced by degenerative change in Operation 1000. Few other arthritis profiles have been generated in the Maya area because preservation rendered too many bones unobservable (e.g., Saul and Saul 1991). However, remains from Playa del Carmen, a Postclassic coastal site in Mexico (Márquez Morfin 1982), commonly exhibited arthritis in the elbows and knees.

What can we say about the health of the individuals in Operation 1000? Although only very general statements might be made, I suggest that these data are incongruent with what one might expect to find if the individuals in the pit all grew up or lived together for a long time prior to death under consistently harsh conditions. No evidence suggests that the life experience of the individuals in Operation 1000 was any harsher than that of individuals included in other mass graves from the Maya area for which paleopathological data are published. Thus, nothing in the paleopathological data might suggest that the individuals in Operation 1000 were, say, a group of slaves. Second, no evidence suggests that the individuals in Operation 1000 suffered a common, chronic disease and were buried together for that reason. Finally, although

I cannot falsify an epidemic, I do not think this is likely either because the Operation 1000 mass grave is a secondary deposit, unlike what one might expect to find if a group of people died within a short period of time and were interred together. Thus, there is currently no reason to think the individuals included in Operation 1000 are a select sample on the basis of health.

The next scenario is death in war. It is clear that warfare and skirmishes were common in the region during the Postclassic. It is also clear that warfare had ritual implications in Mesoamerica, if not a ritual basis. However, war dead seems an unlikely explanation because the assemblage included individuals of all ages including infants, precluding this from being the grave of soldiers. Also, although it cannot be falsified, the grave does not appear to be the resting place of individuals captured and killed in a raid primarily because it was a secondary burial. The Towton mass grave in England, for example, was an interment of individuals killed in warfare, and the bones displayed very high levels of articulation (Margerison and Knüsel 2002). This is inconsistent with Operation 1000.

Sacrifice appears an unlikely scenario for similar reasons: Operation 1000 is a secondary burial. Ultimately, sacrifice cannot be completely ruled out because it is possible that the individuals were sacrificed and their remains used for some other purpose for a period of time prior to interment in Operation 1000. It is clear, though, that the individuals were not simply killed and placed in the ground.

The final scenario, which I regard to be the most parsimonious explanation for Operation 1000, is exhumation and re-interment of enemy ancestors. The grave is clearly a secondary context. There is minimal evidence of carnivore influence on the remains and no evidence of weathering on the bones. All this reveals that the remains were not left exposed for long periods but had been deposited sufficiently earlier to become disarticulated. The discrepancy between right and left forearm bones suggests that at least some of the remains were articulated when selected for inclusion in Operation 1000. The removal and use of remains does not always reflect an act of violation (see earlier discussion); ancestor worship often involves using remains of loved ones in a revered fashion (McAnany 1995). Finally, the context clearly reflects a ritually potent act and deposit. It had been used over and over again since the Middle Preclassic but was abandoned and unused after the remains were placed in the ground, suggesting that the area had become taboo. As I argue later, the discrepancy between right and left forearm elements and trophy taking here likely reflects an attempt to violate the deceased. Thus, the single most parsimonious scenario for the creation of Operation 1000 is the exhumation of previously interred enemy ancestors.

Although exhumation of enemy ancestors' graves is the most likely single scenario, it could be that the remains in Operation 1000 were drawn from a variety of sources. A more complex scenario, which cannot be teased apart archaeologically, may well have led to Operation 1000's formation: for example, the difference in the numbers of left and right forearm bones clearly indicates that some of the bones were drawn from a source where left and right could be distinguished. Because a few right forearm bones are present in the pit, it is possible that some remains included in Operation 1000 were from primary contexts and others were not. We know that bones were ritually potent symbols and were used in different contexts. Thus, it is certainly plausible that while most of the remains were removed from primary contexts, some portion of the bones was taken from other contexts during the creation of the Operation 1000 deposit.

I would argue that although reconstructing exactly what led to the formation of Operation 1000 is potentially murky, the reason why the Xiw/Kowoj might have made this deposit seems clearer. Mortuary practices accomplish a variety of things ranging from disposal of the corpse, to aiding the living in their mourning, to helping the souls of the deceased in the transition to an afterlife (Hertz 1960). For most members of society, funerals accomplish this. This has been described in detail in cultures from Europe, Africa (Goody 1962), the Northwest coast of the United States (Kan 1989), and Mesoamerica (López Austin 1988), among others. However, some individuals—whether deviants, criminals, or individuals who died in a culturally taboo manner—do not receive normal treatment at death. Mortuary practices for these individuals frequently differ in that they do not aid the deceased's soul in its journey to an afterlife (Shay 1985) and they may involve violence. Such mortuary violence is typically manifest in one of two ways (Bloch 1992). The first is to simply deny the soul or animating essence of the deceased entrance to an afterlife or to terminate it outright. Alternatively, the soul or animating essence of the deceased may be appropriated by the living for other purposes. Examples of this include taking scalps of war dead in the Great Plains (Olsen and Shipman 1994) and headhunting in Southeast Asia (Bloch 1992). Teasing apart processes of mortuary veneration and violation in the material record is a long-standing problem in mortuary studies that has recently begun to garner more attention (Rakita et al. 2005).

I have argued elsewhere that mortuary violence occurred in Mesoamerica, but not exactly as Maurice Bloch described it, for at least two reasons (Duncan 2005a). First, in Mesoamerica individuals had multiple animating essences that fall under the western notion of "soul" (Furst 1995; López Austin 1988). Second, and perhaps more important, Bloch's model was based on the Merina in Madagascar, who he suggested have an unchanging and ahistorical sacred component to their worldview. This is not the case for Mesoamerica, where everything exists within a cycle of birth/regeneration and death/termination, including humans and their souls or animating essences (what Marshall Becker [1993] has called a "birth death planting cycle"). As Kay Read (1998) has argued, everything that is born will eventually die, and everything that dies will eventually be reborn. Certainly, this cyclical aspect of time was emphasized particularly in the Postclassic period. Consequently, outright termination of the soul—or denying a soul entrance to a permanent unchanging afterlife (e.g., Bloch's original description of negative predation)—was not likely part of the Mesoamerican worldview. Rather, mortuary violence seems to have been manifest by exercising agency over the animating essences of enemies (or other individuals deserving of such violation) by at least two processes: destruction and isolation.

Destruction and Isolation

Read (1998) has cogently argued that Mesoamericans could control cycles of birth and death, or termination and regeneration, in part through destruction. Destroying things, whether through sacrifice of individuals or smashing of pots, punctuates the cycles within the Mesoamerican worldview and sets the stage for rebirth. In the case of dedicatory sacrifice, Brian Stross (1998) has noted that when houses are built in Tenejapa, Mexico, chickens are killed and placed in the ground under the center pole of the roof. This termination of the chicken allows for the rebirth of the animating essences in the new construction, thereby ensouling it. In this case, by destroying the chicken the builders are able to appropriate the chicken's essences and control the manner of the rebirth animating the building. Most archaeologists working in Mesoamerica are familiar with destruction or termination in this fashion (see Mock 1998a, 1998b for discussion). However, some destructive acts are not part of larger dedicatory or ensoulment processes and reflect no attempt to appropriate the essence of that which was destroyed. I have argued elsewhere (Duncan 2005a) that a second process, isolation, was used—sometimes in conjunction with destruction—to exercise control over cycles of termination and rebirth.

Isolation has been less fully explored as a ritual process in Mesoamerican archaeology than destruction has and deserves explication here. Things may be isolated in a number of ways. One way is by boxing them up and sealing them off to hinder their progression through the normal cycles of termination and regeneration. Doing so does not permanently avoid destruction—everything in Mesoamerica that was created will eventually end—but it can postpone termination. I explore other examples elsewhere (Duncan 2005a: 59–65), but an Itzaj Maya tale of how they dealt with a cave monster is a good illustration:

> Then said the great man, the sorcerer, that no one should be afraid, that he is going to tie the animals inside the caves so they don't come out. And one day, one Friday, (Thursdays and Fridays are days of sorcerers) they say he went to do his work in the mouth of the caves. He bought a new clay plate. Then he filled it with water. Then he took it to leave it in the mouth of the cave. And he sought three arm's lengths of thread. That thread is the one that the old people before made with cotton. They spin it with a spindle. And he got the thread, then he took it, then he tied it. He made a cross with the thread. And as he is a sorcerer, they say, he made his prayer. Thus the animal, when it was feeling that it was hungry, it wants to eat, it begins to roar. And it wants to leave the cave. When it leaves, it comes. It arrives at the mouth of the cave, it sees a lake is formed at the mouth of the cave. And it wants to arrive, to get out of the water. It sticks (is stuck) with the thread placed by the old man, and that thread, it changes into wire with barbs. And there, it sees it can't get out, it returns again, inside his cave. It is roaring when it again enters, they say. And thus, thus, until many years passed, until the day arrived, when the animals died. (Hofling 1991: 187–192)

This is an important example for several reasons. First, it shows that isolation is not a permanent state and death is not avoided. Isolation as a process is not an exception to the Mesoamerican cyclical structure of birth and death. Rather, isolation is a useful way of temporarily dealing with bad things. Second, it shows the connection between caves and isolation: archaeologically, such isolation is seen where sections of caves have been partitioned to seal off harmful things (Prufer 2002). As discussed later, this is relevant to Operation 1000. Third, this is an Itzaj tale told by Itzaj speakers from around the Petén lakes. This confirms the fact that isolation was an important concept for the Itzaj, whose ancestors were contemporaries of the Kowoj. I argue that Operation 1000 reflects mortuary violation through the use of both destruction and isolation.

How Might We Recognize Destruction and Isolation Archaeologically?

Christopher Carr (1995) demonstrated that, cross-culturally, several mortuary variables reflect attempts to influence the deceased's soul or the journey of the soul after death. I modified these for the Maya area specifically to identify four variables that could be used to tease apart veneration and violation: body treatment and preparation, grave characteristics, grave location relative to sacred landscape, and grave goods (Duncan 2005a, 2005b). Operation 1000 reflects destruction and isolation (i.e., some form of violation) for each of these variables. For example, mutilation is characteristic of body treatment associated with violation and destruction. This is seen in the *Popol Vuh* in the gods' destruction of their third attempt to make humans (Tedlock 1996). Archaeologically, it is seen in the skull pit at Colha in northern Belize (Massey 1989), which consists of thirty skulls of adults and children; cutmarks on the faces and skull vaults indicate that processing, such as defleshing, occurred and that vessels were intentionally smashed in the deposit where the skulls were placed. Upon the interment of the skulls and vessels, the building was burned and appears not to have been used again. Although there are different interpretations about exactly what behaviors led to the deposit (cf. Barrett and Scherer 2005; Mock 1998a, 1998b), authors do agree that the deposit reflects an act of violation. The remains in Operation 1000 also exhibited cutmarks that reflect some form of defleshing or processing beyond dismemberment, which is consistent with an act of destruction.

The disproportionate representation of right and left forearm bones also reflects destruction. Joel Palka (2002) recently demonstrated that left and right sides were significant in Maya culture. The Maya associated the right hand with "purity and power," while the left was associated with that which is "weaker, lame, or subordinate" (ibid.: 419). Other researchers (e.g., Houston 1998) had previously noted that subordinate individuals (wearing simpler costumes, having a lowered head, or kneeling or being bound) were more likely to be depicted on the left side in murals. Palka (2002) also noted that subordinates hold objects in their left hand while rulers, victors, and other superordinate individuals hold objects in their right hand. In battle scenes where the victor grabs a defeated enemy, the victor tends to hold the enemy's hair in his left hand with a weapon in his right. More than 82 percent of the images Palka examined on ceramics and 88 percent on monuments exhibited this left/right symbolism. This symbolism is the best explanation for the underrepresentation of the right arm and forearm bones in Operation 1000 and why there are no similar differences among lower limb elements. Side discrepancies also exist in the distribution of deer bones at Seibal (Pohl 1985), but I know of no other examples of caches/burials of human remains in the Maya area that have similar left/right differences.

The emphasis on the mouth as a locus of violence reflects destruction. The power of speech was considerable in Mesoamerica (Gossen 1986). Oration and songs were ways of interacting with the gods; indeed, June Nash (1985) has noted that among Tzotzil speakers the soul exits the body through the tongue after death. The removal of teeth from the jaws in Operation 1000 seems at least to be an attempt to reduce the power of the deceased. The fact that the maxillary molars are underrepresented in conjunction with teeth having drilled roots suggests that these molars were taken as trophies.

Carr (1995) originally distinguished between form of body disposal (e.g., scaffold versus cremation) and other characteristics such as grave dimension. I collapsed these into the more general category of grave characteristics. One such characteristic, the degree to which individuality was maintained, also reflects destruction. In mass graves that appear designed to honor individuals, one principal personage is typically located in a central position or stands out in some way from the other individuals (Robin 1989). In contrast, Operation 1000 has no central or articulated individuals, and there is no reason to think any individual was being honored. Rather, all of the remains are piled in one area of the pit without distinction.

Grave location also reflects an act of violence. Operation 1000 was found on the northwest corner of the Mayapán-style temple assemblage in Group A at Zacpetén. The mass grave at Topoxté was also found on the northwest side of the temple assemblage. West is commonly associated with death and east with rebirth throughout Mesoamerica (Ashmore 1991), and this appears to be an organizing spatial principle on multiple levels of society—from cache, to building, to site, to polity. However, among Tzotzil speakers northwest is associated with violence in houses (Gossen and Leventhal 1993). Pugh (2003b: 409) documented the presence of a *sakbe* dividing the east and west sides of the Group A plaza at Zacpetén. Operation 1000 clearly reflects a concern for cardinal and possibly inter-cardinal directions in its location and an association with termination and violence.

Grave location relative to sacred landscape also reflects attempts to isolate the remains. As demonstrated by the aforementioned Itzaj tale, caves were and are ritually meaningful places that can be used for acts of isolation. William Hanks (1990) noted that Maya shamans in Yucatán place evil spirits they have taken from houses into chultuns. Blood from Tzutujil bloodletting ceremonies is also disposed of in caves. In southern Belize archaeologists found caves partitioned and sealed in what appear to be attempts to isolate harmful spirits (Prufer 2002). Operation 1000 appears to represent such an attempt. This depression on the northwest corner of Group A at Zacpetén had been used repeatedly from the Middle Preclassic to the Late Postclassic. When the human remains were placed in the ground, they were covered with rocks on the west and south sides, and on the north and east sides with limestone chipped from the walls of the pit. Covering the remains marked the cessation of activity for the feature until it was excavated by Pugh in 1997. Above all, the deposit of human remains in Operation 1000 was not associated with an attempt to ensoul something, such as a building, which suggested to Pugh (2001) — and I think rightly so — that a strong taboo was associated with the deposit. This is consistent with an attempt to isolate and sequester the remains, in the same way as is seen in caves.

Finally, the presence of grave goods in the Maya area is associated with attempts to honor or at least provision the deceased in their journey and rebirth after death. No grave goods were associated with the remains in Operation 1000, which is congruent with what one would expect with an act of destruction or violation.

I argue, then, that Operation 1000 was created by exhuming previously interred individuals and possibly including some remains from other contexts (e.g., temples) in an effort to violate the deceased. The creation of the mass grave involved elements of both destruction and isolation, reflecting an attempt to punctuate cycles of birth and death by terminating the animating essences associated with the remains of the deceased. However, the rebirth of the animating essences would have occurred in a context in which the remains were sealed off, thereby reducing their potency to harm the living while simultaneously creating a symbol of the deceased's weakness. Although this is a coherent explanation on its own, I argue that it becomes more cogent when considered in light of the last two questions posed at the beginning of the chapter.

Who was included in the mass grave? How might this inform our understanding of the Xiw/Kowoj interaction with their neighbors? The Kowoj proper claim to have migrated from Mayapán in the early sixteenth century in response to the events of the Spanish conquest, but Mayapán as an indigenous political center collapsed decades earlier, around A.D. 1450. The stratum (Level 7) below the mass grave in Operation 1000 yielded a calibrated radiocarbon date from burned wood between 1389 and 1437, a date that may be closer to a late-fourteenth-century uprising at Mayapán than to the site's collapse (see Rice, Chapter 2, this volume). I argue that the presence of mass graves at Topoxté and Zacpetén, both controlled by the Xiw/Kowoj, and the timing of the creation of the mass graves suggest that these interments were part of their early migration to and emergence as a political force in the Petén lakes region. Although the migration of the Xiw/Kowoj into the region was not likely a single mass event, the political upheavals at Mayapán were significant enough for the Xiw/Kowoj to leave that center. And indeed, there is no reason to think that the collapse of Mayapán did not relate to their emergence as a political power around the Petén lakes. As a faction of Xiw/Kowoj moved into the Petén lakes region or began to emerge as a rival to the Itza already entrenched in the region, they needed a way to claim ownership of their new territory. One way of doing this would have been to exhume the ancestors of the sites' previous occupants (i.e., the ancestors of whoever occupied Zacpetén in the Early Postclassic), violate them, and re-inter them publicly. The violation would have included things like selecting left forearm bones for inclusion and omitting right ones to emphasize the weakness of the previous inhabitants and create an enduring symbol of that weakness. It would not necessarily have done away with the potency of the ancestors' remains, however, which is likely why there would have been a taboo associated with the remains: the remains were only sequestered, not permanently terminated.

Finally, Operation 1000 demonstrates that ritual violence was an important mechanism for creating and constructing social and ethnic boundaries within the political context of the Late Postclassic Petén lakes region. By violating enemies' ancestors through destruction and isolation, the Kowoj established their claim to specific sites and emerged as a significant force that would come to control the eastern half of the lakes region in the Late Postclassic.

Acknowledgments

I would like to thank the editors, Don and Prudence Rice, for inviting me to participate in this volume. I also thank all the members of Proyecto Maya Colonial and the faculty and students of the Centro Universitario del Petén (CUDEP), in particular Lic. Rolando Torres and Lic. Rómulo Sánchez. Their assistance proved invaluable in every stage of this project, from the planning to the fieldwork to the writing. I would like to acknowledge the help I received from the officials at the Instituto de Antropología e Historia in Guatemala, Licda. Sheila Flores and Lic. Boris Aguilar. I thank Drs. Della Cook, Gabriel Wrobel, and Dennis Dirkmaat for permission to cite their work. Finally, I thank Carmen Arendt and the Hernández González family, who were incredibly supportive throughout the fieldwork and writing stages of this project. Two reviewers provided valuable criticism on earlier drafts of this chapter. All remaining errors are my own. This fieldwork was funded in part by NSF Dissertation Improvement Grant 0125311, awarded to W. N. Duncan and P. M. Rice, principal investigator.

The KOWOJ and the LACANDON
Migrations and Identities

—— Timothy W. Pugh ————————————————————————————

Processes of contact, conquest, and colonialism bring about hybridized social configurations built upon the old foundations but molded by new relations of power. Religious systems can be dramatically impacted, especially when colonial powers are obsessed with destroying alternatives to their worldview. This chapter traces transformations of the central ritual space—the god house—in adjacent regions of Petén, Guatemala, and Chiapas, Mexico, from Spanish contact (A.D. 1525) until the present. God house rituals were perduring, reflecting the changing reality and helping those using the ritual spaces to understand a world under physical and spiritual siege.

The A.D. 1697 conquest of Petén resulted in out-migration, and some of the refugees settled in Chiapas, where they mingled with refugees from Yucatán to become the Lacandon (De Vos 1980: 223–224; Pugh 2000, 2001b: 114). The Lacandon did not inhabit their current territory in Chiapas, Mexico, before A.D. 1596. Kowoj ritual practices of sixteenth- and seventeenth-century Petén, as we understand them archaeologically, are remarkably similar to those of the twentieth-century Northern Lacandon.

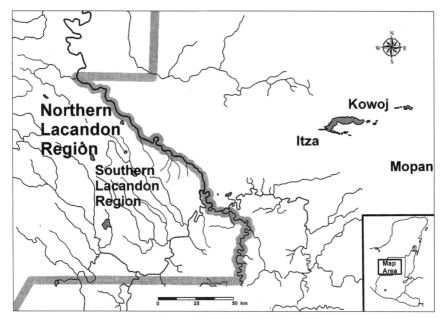

Map 16.1. Lacandon regions in Chiapas, Mexico, and Maya groups in the Petén lakes area.

Petén and the Lacandon at Conquest

The Lacandon live in river- and lakeside communities in Chiapas, Mexico, approximately 150 kilometers due west of Lake Petén Itzá (Map 16.1). They speak Lakantun, a Yukatekan Mayan language or dialect. Before the sixteenth century the area was occupied by speakers of Chol Mayan called Lakam Tun, whom the Spaniards referred to as El Acantun; this was shortened to Lacantun, then Lacandon (Bruce 1977: 185). In A.D. 1586 the Spaniards drove the Lakam Tun from Chiapas, thereby clearing the region for Yukatekan-speaking groups displaced by the conquest of Petén and Yucatán.

To the east, in the seventeenth century the Petén lakes region harbored the last complex polities of independent Yukatekan-speaking Maya, the Itza and Kowoj. Among the Itza, the Kan Ek' dynasty dominated regional politics for at least 172 years and expanded west into the Río Usumacinta by the latter part of the seventeenth century, their reach extending to Kan Itzam in Tabasco, Mexico (Jones 1998: 57). In A.D. 1697, after the Spaniards attacked and seized the Itza capital, they subsequently subdued the Kowoj and resettled the diverse Maya populations at mission settlements, but many groups fled the region (Jones 1998: 253–259, 348–349, 366–372).

The Spaniards encountered refugees at Yucum in Chiapas in 1697, and they claimed to have fled the sacrifice and cannibalism of the Itza (De Vos 1980: 221). This group had Yukatekan patronyms including "Kowoj," which, although common (16.6 percent), was less than the 20.8 percent who had the patronym Chan. In 1709, a group at Petenacte near Palenque had names similar to those at Yucum. This community likely collectively referred to itself as "Kowoj," its most common (23.6 percent) patronym (De Vos 1980: 223). The Yucum and Petenacte groups may have been the same people and the ancestors of the Northern Lacandon (Boremanse 1998: 4; De Vos 1980: 220–231; Hellmuth 1972: 215–216). A small indigenous population settled at San José de García Real near Palenque from 1793 to 1806 to trade with the Spaniards (Boremanse 1998: 4–6). They lived in dispersed settlements, lacked political centralization, and conducted rituals in domestic "temples" comparable to those of the modern Lacandon; in addition, their dress and marriage practices were similar to those of the modern groups (ibid.). Kowoj was, at 50 percent, the most common patronym recorded at San José (De Vos 1980: 229). Another patronym, García, belonged to a Ladino from Tabasco who married into the group; hence, the group was not exclusively Yukateko-speaking (ibid.: 227). In sum, the relative frequency of the name Kowoj increased in Chiapas during the eighteenth century in response to disruptions caused by the Spanish conquest of Petén (ibid.: 223–224).

Lacandon peoples in western Petén interacted with Petén lakes settlements into the nineteenth century (Schwartz 1990: 318). Joel Palka, who is reconstructing gaps in the history of the nineteenth-century Lacandon through archaeological research, has found possible Colonial-period Lacandon settlements in the Petexbatún region of Petén (Palka 1998: 466–468, 2005a, 2005b; also Thompson 1977: 14). Affiliations of these settlements with Northern or Southern Lacandon have not been discerned, although Jacques Soustelle (1935: 334) suggested that they contributed to the Southern populations. The Lacandon incorporated "outsiders" until at least the beginning of the nineteenth century; thus, they certainly were not a pristine group sheltered from colonialism (Boremanse 1998: 9–13; De Vos 1980: 244–257; Palka 1998: 457–458).

The Spaniards identified the names of Colonial-period occupants of Chiapas as patronyms, but they appear to be more complex and tied to social factions and cosmology. When the deity Hachakyum created humans, his Underworld antithesis, Kisin, formed parallel animal souls of humans living in the Underworld forest (Boremanse 1998: 102–104; Bruce 1975: 23; McGee 1990: 32–33, 91). People with matching animal spirits are members of the same unit called an *onen*. *Onen* membership is inherited patrilineally, and the animal name is the patronymic (McGee 1990: 32–33). They were once endogamous, and specific names were tied to places (Tozzer 1907: 40; Boremanse 1998: 102). *Onens* were not totems in the strictest sense (McGee 1990: 31), but because all members have the same species as their animal spirit and its name signifies the group, *onens* were a fuzzy form of totem.

Onens were grouped into larger units of unknown significance, referred to by "ceremonial names," but we know little about them (McGee 1990: 32). The two peccary *onen*, K'ek'en (white-lipped peccary) and Kitam (collared peccary), were combined under the Kowoj ceremonial name, while Ma'ax (spider monkey) and Ba'atz' (howler monkey) were known as Karcia (Boremanse 1998: 104; McGee 1990: 32). It is clear, then, that the fissions in social space had corresponding variations in ritual practice that reflected social interaction as well as differentiation. Karsia likely diverged from "García" (Tozzer 1907: 41) — probably originating from the absorption of the García patronym at San José de García Real. A cacique named Kitam Kowoj lived in a mission town on the Petén lakes around 1704 (Jones 1998: 402), making it possible that *onen* and ceremonial names existed there as well. The names Jaw, Kowoj, Mis, Puk, and Karsia/García appeared as "patronyms" in seventeenth-century Petén, eighteenth-century Petenacte, and Colonial Yucatán (De Vos 1980: 222; Jones 1998: table I.I).

The modern Lacandon, Yukateko, Itzaj, and Mopan Maya speak different dialects of Yukatekan Maya (Hofling 2006b, Chapter 4, this volume). Itzaj speakers descended from the seventeenth-century Itza of the Petén lakes region; thus, this was a recently evolved dialect, whereas Mopan separated earlier (Hofling 2006b, Chapter 4, this volume). Northern and Southern Lacandon speak the Lakantun dialect, but the groups differ: Southern Lacandon is more similar to Yukateko, while Northern groups most closely resemble Itzaj. The close linguistic ties between the Itzaj and Northern Lacandon may be in part the result of trade networks that continued until the twentieth century. However, it also seems likely that some Northern Lacandon ancestors originated in Petén (Pugh 2001: 116-117).

The Northern and Southern Lacandon also differed with respect to ritual, beliefs, kinship, marriage patterns, and material culture (Soustelle 1939: 286). Although varying cultural characteristics do not universally indicate ethnic differentiation (Barth 1969: 14-15), the Northern Lacandon distinguished themselves from Southern groups by referring to the latter as *chukuch nok* ('long tunics'); the southerners referred to the northerners as *naach i winik* ('far-away people') (Boremanse 1998: 8). Each group called itself Hach Winik ('true people'), but neither considered the other Hach Winik (Boremanse 1998: 3-8).

God House Rituals

God houses or temples were used throughout the Lacandon region from the earliest occupation of the area by Yukatekan speakers in the Colonial period until the end of the twentieth century. Buildings nearly identical to Northern Lacandon god houses were constructed in the Kowoj area of Petén from the early fifteenth century until the conquest in A.D. 1697 and perhaps shortly afterward. God houses, god pots, and the rituals enlivening these spaces and objects reflected and contributed to the social being of those who created them. Although they had similar ritual paraphernalia including god pots, the god houses and associated rituals of the Northern and Southern Lacandon differed significantly (G. Soustelle 1961: 59, 1966: 59-60; J. Soustelle 1937: 93).

Northern Lacandon

Various ethnographers have recorded Northern Lacandon rituals from the early twentieth century until recently. Although ceremonials differed according to both their purpose and the human and divine participants, they shared certain characteristics that resulted in consistent patterning in the material items incorporated into the rites (McGee 1991: 455). Lacandon rituals primarily took place in god houses in domestic groups, which were owned by the senior male of the household, but males occasionally shared them. We may see the predecessors of these god houses in Late Postclassic- to Contact-period oratorios.

The Northern Lacandon constructed their residences using modern materials and styles, but god houses were built in archaic forms with a thatched roof, dirt floor, and no walls (McGee 1990: 55). God houses also had differential rules of behavior, including taboos. Objects in the god house were transformed into inverted forms for deities — burned copal became tortillas, palm leaves became benches, small things became large, and so on (Davis 1978: 24–26) — indicating that these were transformative (sacred) places (following Turner 1977). God houses were also places of socialization among males of different households, who rarely interacted in other contexts (Boremanse 1998: 27-28). They were clearly spaces set apart from typical daily activities and helped effect social unity.

At one time, adult males interacting with deities in the god house wore ceremonial tunics and bark headbands (Soustelle 1937: 62; Davis 1978: 57). Extraordinary individuals called *to'ojil* were especially adept at mediating with deities, divination, curing, and oral traditions; they had high community status (Boremanse 1998: 66-68). Except for a cacao preparation performance, initiation rites, and receiving their share of ritual drinks, women were excluded from direct participation in god house rites, although they prepared offerings in the ceremonial cooking house (Davis 1978: 213–215; Pugh 2006: 377–380; Tozzer 1907: 130).

Each god house held a slightly different set of deities (Soustelle 1959: 147–153) and god house rituals focused on "god pots": ceramic bowls with a deity's face modeled on one side (Figure 16.1). God pots were cared for by male heads of household, who often initially used the vessels of their fathers or fathers-in-law (Boremanse 1998: 29), meaning that the veneration of specific deities was influenced by kinship. God pots and associated rituals were important symbols of group solidarity within household clusters and between clusters that shared a god house (ibid.: 28-31). Variation also occurred between *onens*, as each emphasized different deities (McGee 1990: table 3.5; Soustelle 1959: 158). The importance, myths, and attributes of each deity varied regionally as well (Cline 1944: 107-113).

The deities retained "ownership" of their pots, thereby making the vessels sacred and subject to strict taboos (Tozzer 1907: 91). God pots were once reanimated annually, although associated rituals became much less frequent in the later part of the twentieth century (Davis 1978: 75). The person who cared for the vessel also formed and awakened it through a rite involving singing, painting it, striking it with beads, and caching a sacred stone and cacao beans in the bowl (Davis 1978: 77; McGee 1998: 44-45). Awakened or activated pots allowed the Lacandon to communicate with deities and make

Figure 16.1. Recently made Lacandon "god pot," purchased from a Lacandon seller in Mérida in the early 1970s. Decoration is in red and black over white stucco. Collection of Don and Prudence Rice.

offerings to them (Davis 1978: 72–77), including incense, a corn drink called *säk ja'*, tamales, red paint, rubber, and *balché*—a fermented beverage made with tree bark and honey (or sugar) (McGee 1990: 74). *Balché* was the most important offering, and its preparation was a ritual event conducted by males; it was the only edible offering made by males (Davis 1978: 191).

Obtaining the sacred stones that activated new god pots required pilgrimages to the sites and caves believed to be the houses of the deities represented by the particular vessels (McGee 1998: 43). God pots "died" during rites in which their stones were transferred to a new vessel, and recycled stones were linked with the pilgrimages of ancestors (Tozzer 1907: 88). God pots were tied to particular locations and deities though metaphor and metonym, thereby transporting the sacred landscape of caves and ruins into the microcosm of the god house. The bowl of the god pot represented the cave of the deity (Davis 1978: 74, 151–152), and the sacred stone placed in the bowl signified the deity's house, bench, or both (McGee 1990: 52). Because each god house had a unique set of god pots, they evoked slightly different aspects of the sacred landscape.

The Lacandon sacred landscape had many components including god houses, caves, and archaeological sites, all believed to be the homes of deities (McGee 2002: 129–138). In particular, the Classic-period (A.D. 200 to 830) sites of Palenque and Yaxchilán played critical roles in Northern Lacandon mythology (Davis 1978: 19, 244–249). Humans were created at Palenque but the deities moved to Yaxchilán, leaving the traitorous elder sons of Hachakyum at the former site; in consequence, Yaxchilán played a greater role in Lacandon cosmology (McGee 2002: 130). This myth likely reflects the historical movement of the Northern Lacandon and therefore their sacred landscape from Petenacte near Palenque to their present location near Yaxchilán. The elder sons in the myth may represent *tzul,* or "foreigners."

The Northern Lacandon directed the center ridge pole of the god houses toward the North Star Polaris, while the buildings and god pots faced east toward Yaxchilán, thereby tying them into the sacred landscape (McGee 2002: 130–137). Human residences, in turn, mimicked the orientation of the god house (ibid.: 138). A stela carved from a stalactite in a Yaxchilán plaza was the center of the universe, or axis mundi, connecting the earth and sky and a creation place. Not surprisingly, the Lacandon made pilgrimages to "ruins" — especially Yaxchilán — and caves to make offerings directly to deities (ibid.: 129–138).

Several researchers have recorded detailed plans of Northern Lacandon god houses and their contents along with summaries of ritual performances (Tozzer 1907: figure 33; Davis 1978: figure 8; McGee 1990: figure 5.3). The three plans of god houses differ slightly, but they share certain characteristics. For example, one god house plan recorded by Alfred Tozzer (1907: 112) depicts a god pot renewal ritual (Map 16.2): the shelf along the west side held unused god pots; south of the shelf were "dead" god pots facing west; north of the shelf were a drum and a lid used to collect soot for black pigment. Large god pots stood upon a palm leaf–mat altar in front of the shelf; east of the large censers were smaller god pots, representing servants of the gods (ibid.: 89). Among these smaller god pots was a ladle censer representing Akna, the mother of the god pots, whose name parallels that of *ok na,* the name of censer renewal rites in Colonial Yucatán (ibid.: 110–111). A row of *balché* offering cups and tamale offerings lay east of the smaller pots. East of the larger altar was a smaller mat altar with a pot containing *balché* and several cups. Participants sat on wooden benches near the smaller altar. Outside the god house dugout logs contained water, sugarcane, and *balché.* The Lacandon placed the vessel of Sukunkyum, the Underworld deity, outside the god house because it was dangerous to the other god pots (ibid.: 95).

A second god house plan (Map 16.3), dated to 1973, depicts the layout of a *mek'chajal,* ritual payment to the gods for the birth and health of a child (Davis 1978: 59, 264). Two men owned the house, and each had a shelf of pots. Active god pots stood on the west side of a palm altar, with offering cups and a copal

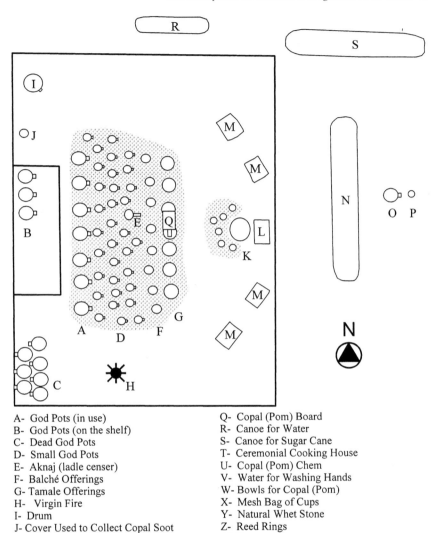

A- God Pots (in use)
B- God Pots (on the shelf)
C- Dead God Pots
D- Small God Pots
E- Aknaj (ladle censer)
F- Balché Offerings
G- Tamale Offerings
H- Virgin Fire
I- Drum
J- Cover Used to Collect Copal Soot
K- Balché Pot and Empty Cups
L- Leader's Stool
M- Participants' Stools
N- Balché Log
0- Sukunkyum's God Pot
P- Sukunkyum's Offering

Q- Copal (Pom) Board
R- Canoe for Water
S- Canoe for Sugar Cane
T- Ceremonial Cooking House
U- Copal (Pom) Chem
V- Water for Washing Hands
W- Bowls for Copal (Pom)
X- Mesh Bag of Cups
Y- Natural Whet Stone
Z- Reed Rings
A1-Prepared Cacao
A2-Cacao Beater and Cup
A3-Secular Fire
A4-Annatto Tree
A5-Offering Cup, Unspecified
- Palm Mat

Map 16.2. Plan of Northern Lacandon god house during god pot renewal rite. Redrawn from Tozzer 1907: 112.

board holding rubber figures to their east. The sacred fire and bowls containing tamales lay south of the altar, and a smaller palm-mat altar held cups,
cacao, a "cacao beater and cup," and a *balché* jug, with the non-sacred fire

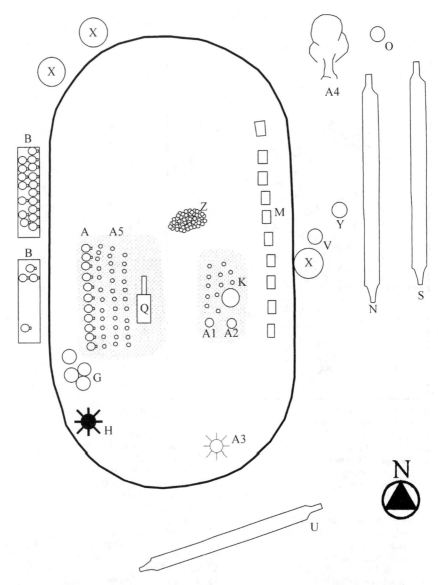

Map 16.3. Plan of Northern Lacandon god house during mek'chajal *ritual. Redrawn from Davis 1978: figure 8.*

burning to its south (ibid.: 59). East of the small mat, the participants sat on wooden benches. Before entering, participants washed their hands with water from a gourd to the east of the god house. Three dugout logs lay outside the house; one contained *balché*, another sugarcane, and the third was reserved for

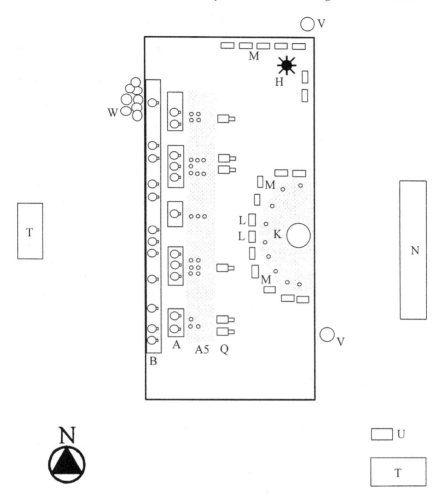

Map 16.4. Plan of Northern Lacandon god house during balché *ritual. Redrawn from McGee 1990: figure 5.3.*

"washing cups and pounding cacao" (ibid.). The god pot of Sukunkyum also stood outside the god house.

The third plan represents a *balché* ritual conducted in the 1980s (Map 16.4) (McGee 1990: 56). Once again, the shelf along the west wall held unused god pots. Participating vessels sat on boards in the west side of the house with offering cups on a palm-mat altar to their east. Boards containing offerings of incense lay east of the altar. The *balché* pot, surrounded by cups, rested on a palm mat on the east side of the house; participants sat on wooden benches around this palm mat. The god pots and the participants were ordered by rank, with the most important in the center flanked by individuals of ever-decreasing relationship and status (ibid.: 55–57). The sacred fire burned in the northeast corner of the structure. Bowls of water for washing hands and a dugout canoe holding *balché* stood outside the structure. Sukunkyum is not depicted outside the house, indicating that this practice may have ceased by the time of this research or that this deity may not have participated in this particular rite.

Another deity, Akyantho', appears as a white male. He created foreigners (*tzul*), diseases, and medicine and guarded "foreign people and objects," including domesticated animals, metal (especially gold), and oranges (Cline 1944: table 1; McGee 1990: 22). His connection with medicine and gold (commerce) parallels Lacandon relations with *tzul* (McGee 1990: 22, 65). The association of Akyantho' with illness may record the historical correlation between the arrival of Europeans and certain diseases (ibid.: 22). Akyantho' is the father of Hesuklistos (Jesus Christ) (ibid.: 70). This deity was not mentioned in earlier accounts and reflects recent interactions with missionaries.

Underlying patterns are obvious in Northern Lacandon god houses. They were oriented to the cardinal directions and were open on the east side (McGee 2002: 137). While living, most god pots rested on the west side of the building, all facing east. Dead god pots were only present during new god pot ceremonies and rested in the southwest corner of the god house, facing west. Ritual participants sat on the east side of the god house near the *balché* pot and cups, which were placed upon a palm-leaf mat. Between the god pots and the participants were various offerings of food, drink, and incense, also placed upon a palm-leaf mat. The god pot of Sukunkyum rested a few meters east and outside of the god house.

Patterning in the god houses reflected the "key ritual" underlying most performances: the *balché* rite (McGee 1991: 455). This ritual was the procedure through which the Northern Lacandon offered *balché*, food, and other items to deities. Participants also consumed *balché*, which purified them and put them in closer proximity to the deities and ancestors (Davis 1978: 111; McGee 1991: 440). The gods also performed the *balché* ritual when communicating with their deity (McGee 1990: 73). The Northern Lacandon considered the ability to conduct the *balché* rite a foundation of their ethnic identity (ibid.: 129).

Some Northern Lacandon conducted "traditional" rituals until 1997, after which the rites were performed for a price for "tourists and filmmakers" (McGee 2002: 125). In the past, foreigners were generally excluded from participation in many rituals, especially pilgrimages (Tozzer 1907: 148–150) and the animation of new god pots (McGee 1990: 51). R. Jon McGee (2002: 150–152) noted several reasons for the decline of indigenous practices: local hospitals ended the need for curing rituals, and the education children receive in schools and the arrival of television displaced cosmology and indigenous knowledge. In addition, many Lacandon are involved in the tourist industry; hence agricultural rites are less critical. God houses that remain in residential groups are also used primarily to perform for tourists and lack the orientation that once tied them to the ritual topography. In 2004 tourists could purchase a non-consecrated god pot for U.S. $4.50. These vessels did not contain a sacred

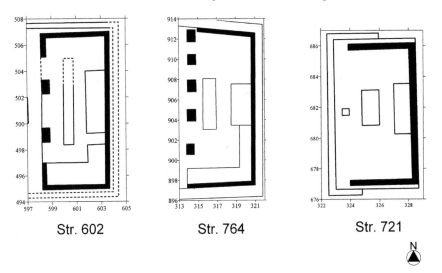

Str. 602   Str. 764   Str. 721

Map 16.5. Plans of excavated temple superstructures at Zacpetén.

stone and therefore lacked connections with the deities. Finally, residences came to be aligned with the road rather than the sacred landscape (ibid.: 48).

Kowoj God Houses

The site of Zacpetén lies within the area controlled by the seventeenth-century Kowoj, who likely contributed to the ancestry of the Northern Lacandon. During the Late Postclassic period, Zacpetén was a small ceremonial center with two central civic-ceremonial groups, Group A and Group C, each of which includes a god house on a high platform (a "temple"). During the Contact period, two elite residential groups outside the two centers also included god houses (Pugh and Rice, Chapter 8, this volume). The domestic god houses were likely reconstructions of the two earlier public houses. Proyecto Maya Colonial excavated three of the four god houses: Structure 602 in Group A, Structure 764 in Group C, and Structure 721 in Group 719. Structure 721 is the latest known god house in Petén (see Chapter 5, Table 5.1, this volume, for radiocarbon dates).

The plans of the god houses at Zacpetén were nearly identical. Both public temples (Map 16.5) had medial altars against their east walls and L-shaped benches in their southeast corners. Between the medial altar and the buildings' rectangular columns lay a long, low interior altar. Structure 721 followed the same basic plan as the other god houses but had no columns or bench—the occupants likely used wooden benches. Late Postclassic temples differ from Lacandon god houses, as they had a formal audience in the plaza. The temple was "open" on the west side toward the audience, but the audience faced east, as did the god pots.

379

Northern Lacandon god houses had a long palm-mat altar in the middle of the structure and a smaller altar on the east side of the building, which were matched by the interior and medial altars of god houses at Zacpetén. The connection between mats and altars is well established, as Late and Terminal Classic carved stone altars, including Altar 1 at Zacpetén (Chapter 13, Figure 13.1, this volume), were often carved with mat motifs. The Lacandon seem to have replaced stone altars with woven palm-leaf mats.

God pots at Zacpetén are Patojo Modeled and Kulut Modeled deity effigy censers, which differ from those of the Lacandon as they are less abstract, with full-figure bodies modeled of clay rather than faces painted on the vessel (Chapters 7 and 9, Figures 7.2 and 9.1, this volume). Late Postclassic- and Contact-period effigy censers were activated through complex rites that tied the vessels to cyclical time and the cardinal directions (Chase and Chase 1988: 72; Landa in Tozzer 1941: 160). The censers were born and died at temporal junctions, and some represented particular cycles themselves. Many were produced by specialists (Landa in Tozzer 1941: 94), but these vessels would have required activation.

Ritual activities at the two Zacpetén temples were identical, to judge from material remains, and also matched those of the Northern Lacandon. The deity effigy censers at Zacpetén were positioned on the west side of the god house like those of the Northern Lacandon (Map 16.6). The east sides of the public temples at Zacpetén had various red-slipped artifacts, including jars and quincunx effigy cups, paralleling the offering vessels of the Lacandon. On the east side of Structure 721, the god house associated with a possible domestic group, were various offering bowls. Public temples had masonry benches on the east side matching the position of the wooden benches of the Lacandon. God houses at Zacpetén and among the Northern Lacandon had the same east/west dichotomy, with god pots on the west of the interior altar and offering materials and participants on the east.

As mentioned, the Northern Lacandon separated the Underworld deity Sukunkyum from the other god pots. At Zacpetén, one deity was also separated from the others: the Kulut Modeled effigy censers were smaller than the Patojo Modeled god pots found in the temples, but they were equally detailed. This deity was placed in its own god house, an oratorio to the north of the temple, and, like his Lacandon parallel, was an elder deity. Whether it had any connections to the Underworld cannot be determined at present.

Late Postclassic Zacpetén differed from Lacandon settlements in that the peninsula's residents placed their god houses with several other ceremonial buildings in patterned assemblages. The ceremonial groups at Zacpetén included a god house, an oratorio containing a single deity, council halls, and ancestral shrines. The Lacandon appear to have collapsed the assembly role of council halls into the god house, much as these roles seem to have been collapsed into Group 719 at Zacpetén. The lack of formal administrative councils among the Lacandon eliminated the need for an independent structure. The god pot of the Lord of the Underworld was placed outside rather than in a separate oratorio — as we may see at Zacpetén.

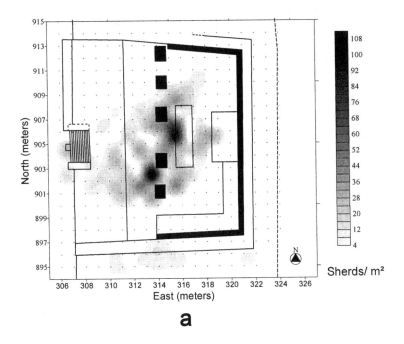

a

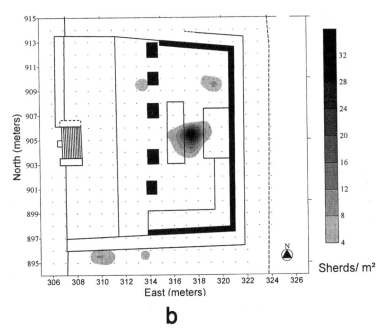

b

Map 16.6. Distribution of ritual artifacts in Structure 764, the temple in Group C at Zacpetén: (a) fragments of effigy censers; (b) fragments of red-slipped offering vessels.

Like the Lacandon, the Kowoj incorporated the sacred landscape into their ceremonial architecture. Several stalactites found in the central ceremonial group at Zacpetén were likely collected during pilgrimages (see Brady et al. 1997: 728–730). Postclassic offerings were found in the temples of Tikal (Adams and Trik 1958: 134), twenty-five kilometers north of Zacpetén, and at other Classic-period sites (Andres 2000; Walker 1990: 472) and caves (Schmidt 1977) throughout the lowlands, indicating that these places were incorporated into Late Postclassic sacred topography. The Petén Kowoj claimed that their place of origin was Mayapán in Yucatán, Mexico, but instead of having their gods and buildings face toward Mayapán, the Kowoj replicated the ceremonial assemblages—including the god houses—of that Yucatán city (Pugh 2002: 319). Later, as public architecture ceased to be constructed, social elites replicated these ceremonial areas in their residential groups in an attempt to co-opt the group's key symbols (ibid.).

The conformity in god house rituals was not restricted to Zacpetén because Topoxté Island, another Late Postclassic site in the Kowoj region of Petén, had identical patterns. God pots lay in the west side of the god house, a bench stood in the east, and redware vessels were smashed between the two (Bullard 1970: 295), indicating that god house activity areas at Zacpetén were characteristic of the Kowoj area in general. The Itza of Petén used god pots, but the rites occurred in council halls rather than in god houses, and the patterns did not follow those defined earlier (Pugh 2001). Christianized Maya in Yucatán no longer use god pots but instead make offerings to *santos*—either crosses or statues of saints. The layout of performances is opposite that of Zacpetén, in that the *santos* stand to the east and the human participants to the west (Hanks 1990: 338). Thus, activity patterns defined in god houses at Zacpetén were repetitive and restricted to the Kowoj area in Petén, and they matched those of the Northern Lacandon, but both differed from the Southern Lacandon and from twentieth-century Yucatán.

Discussion

Late Postclassic temples were much smaller and less well constructed than their Classic-period antecedents. The decrease in temple size followed the so-called Classic-period collapse, which occurred around A.D. 800–950 in central Petén and was marked by a decline in powerful social hierarchies with corresponding decreases in architectural monumentality. Kowoj god pots also differed from those of the Lacandon, as the latter emphasized the head—particularly the mouth—and simply painted the deity's body, while the former included complete modeled bodies. God pots were restricted to public groups and elite residential groups at Postclassic Zacpetén, indicating that social inequality and ritual specialization continued into the Late Postclassic and Contact periods. The god houses of the Petén Kowoj were models for and models of Kowoj identity and social being (following Geertz 1973: 93–95)—their symbolism tied the Kowoj into a larger world and distinguished them from the Itza.

Lacandon god houses lacked any vestiges of monumentality through excessive mass, but they memorialized tradition. The interior of the god house was not restricted to religious specialists; therefore, ritual knowledge was available to all who observed the rites. The ritual assemblage included a god house and a ceremonial cooking house paralleling male and female participation in the rites, respectively, and incorporating gender differences into the god house. The lack of numerous additional ritual buildings such as lineage houses and lineage ancestral shrines may reflect the shift from public ritual to family-based practices. In other words, religious and political ritual was decentralized so that it was practiced almost entirely at the level of the nuclear or extended family. Pre-conquest stratified Maya societies supported a variety of ritual specialists (Tozzer 1941: 111–112) that could not be supported in most households, but the social stratification and religious specialization of the Late Postclassic period did not exist among the decentralized Northern Lacandon.

The underlying pattern of the ritual events associated with the *balché* rite appears relatively constant between Late Postclassic/Contact-period Kowoj and the later Northern Lacandon. Although we do not have direct archaeological evidence (for example, residue analysis of pottery) that the Kowoj performed the *balché* rite, their rituals followed the same pattern. Juan de Villagutierre Soto-Mayor (1983: 84) described *balché* consumption among the Itza. Maya groups throughout the highlands and lowlands used god pots during the Late Postclassic period, but the rituals involving the vessels varied from place to place.

Ties between Late Postclassic- to Contact-period Kowoj and Northern Lacandon ritual performances and language, and an increase in the Kowoj patronym in the Lacandon region during the eighteenth century, together suggest that the Kowoj may have contributed to the population of the Lacandon. Kowoj families likely moved into the area after the conquest of Petén in A.D. 1697 and blended with other migrants. However, if this were the case, one might question why Kowoj-style god house rites persevered.

In 1761 a shaman in Yucatán named Jacinto Uk attempted a nativistic movement he hoped would rid the region of the Spaniards (Patch 2000: 209). He called himself King Kan Ek' Moctezuma, adopting the name of the late ruling dynasty of Petén, Guatemala, as well as the last independent Aztec ruler—thereby situating himself in opposition to the corrupting Spanish interlopers. He further claimed to be the messiah (Patch 2000: 209–210), thus also directing his mythopractice toward the converted. Uk's claims were significant to the masses in Yucatán, who rallied to the revivalist rebellion. Although Jacinto Uk's claims were not based on reality, they were believed by many people and represented a larger historical trend. Maintenance of indigenous ritual practices during the extended conquest of the Maya in Belize and Guatemala was a critical aspect of resistance and identity (Graham, Pendergast, and Jones 1989; Jones 1998: 37–41; Jones, Kautz, and Graham 1986: 41–44). It seems clear that these areas remained centers of resistance, perhaps a source of common pan-Yucatecan opposition to the Spaniards.

In sum, the Lacandon in Chiapas emerged as two of the various ethno-linguistic groups that populated the sixteenth- and seventeenth-century western lowlands. The Lacandon likely descended from a number of Maya populations, and we will never know for certain how much the Kowoj contributed to their ancestry. Nevertheless, we do know that the Lacandon emerged in Yucatan at the time of the conquest of Petén, that the Lacandon and Kowoj spoke similar dialects, and that ritual patterns in their religious buildings were similar. The god house was a place of socialization that contributed to identities based in gender, adulthood, family, community, and ethnicity. The cosmologies inherent in god house practices informed the Lacandon of their sacred landscape, history, and relationships with others. Given the historical link and the similarity in practices, one might reason an analogous function for Kowoj god houses. As places of social unity, god houses and their rituals were key symbols of the Northern Lacandon and the Kowoj. They brought people into contact with their mythic history and the sacred landscape. The rites and associated knowledge differentiated the Northern Lacandon from the Southern Lacandon, just as those of the Kowoj differentiated them from the Itza.

PART VI

CONCLUSIONS

SUMMARY AND CONCLUDING REMARKS
The Kowoj through a Glass, Darkly

—— Prudence M. Rice ————————————————————————

The preceding chapters have been compiled in an effort to begin to answer the question, Who were the Kowoj? Each chapter in this collection has addressed different kinds of evidence in what has come to be known as a conjunctive approach: indigenous written sources, Spanish sources, linguistics, radiocarbon dating, civic-ceremonial architecture, domestic architecture, decorated pottery, incense burners, mortuary practice, and so on. Each chapter has thus provided a window through which to create an image of the Kowoj Maya, but, like all windows, they are bounded by frames. In the case of these chapters, the frames are not only physical limits to the breadth of our vision but also theoretical and methodological boundaries we bring to the study, many of them unconscious. And not all windows (i.e., data sources) have been fully opened yet. So we are resigned to represent the Kowoj to an external audience like the proverbial blind men touching different parts of an elephant. Through a glass darkly, indeed.

As is often the case in research endeavors, Don and I did not begin our work in the eastern Petén lakes in the early 1970s with the question/problem

387

we have tried to answer/solve here, that is, identifying the Kowoj Maya. Instead, it seems the answer arose before the specific question was posed: in the 1990s Grant Jones told us about a little known group, the Kowoj (or Couoh, as the name was spelled by the Spaniards), who, his archival sources revealed, occupied the eastern lakes area in the Contact period and were embroiled in a civil war with the powerful Itza to the west. We realized then that the existence of this ethno-political group could explain striking differences between our archaeological data on the Postclassic in the eastern lakes and others' data around Lake Petén Itzá to the west, which was dominated by the Itza Maya. The darkness of the glass began to lighten. But, as is so often the case, this "solution" only presented more, and more difficult, problems. Among them, we chose to focus our subsequent research on two: (1) Who *were* the Kowoj in the sense of their cultural or sociopolitical identity, as it was manifest or materialized archaeologically, and (2) what was their history in Petén?

After wading through often contradictory evidence and varied interpretations (even among ourselves), we believe we can provide some answers to these questions, and they are the critical conclusions of our studies presented here. The short version is that (1) we accept that the Kowoj, narrowly defined — the "Kowoj proper" — were an elite lineage group that fled the northern Yucatán peninsula for east-central Petén in the mid-1530s. In this regard, Grant Jones (1998, Chapter 3, this volume) asserts that the eastern lakes of Petén — that is, Lakes Macanché, Yaxhá, and Sacnab — constituted the "principal territory" of the Kowoj until the 1630s, at which time the Itza launched a campaign of territorial expansion against their neighbors to the east and south.

More broadly, in the sense of the two central questions motivating our research, we contend that (2) the Kowoj were one (likely the latest) of a number of elite lineages, or *ch'ib'als,* allied with the Xiw in northern Yucatan who fled to Petén, probably in a series of migrations over many generations, as a consequence of conflicts with the Itza and their allies in that region. We also propose, with varying degrees of confidence, that members of the Kowoj lineage/patronym/*ch'ib'al* (3) enjoyed relatively high status at the Late Postclassic city of Mayapán, (4) maintained kinship ties with Champotón/Campeche in southern Campeche, and (5) had deep ancestral ties to the eastern Petén lakes region in the Late or Terminal Classic period. In this chapter I summarize the evidence, direct and indirect, for these propositions.

The "Kowoj Proper"

The first point about the specific and narrow identification of the Kowoj is, for all intents and purposes, indisputable. Grant Jones (1998: 430n24) cites Spanish captain don Marcos de Abalos y Fuentes, who spent several months in Petén in 1699, as "the only source for the time and place of origin of the Kowoj migration." He quotes testimony from Abalos in a document in the Archivo General de Indias in Seville, Spain: "The Couohs are almost one and the same with the Itzas, because they are located in the region to the north of the shores of their lake. Both are descended from Yucatán, the Itzas from

Chichen Itza and the Couohs from Tancab [sic], ten or twelve leagues from this city. These [the Couohs] retreated at the time of the conquest, the others much earlier" (ibid.). Jones goes on to explain that "Tancab" is a transcription error for Tancah, an indigenous name (or epithet: *tancah* 'capital, front town') for Mayapán, and acknowledges that some Kowoj may have fled that city at the time of its earlier (pre-conquest) collapse. The later Kowoj "retreat" at the time of conquest would suggest that their migration to Petén occurred in the early sixteenth century, between about 1520 and 1545. At least one of these movements might have occurred in the mid-1530s, following the Itza/Kokom massacre of Xiw rain priests on a pilgrimage to Chich'en Itza, when one Xiw priest named Na Pot Kowoj was able to escape.

For us as archaeologists, however, this sixteenth-century arrival date of the Kowoj in Petén—and even pegged to a 1450 Mayapán collapse date— provides an unacceptably short timeline for the Postclassic construction and occupation of their territory in the eastern lakes region. We readily grant that there are problems (chiefly a bimodal calibration curve) with radiocarbon dating of remains in the Maya Postclassic period and that chronologies based on ceramic comparisons are inexact; in addition, Postclassic cultures did not erect carved and dated monuments within which to date events (themselves subject to interpretational difficulties) as did their Classic antecedents. Nonetheless, the residential settlement and monumental architecture at the eastern lakes sites of Topoxté and Zacpetén—combined with radiocarbon dates and ceramic chronologies—suggest a period on the order of centuries for the occupation and construction at these sites. By the late seventeenth century, at the time of the Spanish conquest, the Kowoj proper lived on the north shore of Lake Petén Itzá, as Captain Abalos noted, but they also occupied the Yaxhá-Sacnab area to the east (Jones 1998:17)—for example, the community known as Chinoha (or Chiwoja). We believe the Kowoj settlements of this area represented continuities, although perhaps demographically diminished, with the earlier occupation and construction on the Topoxté Islands.

Migrations: The Kowoj and the Xiw

The most parsimonious explanation behind the Itza-Kowoj distinctions (both material and historical) in Petén, we contend, is that the Kowoj proper were long-standing allies of the Xiw in northern Yucatán—the Xiw, in turn, having a history of conflicts with the Itza there. In hindsight, this is rather obvious: the Petén Kowoj claimed ancestry in Mayapán, as Captain Abalos reported, and Mayapán lay within the province of Maní, the home territory of the Tutul Xiw. However, to explain the striking differences in certain aspects of material culture between the east and west lakes region of Postclassic Petén, it is necessary to posit the historical contingencies underlying these differences, as well as the documented hostilities between the Itza and the Kowoj in the region. These contingencies, as stated earlier, rest on postulating historical relations between the Postclassic occupants of eastern Petén with the Xiw of western Yucatán.

The indigenous histories of Yucatán, the various books of the *chilam b'alams* or *k'atun* prophets, are replete with stories of migrations of sectors of the populace in response to various oppressive circumstances. Migrations, of course, are significant elements of the origin myths of peoples everywhere, and this is particularly true of Postclassic Mesoamerica. Most of the migrations reported in the *chilam b'alams* are those of the Itza, who moved from north to south and back again several times. Reference to Xiw (or Tutul Xiw) migrations or demographic shifts in these books, however, emphasizes their origins in the west, possibly from the Chontal area or possibly related to the Toltec ("Tutul") (Roys 1957: 64); they are regarded as "Mexican." Munro Edmonson (1986: 37) noted that there seems to have been a Xiw "incursion" at Chich'en Itza in 1244; a *k'atun* later, in 1264, they are said to have established themselves at Uxmal, in the northwest corner of Maní province, just south of the Puuc hills. Yet another *k'atun* later, in 1283, at the end of a K'atun 13 Ajaw, the Xiw and the Itza jointly seated the *may* at Mayapán (i.e., established the League of Mayapán). The collapse of that seating/league occurred around 1450, when the Xiw attacked, murdered, and expelled their Itza co-rulers from that city.

As has been noted many times, the books of the *chilam b'alams* are not factual histories but rather mythic histories passed down orally over centuries and reworked to suit the circumstances of the present. It seems to be clear that there was a history of conflict between the Itza and the relatively late-arriving Xiw during and after the thirteenth century, and the Maya have a long history of fleeing into the forest in times of social and political stress, along with a cultural tradition of obligation to aid patronym-sharing kinsmen. The wide dispersion of lineage names throughout the Yucatán peninsula, according to sixteenth- and seventeenth-century tributary tax lists (Roys 1957: 8–9), reveals considerable demographic flux. Thus, the absence of references to Xiw emigrations is not evidence that they did not occur, merely that, if and when they occurred, the Xiw did not deem them sufficiently important in their recursivity to record them in their prophetic histories. At the same time, if some or all of the Xiw claimed an origin in the Chontal area of Tabasco and southern Campeche (discussed later), perhaps that region was their destination rather than (or in addition to) the Petén lakes area.

As I suggested in Chapter 2, the books of the *chilam b'alams* might better be considered as expressions of ethnic identity formation or ethnogenesis in Yucatán. They are compilations that express—in part as consciously justified reconstructions and in part as unconscious repetitions of received wisdom— the development of the individual identities of the elite families that maintained them through the centuries. Thus, migration appears to have been an important component of the ethnic histories of the Itza and their allies but not so much for the Xiw and their allies. In any case, it is highly likely that similar family or lineage records were maintained orally during the Preclassic period and committed to writing as perishable codices by nobles during the Classic period. The texts carved on stone stelae relating the accomplishments of rulers and their powerful home territories, then, are mere synoptic moments within this flow of highly personalized dynastic time. Thus, it is not surprising that, as Charles Andrew Hofling documents in Chapter 4, slight dialectical differences are recorded in the ritual language used in these books, much as there are regional and temporal differences in the grammar and signs recorded on the Classic stelae.

The Status of the Kowoj at Mayapán

The Kowoj in Petén claimed to have ancestry in Mayapán, but identifying such a lineage group there is not an easy prospect. Before proceeding, it is important to note that we believe the Kowoj were one of an unknown number of lineages allied with the Xiw, of which the Tutul Xiw were most important; similarly, the "Itza" were not a single monolithic group but rather consisted of an unknown (and probably varying) number of allied lineages, of which the Kokom likely were dominant. In considering Mayapán, then, that city is thought to represent a confederation of sixteen lineages, lineage territories, or both in northern Yucatán, ruled jointly by "the" Xiw and "the" Itza, but archaeological analyses of the site to date have not revealed anything like a spatial divide into Xiw and Itza barrios, much less divisions that can be associated with the specific lineage territories.

That said, three pieces of evidence suggest to us that the Kowoj (or Couoh, Co Uoh) were a relatively high-status lineage. One is that, as discussed, according to the *Chilam Balam of Oxkutzkab*, one Na Pot Kowoj was a priest, one of the "rain priests" who journeyed in the aborted pilgrimage to Chich'en Itza in 1536 but escaped the massacre led by the Itza in Otzmal. Second, according to the *Chilam Balam of Chumayel*, a Kowoj was identified as "the guardian of the spirit of the fort to the east" — that is, the guardian of the East Gate of the Mayapán fortification (Edmonson 1986: 81), apparently holding the title *b'acab'* (ibid.: 39) — and as one of four "counselors" (*jolpops*, "head of the mat") of the south (ibid.: 106). Ralph Roys (1957: 7) commented that the *jolpop* and *b'atab'* appear to have had identical roles, noting that in one ritual described in the *Chumayel* "the holpops appear as presiding over certain lineages, so I infer that he was the head of the most important lineage of a town." The third line of evidence comes from archaeological data, reviewed presently.

Ties to Champotón/Campeche

Despite the focus here on the Kowoj in Petén and Mayapán, the most explicitly attested ties of the Kowoj seem to have been with the southwestern Yucatán peninsula and the areas now known as Champotón and Campeche in the southern part of the Mexican state of Campeche (Chapter 2, Map 2.1, this volume). This region lies south of the western Ah Canul province and northeast of the Chontal area of Gulf coastal Tabasco, which, according to some accounts, was the home of the Xiw. Campeche is the name for the area constituting the province of Can Pech, and Champotón is the current name for the area just to the south, Chanputun, generally thought to be the location of

Chak'anputun ("savanna or plain of the 'Putun,'" as the Chontal Maya might have been known) mentioned in the chronicles. Multiple sources agree that in the sixteenth century, Chanputun was ruled by the Kowoj.

Chak'anputun seems to have been an early key city or region for both the Xiw and the Itza. Both the Xiw-leaning *Chumayel* (Edmonson 1986: 52) and the Itza-sided *Tizimin* (Edmonson 1982: 6) begin with reference to the destruction of Chich'en Itza (around A.D. 948?) after its 200 years of hegemony and the flight of the Itza from there to Chak'anputun, which was their home (*otoch*). The *Tizimin* makes it clear that these Itza were returning to the safety of a homeland, where other Itza already resided, although the *Chumayel* says the Itza "conquered the land." Regardless of the specifics, both sources agree that Chak'anputun seated the *may* cycle and was occupied by the Itza for that entire period of 260 *tuns* (~256 years). Similarly, both sources agree that at the end of the cycle (in a K'atun 8 Ajaw, in 1204) Champotón was destroyed: the *Chumayel* says it was by the Itza (Edmonson 1986: 53), suggesting the ritual termination of cycle seats, whereas in his notes on the *Tizimin* Edmonson (1982: 7) interpreted the destruction as the Xiw having forced the Itza out of Champotón. The Itza then wandered for two *k'atuns*, or 40 years, until ca. 1244 and the establishment of joint government (*mul tepal*) at Mayapán.

Both of these books of indigenous "history" open with this same set of events, colored slightly differently. In each, the record is in the sketchiest and most idiomatic of terms—barely two pages in the modern printed translations. Although well aware of the dangers of taking these prophetic histories literally, especially the earliest accounts, I find the strong similarities between the two intriguing. If, as I have proposed, we consider these books as tracing the establishment of distinct "ethno-historic" identities of the Xiw versus the Itza (or of the main lineages of each), then both are acknowledging a very closely shared—and nearly identically interpreted—early history in the Chontal region.

Significantly, not only the Itza and the Xiw claimed origins in the Chontal area, but so did other lineage groups in Yucatán as well as the K'iche' and Kaqchikel of the Maya highlands (Fox 1987: 18–20). In these various ethno-specific mythistories, Chak'anputun—or the general Acalan-Chontalpa region of the Laguna de Terminos and the modern state of Tabasco—held a pivotal position as a mythic place of origins and legitimization of important lineages in the Postclassic Maya area. Part of the significance of this area seems to be its association with Mexicans, specifically Toltecs, and the location of a *tollan*, a paradigmatic city. That city, the location of which is unknown, may have been referred to as Zuyua (see also Vargas 2001: 85, 88), the language of which is invoked as a ritual language in the Yucatán chronicles.

Tabasco/Acalan experienced its major florescence during the Late and Terminal Classic periods, between A.D. 700 and 950 (Vargas 2001: 87, 110–113). This was a period of major urban construction (e.g., Comalcalco) and the beginning of production of the widely distributed Fine Orange and Fine Gray pottery; in addition, there seem to have been important transitions in external interactions, with less Petén influence in ceramics and more with Yucatán.

Ernesto Vargas (2001: 110) correlated this prosperity and emphasis on trade with the period of Itza occupation of Chak'anputun.

The adjacent territory north of Tabasco/Acalan—the southwestern peninsula area of coastal Canpech and Chak'anputun (Campeche and Champotón)—probably eventually became contested territory. The reasons for this include (1) its importance because of proximity to Zuyua, the mythistorically sacred origin of legitimate Postclassic ruling dynasties; (2) both the Xiw and the Itza would have passed through this region during their apparent migration into northern Yucatán, and undoubtedly groups stopped and settled there instead of moving on; and (3) the increasing competition for power and the fragility of political alliances would have challenged claims to origins and legitimacy. This contested status developed over time such that, by the equivalent of the Late Postclassic period in the indigenous histories, both the allied lineages known as the Itza *and* the allied lineages known as the Xiw claimed the region as ancestral lands. Significantly, in this context this southwestern region was not incorporated into the League of Mayapán.

Ancestral Ties to Petén

I believe that at least some of the Xiw had deep ancestral ties to the eastern Petén lakes region in the Late and Terminal Classic periods and, perhaps more specifically, to Tikal and its allies. Part of this is calendrical: the so-called Tikal or Classic calendar is based on cycles of completing K'atuns 8 Ajaw, the same as observed by the Xiw.

Other kinds of evidence are suggestive. For example, Postclassic construction walls in Group A at Zacpetén were frequently placed directly above and aligned precisely with those of Classic structures, cut stones from Classic buildings were incorporated into Postclassic structures, and carved Classic monuments were incorporated into Postclassic structural facades so as to face out into plazas. On the one hand, it is easy to explain all this away by simple "least-effort" principles: copy the earlier structural alignments and angles rather than measuring anew; reuse old stones—even carved stelae—lying onsite rather than cutting new ones at a distant quarry. But these explanations ignore the fact that the Postclassic temple assemblage of Group A was a sacred landscape, in which buildings and their components are ritually charged and laden with meanings in a group's history. This is most evidenced by Zacpetén Altar 1, set into the front wall of the Structure 606 platform. The inscription references the death of a historical person, probably a Terminal Classic ruler of Zacpetén, and his apotheosis as the new sun on the winter solstice—a metaphor for the birth of the calendar and time itself.

In addition, the known examples of temple assemblages in Petén and nearby Tipu consistently favor the east side of plazas for the siting of temple structures. This is in contrast to the varied orientations of these structures at Mayapán and may relate back to the Tikal Late Classic Plaza Plan 2. This arrangement has a temple structure on the east side of the plaza, typically with a burial within, suggesting ancestor veneration. All of this strongly suggests that the Postclassic occupants of Zacpetén and the builders of at least one of the temple assemblages there were respectful of continuities and regarded their Late and Terminal Classic predecessors (ancestors) as worthy of veneration, incorporating the power of their earlier ideological materializations (stelae, stone buildings) into their own later ones. It also supports the possibility of Xiw/Kowoj/Petén lineage ties between the Classic and Postclassic periods.

The Kowoj and Material Expressions of Identity

This chapter has been a review of our answer to the question, Who were the Kowoj, within a historical framework, largely drawn from primary and secondary documentary sources. But our question was also posed with respect to the identity of the little-known Kowoj in Petén as they can be recognized archaeologically through their material culture.

Because the late Kowoj (the "Kowoj proper") in Petén claimed origins in Mayapán, we need to look to that important city for material data on the Kowoj. First and most obvious are the architectural connections: sites in eastern Petén, which we identify with Kowoj occupation, are characterized by distinctive "temple assemblage" as the focus of their civic-ceremonial architecture, and these have not been found at Itza sites in the west. Temple assemblages were first identified at, and are particularly characteristic of, Late Postclassic Mayapán (Proskouriakoff 1962a), the assumption being that they were first constructed there and copied in Petén. We consider these distinctive complexes to be markers of the earlier in-migration(s) of Xiw-related allies of the Kowoj into eastern Petén from Mayapán.

In addition, Leslie Cecil and I identified very close stylistic similarities between samples of pottery classified as Tecoh Red-on-buff from Mayapán and the red and red-and-black decoration painted on pottery in Clemencia Cream Paste ware, the signature pottery identified with the Kowoj/Xiw–related occupation of the Topoxté Islands in Lake Yaxhá. (Indeed, we have visually identified a few actual sherds of Clemencia Cream Paste ware in those collections.) These similarities are not a new discovery; Robert E. Smith (1971, 1: 231) commented on them almost forty years ago: "The design style [of the Tecoh group] has no immediate Yucatan predecessor. It does not occur with contemporary material at Tulum or in any of the other sites in Quintana Roo. . . . On the other hand, there is a presumably contemporaneous Topoxte Cream Polychrome Type found at Topoxte by W. R. Bullard, Jr. . . . which has certain design similarities. These are based on the use of a similar color scheme" as well as certain design elements (see also Rice 1979: 41; Rice and Cecil, Chapter 11, this volume).

Significant quantities of this unusual pottery were recovered at a Mayapán structure recently excavated by Carlos Peraza Lope of INAH and Marilyn Masson. Structure Y-45a is the largest of a group of three buildings on the south side of Mayapán and represents an elite residence (Masson and Peraza Lope 2005). At the time of the structure's abandonment, large quantities of household vessels were smashed and left in place; they included significant quantities of Tecoh Red-on-buff and Pele Polychrome. As noted, these types are rare throughout the rest of the city and lack local precursors. We interpret this find as indicating that the inhabitants of Mayapán Structure Y-45a were closely related to the people of Topoxté in Petén: as such, they were likely an elite Xiw-related lineage and perhaps even carried the patronym Kowoj, although this probably cannot ever be securely proven.

Identity Politics

Who were the Kowoj? We have opened many windows in our efforts to answer this question, but others remain shuttered. Questions and problems still exist and might be resolved through further archaeological work at Mayapán and at Kowoj, Itza, Mopan, and Kejach sites throughout the peninsula. The Postclassic period in the Maya lowlands was a time of political intrigue, conflict, and uneasy alliances, with the oppressive social and economic circumstances intensifying with the arrival of the Spaniards and the demands—and burden of devastating disease—they imposed. In these circumstances, it is not difficult to imagine that the various Maya lineages, coalitions, and factions wanted to signal their allegiances (or hide them, depending on the situation) in solidarity and as symbols of strength as they negotiated the uncertain future. In this context, the Xiw-related Kowoj in remotest Petén—the builders and occupants of Postclassic Zacpetén and Topoxté—actively created and strategically deployed symbols of their distinct identities, such as temple assemblage architecture and red-on-cream pottery, symbols that tied them to their rich heritage in Mayapán and, even earlier, to the great Classic cities of the region.

REFERENCES CITED

Academia de la Lengua Maya de Yucatán, A.C.
2002   *Diccionario Maya Popular*. Academia de la Lengua Maya de Yucatán, Mérida.

Adams, M. J.
1973   Structural Aspects of a Village Age. *American Anthropologist* 75: 265–279.

Adams, Richard E.W.
1971   *The Ceramics of Altar de Sacrificios*. Papers 63(1). Peabody Museum of Archaeology and Ethnology, Harvard University, Cambridge, MA.

Adams, Richard E.W., and Aubrey S. Trik
1958   Temple I (Str. 5-I): Post-Constructional Activities. Monograph 7. University of Pennsylvania Museum, Philadelphia.

Agrinier, Pierre
1960   *The Carved Human Femurs from Tomb 1, Chiapa de Corzo, Chiapas, Mexico*. Paper 6. New World Archaeological Foundation Publications, Orinda, CA.

Aimers, James J.
2007   What Maya Collapse? Terminal Classic Variation in the Maya Lowlands. *Journal of Archaeological Research* 15(4): 329–377.

Alexander, Rani T.
2000   Patrones de asentamiento agregados en el sudoeste de Campeche: una visión desde la Isla Cilvituk. *Mesoamérica* 39: 359–391.

Alexander, Rani T., and Elena Canché Manzanero
1998   Archaeology and the Cehache: A View from Isla Cilvituk, Campeche, Mexico. Unpublished manuscript.

Andres, Christopher R.
2000   Caches, Censers, Monuments, and Burials: Archaeological Evidence of Postclassic Ritual Activity in Northern Belize. M.A. thesis, Southern Illinois University Carbondale.

Andrews, Anthony P.
1984   Political Geography of the Sixteenth Century Yucatan Maya: Comments and Revisions. *Journal of Anthropological Research* 40(4): 589–596.
1993   Late Postclassic Lowland Maya Archaeology. *Journal of World Prehistory* 7(1): 35-69.

Andrews, Anthony P., E. Wyllys Andrews V, and Fernando Robles Castellanos
2003   The Northern Maya Collapse and Its Aftermath. *Ancient Mesoamerica* 14(1): 151–156.

Andrews, Anthony P., Frank Asaro, Helen V. Michel, Fred H. Stross, and Pura Cervera Rivero
1989   The Obsidian Trade at Isla Cerritos, Yucatán, Mexico. *Journal of Field Archaeology* 16: 355–363.

Andrews IV, E. Wyllys, and E. Wyllys Andrews V
1980   *Excavations at Dzibilchaltun, Yucatan, Mexico.* Pub. 48. Middle American Research Institute, Tulane University, New Orleans.

Aoyama, Kazuo
2001   Classic Maya State, Urbanism, and Exchange: Chipped Stone Evidence of the Copan Valley and Its Hinterland. *American Anthropologist* 103(2): 346–360.
2005   Classic Maya Warfare and Weapons: Spear, Dart, and Arrow Points of Aguateca and Copan. *Ancient Mesoamerica* 16(2): 291–304.
2007   Elite Artists and Craft Producers in Classic Maya Society: Lithic Evidence from Aguateca, Guatemala. *Latin American Antiquity* 18(1): 3–26.

Arnauld, Marie-Charlotte
1997   Relaciones interregionales en el área maya durante el postclásico en base a datos arquitectónicos. In *X Simposio de Investigaciones Arqueológicas en Guatemala*, ed. Juan Pedro Laporte and Hector L. Escobedo, pp. 117–131. Museo Nacional de Arqueología y Etnología and Asociación Tikal, Guatemala City.

Arnold, Dean
1983   Design Structure and Community Organization in Quinua, Peru. In *Structure and Cognition in Art*, ed. Dorothy Washburn, pp. 40–55. Cambridge University Press, Cambridge.

REFERENCES CITED

Ashmore, Wendy
1989   Construction and Cosmology: Politics and Ideology in Lowland Maya Settlement Patterns. In *Word and Image in Maya Culture: Explorations in Language, Writing, and Representation*, ed. William F. Hanks and Don S. Rice, pp. 272–286. University of Utah Press, Salt Lake City.
1991   Site-Planning Principles and Concepts of Directionality among the Ancient Maya. *Latin American Antiquity* 2(3): 199–226.

Atran, Scott
1993   Itza Maya Tropical Agro-Forestry. *Current Anthropology* 34: 633–700.

Atran, Scott, Ximena Lois, and Ediberto Ucan Ek'
2004   *Plants of the Petén Itza' Maya. Plantas de los maya itza' del Petén.* Memoir 38. Museum of Anthropology, University of Michigan, Ann Arbor.

Avendaño y Loyola, Fray Andrés de
1696   Relación de las dos entradas que hice a la conversión de los gentiles Ytzaex, y Cehaches, 29 April 1696. Manuscript on file, Ayer Collection, Newberry Library, Chicago.
1987   *Relation of Two Trips to Peten Made for the Conversion of the Heathen Ytzaex and Cehaches*, trans. Charles P. Bowditch and Guillermo Rivera, ed. and with notes by Frank E. Comparato. Labyrinthos, Culver City, CA.

Aveni, Anthony F.
1981   Archaeoastronomy in the Maya Region: A Review of the Past Decade. *Journal for the History of Astronomy* 11(3): S1–S13.

Ball, Joseph W.
1979   Ceramics, Culture History, and the Puuc Tradition: Some Alternative Possibilities. In *The Puuc: New Perspectives: Papers Presented at the Puuc Symposium, Central College, May, 1977*, ed. Lawrence Mills, pp. 18–35. Central College Press, Pella, IA.

Barker, H., and C. J. Mackey
1959   British Museum Natural Radiocarbon Measurements I. *American Journal of Science Radiocarbon Supplement* 1: 81–86.

Barrera Vásquez, Antonio, and Sylvanus Griswold Morley
1949   *The Maya Chronicles.* Carnegie Institution of Washington Pub. 585. Carnegie Institution of Washington, Washington, DC.

Barrett, Jason W., and Andrew K. Scherer
2005   Stones, Bones, and Crowded Plazas: Evidence for Terminal Classic Maya Warfare at Colha, Belize. *Ancient Mesoamerica* 16(1): 101–118.

Barth, Fredrik
1969   *Ethnic Groups and Boundaries: The Social Organization of Cultural Difference.* Little, Brown, Boston.

Baxter, M. J., and C. E. Buck
2000   Data Handling and Statistical Analysis. In *Modern Analytical Methods in Art and Archaeology*, ed. E. Ciliberto and G. Spoto, pp. 681–746. John Wiley and Sons, New York.

Becker, Marshall J.
1971   The Identification of a Second Plaza Plan at Tikal, Guatemala and Its Implications for Ancient Maya Social Complexity. Ph.D. dissertation, University of Pennsylvania, Philadelphia.

1993   Earth Offerings among the Classic Period Lowland Maya: Burials and Caches as Ritual Deposits. In *Perspectivas antropológicas en el mundo maya*, ed. M. Josefa I. Ponce de León and F. L. Perramon, pp. 45–74. Publicaciones de la SEEM, vol. 2. Sociedad Española de Estudios Mayas, Barcelona.

Behrensmeyer, Anna K.
1987   Taphonomic and Ecologic Information from Bone Weathering. *Paleobiology* 4: 150–162.

Bell, Catherine
1997   *Ritual: Perspectives and Dimensions*. Oxford University Press, New York.

Benavides C., Antonio, and Lorena Mirambell
1991   *Geografía política de Campeche en el siglo XVI*. Instituto Nacional de Antropología e Historia, Mexico, DF.

Bender, Margaret, Reid A. Bryson, and David A. Baerreis
1967   University of Wisconsin Radiocarbon Dates III. *Radiocarbon* 9: 530–544.

Benson, Elizabeth P.
1997   *Birds and Beasts of Ancient Latin America*. University Press of Florida, Gainesville.

Berdan, Frances F., and Patricia R. Anawalt
1997   *The Essential Codex Mendoza*. University of California Press, Berkeley.

Berger, Rainer, Suzanne DeAtley, Rainer Protsch, and Gordon R. Willey
1974   Radiocarbon Chronology for Seibal, Guatemala. *Nature* 252: 472–473.

Berger, Rainer, and Raymond Sidrys
1983   Maya Radiocarbon Dates from the Corozal District, Belize. In *Archaeological Excavations in Northern Belize, Central America*, ed. Raymond Sidrys, pp. 197–199. Monograph XVII. Institute of Archaeology, University of California, Los Angeles.

Bieber Jr., Alan M., D. W. Brooks, Garman Harbottle, and Edward V. Sayre
1976   Application of Multivariate Techniques to Analytical Data on Aegean Ceramics. *Archaeometry* 18: 59–74.

Bill, Cassandra R., C. L. Hernandez, and Victoria R. Bricker
2000   The Relationship between Early Colonial Maya New Year's Ceremonies and Some Almanacs in the Madrid Codex. *Ancient Mesoamerica* 11: 149–169.

Blaha Pfeiler, Barbara, and Charles Andrew Hofling
2006   La variación dialectical en el maya yucateco. *Península* 1(1): 27–43.

Bloch, Maurice
1986   *From Blessing to Violence: History and Ideology in the Circumcision Ritual of the Merina of Madagascar*. Cambridge University Press, Cambridge.
1992   *Prey into Hunter: The Politics of Religious Experience*. Lewis Henry Morgan Lectures. Cambridge University Press, New York.

Blom, Frans
1928   Gaspar Antonio Chi, Interpreter. *American Anthropologist* 30: 250–262.

Boone, Elizabeth H., and Michael E. Smith
2003   Postclassic International Styles and Symbol Sets. In *The Postclassic Mesoamerican World*, ed. Michael E. Smith and Frances F. Berdan, pp. 186–193. University of Utah Press, Salt Lake City.

REFERENCES CITED

Boot, Erik
1995   Kan Ek' at Chich'én Itsá. A Quest into a Possible Itsá Heartland in the Central Petén. *Yumtzilob* 7(4): 333–340.
1997   Kan Ek', Last Ruler of the Itsá. *Yumtzilob* 9(1): 5–21.
2005   *Continuity and Change in Text and Image at Chichén Itzá, Yucatán, Mexico. A Study of the Inscriptions, Iconography, and Architecture at a Late Classic to Early Postclassic Maya Site.* CNWS Publications, Leiden, The Netherlands.

Boremanse, Didier
1998   *Hach Winik: The Lacandon Maya of Chiapas, Southern Mexico.* Monograph 11. Institute for Mesoamerican Studies, State University of New York Albany.

Bourdieu, Pierre
1977   *Outline of a Theory of Practice,* trans. Richard Nice. Cambridge University Press, Cambridge.

Brady, James E., and Keith M. Prufer
1999   Caves and Crystalmancy: Evidence for the Use of Crystals in Ancient Maya Religion. *Journal of Anthropological Research* 55: 129–144.

Brady, James E., Ann Scott, Hector Neff, and Michael Glascock
1997   Speleothem Breakage, Movement, Removal, and Caching: An Aspect of Ancient Maya Cave Modification. *Geoarchaeology* 12(6): 725–750.

Brainerd, George W.
1942   Symmetry in Primitive Conventional Design. *American Antiquity* 8: 164–166.
1958   *Archaeological Ceramics of Yucatan.* University of California Anthropological Records, vol. 19. University of California Press, Berkeley.

Braithwaite, M.
1982   Decoration as Ritual Symbol: A Theoretical Proposal and an Ethnographic Study in Southern Sudan. In *Symbolic and Structural Archaeology,* ed. Ian Hodder, pp. 80–88. Cambridge University Press, Cambridge.

Braswell, Geoffrey E.
2001   Post-Classic Maya Courts of the Guatemalan Highlands: Archaeological and Ethnohistorical Approaches. In *Royal Courts of the Ancient Maya, vol. 2: Data and Case Studies,* ed. Takeshi Inomata and Stephen D. Houston, pp. 308–334. Westview, Boulder.
2002   Praise the Gods and Pass the Obsidian?: The Organization of Ancient Economy in San Martín Jilotepeque, Guatemala. In *Ancient Maya Political Economies,* ed. Marilyn Masson and David Freidel, pp. 285–306. AltaMira, Walnut Creek, CA.
2003   Obsidian Exchange Spheres of Postclassic Mesoamerica. In *The Postclassic Mesoamerican World,* ed. Michael E. Smith and Frances F. Berdan, pp. 131–158. University of Utah Press, Salt Lake City.
2004   Lithic Analysis in the Maya Area. In *Continuities and Changes in Maya Archaeology: Perspectives at the Millennium,* ed. Charles W. Golden and Greg Borgstede, pp. 177–199. Routledge, New York.

Braun, David P.
1985   Ceramic Decorative Diversity and Illinois Woodland Regional Integration. In *Decoding Prehistoric Ceramics,* ed. Ben A. Nelson, pp. 128–153. Southern Illinois University Press, Carbondale.

Bricker, Victoria R.
1989   The Last Gasp of Maya Hieroglyphic Writing in the Books of Chilam Balam of Chumayel and Chan Kan. In *Word and Image in Maya Culture*, ed. William F. Hanks and Don S. Rice, pp. 39–50. University of Utah Press, Salt Lake City.
1990a   *A Morpheme Concordance of the Book of Chilam Balam of Tizimin*. Pub. 58. Middle American Research Institute, Tulane University, New Orleans.
1990b   *A Morpheme Concordance of the Book of Chilam Balam of Chumayel*. Pub. 59. Middle American Research Institute, Tulane University, New Orleans.

Bricker, Victoria R., Eleuterio Po'ot Yah, and Ofelia Dzul de Po'ot
1998   *Dictionary of the Maya Language as Spoken in Hocabá, Yucatán*. University of Utah Press, Salt Lake City.

Briggs, Margaret L., and Alma R. Patt
2005   Osteological and Mortuary Data from Three Burials from the Ehrlington Site (PR9). In *Belize Postclassic Project 2003: Investigations on the West Shore of Progreso Lagoon*, ed. Maxine H. Oland and Marilyn A. Masson, pp. 81–86. Occasional Pub. 10. Institute of Mesoamerican Studies, SUNY Albany.

Brown, Clifford T.
1999   Mayapán Society and Ancient Maya Social Organization. Ph.D. dissertation, Tulane University, New Orleans.

Brown, Linda A.
2000   From Discard to Divination: Demarcating the Sacred through the Collection and Curation of Discarded Objects. *Latin American Antiquity* 11(4): 319–333.

Brown, M. Kathryn, and James F. Garber
2003   Evidence of Conflict during the Middle Formative in the Maya Lowlands: A View from Blackman Eddy, Belize. In *Ancient Mesoamerican Warfare*, ed. M. Kathryn Brown and Travis W. Stanton, pp. 91–108. AltaMira, Walnut Creek, CA.

Bruce, Roberto D.
1975   *Lacandon Dream Symbolism I*. Ediciones Euroamericanas, Mexico, DF.
1977   The Popol Vuh and the Book of Chan K'in. *Estudios de Cultura Maya* 10: 173–209.

Buikstra, Jane, and Douglas H. Ubelaker
1994   *Standards for Data Collection from Human Skeletal Remains*. Research Series no. 44. Arkansas Archaeological Survey, Fayetteville.

Bullard Jr., William R.
1970   Topoxté: A Postclassic Maya Site in Peten, Guatemala. In *Monographs and Papers in Maya Archaeology*, ed. William R. Bullard, pp. 245–308. Papers, vol. 61. Peabody Museum of Archaeology and Ethnology, Harvard University, Cambridge, MA.
1973   Postclassic Culture in Central Peten and Adjacent British Honduras. In *The Classic Maya Collapse*, ed. T. Patrick Culbert, pp. 225–242. University of New Mexico Press, Albuquerque.

Cameron, Catherine M., and Steve A. Tomka
1993   *Abandonment of Settlements and Regions: Ethnoarchaeological and Archaeological Approaches*. Cambridge University Press, Cambridge.

Cano, Agustín
1942 Informe dado al Rey por el Padre Fray Agustín Cano sobre la entrada que por la parte de la Verapaz se hizo al Petén en el año 1695, y fragmento de una carta al mismo, sobre el proprio asunto. *Anales* 19: 65–79. Sociedad de Geografía e Historia, Guatemala City.
1984 *Manche and Peten: The Hazards of Itza Deceit and Barbarity*, trans. Charles P. Bowditch and Guillermo Rivera, with additional comments by A. C. Breton; ed. with notes by Frank E. Camparato. Labyrinthos, Culver City, CA.

Carlson, John B.
1981 A Geomantic Model for the Interpretation of Mesoamerican Sites: An Essay in Cross-Cultural Comparison. In *Mesoamerican Sites and World-Views*, ed. Elizabeth P. Benson, pp. 143–215. Dumbarton Oaks, Washington, DC.

Carlson, John B., and Linda C. Landis
1985 Bands, Bicephalic Dragons, and Other Beasts: The Sky Band in Maya Art and Iconography. In *Fourth Palenque Round Table, 1980*, vol. 6, ed. Merle G. Robertson and Elizabeth P. Benson, pp. 115–140. Pre-Columbian Art Research Institute, San Francisco.

Carmack, Robert M.
1981 *The Quiché Mayas of Utatlan: The Evolution of a Highland Guatemala Kingdom*. University of Oklahoma Press, Norman.

Carmean, Kelly
2008 Limestone and Meaning in the Stone Houses of Sayil, Yucatán, Mexico. Paper presented at the 73rd annual meeting of the Society for American Archaeology, Vancouver.

Carr, Christopher
1995 Mortuary Practices: Their Social, Philosophical-Religious, Circumstantial, and Physical Determinants. *Journal of Archaeological Method and Theory* 2(2): 105–200.

Carrasco, Michael D., and Kerry Hull
2002 Cosmogonic Symbolism of the Corbeled Vault in Maya Architecture. *Mexicon* 24(2): 26–32.

Carsten, Janet, and Stephen Hugh-Jones
1995 Introduction. In *About the House: Lévi-Strauss and Beyond*, ed. Janet Carsten and Stephen Hugh-Jones, pp. 1–46. Cambridge University Press, Cambridge.

Caso, Alfonso
1928 *Las estelas Zapotecas*. Talleres Gráficos de la Nación, Mexico, DF.

Caso Barrera, Laura
2002 *Caminos en la selva: migración, comercio y resistencia. Mayas, Yucatecos e Itzaes, siglos XVII–XIX*. Fondo de Cultura Económica, El Colegio de México, México, DF.

C.D.I.
1898 Colección de documentos ineditos relativos al descubrimiento, conquista y organización de las antiguas poseciones españoles de ultramar. Segunda serie, tomos 11 y 13. Real Academia de la Historia, Est. tipográfico "Sucesores de Rivadeneyra," Madrid.

Cecil, Leslie G.
1997   Pilot Study for the Identification of a Topoxté Red Production Center in the Postclassic Period. Manuscript in possession of the author.
1999   Ceramics from Tipuj: Structures 1–6 of Complex I. Manuscript in possession of the author.
2001a   Technological Styles of Late Postclassic Slipped Pottery from the Central Petén Lakes Region, El Petén, Guatemala. Ph.D. dissertation, Southern Illinois University Carbondale.
2001b   Developing Technological Styles of Petén Postclassic Slipped Pottery with Regard to Clay Mineralogy. In *Archaeology and Clays*, ed. I. Druc, pp. 107–121. B.A.R. International Series 942, Oxford.
2002   Postclassic Decorative Motifs and Social Identity in Petén, Guatemala. Paper presented at the 67th annual meeting of the Society for American Archaeology, Denver.
2004   Inductively Coupled Plasma Emission Spectroscopy and Postclassic Petén Slipped Pottery: An Examination of Pottery Wares, Social Identity, and Trade. *Archaeometry* 46(3): 385–404.

Cecil, Leslie G., Matthew D. Moriarty, Robert J. Speakman, and Michael D. Glascock
2007   Feasibility of Field-Portable XRF to Identify Obsidian Sources in Central Petén, Guatemala. In *Analytical Techniques and Interpretation*, ed. Michael D. Glascock, Robert J. Speakman, and Rachel Popelka-Filcoff, pp. 506–521. American Chemical Society, Washington, DC.

Cecil, Leslie G., and Hector Neff
2006   Postclassic Maya Slips and Paints and Their Relationship to Socio-Political Groups in El Petén, Guatemala. *Journal of Archaeological Science* 33: 1482–1491.

Cecil, Leslie G., Prudence M. Rice, and Michael D. Glascock
2008   The Role of Obsidian at Zacpetén, El Petén, Guatemala. Paper presented at the 73rd annual meeting of the Society for American Archaeology, Vancouver.

Chandler, John B., Russell Kinningham, and Don S. Massey
1963   Texas Bio-Nuclear Radiocarbon Measurements I. *Radiocarbon* 5: 56–61.

Chapman, Anne C.
1957   Port of Trade Enclaves in the Aztec and Maya Civilization. In *Trade and Market in the Early Empires*, ed. Karl Polanyi, Conrad M. Arensberg, and Harry W. Pearson, pp. 114–153. Free Press, Chicago.

Chase, Arlen F.
1983   A Contextual Consideration of the Tayasal-Paxcaman Zone, El Peten, Guatemala. Ph.D. dissertation, University of Pennsylvania, Philadelphia.
1990   Maya Archaeology and Population Estimates in the Tayasal-Paxcaman Zone, Peten, Guatemala. In *Precolumbian Population History in the Maya Lowlands*, ed. T. Patrick Culbert and Don S. Rice, pp. 149–165. University of New Mexico Press, Albuquerque.

Chase, Arlen F., and Diane Z. Chase
1983   La cerámica de la zona Tayasal-Paxcamán, Lago Petén Itzá, Guatemala. Unpublished manuscript.
2004   Terminal Classic Status-Linked Ceramics and the Maya "Collapse": De Facto Refuse at Caracol, Belize. In *The Terminal Classic in the Maya Lowlands: Collapse, Transition, and Transformation*, ed. Arthur A. Demarest, Prudence M. Rice, and Don S. Rice, pp. 342–366. University Press of Colorado, Boulder.

Chase, Arlen F., and Prudence M. Rice
1985a   Introduction. In *The Lowland Maya Postclassic*, ed. Arlen F. Chase and Prudence M. Rice, pp. 1–8. University of Texas Press, Austin.
1985b   (eds.) *The Lowland Maya Postclassic*. University of Texas Press, Austin.

Chase, Diane Z.
1985a   Ganned But Not Forgotten: Late Postclassic Archaeology and Ritual at Santa Rita Corozal, Belize. In *The Lowland Maya Postclassic*, ed. Arlen F. Chase and Prudence M. Rice, pp. 104–125. University of Texas Press, Austin.
1985b   Between Earth and Sky: Idols, Images, and Postclassic Cosmology. In *Fifth Palenque Round Table, 1983*, ed. Virginia M. Fields, pp. 223–234. Pre-Columbian Art Research Institute, San Francisco.
1988   Caches and Censerwares: Meaning from Maya Pottery. In *A Pot for All Reasons*, ed. Charles C. Kolb and Muriel Kirkpatrick, pp. 81–104. Ceramica de Cultura Maya, Temple University, Philadelphia.

Chase, Diane Z., and Arlen F. Chase
1988   *A Postclassic Perspective: Excavations at the Maya Site of Santa Rita Corozal, Belize*. Monograph 4. Pre-Columbian Art Research Institute, San Francisco.
1996   Maya Multiples: Individuals, Entries, and Tombs in Structure A34 of Caracol, Belize. *Latin American Antiquity* 7(1): 61–79.
2004   Hermeneutics, Transitions, and the Transformations in Classic to Postclassic Maya Society. In *The Terminal Classic in the Maya Lowlands: Collapse, Transition, and Transformation*, ed. Arthur A. Demarest, Prudence M. Rice, and Don S. Rice, pp. 12–27. University Press of Colorado, Boulder.

Chowning, Ann
1956   *A Round Temple and Its Shrine at Mayapán*. Pub. 34. Carnegie Institution of Washington, Washington, DC.

Chuchiak IV, John F.
In press *De Descriptio Idolorum*: An Ethnohistorical Examination of the Production, Imagery, and Functions of Colonial Yucatec Maya Idols and Effigy Censers, 1550–1750. In *Maya Worldview at the Time of Conquest*, ed. Leslie G. Cecil and Timothy W. Pugh. University Press of Colorado, Boulder.

Cline, Howard F.
1944   The Lore and Deities of the Lacandon Indians, Chiapas, Mexico. *Journal of American Folklore* 57(224): 107–115.

Cobos Palma, Rafael
2004   Chichén Itzá: Settlement and Hegemony during the Terminal Classic Period. In *The Terminal Classic in the Maya Lowlands: Collapse, Transition, and Transformation*, ed. Arthur A. Demarest, Prudence M. Rice, and Don S. Rice, pp. 517–544. University Press of Colorado, Boulder.

Codex Nuttall
1975   *The Codex Nuttall. A Picture Manuscript from Ancient Mexico*. Dover, New York.

Coe, Michael D.
1965   A Model of Ancient Community Structure in the Maya Lowlands. *Southwestern Journal of Anthropology* 21: 97–114.
1973   *The Maya Scribe and His World*. Grolier Club, New York.
1978   *Lords of the Underworld*. The Art Museum, Princeton University, Princeton, NJ.

Coe, Michael D., and Justin Kerr
1998   *The Art of the Maya Scribe.* Harry N. Abrams, New York.

Coe, William R.
1965   Caches and Offertory Practices of the Maya Lowlands. In *Archaeology of Southern Mesoamerica, Part I,* ed. Gordon R. Willey, pp. 462–468. Handbook of Middle American Indians, Robert Wauchope, gen. ed. University of Texas Press, Austin.

Coggins, Clemency C.
1980   The Shape of Time: Some Political Implications of a Four-Part Figure. *American Antiquity* 45(4): 727–739.

Cohen, Ronald
1978   Ethnicity: Problem and Focus in Anthropology. *Annual Review of Anthropology* 7: 379–403.

Connerton, Paul
1989   *How Societies Remember.* Cambridge University Press, New York.

Cortés, Hernán
1976   *Hernando Cortés: His Five Letters of Relation to the Emperor Charles V,* trans. F. A. MacNutt. Rio Grande Press, Glorieta, TX.
1986   *Hernán Cortés: Letters from Mexico,* trans. and ed. Anthony Pagden. Yale University Press, New Haven, CT.

Cortez, Constance
2002   New Dance, Old Xius: The "Xiu Family Tree" and Maya Cultural Continuity after European Contact. In *Heart of Creation: The Mesoamerican World and the Legacy of Linda Schele,* ed. Andrea Stone, pp. 201–215. University of Alabama Press, Tuscaloosa.

Cowgill, George L.
1963   Postclassic Period Culture in the Vicinity of Flores, Peten, Guatemala. Ph.D. dissertation, Harvard University, Cambridge, MA.

Craine, E. R., and R. D. Reindorp
1979   *The Codex Pérez and the Book of Chilam Balam of Maní.* University of Oklahoma Press, Norman.

Culbert, T. Patrick (ed.)
1973   *The Classic Maya Collapse.* University of New Mexico Press, Albuquerque.
1983   *The Classic Maya Collapse* (2nd ed.). University of New Mexico Press, Albuquerque.

Darish, P.
1989   Dressing for the Next Life. In *Cloth and Human Experience,* ed. Annette B. Weiner and Jane Schneider, pp. 117–140. Smithsonian Institution Press, Washington, DC.

David, Nicholas, and Hilke Hennig
1972   *The Ethnography of Pottery: A Fulani Case Seen in Archaeological Perspective.* Module 21. Addison-Wesley, Reading, MA.

Davis, Virginia D.
1978   Ritual of the Northern Lacandon Maya. Ph.D. dissertation, Tulane University, New Orleans.

REFERENCES CITED

Day, Jane Stevenson
1994   Central Mexican Imagery in Greater Nicoya. In *Mixteca-Puebla. Discoveries and Research in Mesoamerican Art and Archaeology*, ed. H. B. Nicholson and Eloise Quiñones Keber, pp. 235–248. Labyrinthos, Culver City, CA.

Deetz, James
1965   *The Dynamics of Stylistic Change in Arikara Ceramics*. Illinois Studies in Anthropology 4. University of Illinois Press, Urbana.

Deevey Jr., Edward S., L. J. Gralenski, and Väinö Hoffren
1959   Yale Natural Radiocarbon Measurements IV. *American Journal of Science Radiocarbon Supplement* 1: 144–172.

Deevey Jr., Edward S., Don S. Rice, Prudence M. Rice, Hague H. Vaughan, Mark Brenner, and M. Sid Flannery
1979   Maya Urbanism: Impact on a Tropical Karst Environment. *Science* 206: 298–306.

Demarest, Arthur A.
1978   Interregional Conflict and "Situational Ethics" in Classic Maya Warfare. In *Codex Wauchope: A Tribute Roll*, ed. Marco Giardino, Barbara Edmonson, and Winifred Creamer, pp. 101–111. Bureau of Administrative Services, Tulane University, New Orleans.
1997   The Vanderbilt Petexbatun Project. *Ancient Mesoamerica* 8(2): 209–227.
2004   After the Maelstrom: Collapse of the Classic Maya Kingdoms and the Terminal Classic in Western Petén. In *The Terminal Classic in the Maya Lowlands: Collapse, Transition, and Transformation*, ed. Arthur A. Demarest, Prudence M. Rice, and Don S. Rice, pp. 102–124. University Press of Colorado, Boulder.

Demarest, Arthur A., Prudence M. Rice, and Don S. Rice (eds.)
2004   *The Terminal Classic in the Maya Lowlands: Collapse, Transition, and Transformation*. University Press of Colorado, Boulder.

De Vos, Jan
1980   *La paz de Dios y del rey: la conquista de la selva Lacandona 1525–1821*. Fondo de Cultura Económica, Mexico, DF.

Díaz del Castillo, Bernal
1973   *La veradera y notable conquista de la Nueva España*. Editorial Siglo XXI, Mexico, DF.

Dietler, Michael, and Ingrid Herbich
1998   Habitus, Techniques, Style: An Integrated Approach to the Social Understanding of Material Culture and Boundaries. In *The Archaeology of Social Boundaries*, ed. Miriam T. Stark, pp. 232–263. Smithsonian Institution Press, Washington, DC.

Dirkmaat, Dennis C., Luis L. Cabo, James M. Adovasio, and Vicente Rozas
2005   Commingled Remains and the Mass Grave: Considering the Benefits of Forensic Archaeology. Paper presented at the 57th annual meeting of the American Academy of Forensic Sciences, New Orleans.

Divale, William Tulio, and Marvin Harris
1976   Population, Warfare, and the Male Supremacist Complex. *American Anthropologist* 78: 521–538.

Duby, Gertrude, and Frans Blom
1969   Lacandon. In *Ethnology*, ed. Evon Z. Vogt, pp. 276–297. Handbook of Middle American Indians, vol. 7. University of Texas Press, Austin.

Duncan, William N.
2005a   The Bioarchaeology of Ritual Violence in Postclassic El Petén, Guatemala (AD 950–1524). Ph.D. dissertation, Southern Illinois University Carbondale.
2005b   Understanding Ritual Violence in the Archaeological Record. In *Interacting with the Dead: Perspectives on Mortuary Archaeology for the New Millennium*, ed. G. F. M. Rakita, Jane Buikstra, Lane A. Beck, and Sloan R. Williams, pp. 207–227. University Press of Florida, Gainesville.

Durkheim, Émile
1915   *The Elementary Forms of the Religious Life: A Study in Religious Sociology*, trans. Joseph Ward Swain. Macmillan, New York.

Edmonson, Munro S.
1979   Some Postclassic Questions about the Classic Maya. In *Tercera Mesa Redonda de Palenque*, vol. 4, ed. Merle Greene Robertson and Donnan Call Jeffers, pp. 9–18. Pre-Columbian Art Research Center, Palenque, Chiapas, Mexico. (Reprinted in *Ancient Mesoamerica, Selected Readings*, 2nd. ed. [1981], ed. John A. Graham, pp. 221–228. Peek Publications, Palo Alto, CA.)
1982   *The Ancient Future of the Itza: The Book of Chilam Balam of Tizimin*. University of Texas Press, Austin.
1985   The Baktun Ceremonial of 1618. In *Fourth Palenque Round Table, 1980*, vol. 6, ed. Merle Greene Robertson and Elizabeth P. Benson, pp. 261–265. Pre-Columbian Art Research Institute, San Francisco.
1986   *Heaven Born Merida and Its Destiny. The Book of Chilam Balam of Chumayel*. University of Texas Press, Austin.
1988   *The Book of the Year. Middle American Calendrical Systems*. University of Utah Press, Salt Lake City.

Eliade, Mircea
1979   *Tratado de historia de las religiones*. Biblioteca Era, Mexico, DF.

Elson, Christina M., and Michael E. Smith
2001   Archaeological Deposits from the Aztec New Fire Ceremony. *Ancient Mesoamerica* 12(2): 157–174.

Elvatech
2004   *ElvaX 2.4*. Elvatech, Ltd, Kiev, Ukraine.

Farriss, Nancy M.
1984   *Maya Society under Colonial Rule: The Collective Enterprise of Survival*. Princeton University Press, Princeton, NJ.
1987   Remembering the Future, Anticipating the Past: History, Time, and Cosmology among the Maya of Yucatán. *Comparative Studies in Society and History* 29(3): 566–593.

Fash, Barbara W., William L. Fash, Sheree Lane, Rudy Larios, Linda Schele, Jeffrey Stomper, and David Stuart
1992   Investigations at a Classic Maya Council House at Copán, Honduras. *Journal of Field Archaeology* 19(4): 419–442.

Fash, William L.
2001   *Scribes, Warriors, and Kings: The City of Copan and the Ancient Maya*. Thames and Hudson, London.

Fields, Virginia M.
1994 Catalog of the Exhibition. In *Painting the Maya Universe: Royal Ceramics of the Classic Period*, by Dorie Reents-Budet, pp. 313–361. Duke University Press, Durham, NC.

Fiorillo, Anthony R.
1989 An Experimental Study of Trampling: Implications for the Fossil Record. In *Bone Modification*, ed. R. Bonnichsen and M. Sorg, pp. 61–72. Center for the Study of the First Americans, University of Maine, Orono.

Fishman, Bernard, Hamish Forbes, and Barbara Lawn
1977 University of Pennsylvania Radiocarbon Dates XIX. *Radiocarbon* 19(2): 188–228.

Fishman, Bernard, and Barbara Lawn
1978 University of Pennsylvania Radiocarbon Dates XX. *Radiocarbon* 20(2): 210–233.

Foias, Antonia E.
1996 Changing Ceramic Production and Exchange Systems and the Classic Maya Collapse in the Petexbatun Region. Ph.D. dissertation, Vanderbilt University, Nashville, TN.

Follett, Prescott
1932 War and Weapons of the Maya. *Middle American Research Institute Research Papers*, Pub. 4. Tulane University, New Orleans.

Foor, Charles
1994 Analysis of Late Postclassic Censer Materials from Structure II, Negroman-Tipu, Belize. M.S. thesis, Department of Anthropology, Southern Illinois University Carbondale.

Forty, Adrian
2001 Introduction. In *The Art of Forgetting*, ed. Adrian Forty and Susanne Küchler, pp. 1–18. Berg, Oxford.

Fox, John W.
1987 *Maya Postclassic State Formation*. Cambridge University Press, Cambridge.

Freidel, David A
1981 Continuity and Disjunction: Late Postclassic Settlement Patterns in Northern Yucatan. In *Lowland Maya Settlement Patterns*, ed. Wendy Ashmore, pp. 311–332. University of New Mexico Press, Albuquerque.
1986a Maya Warfare: An Example of Peer Polity Interaction. In *Peer Polity Interaction and Socio-Political Change*, ed. Colin Renfrew and John F. Cherry, pp. 93–108. Cambridge University Press, Cambridge.
1986b Terminal Classic Lowland Maya: Successes, Failures, and Aftermaths. In *Late Lowland Maya Civilization: Classic to Postclassic*, ed. Jeremy A. Sabloff and E. Wyllys Andrews V, pp. 409–430. University of New Mexico Press and SAR, Albuquerque.

Freidel, David A., and Jeremy A. Sabloff
1984 *Cozumel Late Maya Settlement Patterns*. Academic Press, Orlando, FL.

Freidel, David A., and Linda Schele
1989 Dead Kings and Living Temples: Dedication and Termination Rituals among the Ancient Maya. In *Word and Image in Maya Culture: Explorations*

in Language, Writing, and Representation, ed. William F. Hanks and Don S. Rice, pp. 233–243. University of Utah Press, Salt Lake City.

Freidel, David A., Linda Schele, and Joy Parker
1993   *Maya Cosmos: Three Thousand Years on the Shaman's Path.* William Morrow, New York.

Fried, Morton H.
1967   *The Evolution of Political Society: An Essay in Political Anthropology.* Random House, New York.

Friedman, Jonathan
1992   The Past in the Future: History and the Politics of Identity. *American Anthropologist* 94(4): 837–859.

Friedrich, Margaret
1970   Design Structure and Social Interaction: Archaeological Implications of an Ethnographic Analysis. *American Antiquity* 35(3): 332–343.

Fry, Robert E.
1987   The Ceramic Sequence of South-Central Quintana Roo, Mexico. In *Maya Ceramics. Papers from the 1985 Maya Ceramic Conference*, Part I, ed. Prudence M. Rice and Robert J. Sharer, pp. 111–122. B.A.R International Series 345(i), Oxford.

Furst, Jill L.
1995   *The Natural History of the Soul in Ancient Mexico.* Yale University Press, New Haven, CT.

Gann, Thomas
1900   Mounds in Northern Honduras. *Nineteenth Annual Report, 1897–1898*, Part 2, pp. 661–692. Bureau of American Ethnology, Smithsonian Institution, Washington, DC.

Gasco, Janine, and Frances F. Berdan
2003   International Trade Centers. In *The Postclassic Mesoamerican World*, ed. Michael E. Smith and Frances F. Berdan, pp. 109–116. University of Utah Press, Salt Lake City.

Geertz, Clifford
1973   *The Interpretation of Cultures: Selected Essays by Clifford Geertz.* Basic Books, New York.

Giddens, Anthony
1984   *The Constitution of Society: Outline of the Theory of Structuration.* University of California Press, Berkeley.

Gifford, James C.
1976   *Prehistoric Pottery Analysis and the Ceramics of Barton Ramie in the Belize Valley.* Memoirs, vol. 18. Peabody Museum of Archaeology and Ethnology, Harvard University, Cambridge, MA.

Gillespie, Susan D.
2000   Rethinking Ancient Maya Social Organization: Replacing "Lineage" with "House." *American Anthropologist* 102(3): 467–484.

Girard, Rafael
1962   *Los mayas eternos.* Antigua Librería Robredo, Mexico, DF.

Glascock, Michael D.
1992   Characterization of Archaeological Ceramics at MURR by Neutron Activation Analysis and Multivariate Statistics. In *Chemical Characterization of Ceramic Pastes in Archaeology*, ed. Hector Neff, pp. 11–26. Prehistory Press, Madison, WI.

Goody, Jack
1962   *Death Property and the Ancestors: A Study of the Mortuary Customs of the Lodagaa of West Africa*. Stanford University Press, Stanford, CA.

Gossen, Gary H.
1986   Mesoamerican Ideas as a Foundation for Regional Synthesis. In *Symbol and Meaning beyond the Closed Community: Essays in Mesoamerican Ideas*, ed. Gary H. Gossen, pp. 1–8. Institute for Mesoamerican Studies, State University of New York Albany.

Gossen, Gary H., and Richard M. Leventhal
1993   The Topography of Ancient Maya Religious Pluralism: A Dialogue with the Present. In *Lowland Maya Civilization in the Eighth Century A.D.*, ed. Jeremy A. Sabloff and John S. Henderson, pp. 185–217. Dumbarton Oaks, Washington, DC.

Graff, Donald H.
1997   Dating a Section of the Madrid Codex: Astronomical and Iconographic Evidence. In *Papers on the Madrid Codex*, ed. Victoria R. Bricker and Gabrielle Vail, pp. 147–167. Pub. 64. Middle American Research Institute, Tulane University, New Orleans.

Graff, Donald H., and Gabrielle Vail
2001   Censers and Stars: Issues in Dating the Madrid Codex. *Latin American Indian Literatures Journal* 17(1): 58–95.

Graham, Elizabeth
1987   Terminal Classic to Early Historic Period Vessel Forms from Belize. In *Maya Ceramics. Papers from the 1985 Maya Ceramic Conference*, Part I, ed. Prudence M. Rice and Robert J. Sharer, pp. 73–98. B.A.R International Series 345(i), Oxford.
1989   Brief Synthesis of Coastal Site Data from Colson Point, Placencia, and Marco Gonzalez, Belize. In *Coastal Maya Trade*, ed. Heather McKillop and Paul F. Healy, pp. 135–154. Occasional Papers in Anthropology 8. Trent University, Peterborough, Canada.
1991   Archaeological Insights into Colonial Period Maya Life at Tipu, Belize. In *Columbian Consequences. The Spanish Borderlands in Pan-American Perspective*, ed. David H. Thomas, pp. 319–336. Smithsonian Institution Press, Washington, DC.

Graham, Elizabeth A., Grant D. Jones, and Robert R. Kautz
1985   Archaeology and Ethnohistory on a Spanish Colonial Frontier: An Interim Report on the Macal-Tipu Project in Western Belize. In *The Lowland Maya Postclassic*, ed. Arlen F. Chase and Prudence M. Rice, pp. 206–214. University of Texas Press, Austin.

Graham, Elizabeth, and David Pendergast
1989   Excavations at the Marco Gonzalez Site, Ambergris Cay, Belize, 1986. *Journal of Field Archaeology* 16: 1–16.

Graham, Elizabeth, David Pendergast, and Grant D. Jones
1989 On the Fringes of Conquest: Maya-Spanish Contact in Colonial Belize. *Science* 246: 1254–1259.

Grove, David
1981 Olmec Monuments: Mutilation as a Clue to Meaning. In *The Olmec and Their Neighbors. Essays in Memory of Matthew W. Stirling*, org. Michael D. Coe and David C. Grove, ed. Elizabeth P. Benson, pp. 49–68. Dumbarton Oaks, Washington, DC.

Guderjan, Thomas
1995 Maya Settlement and Trade on Ambergris Caye, Belize. *Ancient Mesoamerica* 6(2): 147–159.

Guillemin, George F.
1968 Development and Function of the Tikal Ceremonial Center. *Ethnos* 33: 1–35.

Guthe, Carl E.
1921– Report of Dr. Carl E. Guthe. *Carnegie Institution of Washington Yearbook* 20:
1922 364–368. Carnegie Institution of Washington, Washington, DC.

Haglund, William D.
1997a Dogs and Coyotes: Postmortem Involvement with Human Remains. In *Forensic Taphonomy: The Postmortem Fate of Human Remains*, ed. W. D. Haglund and M. Sorg, pp. 367–382. CRC Press, Boca Raton, FL.
1997b Scattered Skeletal Human Remains: Search Strategy Considerations for Locating Missing Teeth. In *Forensic Taphonomy: The Postmortem Fate of Human Remains*, ed. W. D. Haglund and M. Sorg, pp. 383–394. CRC Press, Boca Raton, FL.

Hammond, Norman, and Mathew R. Bobo
1994 Pilgrimage's Last Mile: Late Maya Monument Veneration at La Milpa, Belize. *World Archaeology* 26(1): 19–34.

Hammond, Norman, Rupert A. Housley, and Ian A. Law
1991 Postclassic at Cuello, Belize. *Ancient Mesoamerica* 2(1): 71–74.

Hammond, Norman, Duncan Pring, Rainer Berger, V. R. Switzer, and A. P. Ward
1976 Radiocarbon Chronology for Early Maya Occupation at Cuello, Belize. *Nature* 260: 579–581.

Hanks, William F.
1990 *Referential Practice: Language and Lived Space among the Maya*. University of Chicago Press, Chicago.

Harbottle, Garman
1976 Activation Analysis in Archaeology. *Radiochemistry* 3: 33–72.

Hassig, Ross
1992 *War and Society in Ancient Mesoamerica*. University of California Press, Berkeley.
2001 *Time, History, and Belief in Aztec and Colonial Mexico*. University of Texas Press, Austin.

Headrick, Annabeth
2003 Butterfly War at Teotihuacan. In *Ancient Mesoamerican Warfare*, ed. M. Kathryn Brown and Travis W. Stanton, pp. 149–170. AltaMira, Walnut Creek, CA.

Hellmuth, Nicholas
1972   Progreso y notas sobre la investigación etnohistórica de las tierras bajas mayas de los siglos XVI a XIX. *América Indígena* 32: 197–244.
1977   Cholti-Lacandon [Chiapas] and Peten-Ytza Agriculture, Settlement Pattern, and Population. In *Social Process in Maya Prehistory*, ed. Norman Hammond, pp. 421–448. Academic Press, London.
1987   *Monster Und Menschen In Der Maya-Kunst.* Akademische Druck, Austria.

Hermes, Bernard
2000a   Síntesis y consideraciones finales por período cronológico. In *El sitio maya de Topoxté. Investigaciones en una isla del lago Yaxhá, Petén, Guatemala,* ed. Wolfgang W. Wurster, pp. 289–296. Verlag Philipp von Zabern, Mainz am Rhein, Germany.
2000b   Industria cerámica. In *El sitio maya de Topoxté. Investigaciones en una isla del lago Yaxhá, Petén, Guatemala,* ed. Wolfgang W. Wurster, pp. 164–202. Verlag Philipp von Zabern, Mainz am Rhein, Germany.
2000c   Resúmen de la secuencia constructiva. In *El sitio maya de Topoxté. Investigaciones en una isla del lago Yaxhá, Petén, Guatemala,* ed. Wolfgang W. Wurster, pp. 58–63. Verlag Philipp von Zabern, Mainz am Rhein, Germany.
2000d   Ofrendas. In *El sitio maya de Topoxté. Investigaciones en una isla del lago Yaxhá, Petén, Guatemala,* ed. Wolfgang W. Wurster, pp. 77–91. Verlag Philipp von Zabern, Mainz am Rhein, Germany.
2000e   Vasijas de miniatura y figuras de miniatura. In *El sitio maya de Topoxté. Investigaciones en una isla del lago Yaxhá, Petén, Guatemala,* ed. Wolfgang W. Wurster, pp. 205–207. Verlag Philipp von Zabern, Mainz am Rhein, Germany.

Hermes, Bernard, and Raúl Noriega
1997   El período Postclásico en el área de la Laguna Yaxhá: una visión desde Topoxté. In *XI Simposio de Investigaciones Arqueológicas en Guatemala,* ed. Juan Pedro Laporte and Héctor L. Escobedo, pp. 755–778. Ministerio de Cultura y Deportes, Instituto de Antropología e Historia and Asociación Tikal, Guatemala City.

Hermes, Bernard, Raúl Noriega, Oscar Quintana, and Wolfgang W. Wurster
2000   Sector alto central: la plaza principal y sus accesos; Sector bajo central; Sector alto norte; and Sectores bajos periféricos. In *El sitio maya de Topoxté. Investigaciones en una isla del lago Yaxhá, Petén, Guatemala,* ed. Wolfgang W. Wurster, pp. 35–54. Verlag Philipp von Zabern, Mainz am Rhein, Germany.

Herrera y Tordesillas, Antonio de
1941   Historia general de los hechos de los castellanos en las islas y tierra firme del mar océano. In *Landa's Relación de las Cosas de Yucatan,* ed. Alfred Tozzer, pp. 213–220. Peabody Museum of American Archaeology and Ethnology, Harvard University, Cambridge, MA.

Herrmann, Nicholas
2002   GIS Applied to Bioarchaeology: An Example from the Río Talgua Caves in Northeast Honduras. *Journal of Cave and Karst Studies* 64(1): 17–22.

Hertz, Robert
1960   *Death and the Right Hand,* trans. R. Needham. Cohen and West, London.

Hill, Andrew, and Alan Walker
1972   Procedures in Vertebrate Taphonomy. *Geological Society of London Quarterly Journal* 128: 399–406.

Hill, James N.
1970   *Broken K Pueblo: Prehistoric Social Organization in the American Southwest.* Anthropological Papers, vol. 18. University of Arizona, Tucson.

Hillson, Simon
1996   *Dental Anthropology.* Cambridge University Press, New York.

Hodder, Ian
1977   The Distribution of Material Culture Items in the Baringo District, Western Kenya. *Man* 12: 239–269.
1978   Social Organization and Human Interaction: The Development of Some Tentative Hypotheses in Terms of Material Culture. In *The Spatial Organization of Culture*, ed. Ian Hodder, pp. 199–269. University of Pittsburgh Press, Pittsburgh, PA.
1982   *Symbols in Action.* Cambridge University Press, Cambridge.

Hodell, David A., Rhonda L. Quinn, Mark Brenner, and George Kamenov
2004   Spatial Variation of Strontium Isotopes ($^{87}Sr/^{86}Sr$) in the Maya Region: A Tool for Tracking Ancient Human Migration. *Journal of Archaeological Science* 31: 585–601.

Hofling, Charles Andrew
1991   *Itzaj Maya Texts with a Grammatical Overview.* University of Utah Press, Salt Lake City.
2002   Archaeological and Linguistic Correlations in Yukateko Mayaland. Submitted for a Festschrift for Terrence Kaufman.
2004   Language and Cultural Contacts among Yukatekan Mayans. *Collegium Antropologicum* 28, suppl. 1: 241–248. Zagreb, Croatia.
2006a   A Sketch of the History of the Verbal Complex in Yukatekan Mayan Languages. *International Journal of American Linguistics* 72: 367–396.
2006b   La historia lingüística y cultural del maya yucateco durante el último milenio. In *Los ayas de ayer y hoy: Memorias del Primer Congreso Internacional de la Cultura Maya*, ed. Alfredo Barrera Rubio and Ruth Gubler, vol. 2, pp. 1196–1216. Solar, Servicios Editoriales, S.A. de C.V., Mexico, DF.

Hofling, Charles Andrew, and Félix Fernando Tesucún
1997   *Itzaj Maya-Spanish-English Dictionary.* University of Utah Press, Salt Lake City.

Houston, Stephen D.
1993   *Hieroglyphs and History at Dos Pilas: Dynastic Politics of the Classic Maya.* University of Texas Press, Austin.
1998   Classic Maya Depictions of the Built Environment. In *Function and Meaning in Classic Maya Architecture*, ed. Stephen D. Houston, pp. 333–372. Dumbarton Oaks, Washington DC.

Hubbs, Carl L., George S. Bien, and Hans E. Suess
1962   La Jolla Natural Radiocarbon Measurements II. *Radiocarbon* 4: 204–238.

Hurlbut, Sharon A.
2000   The Taphonomy of Cannibalism: A Review of the Anthropogenic Bone Modification in the American Southwest. *International Journal of Osteoarchaeology* 10: 4–26.

Ichon, Alain, M. F. Fauvet-Berthelot, C. Plocieniak, Robert Hill, Rebecca González Lauck, and M. A. Bailey
1981   *Rescate arqueológico en la cuenca del Río Chixoy.* Centre National de la Recherche Scientifique R.C.P. 500, Guatemala City.

Inomata, Takeshi, Daniela Triadan, Erick Ponciano, Estela Pinto, Richard E. Terry, and Marcus Eberl
2002   Domestic and Political Lives of Classic Maya Elites: The Excavation of Rapidly Abandoned Structures at Aguateca, Guatemala. *Latin American Antiquity* 13(3): 305–330.

Inomata, Takeshi, and Ronald W. Webb
2003   Archaeological Studies of Abandonment in Middle America. In *The Archaeology of Settlement Abandonment in Middle America*, ed. Takeshi Inomata and Ronald W. Webb, pp. 1–10. University of Utah Press, Salt Lake City.

Johnson, Jay K.
1985   Postclassic Maya Site Structure at Topoxté, El Petén, Guatemala. In *The Lowland Maya Postclassic*, ed. Arlen F. Chase and Prudence M. Rice, pp. 151–165. University of Texas Press, Austin.

Jones, Christopher
1969   The Twin-Pyramid Group Pattern: A Classic Maya Architectural Assemblage at Tikal, Guatemala. Unpublished Ph.D. dissertation, University of Pennsylvania, Philadelphia.

Jones, Grant D.
1989   *Maya Resistance to Spanish Rule: Time and History on a Colonial Frontier*. University of New Mexico Press, Albuquerque.
1998   *The Conquest of the Last Maya Kingdom*. Stanford University Press, Stanford, CA.

Jones, Grant D., Robert R. Kautz, and Elizabeth Graham
1986   Tipu: A Maya Town on the Spanish Colonial Frontier. *Archaeology* 39: 40–47.

Jones, Morris R.
1952   Map of the Ruins of Mayapan, Yucatan, Mexico. *Current Reports* 1. Department of Archaeology, Carnegie Institution of Washington, Washington, DC.

Justeson, John S., William M. Norman, Lyle Campbell, and Terrence Kaufman
1985   *Foreign Impact on Lowland Mayan Language and Script*. Pub. 53. Middle American Research Institute, Tulane University, New Orleans.

Kan, Sergei
1989   *Symbolic Immortality: The Tlingit Potlatch of the Nineteenth Century*. Smithsonian Institution Press, Washington, DC.

Kaufman, Terrence
1976   Archaeological and Linguistic Correlations in Mayaland and Associated Areas of Mesoamerica. *World Archaeology* 8(1): 101–118.
1991   Notes on the Structure of Yukateko and Other Yukatekan Languages. Unpublished manuscript.

Kepecs, Susan, and Marilyn Masson
2003   Political Organization in Yucatán and Belize. In *The Postclassic Mesoamerican World*, ed. Michael E. Smith and Frances Berdan, pp. 40–44. University of Utah Press, Salt Lake City.

Kerr, Justin
1989   *The Maya Vase Book: A Corpus of Rollout Photographs of Maya Vases*. Kerr Associates, New York.

1990   *The Maya Vase Book: Volume 2.* Kerr Associates, New York.

1992   *The Maya Vase Book: Volume 3.* Kerr Associates, New York.

1994   *The Maya Vase Book: Volume 4.* Kerr Associates, New York.

1997   *The Maya Vase Book: A Corpus of Rollout Photographs of Maya Vases, Volume 5.* Justin Kerr Associates, New York.

Kertzer, David I.
1988   *Ritual, Politics, and Power.* Yale University Press, New Haven, CT.

Kowalski, Jeff Karl
1989   Who Am I among the Itza? Links between Northern Yucatan and the Western Maya Lowlands and Highlands. In *Mesoamerica after the Decline of Teotihuacan, A.D. 700–900,* ed. Richard A. Diehl and Janet C. Berlo, pp. 173–186. Dumbarton Oaks, Washington, DC.

Krochock, Ruth, and David A. Freidel
1994   Ballcourts and the Evolution of Political Rhetoric at Chichén Itzá. In *Hidden among the Hills. Maya Archaeology of the Northwest Yucatan Peninsula.* First Maler Symposium, Bonn, 1989, ed. Hanns J. Prem, pp. 359–375. Verlag von Flemming, Möckmühl, Germany.

Kubler, George
1985   Aspects of Classic Maya Rulership on Two Inscribed Vessels. In *Studies in Ancient American and European Art: The Collected Essays of George Kubler,* ed. Thomas F. Reese, pp. 334–350. Yale Publications in the History of Art 20, ed. George L. Hersey. Yale University, New Haven, CT [1977].

Laporte, Juan Pedro
1996   Organización territorial y política prehispánica en el sureste de Petén. *Atlas Arqueológico de Guatemala* 4. Instituto de Antropología e Historia, Guatemala City.

2004   Terminal Classic Settlement and Polity in the Mopan Valley, Petén, Guatemala. In *The Terminal Classic in the Maya Lowlands: Collapse, Transition, and Transformation,* ed. Arthur A. Demarest, Prudence M. Rice, and Don S. Rice, pp. 195–230. University Press of Colorado, Boulder.

Larsen, Clark
1997   *Bioarchaeology: Interpreting Behavior from the Skeleton.* Cambridge University Press, New York.

Lawn, Barbara
1974   University of Pennsylvania Radiocarbon Dates XVII. *Radiocarbon* 16(2): 219–237.

Leach, Edmund
1976   *Culture and Communication.* Cambridge University Press, Cambridge.

Lechtman, Heather
1977   Style in Technology—Some Early Thoughts. In *Material Culture: Styles, Organization, and Dynamics of Technology,* ed. Heather Lechtman and Robert S. Merrill, pp. 3–20. West Publishing, St. Paul, MN.

1979   Issues in Andean Metallurgy. In *Pre-Columbian Metallurgy of South America,* ed. Elizabeth P. Benson, pp. 1–40. Dumbarton Oaks, Washington, DC.

1981   Introducción. In *La tecnología en el mundo Andino,* ed. Heather Lechtman and A. M. Soldi, pp. 11–22. Universidad Nacional Autóma de México, Mexico, DF.

1984a   Andean Value Systems and the Development of Prehistoric Metallurgy. *Technology and Culture* 25(1): 1–36.

1984b   Pre-Columbian Surface Metallurgy. *Scientific American* 250(6): 56–63.

1988   Traditions and Styles in Central Andean Metalworking. In *Beginning of the Use of Metals and Alloys*, ed. R. Maddin, pp. 344–378. MIT Press, Cambridge.

1993   Technologies of Power, the Andean Case. In *Configurations of Power in Complex Society*, ed. Patricia J. Netherly and John S. Henderson, pp. 244–280. Cornell University Press, Ithaca, NY.

1994   The Materials Science of Material Culture: Examples from the Andean Past. In *Archaeometry of Pre-Columbian Sites and Artifacts*, ed. D. A. Scott and P. Meyers, pp. 3–11. Getty Conservation Institute, Los Angeles.

LeCount, Lisa, Jason Yeager, Richard M. Leventhal, and Wendy Ashmore
2002   Dating the Rise and Fall of Xunantunich, Belize. *Ancient Mesoamerica* 13: 41–63.

Lefebvre, Henri
1991   *The Production of Space*, trans. Donald Nicholson-Smith. Blackwell, Cambridge.

Lemonnier, Pierre
1986   The Study of Material Culture Today: Toward an Anthropology of Technical Systems. *Journal of Anthropological Archaeology* 5(2): 147–186.

1989   Bark Capes, Arrowheads and Concorde: On Social Representations of Technology. In *The Meaning of Things: Material Culture and Symbolic Expression*, ed. Ian Hodder, pp. 156–171. Unwin Hyman, London.

1992   *Elements for an Anthropology of Technology*. Anthropological Papers 88. Museum of Anthropology, University of Michigan, Ann Arbor.

1993   Introduction. In *Technological Choices*, ed. Pierre Lemonnier, pp. 1–35. Routledge, London.

Leventhal, Richard
1983   Household Groups and Classic Maya Religion. In *Prehistoric Settlement Patterns: Essays in Honor of Gordon R. Willey*, ed. Evon Z. Vogt and Richard M. Leventhal, pp. 55–76. University of New Mexico Press, Albuquerque.

Lévi-Strauss, Claude
1963   *Structural Anthropology*. Basic Books, New York.

1982   *The Way of Masks*, trans. Sylvia Modelski. University of Washington Press, Seattle.

Lincoln, Charles E.
1994   Structural and Philological Evidence for Divine Kingship at Chichén Itzá, Yucatán, Mexico. In *Hidden among the Hills: Maya Archaeology of the Northwest Yucatan Peninsula*. First Maler Symposium, Bonn, 1989, ed. Hans J. Prem, pp. 164–196. Verlag von Flemming, Möckmühl, Germany.

Lind, Michael D.
1994   Cholula and Mixteca Polychromes: Two Mixteca-Puebla Regional Sub-Styles. In *Mixteca-Puebla: Discoveries and Research in Mesoamerican Art and Archaeology*, ed. H. B. Nicholson and Eloise Quiñones Keber, pp. 79–99. Labyrinthos, Culver City, CA.

Long, Austin, and James E. Mielke
1967   Smithsonian Institution Radiocarbon Measurements IV. *Radiocarbon* 9: 368–381.

Longacre, William A.
1970   *Archaeology as Anthropology: A Case Study.* Anthropological Papers, vol. 17. University of Arizona Press, Tucson.

López Austin, Alfredo
1988   *The Human Body and Ideology: Concepts of the Ancient Nahuas.* University of Utah Press, Salt Lake City.

López de Cogolludo, Diego
1688   *Historia de Yucatán.* J. García Infanzón, Madrid.
1954   *Historia de Yucatán,* vol 1. Comisión de Historia, Campeche.
1971   *Los tres siglos de la dominación española en Yucatan, o sea historia de esta provincia.* 2 vols. Akademische Druck- u. Verlagsanstalt, Graz, Austria.

Lounsbury, Floyd
1978   Maya Numeration, Computation, and Calendrical Astronomy. In *Dictionary of Scientific Biography,* vol. 15, suppl. 1, ed. Charles Coulston-Gillispie, pp. 757–818. Charles Scribner's Sons, New York.

Love, Bruce
1994   *The Paris Codex: Handbook for a Maya Priest.* University of Texas Press, Austin.

Lowe, Gareth
1982   *Izapa, an Introduction to the Ruins and Monuments.* New World Archaeological Foundation, Brigham Young University, Provo, UT.

Lyman, R. Lee
2005   Analyzing Cut Marks: Lessons from Artiodactyl Remains in the Northwestern United States. *Journal of Archaeological Science* 32: 1722–1732.

Lyman, R. Lee, and Gregory L. Fox
1997   A Critical Evaluation of Bone Weathering as an Indication of Bone Assemblage Formation. In *Forensic Taphonomy: The Postmortem Fate of Human Remains,* ed. W. D. Haglund and M. Sorg, pp. 223–248. CRC Press, Boca Raton, FL.

MacLeod, Barbara, and Andrea Stone
1995   Hieroglyphic Inscriptions of Naj Tunich. In *Images from the Underworld: Naj Tunich and the Tradition of Maya Cave Paintings,* ed. Andrea Stone, pp. 155–184. University of Texas Press, Austin.

Macri, Martha J., and Matthew G. Looper
2003   *The New Catalog of Maya Hieroglyphs, vol. 1. The Classic Period Inscriptions.* University of Oklahoma Press, Norman.

Malkki, Liisa H.
1997   National Geographic: The Rooting of Peoples and the Territorialization of National Identity among Scholars and Refugees. In *Culture, Power, Place: Explorations in Critical Anthropology,* ed. Akhil Gupta and James Ferguson, pp. 52–74. Duke University Press, Durham, NC.

Manahan, T. Kam
2003   The Collapse of Complex Society and Its Aftermath: A Case Study from the Classic Maya Site of Copan, Honduras. Unpublished Ph.D. dissertation, Vanderbilt University, Nashville, TN.

Marcus, Joyce
  1973   Territorial Organization of the Lowland Classic Maya. *Science* 180: 911–916.
  1992   *Mesoamerican Writing Systems: Propaganda, Myth, and History in Four Ancient Civilizations.* Princeton University Press, Princeton, NJ.

Marcus, Joyce, Kent V. Flannery, and Ronald Spores
  1983   The Cultural Legacy of the Oaxacan Preceramic. In *The Cloud People: Divergent Evolution of the Zapotec and Mixtec Civilizations,* ed. Kent V. Flannery and Joyce Marcus, pp. 36–39. Academic Press, New York.

Margerison, Beverley, and Christopher J. Knüsel
  2002   Paleodemographic Comparison of a Catastrophic and an Attritional Death Assemblage. *American Journal of Physical Anthropology* 119: 134–143.

Márquez Morfin, L.
  1982   *Playa del Carmen: una población de la costa oriental en el posclásico (un estudio osteológico).* Insituto Nacional de Antropología e Historia, Mexico, DF.

Martínez Hernández, Juan de (ed.)
  1969   *Diccionario de Motul Maya-Español,* atribuído a Fray Antonio de Ciudad Real y *Arte de la lengua Maya* por Fray Juan Coronel. Dictionary from 16th-century manuscript, Mérida.

Massey, Virginia
  1989   The Human Skeletal Remains from a Terminal Classic Skull Pit at Colha, Belize. *Papers of the Colha Project,* vol. 3. University of Texas at Austin and Texas A&M University, College Station.

Masson, Marilyn
  1999a   Postclassic Maya Communities at Progresso Lagoon and Laguna Seca, Northern Belize. *Journal of Field Archaeology* 25: 285–306.
  1999b   Postclassic Maya Ritual at Laguna de On Island, Belize. *Ancient Mesoamerica* 10(1): 51–68.
  2000   *In the Realm of Nachan Kan.* University Press of Colorado, Boulder.
  2001   Segmentary Political Cycles and Elite Migration Myths in the Postclassic Archaeology of Northern Belize. In *The Past and Present Maya: Essays in Honor of Robert M. Carmack,* ed. John M. Weeks, pp. 89–103. Labyrinthos, Lancaster.
  2003   The Late Postclassic Symbol Set in the Maya Area. In *The Postclassic Mesoamerican World,* ed. Michael E. Smith and Frances F. Berdan, pp. 194–200. University of Utah Press, Salt Lake City.

Masson, Marilyn A., Timothy S. Hare, and Carlos Peraza Lope
  2006   Postclassic Maya Society Regenerated at Mayapán. In *After Collapse: The Regeneration of Complex Societies,* ed. Glenn M. Schwartz and John J. Nichols, pp. 188–207. University of Arizona Press, Tucson.

Masson, Marilyn A., and Carlos Peraza Lope
  2005   Nuevas investigaciones en tres unidades residenciales fuera del área monumental de Mayapán. In *Investigadores de la Cultura Maya 13,* tomo II, pp. 411–424. Universidad Autónoma de Campeche, Campeche, Mexico.
  2006   Figurines and Social Diversity at Mayapán. Paper presented at the International Congress of Americanists, Seville.

McAnany, Patricia
  1995   *Living with the Ancestors: Kinship and Kingship in Ancient Maya Society.* University of Texas Press, Austin.

McCafferty, Geoffrey G.

1994   The Mixteca-Puebla Stylistic Tradition at Early Postclassic Cholula. In *Mixteca-Puebla: Discoveries and Research in Mesoamerican Art and Archaeology*, ed. H. B. Nicholson and Eloise Quiñones Keber, pp. 53–77. Labyrinthos, Culver City, CA.

1996   The Ceramics and Chronology of Cholula Mexico. *Ancient Mesoamerica* 7(2): 299–323.

2001   *Ceramics of Postclassic Cholula, Mexico: Typology and Seriation of Pottery from the UA-1 Domestic Compound.* Monograph 43. Cotsen Institute of Archaeology, University of California Los Angeles.

McGee, R. Jon

1990   *Life, Ritual, and Religion among the Lacandon Maya.* Wadsworth, Belmont, CA.

1991   The Balché Ritual of the Lacandon Maya. *Estudios de Cultura Maya* 18: 439–457.

1998   The Lacandon Incense Burner Renewal Ceremony: Termination and Dedication Ritual among the Contemporary Maya. In *The Sowing and the Dawning: Termination, Dedication, and Transformation in the Archaeological and Ethnographic Record of Mesoamerica*, ed. Shirley B. Mock, pp. 41–46. University of New Mexico Press, Albuquerque.

2002   *Watching Lacandon Maya Lives.* Allyn and Bacon, Boston.

McGuire, Randall H.

1982   The Study of Ethnicity in Historical Archaeology. *Journal of Anthropological Archaeology* 1: 159–178.

Milbrath, Susan

1999   *Star Gods of the Maya: Astronomy in Art, Folklore, and Calendars.* University of Texas Press, Austin.

2007   Mayapán's Effigy Censers: Iconography, Context, and External Connections. http://www.famsi.org/reports/05025/index.html. Accessed September 28, 2008.

Milbrath, Susan, and Carlos Peraza Lope

2003   Revisiting Mayapan, Mexico's Last Maya Capital. *Ancient Mesoamerica* 14: 1–46.

Miller, Arthur G.

1974   The Iconography of the Painting in the Temple of the Diving God, Tulum, Quintana Roo, Mexico: The Twisted Cords. In *Mesoamerican Archaeology: New Approaches*, ed. Norman Hammond, pp. 167–186. University of Texas Press, Austin.

1982   *On the Edge of the Sea: Mural Painting at Tancah-Tulum, Quintana Roo, Mexico.* Dumbarton Oaks, Washington, DC.

Miller, Mary Ellen

1986   *The Murals of Bonampak.* Princeton University Press, Princeton, NJ.

Miller, Mary, and Karl Taube

1993   *The Gods and Symbols of Ancient Mexico and the Maya: An Illustrated Dictionary of Mesoamerican Religion.* Thames and Hudson, London.

Minc, Leah D., Mary G. Hodge, and James Blackman

1994   Stylistic and Spatial Variability in Early Aztec Ceramics: Insights into Pre-Imperial Exchange Systems. In *Economies and Polities in the Aztec Realm*, ed.

Mary G. Hodge and Michael E. Smith, pp. 133–173. Institute of Mesoamerican Studies, Albany, NY.

Mock, Shirley B.
1997   Monkey Business at Northern River Lagoon: A Coastal-Inland Interaction Sphere in Northern Belize. *Ancient Mesoamerica* 8(2): 165–183.
1998a   Prelude. In *The Sowing and the Dawning: Termination, Dedication, and Transformation in the Archaeological and Ethnographic Record*, ed. Shirley Mock, pp. 3–18. University of New Mexico Press, Albuquerque.
1998b   The Defaced and the Forgotten: Decapitation and Flaying/Mutilation as a Termination Event at Colha, Belize. In *The Sowing and the Dawning: Termination, Dedication, and Transformation in the Archaeological and Ethnographic Record*, ed. Shirley Mock, pp. 113–124. University of New Mexico Press, Albuquerque.

Montgomery, John
2002   *Dictionary of Maya Hieroglyphs*. Hippocrene Books, New York.

Morley, Sylvanus Griswold
1920   *The Inscriptions at Copan*. Pub. 219. Carnegie Institution of Washington, Washington, DC.

Morley, Sylvanus Griswold, and George F. Brainerd
1956   *The Ancient Maya*. Stanford University Press, Stanford, CA.

Morris, Elizabeth H., Jean Charlot, and A. A. Morris
1931   *Temple of the Warriors at Chichen Itza, Yucatan*. Pub. 406. Carnegie Institution of Washington, Washington, DC.

Myers, Thomas P., Michael R. Voorhies, and R. George Corner
1980   Spiral Fractures and Bone Pseudotools at Paleontological Sites. *American Antiquity* 45: 483–490.

Nash, June
1985   *In the Eyes of the Ancestors: Belief and Behavior in a Maya Community*. Waveland, Prospect Heights, IL.

Nations, James D., and John E. Clark
1983   Bows and Arrows of the Lacandon Maya. *Archaeology* 36(1): 36–43.

Neff, Hector
2000   Neutron Activation Analysis for Provenance Determination in Archaeology. In *Modern Analytical Methods in Art and Archaeology*, ed. E. Ciliberto and G. Spoto, pp. 81–134. John Wiley and Sons, New York.

Nelson, Fred W., Raymond Sidrys, and R. D. Holmes
1978   Trace Element Analysis by X-Ray Fluorescence of Obsidian Artifacts from Guatemala and Belize. In *Excavations at Seibal, Department of Peten, Guatemala: Artifacts*, ed. Gordon R. Willey, pp. 153–161. Memoirs 14. Peabody Museum of Archaeology and Ethnology, Harvard University, Cambridge, MA.

Nicholson, H. B.
1960   The Mixteca-Puebla Concept in Mesoamerican Archaeology: A Re-Examination. In *Men and Cultures: Selected Papers from the Fifth International Congress of Anthropological and Ethnological Sciences*, ed. Anthony F.C. Wallace, pp. 612–617. University of Pennsylvania, Philadelphia.

Nicholson, H. B., and Eloise Quiñones Keber (eds.)
1994   *Mixteca-Puebla: Discoveries and Research in Mesoamerican Art and Archaeology.* Labyrinthos, Culver City, CA.

Okoshi Harada, Tsubasa
1995   Tenencia de la tierra y territorialidad: conceptualización de los mayas yucatecos en vísperas de la invasión española. In *Conquista, transculturación y mestizaje: raiz y orígen de México,* ed. Lorenzo Ochoa, pp. 81–94. Instituto de Investigaciones Antropológicas, Universidad Nacional Autónoma de México, Mexico, DF.
1999   Estudio del *cuuchcabal* de Cehpech: el proceso de segmentación del linaje Pech. Paper presented at the 64th annual meeting of the Society for American Archaeology, Chicago.

Oland, Maxine, and Marilyn A. Masson
2005   Late Postclassic–Colonial Period Maya Settlement on the West Shore of Progresso Lagoon: Archaeological Investigations of the Eastern Maya Lowlands. Papers from the 2004 Belize Archaeology Symposium. Institute of Archaeology, National Institute of Culture and History, Belmopan, Belize.

Olsen, Sandra L., and Pat Shipman
1994   Cutmarks and Perimortem Treatment of Skeletal Remains on the Northern Plains. In *Skeletal Biology in the Great Plains: Migration, Warfare, Health, and Subsistence,* ed. R. Jantz and D. W. Owsley, pp. 377–390. Smithsonian Institution Press, Washington, DC.

O'Mansky, Matt, and Nicholas P. Dunning
2004   Settlement and Late Classic Political Disintegration in the Petexbatun Region, Guatemala. In *The Terminal Classic in the Maya Lowlands: Collapse, Transition, and Transformation,* ed. Arthur A. Demarest, Prudence M. Rice, and Don S. Rice, pp. 83–101. University Press of Colorado, Boulder.

Orie, Olanike Ola, and Victoria Bricker
2000   Placeless and Historical Laryngeals in Yucatec Maya. *International Journal of American Linguistics* 66: 283–317.

Ortner, Donald J.
2003a   Infectious Diseases: Introduction, Biology, Osteomyelitis, Periostitis, Brucellosis, Glanders, and Septic Arthritis. In *Identification of Pathological Conditions in Human Skeletal Remains,* ed. Donald Ortner, pp. 179–226. Academic Press, New York.
2003b   Trauma. In *Identification of Pathological Conditions in Human Skeletal Remains,* ed. Donald Ortner, pp. 119–178. Academic Press, New York.

Ortner, Sherry B.
1973   On Key Symbols. *American Anthropologist* 75(5): 1338–1346.

Otterbein, Karl F.
1968   Internal War: A Cross Cultural Study. *American Anthropologist* 70: 277–289.
1973   Anthropology of War. In *Handbook of Social and Cultural Anthropology,* ed. J. Honigmann, pp. 923–958. Rand McNally, Chicago.

Palka, Joel W.
1998   Lancandón Maya Culture Change and Survival in the Lowland Frontier of the Expanding Guatemalan and Mexican Republics. In *Studies in Cultural*

Contact: Interaction, Culture Change, and Archaeology, ed. James G. Cusick, pp. 457–474. Center for Archaeological Investigations, Southern Illinois University Carbondale.

2002 Left/Right Symbolism and the Body in Ancient Maya Iconography and Culture. *Latin American Antiquity* 13(4): 419–443.

2005a Postcolonial Conquest of the Southern Maya Lowlands, Cross-Cultural Interaction, and Lacandon Maya Culture Change. *In The Postclassic to Spanish-Era Transition in Mesoamerica: Archaeological Perspectives, ed. Susan Kepecs and Rani T. Alexander, pp. 183–202.* University of New Mexico Press, Albuquerque.

2005b *Unconquered Lacandon Maya: Ethnohistory and Archaeology of Indigenous Culture Change.* University Press of Florida, Gainesville.

Parsons, Lee A., John B. Carlson, and Peter David Joralemon
1988 *The Face of Ancient America: The Wally and Brenda Zollman Collection of Precolumbian Art.* Indianapolis Museum of Art, Indianapolis, IN.

Patch, Robert W.
2000 Indian Resistance to Colonialism. In *The Oxford History of Mexico*, ed. Michael C. Meyer and William H. Beezley, pp. 183–211. Oxford University Press, Oxford.

Paxton, Meredith
1986 Codex Dresden: Stylistic and Iconographic Analysis of a Maya Manuscript. Ph.D. dissertation, University of New Mexico, Albuquerque.

1991 Codex Dresden: Late Postclassic Ceramic Depictions and the Problems of Provenience and Date of Painting. In *Sixth Palenque Round Table 1986*, gen. ed. Merle Green Robertson, vol. ed. Virginia M. Fields, pp. 303–308. University of Oklahoma Press, Norman.

2001 *The Cosmos of the Yucatec Maya: Cycles and Steps from the Madrid Codex.* University of New Mexico Press, Albuquerque.

2004 Tayasal Origin of the Madrid Codex: Further Consideration of the Theory. In *The Madrid Codex: New Approaches to Understanding an Ancient Maya Manuscript*, ed. Gabrielle Vail and Anthony Aveni, pp. 89–127. University Press of Colorado, Boulder.

Pendergast, David M.
1986 Stability through Change: Lamanai, Belize, from the Ninth to the Seventeenth Century. In *Late Lowland Maya Civilization: Classic to Postclassic*, ed. Jeremy A. Sabloff and E. Wyllys Andrews V, pp. 223–250. University of New Mexico Press, Albuquerque.

1993 Worlds in Collision: The Maya/Spanish Encounter in Sixteenth and Seventeenth Century Belize. *Proceedings of the British Academy* 81: 105–143.

Pendergast, David M., Murray H. Bartley, and George J. Armelagos
1968 A Maya Tooth Offering from Yakalche, British Honduras. *Man* 3(4): 635–643.

Peniche Rivero, Piedad
1987 "Quienes son los Itzá", su identidad, sus dinastías, y su poder sobre Yucatán. In *Memorias del Primer Coloquio Internacional de Mayistas: 5–10 de agosto de 1985*, ed. Mercedes de la Garza et al., pp. 939–952. Universidad Nacional Autónoma de México, Mexico, DF.

Peraza Lope, Carlos, Marilyn A. Masson, Timothy S. Hare, and Pedro Candelario Kelgado Kú
2006   The Late Postclassic Chronology of Mayapan: New Radiocarbon Evidence. *Ancient Mesoamerica* 17(2): 153–176.

Peraza Lope, Carlos, Marilyn A. Masson, and Bradley Russell
2005   Spatial Patterns of Effigy Censer and Sculpture Use at Mayapán. Paper presented at the Second Congress of Mayanists, Mérida.

Peterson, Polly Ann
2006   Ancient Maya Ritual Cave Use in the Sibun Valley, Belize. Unpublished Ph.D. dissertation, Boston University, Boston.

Plunket Nagoya, Patricia
1995   Cholula y su cerámica postclásica: algunas perspectivas. *Arqueología* 13–14: 103–108. INAH, Mexico, DF.

Pohl, John M.D.
1994   *The Politics of Symbolism in the Mixtec Codices.* Vanderbilt University Publications in Anthropology, vol. 46. Department of Anthropology, Vanderbilt University, Nashville, TN.
2003   Ritual and Iconographic Variability in Mixteca-Puebla Polychrome Pottery. In *The Postclassic Mesoamerican World*, ed. Michael E. Smith and Frances F. Berdan, pp. 201–206. University of Utah Press, Salt Lake City.

Pohl, John M.D., and Bruce E. Byland
1990   Mixtec Landscape Perception and Archaeological Settlement Patterns. *Ancient Mesoamerica* 1(1): 113–131.
1994   The Mixteca-Puebla Style and Early Postclassic Socio-Political Interaction. In *Mixteca-Puebla: Discoveries and Research in Mesoamerican Art and Archaeology*, ed. H. B. Nicholson and Eloise Quiñones Keber, pp. 189–199. Labyrinthos, Culver City, CA.

Pohl, Mary
1985   The Privileges of Maya Elites: Prehistoric Vertebrate Fauna from Seibal. In *Prehistoric Lowland Maya Environment and Subsistence Economy*, ed. Mary Pohl, pp. 133–158. Papers, vol. 77. Peabody Museum of Archaeology and Ethnology, Harvard University, Cambridge, MA.

Pollard, Helen Perlstein
1994   Ethnicity and Political Control in a Complex Society: The Tarascan State of Prehispanic Mexico. In *Factional Competition and Political Development in the New World*, ed. Elizabeth Brumfiel and John Fox, pp. 79–88. Cambridge University Press, Cambridge.

Pollock, H.E.D.
1962   Introduction. In *Mayapan, Yucatan, Mexico*, by H.E.D. Pollock, Ralph L. Roys, Tatiana Proskouriakoff, and A. Ledyard Smith, pp. 1–22. Carnegie Institution of Washington, Washington, DC.

Pollock, H.E.D., Ralph C. Roys, Tatiana Proskouriakoff, and A. Ledyard Smith
1962   *Mayapan, Yucatan, Mexico.* Carnegie Institution of Washington, Pub. 619. Carnegie Institution of Washington, Washington, DC.

Proskouriakoff, Tatiana
1954   Mayapan: Last Stronghold of a Civilization. *Archaeology* 7(2): 96–103.

1957   Mayapan Plan of the Main Group of Ruins. In *Mayapan, Yucatan, Mexico* (1962), by H.E.D. Pollock, Ralph L. Roys, Tatiana Proskouriakoff, and A. Ledyard Smith. Pub. 619. Carnegie Institution of Washington, Washington, DC.

1962a   Civic and Religious Structures of Mayapán. In *Mayapan, Yucatan, Mexico*, by H.E.D. Pollock, Ralph L. Roys, Tatiana Proskouriakoff, and A. Ledyard Smith, pp. 87–164. Pub. 619. Carnegie Institution of Washington, Washington, DC.

1962b   The Artifacts of Mayapan. In *Mayapan, Yucatan, Mexico*, by H.E.D. Pollock, Ralph L. Roys, Tatiana Proskouriakoff, and A. Ledyard Smith, pp. 321–442. Pub. 619. Carnegie Institution of Washington, Washington, DC.

Prufer, Keith M.

2002   Communities, Caves, and Ritual Specialists: A Study of Sacred Space in the Maya Mountains of Southern Belize. Unpublished Ph.D. dissertation, Southern Illinois University Carbondale.

Pugh, Timothy W.

1995   Las estructuras defensivas y la distribución del patrón de asentamiento del sitio Zacpetén. Paper presented at the IX Simposio de Arqueología en Guatemala, Guatemala City.

1996   Excavaciones en Estructura 188. In Proyecto Geografía Política del Siglo XVII en el centro del Petén, Guatemala: Informe preliminar al Instituto de Antropología e Historia de Guatemala sobre investigaciones del campo en los años 1994 y 1995, ed. Don S. Rice, Prudence M. Rice, Rómulo Sánchez, and Grant D. Jones, pp. 206–224. Unpublished manuscript on file at Southern Illinois University Carbondale.

1998   An Investigation of Mayapán-Style Ceremonial Groups in Central Petén. Final report to the Foundation for the Advancement of Mesoamerican Studies, Inc.

2000   Ritual Practices of the Contact Period Petén Kowoj and the Modern Lacandon Maya: Evidence of Continuity. Paper presented at the 99th annual meeting of the American Anthropological Association, San Francisco.

2001   Architecture, Ritual, and Social Identity at Late Postclassic Zacpetén, Petén, Guatemala: Identification of the Kowoj. Ph.D. dissertation, Southern Illinois University Carbondale.

2002   Remembering Mayapán: Kowoj Domestic Architecture as Social Metaphor and Power. In *The Dynamics of Power*, ed. Maria O'Donovan, pp. 301–323. Occasional Paper 30. Center for Archaeological Investigations, Southern Illinois University Carbondale.

2003a   A Cluster and Spatial Analysis of Ceremonial Architecture at Late Postclassic Mayapán. *Journal of Archaeological Science* 30: 941–953.

2003b   The Exemplary Center of the Late Postclassic Kowoj Maya. *Latin American Antiquity* 14(4): 408–430.

2003c   Censored Censers: Effigy Censer Deposition at Zacpetén, Petén, Guatemala. Paper presented at the 68th annual meeting of the Society for American Archaeology, Milwaukee.

2004   Activity Areas, Form, and Social Inequality in Late Postclassic Domestic Groups at Zacpetén, Petén, Guatemala. *Journal of Field Archaeology* 29(3–4): 351–367.

2006   Cacao, Gender, and the Northern Lacandon God House. In *The Origins of Chocolate in Mesoamerica: A Cultural History of Cacao*, ed. Cameron L. McNeil, pp. 367–383. University Press of Florida, Gainesville.

Pugh, Timothy W., and Prudence M. Rice
1997   Arquitectura estilo Mayapán y evidencias de organización dual en el sitio Postclásico de Zacpetén, Petén, Guatemala. In *IX simposio de arqueología Guatemalteca*, ed. Juan Pedro Laporte and Hector Escobedo, pp. 521–528. Instituto de Antropología e Historia, Guatemala City.

Pyburn, K. Anne
1989   Maya Cuisine: Hearth and the Lowland Economy. In *Prehistoric Maya Economies of Belize*, ed. Patricia McAnany and Barry L. Isaac, pp. 325–344. *Research in Economic Anthropology*, Supp. 4. JAI Press, Greenwich, CT.

Quezada, Sergio
1993   *Pueblos y caciques yucatecos, 1550–1580*. El Colegio de México, Mexico, DF.

Quezada, Sergio, and Tsubasa Okoshi Harada
1988   Tzucab y cuchcabal: Dos terminos para entender la organización territorial de los mayas yucatecos del tiempo de la invasión española: el caso de la llamada provincia de los Cupul. In *Etnoarqueología: Coloquio Bosch-Gimpera*, ed. Y. Suguira and Mari Carmen Serra Puche, pp. 363–370. Universidad Nacional Autónoma de México, Mexico, DF.

Quirarte, Jacinto
1982   The Santa Rita Murals: A Review. In *Aspects of the Mixteca-Puebla Style and Mixtec and Central Mexican Culture in Southern Mesoamerica*, ed. Doris Stone, pp. 43–59. Occasional Paper 4. Middle American Research Institute, Tulane University, New Orleans.

Rakita, G.F.M., Jane E. Buikstra, Lane A. Beck, and Sloane R. Williams (eds.)
2005   *Interacting with the Dead: Perspectives on Mortuary Archaeology for the New Millennium*. University Press of Florida, Gainesville.

Ralph, Elizabeth K., and Robert Stuckenrath
1962   University of Pennsylvania Dates V. *Radiocarbon* 4: 144–159.

Ramsey, James R.
1982   An Examination of Mixtec Iconography. In *Aspects of the Mixteca-Puebla Style and Mixtec and Central Mexican Culture in Southern Mesoamerica*, ed. Doris Stone, pp. 33–42. Occasional Paper 4. Middle American Research Institute, Tulane University, New Orleans.

Rands, Robert L.
1973   The Classic Maya Collapse in the Southern Maya Lowlands: Chronology. In *The Classic Maya Collapse*, ed. T. Patrick Culbert, pp. 43–62. SAR and University of New Mexico Press, Albuquerque.

Rautman, Alison E., and Todd W. Fenton
2005   A Case of Historic Cannibalism in the American West: Implications for Southwestern Archaeology. *American Antiquity* 70(2): 321–341.

Read, Kay A.
1998   *Time and Sacrifice in the Aztec Cosmos*. Indiana University Press, Bloomington.

Redfield, Robert, and Alfonso Villa Rojas
1934   *Chan Kom: A Maya Village*. University of Chicago Press, Chicago.

Reents-Budet, Dorie
1994   *Painting the Maya Universe: Royal Ceramics of the Classic Period*. Duke University Press, Durham, NC.

Repetto Tío, Beatríz
1985   *Desarrollo militar entre los mayas.* INAH-SEP, Maldonado Editores, Mérida.

Restall, Matthew
1997   *The Maya World: Yucatec Culture and Society, 1550–1850.* Stanford University Press, Stanford, CA.
1998   *Maya Conquistador.* Beacon, Boston.

Rice, Don S.
1976   The Historical Ecology of Lakes Yaxha and Sacnab, El Peten, Guatemala. Ph.D. dissertation, Pennsylvania State University, University Park.
1986   The Petén Postclassic: A Settlement Perspective. In *Late Lowland Maya Civilization: Classic to Postclassic,* ed. Jeremy A. Sabloff and E. Wyllys Andrews V, pp. 301–344. University of New Mexico Press, Albuquerque.
1988   Classic to Postclassic Maya Household Transition in the Central Petén, Guatemala. In *Household and Community in the Mesoamerican Past,* ed. Richard R. Wilk, pp. 227–248. University of New Mexico Press, Albuquerque.
1996   Hydraulic Engineering in Central Peten, Guatemala: Ports and Inter-Lacustrine Canals. In *Arqueología Mesoamericana, Homenaje a William T. Sanders,* vol. II, coords. Alba Guadalupe Mastache, Jeffrey R. Parsons, Robert S. Santley, and Mari Carmen Serra Puche, pp. 109–122. INAH, Mexico, DF.

Rice, Don S., and Prudence M. Rice
1980   The Northeast Peten Revisited. *American Antiquity* 45(3): 432–454.
1981   Muralla de Leon: A Lowland Maya Fortification. *Journal of Field Archaeology* 8: 271–288.
1990   Population Size and Population Change in the Central Peten Lakes Region, Guatemala. In *Precolumbian Population History in the Maya Lowlands,* ed. T. Patrick Culbert and Don S. Rice, pp. 123–148. University of New Mexico Press, Albuquerque.
2005   Sixteenth- and Seventeenth-Century Maya Political Geography in Central Petén, Guatemala. In *The Postclassic to Spanish-Era Transition in Mesoamerica: Archaeological Perspectives,* ed. Susan Kepecs and Rani T. Alexander, pp. 139–160. University of New Mexico Press, Albuquerque.

Rice, Don S., Prudence M. Rice, and Grant D. Jones
1993   Geografía política del Petén central, Guatemala, en el siglo XVII: la arqueología de las capitales mayas. *Ancient Mesoamerica* 26: 281–318.

Rice, Don S., Prudence M. Rice, and Timothy W. Pugh
1998   Settlement Continuity and Change in the Central Petén Lakes Region: The Case for Zacpetén. In *Anatomía de una civilización: approximaciones interdisciplinarias a la cultura Maya,* ed. Andrés Ciudad Riuz, Yolanda Fernández Marquínez, José Miguel García Campillo, Josefa Iglesias Ponce de León, Alfonso Lacadena García-Gallo, and Luis T. Sanz Castro, pp. 207–252. Instituto de Cooperación Iberoamericana, Sociedad Española de Estudios Mayas, Madrid.

Rice, Don S., Prudence M. Rice, Rómulo Sánchez Polo, and Grant D. Jones
1995   *El Proyecto Geografía Política del Siglo XVII en el centro del Petén, Guatemala: informe al Instituto de Antropología e Historia de Guatemala sobre la primera temporada del trabajo de campo.* Center for Archaeological Investigations and Department of Anthropology, Southern Illinois University Carbondale.
1996   *Proyecto Maya-Colonial, geografía política del siglo XVII en el centro del Petén, Guatemala: informe preliminar al Instituto de Antropología e Historia de Gua-*

temala sobre investigaciones del campo en los años 1994 y 1995. Center for Archaeological Investigations and Department of Anthropology, Southern Illinois University Carbondale.

Rice, Prudence M.

1976   Rethinking the Ware Concept. *American Antiquity* 41: 538–543.

1979   Ceramic and Non-Ceramic Artifacts of Lakes Yaxha and Sacnab, El Peten, Guatemala. Part I, The Ceramics, Section B: Postclassic Pottery from Topoxte. *Ceramica de Cultura Maya* 11: 1–86.

1982   Pottery Production, Pottery Classification, and the Role of Physicochemical Analyses. In *Archaeological Ceramics*, ed. Jacqueline S. Olin and Alan D. Franklin, pp. 47–56. Smithsonian Institution Press, Washington, DC.

1983   Serpents and Styles in Petén Postclassic Pottery. *American Anthropologist* 85(4): 866–880.

1984a   Change and Conservatism in Pottery-Producing Systems. In *The Many Dimensions of Pottery: Ceramics in Archaeology and Anthropology*, ed. S. E. van der Leeuw and A. C. Pritchard, pp. 231–288. University of Amsterdam, Amsterdam.

1984b   Obsidian Procurement in the Central Peten Lakes Region, Guatemala. *Journal of Field Archaeology* 11(2): 181–194.

1984c   The Ceramics of Negroman-Tipu: A Preliminary Overview. Paper presented at the annual meeting of the Northeastern Anthropological Association, Hartford, CT.

1986   The Petén Postclassic: Perspectives from the Central Petén Lakes. In *Late Lowland Maya Civilization: Classic to Postclassic*, ed. Jeremy A. Sabloff and E. Wyllys Andrews V, pp. 251–299. University of New Mexico Press, Albuquerque.

1987a   *Macanché Island, El Petén, Guatemala: Excavations, Pottery, and Artifacts.* University Presses of Florida, Gainesville.

1987b   *Pottery Analysis: A Sourcebook.* University of Chicago Press, Chicago.

1989   Reptiles and Rulership: A Stylistic Analysis of Peten Postclassic Pottery. In *Word and Image in Maya Culture: Explorations in Language, Writing, and Representation*, ed. William F. Hanks and Don S. Rice, pp. 306–318. University of Utah Press, Salt Lake City.

1994   La cerámica del Proyecto Maya-Colonial. In *Proyecto Maya-Colonial, Geografía Política del Siglo XVII en el Centro del Petén, Guatemala: informe preliminar al Instituto de Antropología e Historia de Guatemala sobre investigaciones del campo en los años 1994 y 1995*, ed. Don S. Rice, Prudence M. Rice, Rómulo Sánchez Polo, and Grant D. Jones, pp. 247–323. Center for Archaeological Investigations and Department of Anthropology, Southern Illinois University Carbondale.

1999   Rethinking Classic Lowland Maya Pottery Censers. *Ancient Mesoamerica* 10(1): 25–50.

2004a   *Maya Political Science: Time, Astronomy, and the Calendar.* University of Texas Press, Austin.

2004b   Pregnant Female Figurines at Zacpeten, Guatemala. Paper presented at the 69th annual meeting of the Society for American Archaeology, Montreal.

2007a   *Maya Calendar Origins: Monuments, Mythistory, and the Materialization of Time.* University of Texas Press, Austin.

2007b   The Classic Maya "Collapse" and Its Causes: The Role of Warfare? In *Gordon R. Willey and American Archaeology: Contemporary Perspectives*, ed. Jeremy A.

Sabloff and William L. Fash, pp. 141–186. University of Oklahoma Press, Norman.

2008   Time, Power, and the Maya. *Latin American Antiquity* 19(3): 275–298.

in press   Time, History, and Worldview. In *Maya Worldview at Conquest*, ed. Leslie G. Cecil and Timothy W. Pugh. University Press of Colorado, Boulder.

Rice, Prudence M., and Donald W. Forsyth

2004   Terminal Classic-Period Lowland Ceramics. In *The Terminal Classic in the Maya Lowlands: Collapse, Transition, and Transformation*, ed. Arthur A. Demarest, Prudence M. Rice, and Don S. Rice, pp. 28–59. University Press of Colorado, Boulder.

Rice, Prudence M., Helen V. Michel, Frank Asaro, and Fred Stross

1985   Provenience Analysis of Obsidian from the Central Peten Lakes Region, Guatemala. *American Antiquity* 50(4): 591–604.

Rice, Prudence M., and Don S. Rice

1985   Topoxte, Macanche, and the Central Peten Postclassic. In *The Lowland Maya Postclassic*, ed. Arlen F. Chase and Prudence M. Rice, pp. 166–183. University of Texas Press, Austin.

2004   Late Classic to Postclassic Transformations in the Peten Lakes Region, Guatemala. In *The Terminal Classic in the Maya Lowlands: Collapse, Transition, and Transformation*, ed. Arthur A. Demarest, Prudence M. Rice, and Don S. Rice, pp. 125–139. University Press of Colorado, Boulder.

2005   The Final Frontier of the Maya: Central Peten, Guatemala, 1450–1700 C.E. In *Untaming the Frontier in Anthropology, Archaeology, and History*, ed. Bradley J. Parker and Lars Rodseth, pp. 147–173. University of Arizona Press, Tucson.

Ringle, William M.

1990   Who Was Who in Ninth-Century Chichén Itzá. *Ancient Mesoamerica* 1: 233–243.

Ringle, William M., and George J. Bey III

2001   Post-Classic and Terminal Classic Courts of the Northern Maya Lowlands. In *Royal Courts of the Ancient Maya*, vol. 2: *Data and Case Studies*, ed. Takeshi Inomata and Stephen D. Houston, pp. 266–307. Westview, Boulder.

Ringle, William M., Tomás Gallareta Negrón, and George J. Bey III

1998   The Return of Quetzalcoatl: Evidence for the Spread of a World Religion during the Epiclassic Period. *Ancient Mesoamerica* 9(2): 183–232.

Robertson, Donald

1970   The Tulum Murals: The International Style of the Late Postclassic. *Verhandlungen des XXXVIII Internationalen Amerikanistenkongresses* 2: 77–88.

Robicsek, Frances

1975   *A Study in Maya Art and History: The Mat Symbol*. Museum of the American Indian, Heye Foundation, New York.

1990   Weapons of the Ancient Maya. In *Circumpacifica: Festschrift für Thomas S. Barthel*. vol. 1: *Mittel- und Südamerika*, ed. Bruno Illius and Matthias Laubscher, pp. 369–396. Verlag Peter Lang, Bern.

Robin, Cynthia

1989   *Preclassic Burials at Cuello*. B.A.R. International Series 480, Oxford.

Robles Castellanos, Fernando, and Anthony P. Andrews
1986   A Review and Synthesis of Recent Postclassic Archaeology in Northern
         Yucatan. In *Late Lowland Maya Civilization, Classic to Postclassic*, ed. Jeremy
         A. Sabloff and E. Wyllys Andrews V, pp. 53–98. University of New Mexico
         Press, Albuquerque.

Romero, Javier
1970   Dental Mutilation, Trephination, and Cranial Deformation. In *Handbook of
         Middle American Indians*, vol. 9, *Physical Anthropology*, ed. T. Dale Stewart,
         pp. 50–67. University of Texas Press, Austin.

Rosenmeier, Michael F., David A. Hodell, Mark Brenner, and Jason Curtis
2002   A 4000-Year Lacustrine Record of Environmental Change in the Southern
         Maya Lowlands, Petén, Guatemala. *Quaternary Research* 57: 183–190.

Rosenswig, Robert M., and Marilyn A. Masson
2002   Transformation of the Terminal Classic to Postclassic Architectural Land-
         scape at Caye Coco, Belize. *Ancient Mesoamerica* 13: 213–235.

Rovner, Irwin, and Suzanne M. Lewenstein
1997   *Maya Stone Tools of Dzibilchaltún, Yucatán, and Becán and Chicanná, Campeche.*
         Pub. 65. Middle American Research Institute, Tulane University, New
         Orleans.

Roys, Ralph L.
1939   *The Titles of Ebtun.* Pub. 505. Carnegie Institution of Washington, Washing-
         ton, DC.
1943   *The Indian Background of Colonial Yucatan.* Pub. 548. Carnegie Institution of
         Washington, Washington, DC.
1957   *The Political Geography of the Yucatán Maya.* Pub. 613. Carnegie Institution of
         Washington, Washington, DC.
1962   Literary Sources for the History of Mayapan. In *Mayapan, Yucatan, Mexico*,
         by H.E.D. Pollock, Ralph L. Roys, Tatiana Proskouriakoff, and A. Ledyard
         Smith, pp. 25–86. Pub. 619. Carnegie Institution of Washington, Washing-
         ton, DC.
1967   *The Book of Chilam Balam of Chumayel.* University of Oklahoma Press,
[1933]   Norman.
1972   *The Indian Background of Colonial Yucatan.* University of Oklahoma Press,
[1943]   Norman (orig. Pub. 548. Carnegie Institution of Washington, Washington,
         DC).

Ruppert, Karl A., and Ledyard Smith
1952   Excavations in House Mounds at Mayapan. *Current Reports* 1(4): 45–66.
         Carnegie Institution of Washington, Washington, DC.

Russell, Bradley W.
2000   Postclassic Pottery Censers in the Maya Lowlands: A Study of Form, Func-
         tion, and Symbolism. M.A. thesis, State University of New York, Albany.

Sabloff, Jeremy A.
1975   Ceramics. *Excavations at Seibal.* Memoirs of the Peabody Museum of Ar-
         chaeology and Ethnology 13(3). Harvard University, Cambridge, MA.

Sabloff, Jeremy A., and E. Wyllys Andrews V (eds.)
1986   *Late Lowland Maya Civilization: Classic to Postclassic.* University of New Mex-
         ico Press and SAR, Albuquerque.

Sabloff, Jeremy A., and William Rathje
1975a   *A Study of Changing Pre-Columbian Commercial Systems: The 1972–1973 Seasons at Cozumel, Mexico: Preliminary Report*. Monographs, vol. 3. Peabody Museum of Archaeology and Ethnology, Harvard University, Cambridge, MA.
1975b   The Rise of a Maya Merchant Class. *Scientific American* 233(4): 72–82.

Sackett, James
1982   Approaches to Style in Lithic Archaeology. *Journal of Anthropological Archaeology* 1: 59–112.
1986   Isochrestism and Style: A Clarification. *Journal of Anthropological Archaeology* 5: 266–277.

Sanders, William T.
1960   *Prehistoric Ceramics and Settlement Patterns in Quintana Roo, Mexico*. Contributions to American Anthropology and History, Pub. 606, no. 60. Carnegie Institution of Washington, Washington, DC.

Satterthwaite, Linton
1958   The Problem of Abnormal Stela Placements at Tikal and Elsewhere, Tikal Report no. 3. In *Tikal Reports* 1–4, pp. 62–83. University of Pennsylvania Museum, Philadelphia.

Sauer, Norman
1998   The Timing of Injuries and Manner of Death: Distinguishing among Antemortem, Perimortem, and Postmortem Trauma. In *Forensic Osteology: Advances in Identification of Human Remains* (2nd ed.), ed. K. Reichs, pp. 321–332. Charles C. Thomas, Springfield, IL.

Saul, Frank P., and Norman Hammond
1974   A Classic Maya Tooth Cache from Lubaantun, Belize. *Man* 9(1): 123–127.

Saul, Frank P., and Julie M. Saul
1991   The Preclassic Population at Cuello. In *Cuello: An Early Maya Community in Belize*, ed. N. Hammond, pp. 134–158. Press Syndicate of the University of Cambridge, New York.

Schele, Linda
1981   *Notebook for the Maya Hieroglyphic Writing Workshop at Texas*. Institute of Latin American Studies, University of Texas, Austin.

Schele, Linda, and David Freidel
1990   *A Forest of Kings: The Untold Story of the Ancient Maya*. William Morrow, New York.

Schele, Linda, and Nikolai Grube
1997   The Proceedings of the Maya Hieroglyphic Workshop: The Dresden Codex: March 8–9, 1997, transcr. and ed. Phil Wanyerka. Department of Art History, University of Texas, Austin.

Schele, Linda, Nikolai Grube, and Erik Boot
1995   Some Suggestions on the K'atun Prophecies in the Books of Chilam Balam of Chumayel in Light of Classic Period History. In *Texas Notes on Precolumbian Art, Writing, and Culture* 72. Center for the History of Art of Ancient American Culture, Art Department, University of Texas, Austin.

Schele, Linda, and Peter Mathews
1998   *The Code of Kings: The Language of Seven Sacred Maya Temples and Tombs*. Scribner's, New York.

Schiffer, Michael B.
1987   *Formation Processes of the Archaeological Record.* University of New Mexico Press, Albuquerque.

Schmidt, Peter J.
1977   Postclassic Finds in the Cayo District, Belize. *Estudios de Cultura Maya* 10: 103–114.

Scholes, France V., and Ralph L. Roys
1968   *The Maya Chontal Indians of Acalan-Tixchel.* University of Oklahoma Press, Norman.

Schumann Gálvez, Otto
2000   *Introducción al Maya Itzá.* Universidad Nacional Autónoma de México, Instituto de Investigaciones Antropológicas, Mexico, DF.

Schuster, A.M.H.
1999   Redating the Madrid Codex. *Archaeology* 52(1): 26–27.

Schwartz, Norman B.
1990   *Forest Society: A Social History of Peten, Guatemala.* University of Pennsylvania Press, Philadelphia.

Séjourné, Laurette
1966   *Arqueología de Teotihuacan: la cerámica.* Fondo de Cultura Económica, Mexico, DF.

Shanks, Michael, and Christopher Tilley
1987   *Re-Constructing Archaeology: Theory and Practice.* Cambridge University Press, Cambridge.

Sharer, Robert J.
1994   *The Ancient Maya* (5th ed.). Stanford University Press, Stanford, CA.

Sharer, Robert J., and Loa Traxler
2006   *The Ancient Maya* (6th ed.). Stanford University Press, Stanford, CA.

Sharp, Rosemary
1978   Architecture as Interelite Communication in Preconquest Oaxaca, Veracruz, and Yucatan. In *Middle Classic Mesoamerica: A.D. 400–700*, ed. Esther Pasztory, pp. 158–171. Columbia University Press, New York.

Shay, Talia
1985   Differentiated Treatment of Deviancy at Death as Revealed in Anthropological and Archaeological Material. *Journal of Anthropological Archaeology* 4(3): 221–241.

Shook, Edwin
1952   The Great Wall of Mayapan. *Current Reports* 2. Department of Archaeology, Carnegie Institution of Washington, Washington, DC.
1954a   The Temple of Kukulcan at Mayapan. *Current Reports* 20: 89–108. Department of Archaeology, Carnegie Institution of Washington, Washington, DC.
1954b   *Three Temples and Their Associated Structures at Mayapán.* Carnegie Institution of Washington, Washington, DC.

Sidrys, Raymond V.
1983   *Archaeological Excavations in Northern Belize, Central America.* Monograph XVII. Institute of Archaeology, University of California, Los Angeles.

Sidrys, Raymond, and Rainer Berger
  1979   Lowland Maya Radiocarbon Dates and the Classic Maya Collapse. *Nature* 277: 269–274.

Simmons, Scott
  1995   Maya Resistance, Maya Resolve: The Tools of Autonomy from Tipu, Belize. *Ancient Mesoamerica* 6(2): 135–146.

Smailus, Ortwin
  1989   *Gramática Maya*. Wayasbah, Hamburg.

Smith, A. Ledyard
  1950   *Uaxactun, Guatemala, Excavations of 1931–37*. Pub. 588. Carnegie Institution of Washington, Washington, DC.
  1962   Residential and Associated Structures at Mayapán. In *Mayapan, Yucatan, Mexico*, by H.E.D. Pollock, Ralph L. Roys, Tatiana Proskouriakoff, and A. Ledyard Smith, pp. 166–277. Pub. 619. Carnegie Institution of Washington, Washington, DC.

Smith, Michael E.
  2003   Key Commodities. In *The Postclassic Mesoamerican World*, ed. Michael E. Smith and Frances F. Berdan, pp. 117–125. University of Utah Press, Salt Lake City.
  2005   Did the Maya Build Architectural Cosmograms? *Latin American Antiquity* 16(2): 217–224.

Smith, Michael E., and Frances F. Berdan
  2003a   (eds.) *The Postclassic Mesoamerican World*. University of Utah Press, Salt Lake City.
  2003b   Postclassic Mesoamerica. In *The Postclassic Mesoamerican World*, ed. Michael E. Smith and Frances F. Berdan, pp. 3–13. University of Utah Press, Salt Lake City.
  2003c   Spatial Structure of the Mesoamerican World System. In *The Postclassic Mesoamerican World*, ed. Michael E. Smith and Frances F. Berdan, pp. 21–31. University of Utah Press, Salt Lake City.

Smith, Robert E.
  1953   Cenote X-Coton at Mayapan. *Current Report* 12. Carnegie Institution of Washington, Washington, DC.
  1955   *The Ceramic Sequence at Uaxactun, Guatemala*. Pub. 20, vol. 2. Middle American Research Institute, Tulane University, New Orleans.
  1971   *The Pottery of Mayapan*, 2 vols. Papers, vol. 66. Peabody Museum of Archaeology and Ethnology, Harvard University, Cambridge, MA.

Smith, Robert E., Gordon R. Willey, and James C. Gifford
  1960   The Type-Variety Concept as a Basis for the Analysis of Maya Pottery. *American Antiquity* 25(3): 330–340.

Soustelle, Georgette
  1939   Some Observations on the Religion of the Lacandones of Southern Mexico. In *Proceedings of the International Congress of Anthropological and Ethnological Sciences*, pp. 286–287. ICAES, Copenhagen.
  1959   Observations sur la religion des Lacandons du Mexique Méridonal. *Journal de la Société des Américanistes* 48: 141–196.
  1961   Observaciones sobre la religion de los Lacandones del sur de Mexico. *Guatemala Indigena* 1(1): 31–105.

1966   *Collections Lacandons, Série H: Amérique*, vol. 3. Musée National d'Histoire Naturelle, Musée de l'Homme, Paris.

Soustelle, Jacques
1935   Le Totémisme des Lacandons. *Maya Research* 2: 325–344.
1937   La Culture Matérielle des Indiens Lacandons. *Journal de la Societé des Américanistes* 29(1): 1–95.

Stark, Miriam T.
1998   *The Archaeology of Social Boundaries*. Smithsonian Institution Press, Washington, DC.

Stevenson, Marc G.
1982   Toward an Understanding of Site Abandonment Behavior: Evidence from Historical Mining Camps in the Southwest Yukon. *Journal of Anthropological Archaeology* 1: 237–265.

Stipp, J. J., K. L. Eldridge, and R. Cadwell
1976   University of Miami Radiocarbon Dates VI. *Radiocarbon* 18(2): 210–220.

Stone, Doris (organizer)
1982   *Aspects of the Mixteca-Puebla Style and Mixtec and Central Mexican Culture in Southern Mesoamerica*. Occasional Paper 4. Middle American Research Institute, Tulane University, New Orleans.

Stross, Brian
1998   Seven Ingredients in Mesoamerican Ensoulment. In *The Sowing and the Dawning: Termination, Dedication, and Transformation in the Archaeological and Ethnographic Record of Mesoamerica*, ed. Shirley Mock, pp. 31–39. University of New Mexico Press, Albuquerque.

Stuart, David
1985   The "Count of Captives" Epithet in Classic Maya Writing. In *Fifth Palenque Round Table, 1983*, ed. Merle Greene Robertson and Virginia M. Fields, pp. 97–102. Pre-Columbian Art Research Institute, San Francisco.
1987   Ten Phonetic Syllables. *Research Reports on Ancient Maya Writing* 14. Center for Maya Research, Washington, DC.
1996   Stones of Kings: A Consideration of Stelae in Classic Maya Ritual and Representation. *RES: Anthropology and Aesthetics* 29–30: 148–171.
1998   "The Fire Enters His House": Architecture and Ritual in Classic Maya Texts. In *Function and Meaning in Classic Maya Architecture*, ed. Stephen D. Houston, pp. 373–425. Dumbarton Oaks, Washington, DC.
2000   "The Arrival of Strangers": Teotihuacan and Tollan in Classic Maya History. In *Mesoamerica's Classic Heritage, from Teotihuacan to the Aztecs*, ed. David Carrasco, Lindsay Jones, and Scott Sessions, pp. 465–513. University Press of Colorado, Boulder.

Stuart, David, and Stephen D. Houston
1994   *Classic Maya Place Names*. Studies in Pre-Columbian Art and Archaeology 34. Dumbarton Oaks, Washington, DC.

Stuiver, Minze, and Edward S. Deevey Jr.
1961   Yale Natural Radiocarbon Measurements VI. *Radiocarbon* 3: 126–140.

Sugiyama, Saburo
1998   Termination Programs and Prehispanic Looting at the Feathered Serpent Pyramid in Teotihuacan, Mexico. In *The Sowing and the Dawning: Termi-*

nation, Dedication, and Transformation in the Archaeological and Ethnographic Record of Mesoamerica, ed. Shirley B. Mock, pp. 146–164. University of New Mexico Press, Albuquerque.

Talavera González, Arturo, María Elena Salas Cuesta, Luis Alfonso González Miranda, and Juan M. Rojas
1997   Dientes humanos en un área de culto: estudio de un entierro ofrenda de Cuetlajuchitlán, Gurrero. In *Estudios de Antropología Biológica*, vol. 7, ed. Andrés del Ángel E., Carlos Serrano S., and Eyra Cárdenas B., pp. 173–190. Instituto de Investigaciones Antropológicas, Universidad Nacional Autónoma de México, Mexico, DF.

Talavera González, Jorge, Juan Martín Rojas, and Enrique García
2001   *Modificaciones culturales en los restos óseas de Cantona, Puebla: un análisis bioarqueológico*. Serie arqueología, Instituto Nacional de Antropología e Historia, Mexico, DF.

Tambiah, Stanley
1979   A Performative Approach to Ritual. *Proceedings of the British Academy* 65: 113–169.

Tate, Carolyn E.
2001   The Poetics of Power and Knowledge at La Venta. In *Landscape and Power in Ancient Mesoamerica*, ed. Rex Koontz, Kathryn Reese-Taylor, and Annabeth Headrick, pp. 137–168. Westview, Boulder.

Taube, Karl A.
1988   A Prehispanic Maya Katun Wheel. *Journal of Anthropological Research* 44: 183–203.
1989a   The Maize Tamale in Classic Maya Diet, Epigraphy, and Art. *American Antiquity* 54: 31–51.
1989b   *Itzam Cab Ain: Caimans, Cosmology, and Calendrics in Postclassic Yucatan*. Research Reports on Ancient Maya Writing 26. Center for Maya Research, Washington, DC.
1992   *The Major Gods of Ancient Yucatan*. Studies in Pre-Columbian Art and Archaeology 32. Dumbarton Oaks, Washington, DC.
1994   The Birth Vase: Natal Imagery in Ancient Maya Myth and Ritual. In *The Maya Vase Book*, vol. 4, ed. Justin Kerr, pp. 652–685. Kerr Associates, New York.
2001   The Breath of Life: The Symbolism of Wind in Mesoamerica and the American Southwest. In *The Road to Aztlan: Art from a Mythic Homeland*, ed. Virginia M. Fields and Victor Zamudio-Taylor, pp. 102–123. Los Angeles County Museum of Art, Los Angeles.
2003   Maws of Heaven and Hell: The Symbolism of the Centipede and Serpent in Classic Maya Religion. In *Antropología de la eternidad: la muerte en la cultura maya*, ed. A. Ciudad Ruíz, M. Humberto Ruz Sosa, and M. Josefa Iglesias Ponce de León, pp. 405–442. SEEM-CEM, Madrid.

Tedlock, Barbara
1992   *Time and the Highland Maya*. University of New Mexico Press, Albuquerque.

Tedlock, Dennis
1985   *Popol Vuh: The Definitive Edition of the Mayan Book of the Dawn of Life and the Glories of Gods and Kings*. Simon and Schuster, New York.
1996   *Popul Vuh: The Definitive Edition of the Maya Book of the Dawn of Life and the Glories of Gods and Kings*. Simon and Schuster, New York.

Thomas, David Hurst
1978   Arrowheads and Atlatl Darts: How the Stones Got the Shaft. *American Antiquity* 43(3): 461–472.

Thompson, J. Eric S.
1957   *Deities Portrayed on Censers at Mayapan.* Current Reports 40. Carnegie Institution of Washington, Washington, DC.
1960   *Maya Hieroglyphic Writing.* University of Oklahoma Press, Norman.
1962   *A Catalog of Maya Hieroglyphs.* University of Oklahoma Press, Norman.
1970   *Maya History and Religion.* University of Oklahoma Press, Norman.
1977   A Proposal for Constituting a Maya Subgroup, Cultural and Linguistic, in the Peten and Adjacent Regions. In *Anthropology and History in Yucatan*, ed. Grant D. Jones, pp. 3–42. University of Texas Press, Austin.

Thompson, Philip C.
1999   *Tekanto, a Maya Town in Colonial Yucatán.* Pub. 67. Middle American Research Institute, Tulane University, New Orleans.

Tichy, Franz
1981   Order and Relationship of Space and Time in Mesoamerica: Myth or Reality? In *Mesoamerican Sites and World-Views*, ed. Elizabeth P. Benson, pp. 217–245. Dumbarton Oaks, Washington, DC.

Tozzer, Alfred M.
1907   *A Comparative Study of the Mayas and the Lacandon.* Macmillan, New York.
1941   (trans. and ann.) *Landa's Relación de las cosas de Yucatan.* Papers 18. Peabody Museum of Archaeology and Ethnology, Harvard University, Cambridge, MA.

Turner, Christy G., and Jacqueline A. Turner
1999   *Man Corn: Cannibalism and Violence in the Prehistoric American Southwest.* University of Utah Press, Salt Lake City.

Turner, Terence S.
1977   Transformation, Hierarchy and Transcendence: A Reformulation of Van Gennep's Model of the Structure of Rites of Passage. In *Secular Ritual*, ed. Sally F. Moore and Barbara Myerhoff, pp. 53–69. Van Gorcum, Assen, The Netherlands.

Turner, Victor
1967   *The Forest of Symbols: Aspects of Ndembu Ritual.* Cornell University Press, Ithaca, NY.
1969   *The Ritual Process: Structure and Anti-Structure.* Aldine and Gruyter, New York.

Ubelaker, Douglas
1974   *Reconstruction of Demographic Profiles from Ossuary Skeletal Samples.* Smithsonian Contributions to Anthropology 18. Smithsonian Institution Press, Washington, DC.

Vail, Gabrielle
1996   The Gods in the Madrid Codex: An Iconographic and Glyphic Analysis. Ph.D. dissertation, Tulane University, New Orleans.
2000a   Issues of Language and Ethnicity in the Postclassic Maya Codices. *Written Language and Literacy* 3(1): 37–75.
2000b   Evidence of *Haab* Associations in the Madrid Codex. *Revista Española de Antropología Americana* 30: 105–135.

REFERENCES CITED

Valdez Jr., Fred
1987   The Prehistoric Ceramics of Colhá. Ph.D. dissertation, Harvard University, Cambridge, MA.

Vargas, Ernesto
2001   *Itzamkanac y Acalan: tiempos de crisis anticipando el futuro.* Universidad Nacional Autónoma de México, Mexico, DF.

Vayhinger-Scheer, T. (ed.)
1997   Fray Andrés de Avendaño y Loyola: "Relación de las dos entradas que hice a la conversión de los gentiles ytzáex, y cehaches." In *Fuentes Mesoamericanas*, vol. 1. Sauerwein, Möckmühl, Germany.

Villacorta, Carlos A., and J. Antonio Villacorta
1930   *The Dresden Codex: Drawings of the Pages and Commentary in Spanish.* Maya Studies 3. Aegean Park Press, Laguna Hills, CA.

Villagutierre Soto-Mayor, Juan de
1701   *Historia de la conquista de la provincia de el Itza, reduccion, y progresos de la de el Lacandon, y otras naciones de indios barbaros, de las mediaciones de el reyno de Guatimala, a las provincias de Yucatan, en la America septentrional.* N.p., Madrid.
1933   Historia de la conquista de la provincia de el Itzá, reducción y progresos de la de el Lacandón. *Biblioteca "Goathemala" de la Sociedad de Geografía e Historia*, vol. 9. Tipografía Nacional, Guatemala.
1983   *History of the Conquest of the Province of the Itza*, ed. Frank E. Comparato, trans. Robert D. Wood. Labyrinthos, Culver City, CA.
1985   *Historia de la conquista de Itzá*, ed. Jesús María García Añoveros. *Crónicas de América* 13. Historia 16, Madrid.

Vogt, Evon Z.
1964   The Genetic Model and Maya Cultural Development. In *Desarrollo cultural de los mayas*, ed. Evon Z. Vogt and Alberto Ruz. Seminario de Cultura Maya, pp. 9–48. Universidad Nacional Autónoma de México, Mexico, DF.
1969   Introduction. In *Ethnology, Part I*, ed. Evon Z. Vogt, pp. 3–17. *Handbook of Middle American Indians*, vol. 7, gen. ed. Robert Wauchope. University of Texas Press, Austin.

von Winning, Hasso
1961   Teotihuacan Symbols: The Reptile's Eye Glyph. *Ethnos* 26: 121–166.

Voss, Alexander W.
1999   Quienes fueron los Itzaes? La identidad social de un linaje gobernante. Paper presented at the Tercera Palenque Mesa Redonda, Chiapas, Mexico.

Walker, Debra Selsor
1990   Cerros Revisited: Ceramic Indicators of Terminal Classic and Postclassic Settlement and Pilgrimage in Northern Belize. Ph.D. dissertation, Southern Methodist University, Dallas, TX.

Wauchope, Robert
1938   *Modern Maya Houses: A Study of Their Archaeological Significance.* Pub. 502. Carnegie Institution of Washington, Washington, DC.

Webster, David L.
1977   Warfare and the Evolution of Maya Civilization. In *The Origins of Maya Civilization*, ed. Richard E.W. Adams, pp. 335–372. University of New Mexico Press, Albuquerque.

1998   Warfare and Status Rivalry: Lowland Maya and Polynesian Comparisons. In *Archaic States*, ed. Gary M. Feinman and Joyce Marcus, pp. 311–351. School of American Research Press, Santa Fe, NM.

2001   *The Fall of the Ancient Maya: Solving the Mystery of the Maya Collapse.* Thames and Hudson, London.

Weigand, Phil C., Garman Harbottle, and Edward V. Sayre
1977   Turquoise Sources and Source Analysis: Mesoamerica and the Southwestern U.S.A. In *Exchange Systems in Prehistory*, ed. Timothy K. Earle and Jonathon E. Ericson, pp. 15–34. Academic Press, New York.

Whallon, Robert
1968   Investigations of Late Prehistoric Social Organization in New York State. In *New Perspectives in Archaeology*, ed. Lewis Binford and Sally Binford, pp. 223–244. Aldine, Chicago.

White, Tim D.
1992   *Prehistoric Cannibalism at Mancos 5 MTUMR-2346.* Princeton University Press, Princeton, NJ.

Wichmann, Søren
2006   A New Look at Linguistic Interaction in the Lowlands as a Background for the Study of Maya Codices. *In Sacred Books, Sacred Languages: Two Thousand Years of Ritual and Religious Maya Literature*, ed. Gogelio Valencia Rivera and Geneviève Le Fort, pp. 45–64. Acta Mesoamericana, vol. 18. Verlag Anton Saurwein, Germany.

Wiessner, Polly
1983   Style and Social Information in Kalahari San Projectile Points. *American Antiquity* 48: 253–276.

1985   Style or Isochrestic Variation? A Reply to Sackett. *American Antiquity* 50: 160–166.

Willey, Gordon R.
1978   Artifacts. *Excavations at Seibal, Department of Peten, Guatemala.* Memoirs of the Peabody Museum of Archaeology and Ethnology 13(3). Harvard University, Cambridge, MA.

Willey, Gordon R., William R. Bullard Jr., John B. Glass, and James C. Gifford
1965   *Prehistoric Maya Settlements in the Belize Valley.* Papers 54. Peabody Museum of Archaeology and Ethnology, Harvard University, Cambridge, MA.

Willey, Gordon R., Richard M. Leventhal, Arthur A. Demarest, and William L. Fash Jr.
1994   *Ceramics and Artifacts from Excavations in the Copán Residential Zone.* Peabody Museum of Archaeology and Ethnology, Harvard University, Cambridge, MA.

Williams, Ron G., and James W. Boyd
1993   *Ritual Art and Knowledge: Aesthetic Theory and Zoroastrian Ritual.* University of South Carolina Press, Columbia.

Willson, Robert W.
1924   *Astronomical Notes on the Maya Codices.* Papers 6(3). Peabody Museum of Archaeology and Ethnology, Harvard University, Cambridge, MA.

Wobst, Marvin
1977   Stylistic Behavior and Information Exchange. In *For the Director: Research Essays in Honor of James B. Griffin*, ed. Charles E. Cleland, pp. 317–342.

Anthropological Papers 61. Museum of Anthropology, University of Michigan, Ann Arbor.

Wright, Rita P.
1985   Technology and Style in Ancient Ceramics. In *Ancient Technology to Modern Science*, ed. W. David Kingery, pp. 5–25. American Ceramic Society, Columbus, OH.

Wurster, Wolfgang W. (ed.)
2000   *El sitio maya de Topoxté. Investigaciones en una isla del lago Yaxhá, Petén, Guatemala.* Verlag Philipp von Zabern, Mainz am Rhein.

Wurster, Wolfgang W., and Bernard Hermes
2000   Fechas de carbono 14. In *El sitio maya de Topoxté. Investigaciones en una isla del lago Yaxhá, Petén, Guatemala,* ed. Wolfgang W. Wurster, pp. 247–249. Verlag Philipp von Zabern, Mainz am Rhein.

Ximénez, Francisco
1929–   *Historia de la Provincia de San Vicente de Chiapa y Guatemala de la orden de*
1931   *predicadores.* 3 vols. Biblioteca "Goathemala," Guatemala City.

INDEX

Page numbers in boldface refer to figures, maps, and tables.